VOLUME 2

Silent Victory

THE U.S. SUBMARINE WAR AGAINST JAPAN

Volume 2

by Clay Blair, Jr.

J. B. Lippincott Company
Philadelphia and New York

MAPS BY ELIZABETH NICOLL FELTON

All photographs courtesy United States Navy; Submarine Force Library and Museum; Rear Admiral Lewis S. Parks, U.S.N. (Ret.); United States Naval Institute.

The schematic cutaway of a fleet boat is reproduced from *United States Submarine Operations in World War II* by Theodore Roscoe by permission of Fred Freeman.

The excerpts from *Submarine!* by Commander Edward L. Beach, U.S.N., are reprinted by permission of the publishers, Holt, Rinehart and Winston, Inc.

The excerpts from the article "Unlucky in June: *Hiyo* Meets *Trigger*," by Commander Edward L. Beach, U.S.N., are reprinted by permission from *Proceedings*; copyright © 1957 U.S. Naval Institute.

The excerpts from *War Fish* by George Grider and Lydel Sims (copyright © 1958 by George Grider and Lydel Sims) are reprinted by permission of Little, Brown and Co.

The excerpts from *The Codebreakers* by David Kahn (copyright © 1967 by David Kahn) are reprinted by permission of Macmillan Publishing Co., Inc.

The excerpts from *Sink 'Em All* by Charles A. Lockwood are reprinted by permission of Mrs. Charles A. Lockwood.

The excerpts from *Wake of the Wahoo* by Forest J. Sterling (copyright © 1960 by the author) are reprinted with the permission of the publisher, Chilton Book Company, Radnor, Pa.

Contents

VOLUME 1

Photograph sections follow pages 174 and 706.

Maps

By Elizabeth Nicoll Felton

(Surface-force tracks and submarine positions are approximate)

VOLUME 1

VOLUME 2

Part V

Pearl Harbor,
January through April 1944

The U.S. Invasion of the Marshall Islands

After the bloody invasion of Tarawa, General MacArthur reasserted his view that there should be but one road to Tokyo: his own. He argued that all the resources of Nimitz's command—in particular the aircraft carriers—should support his drive up New Guinea to the Philippines, thence to Okinawa and the Japanese home islands.

In Washington, the Combined Chiefs of Staff weighed MacArthur's arguments but held to the "two road" concept. Nimitz would advance across the mid-Pacific to the Marshalls, Truk, the Marianas, the Palaus. MacArthur would push up through New Guinea to Halmahera, then penetrate the soft underbelly of the Philippines by landing on Mindanao and capturing Davao Gulf. The Nimitz and MacArthur forces would meet in the Philippines. British forces staging from India would recapture Burma, Singapore, and Hong Kong. Afterward, the combined Allied forces would drive north from the Philippines to Formosa, Okinawa, and Japan.

Once the "final" strategy had been settled, Nimitz continued with his plans for the jump from the Gilberts to the Marshalls, codenamed Operation Flintlock. The overriding question in Pearl Harbor was, *"Which* Marshalls?" The original plan envisioned simultaneous landings on Maloelap, Wotje, and the main Japanese bastion, Kwajalein. After Tarawa, however, the amphibious experts urged Nimitz to capture the Marshalls in "two bites": first the east-ernmost islands of Maloelap and Wotje, second Kwajalein.

Nimitz weighed the alternatives. The codebreakers provided valu-able intelligence and guidance. The first was that Admiral Koga had written off the Marshalls (and possibly Truk). The new defensive line—to be held at all cost—ran through the Marianas and Palaus to western New Guinea. Admiral Koga's combined fleet was in no shape to do battle. It would not challenge Nimitz in the Marshalls. It would probably withdraw westward to the Palaus or the Philip-pines and challenge Nimitz in the Marianas, where Koga could obtain land-based air support from Guam, Saipan, and Tinian.

The codebreakers also told Nimitz much about the defenses of the various Marshall islands. Admiral Koga, who believed Nimitz would probably follow the "two bite" concept, had reinforced the eastern-most islands: Maloelap, Wotje, and Mili. There were, for example, about 5,000 well-trained troops on Mili. To beef up the eastern is-lands, Koga had stripped Kwajalein, leaving only about 2,200 trained soldiers on that island, plus about 7,000 laborers, administrative per-sonnel, marooned merchant marine sailors, and others. The island of Majuro, which had a large well-protected anchorage suitable for conversion to a fleet anchorage and support base, was virtually unoc-cupied. Based on this information and other intelligence, Nimitz made his decision: U.S. forces would bypass the heavily defended eastern islands (Maloelap, Wotje, Mili) in favor of lightly defended Kwajalein and undefended Majuro.

Accordingly, prior to the landings, carrier and land-based planes from the Gilberts attacked Wotje, Maloelap, Mili, Kwajalein, Majuro, and other islands where Admiral Koga had based planes. With little difficulty, Nimitz achieved total air superiority over the Marshalls.

The amphibious forces landed on Kwajalein and Majuro January 31, as scheduled. Majuro fell without a single U.S. casualty. The fighting on Kwajalein was tougher—it cost the United States 372 dead and 1,582 wounded—but compared to Tarawa these figures were modest. Only 265 prisoners were taken on Kwajalein, 100 Jap-anese and 165 Korean laborers. Within one week, the island was secure and the Seabees had begun an airstrip.

As the codebreakers had predicted, Admiral Koga did not come out to fight; his counterattack was limited to a few aircraft sorties and submarine patrols. The aircraft did no serious damage. The

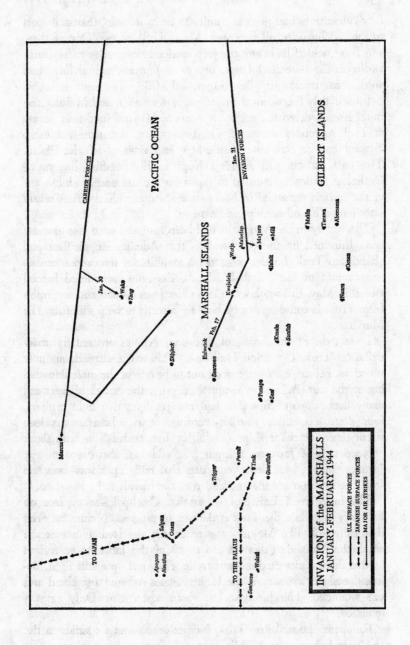

INVASION of the MARSHALLS
JANUARY-FEBRUARY 1944

U.S. SURFACE FORCES
JAPANESE SURFACE FORCES
MAJOR AIR STRIKES

PACIFIC OCEAN

CARRIER FORCES

INVASION FORCES

Jan. 31

GILBERT ISLANDS

Makin
Tarawa
Abemama

Ocean

Nauru

MARSHALL ISLANDS

Majuro
Wotje
Maloelap
Jabit
Mili
Kwajalein

Jan. 30
Wake
Tang

Marcus

Skipjack

Feb. 17
Eniwetok
Searaven

Kusaie
Sunfish

Ponape
Seal

Trigger

Permit
Truk
Guardfish

TO JAPAN

Apogon
Nautilus

Saipan
Guam

TO THE PALAUS

Seahorse
Woleai

four submarines had no opportunity to fire a torpedo; thanks in part to the codebreakers, all four were lost to U.S. forces. (One of these was *I-175*, which had sunk the jeep carrier *Liscome Bay* two months earlier in the Gilberts.) Later, two more Japanese submarines were sunk trying to take supplies to bypassed Mili.

Immediately following the invasion of Kwajalein and Majuro, Admiral Koga ordered the major elements of his combined fleet basing at Truk to retreat westward. On February 3, the giant battleship *Yamato* and several other battleships and cruisers left for Palau. The four carriers and Admiral Koga in his flagship, the super-battleship *Musashi*, returned to Japan for a conference. While some of the carriers remained in home waters, Admiral Koga on *Musashi* later joined his other ships at Palau.

The victory in the Marshalls had been achieved with consummate ease. Informed by the codebreakers that Admiral Koga's fleet had abandoned Truk, Nimitz ordered his amphibious forces to seize the westernmost of the Marshall Islands, Eniwetok, scheduled for invasion in May. Eniwetok was 1,000 miles from Saipan and 670 miles from Truk. It could serve as a base for aircraft to help soften up the Marianas.

In support of the Eniwetok invasion, Nimitz ordered a carrier strike on Truk, Operation Hailstone. This strike, carried out over two days, February 16–17, turned out to be one of the most devastating of the war. Achieving complete surprise, the carrier planes sank many fleet support ships that had not yet left: two light cruisers, four destroyers, three auxiliary cruisers, two submarine tenders, twenty-four merchant ships (including five tankers)—in all, about 200,000 tons of Japanese shipping. In addition, about 250 to 275 Japanese planes were destroyed. After that raid, Truk was scratched from the invasion agenda and added to the islands to be bypassed.

The invasion of Eniwetok—Operation Catchpole—took place on February 17, while the Truk strike was in progress. Nimitz believed that Eniwetok, like Majuro, was practically deserted. However, an amphibious brigade (about 2,200 men) of the Japanese army had landed there undetected on January 4. They put up a stiff fight. Before the island was secure, the United States suffered 195 killed and 521 wounded. The Japanese lost about 2,700 men. Only 64 surrendered.

Following the strike on Truk, Nimitz ordered an air strike on the Marianas February 22. While approaching the islands, the carriers were detected by a Japanese search plane. The Japanese sent out aircraft to attack the carriers, but no ship was hit. On the morning of February 23, U.S. planes struck Saipan, Guam, and Tinian. These raids cost the Japanese about 150 aircraft, including torpedo bombers that had just been sent from Japan to augment Admiral Koga's fleet for the "showdown" battle. The pilots found few ships in the harbor.

Majuro was immediately turned into a major fleet anchorage and support facility. On February 9, a few days after Kwajalein was secure, Lockwood flew there to set up an advance submarine base, picking out a small paradisical island, Enimonetto, renamed Myrna, for a rest camp. When he returned to Pearl Harbor, he ordered Charles Erck, commanding Squadron Ten in *Sperry*, to move from Midway to Majuro. Erck arrived on April 12. Shortly afterward the new tender *Bushnell* joined *Sperry*. *Kingfish*, returning from her seventh patrol on April 7, was the first submarine to receive a refit at Majuro. This new base moved Lockwood's submarines 2,000 miles closer to Japan.

After a brief rest, the carrier forces staging from Majuro once more ranged to the west. They struck again at Truk, then proceeded farther west, launching a massive attack on the Palaus March 31 and April 1, known as Operation Desecrate. The major elements of the Japanese fleet retreated still farther west, to Davao, Tawi Tawi, Surabaya, and Singapore. U.S. planes sank two old destroyers, four small escorts, and twenty naval auxiliaries and merchant ships—in all, about 104,000 tons of Japanese shipping. In addition they destroyed 150 aircraft, most of the planes based on the Palaus. On the return to Majuro, the carriers sideswiped Yap, Ulithi, and Woleai.

During the strike on the Palaus, Admiral Koga decided to shift his headquarters to Davao. On the way there, his plane disappeared. It was the second time within a year that a Japanese commander in chief had died in a plane crash near the front lines. Some U.S. Navy officers believed Koga, like Yamamoto, had been shot down with the help of the codebreakers. It was not so. His plane encountered a fierce storm and was thrown into the sea. Admiral Koga was succeeded by Admiral Soemu Toyoda.

Interceptions in the Marshalls and Other Missions

By January 1, 1944, when Nimitz launched his big push against the Marshalls, Lockwood, Christie, and Fife had a combined force of almost one hundred modern fleet submarines. This was enough to maintain the cyclic war patrols against Japanese merchant shipping and to provide support to U.S. fleet operations. From January onward, enemy-controlled seas were thick with U.S. submarines, on station, going to and from station, or standing by enemy-held islands for fleet support. The Luzon Strait bottleneck became a regular patrol area. More and more wolf packs were sent there and to the usual areas.

During the invasion of the Marshall Islands and the carrier strikes on Truk, the Marianas, and the Palaus, submarines were assigned many missions: (1) interception of Admiral Koga's major fleet units withdrawing from Truk to Palau and Japan; (2) interception of vessels attempting to support the Marshalls; (3) interception of vessels fleeing Truk, Saipan, and Palau during the air strikes; (4) photographic and other reconnaissance; and (5) lifeguarding.

George Garvie Molumphy relieved Howard Stoner, Tommy Withers's son-in-law, on *Skipjack*. Molumphy had commanded *Dolphin* while she was a Pearl Harbor training vessel and then made a PCO cruise on *Finback*. Prior to the invasion, he made his first patrol in the Marshalls. He was criticized for not spending more time close by important harbors.

On his second patrol, during the invasion of the Marshalls, *Skipjack* patrolled off Eniwetok. On the night of January 26, acting on an Ultra, Molumphy intercepted a convoy that included *Okitsu Maru*, a converted seaplane tender of 6,666 tons, escorted by the destroyer *Suzukaze*, bringing more reinforcements to Eniwetok. Molumphy made a submerged approach at radar depth and fired four torpedoes at the destroyer. *Suzukaze* blew up and sank. Shifting targets, Molumphy fired his stern tubes at the seaplane tender but missed it: one hit a merchant ship; others prematured.

During this last attack, one of *Skipjack*'s torpedo tube valves stuck open. A torrent of seawater flooded the after torpedo room. Before the torpedomen could close emergency valves, *Skipjack* took on fourteen tons of water—and a large angle. By fine seamanship, Molumphy overcame the casualty, caught up with the convoy, and attacked the seaplane tender again, sinking it. Thanks to *Skipjack,* the invasion of Eniwetok was easier. After that, Molumphy went over to Truk to intercept Admiral Koga's fleet units leaving the island.

Permit lay off Truk. She, too, had a new skipper, Carter Bennett, who had replaced Moon Chapple. "Relieving Moon," Bennett said later, "was one of the damndest experiences I had in the war. It took me three days to find him. When I finally got him on board for the ceremony, Moon said to his exec, Fred Taeusch, 'Aw, shucks, Fred. You read my orders for me.'"

On his first patrol in *Permit*, Bennett, like Molumphy, went to the Marshalls. He had a busy time off Kwajalein. He damaged a seaplane tender and then attacked a convoy of three "big juicy ships," one of them a tanker bound for Truk. He believed he got hits on the tanker and two freighters. Dodging escorts, Bennett attacked the wounded targets again and again, plus a cruiser that came to the rescue. *Permit* was repeatedly depth-charged, bombed, and almost torpedoed by a Japanese PT boat, but Bennett persisted until he ran out of torpedoes. After this, Bennett took *Permit* back to Mare Island for a long overhaul and then returned to patrol Truk.

After the invasion of the Marshalls, when Admiral Koga ordered his fleet from Truk, Bennett was again a very busy skipper. On February 1, he spotted two battleships, escorted by destroyers, leaving the island at ten o'clock in the morning. Bennett tried to attack but could get no closer than 24,000 yards, so he surfaced within sight of the island, in broad daylight, and got off a contact report stating the battleships were westbound—toward the Palaus. A plane drove him down during the transmission, but he resurfaced and broadcast the message again. One of the battleships was probably *Yamato*.

A week later, February 10, Bennett picked up more big ships coming out of Truk. This time it was night and Bennett closed quickly, preparing to attack. When he got to 4,000 yards, he saw they were two *Mogami*-class heavy cruisers. Bennett submerged ahead, penetrating the destroyer screen. He fired four torpedoes and believed he hit one of the cruisers. Before he could make another attack, however, destroyers pounced on *Permit*, throwing depth charges. Later, Bennett surfaced and got off another valuable contact report.

During the early hours of the following morning, Bennett picked up another contact. He closed to 15,000 yards and saw his contact was an aircraft carrier coming *into* Truk. Bennett moved in to 9,000 yards but could get no closer. In desperation, he fired four torpedoes from this very long range.* All missed. Destroyers tracked *Permit* down and dropped more depth charges. Later, Bennett got off yet another contact report.

The next day, February 12–13, Bennett tangled with two separate convoys. After a long chase, he was preparing to attack when he was picked up by a destroyer. He went deep, hugging a reef to take advantage of "reef noise," but the Japanese destroyer skipper was not fooled. He pinned Bennett down—forcing him to 320 feet—and dropped thirty-five depth charges, many close. Bennett escaped and said later, "With just a modicum of persistence, that destroyer would have had our hide nailed to the barn for sure. It was the roughest time I had during the war."

By this time, *Permit* was low on fuel. Voge inquired if Bennett would like to obtain fuel from *Nautilus*, then entering the Marianas on a regular patrol, but Bennett declined. Instead, he went south to Milne Bay. He hoped to be sent on to Brisbane for a refit, but after his tanks had been filled Fife ordered him to return to Pearl Harbor by way of Palau. He sank no ships on this long and frustrating patrol.

Dusty Dornin and Ned Beach, returning *Trigger* from overhaul at Pearl Harbor, patrolled in the waters between Truk and the Marianas. For the first time, Dusty Dornin found poor hunting. Three weeks dragged by before he made his first contact, and then he botched the attack. The target, discovered on the morning of January 27, was a small RO-class Japanese submarine cruising the surface en route from Guam to Truk. Dornin submerged and moved in close, planning to shoot from 800 yards. However, when Beach raised the periscope for the final look, he found to his consternation that the target had discovered *Trigger* and had zigged directly toward him! The Japanese sub crossed *Trigger*'s bow, then swung stern tubes to bear. Dornin went deep, holding his breath and wait-

* This shot tied Roland Pryce's on *Spearfish*, December 20, 1941, for the longest shot of the war. (Pryce missed also.)

ing for the impact of Japanese torpedoes. Inexplicably, the sub did not fire. Later Dornin surfaced to chase, but the sub got away.

Four days later, January 31, business picked up. *Trigger* found a convoy, and Dornin swung in for a night surface attack. Radar showed three big ships and three escorts. Beach remained on the bridge, feeding bearings through the TBT*; Dornin was in the conning tower, overseeing the attack, checking the TDC and radar plan position indicator (PPI) scope. As the attack developed, *Trigger* would have to fire across the bows of an escorting destroyer at extremely close range. Dornin decided to shoot six torpedoes, three by radar at the biggest ship and three by TBT at the destroyer, now broadside to at 700 yards' range, in a single salvo. On the bridge, Beach saw the three fired at the destroyer spin off erratically just as she finally saw the surfaced submarine and turned to attack. Beach called for flank speed and full rudder, steadied with *Trigger*'s stern on the swinging destroyer, and fired four stern tubes. The destroyer, believing *Trigger* had submerged and possibly confused by the cloud of sudden exhaust smoke from her straining diesels, paused to drop depth charges, and the submarine hauled clear from a near thing.

All torpedoes fired from the stern tubes missed, but one of the initial salvo of three passed through the entire formation and hit one of the other escorts, *Nasami*, a small minelayer, which blew up and sank in minutes. Dornin then ordered a fast end around on the convoy. In a second attack, he again fired at the biggest ship. The ship blew up and went down. Dawn came before Dornin could mount a third attack.

Dornin and Beach returned from this patrol crestfallen. For the first time in many months, *Trigger* returned with torpedoes in her tubes and racks. However, when they reached Pearl Harbor, they received a tremendous welcome from Lockwood. The codebreakers had discovered from Japanese battle-damage reports that the big ship Dornin had sunk in the convoy was a real prize, the 12,000-ton submarine tender *Yasukuni Maru*. Recently overhauled, she was en route to Truk to replace the light cruiser *Katori*, then serving as submarine tender and needed elsewhere. The incoming tender had been loaded with valuable submarine stores and spare parts and the cream of the Japanese navy sub repairmen. There were only forty-three survivors. (Lockwood also believed that his counterpart, Vice Ad-

* Target Bearing Transmitter, a pair of binoculars in a swinging mount designed especially for night surface attacks.

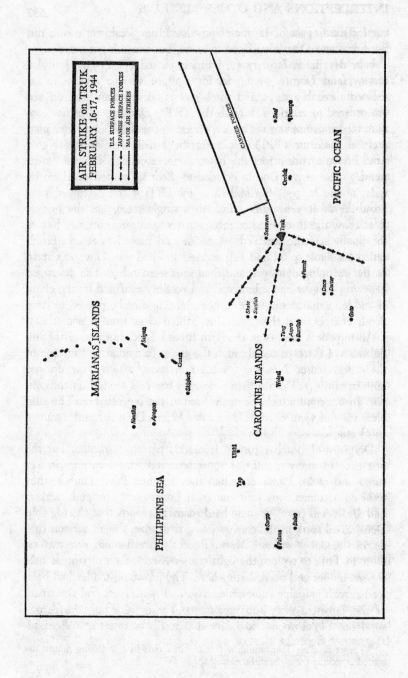

miral Takeo Takagi, commanding the main Japanese submarine force, known as the Sixth Fleet, was on board, but he was mistaken. Takagi was in Truk, flying his flag on a sister ship of *Yasukuni Maru, Heian Maru*).

Dornin found another surprise waiting, a promotion of sorts. He was ordered to relieve C. C. Kirkpatrick in Washington, as aide to Admiral King. Lockwood was happy for Dornin's sake but generally angry at the Bureau of Personnel, and Bob Rice in particular; another first-rate submarine skipper had been removed from his command.

Bub Ward in *Guardfish,* en route from Australia, patrolled south of Truk. On February 1, he picked up a two-ship convoy and began his approach. Just after Ward fired, the destroyer *Umikaze* crossed the torpedo track. One of the torpedoes hit the destroyer, blowing off her stern. She upended and sank. After that, Ward returned *Guardfish* to Pearl Harbor, then on to Mare Island for a long overhaul and modernization.

Skate, with Bud Gruner as her new skipper, patrolled off Truk during the February 16 air strike, Hailstone.

The day before the strike, Gruner found the new light cruiser *Agano*—which Wally Ebert in *Scamp* had damaged off Rabaul in November—coming out of North Pass escorted by two destroyers. In a workmanlike attack, he fired four torpedoes from 2,400 yards. Three hit. Unlucky *Agano* exploded, caught fire, and sank. Her two destroyer escorts picked up 523 survivors and started back to Truk. (One of these was *Oite,* sunk the following day during the air strikes. She went down with her own crew and some *Agano* survivors.)

After that, Gruner took *Skate* westward toward the Palaus. On February 25, off Ulithi, he picked up a Japanese aircraft carrier. Believing the carrier to be coming into Ulithi, he plotted a course to intercept, but it went hurrying off to the north, and Gruner could get no closer than 10 miles.

A new boat joined those patrolling off Truk. This was *Tang,* commanded by Dick O'Kane. His exec was Murray Bennett Frazee, Jr., another from the class of 1939. O'Kane and Morton had been quite a team. How would O'Kane do alone?

Tang came to her area by way of Wake, lifeguarding the air strikes on January 30 and February 5. On the morning of February 17, following the air strike on Truk, O'Kane picked up a fleeing convoy. During the approach, he was driven down but evaded, reapproached, and fired four stern tubes—his first of the war—sinking the big freighter *Gyoten Maru*, 6,800 tons. He trailed the convoy but was not able to get off another shot. After that, *Tang* moved up to Saipan to stand by for the February 22 air strike.

The convoy O'Kane attacked continued westward. Another new boat, *Burrfish*, commanded by William Beckwith Perkins, Jr., patrolled along the path. His exec was Talbot Edward Harper, who had made five war patrols on *Grayback*. Perkins and Harper made contact, but the fire-control party as a whole did not function efficiently and the ships got away. Later, *Burrfish* missed other opportunities. When she returned to port, Shorty Edmunds's endorsement described the patrol as "disappointing" and stated, "The fire-control party needs extensive training."

Melvin Dry in *Searaven* began his patrol off Eniwetok, where he made a photographic reconnaissance; then he shifted to Truk to lifeguard the air strike. The U.S. carrier force approaching Truk went right over *Searaven*. During the operations, Dry received a call for help from the carrier *Yorktown*. A torpedo bomber was down in Northeast Pass. With air cover provided by a carrier fighter, Dry took *Searaven* to the rescue. He picked up three men, the only naval aviators rescued by submarine during the Truk air strike. After that, he moved up to Saipan for the February 22 strike.

After Joe Enright asked to be relieved on *Dace*, following his unlucky first patrol, the ship went to Bladen Dulany Claggett, another member of the class of 1935, who began the war on Klakring's *Guardfish* and later served as exec to Ian Eddy on *Pargo*.

Dace took station south of Truk where, on January 26, she made contact with a tanker with two escorts. Claggett, assisted by his exec, Bill Holman, penetrated the screen and fired at the tanker, but the escorts foiled the attack. After refueling at Tulagi, Claggett returned to Truk for the air strike. On February 11, he made contact with a five-ship convoy but was unable to attack. Claggett concluded the patrol in Milne Bay, where it was declared unsuccessful.

*   *   *

Dace's sister ship, *Darter,* set off on her first patrol in January commanded by an old hand, Shirley Stovall, the ex-codebreaker who had made three war patrols on *Gudgeon* with Dusty Dornin for his exec. Stovall patrolled off Eniwetok and Ponape and then Truk. On January 26, he picked up a tanker with two escorts—probably the one Claggett had fired at—but could not get into attack position. Like *Dace, Darter* dropped down to Tulagi to refuel and then returned to Truk to lifeguard the air strike.

On the way up to Truk, Stovall picked up a ship with four escorts. He fired all six bow tubes. All missed. He swung around and fired his stern tubes. Stovall believed some of these hit and the ship sank, but the evidence was considered too slim and it was denied. Off Truk, after the air strike, he intercepted a big ship under tow but was not able to get around the many escorts for a shot. Stovall returned to Milne Bay for refit.

Slade Cutter, making his second war patrol in command of *Seahorse,* patrolled off the Palaus. His exec was still Speed Currie, but on this trip Cutter took pains to develop the talents of his bright young TDC operator, William Alexander Budding, Jr., then twenty-two.

On the way to the Palaus, while passing near the area where Dornin and Beach were patrolling north of Truk, Cutter picked up a contact—one ship with four escorts. With Budding on the TDC doing "an excellent job," Cutter closed on the surface at night. He maneuvered around the escorts and delivered four electric torpedoes. Two hit, and the freighter went down.*

Continuing onward, Cutter took station on the Palaus-Wewak route. On January 20, he received an Ultra on a convoy and on the afternoon of January 21 picked it up by periscope: two fat freighters "heavily loaded, their decks piled with cargo," and three escorts. After dark, Cutter got into position and attacked. He set up on one freighter and fired three torpedoes from a range of 2,800 yards, obtaining hits in *both* vessels. One sank; one settled low in the water. "The Japs were no more surprised than we," Cutter wrote, "as we entertained no hope whatever of hitting second ship with first salvo. Both targets stopped and commenced firing their deck guns in every direction."

* Lending further credence to the untrue submarine legend that Cutter and Dornin constantly poached on one another's area for the fun of it.

Cutter decided to reattack the settling ship and fired two more torpedoes from a range of 3,120 yards. No hits. Perplexed, Cutter huddled with Budding, then fired two more at 2,600 yards. Again no hits. Another huddle with the fire-control party. The guess was that the TBT on the bridge was either out altogether or putting out erroneous information. They were right and fixed it. "Regretting the waste of precious torpedoes," Cutter turned his stern to the target and fired two more from 2,250 yards. Later, he wrote:

At exactly the correct time (to the second) the first torpedo struck just abaft the stack. The target blew up and burst into flame. With the target brilliantly illuminated, the second torpedo hit forward of the bridge and the ship immediately sank. After she went down explosions were seen on the surface of the water, obviously gasoline drums exploding. During our retirement and for over an hour, the surface of the water where the target had sunk was a mass of burning gasoline. All hands were given an opportunity to witness the spectacular show and enjoy the unique experience of "below-decksmen" actually seeing the results of their work.

After sinking these two ships, Cutter moved *Seahorse* to Palau. On January 28 he spotted three freighters coming out, closely escorted. Cutter tracked this convoy for thirty-two hours before the escorts grew lax and gave him an opening. He fired three torpedoes at one of the freighters, obtaining three hits. The first two set the ship on fire; the third blew her stern off. It sank stern first, vertically.

Harassed by escorts and aircraft, Cutter continued to pursue this convoy for the next forty-eight hours.* Shortly after midnight on February 1, he got into position and fired four stern tubes at a second freighter. All missed. He came around and fired two bow tubes. No hits. With only two torpedoes remaining in his stern tubes, Cutter fired them both in a quick setup from an unfavorable position. He thought he missed and went deep to avoid a charging

---

* During the chase Cutter paused briefly and had his men paint the periscope and shears pink, an idea originated by Sam Dealey, who had painted *Harder*'s periscopes pink on the theory that pink reflected the color of the medium it was in—that is, if the water was blue, the periscopes tended to take on a blue hue; if the sky was overcast and the water a muddy gray, the periscopes tended to take on a muddy-gray hue. Cutter intended to remain on the surface hull down, and hoped the periscopes would take on the prevailing color and be hard to detect. Later, when he returned to patrol off Palau, he repainted them black. (By that time, the hulls of most boats—after much experimentation—were painted grayish black.)

escort. While depth charges exploded around *Seahorse,* Cutter heard his torpedoes hit the target, followed by many light explosions. "They sounded like strings of Chinese firecrackers," Cutter wrote, "and indicated either ammunition or gasoline drums going off." Later he surfaced and observed, "Scene of sinking a mass of gasoline flames with drums still exploding on the surface." In all, the convoy chase had lasted eighty hours, one of the longest and most tenacious on record.

Postwar records credited Cutter with sinking five ships on this patrol. Total score for two patrols: ten confirmed ships sunk.

Philip Weaver Garnett, commanding old *Sargo,* followed Cutter to Palau. Garnett was there when Admiral Koga's ships retreated from Truk, but he failed to intercept them. Later he said, "I was alerted to a task force heading for Palau. I was in position for its daylight position off the south end of Palau, but I was probably detected by their radar. The force passed well outside and around us and entered Palau. The only warship tentatively identified was a *Chitose*-class seaplane tender."

Garnett missed the big targets, but he found plenty of action during his patrol. He made four attacks, firing all his torpedoes. On February 17 he sank the 6,500-ton transport *Nichiro Maru* and on February 29 the 5,300-ton transport *Uchide Maru.*

The Brisbane-based boat *Balao,* commanded by young Cy Cole, en route to Pearl Harbor and refit, patrolled south of the Palaus. Cole sailed under a shadow cast by his previous patrol, during which he botched an attack on two heavy cruisers. On February 23, south of the Palaus, Cole sank his (and *Balao's*) first confirmed ship, *Nikki Maru,* a 5,900-ton transport. On February 28 he sank two more, a 2,700-ton freighter and a 6,800-ton transport. The latter two were probably from the same convoy from which Garnett sank two ships on the same day, a little farther south.

Cutter, Garnett, and Cole in total sank nine ships off Palau in the space of five weeks.

By his performance on this patrol, for which he earned a well-deserved Navy Cross, Cy Cole more than made up for missing the heavy cruisers. But he was unlucky. When *Balao* put into Pearl Harbor for extensive refit, Cole was hospitalized for minor surgery and the boat went to another skipper. When he was ready for duty, Cole had to settle for the only command then available, old *Spearfish.*

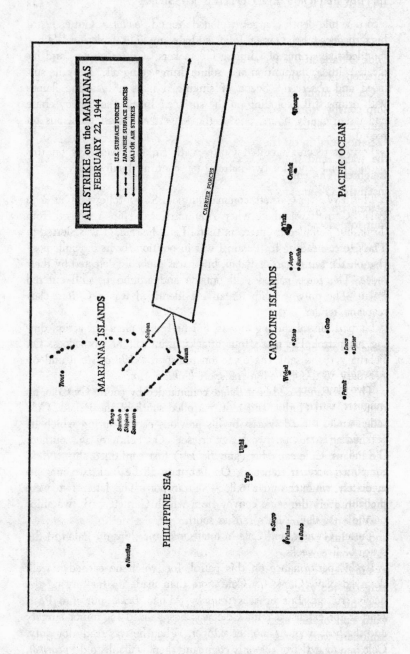

AIR STRIKE on the MARIANAS
FEBRUARY 22, 1944

— U.S. SURFACE FORCES
◄-- --- JAPANESE SURFACE FORCES
········ MAJOR AIR STRIKES

CARRIER FORCES

MARIANAS ISLANDS

Saipan

Guam

Trout

PHILIPPINE SEA

Nautilus

Yap

Ulithi

Sargo
Palau
Balao

CAROLINE ISLANDS

Woleai

Permit

Gato

Dace
Darter

Skate

Aspro
Sunfish

Truk

Onelta

Tange
Sunfish
Skipjack
Searaven

Ponape

PACIFIC OCEAN

*   *   *

By the time U.S. carrier planes struck Saipan on February 22, Dick O'Kane in *Tang* was standing to the westward of the island to intercept fleeing ships.

On the night of February 22, O'Kane found a westbound five-ship convoy: three freighters and two escorts. Going in and out of rainsqualls which made the targets hard to distinguish on radar, O'Kane eased in on the surface to 1,500 yards. With *Tang* "dead in the water, and holding her breath," he fired four torpedoes at a freighter. The ship, 3,600-ton *Fukuyama Maru*, blew up and sank instantly. O'Kane turned back for a second attack on the convoy. Setting up again at close range, he found another target and fired four torpedoes.

The first two were beautiful hits in her stern and just aft of the stack [he wrote], but the detonation of the third torpedo hit forward of his bridge was terrific. The enemy ship was twisted, lifted from the water as you would flip a spoon on end and then commenced belching flame as she sank. The Tang *was shaken far worse than by any depth charge we could remember, but a quick check, as our jaws came off our chests, showed no damage.*

The ship was *Yamashimo Maru*, 6,800 tons.

Two days later, O'Kane picked up another westbound convoy: freighter, tanker, and destroyer. He tracked it during the day, running in and out of rainsqualls, and then moved in to attack after dark, firing four torpedoes at the freighter. "The ship went to pieces," O'Kane wrote, "and amidst beautiful fireworks sank before we had completed our turn to evade. The tanker opened fire fore and aft immediately, while the destroyer . . . closed the scene rapidly, spraying shells in every direction."

While the destroyer nuzzled close to the tanker, O'Kane tracked and got into position for a dawn periscope attack. He looked at both ships from close range, noting every detail, including an estimated 150 lookouts on one side of the tanker. Then, from the point-blank range of 500 yards, he fired four torpedoes at the tanker. "The first three hit as aimed," he wrote, "directly under the stack, at the forward end of his after superstructure and under his bridge. The explosions were wonderful, throwing Japs and other debris above the belching smoke. He sank by the stern in four minutes." This ship was identified in postwar Japanese records not as a tanker but as a freighter, *Echizen Maru,* 2,500 tons.

The next day O'Kane found a third convoy and tracked it, waiting for darkness. Then he surfaced and picked his target carefully, firing his last four torpedoes. He believed he had missed. However, postwar records credited him with sinking *Choko Maru* on that day, a freighter of 1,794 tons. With all torpedoes expended, O'Kane returned to Pearl Harbor.

Following this first sensational patrol, there was no longer any question about how Dick O'Kane would do on his own. He had sunk five ships for 21,400 tons.

Sunfish, now commanded by Edward Ellis Shelby, who had survived the accidental sinking of *R-12* at Key West (and was not blamed for her loss), patrolled near *Tang* during the strike. Shelby began his patrol with a photographic reconnaissance of the island of Kusaie and then shifted to the Marianas. On the night of February 23, fighting the same foul weather as *Tang,* Shelby found a target. At first he believed it might be the light carrier *Unyo,* which had left Saipan under tow several weeks before. Shelby fired six bow tubes from 2,300 yards. Moments later, the target blew up with an explosion so forceful it snapped the heads of personnel on *Sunfish's* bridge and "jerked the boat in the water." It was not a carrier (for which Shelby was credited) but a freighter, *Shinyubari Maru,* 5,354 tons.

A few hours later, Shelby broke out of the rain and found a weird, unmoving sight ahead. He believed it to be the carrier's bow, standing vertically in the water, but someone else said, no, it was a freighter, bows on. Whatever it was, Shelby set up fast and fired three torpedoes down the throat. The target blew up and sank. It was another freighter, 4,000 tons.

Action During the Palaus Air Strike

During the carrier air strike on the Palaus, March 30–31, there were a dozen submarines in the area, seven from Pearl Harbor and from Brisbane (or the advance base, Milne Bay). *Tullibee, Tang, Archerfish, Tunny, Gar, Blackfish,* and *Bashaw* lay offshore to intercept Japanese fleet units fleeing and merchant shipping. *Dace, Dar-*

ter, and *Scamp* patrolled near Davao Gulf to catch ships retreating to that place. *Pampanito* and *Harder* lifeguarded off Yap and Woleai.

John Scott returned *Tunny* from overhaul in advance of the strike. On March 22, he found a convoy and attacked, damaging a freighter. The following night, Scott picked up a Japanese submarine, *I-42*, en route from Palau to Rabaul with supplies. Scott fired four torpedoes from a range of 1,500 yards, then dived to avoid possible counterattack. As *Tunny* went under, Scott and his men heard and felt a violent explosion that lighted the interior of the conning tower. For a brief moment, Scott, fearing the sub had fired at *Tunny*, was not sure "who hit who." He went deep; his sonarman reported breaking-up noises. For Scott, this was the most nerve-racking attack on any of his five patrols to date. He remained submerged all the next day and passed out a ration of whiskey for the crew.

While the U.S. carriers approached the Palaus, Scott took up station near the main pass leading from the islands. At noon on March 29, the day before the carrier planes were scheduled to attack, Scott saw a group of "motley" freighters leaving the Palaus. He violated Lockwood's bird-in-hand policy and let them go by, hoping for bigger game: Koga's *Musashi,* for example.

Scott's gamble paid off. That same night he saw a curious-looking vessel coming out of the pass with destroyer escorts. At first Scott thought the mass was a floating drydock; then, on closer inspection, a *Kongo*-class battleship. In fact, it was Koga's flagship (less Koga), the 63,000-ton *Musashi.* Scott, who had made the classic attack on three aircraft carriers at Truk in April 1943, made a second one: he outwitted the destroyers, closed to 2,000 yards, and fired a salvo of six torpedoes.

One of the destroyer escorts spotted the torpedoes and flashed a warning. While Scott went deep, *Musashi* turned to avoid. One of the torpedoes hit anyway, blowing off part of the bow and killing seven men, but the damage was not serious. By the time the carrier planes hit the Palaus the following day, *Musashi* was gone.

While *Tunny* was standing by on the surface 30 miles off the Palaus, a U.S. torpedo bomber attacked her, dropping a 2,000-pound bomb a few yards off the forward engine room that inflicted serious damage. Scott submerged to make emergency repairs, then surfaced to get off an angry report of the incident to Lockwood. Returning to lifeguard station, Scott found two Japanese aviators floating in the water. One came on board; the other refused. With the remaining torpedoes in the after torpedo room damaged by the U.S. Navy bomb, Scott left station, going to Brisbane by way of Milne Bay for refit.

In squally weather, Charles Brindupke in *Tullibee* made contact with one group of fleeing ships—a convoy consisting of a large troop transport and cargo ship, two medium-sized freighters, two escorts, and a large destroyer. Brindupke set up on the large transport, making several approaches through the rain.

The escorts picked him up and dropped fifteen to twenty depth charges to scare him off, but Brindupke did not scare easily. He maneuvered through the escorts, closed to 3,000 yards, and fired two bow tubes. A couple of minutes later, a violent explosion rocked *Tullibee*. Gunner's mate C. W. Kuykendall, who was on the bridge when the explosion occurred, was thrown into the water, along with some other men. *Tullibee* was nowhere to be seen. Following the explosion she sank immediately, a victim, Kuykendall believed, of a circular run of one of the torpedoes whose contact exploder, unfortunately, worked as designed.

For about ten minutes, Kuykendall heard voices in the water, then nothing. All night long he swam in the ocean. At ten o'clock the next morning a Japanese escort vessel found him. After firing at him briefly with a machine gun, the crew of the escort picked him up. Kuykendall was told that the transport Brindupke fired at was hit by the other torpedo.

Kuykendall suffered the fate of the survivors of Fitzgerald's *Grenadier* and Connaway's *Sculpin*: he was interrogated, beaten, taken to the Naval Interrogation Camp in Ofuna, Japan, and then put to work in the Ashio copper mines. He was the only survivor of *Tullibee*.

Gar, commanded by George William Lautrup, Jr., performed yeoman service as a lifeguard. Popping to the surface within a stone's throw of enemy gun emplacements on the Palau beaches, Lautrup carried out six separate missions, rescuing eight naval airmen.

Six hundred miles to eastward of the Palaus, Sam Dealey and his exec, Tiny Lynch, patrolled off Woleai in *Harder*, returning with new engines. On April 1, the withdrawing U.S. task force hit Woleai but found few good targets. During the strike, an aviator went down near the tiny island west of Woleai. Sam Dealey moved *Harder* in for a rescue.

By the time *Harder* got to the reported position, the aviator, Ensign John R. Galvin, was already stranded high and dry on the beach. Dealey lay to alongside a reef. His third officer, Samuel Moore Logan, and two volunteers jumped in the water with a rubber raft, secured to *Harder* by a line. They fought their way through the surf and coral to the island and picked up Ensign Galvin. As they were attempting to get back to *Harder*, a navy floatplane landed to help. It ran over the line and parted it. Another *Harder* volunteer jumped in the water and swam another line through the surf and coral to the beach. While navy planes circled overhead, providing protection, and Japanese snipers fired away from the foliage, *Harder*'s men pulled the raft and the five men aboard. This rescue was later hailed as one of the boldest on record.

Dealey lay off Woleai for two weeks more. On April 13, a patrol plane spotted *Harder*, forcing her under. Not long afterward, a destroyer that had arrived after the carrier strike nosed out, looking for *Harder*. Dealey decided to attack and closed to 3,200 yards. The destroyer picked up *Harder* on sonar and charged. Dealey let her get within 900 yards and then fired four torpedoes. Later, Dealey noted in his report, "Expended four torpedoes and one Jap destroyer." The ship was *Ikazuchi*, 2,000 tons. She sank within four minutes. Her armed depth charges exploded among her survivors.

Three days later, Dealey spotted a freighter with two destroyer escorts coming out of Woleai. Aircraft circled overhead. Dealey tracked, waiting for dark. Then he surfaced and attacked the formation, sinking his eleventh confirmed ship in four patrols, the freighter *Matsue Maru*, 7,000 tons. Returning to the island, Dealey bombarded it with his new 4-inch gun and then set off for Fremantle to join the other boats of Squadron Twelve.

Pampanito, a new boat, lifeguarded off Yap. She had been commissioned by Charles B. Jackson, Jr. (ex-*Spearfish*), but after an extensive shakedown cruise Jackson arrived in Pearl Harbor in a state of exhaustion and was relieved during training exercises. The exec, Paul Summers, fleeted up to command. After making seven war patrols on *Stingray*, he was one of the first from the class of 1936 to command a fleet boat.

Summers had no opportunity to provide a lifeguard rescue. How-

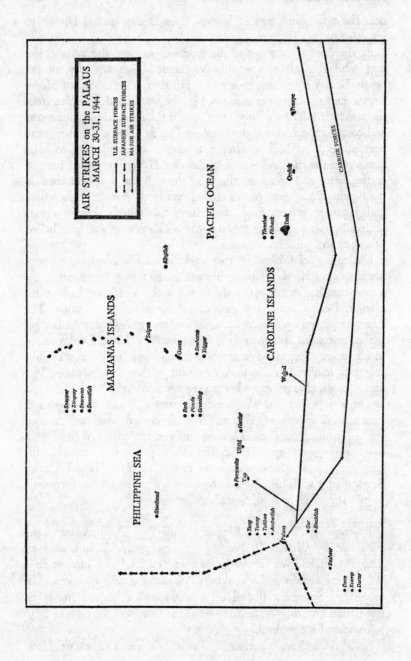

AIR STRIKES on the PALAUS
MARCH 30-31, 1944

U.S. SURFACE FORCES
JAPANESE SURFACE FORCES
MAJOR AIR STRIKES

PACIFIC OCEAN

CAROLINE ISLANDS

MARIANAS ISLANDS

PHILIPPINE SEA

CARRIER FORCES

Ponape

Truk
Trasher
Finback
Oroluk

Kingfish

Saipan

Gunnel
Seahorse
Trigger

Bang
Picuda
Greenling

Wolei

Steelhead

Pampanito
Yap
Harder
Ulithi

Tang
Trump
Tullibee
Archerfish

Palaus

Gar
Blackfish

Bashaw

Dace
Scamp
Dartar

ever, after the air strike he patrolled in the Marianas, where he attacked a destroyer for damage.* In the melee, *Pampanito* was badly depth-charged and incurred damage to her hull. Summers sank no ships, but his superiors labeled this patrol "excellent."

The Brisbane boats lying in wait off Davao Gulf for the major fleet units fleeing Palau had many good opportunities to inflict severe damage on the enemy, but all attacks failed.

A new boat, *Bashaw*, commanded by Richard Eugene Nichols, formerly exec of *Grayback*, found an escort carrier guarded by two destroyers on April 5 near Davao Gulf. Nichols picked it up in the early afternoon while he was submerged, range 17,000 yards. He was able to close to 10,000 yards but no closer. The carrier had an air escort as well (probably land-based planes from Davao), so he refrained from chasing on the surface. On the way back to Brisbane, *Bashaw* was bombed by a U.S. B-24.

The sister ships *Dace* and *Darter* patrolled near Davao Gulf. On April 4, Bladen Claggett in *Dace* saw an aircraft carrier leaving the gulf but was unable to close for an attack. Early in the morning of April 6, *Dace* and *Darter* picked up a grand sight: three heavy cruisers and four destroyers. Claggett went in, firing two torpedoes at one cruiser, two at another, and one at the third. All missed, and he was unable to make another attack. Later he wrote, "Made a mistake, I guess, shooting at three different targets but what a jackpot if we'd collected!"

Shirley Stovall in *Darter* picked up the same set of targets, but by that time they were making 22 knots and Stovall could not overtake.

Another Brisbane boat, *Scamp*, got on the scent. *Scamp* had a new skipper, John Hollingsworth, the officer who had left *Triton* in a huff when his classmate, C. C. Kirkpatrick, was named to command. Since that unfortunate episode, Hollingsworth had been buried at San Francisco in a service unit. He got back into submarine duty and made his way to Brisbane just about the time Wally Ebert returned from his sixth and last patrol, and Jimmy Fife gave Hollingsworth a second chance.

Scamp was nearby when Claggett and Stovall picked up the enemy cruisers. Hollingsworth chased to no avail. The next day,

* Admiral King, wishing to deplete the Japanese fleet in advance of confrontation with U.S. forces, had raised the priority of Japanese destroyers and encouraged Lockwood and Christie to sink them.

while submerged off the mouth of Davao, Hollingsworth picked up a force of six cruisers standing out of the bay and dived for an approach. The sea was glassy calm. While running in, *Scamp* was detected and the destroyer escorts dropped twenty-two depth charges. Hollingsworth remained deep until early afternoon. Then, finding the horizon clear, he surfaced to get off a contact report. While he was so engaged, a Japanese floatplane came directly out of the sun. Hollingsworth dived. Then all hell broke loose inside *Scamp*.

When *Scamp* was passing 40 feet, a bomb landed near her port side. "Terrific explosion jarred boat," Hollingsworth wrote later. She assumed a steep up-angle yet slipped backward to 320 feet. From every compartment of the boat, Hollingsworth received grim news of fire, smoke, damage. To take the up-angle off, Hollingsworth ordered every available man to the forward torpedo room.

For a time *Scamp* bobbed up and down like a yo-yo. Finally, Hollingsworth got her under control. He lay quiet the rest of the day, surfacing after dark to send a distress call to John Haines. Haines ordered Claggett in *Dace* to provide assistance. Claggett escorted *Scamp* back to Milne Bay. From there, Hollingsworth took the boat back to Mare Island for a major overhaul.

After receiving a report, Christie noted in his diary, "A marvelous performance of duty saved the ship from: (1) diving to crushing depth, (2) surfacing under the guns of the enemy. I am sure, as in the case of *Puffer*, that the enemy was certain he had made a kill. Hats off to Hollingsworth and his stout crew."

A new boat, *Flounder*, operated near Halmahera, commanded by Carl Arthur Johnson, who came from *R-12* in the Atlantic. On this, his first Pacific war patrol, Johnson made two attacks against enemy convoys. On the first, he fired his torpedoes from 6,600 yards (over 3 miles) and on the second 7,250 yards (over 3½ miles). When Johnson returned to port, he was dressed down for these attacks and for failing to spend enough time training his crew during the patrol. He was relieved of command and sent to be exec of a new tender, *Apollo*.

Transfers to Fremantle

Early in 1944, Lockwood sent about eighteen boats from Pearl Harbor to Ralph Christie's command in Fremantle. Most were the re-engined H.O.R. boats of Squadron Twelve, replacing the boats of Squadron Six. Others were new boats, to bring Christie's total strength to thirty boats—the figure set by Admiral King.

Angler, a new boat, was commanded by Robert Irving Olsen,* who had been exec to Art Taylor on *Haddock* in 1942. On the way to Australia, Olsen tangled with a convoy north of the Marianas. He was credited with sinking one ship and damaging two, but post-war records confirmed only one of the escorts, an 890-ton net tender. *Angler* developed "structural noises" that made silent running impossible, and Olsen returned to Midway for repairs.

Setting off a second time, Olsen went to Fremantle by way of the west coast of Luzon. While he was there, General MacArthur learned the Japanese had launched a bloodbath on Panay, killing all civilians they could find hiding in the jungles. He requested that a submarine put in at Panay to rescue "about twenty" civilians. Christie gave the assignment to *Angler*.

When Olsen arrived at the rendezvous, he found not twenty but fifty-eight men, women, and children awaiting rescue. After two years in the jungles, most of these people were sick and undernourished, filthy, and full of lice. One woman was pregnant. Olsen took them all, berthing them in the forward and after torpedo rooms. To stretch his limited supply of food, he cut meals to two a day. Toward the end of the patrol, many of the passengers and crew became nauseous—possibly from contamination of the water supply. Altogether, the trip to Australia, through heavily patrolled and shallow waters, was a long and arduous one.

Flasher, a new boat commanded by Reuben Whitaker (who began the war on Bull Wright's *Sturgeon*, commanded S-44 from Brisbane, then made one patrol as exec of *Flying Fish*), went to Fremantle by way of Manila. Whitaker's exec was Raymond Dubois, who had

---

* No kin to Eliot Olsen, ex-*Grayling*. Robert was one of five sons of retired lieutenant Hjalmar E. Olsen. All five graduated from the Naval Academy.

served on the luckless *Snapper* for the first year of the war. Freddy Warder declared *Flasher* the best-trained fleet submarine he had ever seen.

On the way to Manila, Whitaker found his first target, a 3,000-ton ex-gunboat, near Marcus Island and sank it with his first torpedoes. Off the Philippines, he sank three more ships, believed to be tankers but confirmed in postwar records as freighters. Total for *Flasher*'s first patrol: four ships for 10,528 tons.

Victor McCrea, commanding the H.O.R. boat *Hoe*, re-engined at Mare Island, patrolled down the east coast of Luzon to Davao Gulf. On February 25 he found two big tankers, *Nissho Maru* and *Kyokuto Maru*. In an aggressive and well-conducted attack, McCrea sank the first ship, 10,526 tons, and damaged the second.

Another new boat, *Robalo*, was commanded by Stephen Ambruster, who had commanded *Tambor* on four patrols in 1942–43. His exec was a reservist, Charles Woodford Fell, who had graduated with the class of 1934, resigned, and then maintained active reserve status. On the way to Fremantle, Ambruster attacked one ship, firing four torpedoes from 3,100 yards. Christie was disappointed. He wrote Lockwood, "Ambruster is not, in my opinion, of suitable temperament for a commanding officer. On his last patrol he spent thirty-six days submerged in area. He has had one good patrol . . . and three duds. If you have a spot for Ambruster, I think it would be advisable that he leave this area."

Ambruster went to Midway to serve as chief of staff to the base commander. Later, he said, "Ralph Christie and I were not members of the same mutual admiration society. This started long before World War II. . . . I was not the first nor the last submarine skipper to be put on the shelf. . . . My only regret is that I was not given the opportunity to defend my position when it happened."

Junior McCain in *Gunnel*, making his third Pacific patrol, went to Fremantle by way of Manila. On March 18, near Tawi Tawi, McCain picked up an escort carrier and two destroyers, range 9,000 yards. McCain tried to attack, but destroyers found him and forced him off, dropping sixteen depth charges. McCain lay in wait and, four days later, found the same carrier again. He closed to 11,000 yards but could get no closer. It was the second time in as many patrols that McCain had found a Japanese carrier but failed to inflict damage.

Mingo, another ex-H.O.R. boat, had a new skipper, Joseph Jarlathe Staley, who had been one of Herb Andrews's execs on *Gurnard.* Staley took *Mingo* by way of Luzon Strait, where he made several attacks but no hits. During the patrol, *Mingo* suffered a major motor casualty (unrelated to her previous engine problems). Staley requested emergency repairs and took *Mingo* to Milne Bay, the closest repair point, and then to Brisbane. The accident kept *Mingo* out of action for many more weeks.

Lapon, another ex-H.O.R. boat, commanded by Lowell Thornton Stone, patrolled off Hong Kong. On March 8–9, he found a convoy and sank two large freighters. A day or so later, in rough seas, Stone picked up a Japanese task force consisting of two battleships, an aircraft carrier, a heavy cruiser, and several destroyers. It was daytime and Stone was submerged. He set up, but at the last minute the force zigged away. "Thus was lost a submarine officer's dream," Stone wrote later. "The situation could have been avoided had I made a periscope observation at 1210, but the state of the sea, in which a lot of periscope had to be shown, made it imperative to hold exposures to a minimum. With this opportunity irretrievably lost, gloom settled on *Lapon* after our very fine start."

A week later, Stone found the large transport *Hokuroku,* 8,359 tons. He attacked and sank her. His total for the patrol was three ships for 19,500 tons, an excellent performance.

Tommy Dykers in *Jack,* another ex-H.O.R. boat, went to Fremantle by way of Manila. This trip he had a new exec, Miles Permenter Refo III, son of a retired captain. *Jack* was caught by a Japanese plane which dropped three bombs, two of them close. In mid-February, when he reached the South China Sea on a line between Camranh Bay and Manila, Dykers received an Ultra on a convoy of tankers loaded with aviation gasoline. At three o'clock in the morning on February 19, he made contact with this convoy: five large tankers and three escorts in two columns.

Dykers proceeded to conduct one of the most brilliant—and effective—attacks of the war. First he fired three torpedoes at one tanker. Two hit. Dykers wrote, "In about two seconds she exploded with gasoline because flames shot hundreds of feet in the air and the whole area of the sea around the ship was instantly a seething mass of white hot flame."

With daylight coming on, Dykers made an end around and submerged twenty-one miles ahead of the convoy. The ships reached him about dusk, and he fired four torpedoes at two tankers. "Both of them exploded immediately and were completely enveloped in flames."

After dark, Dykers surfaced and fired three torpedoes at another target. All missed. The target fired back with a 5-inch gun, and one shell hit close, shaking *Jack*. Dykers reloaded, swung around, and fired four more torpedoes for three hits on one target that also "exploded and was completely enveloped in tremendous flames instantly." With fourteen torpedoes, four out of the five tankers had been sunk.

For the next ten days Dykers cruised about but could find no other targets. On February 28 he received another Ultra, reporting a *Nachi*-class cruiser coming his way. Dykers picked it up—as it traveled alone at 25 knots—the next day, shortly after lunch. Either *Jack* or the cruiser was slightly off course; Dykers was unable to get closer than 9,000 yards. "This one was a tough one to lose," he wrote.

Next night, Dykers made contact with another convoy, a tanker and three freighters with two escorts. Dykers had only seven torpedoes, four aft and three forward. Assisted by his exec, Miles Refo, he decided to fire the aft tubes first. That plan didn't work out, so he fired the three bow tubes at a freighter. Dykers saw two hits, and the target "exploded violently." Then he fired his last four at another freighter, observing two hits. An escort counterattacked, driving Dykers off, but he believed he had sunk two ships.

All torpedoes expended, Dykers set course for Fremantle. On the way, he sighted another convoy—a freighter and tanker with two escorts—which ran right over him, forcing Dykers to go deep to avoid detection. He wrote, "We sit on station for days with twenty-four torpedoes and see nothing and as soon as we expend them we run into one we can't get out of the way of."

When Dykers reached Fremantle, Christie was prepared. "As soon as the lines went over," Dykers recalled, "he came aboard and gave me a Navy Cross." In a glowing endorsement to Dykers's report, Christie credited him with sinking seven ships—five tankers and two freighters—for 53,486 tons. Postwar analysis reduced this to four ships—all tankers sunk during the February 19 attack—for 20,441 tons.

Later, at headquarters, Christie showed Dykers the text of an Ultra intercept reporting the effect of his attack on Tokyo. The paraphrased text, which Dykers copied, read:

While returning to Japan, a convoy of six tankers was attacked by enemy submarine on February 20th in the waters northwest of the Philippines and five tankers were sunk. Compared to our past losses, the losses sustained by our tankers since the beginning of the year have almost doubled. The present situation is such that the majority of tankers returning to Japan are being lost.

The dockside presentation of the Navy Cross to Dykers annoyed Admiral Kinkaid—and Charles Lockwood. For one thing, it was customary in the navy to go through a series of boards before a medal was finally awarded. In handing out a medal at dockside, Christie seemed to be adopting the technique of General MacArthur, who often gave out medals on the spur of the moment, bypassing army award boards. For another, some believed it might compromise the codebreakers. In meeting Dykers with a Navy Cross, Christie had obviously already confirmed his sinkings through Ultra.

In fact, the medal problem in the Southwest Pacific was even more complicated. Earlier, MacArthur (who had given army medals to Mike Fenno on *Trout* and Mush Morton on *Wahoo,* among others) had told Christie he was anxious to give army medals to other submariners. After Walt Griffith's famous first patrol commanding *Bowfin,* Christie had recommended Griffith (who received a Navy Cross) to MacArthur for further award, perhaps thinking of a Medal of Honor. Kinkaid had taken a dim view of this recommendation and may have taken steps with MacArthur's staff to prevent it. In any case, Christie had not heard from MacArthur about it.

Kinkaid gave Christie orders to stop the dockside presentations. In addition, he forbade Christie and other naval officers to recommend the award of army medals to naval personnel by MacArthur. This order would lead to further serious conflict between Kinkaid and Christie.

John Coye, who had made three fine patrols in *Silversides,* took the boat to Fremantle on his fourth. He patrolled through the Marianas and on to Palau and the area near Halmahera. On March

2 he picked up two heavy cruisers with destroyer escorts, moving at high speed. Coye withheld fire, believing the ships were moving too fast. They passed him at 2,800 yards. (Later, John Haines criticized Coye's decision.) On March 16 Coye sank a 1,900-ton freighter and later fired four torpedoes at a damaged ship under tow. Angry escorts prevented a second attack, and the ship got away.

Paddle, another ex-H.O.R. boat, was commanded by Byron Horne Nowell, who went to Fremantle by way of the Celebes Sea and Ambon. On the night of April 16, Nowell attacked a three-ship convoy with four escorts, sinking two freighters and damaging a tanker that later joined the formation. Nowell was credited with sinking a destroyer, but it was not confirmed in postwar records.

Ian Eddy in *Paddle*'s sister ship, *Pargo,* patrolled by way of Davao Gulf, where he sank a small net tender. On April 26, Eddy picked up two cruisers—one heavy, one light—off the entrance to the gulf. He closed to 1,400 yards, but a plane spotted him and dropped a bomb, alerting the formation. The cruisers turned toward *Pargo* and dropped eight depth charges, forcing Eddy to go deep and lose contact. "Certainly hated to let them get away with this," Eddy wrote later. He was sorely tempted to follow them right into the gulf but decided discretion was the better part of valor.

Empire and East China Sea Patrols

Other Pearl Harbor boats patrolled the usual stations in Empire, East China Sea, and Kurile waters. During January and February, the weather was foul everywhere; typhoons and near-typhoons in many cases interfered with attacks. Lockwood placed high priority on interdicting convoys en route to reinforce the Marianas.

Batfish, commanded by the unstable Wayne Merrill, underwent a trauma. The exec, Molteni, who refused to return to sea with Merrill after the abortive attempt to attack *Yamato* on the first patrol, made good his promise and got off the boat, and Jim Hingson fleeted up to exec. Merrill took *Batfish* to Empire waters for the second patrol but spent most of the time fighting heavy seas rather than Japanese. He made no attacks.

Batfish refitted in Midway and then set off on a third patrol. En route to the area, Hingson determined that Merrill was emotionally unfit and in a kind of Caine Mutiny procedure relieved him of command, reporting the fact to headquarters. *Batfish* was ordered to return to Midway, where Merrill was relieved of command and ordered out of submarines for good. "He was relieved at the same time they pinned a Silver Star on him for the first patrol," Hingson said later. "The same officer tore his dolphins from his chest."*

Chuck Triebel in *Snook*, making his fifth patrol, returned to the East China Sea, still with reservist Vard Stockton as his exec. On this trip Triebel decided to give Stockton more responsibility.

On the way to station, south of Honshu, while running on the surface at night, Triebel picked up a target. It was a dark, rainy night, visibility zero. Triebel fired six torpedoes into the void. Two hit, and the ship went down. "There were three more violent explosions aboard before he sank," Triebel reported. It was *Magane Maru*, 3,120 tons.

Arriving on station, Triebel found another convoy on February 8. After a long chase, *Snook* caught up. Triebel gave the attack to Stockton and took over as diving officer. Stockton fired four torpedoes at two ships. One, *Lima Maru*, 6,989 tons, went down. Escorts charged and *Snook* went deep to evade.

On February 10 Triebel fired four torpedoes at a passing destroyer. All missed. Four days later he found a freighter, *Nittoku Maru*, sailing alone, not zigzagging. Triebel fired three torpedoes. The ship went down. The following morning he sank his fourth ship, *Hoshi Maru II*, 875 tons.

On February 19 Triebel received an Ultra from Lockwood on an aircraft carrier. Triebel moved in to intercept. About noon, February 20, he sighted the carrier and two destroyer escorts making 19 knots. However, *Snook* was 9,000 yards off the track and going the wrong way. Triebel bent on flank speed but could get no closer than 7,000 yards. A plane from the carrier came back to circle *Snook*. When it left, Triebel surfaced and got off a report to Lockwood. Just as the message cleared, another plane came over, driving him down. Later that evening Triebel set course for Midway.

En route, Triebel was directed to intercept a convoy headed south

* In postwar years, Merrill got into serious difficulties; Hingson, a Pentagon staff officer, saved him from a general court-martial by seeing that he was "surveyed out" of the navy.

from Tokyo toward the Marianas. Benny Bass, who was making his sixth fine patrol as skipper of old *Plunger* in the same area, also received an Ultra from Lockwood on the convoy. Bass had sunk two freighters and, running low on fuel, was making his way back to Pearl Harbor. He had only one torpedo remaining on board.

Triebel, Bass, and the convoy all converged in mid-ocean early on the morning of February 23. Bass, unaware that Triebel was in the vicinity, headed southward on the surface to the point where he figured he would intercept the convoy. Triebel, who had submerged, watched *Plunger* go by close aboard. Then—partly as a joke—Triebel popped to the surface about 1,000 yards off *Plunger*'s port quarter. "He scared me to death," said Bass later. "I was surprised, shocked. . . . I didn't know what to do. Some joke!"

Triebel manuevered close to *Plunger* and talked to Bass by megaphone. "I just wanted to let him know I was there," Triebel said later with a straight face.

As the two skippers were exchanging information, radar picked up the convoy. Moments later, one of Bass's men saw smoke through the high periscope. Bass went north; Triebel went south.

It was a large convoy, six ships with many small escorts and one old coal-burning destroyer. Bass moved in with his one stern torpedo, picked out the biggest ship he could find, and fired. In one of the best shots of the war, he sank the cargo ship *Kimishima Maru,* 5,200 tons. The escorts jumped on *Plunger* and held her down for hours.

Watching from a distance, Triebel later wrote, "Observed one hit on ship in enemy convoy. . . . Later heard numerous explosions and observed two large distinctively separated smoke columns indicating two ships were hit."

Triebel was not able to reach firing position during the day. After dark, however, he surfaced and chased. He caught up and fired five torpedoes at two ships. He wrote, "Observed two good hits two minutes later. Eight minutes after firing felt a terrific explosion which shook the boat . . . target radar pip had just disappeared . . . evaded to the north for an hour and then set course for Midway." It was *Koyo Maru,* 5,471 tons.

On return to Pearl Harbor, both Triebel and Bass received high praise for these patrols. Triebel had sunk five confirmed ships for 21,046 tons; Bass three for 9,600 tons. Both men stepped down from command. In his six patrols on *Plunger,* Bass had sunk nine ships for about 38,000 tons, a remarkable achievement considering *Plunger*'s age and infirmities. He returned to Portsmouth to fit out and command a new boat.

When Triebel, who had sunk a total of fourteen ships, left, his division commander wrote, "It is with regret that . . . Triebel is being detached. It is hoped this valuable submarine skipper will not be lost to the submarine service." He was. Like Oliver Kirk and Eli Reich, Triebel had earlier written an official letter complaining about poor torpedo performance. "I practically accused the Bureau of Ordnance of sabotage," he said later. Lockwood had stopped the letter at his desk but later used it to advantage in private showings. Now he sent Triebel to the Bureau of Ordnance. Thus Triebel became the first truly outstanding submarine skipper to go to the Gun Club. He remained there for the rest of the war.

Before leaving *Snook*, Triebel did his best to help his exec, reservist Vard Stockton, move up to command and declared him qualified. Triebel's division commander agreed, writing of Stockton in the endorsement to Triebel's last patrol, "This officer has been previously observed during the training period and the Division Commander concurs with the C.O. that this officer be recommended for command of his own at an early date." Nothing came of it. At Lockwood's insistence, all fleet boats remained in the hands of Naval Academy graduates for the first three years of the war. He reasoned that reservists, by now composing about 50 percent of all wardrooms, were not nearly so experienced as Academy graduates. Few reservists had held down responsible jobs in the boats, such as exec, and Lockwood believed it was unfair to give command to a reservist when able men then serving as execs—from the class of 1939, for example—with five, six, or seven war patrols under their belts (plus two years in peacetime surface forces) were still being denied.

When the Gilberts and Marshalls were captured, thousands of classified Japanese documents had fallen into the hands of the U.S. Navy. Among these were some secret red-bordered "Notices to Mariners" showing the exact locations of Japanese minefields—vital information to U.S. submarines. The red borders made the documents easy to find. Jasper Holmes set up a special unit under a reserve officer, Edward McCormick Blair, to hunt out these valuable papers and get them translated. The results were then issued to submarine skippers in booklet form.

Holmes and Blair discovered from the red-bordered notices that the

Japanese had laid new and extensive minefields in the East China Sea. One boat—*Scorpion*, commanded by Maximilian Gmelich Schmidt, making his second patrol—presumably hit one of these new mines and sank with all hands.

Grayback was lost about the same time. Her commander, the aggressive Johnny Moore, had been ordered to begin his patrol in the Formosa Strait. On February 19, he found a convoy and attacked, sinking two ships for 6,600 confirmed tons and damaging others. Moving north along the east coast of Formosa five days later, he sank a large tanker, *Nampo Maru*, 10,000 tons. After this attack, Moore radioed Lockwood that he had sunk or damaged 44,000 tons of Japanese shipping and had only six torpedoes left, five aft and one forward. The next day, February 25, Moore reported firing four torpedoes and damaging two more ships, leaving him with only two torpedoes. Upon receipt of this message, Lockwood ordered Moore to return to Pearl Harbor. Nothing further was ever heard from him.

Japanese records state that on February 26 a carrier plane near Okinawa discovered a submarine on the surface about 300 miles east of *Grayback*'s last reported position. According to the Japanese records, the plane "gave a direct hit at the sub, which exploded and sank immediately." If Moore received the message from Lockwood and headed home immediately, he would have been in the approximate position reported in the Japanese attack.

John MacGregor on *Shad*, Moore's wolf-pack mate in the fall of 1943, was inclined to believe that Moore, low on torpedoes, may have lost the boat by using his 5-inch gun on some targets. He said later, "I did feel that John was in a frame of mind to use that five-inch gun in cases where the risk to the submarine and crew did not warrant it."

In three patrols, Moore had sunk nine confirmed ships.*

Following his aggressive patrol to the Palaus, Ralph Metcalf in *Pogy* went to Luzon Strait and then up the east coast of Formosa and on to the Okinawa area. On February 10, he found a convoy and attacked, sinking *Malta Maru*, 5,500 tons, and one of the escorts, the destroyer *Minekaze*, 1,300 tons. Ten days later, off the east coast of

---

* JANAC credited Moore with sinking yet another ship, *Ceylon Maru*, 5,000 tons. According to JANAC, it sank about 300 miles to the north of *Grayback*'s last reported position, however, so it could not have been sunk by Moore. This is merely one of many errors that have cropped up in JANAC.

Formosa, he penetrated another convoy, sinking two more ships: *Taijin Maru,* 5,154 tons, and *Nanyo Maru,* 3,610 tons. Three days later, he sank *Horei Maru,* 5,588 tons. His total for the patrol: five ships for 21,150 tons.

On his third patrol, Metcalf took *Pogy* to Empire waters with a new exec, Richard Thomas Fahy. On the night of April 28 off Bungo Suido, Metcalf and Fahy picked up the Japanese submarine *I-183.* After a tedious three-hour end around, Metcalf got into a favorable position and fired. One torpedo hit, and *I-183* went down for the last time. When Metcalf steamed through the area where she sank, he could smell gasoline and assumed she was a supply boat, taking gasoline to the Marianas or elsewhere.

Shortly afterward, Metcalf received an Ultra from Dick Voge stating, in effect, INDICATIONS ARE THAT JAPANESE SUBMARINES ARE LEAVING VIA BUNGO SUIDO EVERY NIGHT ON RESUPPLY MISSIONS. Metcalf responded, YES, YOU'RE RIGHT. I GOT ONE.

That was not all. On the night of May 5 he sank a 2,800-ton cargo vessel and on May 13 another freighter for 4,600 tons. One of the freighters was being used as a coastal tanker. It "burned like a Roman candle," Metcalf said later. Returning from this patrol, Metcalf took *Pogy* to San Francisco for overhaul and stepped down as skipper. In three patrols, he had sunk ten confirmed ships for about 40,000 tons, making him one of Lockwood's high scorers.

The Imperial Japanese Army ordered that Saipan and Guam be reinforced by the crack 29th Division, then based in Manchuria. It was lifted in four big transports escorted by what Jasper Holmes later described as three of Japan's "best" destroyers: *Kishinami, Okinami,* and *Asashimo.*

As this important convoy approached the Marianas, Lockwood sent several boats to intercept. One was *Rock,* commanded by John Jay Flachsenhar, who had made eight war patrols on *Permit. Rock,* en route to Formosa, was redeployed along the convoy's path. On February 29 *Rock* picked it up, and Flachsenhar prepared to attack. One of the escorts spotted *Rock* and fired a 5-inch gun. A shell hit the port-side shears, shattering both periscope prisms and causing other damage. Flachsenhar got off a contact report and turned back to Midway.

On the same day, *Trout,* now commanded by Albert Clark, returning from long overhaul, also intercepted the convoy. Clark sank one of the big transports, *Sakito Maru*, 7,100 tons, and damaged another, 11,400-ton *Aki Maru*. On *Sakito Maru*, 2,300 of 4,000 troops were drowned and all the equipment was lost. Then the three skilled Japanese destroyers counterattacked. They claimed a kill, probably correctly. The famous *Trout* was never heard from again.

Nautilus, reconverted for regular duty, patrolled nearby, commanded by Bill Irvin. While other boats searched for the convoy without success, he intercepted it on March 1. Setting up, he fired six torpedoes, damaging two of the ships.

A few days later, Irvin received an Ultra on a convoy leaving Saipan. He found it on March 6 in the northernmost Marianas: three ships in "irregular column." Irvin fired four torpedoes at two of the ships. All four hit. The first ship was damaged; the second ship, which Irvin identified as *America Maru*, had its stern blown off. "Don't see how she can stay afloat," Irvin noted in his report. Irvin had no chance to watch her sink because escorts quickly moved in, dropping thirty depth charges that were, Irvin reported, deep, heavy, and close. Irvin escaped by taking big old *Nautilus* to 280 feet.

After the war, Japanese reports confirmed that *America Maru* was indeed sunk by *Nautilus* at this time and place. She had left Saipan three days earlier, loaded with 1,700 old people, women, and children—families of construction workers on Saipan—who had been ordered back to Japan. How many perished is not known.

One Pearl Harbor boat that did not make it on patrol was a new one, *Flier,* commanded by John Daniel Crowley, who came from five patrols on *S-28* in the Aleutians. *Flier* was commissioned at Electric Boat Company in October 1943. After trials, she had a naval baptism by fire on the way to Panama and the Pacific; a friendly merchant ship saw her and fired thirteen shells before Crowley evaded in a rainsquall. She got under way from Pearl Harbor on January 12 for her maiden war patrol, planning to stop off at Midway. She arrived at the island during a bad storm on January 16 and, while attempting to get inside, ran aground on a reef.

Crowley gave the alarm. Out came the submarine rescue vessel *Macaw* to pull *Flier* off. However, the storm winds and currents also drove *Macaw* on the reef. Both ships remained stuck fast, with heavy seas breaking over them, until the storm abated six days later. A floating derrick engaged in construction work at Midway finally pulled *Flier* to safety.

Macaw was not so fortunate. Every effort to get her off the reef failed, and she remained stuck until the night of February 12–13. That night, she broached and slid into deep water. During this disaster, her commanding officer, Paul Willits Burton, and four crew members were killed.

Lockwood sent another submarine rescue vessel from Pearl Harbor. This was *Florikan,* commanded by George Sharp (ex-*Spearfish*), whose divers had salvaged valuable documents from the Japanese submarine *I-7* in Kiska in the fall. Sharp had orders to tow *Flier* back to Pearl Harbor for drydocking. On the way, he encountered heavy seas. The tow line parted, and for five hours *Flier* drifted helplessly. Finally the tow line was remade and Sharp got *Flier* back to Pearl Harbor, where it was found that her screws and bottom were badly damaged. The workers fixed up the starboard shaft and *Flier* limped to San Francisco for extensive repairs.

In San Francisco, yet another problem developed. Crowley and his exec, Benjamin Ernest Adams, Jr., fell into an irreconcilable dispute. "It became a very bad situation," the senior officer in San Francisco reported. He considered sending Adams to surface forces because Adams, he said, was not willing to work. The situation was resolved by transferring Adams to Jim Blanchard's *Albacore,* then in San Francisco for overhaul. Blanchard's exec, Ralph De Loach, was due for new construction. Adams was replaced in *Flier* by James Liddell, the former All-American football player from Northwestern who began the war on *Snapper.* Many months would drag by before *Flier* was again ready for combat.

As a reward for the fine job he had done in bringing *Flier* safely through the storm, George Sharp got a second chance at submarine command. He was named to replace Irvin on *Nautilus.* His exec was Ben Jarvis, who had become involved in the dispute on Lefavour's luckless patrol in *Sailfish. Nautilus* was shifted to Darwin to help her sister ship, *Narwhal,* with special missions to the Philippines.

John Tyree, making his fifth patrol in *Finback,* patrolled the East China Sea in foul weather with his usual aggressiveness. In spite of hard hunting, he found only a few targets worth torpedoes. In four attacks he damaged three ships (and sank a trawler by gunfire) but sent nothing big to the bottom.

When Tyree returned from patrol, Lockwood (in keeping with his policy of rotating skippers to the States for rest after five war patrols) sent him to new construction. Tyree reported to Portsmouth to fit out and commission the new boat *Tigrone*. About that time, President Roosevelt's naval aide, Admiral Wilson Brown, requested the Bureau of Personnel to assign a man with a good combat record to the White House. Bob Rice picked Tyree.

Lockwood exploded. Here again another fine, aggressive submarine skipper had been yanked from the force to serve in what Lockwood considered a "coat holder's" job. First C. C. Kirkpatrick, then Dusty Dornin, then John Tyree (among many others). Lockwood wrote blistering letters to Bob Rice and Louis Denfeld, protesting Tyree's reassignment, but it did no good. BuPers, then as now, had immense power over the destiny of the professional naval officer, and it was not about to yield to Lockwood. In spite of all objections, the bureau continued to siphon off aggressive (as well as not-so-aggressive) skippers. Lockwood complained to Christie, "Possibly after we get the entire navy manned by submarine personnel we will be allowed to retain a few of our good men."

The Polar Circuit

A new boat, *Sandlance*, commanded by Malcolm Everett Garrison, made the polar circuit. Garrison had helped fit out and commission *Trout*. In May 1943 he had reported to Portsmouth to put *Sandlance* in commission. Caught up in the backwaters of Portsmouth, Garrison had never made a real war patrol.

Garrison traveled far north to Kamchatka. The weather was bitterly cold, and the seas were full of floating ice. Garrison struck an ice floe with his periscope and it jammed in the fully elevated position, a serious handicap. Later he wiped off a sonar head in shallow water while attempting to look in a harbor.

Garrison picked up a ship which, he said later, "I positively identified as the *Florida Maru*." He fired and the ship sank while Garrison took photographs through the periscope. It was not *Florida Maru* but *Bella Russa*, a Soviet ship. It had no markings and was "not within the safe conduct lane" given the Russians. With that, Garrison joined the exclusive club of Russian-ship sinkers, founded by Eugene Sands in *Sawfish* and Moon Chapple in *Permit*.

During the days following, Garrison found many targets. He sank two freighters in the far north: *Kaiko Maru*, 3,548 tons, and *Akashisan Maru*, 4,541 tons. In addition, he wasted five torpedoes on what he concluded later was a shallow-draft decoy vessel. With only six torpedoes remaining, Garrison dropped southward to patrol off Honshu.

On March 12, Voge notified Garrison of a big convoy that had left Tokyo crammed with men and supplies to reinforce the Marianas. Garrison found the convoy in moonlight on the night of March 13, right on schedule. It consisted of five big freighters and several smaller ships, escorted by several destroyers and the 3,300-ton light cruiser *Tatsuta*. Regretting the wastage of five torpedoes against the decoy, Garrison prepared to attack with his remaining six.

Coming in submerged with the jammed periscope, Garrison chose the cruiser and one big freighter, planning to fire two stern torpedoes at each and then swing around and fire his last two bow torpedoes at another freighter. He executed his plan with cool precision. Two torpedoes hit *Tatsuta*, which sank immediately. The other two hit *Kokuyo Maru*, a 4,667-ton cargo vessel. The two bow torpedoes hit another freighter for damage.

In the confusion, the escorts could not at first find *Sandlance*. Garrison remained at periscope depth for a while, surveying his work with satisfaction. Then two escorts charged, and Garrison took *Sandlance*, a thick-skinned boat, to 550 feet. For the next eighteen hours, the destroyers zipped back and forth, dropping a total of 105 depth charges. But the charges were set to go off for 250 feet, 300 feet above *Sandlance*, and no damage was done. With all torpedoes expended, Garrison returned to Pearl Harbor from his first patrol. He had sunk a light cruiser, three Japanese freighters, and one Russian ship. Damage to the Japanese: four confirmed ships for 16,000 tons.

On his next patrol, Garrison went to Fremantle by way of the Marianas. Between May 3 and May 11, he sank three confirmed ships: *Kenan Maru*, 3,129 tons; *Mitakesan Maru*, 4,441 tons; and *Koho Maru*, 4,291 tons. On May 17 he joined forces to attack a convoy with John Scott in *Tunny*, coming up from Milne Bay. Garrison sank two more ships, one for 3,834 and one for 2,633 tons. John Scott sank one for 5,000 tons.

At about this time *Gudgeon* was lost. Scott in *Tunny* and Garrison in *Sandlance* were looking for a convoy near Saipan, and *Gudgeon* was in the area, presumably looking for the same convoy.

Scott and Garrison may have heard the fatal attack on *Gudgeon*; Garrison reported "about forty depth charges eight to ten miles away." Since no other submarine reported being under attack at that time and place, Lockwood and Voge presumed the attack Garrison heard was on *Gudgeon*. Nothing was ever heard from her again. She was skippered by Robert Alexander Bonin, class of 1936, making his first patrol in her without benefit of a PCO cruise. (Bonin had formerly been exec on *Grayling*.) *Gudgeon*'s young exec was Donald Raymond Midgley, class of 1941.

Scott remained in the Marianas. Garrison, who had shot off all his torpedoes, proceeded to Fremantle, arriving thirty-five days after leaving port. Total for the patrol: five ships for 18,328 tons. In two brief patrols, Garrison had sunk nine ships—and he submitted two of the briefest patrol reports on record (five or six pages), describing the action.

Tautog, commanded by Barney Sieglaff going on his sixth patrol, followed *Sandlance* on the polar circuit. On board for a PCO run was Tom Baskett, who had made two patrols in *S-44* as exec to Dinty Moore and then commanded *S-37* for one patrol. Baskett had been trapped in San Diego for a long time, trying to get cranky old *S-37* in working order. Now he was making his first patrol in a fleet boat.

On the way to station, Sieglaff paused at sea to make some topside repairs. During the pause, a new sailor on *Tautog*, R. A. Laramee, a motor machinist mate, was swept over the side. Sieglaff spent a futile half hour circling the vicinity, but nothing was ever seen of Laramee—a needless death, it seemed to Sieglaff, and it cast a pall over the crew.

Tautog spent a week in northwestern waters before finding a target worthy of a torpedo. It was cold. "At times," Sieglaff wrote, "*Tautog* was completely surrounded by a solid mass of floating ice about two inches thick." Snow fell from time to time.

On March 13, Sieglaff found two ships. He closed to 1,500 yards and fired three torpedoes. Two hit one of the targets, and the Japanese began to abandon ship. Observing that the ship had not yet sunk, Sieglaff put another four torpedoes into her, one at a time. Still the ship would not sink. (Sieglaff later called it a "rubber ship.") He then battle-surfaced with his 5-inch deck gun.

While he was busy, the other ship came up to rescue survivors of the first. Sieglaff submerged, approached, and fired three torpedoes at her. She "sank in short order." In time, the first ship also sank.

Following this action, Sieglaff dropped south to patrol the northeast coast of Honshu. On March 16, he found a seven-ship convoy. He set up and fired four torpedoes at one freighter, another spread of three at a second, then another of four at a third. With explosions going off and escorts charging, Sieglaff was not positive of what he hit; postwar records revealed that he sank a freighter and one of the escorts, the destroyer *Shirakumo*. His total for the patrol was four ships for about 11,000 tons.

Following this patrol, Sieglaff stepped down as skipper of *Tautog* and returned to new construction. In six patrols, he had sunk thirteen confirmed ships, including two destroyers.

Replacing Sieglaff as skipper, Tom Baskett returned to the polar circuit for *Tautog's* eleventh patrol. On May 2, Baskett found a big ship at anchor near Matsuwa and fired six torpedoes. Down went *Ryoyo Maru*, 6,000 tons.

The next day at dawn Baskett stumbled across a large unescorted freighter in the fog near Matsuwa. He remained on the surface, using the fog for protection, and fired four torpedoes. Two hit, and *Fushimi Maru*, a 5,000-ton transport, sank.

Following this, Baskett dropped down to the northeast coast of Honshu, reaching the area May 8. He found swarms of ships. He set up on one 4,000-ton freighter, fired five torpedoes, and watched it sink. The next day at dawn he fired two torpedoes at a small freighter but missed. On May 12, he fired his last three torpedoes at a small freighter of 1,100 tons. It sank. Baskett returned *Tautog* to Pearl Harbor. The total for his first patrol: four confirmed ships for 16,100 tons.

Wolf Packs Four and Five

In March and April Lockwood organized two more wolf packs. The first consisted of *Parche*, *Bang*, and *Tinosa*. *Parche*, commanded by Red Ramage from *Trout*, was a new boat. *Bang*, also new, was commanded by a new skipper, Anton Renki Gallaher, who came from command of *R-13* in the Atlantic but had never served in a fleet boat. *Tinosa* had been brought back from Fremantle by Don Weiss, who—in a brilliantly daring action—had sunk four confirmed ships for 15,600 tons on the way.

The pack was led by George Edmund Peterson, 1924, commanding SubDiv 141. Peterson had spent most of the war in the Atlantic, serving with the boats operating out of Scotland, and had never made a Pacific war patrol. Before setting off, the pack developed new and simplified techniques to facilitate communications.

The three boats took up station in Luzon Strait in mid-April, and for the next two weeks they milled about without any contacts. Red Ramage was so bored he filled his patrol report with humorous entries, such as the one on April 18: "Picked up sky lookout—bird—which took station on Number One Periscope going round and round and up and down, hanging on with dogged determination over four hours. Genus: unknown. Sex: undetermined. Habits: not altogether proper."

In the late afternoon of April 29, J. W. Champ, a keen-eyed quartermaster on *Bang*, alternating periscope watch with the officer of the deck, picked up smoke on the horizon. The smoke developed into a huge southbound convoy: fifteen to twenty ships and numerous destroyer escorts. Gallaher surfaced and got off contact reports—repeated every hour—to *Parche* and *Tinosa*, some 60 to 70 miles northwest of the convoy. *Tinosa* receipted after one hour, *Parche* after three hours.

Gallaher submerged again for a night periscope attack, selecting a tanker and two freighters for his initial ten-torpedo salvo. He was all set to fire when one of the destroyers, looking as big as a heavy cruiser to Gallaher, got in the way. In a change of tactics, Gallaher fired four torpedoes at the destroyer and two at the tanker. He missed the destroyer, which turned out of the way, but one or two torpedoes hit a freighter behind it. Another destroyer charged *Bang*, and Gallaher went deep to evade.

An hour or so later, after the escort broke off, Gallaher surfaced to chase. He caught up with the convoy in an hour, threaded through the escorts, and set up on a big freighter, firing six torpedoes. All missed. He swung around and fired his four stern tubes. There was confusion in the fire-control party; all four stern tubes also missed. Gallaher began reloading his tubes and making an end around.

Shortly after five o'clock in the morning, April 30, he caught up again and fired his four remaining bow tubes at a big freighter. Gallaher wrote, "The first explosion caused a tremendous flash. . . . The concussion was so great on the bridge that it felt as if there had been a bodily push away from the target. The second hit caused a ripple of flame. . . . Target sank amid a cloud of dense smoke." The escorts charged again and drove *Bang* down for eleven hours.

In these attacks, Gallaher had fired twenty torpedoes. He sank two confirmed ships.

All the while, *Tinosa* and *Parche* were hurrying down from the northwest at full speed, trying to find the convoy. At 4:20 A.M., Ramage saw flames on the horizon, the result of Gallaher's earlier attacks. About the time Gallaher made his dawn attack, Ramage picked up the convoy on radar. He counted ten large ships. Ramage and Weiss ran around the convoy to get ahead for a day periscope attack; Gallaher, with only four torpedoes left, was ordered to trail and sink any stragglers.

Ramage and Weiss dived in front of the convoy and waited. At about nine o'clock in the morning, it came into Weiss's range. He saw a "dream setup": five overlapping ships. He fired all six bow tubes, hearing and feeling four hits. With destroyers charging, Weiss went deep and remained there, losing contact. An hour later, Ramage set up and fired four torpedoes—two each at two freighters. All missed. Aircraft and destroyers charged *Parche,* and Ramage went deep for the rest of the day, also losing contact. The convoy ran into Lingayen Gulf, and none of the three boats could make another attack on it. Neither Weiss nor Ramage received credit in postwar records for a sinking on this day.

Three days passed. About daylight on May 3, Weiss in *Tinosa* picked up another convoy and flashed the word. It consisted of twelve ships. The pack tracked it submerged during the day and surfaced after dark to chase. The boats caught up about midnight. Weiss attacked first, firing six torpedoes at a tanker and freighter. He saw two hits on the tanker and hits on the freighter, but destroyers drove him under before he could make a follow-up attack. Ramage attacked next, firing six bow tubes—four at one freighter and two at another. He saw three hits in the first ship, which "appeared to blow up" and sink immediately, and two hits on the second, which began settling in the water. He swung around and fired his four stern tubes at another freighter, observing two hits.

Gallaher on *Bang,* meanwhile, set up on another target with his last four stern torpedoes. When he fired, he believed he obtained two hits on a freighter and one hit on a destroyer. Both, he reported, "sank."

Weiss in *Tinosa* surfaced and prepared to attack again. He fired six torpedoes at a big freighter, obtaining three hits which seemed to disintegrate the target, and then fired four more for misses. He submerged for a daylight attack on another ship, firing his last four torpedoes—all misses. During the day the remnants of the convoy eluded *Parche*, the only boat of the three with any torpedoes left. In this combined attack the three boats sank five ships, almost half the convoy.

After *Tinosa* and *Bang* reported all torpedoes expended, the pack commander, Peterson, ordered them to return to base. Ramage hung around a few more days but found no further opportunity to shoot. In total, Pack Number Four sank seven confirmed ships for about 35,300 tons. Gallaher was credited with three freighters for 10,700 tons, Ramage two for 11,700 tons, and Weiss two for 12,900 tons.

Wolf Pack Number Five set off in April for Luzon Strait. It consisted of Albert Raborn commanding *Picuda*, Paul Van Leunen, Jr., on *Peto* (both making their second patrols), and a brand-new boat, *Perch II*,* commanded by Blish Charles Hills, who had been Dick Lake's exec on *Albacore* for the first four patrols. The pack, known as "Fenno's Ferrets," was commanded by Mike Fenno (making his eighth patrol of the war) in *Picuda*.

Fenno's Ferrets had bad luck. On May 22, Raborn in *Picuda* picked up a convoy and sank the 1,200-ton river gunboat *Hashidate* and damaged a freighter with the same salvo. On May 24, Hills in *Perch* attacked a convoy, firing four torpedoes at a medium-sized tanker. In the counterattack, *Perch* was almost lost. She flooded her pump room, putting the air compressors out of commission, and was forced to return early. On June 2, Raborn found a twelve-ship convoy. He damaged one tanker but was not able to sink anything. Van Leunen in *Peto* saw six ships but delivered no attacks. Net results: one boat almost lost, one 1,200-ton river gunboat sunk.

During the course of this luckless patrol, a fourth boat joined the pack briefly. It was a new one, *Guitarro*, on the way to Fremantle, commanded by Enrique Haskins, who had commissioned *Flying Fish* and served as Donaho's first exec. On May 30 Haskins sank a 2,000-ton freighter and on June 2 the frigate *Awaji*. Then he went on to Darwin and Fremantle.

On return to port, Paul Van Leunen in *Peto* received harsh en-

* Named for Dave Hurt's boat, lost in the retreat from Manila.

dorsements on his patrol report, being criticized for not pressing attacks home and for failing to intercept a *Picuda* contact report. He was relieved of command and went to serve on Lockwood's staff. Al Raborn—who was praised for his aggressiveness—stepped down voluntarily, going to a shore job on the West Coast.

Patrols to the Marianas

Slade Cutter took *Seahorse* to the Marianas for his third patrol. This trip he had a new exec, Elbert Crawford ("Spud") Lindon, replacing Speed Currie. Young William Budding manned the TDC. *Seahorse*'s mission was to stop the Japanese from reinforcing Guam and Saipan.

On March 31, Cutter rendezvoused with *Stingray* in the northern Marianas. *Stingray*, returning from overhaul, was now commanded by Sam Loomis, who had been exec to Chuck Triebel in *Snook*. Loomis had got on the trail of a convoy and sunk a 4,000-ton freighter the previous day. The two classmates (they had been to the same secondary schools and roomed together at the Naval Academy) exchanged information; then Cutter headed south, in pursuit of a convoy thought to be headed for Saipan. He took station at the normal channel, but the convoy gave him the slip and went into Saipan by a new route.

Another convoy soon came along. Cutter found it on April 8 and attacked, firing three torpedoes each at two freighters. He sank two ships: *Aratama Maru*, a 6,784-ton converted submarine tender, and *Kizugawa Maru*, a 1,915-ton freighter. Both were loaded with troops and supplies for the defense of the Marianas.

Meanwhile, *Trigger*, with a new skipper, Fritz Harlfinger, set off for patrol at Palau. His exec was the seemingly indefatigable Ned Beach, who had made all eight of *Trigger*'s patrols under Jack Lewis, Roy Benson, and Dusty Dornin. Lockwood detoured *Trigger* to the Marianas to lend Cutter a hand.

On April 8, while Cutter was sinking his two ships, Harlfinger found one of the largest convoys anyone in the submarine force had ever seen. Manning the periscope, Ned Beach counted four columns of ships—tankers, freighters, transports, and auxiliaries—with about five ships in each column surrounded by ten or more escorts. *Trig-*

ger's fire-control party set up to fire a ten-torpedo salvo at a tanker and two other targets.

After Harlfinger had fired four torpedoes, a destroyer charged in, firing machine guns at the periscope. It was so close that it blanked out Beach's vision. Harlfinger ordered a deep dive, but nobody in the conning tower believed *Trigger* would make it in time; the destroyer was too close. Beach thought, "How long does it take a depth charge to sink fifty feet?"

Apparently it had all happened too fast for the depth-charge team on the destroyer. The first explosion the men in *Trigger's* conning tower heard were "four solid torpedo hits" which were, Beach believed, two in the tanker and two in a freighter. By then *Trigger* had reached 300 feet.

A nightmare followed. The destroyer dropped twenty-five depth charges. They were, Beach wrote, "absolute beauties. . . . How *Trigger* managed to hold together we'll never know." Lights went out. Cork insulation flew. Switches came undone. Valves leaked. The hull buckled in and out.

Then, as Beach remembered later, six of the escorts formed a ring around *Trigger*, keeping the submarine at the center. Every half hour or so, one charged in to pummel *Trigger* with a new series of charges. The attack went on for eighteen hours. Water leaked up to the level of the floor plates in the forward torpedo room. The temperature in the boat rose to 135 degrees. It was, Beach reported, a "long and horrible day," the worst beating *Trigger* had ever received, and one of the worst on record.

During the late afternoon, Harlfinger and Beach decided to surface and fight their way clear. They would make ready all torpedoes and man the deck gun. However, around sunset the escorts became lax, and *Trigger* slipped out of the deadly circle. That night, Harlfinger surfaced and set a course for the Palaus.

On the following day, April 9, Slade Cutter intercepted this same large convoy as it neared Saipan. It was, Cutter estimated, a fifteen-to-twenty ship convoy, the "largest we have ever seen." Cutter set up and fired four torpedoes from a range of 1,800 yards. "There were four ships overlapping in the field of the periscope with no open water between them," Cutter reported. However, just as Cutter fired, the targets zigged and all four torpedoes missed. One of the four made a circular run and, Cutter reported, "passed close aboard several times." Cutter fired two more at a freighter and obtained two hits. He lost depth control and went deep, just as two destroyers swung over dropping depth charges. Cutter went deeper.

Later that night, when Cutter came up, he found the freighter he hit still afloat, guarded by two destroyers. "Most discouraging," Cutter wrote. He moved in for another attack, but planes drove him under. Postwar records showed that the ship, *Bisaku Maru*, a 4,467-ton freighter, sank anyway.

On April 20, while Cutter was patrolling submerged off Saipan, he suddenly sighted a small RO-class Japanese submarine. Setting up fast, he fired two torpedoes from 1,800 yards. Again he lost depth control and went unavoidably deep. He reported one very loud explosion, "the loudest we have ever heard or felt." Cutter believed, "It must have been helped by an explosion in the target." The submarine was *RO-45*.

A week later, April 27, Cutter picked up yet another convoy about forty-five miles west of Saipan. It consisted of four freighters, a destroyer, and three smaller escorts. He attacked, firing four torpedoes at a freighter. Three hit, and down went 5,244-ton *Akigawa Maru*. Cutter's score: five ships (including *RO-45*) for 19,500 tons. In three patrols, Cutter had sunk fifteen ships—five on each time out.

Arriving at Palau on April 14, *Trigger* rendezvoused with Dick O'Kane in *Tang*. Following the air strike on the Palaus, Operation Desecrate, O'Kane had had a discouraging two weeks. The seas were empty of targets. He gave *Trigger* some spare parts to repair her damage and headed eastward toward Truk.

Patrolling off the Palaus, Harlfinger and Beach picked up a six-ship convoy on the night of April 26. Harlfinger attacked, firing six torpedoes at overlapping targets and obtaining four hits. He believed he had sunk two freighters and an escort. He chased the remaining three, attacking again, believing he sank two more and damaged the other. Harlfinger received credit for sinking five ships for 33,200 tons, but JANAC reduced that to one ship sunk off the Palaus, the large 11,700-ton transport *Miike Maru*.

When *Trigger* returned from patrol, she was found to be so weakened by her encounter with the escorts off the Marianas that she required a lengthy overhaul. During that period, Ned Beach went to new construction.

Herbert Jukes, who had sunk three tankers on his first patrol on *Kingfish*, en route from Fremantle to Pearl Harbor, took the boat to the Marianas. The patrol was unsuccessful. The endorsements pointed out that "opportunities to attack were missed on three occasions." One of these was a convoy. The endorsement stated, "The Commanding Officer apparently became confused and went deep, losing an opportunity to attack. The convoy passed over *Kingfish* fifteen minutes later."

Jukes—who had lost *S-27* in Alaska—retained command for one more patrol, also unsuccessful. Then he was relieved of command.

Patrols to Okinawa

When Donc Donaho finally left *Flying Fish*, Lockwood gave the boat to an officer far different in character and turn of mind. This was Robert Risser, who had made two patrols as exec to Roy Gross in *Seawolf*. Risser, who had a master's degree in ordnance, had graduated in the top 10 percent of the class of 1934; Donaho had graduated in the bottom 10 percent of the class of 1927. Where Donaho had been indifferent to personal relationships and the welfare of his men, Risser was thoughtful, easygoing, self-effacing. He inherited one of the best-trained crews in the submarine force. Walt Small, class of 1938, remained as exec.

On his first patrol, Risser had taken the boat to Formosa Strait and sunk two ships, a large tanker, 10,171 tons, and a large transport, 8,613 tons. On his second patrol, he went to the area near Okinawa. On the way out, he sank a ship near Iwo Jima. Off Okinawa, he dodged torpedoes from a Japanese submarine and attacked a convoy, sinking a 5,439-ton transport. Returning home, he found a freighter at anchor off Daito Jima, a tiny island east of Okinawa, sank it, and then returned to Majuro for refit. In two skillful patrols, Risser had sunk five ships for 28,712 tons.

Beetle Roach in *Haddock*, going on his second patrol, became involved in one of the most unusual Ultra episodes of the submarine war. On board for this patrol for a PCO cruise was William Joseph Germershausen, who had served in peacetime on *Nautilus* and then demothballed and commanded *O-6*. Since the outbreak of the war, Germershausen, like Jim Blanchard on *Albacore*, had been stuck at the Submarine School "hollering like hell to get out." He reached Pearl Harbor in January 1944 and was assigned to *Haddock*.

The patrol, also conducted in the Okinawa area, was long and dull. Roach made two attacks on small vessels, claiming to have sunk one escort for 1,000 tons, but there had been nothing big or challenging.

On the way home, Roach received an Ultra. As Germershausen remembered it, the message ordered *Haddock* to intercept a small supply boat which was taking food and "many classified documents" to Wake Island; the documents might have included new codebooks for the Japanese garrison stationed there. The Ultra gave specific times and positions for the ship. On the way to the intercept, Roach and Germershausen planned to capture the ship intact and sail it back to Pearl Harbor, like privateers. They argued over who would take command of the captured vessel.

Unknown to Roach and Germershausen, Lockwood had also alerted another boat to intercept this important little ship. This was *Tuna*, commanded by James Hardin, who had just returned from long overhaul and was setting off on his second patrol. Hardin made contact first and attacked with his 5-inch deck gun.

Germershausen recalled:

We reached the intercept point and suddenly Roach, who was at the periscope, saw the little ship—and shells hitting it. It burst into flames. We surfaced immediately and joined in the fun. She was already on her way down. We put a rubber boat in the water. An officer and an enlisted man from Haddock went in the rubber boat to pick up classified documents which were floating out of the sinking ship all over the water.

I was then the Officer of the Deck. I asked Roach if I could join the fellows in the water. He said, "Yes, go ahead." I took off my clothes and jumped over the side and grabbed some of the papers. Books and things. Meanwhile, people from the Tuna were doing the same thing. We were all in the water together, the Japanese, ourselves, the floating documents and the sinking ship.

When I got back to the boat, we watched the officer and the enlisted man in the raft from Haddock. They had found two Japanese whom they wanted to take as prisoners. The Japanese didn't want to come on board. So the officer whacked them across the head with a paddle and then they came aboard.

During the efforts to salvage the ship's papers, Hardin lost one of his men. The chief of the boat, John Kirkman Huff, apparently a non-swimmer, fell over the side and disappeared.

Tuna and *Haddock* recovered only about thirty documents apiece. Roach took these—and the two prisoners—and turned them all over to the intelligence center at Pearl Harbor. Germershausen was disappointed that Hardin had attacked and sunk the vessel. Had *Haddock* captured it, he believed, they could have gotten much more classified material. The little trawler—*Takima Maru*—would have been a fine trophy for Admiral Lockwood.

Hardin took *Tuna* on to patrol near the Palaus but made no attacks. After his third patrol—again, with no attacks—his division commander, Dutch Will (who had come up from Australia on *Tuna*), wrote Lockwood, "I again wish to state that I do not recommend Hardin for another patrol nor do I recommend him for new construction." Hardin was relieved after these three patrols on *Tuna* and went to be exec of the tender *Bushnell*. Hardin said later, "It is true that we had poor results on the three patrols when I had command."

27

Australia, January through March 1944

Codebreaking and the New Guinea Campaign

In the Southwest Pacific, General MacArthur continued his portion of the "two roads" to Tokyo strategy, the reconquest of New Guinea. There had been one important revision in his plan: Rabaul and Kavieng would be bypassed. He concentrated on north New Guinea.

On the eve of this push, the general became the beneficiary of a valuable intelligence legacy from the Japanese. In January 1944, following a landing on the northeast coast of New Guinea, one of MacArthur's army units found a trunkful of Japanese army codebooks, buried in the sand along the beach. The covers had been carefully removed and perhaps sent to Tokyo as "proof of destruction," but the books were intact. They were rushed to MacArthur's intelligence center in Brisbane and turned over to MacArthur's Navy Intelligence Chief and Japanese linguist, Arthur McCollum.

McCollum discovered to his delight that the books were still current. To help with the translations, he put in a call to the codebreaking unit, FRUMEL, to ask for the loan of two linguists.

There had been changes in the unit at FRUMEL. In September 1943 the Naval Communicators in Washington sent out Ernest Sidney Goodwin to relieve Rudolph Fabian as commander of the unit. In January 1944, following the turnover, Fabian was transferred to serve with the Commander in Chief, British Eastern Fleet in India,

580 AUSTRALIA, JANUARY–MARCH 1944

to coordinate the codebreaking functions of the United States and the Allies. Swede Carlson returned to duty in Washington.

On the lower levels there had also been changes. Rufus Taylor had returned to Washington for duty. Forrest Rosecrans ("Tex") Biard moved down from FRUPAC to FRUMEL to help Tom Mackie with the heavy hauling. Gill Richardson and John Lietwiler were still the leading codebreakers for the unit. They were now assisted by many of the former enlisted men on Corregidor who had been field-promoted to officer rank.

In response to McCollum's call, Goodwin picked his two best linguists, Tom Mackie and Tex Biard. Mackie and Biard traveled to Brisbane and reported to McCollum, who turned over the books and sent the two men to work with army intelligence officers. "The books were beautiful," Mackie recalled. "I guess the Japanese general who had charge of them couldn't bear to see them destroyed."

For the next twelve days Mackie and Biard, using the codebooks, eavesdropped on conversations between the Japanese generals in charge of defending New Guinea. "They were arguing back and forth," Mackie recalled, "about which places should be heavily defended and which places they ought to ignore." When the Japanese generals finally resolved the debate, MacArthur knew not only the places marked for defense concentrations but how many soldiers and aircraft would be assigned to each. His staff then laid plans to move up the New Guinea coast by invading the lightly defended areas and bypassing those that were heavily defended.

The outcome was one of the most remarkable chapters in the history of the Pacific War. Having slogged painfully up through the Solomons for seventeen long months, the Allies conquered much of the northern coast of New Guinea in a few weeks with almost no casualties.

Bypassing Japanese strongholds at Wewak and Hansa Bay, MacArthur's troops prepared to strike the Hollandia area on April 22, landing at three points: Aitape, Humboldt Bay, and Tanahmerah. As a preliminary to these landings, Admiral Nimitz sent fast carrier task forces (a total of twelve carriers) from Majuro for an air strike. On the way back, April 30, the carriers hit Truk again, wiping out the last of the Japanese aircraft based there and sinking most everything left afloat in the harbor.

During this raid, there were several Pearl Harbor boats lying off Truk lifeguarding: Dick O'Kane's *Tang*, returning from his long

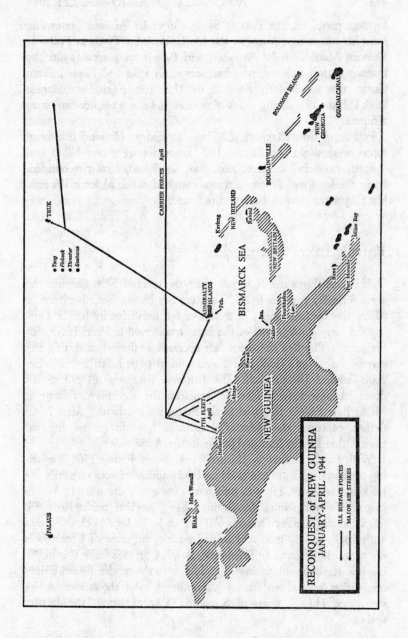

RECONQUEST of NEW GUINEA
JANUARY-APRIL 1944

U.S. SURFACE FORCES
MAJOR AIR STRIKES

CARRIER FORCES April

TRUK

• Tang
• Finback
• Threadfin
• Seahorse

ADMIRALTY
ISLANDS
Feb.

BISMARCK SEA

Kavieng

NEW IRELAND

Rabaul

NEW BRITAIN

SOLOMON ISLANDS

GUADALCANAL

NEW GEORGIA

BOUGAINVILLE

7TH FLEET
April

Hollandia

Aitape

Wewak

Hansa
Bay

Saidor

Finschhafen
Lae

Madang

Buna

Port Moresby

Milne Bay

NEW GUINEA

PALAUS

BIAK

Mios Woendi

luckless patrol off the Palaus; Slade Cutter in *Seahorse*, returning from his spectacular patrol in the Marianas; John Tyree in *Finback*; Duncan MacMillan in *Thresher*; and *Permit*, now commanded by Donald Arthur Scherer, who had served on *Pike* and *Lapon*. Slade Cutter was accidentally bombed by U.S. forces (slight damage); Dick O'Kane in a daring series of rescues picked up twenty-two naval airmen.

Following this, MacArthur's forces landed at Hollandia. Enemy forces were slight. At Aitape, U.S. casualties were two killed and thirteen wounded; at Humboldt Bay, six killed, sixteen wounded. After the landings, Japanese troops marched overland from Wewak, but they were thrown back and defeated.

Patrols from Fremantle

As MacArthur's troops advanced up the coast of New Guinea, the areas formerly covered by U.S. submarines basing from Brisbane or Milne Bay became empty of targets or fell into friendly hands. During the early spring, most of the boats transferred to Pearl Harbor or Fremantle. The few that were left operated as lifeguards during the carrier strikes on Truk and Palau and patrolled farther to westward—around Davao Gulf. The Brisbane base was all but closed down. A new tender, *Eurayle*, replaced the workhorse *Fulton* at Milne Bay; *Fulton* returned to the States for overhaul.* After MacArthur captured the Admiralty Islands, *Eurayle* moved forward from Milne Bay to Manus Harbor in the Admiralties.

With the reduction in Brisbane operations, Jimmy Fife (an acting commodore) had little to do and not sufficient forces to justify his rank and seniority. He was transferred back to shore duty in Washington as a war planner for Admiral King, working under Rear Admiral Donald Bradley Duncan. All the while, he kept in close contact with Lockwood by mail and helped push along some of Lockwood's pet technical projects. In Fremantle, Ralph Christie's force was building toward thirty submarines. In addition to the tender *Pelias*, a new one, *Orion*, arrived on January 5. Another, *Griffin*, the tender for the re-engined H.O.R. boats of Squadron Twelve, came later in the spring.

* Administratively, Squadron Eighteen, commanded by Eliot Hinman ("Swede") Bryant, replaced Squadron Eight.

Fife's departure created some changes in Christie's command. John Haines, commanding Squadron Sixteen in *Pelias*, was named to succeed Fife as overall boss of submarine operations at Brisbane–Milne Bay–Manus Harbor. Upon Haines's departure, Tex McLean, Christie's waterfront boss, assumed additional duties as commander of Squadron Sixteen. The other key men, P. G. Nichols (chief of staff) and Murray Tichenor (operations), remained in place. Frederick Kent Loomis filled the post vacated by Dutch Will as chief maintenance officer.

During the early months of 1944, Christie continued the war on Japanese shipping—with priority on tankers—in much the same manner as in the late months of 1943. With refueling facilities available in Darwin, many boats made double-barreled patrols. Many edged up into Luzon Strait, where skippers exchanged information on convoys with Pearl Harbor boats operating in the same area. In February, when Admiral Koga ordered his major fleet units to abandon Truk and withdraw to the west, many of these went to Davao, Tawi Tawi, Surabaya, and Singapore—all ports in Christie's area. As the spring progressed, Christie's boats spent much time lying in wait for these units, helped by information from the codebreakers. He also continued the many special missions requested by General MacArthur. Most were carried forward by *Narwhal* (joined at Darwin by *Nautilus* in April), but many fleet boats were also diverted for this purpose.

Although Christie had ordered his submarines to deactivate the magnetic exploder on January 20, he was not yet ready to let go entirely. He set two officers in the PCO pool to work on a study of the exploder: young Chester Nimitz and James Lowell Page McCallum, who had a master's degree in ordnance. After an exhaustive technical study, Nimitz and McCallum evolved some new ideas for improving the reliability of the exploder. Christie ordered the torpedo shops to modify some exploders along the lines they suggested and then sent them to sea, but many of them exploded prematurely, and they proved as unreliable as any of the earlier versions.

A new boat, *Redfin*, commanded by Robert Donovan King,* reported from the States in January. His exec was Mike Shea, who had served on *Gar* and *Gudgeon*. *Redfin* went on patrol from Darwin. On January 9, King found a convoy and fired a salvo of three tor-

* No kin to Chief of Naval Operations Admiral King.

pedoes, his first war shots. All three exploded prematurely. After surfacing, King found pieces of his own torpedoes scattered along his deck.

A week later King found a destroyer, *Amatsukaze*. He fired four torpedoes down the throat from a range of 2,900 yards. King believed he got four hits and that the destroyer sank. However, *Amatsukaze* survived the encounter and limped into the nearest port with eighty of her crew dead from the explosions. The ship was out of action for a full year.

On return to Fremantle, King complained of eye trouble. He had a blind spot on his retina, perhaps caused by not using a sunshade on the periscope while looking into the sun. Christie relieved King of command and sent him to a hospital for treatment. Later the spot diminished, and King took command of the submarine repair unit in Brisbane.

Tom Hogan in Christie's flagship, *Bonefish*, conducted a third aggressive patrol off Indochina. On the way out, he received an Ultra from Christie cautioning him that Balabac Strait had just been mined. Hogan went through anyway, taking care to remain in deep water. All the boats that followed him did likewise.

While south of Camranh Bay, Hogan received another Ultra, reporting the movement of an important tanker convoy. "It was coming down the coast and going into harbors to anchor for the night," Hogan said later. Actually, the convoy turned out to be two days late. When Hogan found it, he set up on a huge whale-factory tanker. "The area between the bridge and the after superstructure had been decked over," Hogan recalled. "I counted twenty aircraft as cargo."

Hogan penetrated the screen and fired three torpedoes at the tanker. A destroyer charged, forcing *Bonefish* to the bottom, where Hogan wiped off a sonar head. Hogan heard three hits in the tanker, but she did not sink. After dark, Hogan surfaced and tried to find the convoy again, but it was gone.

Jim Dempsey in *Cod* patrolled the same area. On the way out, he sank two ships, including a 7,350-ton tanker. After that, most of the crew came down with poisoning from tetrachloride or food. Christie sent Dempsey an Ultra on an important tanker convoy, but Dempsey and the crew were so ill they were not able to carry off an attack.

"The commanding officer accepts full responsibility for this fiasco," Dempsey wrote later. "The officers and crew, nearly all of whom are still suffering from the effects [of the] poisoning, did the best they could. Nothing seemed to click and each unsuccessful attempt to gain attack position made the next try more difficult."

Walt Griffith in *Bowfin* made a double-barreled patrol. On the first half, he patrolled the South China Sea. In a furious few days of action, Griffith fired off most of his torpedoes, sinking one confirmed freighter for 4,408 tons and damaging several other ships.

After a mere fourteen days, Griffith was back in Darwin to obtain a load of torpedoes and more fuel. In addition, he received some mines and orders to plant them off the coast of Borneo. Ralph Christie, still eager to make a brief submarine war patrol, decided to go with Griffith on this second leg. Not wanting to risk another turndown, he did not ask permission of his new boss, Admiral Kinkaid.

Leaving P. G. Nichols and Murray Tichenor in charge, Christie flew to Darwin on January 29 and joined *Bowfin*. The mines had been loaded on board. In addition, Griffith carried sixteen torpedoes. The boat got under way immediately. Christie established his quarters in the wardroom, sleeping in a pull-down bunk over the wardroom table. He was quite pleased with himself. "If I came back," he wrote later, "I would be congratulated. If I did not, well . . ."

On the evening of the second night out, Griffith found a 4,300-ton merchant ship en route from Ambon to Timor, bringing food and supplies to the Japanese garrison. While Christie stood on the bridge looking on from a "box seat," Griffith swung and fired two torpedoes. Both hit, Christie reported later, and "sank the enemy ship in less than one minute." There was, he reported, "no applause—just silence —and everybody went about his own business." Postwar records failed to credit Griffith with sinking a ship on this day and at this place.

On the way to Borneo to lay the minefield, Griffith received an important Ultra from P. G. Nichols. A Japanese seaplane tender, the 17,000-ton *Kamoi*,* was en route to Makassar City. Griffith found her in the shallow waters of Salajar Strait the next night and trailed. She had three small escorts and air cover. Griffith could not achieve a firing position that night. He tracked her all the following day on the surface, diving eight times to avoid detection by Japanese

* Converted from a 20-knot tanker originally built in the United States.

aircraft. During the afternoon, Rear Admiral Christie stood watch as officer of the deck so the officers could rest up for the long night ahead.

That night about eleven o'clock, Griffith maneuvered around the escorts and attacked, firing six bow tubes. Owing to a fire-control error, all missed. The torpedoes alerted the escorts. They thrashed about, dropping depth charges at random to scare Griffith away. *Kamoi* began twisting and turning with radical zigs and zags to complicate Griffith's problem.

Griffith remained on the surface, maneuvering slowly for a second attack. Christie, who was on the bridge watching, became uneasy. "We were very close to him," Christie wrote. "Too close, within machine gun range. I thought we would dive, but [Griffith] chose to hold the initiative by remaining on the surface. . . . I thought surely he must see us. . . . I was most uncomfortable. . . . The enemy could easily have sunk us with gunfire or at least swept our bridge with machinegun fire."

Griffith swung around and fired two stern tubes from a range of about 1,000 yards. Christie heard the first torpedo leave the tube. He wrote, "I could see the luminous wake and WHAM! an enormous detonation which shook us up as though our own ship had been hit. We got two hits smack under his bridge this time. Debris was thrown skyward in a background of fire and smoke. I was slammed against the bridge railing by the force of the explosion and broke my binocular strap and lost my cap."

About then, the target responded with searchlights and gunfire. To Christie, the light seemed like a "million flashbulbs." After it came whizzing shells: 4-inch, 40-mm., and 20-mm. Griffith raced away from the target and then cleared the bridge of all personnel except himself. Admiral Christie lunged for the hatch like any lookout. "I don't think I hit a rung of the ladder to the conning tower."

There was one torpedo remaining aft. Griffith was determined to put it in *Kamoi*. He outran the guns, then swung around in the darkness, avoiding the searchlights. He set up and fired. Christie, taking station in the forward torpedo room, believed he heard a hit, but it was drowned out by the diving alarm. Griffith took *Bowfin* to 442 feet to evade. No depth charges followed. For that, Christie was grateful.

Kamoi did not sink. Christie learned from Ultra reports that, following the attack, the Japanese beached her. Later, they towed her into Surabaya for temporary repairs. Months later, according to Christie, she was towed to Singapore for major repairs.

Following this action, Griffith took *Bowfin* to the approaches to Balikpapan, where he planted the small minefield. On the way home, he shot up two sampans "loaded with cement." Then he dropped Christie at Exmouth Gulf, where a plane was waiting to fly him back to Fremantle. Christie arrived back at his office nine days after departing, the second oldest officer* and first force commander—and admiral—in the history of the U.S. Navy to make a submarine war patrol. In this two-part patrol, Griffith had fired a total of thirty-five torpedoes, achieving sixteen hits.

After a brief refit, Griffith went out again for his third patrol, another double-barrel. This time he carried a special load of the "modified" exploders recommended by young Nimitz and McCallum. They did not work very well. During his thirty-three days at sea, Griffith attacked seven ships, firing forty-one torpedoes. Of these, *eight* of the first twenty-four prematured; fourteen hit, sinking three big freighters for 15,000 tons; others caused damage to two ships. During the patrol, Griffith took *Bowfin* into narrow, shallow, and restricted waters, received six close depth-charge attacks and three close bombs from aircraft, and was twice shot at by shore guns.

When Griffith came in from this patrol, Christie decided he should return to the States for new construction and rest. To replace him, Christie picked Frederick Williams Laing, who came from command of S-30 in Alaska. However, Laing was found to be suffering from gout, so the boat went to John Corbus, whom Christie had relieved in *Haddo* but believed deserved a second chance.

Gordon Selby, taking *Puffer* out for his second patrol, hunted north of Singapore. Shortly after sunset on the night of February 20, Selby found a ten-ship convoy made up of large ships, southbound. "Three of the first four ships sighted," he wrote later, "were very large, their superstructures having the triangular appearance of battleships and cruisers. . . . The night was too dark and the horizon too hazy to make out any definite type characteristics on the larger ships but the overall silhouettes were those of men-of-war and not freighters, tankers or transports."

Unaware at first that he had intercepted fast-moving combatant

* After Babe Brown in *Narwhal*, supporting the 1943 Sea of Japan foray.

ships, Selby underestimated the convoy's speed. He gave chase, but the formation soon pulled out of range. These ships were probably units of the Japanese main fleet, en route to Singapore from Truk or Japan to be closer to the oil supply.

In midafternoon on February 22, Selby picked up another convoy. This one was northbound and consisted of several medium or small freighters. Selby began chasing, looking for deeper water to make his attack. Meanwhile, high-periscope lookouts reported two more ships; Selby moved his periscope around and saw what appeared to be a large camouflaged transport with one escort, zigzagging.

Turning to attack, Selby fired two torpedoes at the transport and two at the escort. One torpedo hit the transport, throwing up a column of smoke and debris. Closing in, Selby saw lifeboats being lowered into the water. Selby fired two more torpedoes into the transport. Both hit. As the ship began to sink slowly by the stern, Selby took periscope pictures.

The ship, which soon slid beneath the waves, was later identified from Selby's excellent photographs as an ocean liner, *Teiko Maru*, 15,100 tons—which, as the French liner *D'Artagnan*, had been captured in the early days of the war. She was the third largest Japanese merchant ship sunk to that time, after Post's 17,526-ton liner *Kamakura Maru* and Tom Wogan's 16,975-ton liner *Tatsuta Maru*.

The rest of this patrol was frustrating. Selby found two more convoys, one of which he attempted to attack on three separate occasions but failed for one reason or another. "Except for *Teiko*, I was not too happy with our third patrol," Selby said later. "I should have had a big haul—too cautious I guess." When he returned to Fremantle, Selby received a "rude shock." After three days of "letting off steam," he went down to the docks and saw what appeared to be *Teiko* moored in a slip. It turned out to be her sister ship, *Porthos*, still in Allied hands.

Willard Laughon, making his second patrol as skipper of *Rasher*, got under way from Fremantle February 19, a day after James Davis left for his third patrol in *Raton*. Just north of Lombok Strait, Laughon received an Ultra on a convoy going from Surabaya to Ambon. Davis received the same report and joined with Laughon in a coordinated search. On February 25 the two boats rendezvoused and agreed on a battle plan. One and a half hours later, they found the convoy: two freighters with two escorts.

Laughon attacked first, just after dark, firing four torpedoes at one freighter from 1,000 yards and another four torpedoes at the second from 1,300 yards. He obtained three hits in each target, and both sank. They were *Tango Maru,* 6,200 tons, and *Ryusei Maru,* 4,800 tons. Laughon then noted in his report, "Told *Raton* that there were no more targets and that we were clearing the area and apologized for hogging the show."

Laughon took *Rasher* north through Molucca Passage to the Celebes Sea. On March 3, he picked up a big convoy: six freighters, three escorts. After a hard chase, during which his SJ radar went out of commission, he attacked at night, firing three torpedoes at one ship, three at another. Escorts drove him under, preventing another attack. One of the freighters, *Nittai Maru,* 6,400 tons, went down.

On the night of March 4, Laughon chased and attacked another convoy, firing two torpedoes at one ship and four at another. All missed or ran under. He swung, maneuvered, and fired his last four at another ship. It was a bad setup; all missed. Laughon returned to Darwin to take on another load of torpedoes and resume the patrol.

Davis in *Raton* went on to Indochina, where he joined in a loosely coordinated search with Brooks Harral in *Ray* (who had laid a minefield off Saigon), *Bluefish* (now commanded by Charles Mitchell Henderson, who had served on *Sculpin* and *Cabrilla*), and Selby in *Puffer.* On March 3, Christie sent all four boats an Ultra on a tanker convoy. Henderson in *Bluefish* sank one tanker for 10,500 tons, but the other three boats did not fare so well. Neither Davis nor Harral sank a confirmed ship on their patrols.

Haddo, brought down from Pearl Harbor by John Corbus, went to young Chester Nimitz, the first from the class of 1936 in Fremantle to get a command. Like Griffith, Nimitz carried a load of torpedoes with the modified magnetic exploders he and McCallum had designed. Nimitz went up through Lombok Strait in early March.

While Nimitz was en route, Ralph Christie received "evidence of a movement" (as he noted in his diary) of many Japanese men-of-war from Singapore to Surabaya, possibly a carrier, two battleships, three heavy cruisers, and many destroyers. The information—obtained from the codebreakers—led Christie to believe that the Japanese might be planning a hit-and-run attack against Fremantle, so he alerted Nimitz to patrol the north end of Lombok Strait and watch for a possible sortie south.

Early on the morning of March 12, while *Haddo* was slowly cruising 12 miles east of Bali, Nimitz noted in his log, "We are relying on our SJ radar to prevent somebody from running our blockade." That same morning, radar produced several large pips at ranges of 6,700 to 16,000 yards. Nimitz bent on full power, turning toward the bearings of the pips. They disappeared mysteriously.

Nimitz was torn: report these pips or not? He wrote later, "Finally decided to send message reporting possibility of enemy ships passing through Lombok. 'Remember Pearl Harbor' was the message that kept sticking in my mind."

In Fremantle, the Nimitz message touched off a monumental flap. Christie was now certain the Japanese were headed his way. He noted in his diary, "We are busy making 'Estimates of the Situation' and studying our defenses against a probable air raid by carrier planes." He ordered all submarines in refit except *Crevalle*, revamping her conning tower and lacking periscopes and radar, to stop work and get into "fully ready" status. *Flasher, Hoe, Robalo, Hake,* and *Redfin* got under way and stood out to sea to attack the incoming Japanese. Many aircraft were concentrated at Fremantle. The tenders there—*Pelias* and *Orion*—were sent to Albany. At sea, Laughon in *Rasher,* having just taken on board a new load of torpedoes at Darwin, was ordered to take position in Lombok Strait. William Thompson (who had been Griffith's exec on *Bowfin*), starting off on his first patrol in *Cabrilla,* was ordered to guard Sunda Strait and later to reconnoiter Christmas Island. Other boats were ordered to likely points of intercept, to catch the Japanese task force on the way back.

Tom Hogan in *Bonefish,* returning from Indochina, still had thirteen torpedoes on board but little fuel and food. He put into Exmouth Gulf, picking up fuel and ten sheep and fifteen lambs. Returning to sea, to stand watch off the approaches to Fremantle, *Bonefish* ran into a tremendous hurricane with winds as high as 120 knots. The storm lasted three days. Hogan's men got seasick. The cook prepared lamb and mutton sandwiches, all that he could put out in those mountainous seas. "It was the worst thing you can imagine," Hogan wrote later. "And when we got into Fremantle and got to the hotel, the first meal they served us was lamb stew!"

MacArthur did not send as many aircraft as Christie would have liked. On March 10 he noted in his diary, "So we face zero hour—dawn Saturday, March 11—without much help from Mr. Kenney's [General George C. Kenney] famed 5th Air Force. Despite the tremendous development of aircraft, they are not yet that independent of the weather to the extent that ships are. Twenty-three aircraft arrived out of 82 ordered."

Zero hour passed without an attack. Christie delayed zero hour another day, thinking perhaps the Japanese task force had been slowed by the storm. On Sunday, March 12, he noted, "No Japs this morning as expected."

The Japs never did appear; it had all been a false alarm. Christie wrote Lockwood, "The 'threat to Fremantle' was a lot of fun and of value to the area. The highlight, in my opinion, was the remarkable performance of the tenders in getting out seven boats under refit to sea fully ready for offensive operations within twelve hours."

Laughon in *Rasher* spent eighteen terrible days on station in Lombok Strait to intercept the expected forces, constantly harassed by Japanese patrol boats. After being released from this hazardous assignment, he went on to sink another ship for 2,700 tons. In all, his total for this double-barreled patrol was four ships for 20,100 tons.

Unaware of the commotion he had stirred up, Nimitz continued his patrol. On March 8, two nights after his encounter with the mysterious pips in Lombok Strait, he came upon a submarine tender and escort. Nimitz set up and fired three torpedoes with his modified magnetic exploders. Two of the three prematured after twenty-three seconds, and the third missed aft when the tender, alerted by the premature explosions, veered away. After that, Nimitz deactivated the experimental magnetic exploders. Later he said, "I told Christie that night by [radio] dispatch that I was inactivating all of my remaining exploders and suggested that somebody get back to the drawing board."

On March 12, Christie noted in his diary, "We have reached the positive end of the long trail with the magnetic exploder. . . . From now on BuOrd can do the experimenting. . . . Finis!"

Nimitz went up Makassar Strait. On the night of March 14, off Balikpapan, he found a tanker escorted by a destroyer and fired three torpedoes at each, but missed. Off Indochina on March 29, he attacked a seven-ship convoy, damaging at least one large freighter but achieving no sinkings. On April 1 he fired at a shallow-draft coastal steamer, but the torpedoes ran under. On April 5 he found another tanker but was driven off by accurate gunfire. On the way home, he was ordered to pick up a group of guerrillas on the northeast coast of Borneo, but the rendezvous misfired and he could not find them.

In addition, Nimitz was alerted to yet another special mission. Rumors came down from the Philippines that Admiral Koga had not been killed in the plane crash after the U.S. raid on the Palaus but was in fact being held prisoner by MacArthur's guerrilla chief on Cebu, Lieutenant James Cushing. MacArthur requested a submarine to pick up Admiral Koga. Christie, thinking what a fine story it would make if young Nimitz "delivered" Admiral Koga to Australia, ordered Nimitz to stand by in the Sulu Sea. As it turned out, Cushing had captured not Koga (who was definitely dead) but Koga's chief of staff, Admiral Shigeru Fukudome. However, Fukudome escaped and the Nimitz mission was cancelled.

John Broach in *Hake* and Marshall Harlan ("Cy") Austin, new skipper of *Redfin*, both found important Japanese men-of-war.

On April 3, Broach in *Hake*, patrolling off the west coast of Borneo on the Singapore-Manila traffic lanes, picked up a *Shokaku*-class aircraft carrier escorted by two destroyers. The force was making 22 knots, and Broach was unable to gain a favorable attack position. Later that morning he found two light cruisers and fired four stern tubes at one, believing he obtained a hit. On April 8 he picked up four cruisers and five destroyers but was unable to close.

Cy Austin, patrolling on the other side of Borneo in the Celebes Sea, also sighted several cruisers. He picked up the first, a light cruiser, on April 1 and closed to 8,000 yards, but the ship got away. On April 8, he sighted two cruisers, one heavy and one light. He closed to 10,000 yards, but again the men-of-war slipped out of range. On April 12, he sighted yet another light cruiser escorted by destroyers. Austin went in, closing the range to 2,800 yards. During the approach, the TDC went out of commission, fouling the attack, but Austin fired four stern tubes anyway. All missed.

Both Broach and Austin got bags of a different kind. Off Borneo, Broach sank a tanker, *Yamamizu Maru*, 5,174 tons, and damaged others. Austin sank two medium-sized freighters and the destroyer *Akigumo* for 10,300 confirmed tons. On the way home, Austin was ordered to pick up the guerrillas on northeast Borneo that Nimitz had missed. His small boat was ambushed by the Japanese, who very nearly killed four of his men. He had to leave the guerrillas behind.

28

Australia,
April through June 1944

Showdown in the Marianas

In May 1944 the Allied juggernaut in the Pacific—reinforced by more carriers, amphibious craft, soldiers, marines, and airmen—rolled swiftly down the twin roads to Tokyo. At Pearl Harbor, Admiral Nimitz laid final plans for the invasion of the Marianas. As a preliminary, the carrier task forces prepared to make air strikes. In western New Guinea, MacArthur's forces, supported by Admiral Kinkaid's growing naval force, leaped from Hollandia to Wakde and Sarmi (May 18) and then to the island of Biak (May 27). During these operations, a British-U.S. task force conducted an air strike on Surabaya (May 17).

Admiral Toyoda, who had replaced Admiral Koga as commander in chief of the Japanese combined fleet, was determined to make a stand in the Marianas and the Palaus, to blunt any further westward movement of Allied forces. His battle plan, issued on May 4, was known as A-Go. It called for the Japanese army and navy to reinforce the Marianas, Palau, and the Philippines with troops and aircraft. All Japanese forces would fight to the death. Toyoda (like Koga before him) hoped to draw the U.S. Pacific Fleet into a decisive battle near the Palaus which he would win with the help of land-based aircraft supplementing his inferior carrier forces. In addition, he established a line of submarines between Truk and New Guinea to intercept the fleet.

Toyoda ordered the major units of the Japanese fleet to assemble at Tawi Tawi, the big anchorage off the northeast coast of Borneo. Carriers, battleships, and cruisers steamed down from Japan and over from the anchorage at Lingga Roads near Singapore. With them came a steady stream of fleet tankers and auxiliaries. While the fleet was staging at Tawi Tawi, the tankers shunted back and forth between Tawi Tawi and Borneo, hauling oil. The codebreakers followed these movements, predicting courses, speeds, and rendezvous points with a high degree of accuracy.

Both submarine forces—Christie's in Australia, Lockwood's in Pearl Harbor—geared for the coming showdown. Their primary missions: (1) to intercept, report, and attack Japanese fleet units, troop convoys, and tankers based on Ultra information; (2) to report movements of major Japanese fleet units and other vessels discovered without the help of Ultra information, and then attack; and (3) to provide advance reconnaissance on islands to be struck or invaded and lifeguard support during preliminary raids.

Christie's submarines carried out all three missions with much success.

Eric Lloyd Barr, Jr., son of a noted World War I submariner who had commanded *E-1*, arrived at Milne Bay in a new boat, *Bluegill*. Barr, who had served as exec to Rebel Lowrance on *Kingfish*, was notoriously aggressive and determined to uphold the family's fine name in submarines.

Barr patrolled near Halmahera. On about April 26 he received an Ultra: the light cruiser *Yubari* and destroyer escorts were en route from Davao with 900 troop reinforcements for the tiny island of Sonsorol, lying between Halmahera and Palau. Another boat, *Blackfish*, commanded by Robert Sellars, was also directed to the scene. Early on the morning of April 27, *Bluegill* and *Blackfish* met off Sonsorol.

At about 4:20 A.M., Barr's radar operator reported two high-speed pips on radar headed for Sonsorol. Barr moved to intercept. At 7:07, he spotted the tops of ships coming out of a rainsquall, range 13 miles. Barr dived, but the ships eluded him and reached the island, where they unloaded troops. Later in the morning, Barr saw a destroyer lying to off the island. He was preparing to attack it when suddenly *Yubari* appeared. Undeterred by two depth charges from Japanese aircraft, Barr set up quickly and fired six torpedoes at the cruiser, range 2,600 yards. Three hit and *Yubari*, 3,300 tons, often shot at by U.S. submarines, went down.

The destroyer, *Samidare*, charged at *Bluegill*. Barr swung his stern tubes to bear and fired four torpedoes down the throat. All missed. *Samidare* unleashed a persistent depth-charge attack, driving *Bluegill* deep. Later, three other destroyers joined *Samidare*, and Barr, believing in discretion, eased away.

Eric Barr was the third skipper within a period of a few weeks to sink a light cruiser on his first war patrol. The others were Bud Gruner in *Skate* (*Agano*, February 16) and Malcolm Garrison in *Sandlance* (*Tatsuta*, March 13).

The Japanese organized a convoy at Shanghai for the purpose of lifting two divisions of reinforcements to New Guinea. The convoy, commanded by Rear Admiral Sadamichi Kajioka, who had captured Wake and led the Port Moresby invasion forces during the Battle of the Coral Sea, headed for Manila. Kajioka's flagship was a coal-burning minelayer, *Shirataka*, which gave off heavy smoke. The convoy left Shanghai on April 17, its progress followed closely by the codebreakers.

Two of Christie's boats were patrolling near Manila as the convoy approached: Tommy Dyker's *Jack* and Jim Dempsey's *Cod*. On the morning of April 26, *Jack* intercepted the convoy off the northwest coast of Luzon. As Dykers was taking up position, he spotted a Japanese submarine and evaded at high speed. A few minutes later, a plane came over and dropped a bomb. Dykers was certain the Japanese would route the convoy around him, but they didn't; at noon, Dykers picked up the heavy smoke of the flagship *Shirataka* again and trailed. An hour before sunset he surfaced to make an end around, but a plane came over and drove him down.

After dark, Dykers again surfaced and tracked the convoy, waiting for moonset. When it came, he moved in to attack. The escorts were more alert than usual, and Dykers, trying one side and then the other, couldn't find a hole. Finally he decided to shoot spreads of low-speed torpedoes under the escorts at the mass of overlapping targets in the convoy. In three separate attacks, he fired off nineteen torpedoes. They appeared to hit, and Dykers believed he had sunk one or more, but Christie only credited Dykers with damage to five ships.

In the postwar accounting, however, it was discovered that Dykers had hit and sunk a very valuable target, the 5,425-ton freighter *Yo-*

shida Maru I, packed with an army regiment of 3,000 men. She sank quickly, and all the troops, including the regimental commander, drowned. After that disaster, the convoy put into Manila, where it received more escorts before setting off again.

Jim Dempsey in *Cod* was unable to attack this convoy, but he made his presence felt later; on May 10, he attacked a convoy off the west coast of Luzon, sinking an old 820-ton destroyer and a big 7,200-ton freighter and damaging two other ships. Upon return to Fremantle, Dempsey stepped down as commander of *Cod,* going to serve as operations officer on Freeland Daubin's staff. Jim Dempsey had made a record ten Pacific war patrols as commanding officer, three on *S-37,* four on *Spearfish,* and three on *Cod.*

Herb Andrews in *Gurnard,* one of the last of the re-engined H.O.R. boats to shift from Pearl Harbor to Fremantle, went by way of Manila. Andrews had yet another new exec, his fourth in four patrols, George Stuart Simmons III. By then, Admiral Kajioka's convoy was under way from Manila, bound for New Guinea, now re-inforced by more destroyers. Christie put Andrews on the track.

Andrews intercepted on May 6 in the Celebes Sea. He submerged and began a slow, cautious approach to avoid detection by aircraft. Four hours later, the convoy bore down on him: eight transports in three columns with many escorts.

Andrews let a destroyer escort go by, then fired a salvo of six bow tubes at two of the transports in the near column. One torpedo of his first salvo hit his first target, but the second salvo missed the second target and traveled on to the far column, hitting another transport. Andrews swung around and fired his stern tubes, which hit the second target. An escort charged up, and Andrews went deep as about a hundred depth charges rained down, none close. Two hours later, Andrews came up cautiously, raising the periscope to find three sinking ships and a massive rescue operation in progress. He cruised around for a while, taking photographs through the periscope, and later that night he fired at one of the cripples which was still afloat.

In all, Andrews had sunk three big ships crammed with soldiers and equipment, the transports *Aden Maru,* 5,824 tons, and *Taijima Maru,* 6,995 tons, and a cargo ship, *Tenshinzan Maru,* 6,886 tons. (Andrews was told later that about 6,000 Japanese troops drowned that day. It is possible but not probable. Jasper Holmes reported after the war that the rescue operations had been unusually efficient, with the Japanese even lashing field guns to floating rafts.)

Since leaving Shanghai, the convoy had lost four valuable ships: one to Tommy Dykers on *Jack* and now three to Herb Andrews on *Gurnard*. What remained of the force went not to New Guinea, as planned, but to Halmahera, where efforts were made to transship them to New Guinea by barge. These efforts either failed or came too late. Between them, Dykers and Andrews stopped the better part of two army divisions from reaching New Guinea.

Frank Walker, exec to Hank Munson on *Crevalle,* moved up to command when Munson stepped down. On his first time out as skipper, Walker patrolled off the west coast of Borneo. On April 25 he sank a small 1,000-ton freighter, but the next two weeks were a time of utter frustration. On April 26 he tried to attack an eight-ship convoy, but a destroyer beat him off. On May 3 he picked up two ships with one escort, tracked them in driving rain, and attacked after dark, firing eight torpedoes. (Walker believed he sank one ship, but postwar records failed to confirm it.) On May 4 he found a six-ship convoy, but it went into shallow water before he could attack.

On May 6—the day Herb Andrews sank three ships from the troop convoy—Walker's luck changed. He picked up an eleven-ship convoy with several destroyer escorts. With these ships was *Nisshin Maru,* 16,801 tons, a huge tanker (once a whale factory) similar to *Tonnan Maru III,* which Dan Daspit had tried to sink off Truk. Maneuvering in shallow water, less than 200 feet, Walker expertly outguessed swarms of escorts and circling planes and fired three torpedoes at *Nisshin Maru.* Two hit, and the great ship blew up and sank. It was the third largest Japanese merchant ship sunk to date.

The escorts counterattacked violently, dropping sixty-one close depth charges and aerial bombs. Walker took *Crevalle* to the bottom —only 174 feet—and lay still. A little later, there was a terrifying scraping sound along the outer hull. The Japanese, Walker believed, were trying to snare *Crevalle* with grappling hooks. This was more than anybody could stand. Walker got off the bottom and cleared the area safely.

After that, Walker was ordered to a special mission: proceed northward to Negros Island to evacuate refugees. He took aboard a total of forty-one, including thirty-five women and children. Four of the men were survivors of the Bataan Death March who had escaped into the Philippine jungles. On the way home with his passengers, Walker picked up a six-ship convoy with five escorts. He went to battle stations to attack, but before he could get off any torpedoes a destroyer attacked *Crevalle*, dropping eight depth charges right on top of the boat. It was the worst working over *Crevalle* had ever received and a near thing. The damage was heavy and the passengers were terrified. Afterward, Walker set course for Darwin.

When the Japanese fleet left Singapore to shift to the anchorage at Tawi Tawi, Christie, thanks to the codebreakers, could deploy his submarines to intercept and confirm its movements.

The first to make contact was Lowell Stone in *Lapon*, lying off the west coast of Borneo. At eight on the morning on May 13, Stone saw at least three aircraft carriers, five cruisers, and several destroyers, range 6 miles. He submerged, hoping for a shot, but got no closer than 5,000 yards and didn't shoot. That night he sent out a contact report. He then shifted to Indochina for a regular patrol.

Tom Hogan in Christie's flagship, *Bonefish*, patrolled in the Sulu Sea, where he had attacked several convoys, shooting off all his torpedoes but six. He had been bombed by a Japanese plane that damaged his periscope and radar. Christie ordered Hogan to look into Tawi Tawi to see if the fleet had arrived, and Hogan went south at full speed. At about 2 A.M. on May 14, Hogan picked up a convoy of three big tankers and three destroyers, apparently headed for Tawi Tawi. Hogan closed and fired five of his six torpedoes, range 1,300 yards. He got two hits—one in a tanker and one in the destroyer *Inazuma*, which blew up and sank. The other destroyers worked over *Bonefish*, but Hogan slipped away submerged.

The following morning at about eleven, while Hogan was submerged about 40 miles northwest of Tawi Tawi, he saw through his periscope the Japanese fleet reported by Stone in *Lapon*: a large carrier, two battleships, many heavy or light cruisers, and about ten destroyers. That night, Hogan withdrew into the Sulu Sea and sent off a contact report.

After sending his message, Hogan returned to Tawi Tawi during the night. The next morning, lying off the coast, he raised his periscope and saw a grand sight inside the anchorage: "six carriers, four or five battleships, eight heavy cruisers, light cruisers, and many destroyers." That night, Hogan moved south a little and sent off another contact report. The report was evidently DF-ed because two destroyers charged out to attack. Hogan, who had no torpedoes (the one left was defective), eluded and waited for Christie to send a relief submarine.

Brooks Harral in *Ray* patrolled off Davao Gulf. On May 14, he picked up a task force heading into the gulf: a big aircraft carrier, a heavy cruiser, and a light cruiser, escorted by many destroyers. Harral could get no closer than 9,000 yards. That night he withdrew to sea and got off a contact report. Two days later, May 16, he saw the same force standing out of Davao Gulf at high speed but could get no closer than 6,500 yards. He did not shoot. "It was a sad disappointment," he wrote, "to see a plum like this go by just out of reach." He remained on station. These ships also went to Tawi Tawi.

After Christie had relieved Ambruster on *Robalo*, he gave command of the boat to Manning Kimmel, a son of the admiral. The exec, Charles Fell, remained. Christie sent Kimmel to the South China Sea to interdict Japanese tankers resupplying the fleet at Tawi Tawi.

Kimmel conducted a wildly aggressive patrol. In four attacks, he fired twenty torpedoes. He was credited with sinking a tanker, but it was not confirmed in postwar records. During one attack, Kimmel was caught by a Japanese plane. On diving, the main induction flooded "due to personnel error" and *Robalo* plunged toward the bottom, out of control. Kimmel caught the boat at 350 feet. The bombs badly damaged *Robalo*'s periscopes, shattering and flooding number one and ruining the low-power adjustment on number two. "High power is usable but not clear," Kimmel noted. In addition, the bombs sprung the conning tower hatch and knocked out the SJ radar. In spite of all this, Kimmel remained on station.

When he finally returned to Fremantle, Tex McLean was upset. Later he said, "Anybody else would have come home long before. I worried that Kimmel was a little too anxious to put the name of Kimmel high in Navy annals." Christie and McLean thought maybe they should replace Kimmel, to save his neck, but since Kimmel was Admiral Kinkaid's nephew it might prove awkward.

Herb Andrews in *Gurnard*, still in the Celebes Sea, was ordered up near Davao Gulf. On May 18, about eight o'clock in the morning, Andrews intercepted a battleship escorted by destroyers. The enemy force was clocked at 23 knots. Andrews set up and fired six torpedoes, range 2,300 yards. Destroyers charged at *Gurnard* and Andrews went deep. He heard two solid hits. Later, he was credited with damage to the battleship for 32,700 tons. Andrews was only the fourth submarine skipper to have hit and damaged a battleship, after Donaho on *Flying Fish*, Gene McKinney on *Skate,* and John Scott on *Tunny.*

Victor McCrea in *Hoe* patrolled off Indochina and Luzon. On May 8, while off the northwest coast of Luzon, he made contact with a convoy en route from Formosa to Manila with troop reinforcements. The convoy was escorted by a light carrier. McCrea could not get position on the carrier, but he attacked a tanker and a freighter, causing damage. He got off a contact report (Dempsey in *Cod* was still near Manila) and trailed. Off Lingayen Gulf and Manila, McCrea found several more convoys to attack. He was credited with sinking one ship and damaging four, but postwar records failed to credit the sinking.

Reuben Whitaker in *Flasher* patrolled off Indochina. On April 29, he found a convoy and sank two ships, a 644-ton gunboat and a 1,000-ton freighter. After several more actions, Whitaker set course for Fremantle. On May 3, in the Sulu Sea, he sank a 6,709-ton freighter, *Teisen Maru.* Three days later, Whitaker expended the last of his torpedoes against another freighter for damage.

The Joint Strike on Surabaya

In early May, the U.S. carrier *Saratoga*, detached from Nimitz's force and assigned to Kinkaid, arrived in southwest Australia. After intelligence had confirmed the relocation of major Japanese fleet units to Tawi Tawi, Christie conceived a mission for *Saratoga*: a strike on the antisubmarine shore batteries at Lombok Strait and the Wanikroma Oil Refineries, the navy yard and the Bratte Engineering Works in Surabaya. The strike would be launched from Indian Ocean waters.

Christie believed that, with radio silence, *Saratoga* could carry out

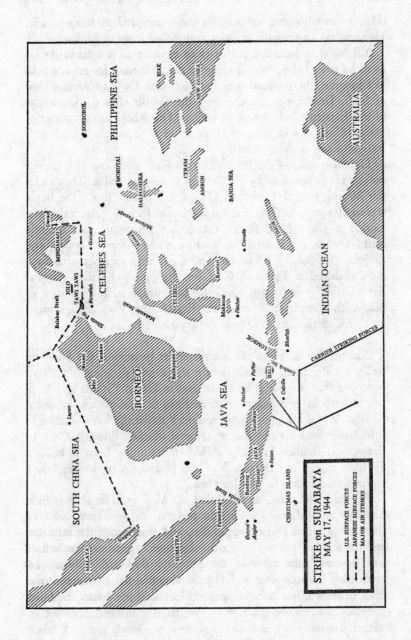

STRIKE on SURABAYA
MAY 17, 1944

U.S. SURFACE FORCES
JAPANESE SURFACE FORCES
MAJOR AIR STRIKES

CARRIER STRIKING FORCES

this mission with complete surprise and then withdraw to Fremantle. He drew up an operational order and passed it up to Kinkaid.

Although Kinkaid had authority to conduct such a strike on his own, he passed the proposal along to Admiral King for approval. In Washington, the proposal was discussed with the Combined Chiefs of Staff. During these discussions, the British offered the services of the Eastern Fleet, basing in India. "The whole thing got out of hand," Christie said later. "So instead of a nice neat operation, it became almost a major effort."

The main units of the British Eastern Fleet made available for the strike were commanded by Admiral Sir James Somerville. They were: the World War I battleship *Queen Elizabeth* (flag); the battle cruiser *Renown;* the Free French battleship *Richelieu,* recently overhauled in the United States; the carrier *Illustrious,* also recently refurbished in the United States; the cruisers *Valiant, London,* and *Suffolk;* plus destroyers and tankers. This force, together with *Saratoga,* gathered at Exmouth Gulf for the proposed strike. Admiral Kinkaid flew over from Brisbane for last-minute strategy talks, stopping with Christie at "Bend of the Road." The two men then went up to Exmouth Gulf to inspect the combined force.

Christie ordered eight of his submarines to support the Surabaya strike—as lifeguards, to sink fleeing ships, and to guard the major entrances from the Java Sea to the Indian Ocean (Sunda and Lombok straits) in case Japanese submarines or men-of-war attempted to move into the Indian Ocean to attack the strike force. The eight submarines were *Rasher, Puffer, Gunnel, Angler, Bluefish, Cabrilla, Raton,* and Reuben Whitaker's *Flasher,* returning from Indochina. (Whitaker put into Darwin May 13, picked up twelve torpedoes, and reversed course for the Java Sea.)

The raid took place, as scheduled, on May 17. The aircraft from *Saratoga* and *Illustrious,* Christie reported in his diary, achieved complete surprise, met no opposition, and demolished the refineries and the engineering works "for the duration." However, they missed five Japanese submarines in the Surabaya dockyards. Christie believed that if a second strike had been mounted those too could have been destroyed, but Admiral Somerville, the senior officer, declined.

None of the eight submarines diverted for this sideshow accomplished anything—no rescues, no ships sunk fleeing the raid. Many valuable patrol days were lost. The submarines probably would have accomplished far more had they been stationed off Tawi Tawi while the Japanese fleet was gathering.

Junior McCain in *Gunnel* and Robert Olsen in *Angler* stood guard in Sunda Strait. During *Angler*'s refit, Olsen had asked that special attention be given his fresh-water tanks; the water had tasted strange and many people (including those rescued from Panay) had become sick on his last patrol. "When I got back from the hotel," Olsen said later, "I found out they hadn't had time to do anything about the water tanks. I went up to see my division commander to tell him they were dangerous—too much chlorine had been added to the water originally in Pearl Harbor and I thought some of it might have settled in the concrete lining of the tanks. The division commander said it looked O.K. and that if I didn't want to take the boat on patrol he'd find somebody else."

While lying in Sunda Strait, Olsen found a freighter and attacked, sinking it. Afterward, escorts gave *Angler* a bad pounding. On the following day, everybody on *Angler* once again became nauseous. "I figured the depth charges shook up the chlorine in the concrete," Olsen said later. He reported the calamity to Christie, who ordered *Angler* to return to Fremantle at once.

On the way home, the situation worsened. On May 22, Olsen noted in his log, "Physical condition of officers and crew is so bad that it is difficult to maintain watch, either surface or submerged. Put crew on fruit juice alone, no water. Held thorough field day in case boat is contaminated. Exercised special supervision in cooking, dishwashing." On May 23 he wrote, "Decided to run submerged as we did not have enough able-bodied people to maintain proper surface watch."

Christie ordered *Flasher*, returning to Fremantle, to intercept *Angler* and lend assistance. In addition he sent U.S.S. *Childs*, an ancient destroyer converted to patrol plane tender. Frank Walker in *Crevalle*, who had just unloaded his forty-one refugees from Negros at Darwin and embarked a doctor for passage from Darwin to Fremantle, also went to intercept *Angler*. On May 24, *Flasher, Crevalle, Childs,* and *Angler* met at sea. The doctor on *Crevalle* went on board *Angler* to help the busy (and ill) pharmacist's mate, L. M. Neidlinger, with the sick officers and crew. *Flasher, Crevalle,* and *Childs* gave *Angler* fresh water. *Angler* continued to Fremantle, arriving after a patrol of twenty-seven days.

Debarking at Fremantle to make his report to Christie, Olsen noted that the gangway put over was old and rickety. He told the officer of the deck to get a new one, "before someone falls and breaks their neck." About an hour later Olsen returned to the boat, and as he boarded the gangway gave way. Olsen fell, fracturing his skull, and—the final irony—was sent to a hospital in Sydney for three months, losing command of *Angler*.

While he was gone, Christie's men conducted an investigation into the illness. During the taking of testimony, it was determined that one of the electricians had brought a can of carbon tetrachloride on board as a cleaning agent—strictly prohibited. The illness was laid to that. "But that was a lot of bunk," Olsen said later. "A cover-up. That can was *never* opened. The cause was the same cause as the illness on the previous patrol: bad water. They blamed it on the carbon tet to cover up the fact they hadn't cleaned the fresh-water tanks."

For Junior McCain too this patrol was a frustrating one. *Gunnel* left Sunda Strait after the raid and went up to patrol off Indochina. On June 8, McCain picked up a convoy. It was guarded by a small escort carrier, perhaps the same McCrea in *Hoe* had seen the previous month near Manila. McCain commenced tracking on the surface from 15 miles. In the middle of the chase, the officer of the deck "inadvertently dived on an aircraft contact at 24 miles." McCain lost contact and was not able to regain it. It was the third time in as many patrols that McCain had seen an aircraft carrier and failed to damage it. When he returned to Fremantle, he was sent to new construction, having achieved little on *Gunnel* in five patrols.

At the time of the Surabaya strike, James Davis in *Raton* life-guarded at a station south of Java. Afterward, he went to patrol off Indochina near *Gunnel* and Lowell Stone's *Lapon*, which had gone there after making the initial contact with the Japanese fleet, May 13. On the way up, Davis sank an 800-ton frigate.

Stone in *Lapon* found good hunting off Indochina. On May 23–24 he got into a convoy, sinking two large freighters confirmed in postwar records at about 6,500 and 4,600 tons. Three days later, Stone found what he believed to be an I-class Japanese submarine. (In fact, it was James Davis in *Raton*.) He went to battle stations, turning away to fire all four stern tubes. At 5:13, Stone fired two torpedoes at *Raton*, range 1,400 yards. He was on the point of firing two more when he suddenly had doubts and checked firing. Was his target a U.S. submarine? Stone went to 200 feet and heard two explosions that sounded like torpedoes reaching the end of their run.

On *Raton,* meanwhile, Davis felt two violent explosions which shook the ship "considerably." He was puzzled, believing at first that he might have run aground, and changed course radically, moving ahead full speed and clearing the area.

After this episode, Stone in *Lapon* returned to Fremantle. Davis remained in Indochina waters for another two weeks, sinking a second small frigate before returning to Fremantle. Later, when the two skippers compared notes—and patrol reports—they discovered Stone had fired at Davis. It was the only confirmed instance of one U.S. submarine firing at another during the war.

On the way to lifeguard station north of Surabaya, Willard Laughon in *Rasher* made contact with a five-ship convoy near Ambon on the afternoon of May 11. For the next eighteen hours, Laughon attacked repeatedly, firing off all twenty-four of his torpedoes. Many torpedoes ran under targets without exploding or otherwise malfunctioned. Although many of the ships were damaged, Laughon received credit for sinking only one.

After that—all torpedoes expended—Laughon took station north of Surabaya for the strike. When it was done, he returned to Darwin, took on eighteen more torpedoes, and went north near Halmahera for further action.

Patrols to Tawi Tawi and Davao

While standing watch off Surabaya during the air strike, Gordon Selby in *Puffer* had sunk a 3,000-ton freighter that happened along. Following this, he was ordered up Makassar Strait to Tawi Tawi with Henderson's *Bluefish.*

In the north end of Makassar Strait on May 22, approaching Tawi Tawi, Selby picked up a portion of the Japanese main body conducting maneuvers to train the many green pilots in the air wings. Selby found the force at 9:12 A.M. while submerged, range 7,000 yards. It consisted of two aircraft carriers and three destroyers, all "milling around." (*Bluefish* was nearby but did not see the carriers.) While Selby was concentrating on one carrier, the other passed five hundred yards astern! "The general effect," Selby wrote later, "was similar to the dazzling speed with which the participants in a Walt Disney cartoon sizzle past and disappear in a cloud of vapor."

Having missed several opportunities, Selby "settled down" and prepared to make another approach at 10:24. He closed to 1,400 yards and fired six torpedoes. Only one hit, but Selby was later credited with damage to a 26,900-ton aircraft carrier. The destroyer escorts counterattacked *Puffer*, dropping many depth charges, but Selby evaded and slipped away. Postwar Japanese records did not confirm damage to a carrier that day; however, the destroyer *Yukikaze* was damaged by a submarine at that time and place. Later Selby concluded that he had "used the wrong ranges."

Puffer and *Bluefish* arrived at Tawi Tawi, joining Tom Hogan in *Bonefish*. Both Selby and Henderson observed the many men-of-war in the anchorage. With their arrival, Hogan left Tawi Tawi to proceed to Fremantle. On May 25, his radioman picked up a puzzling plain-language message, addressed to all naval vessels: WHAT HAS GOD WROUGHT? Hogan examined the message for codes. He then decided it could have meant one of the following (as he noted in his log): (1) a national calamity had occurred; (2) Hitler was dead; (3) prohibition was back in effect. "Decided no action required this vessel," Hogan wrote. An hour later, another message clarified the first; it had been sent in commemoration of the centennial of the telegraph. "Entire crew vastly relieved," Hogan wrote.

Other boats converging on or guarding at Tawi Tawi, or off Davao or in the Celebes Sea, found targets. William Thompson in *Cabrilla* sank the ex-seaplane tender *Sanyo Maru*. On June 5, Gordon Selby in *Puffer* sank two tankers in the north end of Sibutu Passage: *Ashizuki*, 2,100 tons, and *Takasaki*, 2,500 tons. Eric Barr in *Bluegill* sank an 8,800-ton freighter off Davao and another off Halmahera. Edward Farwell Dissette in *Cero* sank one off Halmahera and damaged two others. And Willard Laughon in *Rasher*, on the second half of a double-barreled patrol, sank a 2,600-ton converted gunboat near Halmahera.

Brooks Harral in *Ray* and Herb Andrews in *Gurnard* patrolled off Davao. On the afternoon of May 21, Harral in *Ray* sighted a nine-ship convoy with surface and air escorts. In a furiously aggressive series of attacks, Harral believed he sank six of the nine. Something must have gone drastically wrong with his torpedoes; postwar records confirmed only one sinking, a freighter of 6,000 tons. Undoubtedly many other ships were damaged. Harral was driven off by land-based aircraft.

Shortly after this, Herb Andrews in *Gurnard* picked up a tanker convoy and attacked, sinking one of the fleet tankers, *Tatekawa Maru,* 10,000 tons.

Thompson in *Cabrilla,* taking station south of Tawi Tawi in the same area Selby had found the carriers in training, found another training operation in progress. This force consisted of three battle-ships and three carriers. Thompson closed, setting up on a battle-ship. He made one long (forty-five-second) observation, which he later called an "error," dipped the periscope, then went back for a final look. A Japanese plane dived at *Cabrilla,* dropping a "close and violent" depth charge which shook the ship badly. A second close string drove *Cabrilla* off, and the battleships and carriers veered out of range. Thompson evaded but later that night he surfaced, chased, and got off a contact report. The Japanese ships—out for a day's training—slipped back into Tawi Tawi.

The Japanese Reinforcement of Biak

Meanwhile, Admiral Jisaburo Ozawa, who had been named to command the Japanese naval forces in battle, waited in Tawi Tawi to execute Plan A-Go, hoping for a decisive battle with the Pacific Fleet off the Palaus. The plan was thrown into jeopardy when Mac-Arthur's forces landed on Biak on May 27. An airfield on Biak in Allied hands would place U.S. land-based bombers within 500 miles of the Palaus and the seas where Ozawa hoped to meet the Nimitz forces. Ozawa was determined to reinforce Biak and throw out the invaders.

The Japanese reaction to Biak, known as Plan Kon, was spliced into the middle of Plan A-Go. It called for men-of-war to deliver about 2,500 troops to Biak. The first effort was a task force consisting of the battleship *Fuso,* four cruisers, and eight destroyers. They would embark troops at Zamboanga in western Mindanao and de-liver them to Biak, going by way of Davao.

On the night of May 30, some ships of this force left Tawi Tawi

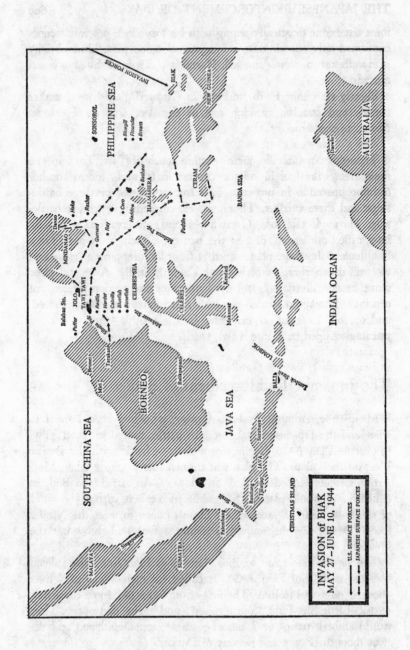

INVASION of BIAK
MAY 27 – JUNE 10, 1944
U.S. SURFACE FORCES
JAPANESE SURFACE FORCES

for assigned missions. William Thompson in *Cabrilla* and Charles Henderson in *Bluefish* spotted them leaving the anchorage.

Henderson in *Bluefish* saw a battleship (*Fuso*), four heavy cruisers, and three of the eight destroyers. He went to battle stations but could get no closer than 6,000 yards. "Everybody was ready," he wrote later, "but could only watch helplessly as they went by out of range." That night, Henderson got off a contact report.

The Kon force for the relief of Biak continued toward Mindanao to pick up troops. Herb Andrews in *Gurnard* and Brooks Harral in *Ray* moved to intercept. They made contact at 8:57 on the morning of May 31, south of Mindanao. Andrews thought it was three battleships and five other vessels. They were on an easterly course (toward Davao Gulf), making 18 knots. Andrews tried to maneuver into firing position but could get no closer than 5 miles. He wrote, "To have in sight the targets all submariners dream of yet be unable to close in to firing range remains a bitter disappointment." After this encounter, Andrews got off a contact report and headed for Fremantle. Altogether, Andrews had sunk four ships for 29,795 tons, making this—in terms of confirmed tonnage—the best patrol of the war to date.

Harral in *Ray* believed the force to be one battleship, one heavy and one light cruiser, and three destroyers. The cruisers passed him at 8,000 yards, but Harral was not able to close. He picked up the battleship at 16 miles and got within 7 miles—but no closer. Harral tracked the force toward Davao Gulf on June 1, sending off a contact report. Then he headed for Fremantle, pausing near Talaud Island, where Laughon in *Rasher* was patrolling.

The Kon force stopped at Davao as planned, then got under way for Biak in two separate units. On the morning of June 3, Willard Laughon in *Rasher* picked up part of the force, what he believed to be two heavy cruisers, a light cruiser, and several destroyers. He could not gain firing position, but he got off a contact report which the Japanese heard. The Japanese, distressed that they had been spotted so soon and so far from their destination, called off Kon and drew up another plan. *Fuso* and two cruisers went back to Davao. Two cruisers proceeded to disembark troops on New Guinea. Two other cruisers went directly from Davao to Batjan with troops.

Laughon in *Rasher* moved up to Davao Gulf, replacing *Gurnard* and *Ray*. On June 4 he spotted the retiring Japanese cruisers returning to Davao but was unable to attack. A little later, a destroyer picked up *Rasher* and closed to 100 yards. Laughon went deep, while the destroyer—soon joined by another—dropped depth charges. After dark, Laughon surfaced and got off a contact report on the cruisers.

After that, Laughon withdrew to seaward to patrol the traffic lanes. On June 7 he found two merging convoys but was unable to gain attack position. The following day he found another convoy and fired six of his eighteen torpedoes at the 4,000-ton tanker *Shioya*. It caught fire and sank.

Laughon was replaced at Davao by John Broach in *Hake* and by young Chester Nimitz in *Haddo*, who had been patrolling off Halmahera. On the night of June 8, Broach picked up a task force—part of the retiring Kon force—of two cruisers and several destroyers. He attacked one of the destroyers, *Kazegumo*, and sank it. Later, he saw another cruiser and several destroyers inside Davao Gulf. He penetrated the gulf but could get no closer than 6,000 yards to the ships.

Nimitz had no major contacts. He was shifted from the Davao area to Tawi Tawi.

Sam Dealey in *Harder,* going on his fifth patrol, was ordered to Tawi Tawi. Christie's operations officer, Murray Tichenor, who had never made a war patrol, went along for the ride. In addition to a regular patrol, Dealey was asked to try to pick up the guerrillas on northeast Borneo that both Chester Nimitz in *Haddo* and Cy Austin in *Redfin* had missed. Dealey agreed to the special mission—reluctantly.

On the night of June 6, while going into Sibutu Passage just south of Tawi Tawi on his way to pick up the guerrillas, Dealey ran into a convoy of three empty tankers and two destroyers headed for Tarakan for a refill. One of the destroyers picked up *Harder* and charged. Dealey let it get within 1,100 yards, then fired three torpedoes. *Minatsuki* blew up and sank immediately.

Dealey chased the convoy, making an end around. He submerged to radar depth and prepared to attack. A second destroyer peeled off and charged at *Harder*. Dealey let it get within 1,200 yards before firing six bow tubes. All missed. Dealey went to 300 feet to evade. One of his diving plane operators, a new man, misread his instruments and took *Harder* to 400 feet by mistake. As a result, Dealey lost another opportunity to attack the convoy.

Dealey turned back for Sibutu Passage, submerging for the transit shortly after 8 A.M. on June 7. At 11:43, he sighted another destroyer. Dealey let it get within the point-blank range of 650 yards and then fired three torpedoes at five-second intervals. All three torpedoes hit *Hayanami*.

Dealey went ahead full with hard right rudder to get out of the path of the destroyer. He later wrote, "At a range of 300 yards we were racked by a terrific explosion believed to have been the destroyer's magazine. Less than one minute after the first hit and nine minutes after it was sighted, the destroyer sank tail first."

A sister ship of the *Hayanami* came over and dropped seventeen depth charges in the next two hours. Shortly after 3 P.M., Dealey returned to periscope depth and found two more destroyers. They went away, but he found another, about 5:30, and then a line of eight. Feeling he had worn out his welcome, Dealey withdrew to pick up the guerrillas.

On the night of June 8, Dealey nosed *Harder* near the appointed rendezvous and sent two small boats ashore into the gloom. The boats picked up the guerrilla force and returned to *Harder*. Dealey cleared the area and went through Sibutu Passage to see what he could turn up at Tawi Tawi.

The following night he found two more destroyers. He submerged for an approach, firing four torpedoes at overlapping targets. Two of the four hit *Tanikaze*, which blew up and sank. Dealey thought one of his other torpedoes hit the other destroyer, but he must have been mistaken. There is no record of a second Japanese destroyer being lost on June 9 off Tawi Tawi.

During this time, the Japanese mounted a second Kon effort to reinforce their besieged troops on Biak. Two cruisers and six destroyers embarked troops from Sorong, on the northwestern tip of New Guinea, with the intent of landing them on Biak. Allied aircraft discovered this force, sank the destroyer *Harusame*, and damaged three others, one seriously. The air attack was followed up by cruisers and destroyers of Kinkaid's Seventh Fleet supporting the Biak landings. Kinkaid's surface forces—in a minor engagement known as the Battle of Biak—drove the remaining Japanese forces back into ports.

Following this the Japanese made a third Kon attempt, this time with a major force consisting of the huge battleships *Yamato* and *Musashi*, five cruisers, seven destroyers, and other miscellaneous craft. The plan was to send this force to Batjan, south of Halmahera, embark troops, and then fight into Biak. *Yamato* and *Musashi* got underway at Tawi Tawi on the evening of June 10.

Sam Dealey in *Harder* was patrolling off Tawi Tawi that evening. At about 5 P.M., he sighted *Yamato* and *Musashi* coming out of the anchorage. While Dealey maneuvered *Harder* for an approach, a Japanese pilot spotted his periscope and dropped a smoke bomb and a destroyer peeled off and headed for *Harder*. Dealey let him close to 1,200 yards, fired three torpedoes down the throat, and then went deep.

Going down, Dealey was positive that at least two of the torpedoes hit; he heard explosions far louder than depth charges. Passing 80 feet, he later wrote that "all hell broke loose. It was not from his depth charges—for if they had been dropped, this report would not have been completed—but a deafening series of progressive rumblings that seemed to almost blend with each other. Either his boilers or his magazine, or both, had exploded and it's a lucky thing that ship explosions are vented upward and not down."

Dealey took *Harder* to 400 feet to evade. The escorts—and land-based aircraft—delivered a violent counterattack that kept him down until after dark. Dealey wrote in his log, "It is considered amazing that [*Harder*] could have gone through such a terrific pounding and jolting around with such minor damage. Our fervent thanks go out to the workmen and designers at the Electric Boat Company for building such a fine ship." In the postwar records, there was no evidence that a Japanese destroyer was lost this day off Tawi Tawi. The noise Dealey heard might well have been close aerial bombs or depth charges.

After dark, Dealey surfaced and got off a contact report on the departure of *Yamato* and *Musashi*, which continued on to Batjan without further interference from U.S. submarines.

Dealey remained off Tawi Tawi for another day, watching the anchorage and reporting the ships he saw. On the evening of June 12, Christie ordered him to patrol northward along the Sulu Archipelago. Going north, Dealey rendezvoused with Chester Nimitz in *Haddo*, who was having another frustrating patrol. So far, Nimitz had found nothing to shoot at except a couple of mangy sampans, sunk by deck gun. Dealey continued on to Zamboanga, then to Davao, then back south through Molucca Passage to Darwin.

When Dealey reached Darwin, Christie was ecstatic. He credited him with sinking five destroyers, and the endorsements called the patrol "epoch-making" and "magnificent." Since Dealey had sunk a destroyer on his previous patrol off Woleai, his total was thought to be six. For this reason, he was nicknamed "The Destroyer Killer."

John Crowley finally got *Flier*—the boat that had gone aground at Midway in January—ready for his first patrol. With his exec, Jim Liddell, the onetime All-American from Northwestern, he patrolled from Pearl Harbor to Fremantle by way of Lingayen Gulf. They were anxious to make up for the five months they had lost because of the grounding. Crowley offered a prize to the lookout who spotted the most ships—$15 and a bottle of Old Taylor bourbon.

On June 4, while west of the Bonins, Crowley picked up a convoy en route from the Marianas to Japan. After dark, he closed to attack, misjudged the enemy course, and dived in the wrong place. He surfaced and chased, making an end around, and then dived for a dawn attack. Crowley got between the columns in the convoys and fired all bow tubes, three each at two ships. He was about to fire stern tubes at the other column when he saw one of the freighters boring in to ram. He went deep and the convoy got away. Postwar records credited him with a fine sinking, *Hakusam Maru*, a 10,400-ton transport.

Crowley took up station on the west coast of Luzon near Subic Bay about June 12. There was another submarine in the vicinity, *Jack*, now commanded by a new skipper, Arthur Elmer Krapf. Both Crowley and Krapf had orders to report any movement of Japanese fleet units they detected and then attack. They were also free to attack convoys.

On June 13 Crowley spotted a large convoy, eleven ships and six escorts. The sea was flat calm, the sun bright. Yet Crowley and Liddell slipped inside the escorts and attacked, firing stern tubes at a medium-sized tanker. When Crowley got ready to fire his bow tubes, he found he was too close. Escorts charged in and blasted *Flier* with over a hundred "moderately well placed depth charges." After dark, Crowley attempted an end around, but the convoy got into Subic Bay before he could attack again.

Next, Crowley was ordered to drop down to Tawi Tawi. Going through Mindoro Strait he picked up another convoy "quite by accident." He let the convoy pass and then surfaced after dark, caught up, and fired all six bow tubes at two ships, obtaining two hits in each. After reloading, Crowley fired his remaining four bow torpedoes at a freighter, obtaining three hits. With only four stern torpedoes remaining, Crowley closed in on a cripple, but before he could fire, he reported later, the ship "obligingly sank."

When Crowley reported this encounter to Fremantle, Christie ordered him to head for the barn. On his arrival, Crowley was credited with sinking four ships for 20,000 tons and damaging two for 13,000 tons, but postwar records credited only the transport sunk west of the Bonins on June 4.

All these activities by Christie's submarines cost Admiral Ozawa and his A-Go plan for annihilating the U.S. Pacific Fleet dearly. Almost every movement of his fleet units—from Singapore to Tawi Tawi, maneuvers outside Tawi Tawi, plan Kon for Biak—had been spotted and reported by submarines. Submarine activity off Tawi Tawi forced the Japanese to curtail valuable training for new air wings. Two major men-of-war, a carrier and a battleship, had been attacked by torpedoes, the carrier by Selby, the battleship by Andrews. Seven men-of-war had been sunk: the light cruiser *Yubari* (Barr), five fleet destroyers (three by Dealey, one by Hogan, one by Broach), and an old destroyer (Dempsey). In addition, twenty-four important merchant ships had been sent to the bottom: six tankers (two by Selby and one each by Andrews, Laughon, Walker, and Cy Austin in *Redfin*), four troopships (three by Andrews, one by Dykers), and fourteen freighters. Dozens of other merchant ships had been damaged; convoys had been thrown into confusion and, in some cases, forced to return to port.

In addition, Admiral Ozawa's submarine line, stretching from Truk to New Guinea, was devastated, thanks to marvelous information furnished by the codebreakers. Having been given the precise location of the line, U.S. destroyer hunter-killer groups (equipped with forward-throwing depth charges) sank nine out of about a dozen Japanese submarines. In the most remarkable antisubmarine operation of the war, one destroyer, *England*, was directly responsible for sinking six of the nine. This feat led Admiral King to say, "There'll always be an *England* in the United States Navy."*

* The pledge was not completely kept. *England* was decommissioned in 1945 and sold in 1946. There was no *England* in the navy until 1960, when the guided missile frigate *DLG-22* was christened *England*.

29

Pearl Harbor,
May and June 1944

Patrols to the Marianas

In Pearl Harbor Admiral Nimitz gave the final green light for Operation Forager, the invasion of the Marianas, with the sequence of landings to be Saipan, then Guam, then Tinian.

Nimitz had no illusions about the Marianas. He knew it would be a tough fight all the way, perhaps as tough as Tarawa. But victory would be worth the price. The Marianas were decisive to the control of the western Pacific. Saipan and Guam would provide a staging base for another leap in any direction: the Palaus, the Philippines, Formosa, Okinawa, or the Bonins. In addition, the air force wanted the Marianas as a base for a new bomber, the B-29 Superfortress, which could reach the Japanese mainland. Finally, the Marianas would provide Lockwood with an advance submarine base—3,300 miles beyond Pearl Harbor and only 1,500 miles from Luzon Strait.

Before the invasion, Nimitz merged the forces under his command with those of Admiral Bull Halsey, who had been basing in Noumea. In effect, he combined the Fifth Fleet under Raymond Spruance with Halsey's Third Fleet. Thereafter, Spruance and Halsey alternated in command. The main striking force—known as the Fast Carrier Force—was commanded by Marc Andrew Mitscher. When Halsey had overall command, the Fast Carrier Force was called Task Force 38; when Spruance had overall command, Task Force 58.

Nimitz named Spruance to lead the invasion of the Marianas. He commanded a huge armada: 535 ships and auxiliaries that would land 128,000 troops, two thirds marines and one third army. The Fast Carrier Force—Task Force 58—now numbered fifteen heavy and light carriers. It would soften up the islands and stand by for battle, should Admiral Ozawa elect to sortie from Tawi Tawi and oppose the landings.

While this armada was assembling for the voyage west, Lockwood sent a last wave of submarines into the Marianas to interdict Japanese attempts to reinforce the islands.

John Coye in *Silversides*, coming up from Fremantle, entered the Marianas shortly after Malcolm Garrison in *Sandlance* departed. Coye performed like a one-boat wolf pack. On May 10 he intercepted a convoy and sank three ships: the freighter *Okinawa Maru*, 2,254 tons; the transport *Mikage Maru No. 18*, 4,310 tons; and the converted gunboat *Choan Maru II*, 2,631 tons. On May 20, while attacking a freighter off Guam, Coye missed the freighter but hit one of the escorts, the converted gunboat *Shosei Maru*, 998 tons. On May 29 he found another convoy bringing aviation gasoline into Saipan and sank two ships from it: *Shoken Maru*, 1,949 tons, and *Horaizan Maru*, 1,999 tons. With only two torpedoes remaining, Coye looked for other targets, along with John Scott in *Tunny*.

In addition, Lockwood sent a three-boat wolf pack to the Marianas. All three boats were new, all commanded by new skippers who were classmates from 1934: *Pilotfish*, commanded by Robert Hamilton ("Boney") Close, who had been Spike Hottel's exec on *Grouper*; *Pintado*, commanded by Chick Clarey, who began the war as exec of *Dolphin* and then made two patrols on Bole's *Amberjack* and a PCO run; and *Shark II*, commanded by Edward Noe Blakely, who had made seven patrols on *Tuna* under Johnny DeTar and Ike Holtz. The pack was commanded by Leon Blair, Commander, Submarine Division 44, making his first war patrol. Blair rode with Clarey in *Pintado*. The pack was dubbed "Blair's Blasters."

When the pack reached the Marianas on May 31, John Coye in *Silversides* was trailing—and giving contact reports on—an outbound convoy. Blair's Blasters were ordered to close Coye's convoy and take over.

When the pack made contact, they found three freighters and two escorts. Blakely in *Shark* and Coye in *Silversides* wound up on one side of the convoy. Blakely held back so that Coye could go in and fire his last two torpedoes. Both missed. By allowing Coye to go in, Blakely deprived himself of a chance to attack. On the other side of the convoy, Clarey in *Pintado* tried to get in but was chased off by gunfire from one of the escorts. He trailed and then mounted a second attempt near daybreak, firing six torpedoes. All six hit *Toho Maru*, 4,700 tons. The ship, Clarey wrote, "disintegrated before my eyes and sank immediately."

Meanwhile, Coye, having sunk six ships, set off for Pearl Harbor and found a second convoy—inbound—of five ships and several escorts. Boney Close in *Pilotfish* gave up trying to attack Convoy Number One in favor of Convoy Number Two. In the late afternoon of June 1, Close reported he had the convoy in sight. Blair, knowing an outbound convoy to be less valuable than an inbound one with reinforcements, ordered all boats to break off from the first and concentrate on the second. Boney Close trailed but was not able to get in an attack. Nor were the other boats. Convoy Number Two, which was carrying half of the Japanese 43rd Division, reached Saipan without damage.

In the meantime, Close found yet another convoy, Number Three. It was outbound. On the evening of June 2, Blakely in *Shark* also made contact with this convoy. He set up and fired four torpedoes at a freighter, and all four hit. Down went *Chiyo Maru*, 4,700 tons. Clarey in *Pintado* tried to get in from the other side but was driven down by an escort and received a stiff depth-charging. Close was also unable to attack.

During the early hours of June 3, while chasing Convoy Number Three for another attack, Blakely found a fourth convoy, also inbound. It consisted of about seven big freighters and four or five escorts. Again, knowing that an inbound convoy was a more significant target than an outbound one, Blair ordered his three boats to close Convoy Number Four.

It took the boats twenty-four hours to get into shooting position. Late on the afternoon of June 4, *Shark* made the first attack. Blakely took the boat submerged into the middle of the convoy, watched an escort pass about 180 yards down his side, then set up on a freighter at 1,500 yards. "In the few brief looks taken on this target," Blakely reported, "it was noted that the topside, forecastle in particular, was heaped high with military packs and what appeared to be landing force equipment, the topside was jammed with personnel, apparently troops." As he learned later, Convoy Number Four was carrying the other half of the 43rd Division.

Blakely fired four torpedoes. All hit. During the attack, he lost depth control and went deep. An escort charged over, dropping four depth charges very close. *Shark* remained deep while the escorts unleashed another forty-nine charges in the next two hours, none close. After dark, Blakely surfaced to chase. Neither Clarey in *Pintado* nor Close in *Pilotfish* was able to get in an attack. After dark, they too surfaced to chase.

Next day, it was Blakely who again got in the lucky position. Late in the afternoon of June 5, he made a submerged attack, firing six torpedoes at two freighters. Three torpedoes hit each target. Blakely paused a moment to swing the periscope on an escort, then back to the first freighter. "There was nothing left except his masts in a swirl of water sticking out," Blakely wrote. "It was unbelievable to me that a ship could sink so fast." Blakely had sunk two ships in this attack: *Tamahime Maru*, 3,000 tons, and *Takaika Maru*, 7,000 tons. He then went deep and received another drubbing, one which damaged his port shaft.

That night, all three submarines again surfaced to chase. Shortly after midnight, Clarey got into position and fired four torpedoes at overlapping targets. All four slammed into *Kashimasan Maru*, 2,800 tons, which was loaded with gasoline and burned far into the night before sinking. The escorts drove Clarey down before he could confirm that she sank or mount a second attack. He came up shortly and began an end around to get ahead of the convoy for a daylight periscope attack.

The opportunity came just before noon. Clarey got inside the escorts and fired six torpedoes at two overlapping targets. He heard six hits and then looked through the periscope. He wrote:

What was left of the near ship was burning furiously; she had broken in two and her bow and stern both projected up in the air as she sank. The second target was partially obscured by fire from the first ship. I could see that her stern was all under water and she had listed over to port about 40 degrees. She was enveloped in the most tremendous fire I have ever seen.

Five escorts closed on Clarey and drove him under, dropping fifty depth charges. Postwar assessment gave him only one of the ships, *Harve Maru*, 5,600 tons.

After this attack, Blair ordered the boats to break off and regroup. When the score was tallied up in the postwar Japanese records, it was found that, in the four convoys, Clarey and Blakely had sunk a total of seven ships for about 35,000 tons: one each out of outbound convoys One and Three and Blakely three and Clarey two out of the important inbound Convoy Four. In all this action, Boney Close in *Pilotfish* had not shot a single torpedo. His patrol was declared "nonsuccessful."

The virtual destruction of the inbound Convoy Four—five out of seven ships sunk—made the invasion of Saipan and Guam an easier task for the U.S. Navy. Most of the Japanese troops were rescued, but their equipment had been lost and the troops did not arrive in time to be integrated into the defense plan.

With the invasion forces bearing down on the Marianas, Lockwood ordered Blair's Blasters out of the area. Blakely in *Shark* went back to base for battle-damage repairs; John Scott in *Tunny*, still in the area, joined Clarey and Close; and Blair took the pack west toward Luzon Strait to watch for major Japanese fleet units.

After Blair's Blasters cleared out of the Marianas, Lockwood sent four boats there for lifeguard duty during the reconnaissance and air strikes preceding the invasion. These were: *Growler*, commanded by a new skipper, Thomas Benjamin Oakley, Jr., who had served on Daspit's *Tinosa* and commanded *Tarpon* for one patrol; a new boat, *Pipefish*, commanded by William Deragon, who had made seven patrols as exec of *Seawolf*; Sam Loomis's *Stingray*; and *Finback*, commanded by a new skipper, James Langford Jordan, who had made eight war patrols on *Greenling*.

Planes of Task Force 58 struck the Marianas on June 11 and every day thereafter, destroying dozens upon dozens of aircraft. During the strikes on Guam and Saipan, only Sam Loomis in *Stingray*, maneuvering boldly and close to shore, made any rescues; he picked up five airmen. In one case he employed a novel technique: he approached Ensign Donald Carol Brandt's raft submerged, ran up the periscope, and had Brandt tie his life raft to the periscope with a line. Loomis then moved out to sea beyond range of Japanese shore-based guns, surfaced, and took Brandt below.

After the air strikes, Lockwood ordered the four boats away from the Marianas. Oakley in *Growler* moved west to Surigao Strait to keep watch for enemy fleet units; *Pipefish*, *Finback*, and *Stingray* took positions on a scouting line west of the Marianas, joined by two other boats, Jim Blanchard's *Albacore*, returning from overhaul, and Anton Gallaher in *Bang*. *Finback*, *Albacore*, *Bang*, and *Stingray* were positioned in a "square" 60 miles on a side, while *Pipefish* roved to the south.

Other Pearl Harbor submarines took stations at various islands. *Gato*, commanded by a new skipper, Dixie Farrell, lifeguarded off Truk, along with *Snapper*, commanded by William Warren Walker. Michael Peter Russillo, returning the last H.O.R. boat to get new engines, *Muskallunge*, patrolled near Ulithi. *Seawolf*, back from long overhaul with a new skipper, Ozzie Lynch, went to Peleliu, an island in the Palaus, to make photos of the beaches. James Hardin in *Tuna* lifeguarded at Woleai.

Flying Fish, commanded by Robert Risser, went to the Palaus, where John Corbus in *Bowfin*, coming up from Fremantle, and William Stevenson in *Aspro*, going to Fremantle, had been patrolling. After sinking a Japanese submarine, *I-43*, the first confirmed ship sunk by *Aspro*, Stevenson had gotten a freighter of 6,440 tons. When Risser arrived, Stevenson and Corbus were making a joint attack on a convoy which resulted in the sinking of another freighter of 4,500 tons, for which they shared equal credit. Corbus, chasing the convoy to the northwest, inflicted further damage but no more sinkings. Risser heard the explosions and the ensuing counterattack by the escorts.

On May 24 Risser picked up a southbound convoy, two freighters and two escorts. He closed for a night surface attack, firing four torpedoes at one of the freighters. At the moment of firing, the Japanese saw *Flying Fish* and maneuvered wildly to avoid being hit. One minute and twenty seconds after firing, Risser felt "the biggest explosion I have felt to date." He believed it was a circular run of one of his own torpedoes which blew up close aboard. The escorts turned toward *Flying Fish* and opened fire, driving the boat under.

During the night, Risser made an end around and dived for a daylight attack. The convoy came directly at him. When the range closed to 3,300 yards, Risser fired four more torpedoes at one of the freighters. Three torpedoes hit the main target, and one hit the other freighter. Both sank. They were two transports taking supplies and troops to reinforce the Palaus: *Taito Maru*, 4,500 tons, and *Osake Maru*, 3,700 tons. The escorts delivered a vicious counterattack. When he finally got back to the surface, Risser sent off a contact re-

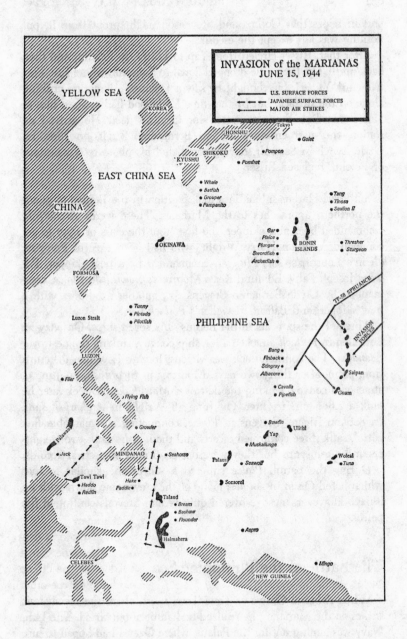

INVASION of the MARIANAS
JUNE 15, 1944

→ U.S. SURFACE FORCES
⟵--→ JAPANESE SURFACE FORCES
········· MAJOR AIR STRIKES

YELLOW SEA

KOREA

EAST CHINA SEA

CHINA

HONSHU

Tokyo

• Golet

KYUSHU   SHIKOKU

• Pompon

• Pomfret

• Whale
• Batfish
• Grouper
• Pampanito

• Tang
• Tinosa
• Sealion II

Gar •
Plaice •
Plunger •
Swordfish •
Archerfish •

BONIN
ISLANDS

• Thresher
• Sturgeon

OKINAWA

FORMOSA

PHILIPPINE SEA

TF-58 SPRUANCE

• Tunny
• Pintado
• Pilotfish

Luzon Strait

LUZON

Bang •
Finback •
Stingray •
Albacore •

INVASION FORCES

Saipan

• Cavalla
• Pipefish

Guam

• Filer

Flying Fish

• Bowfin

Yap   Ulithi

• Growler

• Muskallunge

Palawan

MINDANAO

• Seahorse

Palaus •

• Seawolf

• Woleai
• Tuna

• Jack

Tawi Tawi
• Haddo
• Redfin

Hake •
Paddle •

• Sorsorol

Talaud
• Bream
• Bashaw
• Flounder

• Aspro

Halmahera

CELEBES

NEW GUINEA

• Mingo

port in hopes that Corbus and Stevenson might profit from it, but nothing was left except the escorts.

After that, Risser circled from Yap to Ulithi, to Peleliu, and then back north. On June 9 he dropped down to Sonsorol, where Eric Barr had sunk *Yubari*. He thought he saw a Japanese submarine cruising alone on the surface, but by that time Lockwood had ordered him to San Bernardino Strait to watch for Ozawa's fleet. He arrived on station—the west entrance of San Bernardino Strait—on June 12. Ozzie Lynch in *Seawolf*, having completed his photo reconnaissance of Peleliu, replaced Risser.

Six Pearl Harbor submarines took position in the Bonins to guard the northern approaches to the Marianas. These were: *Archerfish*, commanded by a new skipper, the first from the class of 1937 to get command, William Harry Wright, who had been exec of *Pompon*; George Lautrup's *Gar; Plunger*, commanded by a new skipper, Edward Joseph Fahy; Edmund Keats Montross's *Swordfish; Plaice*, commanded by Clyde Benjamin Stevens, Jr., another new boat with a new skipper; and Bafford Lewellen's *Pollack*.

Three of the six boats in the Bonins sank seven ships. On May 22 Lewellen in *Pollack* attacked a ten-ship convoy, sinking the destroyer *Asanagai*. The counterattack was vicious, forcing Lewellen to return from patrol after thirty-two days. Montross in *Swordfish*, on June 9, attacked a convoy, sinking the destroyer *Matsukake*. A week later he sank a 4,800-ton freighter. On June 28 Wright in *Archerfish* sank an 800-ton frigate. Stevens in *Plaice*, conducting a remarkable first patrol, sank three confirmed escorts and thought he sank two freighters and a transport, but they were not confirmed in postwar records.

During the patrol, *Plaice* suffered a misfortune similar to that which befell Olsen in *Angler*; many of the crew came down with an illness. However, most recovered quickly and Stevens continued the patrol.

The Battle of the Philippine Sea

When Admiral Ozawa at Tawi Tawi heard about the massive air strikes on the Marianas, he realized he had been outwitted. The U.S. Navy was aiming not for the Palaus, where Ozawa had hoped to lure it, but Guam and Saipan. Ozawa "temporarily" postponed Plan Kon, the reinforcement of Biak, and ordered the execution of Plan A-Go, the annihilation of the U.S. Pacific Fleet "with one blow." From naval headquarters in Japan came this exhortation: "This operation has immense bearing on the fate of the Empire. It is hoped that the forces will exert their utmost and achieve as magnificent results as in the Battle of Tsushima."*

Ozawa was confident of victory. He had fewer carriers—nine to fifteen for the United States—but he was counting on the support of not less than 500 land-based aircraft from Guam, Rota, Yap, and other bases. His carrier planes could also use these bases for refueling and rearming, shuttling between the bases and the carriers. The United States would have no land-based planes. Japanese carrier-based aircraft had longer ranges, giving Ozawa a slight edge in searching out his foes. The wind (important for launching and re-covering carrier aircraft) was in Ozawa's favor.

At ten on the morning of June 13, the Japanese fleet steamed out of Tawi Tawi, with destroyers and two heavy cruisers in the van. Cy Austin in *Redfin* saw them come out. He went to battle stations, but the cruisers commenced zigzagging radically; he tried to follow and attack but could not close the range. Two hours later, Austin saw most of the main body of the fleet come out: at least six carriers, four battleships, five heavy cruisers, one light cruiser, and destroyers. He tried to attack a battleship, but the earlier chase of the cruisers had pulled him out of position and again he was not able to close the range. That night at eight, however, he got off a vital radio report announcing that the Japanese fleet was on the move.

Austin trailed the fleet, but it soon outran him, so he turned north-east to take station in the western end of Surigao Strait, hoping to catch cripples returning to Tawi Tawi from the battle.

Admiral Ozawa took his fleet through Sibutu Passage, northward into the Sulu Sea. He stopped at Guimaras on June 14 to refuel. At 8 A.M. on June 15, he got under way again, crossed the small Visayan Sea, then headed for San Bernardino Strait, lying between the southern tip of Luzon and Samar. Meanwhile, a supply force set out from Davao, and the last Kon elements—*Musashi* and *Yamato* plus supporting vessels—left from Batjan. Both the latter sailed to the east of Mindanao, directly into the Philippine Sea. The plan was

---

* The 1905 battle of the Russo-Japanese War in which the Japanese navy virtually destroyed the Russian fleet.

that all three forces would rendezvous in the middle of the Philippine Sea on June 16.

At 4:22 on the afternoon of June 15, while patrolling submerged in San Bernardino Strait, Robert Risser in *Flying Fish* picked up Ozawa's fleet, hugging the coastline 11 miles away. Risser could see three carriers, three battleships, and several cruisers and destroyers. It was a beautiful group of targets, but Risser had orders to report first, then attack. He watched the ships go by; then, after dark—at 7:25 P.M.—he surfaced and commenced transmitting and trailing. Risser's valuable report was received, although he didn't know it. After this, Risser, low on fuel, was ordered to Brisbane for refit.

Slade Cutter, who had taken *Seahorse* to Brisbane following his tough third patrol in the Marianas, got under way on June 3. He topped off his fuel tanks in the Admiralties and proceeded northwestward toward Surigao Strait to join Ben Oakley in *Growler*, who had moved to that station after his lifeguard duty in the Marianas. These boats were to guard the east entrance of the strait in case Ozawa's fleet—or parts of it—came out that way.

At 6:45 P.M. on June 15, the same day and almost the same hour that Risser picked up the Ozawa force in San Bernardino Strait, Cutter saw smoke on the horizon about 200 miles due east of Surigao Strait. At first it appeared to be coming from "four large unidentified men-of-war."

Cutter immediately commenced tracking at maximum speed, setting up to attack, and obtaining the enemy course, speed, and zigzag plan. He had closed to 19,000 yards when one of his main motors began sparking badly, forcing him to reduce speed to 14½ knots. *Seahorse* gradually fell behind the formation. At 3 A.M. the following day, he got off a vital contact report to Lockwood.

AT 1330 ZEBRA [Japanese] TASK FORCE IN POSITION 10–11 NORTH, 129–35 EAST. BASE COURSE 045, SPEED OF ADVANCE 16.5. SIGHT CONTACT AT DUSK DISCLOSED PLENTY OF BATTLESHIPS. SEAHORSE WAS ASTERN AND COULD NOT RUN AROUND DUE TO SPEED RESTRICTIONS CAUSED BY MAIN MOTOR BRUSHES. RADAR INDICATES SIX SHIPS RANGES 28,000 TO 39,000 YARDS. CRUISERS AND DESTROYERS PROBABLY COULD NOT BE DETECTED AT THESE RANGES WITH OUR RADAR. POSSIBLE CARRIER PLANE FORCED US DOWN THIS MORNING. SEAHORSE TRAILING.

The unit Cutter found was the last Kon force, built around the super-battleships *Musashi* and *Yamato*. The force soon outdistanced Cutter. He got off a final contact report which stated in part:

SEAHORSE LOST CONTACT 15 HOURS ZEBRA FIFTEEN [3 P.M. June 15, local time] DUE TO MOTOR FAILURE. REGRET UNABLE TO CLOSE TO AMPLIFY PREVIOUS REPORT. SIGHTED TOPS OF FOUR UNIDENTIFIED LARGE MEN-OF-WAR AND SIX OTHER SOURCES OF SMOKE AT DUSK FIFTEENTH.

By the time these reports from Risser and Cutter were received, U.S. troops were storming ashore against heavy opposition at Saipan. The invasion of Guam was set for June 18. However, it was now clear to Admiral Spruance that Admiral Ozawa was on the way to fight with all he had. Spruance postponed the invasion of Guam and redeployed Task Force 58 to meet the oncoming threat from the west.

A brand-new Pearl Harbor submarine, *Cavalla*, with a new skipper, Herman Kossler, who had been exec to Burt Klakring for *Guardfish*'s first five patrols, left Midway on June 4 to relieve Risser at San Bernardino Strait. On the way to station June 9, *Cavalla*, under way on the surface, collided with a whale, which broached in a pool of blood. Kossler was concerned that the collision might have bent one of his shafts or a screw. However, he felt no vibrations or other defects and continued on his way. On June 11 he passed Corbus in *Bowfin*, who had left Palau and was headed for Majuro for refit.

On June 15, after Lockwood received the contact reports from Risser and Cutter, he shifted *Cavalla* and Deragon's *Pipefish* to advance scout stations along the probable track of the main body. The two boats rendezvoused about 8 A.M. June 16, directly on the "estimated track" and about 360 miles due east of San Bernardino Strait. According to the arrangement made between them, Kossler would patrol 5 miles north of the estimated track and Deragon 5 miles south. The two boats searched all day without finding anything. At about 8 P.M., Kossler got off a negative search report and informed Lockwood that he was proceeding to San Bernardino Strait to relieve Risser.

Three hours later, at 11:03 P.M., Kossler picked up a contact on radar. It was four ships. This was not the main body—which had veered southeastward off the estimated track—but a supply force which had continued due east from San Bernardino. Kossler made an end around and dived about 3:40 A.M. He went in to attack, setting up stern tubes on one of the tankers. As he was about to fire, one of the destroyers charged at *Cavalla*, forcing Kossler to break off the attack and go deep to avoid a collision. Kossler later estimated that the destroyer came over *Cavalla*'s engine room as he was passing 75 feet.

When he came up again about 5 A.M. Kossler could not see the convoy. He decided not to chase, reasoning that his relief of Risser took priority. He had already expended much fuel and a full day looking for Ozawa; to chase the tanker convoy would take at least another day and more fuel. Kossler radioed Lockwood his decision.

When Lockwood received the message, he was of a different mind. Risser had already reported the fleet coming out; his relief was not urgent. Obviously these tankers had come to the area to refuel Ozawa's fleet. If Kossler trailed the tankers, they might lead him to the carriers and battleships. If they were sunk, Ozawa's fleet could not refuel and would be left sitting ducks. At 7:04 A.M. on June 17, Lockwood radioed Kossler: "CAVALLA IS [TO TAKE] ACTION. COM-SUBPAC ALSO SENDS TO MUSKALLUNGE, SEAHORSE AND PIPEFISH FOR INFO. . . . DESTRUCTION THESE TANKERS OF GREAT IMPORTANCE. TRAIL, ATTACK, REPORT."

Kossler spent thirteen seemingly fruitless hours running down the track of the tankers. However, at about eight that night, June 17, he ran into a Japanese task force. At about 20,000 yards, his radar showed seven good-sized pips, which Kossler presumed to be a carrier, battleships, and cruisers. He submerged and ran in.

Believing it more important first to report this force, then attack if possible, for the next hour or so Kossler remained submerged, letting the task force pass by. At 10:45 P.M. he surfaced and got off a contact report—"fifteen or more large combatant ships"—to Lockwood and attempted to trail. Upon receiving this information, Lockwood told Kossler—and all other submarines—to shoot first and report later. To Kossler he said: HANG ON AND TRAIL AS LONG AS POSSIBLE REGARD-LESS OF FUEL EXPENDITURE. . . . THEY MAY SLOW TO FUEL FROM YOUR PREVIOUSLY REPORTED TANKERS AND YOU MAY HAVE A CHANCE TO GET IN AN ATTACK. But by then Kossler had lost track of the force.

The contact report from Kossler puzzled Admiral Spruance. From the time of Risser's report to the time of Kossler's report, Admiral Ozawa had advanced only 500 miles for a very low average speed of about 8.8 knots. Moreover, Kossler had only reported "fifteen or more" large ships, and Spruance believed Ozawa capable of sending over forty. Spruance was suspicious. The idea took root that Ozawa had split his force and would attempt to flank Task Force 58 and break up the landing on the beaches at Saipan. But Ozawa had not split his forces. He was killing time. Admiral Toyoda had got him under way a day too early. He was waiting for land-based aircraft to congregate in the Marianas to help him attack.

Based on Kossler's several reports, it appeared to Lockwood that the four submarines—*Albacore, Bang, Finback,* and *Stingray*—in the "square" scouting line west of the Marianas were too far north. At eight on the morning of June 18, he ordered all four to shift position 100 miles southward. During the morning hours, the four boats carried out these orders.

All day on June 18 the two carrier forces lay back, trying to find one another with search aircraft. None of the U.S. planes found the Japanese forces. Ozawa's planes found Spruance's forces, about 250 miles southwest of the Marianas, and he decided that the next day—June 19—he would launch the "decisive" battle.

Spruance was still concerned that Ozawa might have split his forces to make an end run against the amphibious forces at Saipan. Another submarine report seemed to lend credence to that theory. At about eight on the night of June 18, Sam Loomis in *Stingray,* one of the "square" submarines, tried to get off a routine report on a minor fire in his radio antenna. The Japanese jammed his transmission, making it unreadable. Spruance thought Loomis might have found the Japanese and his radio transmission was a contact report. If so, it put the Japanese much farther *east* than anyone had guessed, possibly making the end run Spruance feared. Accordingly, Spruance took up an easterly course—back toward Saipan and away from Ozawa—during the night.

Shortly after Spruance gave these orders, Ozawa broke radio silence. He called headquarters on Guam to make arrangements for land-based air support for the morrow's attack and to tell Guam to be prepared to service carrier planes that might land there to refuel and rearm after hitting the enemy. Spruance's radio intelligence specialists DF-ed these transmissions, obtaining an accurate fix. The fix placed Ozawa's forces much farther *west* of *Stingray*'s position. But Spruance did not trust DF-ing and preferred to be guided by *Stingray*'s unreadable message.

About this time James Jordan in *Finback,* patrolling the northwest corner of the square, saw two searchlight beams on the southern horizon. Jordan charged south toward the beams at full speed but could not get close enough to pick up whatever it was on his SJ radar. Six hours later—11 P.M.—Jordan reported what he had seen to Lockwood. Another three hours went by before the message reached Spruance. Jordan had probably detected the main body, but his six-hour delay in getting off the report and the further three-hour delay in relaying the message to Spruance—a total lapse of nine hours—had rendered the contact meaningless.

When dawn broke on the morning of June 19, Ozawa had 430 aircraft on his nine carriers. He launched these against Task Force 58 in four major raids, all the while expecting massive raids from his land-based aircraft on Guam. Unknown to Ozawa, none of the four raids went well. His planes were pounced upon by U.S. carrier aircraft or chewed to pieces by barrages of antiaircraft fire. On that day, which would become famous as "The Great Marianas Turkey Shoot," Ozawa lost about 330 planes without sinking a single U.S. ship. Nor did he receive much support from land-based aircraft, most of which had already been destroyed by U.S. carrier raids.

At about eight on the morning of June 19, as Ozawa was preparing Raid One, Jim Blanchard in *Albacore*, working the southwest corner of the square, raised his periscope. Thanks to Lockwood's decision the day before to shift the square 100 miles south, Blanchard found himself right in the midst of Ozawa's main carrier group.

Blanchard let one carrier go by and selected a second one for his target. The initial range was 9,000 yards. A destroyer loomed in his crosshairs. Blanchard coolly changed course to allow the destroyer to pass ahead. The range to the carrier closed to 5,300 yards. As Blanchard went in, he took another periscope look. It was immediately apparent that something had gone wrong with the TDC. Cussing his luck, Blanchard fired six bow tubes by "seaman's eye."

At least three destroyers immediately charged *Albacore*. Blanchard went deep. Going down he heard—and felt—one solid torpedo explosion which timed perfectly for the run of his number-six torpedo. About that time, twenty-five depth charges rained down, many so close that cork flew off the overhead. Then Blanchard heard "a distant and persistent explosion of great force." Then another.

One of Blanchard's torpedoes had hit the carrier. It was Ozawa's flagship, *Taiho*, 31,000 tons, newest and largest in the Japanese fleet.

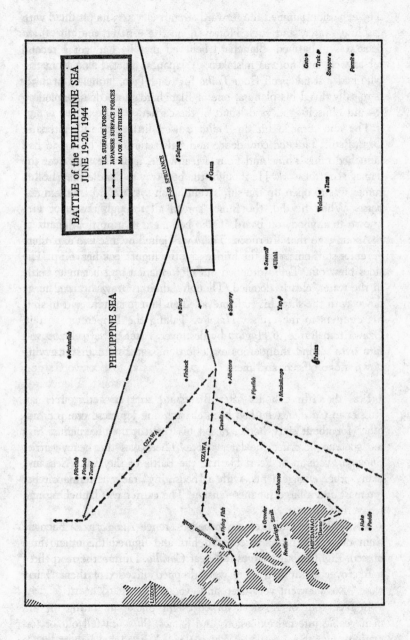

BATTLE of the PHILIPPINE SEA
JUNE 19-20, 1944

U.S. SURFACE FORCES
JAPANESE SURFACE FORCES
MAJOR AIR STRIKES

PHILIPPINE SEA

TF-58 SPRUANCE

OZAWA

OZAWA

•Saipan

•Guam

•Woleai   •Truk

•Seawolf
•Ulithi

•Yap

•Palau

•Bang

•Saigray

•Finback

•Albacore

•Cavalla

•Pipefish

•Muskallunge

•Seahorse

•Flying Fish

•Growler

•Redfin

Surigao Strait

San Bernardino Strait

MINDANAO

•Davao

•Hake

•Paddle

•Pilotfish
•Pintado
•Tunny

•Archerfish

LUZON

•Gato   •Truk
•Snapper

•Permit

•Tuna

The explosion jammed the forward aircraft elevator; its pit filled with gasoline, water, and fuel. However, no fire erupted and the flight deck was unharmed. Blanchard believed that he had got a second hit as well, but he was mistaken. A Japanese pilot, Sakio Komatsu, who had just taken off from *Taiho* for Raid Two, launched at 8:56, heroically dived his plane at one of Blanchard's torpedoes, exploding it—and himself—100 yards short of the carrier.

The one torpedo hit on *Taiho* caused little concern on board. Ozawa still "radiated confidence and satisfaction" and by 11:30 had launched raids Three and Four. Meanwhile, a novice took over the damage-control work. He thought the best way to handle the gasoline fumes was to open up the ship's ventilation system and let them disperse. When he did, the fumes spread all through the ship. Unknown to anybody on board, *Taiho* became a floating time bomb.

About 3:30 that afternoon, *Taiho* was jolted by a severe explosion. A senior staff officer on the bridge saw the flight deck heave up. The sides blew out. *Taiho* dropped out of formation and began to settle in the water, clearly doomed. Though Admiral Ozawa wanted to go down with the ship, his staff prevailed on him to survive and to shift his quarters to the cruiser *Haguro*. Taking the Emperor's portrait, Ozawa transferred to *Haguro* by destroyer. After he left, *Taiho* was torn by a second thunderous explosion and sank stern first, carrying down 1,650 officers and men.

Less than three hours after Blanchard shot at *Taiho*, Herman Kossler in *Cavalla*, who had been chasing one Japanese group or another for about sixty hours, raised his periscope. "The picture was too good to be true," he later wrote. There was the heavy carrier *Shokaku*, veteran of Pearl Harbor, the Battle of the Coral Sea, and many other engagements, with a "bedspring" radar antenna on her foremast and a large Japanese ensign. The carrier was launching and recovering aircraft.

Kossler closed and fired six torpedoes, range 1,200 yards. Then he went deep. He heard three solid hits and figured the other three missed. Eight depth charges fell near *Cavalla*. During the next three hours, over a hundred more were dropped, fifty-six of them "fairly close." Kossler went very deep and evaded.

In fact, four of Kossler's torpedoes hit *Shokaku*, setting off unmanageable internal explosions and flames. *Shokaku* fell out of formation. Her bow settled. Water flooded into the hangar space through an elevator. Shortly after three o'clock in the afternoon, she turned over and plunged beneath the waves.

After sinking *Shokaku*, Kossler took *Cavalla* to her original destination, San Bernardino Strait, to relieve Risser in *Flying Fish*. On June 26 he picked up an eight-ship convoy but bungled the attack. He tried to recover with an end around but lost the convoy and was not able to find it again.

Kossler returned a hero from this, his first war patrol. Lockwood knew from the codebreakers that *Shokaku* had sunk.

Neither Jim Blanchard nor anyone else on *Albacore*—and not even Lockwood—believed *Taiho* had sunk. Rather, Blanchard was angry at himself for "missing a golden opportunity." After the action, he was sent on to lifeguard for follow-up carrier strikes on Yap and Ulithi. During a raid on June 29, *Albacore* was strafed by a Japanese plane, which left several holes in the superstructure but did no major damage. On July 2, Blanchard shifted over to intercept traffic between Yap and Palau.

Shortly after eight the following morning, Blanchard picked up a ship and dived to attack. On closing, he saw it was a "wooden interisland steamer, approximately 900 tons." It was not worth torpedoes, Blanchard decided, so he surfaced for a gun attack. He set the ship on fire, ensuring its destruction, but was driven down by Japanese aircraft.

After the plane went away, Blanchard surfaced and picked up five wounded survivors, clinging to wreckage. When their wounds had been attended to by the pharmacist's mate, Blanchard had them locked up in the empty 4-inch ammo magazine locker, a tiny cell beneath the crew's mess. Later, he found a half-submerged lifeboat. He wrote, "When close aboard saw two women clinging to side of boat and a child four to five years old lying on the forward thwart." Blanchard—shaken by the sight—ordered a rubber raft put over the side alongside the lifeboat. It contained food, water, and fruit juices.

As Blanchard recalled the sorry episode years later, the interisland freighter he sank, *Taimei Maru*, was loaded with "lots of civilians . . . construction workers and their families . . . who were returning to the mainland." The survivors who reached Japan claimed that Blanchard had treated them ruthlessly. Emperor Hirohito, Blanchard recalled, lodged an official protest with the United States, one of the rare cases a Japanese ship sinking was officially protested.

After that, Blanchard put into the Admiralty Islands, unloaded his prisoners, refueled, and returned to Majuro for refit, arriving July 15. He was praised for an aggressive patrol and received credit for damaging a "*Shokaku*-class" carrier. For this, he was awarded only a Commendation Ribbon. Between "missing" *Taiho* and sinking a ship that drew a protest from the Emperor, Blanchard was less than pleased with this patrol.

As Blanchard recalled, the codebreakers lost track of *Taiho* after this battle. They were puzzled but did not think she had been sunk. "Months and months went by," Blanchard recalled. "Then they picked up a POW someplace who said *Taiho* went down in the Battle of the Philippine Sea. Even then, intelligence was doubtful. So I said, 'Keep him alive until he convinces them.'"

When the confirmation finally was obtained, Lockwood substituted a Navy Cross for Blanchard's Commendation Ribbon.

During the night of June 19, Admiral Ozawa on *Haguro* retired his forces and regrouped for refueling on the following day and then shifted his flag to *Zuikaku*. Even though he had lost two carriers to U.S. submarines, most of his planes had failed to return, and he had had no help from land-based aircraft, he was not dispirited. He believed that many of the aircraft which failed to return had gone on to bases in the Marianas and would be ready for battle again soon. Ozawa prepared for a second strike on June 21 which would truly annihilate the U.S. Pacific Fleet.

That night at 9:21, James Jordan in *Finback*, patrolling the northwest corner of the square, again sighted searchlights on the horizon. These must have come from Ozawa's force, which passed close to *Finback*'s area. Again Jordan charged in, and this time he made radar contact. He had closed to 14,000 yards when four destroyers came up astern, seemingly attacking *Finback*. Jordan submerged. Later he said, "The destroyers passed over us without attacking, followed closely by the major ships, which numbered more than twenty-five."

Three hours later, Jordan surfaced with all these ships still in sight. He trailed and tried to get off a contact report, but the radio transmitter was out of commission. Jordan said later, "We continued to track on the surface, hoping the transmitter could be quickly repaired, but were again forced down by one or more high-speed ships. The pattern continued all night. Each time we surfaced we were forced to dive by returning aircraft or surface ship, although none stayed to attack us."

Jordan's radio transmitter remained out of commission for several days. Later, when *Finback* returned from patrol, Jordan's squadron commander wrote in despair, "*Finback*'s inability to transmit information on contact with enemy force on June 19 was one of the costly misfortunes of the war." The episode left Jordan in a deep depression, and he requested immediate relief.

I was despondent and morose after making nine patrols in less than three years [he wrote later]. I felt my next one would be my last. . . . I now believe I had a simple case of combat fatigue and should have turned myself in for treatment. Instead I represented to my superior that I felt unfit and unsafe to command the boat any longer and feared for the safety of the ship and its crew. My boss was most understanding and urged me to take two weeks to reconsider my decision since the consequences of such an act can be disastrous to an officer's career. I understood this but stuck with my decision. It caught up with me about fifteen years later when I failed of selection [i.e., was not promoted].

That same night, Admiral Spruance made a move that was strangely reminiscent of his move in the Battle of Midway: he again let the surviving and badly mauled Japanese fleet slip away. At Midway he may have been lucky; this time it was, beyond doubt, a tactical error. He lost contact with Ozawa's forces, now maintaining strict radio silence. Nobody sent out night search planes to find it. While Ozawa retired to the northwest to rendezvous with his tankers, Spruance steamed east. Hour by hour the distance between the two forces grew greater.

Had Spruance followed up more aggressively and obtained a position report on Ozawa, U.S. submarines might have inflicted even more damage on the Japanese. Lockwood had three boats to the north of the battle scene ideally positioned to intercept: the wolf pack Blair's Blasters, composed of *Pilotfish*, *Pintado*, and *Tunny*. If Spruance had determined earlier that Ozawa was retiring northwestward toward Okinawa, these three boats could have intercepted. Having no positive information on Ozawa's movements, Lockwood kept the pack in place to the north, hoping Ozawa would head for Japan, passing through the pack's area. In addition, he moved

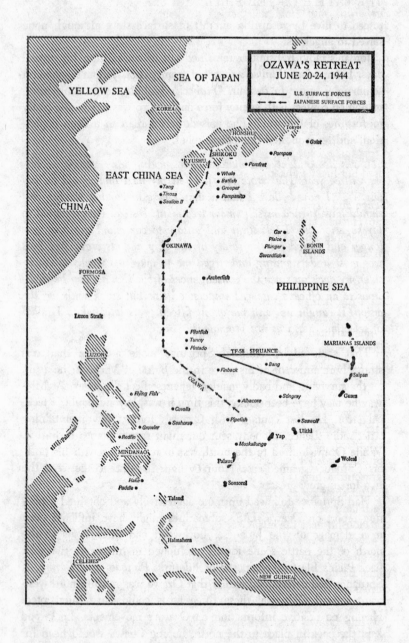

OZAWA'S RETREAT
JUNE 20-24, 1944

→ U.S. SURFACE FORCES
⟵--- JAPANESE SURFACE FORCES

SEA OF JAPAN

YELLOW SEA

KOREA

HONSHU

Tokyo

• Golet

SHIKOKU

• Pompon

KYUSHU

• Pomfret

EAST CHINA SEA

• Whale
• Batfish
• Grouper
• Pampanito

• Tang
• Tinosa
• Sealion II

CHINA

Gar •
Plaice •
Plunger •
Swordfish •

BONIN
ISLANDS

OKINAWA

FORMOSA

• Archerfish

PHILIPPINE SEA

Luzon Strait

• Pilotfish
• Tunny
• Pintado

MARIANAS ISLANDS

TF-58 SPRUANCE

LUZON

• Bang

Saipan

• Finback

OZAWA

Guam

• Flying Fish

• Albacore

• Stingray

• Cuvalla

• Pipefish

• Seawolf

• Seahorse

Ulithi

• Growler

Yap

• Redfin

MINDANAO

• Muskallunge

Woleai

Palaus

Haka

• Paddle

• Talaud

Sonsorol

Halmahera

CELEBES

NEW GUINEA

Archerfish west from the Bonins to cover a northward retreat to Japan.

On June 20, Spruance belatedly headed west, launching the hunt for Ozawa. That afternoon, at about four, a search plane from *Enterprise* found Ozawa 275 miles away. It was the first time in the whole battle that a U.S. carrier plane had even *seen* the Japanese surface forces. Although it was late in the day and the Japanese lay almost at the extreme range of U.S. aircraft, Spruance gave the go-ahead for an all-out attack.

The planes reached the Japanese shortly before sunset. In a confused but lucky fight, they sank the carrier *Hiyo* (which Roy Benson had damaged off Tokyo Bay in June 1943) and two fleet tankers, *Genyo* and *Seiyo Maru*. They inflicted heavy damage on the battleship *Haruna* and the cruiser *Maya* and light damage on Ozawa's new flagship *Zuikaku* and the carriers *Junyo*, *Ryuho*, and *Chiyoda*. In addition, they shot down another twenty-two Japanese planes, leaving Ozawa with only about thirty-five operational aircraft.

The U.S. carrier planes involved in this long-range sunset action had a rough time getting home. One hundred of the 216 that took off for battle failed to make a safe return. Twenty were shot down or unaccounted for. The other eighty ran out of fuel and had to ditch or make crash landings on the carriers. To help them find the way home, Marc Mitscher ordered his carrier captains to turn on their lights. But for that bold action, many more might have been lost.

Following this attack, Ozawa realized he was in no position to make a second strike against Spruance. He retired to Okinawa at best speed, and offered his resignation, which was not accepted. Spruance ordered up a stern chase, but Ozawa, who had a good head start, outran him.

After stopping at Okinawa to refuel, Ozawa returned his fleet to the Inland Sea. Lockwood had four submarines patrolling off southern Honshu near the entrances to the Inland Sea: *Batfish*, *Grouper*, *Whale*, and *Pampanito*. None made contact with Ozawa's forces. In this greatest carrier air battle in history, later to be known officially as the Battle of the Philippine Sea, Ozawa had lost three of his nine carriers: *Shokaku*, *Taiho*, and *Hiyo*—two to submarines.

While Ozawa was beating his retreat, Admiral Toyoda ordered the Japanese submarine commander, Admiral Takagi, to throw every submarine he could lay his hands on into a close-in defense of the Marianas, an order reminiscent of Bob English's abortive plan to save Midway from Japanese invaders in 1942. With the help of code-breakers, DF experts, radar, and sonar, U.S. forces sank a dozen RO- and I-class boats in June and July, mostly in the waters of the Marianas. After the battle, Admiral Takagi himself was missing, perhaps lost escaping from Saipan in one of his boats. Other Japanese submarines trying to bring supplies to Saipan and Guam were driven off and were unable to complete their missions.

Thus far in the year 1944, Japan had lost about forty submarines from all causes. Counting the forty-five boats lost in 1942 and 1943, the total was about eighty-five. The force had been, in truth, cut in half. In Japan's increasingly desperate shipbuilding program, sub-marine replacement held a relatively low priority. The Japanese sub-marine force never recovered from the June–July holocaust. From that point forward, submarine construction was aimed in a different direction: the production of scores of midget submarines to be used in Japanese home waters against an anticipated Allied invasion force and the equipping of the remaining (and replacement) I-class with suicidal man-guided torpedoes called *kaitens*.

30

Pearl Harbor and Australia, June to July 1944

The Fight for Saipan

Saipan was invaded June 15, and the fighting there was indeed bloody. For once, the codebreakers and other intelligence forces failed Nimitz. There were 32,000 Japanese on the island, twice as many as intelligence had estimated. The resistance was suicidal. The island was not "secure" until July 9. After that, the invasion forces landed on Guam and Tinian, where the Japanese also put up fanatical resistance. By August 10, all three islands were in U.S. hands, but to capture them the United States lost about 5,000 killed and 20,000 wounded.

The invasion of the Marianas turned out to be even more decisive than Nimitz had foreseen. The battle not only cost Toyoda three aircraft carriers but also most of his carrier air wings, a blow from which the Japanese naval air arm never really recovered. The remaining carriers were relegated to the role of divisionary forces for the future, and Japan began training pilots for its kamikaze corps: flying bombs, piloted by humans who would achieve everlasting fame by diving their craft into U.S. warships.

In Tokyo, the loss of the Marianas brought shock on an unprecedented scale. "Saipan was really understood to be a matter of life and death," said Vice Admiral Paul H. Wenneker, German naval attaché to Tokyo. Said Marine General Holland M. Smith, "Its loss caused a greater dismay than all her previous defeats put together."

And Admiral King noted, "Saipan was the decisive battle of the war."

On July 18, the day the loss of Saipan was announced to the Japanese people, Prime Minister Tojo and his entire cabinet resigned. General Kuniaki Koiso formed a new cabinet. "And, although Koiso took office with a promise to prosecute the war vigorously and issued a defiant statement," Samuel Eliot Morison later wrote, "everybody who understood Japanese double-talk knew that a change in ministry meant an admission of defeat and a desire for peace. Yet nobody in Japanese military or political circles would accept the onus of proposing peace, so the Pacific war dragged on for another twelve months."

Patrols from Pearl Harbor

While the big battle in the Philippine Sea was in progress—and in the days and weeks following—Lockwood and Christie sent other boats on patrol to the usual areas. Most of these were single boats, operating alone, but both commanders organized more wolf packs.

A Lockwood pack went on the polar circuit. It was a twosome made up of *Herring*, commanded by another Naval Academy football star, David Zabriskie, Jr., and *Barb*, now commanded by Eugene Bennett Fluckey.

Fluckey had been caught up in backwater assignments since the beginning of the war. After making five patrols out of Panama on the ancient *Bonita*, he had returned to the States for a postgraduate course in naval engineering. During *Barb*'s seventh war patrol (the second in the Pacific), Fluckey had made a PCO cruise.

While Fluckey was preparing to get under way from Midway, Lockwood flew out for an inspection. Fluckey said later, "I had never known the man but I did know he was a tough one and he wanted good skippers and good producers. I liked his methods. . . . If you produced, he supported you and gave you everything he could possibly give you. If you failed, he would give you another opportunity, but if you came back the second time with an empty bag, you usually were forced out of command."

For a brief moment, Fluckey feared he might be forced out of command before he set sail. "As he walked down the dock with my crew at quarters," Fluckey said later, "I had my heart in my throat for fear that he was coming aboard to tell me he didn't think I had enough experience and that he was going to remove me from command until I had proven myself. On his arrival on board, after saying hello, I immediately took an aggressive attitude and said, 'Admiral Lockwood, how many ships would you like us to bring back in our bag this time?' He looked at me with a smile and replied, 'How many do you think you can sink?' and I said, 'Would five be enough?' Lockwood said, 'I think five would be enough.' Then I said, 'What types do you want?' Lockwood said, 'Forget the types, you just get five. Now get out there and give 'em hell.'"

The two boats proceeded north. On the way, Lockwood sent them an Ultra about a three-ship convoy departing Matsuwa To in the Kuriles. Fluckey, the senior skipper, laid out the intercept plan: *Herring* close in, *Barb* to seaward. The convoy came out right on schedule. Zabriskie set up and sank an escort, then a 2,000-ton freighter. The remaining ships scattered and ran—directly toward Fluckey in *Barb*. Fluckey moved fast and fired three torpedoes; a freighter blew up and sank while he took pictures. It was *Koto Maru*, 1,000 tons.

After that, Fluckey surfaced to chase. He caught up with *Madras Maru*, 3,800 tons, and fired three stern tubes. This ship also blew up and sank. Fluckey then returned to the scene of his first sinking to capture a survivor for intelligence purposes.

He wrote, "It was a gruesome picture . . . an unholy sight . . . it was getting dark, the atmosphere was much like one you'd expect from Frankenstein. The people were screaming and groaning in the water. There were several survivors on rafts. The water at that time was very cold, about 27 degrees. These people were gradually freezing and dying. We took the most lively looking specimen aboard."

Meanwhile Dave Zabriskie closed in on Matsuwa and found and sank two ships at anchor in the harbor, *Iwaki Maru*, 3,100 tons, and *Hiburi Maru*, a transport of 4,400 tons.

Immediately after his torpedoes exploded, the shore batteries on Matsuwa* opened fire on *Herring*. The Japanese evidently scored two direct hits on *Herring's* conning tower, destroying the boat. The Japanese reported "bubbles covered an area about 5 meters wide and

* The same batteries that had shot at Frank Latta and Babe Brown in *Narwhal*, July 1943, when they were assigned to create a diversion so that *Lapon*, *Plunger*, and *Permit* could leave the Sea of Japan.

heavy oil covered an area of approximately 15 miles." Nothing further was ever heard from Zabriskie.

On his first patrol, Zabriskie had not sunk a confirmed ship and had been roasted for inadequacies in the fire-control party. On this, his second, he sank four confirmed ships for almost 10,000 tons within a two-day span and gave Fluckey an opportunity to sink two other ships fleeing his attack.

Fluckey wrote later that his POW turned out to be a "traitor to his country." Using sign language, he poured out valuable intelligence on Japanese ships and minefields. Fluckey radioed some of this—information on minefields off Hokkaido and northeast Honshu—to Lockwood.

Lockwood relayed it to Fluckey's classmate, James Seerley Clark, who was making his first patrol as skipper of *Golet* to the south. *Golet*, a new Manitowoc boat, had arrived in the Pacific earlier in the year, commanded by James Markland Clement. After an inspection cruise, Lew Parks decided the wardroom was ill-trained and ill-led and that it should be scattered. Mike Fenno, who also went to sea on her, thought they might get by with relieving the skipper. In the end, it was decided to relieve Clement and his exec and make do with the others.

Phil Ross was drafted from his job in operations at the Training Command to take *Golet* on her first war patrol and bring her up to snuff. His new exec—and prospective commanding officer—was James Clark, who had served on Chet Smith's *Swordfish* and then made one patrol on *Archerfish*. When *Golet* returned to port, Ross was still not satisfied with her wardroom and crew. Clark passed with flying colors, but Ross recommended that four other officers and two senior chiefs (from the original group) be sent to shore duty. His recommendation was not followed.

Despite the information on minefields, Clark ran into trouble. On June 14, two weeks after *Herring* had sunk, the Japanese attacked and sank a submarine off northeast Honshu—evidently *Golet*. The Japanese report stated, "On the spot of fighting, we later discovered corks, raft, etc., and a heavy oil pool." Clark was never heard from again.

Now alone, Fluckey shifted northwest to the Sea of Okhotsk, cutting among icebergs, bedeviled by mirages. He found some trawlers out sealing and sank them with his deck gun. On the night of June 11, he picked up two more ships and sank both with torpedoes; they were *Toten Maru,* 3,800 tons, and *Chihaya Maru,* 1,100 tons. Two nights later, Fluckey found another ship with a small escort. He fired two torpedoes and sank the large transport *Takashima Maru,* 5,600 tons. After that Fluckey returned to Matsuwa, poking *Barb*'s nose into the anchorage there and at other islands, threading through dozens of sampans. Twice Fluckey got caught in Japanese fishing nets. The first time he backed down submerged and got out. The second time, *Barb* was hooked solidly and Fluckey had to surface to cut himself loose.

When Fluckey returned to base, he was showered with congratulations. Later he said, "Admiral Lockwood reminded me that, by God, I was the only skipper during the war that told him exactly how many ships I was going to sink and then went out and did it."

Pomfret, a new boat, was commissioned by Frank Clements Acker, who came from *S-15*. Acker had always prided himself on keeping physically fit, but shortly after the commissioning ceremony he experienced a severe backache. It was diagnosed as an extended disc pressing on a nerve. Acker spent ten days in the hospital and then returned to his ship, as he said later, "back to normal nicely."

After reporting at Pearl Harbor, Acker went off on his first Pacific war patrol to Bungo Suido. One day, the watch spotted two freighters coming out of the channel. Acker plotted an intercept course, but the two ships went behind a minefield and anchored. Acker ordered *Pomfret* to close the minefield. His exec, Fredric B. Clarke, who had come from *Sawfish,* asked Acker what in the world he was doing. Acker replied that they had been sent out to sink Jap ships and that was what he intended to do.

Later, Clarke wrote, "Now I think that I am as brave a guy as many, but my stomach flipped over. Any submariner in the world is afraid of minefields—if you strike one while submerged, death is instantaneous. There is no chance of survival."

Clarke prevailed on Acker to stop the headlong pursuit into the minefield and wait to see what the ships would do next. After dark, they got under way, hugging the dark coast. Acker tracked, skirting the minefield, and then fired six torpedoes—three at a freighter, three at an escort. All missed, probably running under.

Early on the morning of June 14, while the moon was bright, radar reported a big contact at 23,000 yards. It was zigzagging, heading for Bungo Suido. Acker put on full power to intercept. At 14,000 yards, there was no longer any doubt about the target. It was a battleship, looking "big as the Empire State Building," escorted by a cruiser and some destroyers.

By good luck and good seamanship, Acker got position 2,000 yards off the target's projected track, with a fair chance at a shot. Acker thought they should dive and wait, while Clarke suggested holding on for ten more minutes. The officer of the deck swore at the brilliance of the moon. Two or three minutes after Acker agreed to remain on the surface, the battleship, which had probably picked *Pomfret* up on its own radar, beamed a searchlight on the bridge of *Pomfret*. Clarke wrote later, "It gave me the most naked feeling I have ever had."

Acker dived, while everybody waited for the splash of big shells from the battleship, the cruiser, or the destroyer escorts. None came, so Acker poked up the periscope. The formation had zigged and then turned back toward *Pomfret*. Acker set up and fired six torpedoes at the battleship at extremely long range. All missed.

Acker continued the patrol—aggressively. On the last night on station, he closed to 3,000 yards of the Japanese coast to bombard a small town with his deck gun. *Pomfret* ran aground and stuck fast in the mud. After several spine-tingling hours Acker got her loose and made flank speed for deep water. During this patrol, he experienced no further difficulty with his back.

Search for the Nickel Ship

After the Battle of the Philippine Sea, and while the fight for Saipan was in progress, Ralph Christie decided to make a second war patrol. Looking at the schedules, he saw that Enrique Haskins in *Guitarro* would be arriving in Darwin about June 19 from Pearl Harbor. Christie decided that Haskins could refuel and get a new load of torpedoes at Darwin and take him out for a "three-week patrol."

On June 21, Christie flew up to Darwin. Upon arrival, however, he discovered that *Guitarro* had engine problems that required immediate repairs in Fremantle. What to do? There was one possible answer. That same day, Sam Dealey in *Harder* arrived in Darwin from his epic destroyer-killing patrol off Tawi Tawi. His crew was worn out from this arduous cruise. Yet when Christie asked, Dealey agreed to make a brief extension. Thereafter, the forepart of the patrol would be known unofficially as 5A and the extension as 5B.

According to some accounts, the extension did not sit well with the crew. Lockwood later wrote that the news caused "bitter disappointment," and he quoted one of *Harder*'s radio technicians: "After blowing up the last destroyer on June 10, everyone was overjoyed, figuring on a short patrol and then back to Rest Camp in Perth. Unfortunately we pulled into Darwin and Admiral Christie wanted to go out with us. The crew was pretty sore."

In effect, Christie changed places with his operations officer, Murray Tichenor, who had gone along for the ride on 5A. Dealey got under way that same day, June 21. Christie wrote later, "The primary purpose of this short patrol was to intercept and sink what we called the 'Nickel Ship,' which left from Pomalaa in the Gulf of Boni, Celebes, about once a month. This was the sole source of nickel for the Japanese. We generally knew when it was leaving."

On the way to the Gulf of Boni, *Harder* received an Ultra. A damaged Japanese cruiser with two escorts, returning from the Battle of the Philippine Sea en route to Surabaya or Singapore, would pass their way, probably through Salajar Strait, south of Celebes. Dealey took up station 5 miles east of the strait.

On the morning of June 27, Dealey, expecting the cruiser any moment, dived at dawn. Christie, who was standing junior-officer-of-the-deck watch, manned the periscope. At 7:30 A.M., Christie sighted the cruiser and two destroyer escorts, right on schedule. However, as happened so many times with Ultra intercepts, *Harder*—or the cruiser—was slightly off course. The range was 9,000 yards. Dealey rang up flank speed, but he could get no closer than 5,600 yards.

After the cruiser and destroyers disappeared over the horizon, Christie turned to Dealey and said only half jokingly, "Why didn't you expose your conning tower and lure the destroyers in and sink them?"

Later, in private, Dealey asked Christie, "Admiral, were you serious about luring them in?"

Christie, who had unbounded faith in Dealey, replied, smiling, "Well, Sam, you're the Destroyer Killer." He explained later, "I was neither criticizing nor directing . . . the way we felt about Sam and *Harder*, the risk was not great."

Christie and Dealey then turned their attention to the Nickel Ship, going north into the Gulf of Boni to patrol off Pomalaa. Christie said later, "We could see the Nickel Ship being loaded under lights at night. However, we couldn't do anything then because there was a breakwater between *Harder* and the target. The only thing to do was withdraw to Salajar Strait and wait for it to come out."

On June 30, *Harder* submerged at the east entrance of Salajar Strait, waiting. About 7:15 that morning, the periscope watch picked up a ship coming eastward through the strait. Dealey and Christie had a look. The ship was close to shore, merging with the backdrop, making it difficult to identify. Both men agreed it was small, a tugboat, fishing trawler, or small freighter.

Dealey thought whatever it was might be worth attacking, either by torpedo or deck gun. Christie agreed. Dealey ordered the gun crew to stand by below, then surfaced and ran in at 17 knots. On the way in, a lookout spotted an aircraft. Dealey dived for twenty-four minutes. Seeing no further sign of the aircraft, he surfaced to resume the chase.

When they came to within 5 miles of the target, Christie and Dealey received a jolt. There were now two ships: the small one they had been chasing and the Nickel Ship. Both were westbound, the smaller ship trailing. Belatedly, it dawned on Christie and Dealey that the "trawler" was in fact a small escort vessel which had come to meet the Nickel Ship. Moreover, there were two aircraft circling overhead. They banked and headed for *Harder*.

Dealey dived. The planes dropped three small bombs, none close. Afterward, the men in the after section of the ship reported they could hear something rolling around on the deck topside. An unexploded bomb? Dealey put the rudder hard over and rang up full speed. The rolling noise stopped. "Whether the sound was caused by an imagination or by a dud," Dealey wrote, "it now ceased."

The escort churned over to help the aircraft. For the next two and a half hours, depth charges fell at a distance. This was not a real attack, Dealey thought, but rather a harassing action to keep them from getting at the Nickel Ship. The tactic worked. The escort and the planes kept Dealey down all day, and the ship got away.

Christie and Dealey were chagrined. They had been faked out. Had Dealey ignored the escort, he might easily have maneuvered around it to sink the Nickel Ship. It was, Christie wrote later, "one of the very rare instances in which Sam was fooled." Dealey wrote, "We had been maneuvered into trying to stop the ball carrier on an end run while he made an off-tackle play."

Having missed both these Ultra contacts, Dealey set course for Darwin. On the night of July 1, while passing close to Timor Island on the surface, the sky around *Harder* was suddenly illuminated "bright as day." The officer of the deck, scared out of his wits, dived *Harder* instantly. A Royal Australian Air Force Catalina patrol plane pilot had picked them up on radar and dropped a magnesium flare to see what he had found. Fortunately he dropped no bombs. An angry Sam Dealey kept *Harder* submerged four hours. Then he continued on to Darwin without incident, arriving July 3.

On the way to Darwin, Christie and Dealey had a long discussion about what to do with Sam Dealey and *Harder*. Dealey had made his five patrols. It was time for him to step aside. As Christie saw it, Sam's exec, Tiny Lynch, should take command of *Harder*; Sam should return to the States for thirty days' leave, after which he could go to new construction or back to Christie's staff to serve as Tichenor's assistant, or possibly to command a division if BuPers was ready to give the class of 1930 that responsibility.

Sam had other ideas. He agreed that Lynch should take command of *Harder* but thought that Lynch, who had also made five patrols, ought to have shore leave before taking on the heavy responsibilities of command. There were eighteen or twenty men scheduled to leave *Harder* after the fifth patrol; it was not fair to have Lynch assume command and train a new crew all at once. Dealey wanted to take *Harder* on one more patrol, shape up the new men, and then turn over the boat to Lynch.

Christie replied, "Sam, let's don't try to decide all this now. When you get to Fremantle, I want you to be my guest at Bend of the Road, if you want. It will be quiet and you can think it all out."

Dealey agreed.

While Christie was at sea on *Harder* his staff was preparing for a momentous political event in the submarine war, a summit conference between Admirals Lockwood and Christie. The two men had not talked face to face for sixteen months. The last time had been in February 1943 at Pearl Harbor, after Lockwood had come up from Fremantle to replace Bob English and Christie was en route to Fremantle to replace Lockwood.

The idea for the meeting had originated with Admiral Nimitz, who believed that as the "two roads" to Tokyo began to merge, Lockwood and Christie should integrate submarine activities more closely. In a letter to Christie May 29, Lockwood passed along the Nimitz idea, proposing that they meet at Pearl Harbor since it was "inconvenient" for him to come to Australia.

But Lockwood's own staff disagreed with this proposal. Without exception, every man who would attend the conference—Merrill Comstock, Dick Voge, Joe Grenfell, Art Taylor, Pete Ferrall, Bill Irvin—voted to meet in Perth. This vote, Lockwood wrote Christie, "shows what a lure your city has." A compromise was worked out. All hands would meet in Brisbane, July 5.

Immediately after leaving *Harder*, Christie boarded Admiral Kinkaid's plane at Darwin and flew to Brisbane for the conference, arriving in a driving rain on July 4. Lockwood flew in the following day. The two submarine force commanders instantly locked horns. Christie later noted in his diary, "Charlie as insufferably smart aleck as ever. . . . Almost impossible to discuss anything with him without his witless jokes and personal remarks. That bird has gotten away with 'moider.'"

After Christie got back to Fremantle, he wrote Lockwood, "I am extremely sorry that we had a personal spat of words at the outset. I felt I was being subjected to ridicule and lost my temper. It would be most unfortunate if such a thing could react on our official relations, in which we are substantially in accord. I regret it and do apologize." Lockwood replied, "As to your flare-up the other night, maybe my sense of humor is a bit unhumorous at times. Almost had a fight with Gnu Mayer [Andrew DeGraff Mayer, class of 1916] in almost the same way. Your apology is accepted."

The conference dealt with many technical matters, among them exchange of areas, rotation of boats for overhaul, radio frequencies, combat awards, spare parts, and officer and enlisted personnel. In the evenings, there were cocktail parties and formal dinners for all the visitors.

The most important matter was the creation of advance submarine bases. Lockwood had obtained permission from Admirals King and Nimitz to put a base on Saipan as soon as it was feasible. The old *Holland* would provide the first refit and refueling services beginning later in the month. In September, Christie would move *Orion* forward from Fremantle to Mios Woendi, a small island on the eastern end of Biak. Mios Woendi and Saipan were only 1,000 miles apart. With the creation of these advance bases, the submarines of both commands could shift back and forth with little difficulty.

Throughout the conference, Lockwood and Christie remained more or less at arm's length. One factor that may have helped open the distance was Christie's recent ride on *Harder*. Some in the Lockwood camp believed it had been a "stunt," an unnecessary strain on Dealey and the *Harder* crew. Lockwood may have been jealous. Christie had now made two brief patrols, where he had made none.

After Lockwood had departed, Christie, through no real fault of his own, got into hot water with his boss, Admiral Kinkaid. Christie paid his customary call on General MacArthur, during which he briefed the general on Sam Dealey's patrol 5A at Tawi Tawi and the sinking of what was then believed to be five destroyers. This reminded MacArthur that Christie had not yet accepted his offer to give army awards to submarine skippers. Christie corrected MacArthur politely, reminding him that he had already put forward such a recommendation for Walt Griffith in *Bowfin*. The recommendation, MacArthur replied, had never reached his desk.

It was now clear to Christie that his proposal for Griffith had been killed by Admiral Kinkaid. Christie later wrote, "Then to my embarrassment, surprise, astonishment, etc., he said he was going to give me a Distinguished Service Cross and Sam Dealey a Silver Star regardless of [Kinkaid's] policy of no Army awards to Navy personnel. . . . This turn of events put me rather on the spot because I had run counter to Admiral Kinkaid on the recommendation for an Army award to Commander Griffith. So I at once reported the whole affair to Kinkaid in his quarters where he was confined for a day with a severe cold."

What was said in this meeting has not been revealed. However, MacArthur was determined to present both Dealey and Christie an army medal. In the end, he quite properly reversed the order, presenting Dealey the higher award, the Army Distinguished Service Cross, and Christie the Army Silver Star. Kinkaid was not pleased.

Wolf Packs in Luzon Strait

Immediately following the Battle of the Philippine Sea, Lockwood improvised a wolf pack for Luzon Strait composed of boats that had been deployed for the battle. These were Slade Cutter's *Seahorse*, Anton Gallaher's *Bang*, and Ben Oakley's *Growler*. The three boats met in the strait on June 25. Gallaher was senior, so he took command. Cutter and Oakley went on board *Bang* to plan tactics.

Shortly after midnight on June 27, Cutter picked up a ten-ship convoy: five big ships, five escorts. In keeping with pack policy, he prepared a contact alert but deferred sending it in the belief that both *Growler* and *Bang* were too far away to help. Cutter dived for a submerged attack, firing six torpedoes at a tanker and two freighters. He believed he got five out of six hits—three in the tanker, one each in two freighters. He wrote, "First hit in tanker at point of aim, forward of bridge. It was a beautiful hit, producing a huge sheet of flame and setting the ship on fire." Cutter was positive that the tanker and a freighter sank, but postwar records credited him only with the tanker, *Medan Maru*, 5,000 tons.

Gallaher in *Bang* was not as far away as Cutter thought. He saw the tanker burning on the horizon and closed in. But he was too late. The following night, Cutter and Gallaher rendezvoused again. Later, Cutter wrote, "*Bang* told us that they had seen the fire from our tanker last night and believed that they could have gotten in had we notified them early enough. If that is so, we made a grave error in judgment, and deeply regret the decision to maintain radio silence. We apologize to *Bang* for what they may consider a lack of cooperation on the part of *Seahorse*."

The next day, *Growler,* by now seriously low on fuel, departed for Midway, leaving Cutter and Gallaher as a two-boat pack. Oakley's fuel problem was so acute he was forced to proceed on only one engine. Nevertheless, on the day he left he found a cargo ship with four escorts and managed to track and attack. He sank *Katori Maru*, 2,000 tons, early on the morning of June 29. The ship was evidently carrying gasoline. It blew up with an awesome explosion, "like a 4th of July flowerpot."

Cutter and Gallaher went on patrolling the strait. Near dawn on June 29, Gallaher picked up another convoy. He made a long end around in daylight, getting off a contact report to Cutter. But *Seahorse* did not receive the report. About 3 P.M. Gallaher attacked the convoy submerged, firing ten torpedoes at three ships. Gallaher believed he had sunk one or two of the ships, but postwar records failed to confirm his estimate.

That night, Cutter noted in his report, "Received the rebroadcast of *Bang's* dispatch reporting her brilliant attack this afternoon. Our radio had been manned continuously, but the contact reports the

Bang sent out were not received. Cannot understand this as we were hearing Jap stations clearly on the assigned frequency. We were particularly happy to hear of *Bang*'s good fortune in view of what happened the night before last."

On the night of July 3, Cutter picked up another convoy and flashed an alert to Gallaher. Then he closed in and fired at two freighters loaded with troops and equipment. He hit both. They each gave off many secondary explosions, probably caused by exploding gasoline drums. An escort charged in, forcing *Seahorse* deep. Forty minutes later, Cutter returned to periscope depth to find one ship sunk and the other severely damaged and lying to.

Meanwhile, Gallaher in *Bang*, receiving the contact report from Cutter, moved in to attack. He tried to torpedo the cripple, but a destroyer got in the way. Gallaher fired three torpedoes down the throat at the destroyer and went deep. At the last minute, the destroyer turned and avoided. Then it attacked *Bang*, dropping twenty depth charges.

After daylight, both Cutter and Gallaher made end arounds, gaining position ahead of the convoy. About noon, Cutter, who had ignored aircraft flying over him all morning, submerged ahead of the convoy to attack. He let the ships come close, so close that one passed directly over *Seahorse*. Cutter came up to periscope depth for a look at her stern. He wrote, "Troops were packed tight on the fantail and sitting up on the canvas-covered deck cargo. Every bit of deck space appeared to be utilized. . . . It was a fascinating picture."

Cutter fired at two of the freighters; he hit one and missed the other. Gallaher, harassed by aircraft and escorts, was not able to make an attack. Later he was commended for drawing off some of the escorts, enabling Cutter to make his attacks without excessive interference.

Following this attack, Cutter departed for Pearl Harbor, leaving Gallaher alone. Cutter had sunk four ships for about 11,000 tons. His total score in four patrols: nineteen ships. In his endorsement to Cutter's patrol report, Lockwood stated, "This was the fourth successive brilliantly conducted war patrol for *Seahorse*." He presented Cutter with his fourth Navy Cross.

When Cutter returned to Midway for refit, he was exhausted and asked for two weeks' leave to return to the States to see his wife and young daughter. Babe Brown gave him thirty days, turning *Seahorse* over to Weary Wilkins, who had come from BuPers and was anxious to make one more war patrol in a "modern boat." "Weary was wonderful," Cutter said later, "and said *Seahorse* was my boat and he was only borrowing it for one run. He said he would change nothing and didn't—including taking along young Budding, whom I had promised to be exec."

After Cutter had been home for a while, he received unexpected orders to new construction—*Requin,* which his wife was to sponsor at commissioning. "By this time," Cutter said later, "I had accepted the new situation and was perfectly willing to remain with my family."

Like the late Mush Morton, Slade Cutter had been an inspiration to the submarine force, a skipper's skipper and Lockwood's pride and joy. Like Burlingame and Triebel, Cutter was sometimes a terror while unwinding on the beach. But at sea he was awesomely cool and able, and possessed of an uncanny ability to find Japanese ships. (Lockwood wrote, in jest, that he believed that, if asked, Cutter could even find Japanese ships in Pearl Harbor.) In the postwar accounting, his nineteen confirmed ships sunk put him in a tie for second place with Mush Morton for the greatest number of ships sunk by a U.S. skipper. For years afterward, whenever submariners gathered to recount the war and spin yarns, the name of Slade Deville Cutter—football star, heavyweight boxer, and submariner extraordinary—would soon surface.

Three other wolf packs patrolled Luzon Strait during this period. Between them they sank twelve ships, by postwar accounting.

One of them began as a four-boat pack: *Apogon,* commanded by Walter Schoeni; a new boat, *Piranha,* commanded by Harold Eustace Ruble; *Thresher,* commanded by Duncan MacMillan; and *Guardfish,* back from a long overhaul and still commanded by Bub Ward. The commander was William Vincent ("Mickey") O'Regan, who called his pack the "Mickey Finns." O'Regan, who commanded Submarine Division 42, rode in *Guardfish.*

Late in the evening of July 11, the Mickey Finns moved in on a convoy. Harold Ruble in *Piranha* sank one ship for 6,500 tons, but Schoeni's boat, making a submerged attack, was rammed: the leading freighter in the center column hit *Apogon* on the starboard side, bending the periscopes and shears 45 degrees, tearing off the number-one periscope, and flooding the conning tower. Seven depth charges rained down. Schoeni managed to hold everything together, and *Apogon* escaped to go to overhaul. Schoeni, congratulated for saving his boat, went to shore duty.

Now short one boat, O'Regan received an Ultra on July 15 on an important southbound convoy. The pack changed course to intercept—all but *Piranha*, which didn't receive the message. Ironically it was *Piranha*, off course, that found the convoy at 4 A.M. and flashed the word. While *Guardfish* and *Thresher* were coming up, Ruble sank another ship.

That night—July 16—Ward in *Guardfish* closed the convoy for a night surface attack. He counted ten ships and several escorts. He fired six torpedoes at five overlapping ships, including a tanker. As he later described it, "The tanker was loaded with gas and blew up immediately, sending flames thousands of feet high. The large freighter was also loaded with combustibles, commencing to burn aft, and later blew up. The third ship in line, a freighter, broke in two in the middle and sank, and the fourth ship in line went down bow first. The scene was lit up as bright as day by the explosions and burning ships."

Ward then maneuvered around for a stern shot, firing three torpedoes at a freighter. One torpedo missed, two hit. Ward wrote, "Target leaned over on its starboard side and disappeared from sight and SJ [radar] screen." Finding another target, Ward "became impatient" and fired two torpedoes which missed. He turned around and fired two more at the same target. Both hit. Ward believed the ship sank, but he claimed only damage. He hauled clear to reload and rest, noting, "Everyone in the control party was beginning to show fatigue after six hours at battle stations under constant tensions. . . . Commanding Officer had had no rest for over fifty hours."

In action no less furious, MacMillan in *Thresher* attacked the convoy from another quarter, firing off twenty-three torpedoes. He believed he had sunk four ships and two destroyers, but postwar records credited him with only two ships: *Sainei Maru*, 5,000 tons, and *Shozan Maru*, 2,800 tons. Ward believed he had sunk five ships during his series of attacks, but postwar analysis gave him credit for three: *Jinzan Maru*, 5,200 tons; *Mantai Maru*, 5,900 tons; and *Hiyama Maru*, 2,800 tons. There was no record of a tanker sunk on this night at this place.

When Ward came back up at 6 P.M. on July 18, having rested himself and his crew, he found that a gale had kicked up huge seas. But he had surfaced in the middle of a massive convoy: two aircraft carriers (type unknown), two large tankers, one transport, one seaplane tender, and a naval auxiliary—all southbound. Ward fired three bow tubes at the naval auxiliary, range 1,370 yards. He swung to set up on a tanker, but it was coming in to ram, so Ward had to go deep to avoid and lost contact.

At dawn the following morning, July 19, he found yet another convoy. He submerged and fired four torpedoes at a target. One of them made a circular run around *Guardfish*; two hit. "Target broke in half immediately," he reported later. In these two attacks, according to postwar records, Ward sank only one ship, *Teiryu Maru*, 6,500 tons.

Following Bub Ward's attack, the Mickey Finns, out of torpedoes, left the area and returned to Midway. In all, the pack had sunk eight confirmed ships for about 40,000 tons, making it the best wolf-pack performance to date. Bub Ward, who had fired twenty torpedoes in the space of fifty-six hours, sank half: four ships for 20,400 tons.

A second pack operating in the strait arrived to attack Ward's convoy of the nineteenth. It consisted of three boats: John Flachsenhar's *Rock*, Alan Boyd Banister's *Sawfish*, and Roger Keithly's *Tilefish*. (Gallaher in *Bang* had come down from Formosa to join the pack for about nine days and had returned to base independently.) The pack, "Wilkin's Wildcats," was commanded by Warren Dudley Wilkin, head of Division 142, in *Tilefish*. All three boats closed and inflicted damage, but postwar records credited no ships sunk.

More significant action came a week later, when they were alerted by Ultra to an important contact. A Japanese submarine, I-29, was returning from a sea voyage to Germany, bringing a "precious cargo" (as Jasper Holmes later put it) of "German technical material." *Tilefish*, *Rock*, and *Sawfish* formed an ambush. The prize fell to Banister in *Sawfish*. When a submarine came along, right on schedule, Banister fired four torpedoes, three of which hit. Keithly in *Tilefish* was beginning an approach when he saw the explosion.

There was no immediate rejoicing in Pearl Harbor when Banister reported sinking what he assumed to be I-29. Nothing had been heard from Ruble's *Piranha* since the Mickey Finns had cleared the area, and Lockwood and Voge were convinced that, by a tragic error, Banister had actually sunk *Piranha*. It wasn't till a few days later that Ruble spoke up with a radio dispatch and Lockwood breathed easier.

* * *

The third wolf pack in the Luzon Strait in July was commanded by Lew Parks, riding Red Ramage's *Parche*. Besides *Parche,* the pack was made up of Dave Whelchel's *Steelhead* and a new boat, *Hammerhead,* commanded by John Croysdale Martin.* "Parks' Pirates," as the pack was called, had spent much of its patrol in frustration since leaving Midway on June 17. En route, Red Ramage had bagged just one small patrol craft with *Parche*'s deck gun. In the strait on July 5, when Ramage was moving in to attack what appeared to be two cruisers and a destroyer, he had to take his boat deep when one of the cruisers opened fire and he lost contact. After many days of bad weather and no targets, Parks received a report from Ward, on the Mickey Finns' boat *Guardfish,* of the massive convoy Ward had discovered on July 18, when he'd surfaced in its midst. Parks' Pirates never made contact with it. On the way to intercept, Parks and Ramage came upon an unescorted aircraft carrier—"the perfect dream come true"—only to have this vulnerable target zig and escape them.

It was only after eleven empty days that Parks' Pirates made their next convoy contact, and again bad luck plagued them. In the early hours of July 30, Martin in *Hammerhead* picked up a big convoy—twelve to fifteen freighters and tankers and many escorts—and flashed the alert. While Martin trailed, Red Ramage and Dave Whelchel moved in. With daylight fast approaching, Martin attacked, firing ten torpedoes at two big ships. He believed he sank one and damaged another, but postwar records showed no sinking at this time and place. Martin then attempted to trail the convoy submerged, but it got away. That night, running low on fuel, he surfaced and set course for Fremantle.

The contact reports that Martin flashed to Parks and Ramage were confused, erroneous, and niggardly. While Martin attacked, both Ramage and Whelchel thrashed around the dark seas, unable to make contact. They were somewhat puzzled, then angry. Ramage wrote bitterly, "As the sun came up, it finally dawned on us that we were the victims of another snipe hunt. That was bad enough

---

* Since Academy days, Martin had been nicknamed "Hammerhead." When he wound up on *Steelhead* for two patrols as exec, and then on *Hammerhead* itself, it seemed that either fate or a pixyish detail officer in BuPers was taking a hand in his assignments. It is not true, as widely believed in the submarine force, that Martin also served on *Marblehead* and the submarine *Hardhead.*

but we never expected to be left holding the well known burlap bag by one of our own teammates."

During the day, July 30, Whelchel and Ramage kept up the hunt, both harassed by planes. At 10:30 A.M., Whelchel spotted smoke and sent off a contact report. At about noon, Ramage saw the smoke, trailed, then lost it. After dark, Whelchel, who was still in contact, vectored Ramage into position. At 2:40 A.M. on the morning of July 31, Ramage made radar contact and went to battle stations.

Meanwhile, Whelchel attacked. At 3:32 A.M. he fired ten torpedoes at a tanker and two freighters. He observed a hit in the first freighter and black smoke near the waterline of the tanker. He missed the second freighter. He pulled off and began reloading his torpedo tubes.

The next forty-eight minutes were among the wildest of the submarine war. Ramage cleared the bridge of all personnel except himself and steamed right into the convoy on the surface, maneuvering among the ships and firing nineteen torpedoes. Japanese ships fired back with deck guns and tried to ram. With consummate seamanship and coolness under fire, Ramage dodged and twisted, returning torpedo fire for gunfire.

After Ramage hauled clear, Whelchel came in again. At 4:49, he fired four stern tubes at a freighter. He heard two explosions and saw a flash under the stacks. At 5:16, he fired four bow tubes at another freighter, observing two hits amidships. Escorts charged, forcing Whelchel under. He received a bone-jarring depth-charging.

Both boats remained submerged the following day, and that night Parks gave orders to leave the area. When the pack returned to Pearl Harbor, Lockwood credited Ramage with sinking five ships for 34,-000 tons, Whelchel two ships for 14,000 tons. In the postwar reckoning, Ramage received confirmation for sinking two ships for 14,700 tons, Whelchel two for 15,400. In addition, each skipper received half credit for sinking the 9,000-ton transport *Yoshino Maru*. Total for both: five ships, 39,000 tons.

The attack mounted on the convoy by Red Ramage was the talk of the submarine force. In terms of close-in, furious torpedo shooting, there had never been anything like it. Although the score was no record, Lockwood's staff believed Ramage deserved more than a Navy Cross. Accordingly, the recommendation went forward that Ramage be awarded the Medal of Honor. The recommendation was subsequently approved and Ramage became the third—and at the time the only living—submariner, after Howard Gilmore and John Cromwell, to receive this recognition.

Patrols in the East and South China Seas

Three boats went to the East China Sea. They were not a formal wolf pack, since they operated in separate—but adjacent—areas, but they mapped out a semicoordinated attack plan. The boats were Dick O'Kane's *Tang,* Donald Weiss's *Tinosa,* and a new boat, *Sealion II,* commanded by Eli Reich.

Weiss in *Tinosa* went to the area by way of the Bonins. On the night of June 15 he sighted a five-ship convoy: two tankers, a small transport, and two destroyer escorts. He tracked and dived for a daylight attack, firing six torpedoes at the two tankers. All missed and the destroyers charged in, forcing Weiss deep. He was not able to make another attack.

On the night of June 18, Weiss battle-surfaced on a fishing sampan, riddling the craft with small-arms fire and getting an occasional hit with the deck gun. When the sampan stubbornly refused to sink, Weiss decided on more drastic action. Later he wrote, "Tommy guns, hand grenades, rags and fuel oil were mustered topside. Moving close aboard the sailer, rag firebrands and about a half a dozen buckets of fuel oil were tossed on board. . . . The target quickly became a raging mass of flame."

On the night of June 24, the three boats rendezvoused about 120 miles southwest of Nagasaki. Since Donald Weiss was the senior skipper, O'Kane and Reich sent their execs, Murray Frazee and Henry Conrad Lauerman, to *Tinosa* for a strategy meeting.

The next night O'Kane picked up a large convoy heading into Nagasaki. He flashed the word to *Tinosa* and *Sealion,* but neither boat was able to close, so O'Kane had this one all to himself. It consisted of six large ships with an enormous number of escorts, probably sixteen. O'Kane came in on the surface, firing six torpedoes at a freighter and tanker. Later, he wrote, "Observed two beautiful hits in the stern and amidships of the freighter. . . . The explosions appeared to blow the ship's sides out and he commenced sinking rapidly. . . . Our fourth and fifth torpedoes hit under the stack and just forward of the superstructure of the tanker. His whole after end blazed up until extinguished as he went down by the stern." Escorts drove *Tang* under.

O'Kane claimed two sinkings for that night and Lockwood so credited him, but O'Kane's torpedoes evidently did far more damage than he thought. Postwar Japanese records revealed that four ships of the convoy went down: two transports and two freighters, totaling 16,000 tons. If the records are accurate, it means that O'Kane sank four ships with six torpedoes, making this the single best attack of the war. If his report that he saw two torpedo hits in both the freighter and tanker is correct, then the other two torpedoes got one ship each.

After that, the three boats moved northward, taking station off the southwest coast of Korea in the shallow waters of the Yellow Sea. On June 26, O'Kane picked up a lone freighter and fired four torpedoes. All missed. On June 28, Eli Reich in *Sealion* sank a 2,400-ton ship near the minefields in Korea Strait. The next day, O'Kane picked up another single, fired two torpedoes, and missed again. He attacked this ship a second time, firing a single torpedo. Down went *Nikkin Maru*, a 5,700-ton freighter. On July 1, O'Kane sank a small freighter and a small tanker.

Two days later, O'Kane and Reich rendezvoused again to compare notes. (Weiss in *Tinosa* had moved south.) Reich decided to have a look near Shanghai; O'Kane would stay off the coast of Korea. The following day, July 4, O'Kane sank two large freighters: 6,886-ton *Asukazan Maru* and 7,000-ton *Yamaika Maru*, from which he took a prisoner. On July 6, he fired his last torpedoes at a 1,500-ton freighter. It sank immediately.

While O'Kane and Reich were conferring on July 3, Weiss found a convoy and sank two ships: *Kosan Maru*, 2,700 tons, and *Kamo Maru*, 8,000 tons. Reich also found other ships. On July 6, off Shanghai, he sank a 2,000-ton freighter; moving up into the shallows of the Yellow Sea on July 11, he sank two more ships, one for 2,400 tons and one for 1,000 tons.

One by one the three boats left the area and returned to base. When *Tang* reached Midway, Lockwood credited O'Kane with sinking eight ships for 56,000 tons. In the postwar accounting, the number of sinkings was readjusted upward to ten and the tonnage cut to 39,100. In terms of confirmed ships sunk, this was the best war patrol by any submarine in the war. For it, O'Kane received his third Navy Cross.

Eli Reich in *Sealion II* turned in an excellent maiden patrol; he had sunk four confirmed ships for 7,800 tons. Weiss sank two confirmed ships. After this patrol, he took *Tinosa* back for an overhaul and then moved up to command a division. In three patrols on *Tinosa*, Weiss had sunk eight confirmed ships for 40,000 tons.

Altogether, the three-boat foray into the East China Sea cost the Japanese sixteen confirmed ships for 58,000 tons.

Ralph Christie's first formal wolf pack put to sea in June shortly after the Battle of the Philippine Sea. It consisted of three boats: Reuben Whitaker's *Flasher*, Frank Walker's *Crevalle*, and *Angler*, now commanded by Franklin Hess, who had been Jensen's exec on the disastrous first patrol of *Puffer*. Whitaker, the senior skipper, commanded the pack. To avoid a concentration in Lombok Strait, the boats left for patrol in the South China Sea independently.

Whitaker went up through Lombok Strait into the Java Sea. He traveled along the southern coast of Borneo, going through Karimata Strait, until he reached the equator, directly on the Surabaya–Singapore traffic lanes. Shortly after sunset on June 28, he picked up a thirteen-ship convoy bound for Singapore. Because the water was shallow and pitted with uncharted shoals and reefs, Whitaker elected to attack on the surface. He fired six torpedoes at two freighters, obtaining hits in both. "The first target," he later wrote, "with three hits, was seen to break in two and sink almost immediately." It was *Nippo Maru*, a 6,000-ton freighter. Whitaker believed the second also went down, but postwar records failed to bear him out.

While waiting for the other members of his pack to arrive, Whitaker took up station north of Camranh Bay. On the night of July 7, he saw a freighter with one escort. He sank the freighter, *Koto Maru*, 3,500 tons, with four stern tubes. The escorts zipped back and forth menacingly but never did find *Flasher*.

On July 13, *Angler* and *Crevalle* arrived and the pack was officially formed up. For five days, the boats rotated between the middle of the South China Sea and the Indochina coast, finding nothing. Whitaker, somewhat discouraged, got off a message to Christie stating that in view of the lack of traffic he doubted the need for three submarines to patrol the area; then he ordered a routine surface patrol on July 19 in the middle of the South China Sea.

At 10:46 that morning, Whitaker's officer of the deck saw a ship approaching through the haze and dived immediately. When Whitaker got a look through the periscope, his heart skipped a beat; the target he saw was a Japanese light cruiser escorted by a single destroyer, approaching at 18 knots. Whitaker set up quickly. Twenty-four minutes after diving, he fired four stern tubes at the cruiser. The destroyer was a mere 500 yards distant, headed dead on. "Don't think he saw us," Whitaker recorded, "but he sure looks mean."

Whitaker went deep, hearing two torpedoes hit. The destroyer dropped fifteen depth charges, but Whitaker outwitted him and eased away. An hour and twenty minutes after shooting, Whitaker came to periscope depth for a look. He saw the cruiser stopped dead in the water, down by the stern with a port list. At 1:26 P.M., Whitaker moved in for another attack, firing four bow tubes. The destroyer charged again, forcing Whitaker deep. Something went wrong with the attack. "I didn't see how we could miss," Whitaker wrote, "but we did." Whitaker took *Flasher* deep. The destroyer dropped thirteen more charges, none close.

While down, Whitaker was forced to reload, a time-consuming process, since it had to be carried out with absolute silence. When he came up again at 4:08, the destroyer was there but the cruiser was gone. Whitaker did not know whether the cruiser had sunk or had crept off toward Saigon. Assuming the latter, Whitaker surfaced after dark and alerted *Angler* and *Crevalle* to watch for a damaged cruiser heading for Saigon. For the next twenty-four hours, Whitaker jockeyed the boats around, looking for the cruiser. It was all wasted effort. Whitaker's first salvo had been successful, and the light cruiser *Oi*, 5,700 tons, had gone down while he was reloading.

Christie next ordered the pack to move up the South China Sea to a position off the west coast of Luzon, north of Manila. About dawn on July 25, Hess in *Angler* picked up a large northbound convoy and flashed the word. An hour later, Whitaker found it and got off a contact report but was driven down by an airplane. An hour and a half later, the entire convoy passed directly over Whitaker. He raised his periscope to find one escort passing over his after torpedo room, 100 feet away from the periscope. In his look, Whitaker counted fourteen large ships plus half a dozen escorts.

At that time, Whitaker had only six torpedoes. Since both *Crevalle* and *Angler* had a full load, Whitaker believed it would be better if Walker and Hess attacked first; then he could pick off what was left. He let the convoy go by and trailed. At 12:22, Walker in *Crevalle* submerged in a driving downpour, made a snap setup, and fired four stern tubes at one of the largest freighters. At the moment of firing, Walker sighted an escort carrier which was evidently providing the convoy air protection. After the torpedoes left the tubes, he lost depth control, almost broached, then went deep. Escorts found him and dropped fifty-two depth charges.

After dark, Whitaker surfaced, regained contact with the convoy, and flashed a report to his packmates. At 2:11 on the following morning, July 26, he attacked, firing his last six torpedoes at two ships, obtaining two hits in one freighter and one in another. He was feeling pretty good about that, he reported later, but then "our feeling of security" came to an abrupt end. One of his torpedoes had run through the near formation and hit a tanker beyond. Whitaker wrote that

the whole scene was lighted up as bright as daylight by the explosion of a tanker in the center column. One of our torpedoes which had missed the second target hit this large tanker about amidships. The ocean appeared full of ships and we were in an uncomfortable position. We cleared the bridge immediately and started down. By the time we hit fifty feet we could hear shells landing all around where we had been. We felt that we must have been seen and went to three hundred feet, turning at high speed and expecting an immediate depth charge attack. Although many high speed screws passed over us, and although escorts were pinging in our vicinity for a long time, it appears that they still thought we were on the surface as they dropped no depth charges. We were giving out a tremendous cloud of smoke when we submerged, and I believe that they were firing at our smoke thinking that we were still on the surface. We took a southerly course to clear the vicinity in order to surface and trail.

The tanker, which blew up and sank, was *Otoriyama Maru,* 5,280 tons.

After Whitaker withdrew, Frank Walker moved in for a second attack, firing nine torpedoes at two freighters just before dawn. He believed he hit and sank both targets, but postwar records failed to credit him. Escorts drove *Crevalle* deep. When Walker came up again, he saw a ship Whitaker had damaged. He fired four torpedoes, obtaining four hits. The ship, *Tosan Maru,* an 8,700-ton transport, sank quickly, while Walker snapped pictures of it through the periscope. Escorts again drove Walker deep, delivering many depth charges.

That night, when all the boats surfaced, Whitaker reported he was out of torpedoes and returning to Fremantle. The next-senior skipper, Frank Walker, took command of the pack. Two days later, Walker and Hess picked up another convoy: eight ships, four escorts. Walker fired his last six torpedoes, sinking the 6,600-ton transport *Hakubasan Maru*. Hess made two attacks but failed to achieve any sinkings.

This first formal Fremantle pack had done well. Whitaker had sunk four and a half confirmed ships for almost 25,000 tons (sharing credit with Walker for *Tosan Maru*); Walker had sunk one and a half ships for almost 11,000 tons. (Hess had sunk no confirmed ships.) The pack as a whole got six ships for about 36,000 tons.

Manning Kimmel in *Robalo* was sent to Indochina via Balabac Strait, a maze of waterways and islands. By that time, the code-breakers had given Christie at least four intercepted messages regarding Japanese minefields in Balabac Strait, containing specific details on which waters were mined—or likely to be mined. Kimmel's Operations Order contained specific information on how to transit the strait and what to avoid. Since the Japanese mined the strait in March 1943, it had been used about forty times by U.S. submarines. In 1944 *Crevalle*, *Tinosa*, *Puffer*, *Ray*, *Bluefish*, and *Lapon* (among others) had passed through safely. Kimmel himself in *Robalo* had passed through it in April, westbound to Indochina on his first patrol.

On July 3 Kimmel again made the transit, passing into the South China Sea. That same night, he received an Ultra and intercepted a *Fuso*-class battleship. He got off a contact report but did not state whether or not he had attacked it—probably not. It was the last message received from Kimmel. He then apparently patrolled his assigned area off Indochina without success. On July 26 he set course for Australia, returning via Balabac Strait. That night, while traveling on the surface, Kimmel evidently strayed into shallow waters. *Robalo* struck a mine, blew up, and sank swiftly.

Kimmel and perhaps half a dozen men—probably flung from the bridge into the water—may have survived the explosion. They made their way through the jungle up the east coast of Palawan, looking for friendly guerrillas. Instead, the Japanese found them and put them in jail at the Puerto Princesa prison camp, on the island. A few days later one of the *Robalo* prisoners managed to drop a note from a window to a U.S. Army prisoner who was on a work detail outside. The note described the loss of *Robalo* (by mine) and named four survivors held in that part of the prison. The army POW turned the note over to a U.S. Navy POW, who later made contact with the wife of a guerrilla leader. Her husband, a Dr. Mendosa, in turn relayed word that ultimately reached Christie.

None of *Robalo*'s survivors—the exact number has never been determined—survived the war. Many, perhaps all, were murdered by the Japanese on Palawan.

There were two versions of Manning Kimmel's death. During the war, Christie's command put out the word (and told his family) that he went down with the boat. After the war, Christie gave a grimmer version. He said that he received word from intelligence (probably from the guerrillas on Palawan) that when some Allied aircraft attacked Palawan, the Japanese became enraged, "went into a frenzy, pushed Kimmel and some other POWs in a ditch, then poured gasoline into the ditch and set it on fire." According to this version, Manning Kimmel died in the blaze.

Manning's brother Thomas, who had just returned to Christie's command as exec of a new boat, was summoned to Christie's office after one patrol. Christie informed Thomas that he was being relieved and sent to shore duty and that he could not and would not change the orders. Later Thomas recalled, "Dusty Dornin told me that Admiral King had directed I be ordered home when he found out about my brother being lost." This was a great disappointment to Thomas, who had hoped to move up to command before the war ended. (In the final days, he was ordered to command *Bergall*—too late to make a war patrol.)*

All this submarine activity had a devastating impact on Japan. Now that wolf-packing had been formalized and perfected and the torpedoes fixed, Japan was losing an average fifty merchant ships a month for about 200,000 tons. There was no way the shipbuilding yards could keep pace. Imports—especially oil imports—fell off drasti-

---

* Years later, Thomas held the opinion that *Robalo* had not strayed off course but that the Japanese had probably changed the position of the minefield. He doubted Christie's wisdom in continuing to use Balabac Strait this late in the war. Wrote Thomas, "The Japanese were obviously in retreat and the urgency for transiting a dangerous strait with known minefields was certainly greatly reduced if not nonexistent."

cally. There was a critical shortage of escorts for the convoys, and mounting chaos in the ranks of Japanese merchant seamen. Many hundreds were shipwrecked and marooned in southern waters, unable to get home. Others feared to leave Japanese home waters and sail off into the crosshairs of a hundred U.S. periscopes, almost certain of attack and perhaps a terrifying death at sea.

31

Washington, Summer 1944

In Washington, the breaking of Japanese and German codes had become a huge enterprise and a massive bureaucracy. By mid-1944 there were well over 5,000 people engaged directly or indirectly in the task. The navy had established a Japanese language school; it had recruited hundreds of reserves to help with codebreaking—including people such as the famous bridge expert Oswald Jacoby. Thanks to a combination of codebreaking and direction finding, U-boats in the Atlantic were being hounded and sunk by the dozens.

That summer, two episodes shook the bureaucracy to its foundations and threatened to blow the whole operation.

The first was an unknowing blunder by a navy captain, Daniel Vincent Gallery. Gallery commanded a navy hunter-killer group in the Atlantic whose mission was to sink U-boats. In the spring of 1944, Gallery conceived a plan to capture one of these U-boats intact. With this in mind, he trained a special boarding team that would rush inside a U-boat, close the sea cocks, and prevent scuttling.

On May 31, 1944, Gallery was put on the trail of *U-505*, which was returning to base in Brest, France, from war patrol. On the morning of June 4, one of Gallery's vessels found it off Cape Blanco, French West Africa, and forced it to the surface with depth charges. The Nazi captain abandoned ship. One of Gallery's destroyers, *Pillsbury*, quickly lowered a whaleboat carrying the boarding team, led by Lieutenant (j.g.) Albert L. David. David and his men performed brilliantly, shutting off sea cocks and dismantling demolition charges. *U-505* was seized intact, the first enemy man-of-war captured by the U.S. Navy since the War of 1812. David later received a Medal of Honor, his teammates the Navy Cross.

Although Gallery's accomplishment has survived in navy annals as one of the more brilliant feats of World War II, Admiral King and the codebreakers viewed it otherwise. When they learned of the capture of *U-505* they were thunderstruck—and furious.

If word got back to Admiral Doenitz that one of his U-boats had been captured intact, he would assume that the codebooks had fallen into U.S. hands (as they had) and would undoubtedly completely change the U-boat codes, requiring another massive (and perhaps unsuccessful) attempt to break them.* According to Al McCann, who was then commanding the 10th Fleet (the paperwork fleet charged with wiping out the U-boats), King was angry enough to want to court-martial Gallery.

Gallery had planned to tow the U-boat into a U.S. base in North Africa. Admiral King immediately sent orders to tow it to Norfolk and to swear the whole hunter-killer group to strictest secrecy. This was a monumental task, since there were about 3,000 men in the group, but Gallery managed to do it and his career was saved. No word leaked out. Doenitz never knew *U-505* had been captured; he assumed it was sunk.†

The second episode was political.

The Republican Party, led by Governor Thomas E. Dewey of New York, the presidential candidate in 1944, sought a powerful issue with which to unseat the entrenched Roosevelt, then running for a fourth term. The many secret investigations into the Pearl Harbor attack conducted up to that time had led to the impression in some circles that Roosevelt had had, through codebreaking, ample warning of the Japanese attack and had been derelict in preventing it. Admiral Kimmel and his anti-Roosevelt backers (which included the

---

* In 1943, operatives of the Office of Strategic Services (OSS) broke into the Japanese Embassy in Portugal without first informing Marshall, King, or the codebreakers. As a result, the Japanese had changed the entire military attaché code. It had not yet been broken again, and the United States had lost an important source of information, particularly regarding the European situation.

† After the war, *U-505* was towed to Chicago and wound up as a display outside the Museum of Science and Industry.

Chicago Tribune) were eager to foster that impression, which Kimmel sincerely believed to be fact. Some extremist Republican isolationists (and a few extremist naval officers) even professed to believe that Roosevelt had deliberately invited the Japanese attack in order to involve the United States in the war.

To many Republicans, all this seemed a heaven-sent issue. Some hinted at it publicly: for example, Congressman Forest A. Harness of Indiana, who said on the House floor that "the government had learned very confidentially that instructions were sent out from the Japanese government to all Japanese emissaries in this hemisphere to destroy the codes."

Would Dewey go all the way and break the secret? Admiral King and General Marshall feared he might. General Marshall, with King concurring, took it upon himself to warn Dewey that any disclosure about codebreaking at that point in the war would be a grave disservice to the country and the war effort. He wrote a three-page single-spaced letter to Dewey, which stated that none of the codebreaking information obtained prior to the Pearl Harbor attack disclosed Japanese intentions on Hawaii. Marshall went on to say:

Now the point to the present dilemma is that we have gone ahead with this business of deciphering their codes until we possess other codes, German as well as Japanese, but our main basis of information regarding Hitler's intentions in Europe is obtained from Baron Oshima's messages from Berlin reporting his interviews with Hitler and other officials to the Japanese government. These are still in the codes involved in the Pearl Harbor events.

To explain further the critical nature of this set-up which would be wiped out almost in an instant if the least suspicion were aroused regarding it, the battle of the Coral Sea was based on deciphered messages and therefore our few ships were in the right place at the right time. Further, we were able to concentrate our limited forces to meet their naval advance on Midway when otherwise we almost certainly would have been some 3,000 miles out of place. We had full information of the strength of their forces in that advance and also of the smaller force directed against the Aleutians which finally landed troops on Attu and Kiska.

Operations in the Pacific are largely guided by information we obtain of Japanese deployments. We know their strength in various garrisons, the rations and other stores continuing available to them, and what is of vast importance, we check their fleet movements and movements of their convoys. The heavy losses reported from time to time which they sustain by reason of our submarine action largely result from the fact that we know the sailing dates and routes of their convoys and can notify our submarines to lie in wait at the proper points. . . .

The conduct of General Eisenhower's campaign and of all operations in the Pacific are closely related in conception and timing to the information we secretly obtain through these intercepted codes. They contribute greatly to the victory and tremendously to the saving in American lives, both in the conduct of the current operations and in looking towards an early termination of the war.

I am presenting this matter to you in the hope that you will see your way clear to avoid the tragic results with which we are now threatened in the present political campaign.

After reading this letter, Dewey decided against making the Pearl Harbor attack a political issue. The codebreakers breathed easier.

32

Pearl Harbor and Australia, July and August 1944

Debate over Pacific Strategy

After the Marianas were secure, the next steps on the dual road to Tokyo were for MacArthur's forces to invade Morotai, an island off the northeast tip of Halmahera, and for Nimitz's forces to invade the Palaus. After that, the two roads would merge into one for an assault on the Philippines: Mindanao, then Luzon. Once the Philippines had been recaptured, fulfilling MacArthur's promise to return, the merged forces would push northward to Formosa and the Japanese homeland, securing the western flank by capturing bastions along the coast of China.

In Washington, Admiral King and his war planners (who now included Jimmy Fife) began to have second thoughts. King objected to the idea of "battering our way through the Philippines." He proposed that the Philippines be bypassed altogether and that Allied forces move directly against Formosa. With Formosa in Allied hands, the navy could "put a cork in the bottle" of Japanese sea communications, choking off shipping between Japan and the southern possessions. King believed Japan could be strangled by submarine blockade while U.S. carrier units and B-29s basing from the Marianas pounded her warmaking potential to rubble.

This was a bold and imaginative idea. While it is doubtful that air strikes on the Japanese homeland would have inflicted sufficiently severe damage (as time would prove), a submarine blockade could have been decisive. Between them, Lockwood and Christie now had almost 140 fleet boats (roughly 100 at Pearl Harbor and 40 in Australia) manned by combat-wise officers and crews. The torpedo problems had finally been licked: both the Mark XIV steam and Mark XVIII electric were completely debugged and the production bottleneck had been overcome.* The codebreakers were tracking most major Japanese ship and convoy movements. They knew the precise location and composition of Japanese minefields. Japanese antisubmarine warfare tactics had been proven relatively ineffective. After a fumbling, inept, and much-belated beginning, Lockwood had worked out the search, communications, and attack problems of wolfpacking. The Marianas were merely a three-day voyage from Tokyo and the gateway to the East China Sea.

With Formosa in Allied hands and a submarine blockade imposed on the homeland, the flow of oil and other strategic materials to Japan could have been shut off completely. Under conditions of total sea blockade, Japan would soon have used up her remaining oil reserves, immobilizing ships, aircraft, automobiles, electrical plants and production lines. Conceivably, Japan could have been "starved out" and demoralized to the point of surrender within a matter of two or three months. "In every phase of the war," the U.S. Strategic Bombing Survey reported, "oil determined Japan's strategy and governed the tactical operations of its Navy and Air Forces."

When MacArthur heard about this new idea, he was outraged. For one thing, it was clear that if the new strategy were adopted General MacArthur would play only a minor role. For another, MacArthur had promised to return to the Philippines, and now that promise might not be carried out. Some sixteen million Filipinos, MacArthur complained, would be left to "wither on the vine" until Japan was defeated. He argued that if the new strategy were adopted the Filipinos would continue to suffer unspeakable hardship for an indefinite period, and all Asia would lose faith in American honor. Admiral King rejoined that he was reluctant to slow up the war and shed American blood for mere sentimental reasons.

The debate was dumped into President Roosevelt's lap. On a trip to Honolulu, he met with Nimitz and MacArthur, who flew up from Brisbane. During these meetings, MacArthur eloquently presented

---

* Beginning in July 1944, boats going on patrol carried 75 percent electrics, 25 percent steam. The speed of the electric had been increased to about 40 knots, depending on water temperature.

his case. Nimitz, who was not wholly in favor of the direct thrust at Formosa, did not strongly oppose MacArthur, and years later he said he thought MacArthur was correct. Roosevelt made no hard and fast decision in Honolulu. In the weeks following, the Joint Chiefs of Staff, vastly overrating Japan's ability to continue the war of production and strongly influenced by General Marshall, who finally backed MacArthur's concept, decided the original plan for liberating the Philippines should be adhered to. The dual roads would merge at the Palaus and Morotai on September 15, as scheduled, and then point toward Mindanao, Leyte, and Luzon.

In the final analysis, Pacific strategy was dictated by political expediency and the considerable ego of General MacArthur. In giving way to his arguments, the Joint Chiefs committed the United States to tens of thousands of unnecessary casualties. Even though Britain had twice been brought to the point of collapse by German submarines in two wars, they overlooked the tremendous potential of the existing submarine force. Not only that; from this decision onward, the submarine force was called upon more and more to provide support for Allied invasion forces—guerrilla activity in the Philippines, photographic reconnaissance, lifeguard duty, scouting for enemy fleet units—all of which reduced the number of submarines on anticommerce patrol and needlessly prolonged the war.

Patrols from Pearl Harbor

In the lull between the invasion of the Marianas and the invasion of the Palaus and Morotai during July and August 1944, Lockwood and Christie mounted over ninety war patrols. Many were special missions in the Philippines or in support of fleet operations; many others were wolf packs; one boat, William Perkins's *Burrfish*, took a team of eleven frogmen to explore the beaches at Peleliu and Yap. A few of Lockwood's boats used the facilities at Saipan provided by *Holland*; Christie's Brisbane-based boats left from the new base at Manus Island in the Admiralties and resupplied at the new base in Mios Woendi. Many boats went to Luzon Strait to shut off the flow of reinforcements from Japan to the Philippines and the flow of oil from the south to Japan. In order to give Lockwood's submarines more legroom in the strait, the boundary separating the two commands was moved 90 miles south. In some cases, Lockwood's submarines and Christie's submarines attacked the same convoys, passing along information.

A new boat, *Hardhead*, commanded by a colorful character, Fitzhugh McMaster, set off from Pearl Harbor for Fremantle. Along the way McMaster was assigned to patrol San Bernardino Strait. Shortly after midnight on August 18, he picked up two large pips on his radar. About an hour and a half later, he could see the targets through binoculars at 8,000 yards. He—and others on *Hardhead*—believed them to be one battleship and one light cruiser. *Hardhead* maneuvered to intercept.

At 2:37 A.M., from 2,800 yards, McMaster fired at the "battleship"—five bow torpedoes and then four stern tubes. The bow tubes missed, but one or two of the stern-tube shots hit, causing an explosion and flame. In the glow, McMaster believed he had hit and sunk a battleship. He then chased the "cruiser," achieving attack position just before dawn and firing six more torpedoes. He believed that some of these hit and the "cruiser" went down too.

In all, McMaster had fired fifteen torpedoes, claiming ten hits which sank a battleship and a cruiser. He got off a triumphant contact report which mystified everybody. According to the codebreakers, all the battleships were still in Singapore or Empire waters.

The mystery was cleared up two weeks later by Sam Loomis in *Stingray*, who was taking his boat to Australia for special missions. About 600 miles due east of Surigao Strait, Loomis came upon a rubber raft painted with red and white stripes. In it were four Japanese, one naval officer and three ratings. All were seriously ill from exposure and lack of food.

When questioned, the four men reported they were survivors of the Japanese light cruiser *Natori*, 5,700 tons, torpedoed off Surigao Strait on the morning of August 18. They reported that *Natori* had received one hit from McMaster's first attack, that they had tried to retreat to eastward, but that heavy seas caused flooding. The other vessel in the formation had been a 1,000-ton transport, similar in appearance to a destroyer. It was undamaged and fled the scene.

Meanwhile, McMaster, replaced at Surigao by *Gar*, took *Hardhead* into Fremantle, where he staged a legendary party to celebrate his victory. He was, he believed, the first U.S. submarine skipper in the war to sink a battleship. Christie was not much impressed with McMaster or his celebration. He wrote in his diary, "He appeared at lunch Saturday in such condition [that the] Chief of Staff had him sent away before I arrived. This young man didn't get a battleship and may lose a submarine."

McMaster said later, "I did have a run-in with Captain Nichols who was Admiral Christie's Chief of Staff. . . . Anyhow, with the firewater in me talking, I told Nichols that if the Admiral didn't believe that we had sunk a battleship, he could get a new 'boy' for the *Hardhead* and to stick both the Navy Cross (for which I had been recommended) and the *Hardhead*. . . . He got a new boy!" (In about 1950, McMaster was awarded a Bronze Star for sinking *Natori*.)

Pollack, Tambor, and *Pompon* were among the boats leaving Pearl Harbor in July. Old temperamental *Pollack,* commanded by a new skipper, Everett Hartwell Steinmetz, lifeguarded off the Palaus and Yap during some air strikes and then refueled at Manus and continued to Pearl Harbor. On August 27 *Pollack* was strafed by a friendly B-24, causing Steinmetz to note wryly in his report, "I now have positive proof that four men can go through the conning tower hatch simultaneously." This was the last war patrol for *Pollack.* She was sent to serve as a training vessel for U.S. antisubmarine forces.

Tambor, commanded by William Germershausen (a star boxer at the Naval Academy), and *Pompon,* commanded by Steve Gimber, ex-*Trigger,* made the polar circuit, each sinking one ship. Germershausen also attacked a tanker and another ship, probably Russian. "I knew she was Russian but she didn't have proper markings," he said later. "I thought it sank but I must have missed."

Leaving in August were *Batfish, Bang, Plaice, Scabbardfish,* and *Bowfin,* among others. *Batfish,* now commanded by John Kerr ("Jake") Fyfe (who retained Jim Hingson as his exec), having made one extremely aggressive patrol off Honshu, where Fyfe sank one confirmed ship, patrolled the Palaus during some preliminary air strikes. Fyfe put six torpedoes into the destroyer *Samidare,* damaged by the air strike, leaving her "sinking fast and smoking heavily" and blowing off her stern. He was credited with half the destroyer, plus a 500-ton minesweeper which was assisting in the salvage operations.

In a patrol Lockwood called "brilliant," Anton Gallaher in *Bang* picked up three convoys off the north end of Formosa, sinking three ships for 4,200 tons and damaging others.

Plaice, patrolling off the south coast of Kyushu under Clyde Stevens, picked up a set of targets one morning that brought her skipper's heart into his throat: two *Fuso*-class battleships escorted by four destroyers "coming out of the mist": range 7½ miles, speed 15 knots, course south. Stevens set up on the lead battleship, let it close until it "filled three fourths of the periscope," and fired six torpedoes. On the way down to avoid being hit, he heard explosions, four of which he judged to be torpedo hits and one an "internal explosion" on the target; he later received credit for damage to a battleship of 30,000 tons, but postwar records did not verify it.

Frederick Arthur Gunn in a new boat, *Scabbardfish*, was patrolling to the south of *Plaice*. That evening, when Stevens got off a contact report, Gunn tried to plot an intercept course but failed to make contact. Both battleships were en route to Singapore, to be closer to the oil supply. They made it without further submarine attack.

In a brilliant attack on July 22, John Corbus in *Bowfin*, patrolling to the south near Okinawa, zipped in and out of a seven-ship convoy and shotgunned eighteen torpedoes left and right. When it was all done, Corbus believed he had wiped out the whole convoy: five big ships, two destroyers. However, postwar records gave him credit for only one ship, a 6,754-ton transport, *Tsushima Maru*.

Later in that same patrol, approaching Minami Daito, a small island east of Okinawa, Corbus daringly put *Bowfin's* nose in the mouth of the harbor and fired six torpedoes at two freighters, one anchored, one at the wharf. All torpedoes appeared to hit, blowing up both ships and the wharf, including a bus which was embarking a liberty party, but none was confirmed in postwar accounting.

Chick Clarey in *Pintado* and the old hand John Lee (ex-*Grayling*) in a new boat, *Croaker*, were sent to the East China Sea as a loosely coordinated twosome, and together they sank five ships for 38,500 tons.

On the way to station, Lockwood sent them an Ultra on a convoy southbound from Japan to the Bonins. Clarey and Lee made the intercept near Lot's Wife, but neither was able to achieve attack position, so after trailing and sending off contact reports to the boats in the Bonins, they took station along the approaches to Nagasaki.

On August 4 Clarey saw a light cruiser that appeared to be going in and out of Nagasaki on training cruises. He lay in wait, hoping it would come out the following day or the next, while Lee in *Croaker* patrolled nearby.

On August 6 Clarey picked up a large southbound convoy. He

attacked, firing six torpedoes—three each at two ships—and thought both sank, but postwar records credited only one, a 5,400-ton freighter. Shortly after this attack, *Pintado* suffered a freak accident: while reloading a torpedo, the forward torpedo room gang accidentally tripped the starting switch, flooding the compartment with steam and gas.

This was a grave matter. Clarey ordered all air lines and doors to the compartment shut. In order to get the men out, he was forced to surface in broad daylight, immediately following his attack on the convoy, within sight of the Japanese mainland. Clarey's exec ran forward on the deck and battered open the forward torpedo room hatch with a maul. In this manner, the compartment was evacuated. Meanwhile, Clarey ordered the main induction and conning tower hatch shut and "took a suction" through the boat to get rid of the gases. "Papers, dust, curtains and loose rags sailed towards the engine rooms in the hurricane winds," he reported later.

The next day at about eleven o'clock in the morning, John Lee in *Croaker* spotted the light cruiser coming out of Nagasaki for another training cruise. It was zigzagging. Lee let it close to 1,300 yards and then fired four stern tubes. Some hit and, Lee reported, "flames and water rose to the mast top." Soon the ship began to settle by the stern. While Lee took color movies through the periscope eyepiece, he heard a "tremendous explosion," followed by breaking-up noises. *Nagara*, 5,700 tons, went to the bottom. In the next week, Lee sank two more ships for 8,200 tons.

On August 21, Clarey received an Ultra reporting a convoy in the middle of the East China Sea. It showed up right on schedule: a whale-ship tanker, half a dozen other tankers and freighters, and many escorts. Clarey picked the whale factory for his main target and fired ten torpedoes. Several hit the target, and several went on to hit another tanker. The whale factory blew up and caught fire, an "incredible sight," Clarey reported. She was *Tonan Maru II*, 19,-262 tons, the largest merchant ship sunk thus far by U.S. submarines. By a curious coincidence, Clarey had helped "sink" this ship once before; when he was exec of Bole's *Amberjack* they had caught *Tonan Maru II* in Kavieng Harbor, October 10, 1942, but she had been salvaged to fight on.

Patrol scores in Empire waters had been declining during the summer of 1944. Dick O'Kane suspected the reason might be that Japanese merchant ships were running very close to the beach in shoal water. He postulated that this might be an advantage for the submarine; running close to the beach cramped zigzagging, forcing ships to steer a more or less straight course.

When he took *Tang* to Empire waters, therefore, he patrolled only a mile and a half (3,000 yards) off the shore of Nagoya, in less than 250 feet of water. He proved his point.

On August 10 he found an old tanker, hugging the beach. He fired three torpedoes. All missed. Seeing aircraft, O'Kane turned away to evade, bouncing off an uncharted upturn on the bottom. The following day, O'Kane picked up two freighters, escorted by a gunboat. He crept into position 1,800 yards away and fired six torpedoes, three at each freighter. One freighter, *Roko Maru,* 3,328 tons, "disintegrated with the explosion." The other was damaged. The gunboat jumped on *Tang,* dropping twenty-two close depth charges, trying to force O'Kane toward the beach. O'Kane evaded to seaward and deep water.

A week went by with no targets in sight. Then on August 20 O'Kane found a freighter coming out of the mist with two small escorts. He closed to 900 yards and fired two torpedoes. The first missed astern and exploded on the beach. The second "left the tube with a clonk but did not run," O'Kane reported later. The next day, O'Kane found another freighter "unbelievably close to the beach" with two small escorts. O'Kane eased into 200 feet of water and fired three electrics. All missed and exploded on the beach.

The next night, O'Kane found one of the escorts anchored in a cove. O'Kane stuck *Tang's* nose in the cove and fired one electric torpedo. The torpedo ran erratically and sank, hitting bottom, where it blew up "with a loud rumble." O'Kane fired two more electrics, one at a time. The first evidently ran under; the second missed astern. O'Kane—now whispering orders from the bridge—closed to 900 yards and fired another electric. Forty seconds later the escort blew up. "The explosion," O'Kane reported later, "was the most spectacular we've ever seen, topped by a pillar of fire and more explosions about five hundred feet in the air. There was absolutely nothing left of the gunboat." O'Kane estimated her at 1,500 tons, but she must have been under 500 because the sinking was not listed in postwar Japanese records.

The next day, hugging the beach, O'Kane found two more freighters. He couldn't get into position to attack them, but a few hours later he found a ship, well escorted by surface ships and aircraft, standing out to sea. "The decks on his long superstructure," O'Kane reported, "were lined with men in white uniforms, as was his upper bridge." This indicated a navy auxiliary. He closed to point-blank range of 800 yards and fired three torpedoes. "The first and third torpedoes hit beautifully in his short well deck forward and the after part of his long superstructure, giving him a 20 degree down-angle which he maintained as he went under with naval ensign flying." It was a navy transport, *Tsukushi Maru*, 8,135 tons.

In the following days, O'Kane (with three torpedoes left) kept close to the beach, searching. On August 25 he closed to 600 yards of the beach and fired his three torpedoes at a tanker, heavily escorted. O'Kane believed that two hit the tanker and sank it and one "blew hell out of the leading escort," but neither ship was listed in postwar accounts.

O'Kane returned to Pearl Harbor after a mere thirty-four days at sea. He was credited with six ships sunk for 31,000 tons, a total trimmed by postwar records to two ships for 11,500 tons. Squadron Commander Charles Erck commented, "As the wide open sea areas diminish by reason of further U.S. Naval conquest, it is incumbent upon all submariners to develop the tactic of attack and evasion in shoal water. The tactics used in this patrol point the way."

Not many would follow. Many believed O'Kane was simply nuts.

Four Wolf Packs in Luzon Strait

Lockwood sent Stan Moseley to command a three-boat wolf pack in Luzon Strait: Vernon Clark Turner's *Billfish*; Bob Ward's *Sailfish*, returning from a long overhaul and modernization; and *Greenling*, with a new skipper, Jack Gerwick, who had made a patrol on *Cuttlefish* with Steam Marshall and on *Gurnard* as exec to Herb Andrews. The pack was known as "Moseley's Maulers."

The Maulers had bad luck. August storms with gale-force winds lashed the strait, making patrol difficult. On August 7 Bob Ward picked up a convoy and attacked in cooperation with Gerwick in *Greenling*. Ward fired three torpedoes at a medium-sized tanker; he believed it sank, but postwar records did not credit it. Gerwick also believed he had got a ship, but neither Lockwood nor postwar records credited it.

On August 18, shortly after midnight, Ward picked up another contact on radar: one very large pip and three small ones. Ward flashed the word to his packmates and began maneuvering at maximum speed to attack. The target group turned out to be a battleship with three escorts moving at high speed. By 1:35 A.M. August 19, Ward had got as close as he could: 3,500 yards. It was a long shot but worth a try. He fired all four bow tubes. One of the escorts crossed his path and caught two of the torpedoes. The others missed. Ward went deep, expecting a terrible pasting, but no depth charges fell. He resurfaced to chase, but the battleship quickly outpaced him. Ward was credited with sinking the escort, but postwar records showed no sinking for that night at that place.

Six days later, August 24, Ward picked up another convoy during the early morning hours. He flashed the word and moved to attack, firing four torpedoes at a freighter. He saw two hits and was certain the ship sank. He dived and attacked a second ship, firing another four torpedoes. He saw and heard hits, but postwar records credited only the first, Toan Maru, 2,100 tons. Neither Greenling nor Billfish was credited with a sinking.

A new Lockwood pack under Donc Donaho (who took temporary command of Picuda from Al Raborn), patrolled Luzon Strait also and turned in a smashing success. This was Donaho's seventh war patrol. The other boats were new ones: Spadefish, commanded by Gordon Waite Underwood, who had made two patrols in Scott's Tunny as PCO and exec, and Redfish, commanded by Sandy McGregor, who had commanded Pike on her last two patrols.

The pack, known as "Donc's Devils," departed Pearl Harbor on July 23, reaching station August 11 in stormy seas. Sandy McGregor thought it was a typhoon. He estimated the winds at 100 knots. The heavy seas jarred loose many plates in the superstructure of Redfish.

On the evening of August 17, when the seas had abated, McGregor picked up a very large southbound convoy. He did not know it, but this was a special convoy, HI-71, consisting of about a dozen big tankers and freighters, escorted by the small carrier Taiyo (Otaka) often shot at by U.S. submarines.* McGregor passed the word to his packmates and attacked.

By about 5:00 A.M. on the morning of August 18, McGregor was

* Not to be confused with the large carrier Taiho, sunk by Blanchard in Albacore June 19 during the Battle of the Philippine Sea.

in position. He fired four torpedoes at a big unidentified ship; then he saw *Taiyo (Otaka)*. He shifted targets quickly—perhaps too quickly—and prepared to fire two torpedoes at the carrier. He got the first one off, but then the solution light on the TDC went out, forcing him to withhold fire. With daylight fast approaching, McGregor submerged. Four hours later, he saw a tanker riding high. He surfaced and chased it in a driving rain, firing two torpedoes that missed. Then he lost the target and hauled clear.

"Decided it was time to think things over," he wrote later, "and find out where we went wrong. Already muffed the ball twice."

Meanwhile, all submarines in the vicinity were converging on HI-71 to capitalize on McGregor's contact report. Hank Munson, who relieved Willard Laughon in *Rasher*—south of the boundary—picked up the alert and in turn alerted his packmate Charles Henderson in *Bluefish*, plus Mike Shea commanding *Raton* in the adjacent area. Because he had not been able to obtain a good navigational fix for several days, McGregor's position report was inaccurate. Donaho in *Picuda* and Underwood in *Spadefish* tore around for many hours, unable to make contact.

Munson in *Rasher* moved northward in a blinding rain. At 8 P.M. on August 18, Munson ran right into the southbound HI-71. He counted about twenty ships and fifteen escorts. The dark, rainy night was "absolutely ideal for night attack," he wrote.

At 9:22 P.M., Munson commenced firing four torpedoes. After two had left the tubes, he ordered cease fire, thinking that the gyros were not matching properly. He drew off and ran along the starboard flank of the convoy to make another attack. As he was steadying down, he saw that both torpedoes had hit the target. It was apparently a tanker. It blew up with "an appalling explosion" that sent a column of flame 1,000 feet into the sky. Later Munson wrote:

The entire sky was a bright red momentarily and the target and the whole convoy was seen for an instant. Part of the ship blew off and landed about 500 yards from the remainder of the tanker and both parts burned fiercely for about twenty minutes and then disappeared from sight in one grand final explosion. The near escort decided something was wrong, he fired his guns at all points of the compass, reversed course and fiercely depth charged something or other two miles astern of us. Pandemonium reigned in the convoy, lights flashed on and off, side lights turned on, depth charges fell in every direction, gun fire broke out all over and some badly aimed 40mm tracer passed astern of us about 100 yards wrong in deflection and way over. Two ships appeared to indulge in a spirited gun duel for a few moments. We proceeded up the starboard side of the convoy about 4000 yards off reloading and enjoying the spectacle.

The ship Munson hit was not a tanker but the escort carrier *Taiyo* (*Otaka*). While she was sinking, Munson went in for a second attack, firing ten torpedoes at two big freighters. He saw and heard three hits in the bow tube target. He believed one of the bow torpedoes ran on and hit another ship in the far column. Two of the stern tubes slammed into the other target. Munson believed one of the stern torpedoes also ran on and hit a ship in the far column. He then hauled clear to reload, broadcasting for help.

Following the reload (he had only six torpedoes left, four forward, two aft), Munson came in for another attack. He fired all six torpedoes at two targets and believed he hit both.

After Munson finished this attack and was out of torpedoes, he received orders to go on to Pearl Harbor. When he arrived there, he was credited with sinking four ships that rainy night, plus one sunk earlier, on August 6, for a total of five for 45,700 tons. In addition, he was credited with damaging four ships for 22,000 tons. Later, when it was discovered that he had sunk not a tanker but *Taiyo* (*Otaka*), the tonnage figure was revised upward to 55,700 tons. Postwar Japanese records credited five ships for 52,600 tons, making this patrol, in terms of confirmed tonnage sunk, the best of the war to date.

All the while, two other submarines were nibbling at the convoy. Henderson in *Bluefish*, who came up too late to make a coordinated attack with Munson, found two tankers. He attacked, believing he sank both, but postwar records credited him with only one, *Hayasui*, 6,500 tons.

Shortly after midnight on August 19, Gordon Underwood in *Spadefish*, who was stern-chasing the convoy, found several large ships, evidently some that had reversed course and fled northward after Munson attacked. Underwood fired four torpedoes—his first as commanding officer—from a range of 3,000 yards. All missed. He went deep, then came up again, to receive a report of Munson's attack on the convoy. "This explained the mystery," Underwood later wrote, "of unescorted ships running all around the ocean."

At 3:33, Underwood picked another target and fired six bow tubes. He reported, "Loud explosion from target. Radar pip died down and disappeared. No doubt about this fellow." He surfaced and ran through the place where the ship had been, reporting "wreckage and oil slick of our target." The ship Underwood had sunk was the large transport *Tamatsu Maru*, 9,500 tons.

Munson, Henderson, and Underwood had riddled convoy HI-71. Munson sank three big freighters plus *Taiyo* (*Otaka*); Henderson sank one tanker; Underwood sank one 9,500-ton troopship. Total: six ships. There are no existing records about what went down with these ships. Whatever it was—troops, ammunition, supplies, guns, gasoline—it would not be in the Philippines to face MacArthur's armies when he landed.

Donc's Devils continued on patrol. On August 22 Underwood picked up another convoy, two large empty tankers with escorts. Underwood fired three torpedoes at each, sinking *Hakko Maru II*, 10,-000 tons. The second tanker, severely damaged, ran into Pasaleng Bay on the coast of Luzon, where a destroyer was patrolling. Underwood coolly took *Spadefish* into the glassy waters at the entrance of the bay, intent on sinking the destroyer and firing again at the beached tanker. For three uneasy hours he played cat and mouse with the destroyer, trying to get into position to fire electrics from his stern tubes. Finally, at 10:15 A.M., he shot four. All missed. Later in the afternoon, Underwood again tried to penetrate the bay submerged, but the destroyer began dropping depth charges and Underwood prudently hauled clear. Donaho called for a rendezvous of his three boats and ordered Underwood to put into Saipan, get a new load of torpedoes from *Holland*, and then return to station.

On August 25, Donaho in *Picuda* picked up a ten-ship convoy hugging the coast of Luzon. He slipped past five escorts, got in close, and sank the 2,000-ton transport *Kotoku Maru*. A destroyer charged. Donaho turned and fired down the throat, sinking 1,200-ton *Yunagi*. Hearing all this racket, Sandy McGregor in *Redfish* picked up the convoy, maneuvered between it and the beach—some 3,000 yards distant—and fired four torpedoes at a freighter. This time, McGregor did not muff the ball; as he went deep he heard three hits, then breaking-up noises. The ship he sank was the 6,000-ton *Batopaha Maru*. Escorts delivered forty-three depth charges, none close.

After this attack, Donaho and McGregor followed Underwood

into Saipan to refuel and get a fresh load of torpedoes. By September 5, they were en route back to the area.

Slightly ahead of his packmates, Underwood arrived back at Luzon Strait on September 5. Three days later, he picked up another convoy: eight big ships, three escorts. In a flawless series of attacks, Underwood fired twenty torpedoes and sank four ships for 12,000 tons. He followed the rest of the convoy to a harbor and then sent a call for help to Donaho and McGregor, who were coming back into the area. After Donaho and McGregor arrived on station, Underwood was ordered back to Pearl Harbor.

Donaho and McGregor went back to work. On September 12 McGregor picked up a small ship and fired three torpedoes, but they all ran under. On September 16 Donaho found an eight-ship convoy from which he sank one ship, the 6,000-ton *Tokushima Maru*. Part of the convoy came McGregor's way. He sank *Ogura Maru II*, a 7,300-ton tanker. On September 21, Donaho and McGregor attacked another convoy. Donaho sank a 2,000-ton freighter, McGregor an 8,500-ton transport.

Donc's Devils turned out to be one of the most successful double-barrel packs of the war. In the two forays, Donaho, McGregor, and Underwood sank thirteen confirmed ships for almost 65,000 tons. Underwood got six for 31,500 tons, Donaho four for 11,270 (including the destroyer *Yunagi*), McGregor three for 21,800. The advance base at Saipan, which enabled all three boats to refuel and reload, had already paid for itself.

In August, Lockwood sent two more packs to Luzon Strait. The first was commanded by his flag secretary, Edwin Robinson Swinburne, class of 1925, who had never made a war patrol. Known as "Ed's Eradicators," it consisted of Gene Fluckey's *Barb* (flag); a new boat with a new skipper, *Queenfish*, commanded by Charles Elliott Loughlin, an All-American basketball player who had been stuck in Panama commanding the old *S-14*; and an old boat with a new skipper, *Tunny*, commanded by George Pierce (brother of Jack Pierce, lost on *Argonaut*), who had made a PCO run in *Steelhead*.

Ed's Eradicators went to Luzon Strait by way of the Bonins. On August 18 they encountered Gordon Selby in *Puffer*, returning to Pearl Harbor. At first Fluckey thought he was a Japanese submarine, and the pack evaded at high speed. Three days later the pack passed

Hank Munson in *Rasher*, also returning to Pearl Harbor. On August 24, the pack arrived on station.

The second pack departed Midway on August 17. It consisted of three boats: Ben Oakley's *Growler*, Paul Summers's *Pampanito*, and Eli Reich's *Sealion*. Ben Oakley, the senior skipper, named his pack "Ben's Busters." They reached Luzon Strait on August 29.

A day later, both packs received an Ultra on a southbound convoy, and all six boats rushed to intercept. Elliott Loughlin in *Queenfish*, who had never fired a torpedo in anger, made the first attack at 2:23 A.M., shooting three torpedoes at a freighter and three at a tanker. The tanker blew up and sank. Eli Reich in *Sealion*, who was watching, wrote that it "burned with an immense flame and heavy black smoke—silhouettes of ships could be seen against the backdrop of the burning ship." It was *Chiyoda Maru*, 4,700 tons.

With that, the convoy scattered in all directions. Ben Oakley in *Growler* fired his stern tubes at a destroyer for damage. Eli Reich in *Sealion* fired ten torpedoes at a tanker and a freighter for damage. Then Reich fired three at a freighter and three at what he believed to be a destroyer. He hit both, sinking the minelayer *Shirataka*, 1,300 tons. Later he fired three more torpedoes at a patrol craft. All missed. Gene Fluckey in *Barb* fired three stern tubes at a freighter and tanker, sinking the freighter, *Okuni Maru*, 5,600 tons. (He believed he sank another freighter with three torpedoes, but it was not confirmed in postwar records.) All that night and the next day, depth charges and aerial bombs rained down on the submarines.

The convoy turned around and headed back to Formosa. Whatever it was carrying never reached the Philippines. In the confusion of this six-boat attack against a multiplicity of scattering targets, the postwar accounting may not have been accurate; it credited three ships: Reich's minelayer, one of Fluckey's freighters, and Loughlin's tanker. Afterward, the two packs regrouped and went to separate areas.

Ed's Eradicators—*Barb*, *Tunny*, and *Queenfish*—patrolled the strait near the northwest coast of Luzon. Radar-equipped antisubmarine aircraft attacked the group relentlessly. Shortly after dark on the evening of September 1, the planes caught *Tunny* and delivered a devastating bombing attack. Fluckey in *Barb* submerged about 4 miles away and watched. The bombs dished in *Tunny*'s hull. Pierce was granted permission to withdraw and go home for repairs.

About noon on September 8, Loughlin in *Queenfish* picked up a convoy and trailed. After dark, he surfaced and flashed word to Swinburne and Fluckey in *Barb* and then made an end around, submerging in bright moonlight. At about 2 A.M. September 9, the convoy came right over Loughlin. He fired ten torpedoes at four targets, sinking the 7,000-ton transport *Toyooka Maru* and the 3,000-ton transport *Manshu Maru*. Fluckey in *Barb* fired three torpedoes at what he believed to be a destroyer. One made a circular run over *Barb*; the other two missed. Aircraft, dropping close bombs, prevented Fluckey from firing any more torpedoes.

The other pack, Ben's Busters—*Growler, Pampanito,* and *Sealion* (after a quick dash to Saipan for more torpedoes)—moved 300 miles to the west and lay in wait along the Singapore-Formosa convoy routes. On September 6, an important convoy consisting of six ships and five escorts had departed Singapore for the Empire. There were 1,350 British and Australian POWs crammed in the hold of one ship, *Rakuyo Maru,* and 750 in another. These POWs, survivors of a large group of slave laborers who had built a railroad for the Japanese in Malaya, were being shipped to Japan to work in the factories and mines. Three ships from Manila joined the convoy, making a total of twelve big ships plus escorts.

Dick Voge had information on this convoy from the codebreakers, but not on the POWs aboard. He gave Oakley the position reports. On the night of September 11–12, the Busters made contact. Oakley opened the attack by sinking the lead escort, a frigate, *Hirado,* 860 tons. He then pulled around and sank the destroyer *Shikinami,* 2,000 tons. Eli Reich in *Sealion* followed up, firing six torpedoes at a big transport and a tanker. The transport was *Rakuyo Maru,* 9,400 tons. His torpedoes hit her and the tanker and another transport, *Nankai Maru,* 8,400 tons. Both transports sank. Although many Japanese were rescued from the two transports, the POWs on *Rakuyo Maru* were left to fend for themselves. They went into the water; some found small life rafts.

The convoy turned west to flee toward Hainan, 200 miles away. The three boats followed. Oakley in *Growler* fired off all his torpedoes and then broke off to go down to Fremantle. Reich, the next-senior officer, took charge of the pack. Summers in *Pampanito,* who had not yet been able to attack, trailed the convoy westward. Reich, driven down by escorts, lost contact. When he surfaced, he wrongly assumed the convoy would continue its general route toward Formosa and planned an interception course to the north.

Summers trailed the convoy to the coast of Hainan and then attacked, firing nine torpedoes at three targets after dark and sinking a 5,000-ton tanker and a big transport, *Kachidoki Maru*, 10,500 tons. The remnants of the convoy evidently rounded the north coast of Hainan and scurried into Hainan Strait.

All the next day, September 13, Reich headed westerly in an effort to correct his mistake. Near midnight he found Summers's tanker, which was still on fire. He continued north to parallel the east entrance of Hainan Strait, where he patrolled all the following day. The convoy did not come out. Early on the morning of September 15, Reich rendezvoused with Summers and laid out a search plan that would take them east, back to Luzon Strait.

That afternoon about four o'clock, Summers, who was patrolling to the south of Reich, re-entered the area where the pack had first attacked the convoy. For miles the water was filled with debris and dead bodies held afloat by oily life jackets. Then Summers began finding live survivors—the British and Australians left behind by the Japanese. They had now been in the water four days and three nights. Those still alive, Summers reported later, were "a pitiful sight none of us would ever forget." He sent a call for help to Reich, who came barreling south at full speed.

Summers maneuvered *Pampanito* from raft to raft, gingerly taking on board survivors. He picked up seventy-three men. When Reich came on the scene, he rescued another fifty-four. By ten that night, no more could be safely taken aboard either submarine. Reich got off a report to Lockwood, then ordered both boats to head for Saipan. "It was heartbreaking to leave so many dying men behind," Reich wrote. On the way, four of his passengers died and were buried at sea.

Upon receiving Reich's report, Lockwood ordered the two boats remaining in Ed's Eradicators—Fluckey's *Barb* and Loughlin's *Queenfish*—to head immediately to the scene and rescue as many survivors as they could find. The scene was 450 miles away. The two boats rang up flank speed and proceeded southward at 19 knots. At midday they passed Reich in *Sealion* heading north. The seas were rising, the barometer falling.

At about 9:40 P.M. September 16, when they were within 150 miles of the scene, Loughlin in *Queenfish* picked up a northbound convoy. A few moments later, Fluckey found it too. The pack commander, Ed Swinburne, ordered an attack; the POW survivors would have to wait. Loughlin shot first, firing his last four torpedoes for damage. Twenty minutes later, Fluckey moved in, maneuvering through escorts at very close range. He could see "several large, deeply laden tankers." Then he saw something else in the darkness, the target of a lifetime:

> *Ye Gods, a flat top! This was the large pip about 300 yds to port and just ahead of the very large after tanker in the starboard column. Range 4900 yards. Went ahead standard to close for a good shot.*

2328   *Working for an overlap. This is undoubtedly the prettiest target I've ever seen.*

2331   *At 2000 yds slowed to 10 kts. We have a perfect overlap of the tanker and just beyond, the flat top. About 1000 feet of target.*

2332   *Commenced firing all bow tubes, point of aim bow of tanker, range 1820 yards. First torpedo broached badly. Other torpedoes normal. As soon as all fish fired went ahead emergency with full right rudder to put the stern tubes into the carrier. Can't make it without being rammed by escort.*

2333   *Dived. Rigged for depth charge, going deep.*

2334–16   *First hit in tanker.*

2334–24   *Second hit in tanker.*

2334–53   *First hit in carrier.*

2335–01   *Second hit in carrier.*

2335–10   *Third hit in carrier.*

2337   *Breaking up noises, very heavy underwater explosions, whistlings, cracklings. One ship sunk. Random depth charges started.*

In retrospect, Fluckey was critical of his attack. He said, "Being so excited, I fired a continuous salvo with my point of aim on the bow of the tanker, so that three torpedoes were to hit the tanker and three [were] to hit the carrier . . . if I had been in my normal senses . . . I would have fired all six at the carrier. That is what I should have done."

The carrier Fluckey hit was *Unyo*, 20,000 tons, an escort type that had often been a target for U.S. submarines. This time she blew up and sank. At the same time, the tanker went down. It was *Azusa*,

11,000 tons. In one famous salvo—nobody had ever sunk two huge ships with one shot—Fluckey had sunk two ships for 31,000 tons.

Fluckey had three torpedoes left and was sorely tempted to try to sink another ship, but he broke off and continued on the rescue mission. He and Loughlin reached the scene about dawn the following morning. By then the survivors had been in the water six days and five nights. The seas were steadily rising. Fluckey and Loughlin searched all that day and the next. In all, Fluckey picked up fourteen men, Loughlin eighteen. On the evening of September 18, with a typhoon coming on, they gave up the search and headed for Saipan.

Both these packs were extremely successful, demonstrating what aggressive, well-coordinated packs in Luzon Strait could do. Ed's Eradicators—*Barb*, *Queenfish*, *Tunny*—had sunk six ships for 51,600 tons: Fluckey three for 36,800, including *Unyo*, and Loughlin three for 14,800 tons. Ben's Busters—*Growler*, *Pampanito*, *Sealion*—had sunk seven ships for 37,500 tons: Reich three for 19,100 tons, Summers two for 15,600 tons, and Oakley two for 2,800 tons, including the destroyer. Total for both packs: thirteen ships for 89,100 tons.

Patrols from Australia

Christie's boats, staging from Fremantle, Mios Woendi, and Manus, also chipped away at the shrinking target list, concentrating on the convoys trying to reach Manila and Indochina.

Gordon Selby in *Puffer* turned in another aggressive patrol en route to Pearl Harbor for refit. On August 1, north of Sibutu Passage, he attacked and believed he sank a ship, but postwar records did not credit it. On August 12 he attacked a convoy, sinking the 5,000-ton tanker *Teikon Maru* and severely damaging another tanker, *Shimpo Maru*, 5,000 tons. The captain of *Shimpo* beached his ship. Selby, who had run out of torpedoes, could not follow up. He reported this to Christie, who sent Charles Henderson in *Bluefish* to finish the job.

Selby took *Puffer* on to Pearl Harbor and Mare Island for overhaul and then stepped down as skipper, going to work for Dick Voge as an assistant operations officer. On four patrols in *Puffer*, Selby had not only restored the fighting spirit of the boat but also sunk seven and a half ships for about 38,000 tons.

*   *   *

James Alvin ("Caddy") Adkins, who had been Freddy Warder's exec in peacetime on *Seawolf*, replaced Jim Dempsey on *Cod*. Adkins, disqualified from submarines after an unfortunate patrol in the Atlantic on *S-21*, had arrived in Australia in the latter part of 1943 as a navigator on the cruiser *San Diego*. When Warder found him in that job, he put him back into submarines, sending him with John Broach in *Hake* for a PCO cruise.

On his first patrol, Adkins (an "oldster" from 1930) patrolled near Surabaya and Makassar Strait. In a series of aggressive attacks, he fired off most of his torpedoes and returned to Darwin for a reload. There, John Griggs, commanding Squadron Twelve, joined the boat for the second leg. During this double-barreled patrol, Adkins was credited with sinking four ships and damaging one. Postwar accounting reduced the sinkings to two, but Warder was proud at having found this "lost sheep."

Enrique Haskins in *Guitarro* took station near Manila. On August 7 he picked up a large convoy and attacked. After missing his main target, he fired three torpedoes at an escort, the frigate *Kusakaki*, blowing off her bow, after which she sank with a "spectacular explosion." The other escorts drove Haskins deep and the convoy got away.

Three days later off Lingayen Gulf, Haskins, joining forces with Mike Shea in *Raton*, found another convoy. It was an impressive sight: a light cruiser and several destroyers leading tankers and freighters. Haskins fired four stern tubes at the cruiser and saw two hits. Shea in *Raton* later reported the cruiser "burning furiously"— but she did not sink. Haskins then fired four torpedoes and sank a freighter, *Shienei Maru*, 5,000 tons. Escorts attacked, dropping charges that smashed part of *Guitarro*'s superstructure but did no internal damage. Shea was not able to fire.

Malcolm Garrison, who had brought *Sandlance* to Fremantle following two sensational patrols for Lockwood, was nearly lost. On July 3, he left to patrol the Celebes Sea. On the way, he sank a 3,000-ton freighter south of Celebes. It was his tenth and last ship.

In the Celebes, Garrison found a convoy and tried to attack. A Japanese plane spotted him. Later, Garrison wrote:

When at 70 feet, I heard something I don't care to have repeated. Everyone in the conning tower distinctly heard the splash of a bomb about three seconds before the explosion. Two bombs went off directly under the stern and blew the whole ship about three feet in the air. I started down and as we passed 300 feet, the escorts started depth charging. The port reduction gear sounded like a cement mixer. So that shaft was secured. The starboard controls were jammed by a broken washer. At 430 feet, we discovered that No. 8 torpedo was running hot in the tube and was so hot it couldn't be touched by naked hands. It couldn't be fired that deep. So, in spite of the escorts, we had to come up to 150 feet. Torpedo was jammed. Couldn't be fired. At 100 feet, it was fired and the torpedo prematured 8 seconds after firing, which did not help our already battered stern. After dark we surfaced and cleared the area.

Sandlance was so badly smashed up she had to return to port. After looking her over, Christie's engineering chief, Kent Loomis, recommended a complete navy yard overhaul. Eight months would go by before *Sandlance* returned to combat. When it did, one of the junior officers was the reservist R. Sargent Shriver, who later married Eunice Kennedy, served as ambassador to France, and was the Democratic Vice-Presidential candidate in 1972.

Eric Barr in *Bluegill* patrolled off Davao Gulf. On July 20, close to shore, Barr picked up a *Natori*-class light cruiser boiling along at 26 knots. Barr, who had sunk the light cruiser *Yubari* on his first patrol, was eager to sink another on his second. He rang up flank speed but was unable to gain a favorable firing position. Later he wrote, "Oh boy! . . . Damnation. . . . Radical zig. Twenty-six knots. She's not coming any closer." Barr fired six torpedoes anyway. All missed.

Farther along on this aggressive patrol Barr sank three confirmed ships, two freighters and a subchaser, raising his total in two patrols to six ships, including *Yubari*. During the patrol, Barr (like Walt Griffith and many other Australia-based skippers) battle-surfaced on a native sailing craft and sank it. This prompted Christie to change policy. He wrote, "The destruction of a small sailing vessel is regretted. We are not at war with inhabitants of the Netherlands East Indies and Philippine Islands. The destruction of their craft does the enemy little or no harm and is forbidden."

*   *   *

Carl Tiedeman in *Guavina*, patrolling along the west coast of Mindanao, found what he believed to be a light cruiser anchored in a cove and "swarming with men," so he eased his boat to the mouth of the cove, closed to 2,000 yards, and fired four torpedoes. The first missed astern and smashed against the beach, blowing up. The excited Japanese "started shooting at it," Tiedeman wrote. The second and third hit the "cruiser" on the stern; the fourth missed ahead, also striking the beach.

There was, Tiedeman reported, a "tremendous explosion" that evoked "huge flames and black clouds." Tiedeman set up and fired two more torpedoes. Both hit, sending up more smoke and flame. Tiedeman eased out of the mouth of the cove, opening the range to 2,500 yards. From there, he fired electrics. Some missed, some hit, causing further damage. One blew the bow off the ship. In all, twelve torpedoes, eight hits. When Tiedeman left the scene, the "wreckage left above water was a jumbled twisted mass."

When Tiedeman returned to port with photographs, his target was something of a mystery. Headquarters did not think it was a cruiser but rather a minelayer that resembled a cruiser. However, postwar records showed that it was a new type of landing craft, estimated at a mere 1,500 tons.

John Crowley in *Flier*, the unlucky boat that had grounded at Midway, got under way at Fremantle for his second patrol in company with Michael Russillo's *Muskallunge*. Crowley and Russillo were to go up through Lombok and Makassar straits, Sibutu Passage, and Balabac Strait into the South China Sea, conducting patrols off the coast of Indochina.

On about August 12, while Crowley was still in the Sulu Sea preparing to go through Balabac, Christie sent him an Ultra on a convoy in the South China Sea. In order to make the intercept, Crowley had to put on more speed. The weather had been bad and Crowley did not have a precise navigational fix. In his eagerness to get at the Ultra targets, he ran through Balabac at 15 knots and strayed off the usual safe course into shallow water—40 fathoms. *Flier* struck a mine and, like Manning Kimmel's *Robalo*, blew up with a thunderous explosion.

Crowley was on the bridge when the disaster occurred. "The force of the explosion dazed me," he said later. "It injured several of the personnel on the bridge and caused the vessel to start down with astounding rapidity, sinking in 20 or 30 seconds. . . . When I came to I was on the after part of the bridge holding on to the rail. I immediately ran forward to sound the collision alarm. . . . There was a very strong smell of fuel oil, terrific venting off of air through the conning tower hatch, the sounds of flooding and the screams of men from below. Personnel were pouring out of the conning tower hatch as fast as they could . . . At that point the water came over the bridge deck with a force that was positively amazing. . . . It swept me out of the after section of the bridge, and thereafter I did not see nor feel any part of the *Flier* again."

Crowley's exec, Jim Liddell, was one of those in the conning tower when *Flier* blew up. Liddell heard a muffled explosion and started to go up to the bridge to ask Crowley what was going on. "The air started running through the conning tower with tremendous pressure," he said later, "and lifted me bodily to the bridge, tearing my shirt off. I walked aft to the cigarette deck and when I got there the water was waist deep and the next thing I knew I was swimming."

There were about fifteen men in the water: Crowley, Liddell, lieutenants W. L. Reynolds, J. E. Casey, and P. Knapp, ensigns A. E. Jacobson, Jr., and P. S. Mayer, and about eight enlisted men. They banded together to swim to the coral reefs lying to the northwest. "It was extremely difficult to keep going in the proper direction," Liddell said later. "I think we swam back and forth through the oil slick several times. . . . After moonrise we were able to orient ourselves and head for land. At dawn we were able to see an island ahead, and at this time the seas and wind began to pick up and the party began to disperse—all of them could see the island closely."

During the night, some of the injured and weak swimmers drifted off, never to be heard from again. Among these were four of the five junior officers, Reynolds, Casey, Knapp, and Mayer. During the forenoon, Liddell saw what he believed to be a native boat and swam toward it. The boat turned out to be a floating palm tree. When Liddell reached it, he found three survivors, including the other officer, Ensign Jacobson. Crowley, a notoriously poor swimmer at the Naval Academy, came to the tree about half an hour later. The five men pushed the tree along toward the island, reaching it about 3 P.M. after seventeen hours in the water. They found three more enlisted men already there.

For the next few days, *Flier*'s eight survivors lived on land—it was Manatangule Island—as castaways, building lean-tos of palm fronds and foraging for seafood among the coral reefs. Then they built a raft of driftwood and set off for Palawan, working from island to island. On August 19, they made contact with some friendly natives who took them to a group of commandos who had been landed some weeks before by Cy Austin in *Redfin*. The commandos notified Australia, and arrangements were made for *Redfin* to evacuate the *Flier* survivors. (While being cared for by these underground agents, Crowley heard the news about *Robalo* and was told that Kimmel was a POW.)

The rendezvous was set up for the night of August 30. Crowley and his men put out to sea in small boats, quietly skirting a Japanese ship anchored near the rendezvous point. Early on the morning of August 31, Austin's men hauled them aboard *Redfin* and set course for Darwin, where they arrived about a week later.

Since there were survivors of *Flier*, by navy regulation there had to be an official investigation into the loss. It was broadened to include *Robalo*, lost in the same area and apparently by the same cause. Inasmuch as *Robalo* and *Flier* were following operational orders from Christie, Christie named himself an "interested party," in order that he might get on the record his own version of events. He then asked Admiral Kinkaid to name a submarine officer senior to himself to conduct the investigation. There was no submariner in Kinkaid's command senior to Christie. Kinkaid asked Admiral King to name a man. King chose Freeland Daubin, Commander, Submarines Atlantic.

Daubin arrived in Fremantle about September 12. Christie got him rooms at the Weld Club, a private hostelry in Perth. Daubin found this place extremely uncomfortable. "There was nobody in the Weld Club under age 80," Christie said later. "Daubin wanted out so bad I believe he would have stayed in a hall closet in Bend of the Road." At Christie's invitation, Daubin took over P. G. Nichols's room there.

The investigation took on the aspect of a formal legal proceeding. John Crowley, who was technically a defendant, retained Herb Andrews as his counsel. P. G. Nichols, Murray Tichenor, and Tex McLean (who had prepared the operational orders for *Robalo* and *Flier* while Murray Tichenor was at sea on *Harder*'s Patrol 5A) all testified.

As the investigation went along, Herb Andrews, no admirer of

Daubin's, gained the impression that Daubin was "using" the proceedings. He said later, "I felt pretty certain that Daubin had in mind trying to get Christie's job. He tried to develop a case that Christie had been careless, or negligent in operating his boats, that he had not paid enough attention to his job. Later on, I saw Dusty Dornin, Admiral King's aide. He said King was annoyed at the way Daubin handled the thing, saying, 'Goddammit, I sent Daubin out there to get facts, not to get in a pissing contest with Christie. I ought to relieve them both.'"

Officially, at any rate, Daubin found no fault with Christie or his staff. "We got a clean bill of health," P. G. Nichols recalled later. "Daubin had nothing but praise for the way we conducted our operations," Christie said. However, after the investigation Christie declared Balabac Strait off limits and routed his boats into the South China Sea by way of Karimata Strait.

The Loss of *Harder*

After a two-week vacation at "Bend of the Road" following his extended patrol with Christie aboard, Sam Dealey had decided he was sufficiently rested to make another patrol in *Harder*, while Tiny Lynch, who was to assume command of *Harder* on the next patrol, stayed for a longer rest. Samuel Moore Logan, the third officer, who had graduated first in the class of 1942 and had made all five patrols on *Harder*, would move up to be exec.

This decision did not sit well with Lynch, who believed that Sam Dealey was mentally exhausted and that Lynch, not Dealey, should take the boat out. "Sam was showing unmistakable signs of strain," Lynch said later. "He was becoming quite casual about Japanese antisubmarine measures. Once, on the previous patrol, I found Sam in a sort of state of mild shock, unable to make a decision." Dealey's former roommate at the Academy later reported receiving a letter from Dealey written from "Bend of the Road" that, he believed, showed signs of extreme fatigue; the letter was incoherent and the penmanship almost unreadable.

Christie himself was not fully convinced that Dealey should go out again. He said, "Sam, I give great weight to whatever you say, but I want you to know that I stand ready to send you to the States for thirty days' leave. Whatever job you want, I'll try to get it for you." Christie remembers that Dealey said, "I've got to make this patrol."

Christie's operations officer, Murray Tichenor, later wrote, "I believe that when he came in from his fifth patrol, Sam was quite tired and Admiral Christie seriously considered taking him off. However, Dealey had marvelous recuperative powers and bounced back to real health and fighting spirit in a very few days."

Dealey was to command a three-boat pack. In addition to *Harder* there would be Chester Nimitz's *Haddo*, and *Hake*, commanded by a new skipper, Frank Edward Haylor. Dealey and Haylor got under way on August 5; Nimitz departed three days later. The boats were to rendezvous near Subic Bay and concentrate on the traffic south of Luzon Strait.

Just before they left Fremantle, Bill Kinsella, a new skipper on *Ray*, patrolling off southwest Borneo, had received an Ultra on an important northbound convoy and had moved in to intercept. Kinsella already had had a busy patrol; he had fired twenty-two torpedoes at a single tanker (*Janbi Maru*, 5,250 tons) before she finally sank. After sinking three ships of this convoy—a troop transport, a freighter, and a tanker—he had only four torpedoes left of his second load, so he sent out a call for help. By that time he had tracked the convoy up the western coast of Borneo, past the entrance to Balabac Strait, and north to Mindoro, where he watched it go into Paluan Bay.

Sam Dealey and Chester Nimitz answered the call first, arriving alongside *Ray* about eight on the night of August 20. In addition, Enrique Haskins in *Guitarro* and Mike Shea in *Raton*, patrolling off Manila, came southward to join the group. There were now five submarines lying in wait for the convoy holed up inside the harbor: *Harder*, *Haddo*, *Ray*, *Guitarro*, and *Raton*. Sam Dealey, the senior skipper, deployed the boats for action.

The convoy came out at 5:45 the following morning. Kinsella was in the most favorable position to attack. He fired his last four torpedoes at a 7,000-ton transport, *Taketoyo Maru*, which sank immediately. Kinsella went deep, withdrew, and returned *Ray* to Fremantle, having sunk five confirmed ships on his double-barreled first patrol.

Kinsella's attack evoked a tremendous counterattack by the escorts. Chester Nimitz wrote, "Depth-charging was started on all sides and it kept up, almost without interruption, until 0616. I have never heard such a din, nor would I have believed it possible for the whole

Jap fleet to unload so many charges so rapidly. . . . I had to shout to make myself heard in *Haddo*'s conning tower."

When Kinsella sank his ship, others in the column veered off, presenting a perfect target for Nimitz. He fired six bow tubes at two targets, sinking his first ships, two large transports: *Kinryo Maru*, 4,400 tons, and *Norfolk Maru*, 6,600 tons. Haskins in *Guitarro* sank the 4,400-ton transport *Naniwa Maru*. Neither Dealey nor Shea could get into position to attack, but in one morning the five submarines had sunk four more ships from the convoy for 22,400 tons. After this action, Haskins and Shea separated from the Dealey pack and went south to the Sulu Sea.

Dealey and Nimitz moved northward to the mouth of Manila Bay, arriving the same evening, August 21. Shortly after midnight, they picked up three small pips on radar heading into the bay. Nimitz sent Dealey a message stating the targets were too small to bother with. Dealey responded succinctly: NOT CONVINCED.

The three vessels were small 900-ton frigates, escorts from the battered convoy HI-71. Dealey directed an attack. About 4 A.M. he fired a bow salvo at two, stopping *Matsuwa* and *Hiburi*. Nimitz stopped the third, *Sado*. At dawn's first light, Dealey fired again at *Matsuwa*, sinking it. Nimitz attacked the two remaining frigates, sinking *Sado* but missing *Hiburi*. Dealey fired again and sank *Hiburi*.

The two boats moved northward along the west coast of Luzon with plans to rendezvous with the third boat of the pack, Haylor's *Hake*, which had come a roundabout way and had missed all the action so far. That night, August 22, Nimitz picked up a destroyer and attacked. The destroyer saw *Haddo* and turned to counterattack, forcing Nimitz to fire four down-the-throat shots which missed. Near daybreak the following day, Nimitz picked up a tanker escorted by another destroyer. He fired four torpedoes at the destroyer, blowing off her bow. He fired another but missed. Two trawlers and another destroyer came out to tow the crippled ship into Dasol Bay, south of Lingayen on the gulf. But unknown to Nimitz the destroyer (*Asakaze*, 1,500 tons) slid beneath the sea before they could help. Having shot off all his torpedoes, Nimitz set course for the new advance base at Mios Woendi to refuel and reload.

Dealey in *Harder* and Frank Haylor in *Hake*, meanwhile, rendezvoused off Dasol Bay. Believing *Asakaze* had been towed inside and that the Japanese might tow her down to Manila the following day, Dealey decided he and Haylor should lie in wait. Dealey graciously offered Haylor first crack.

At 5:54 the following morning, August 24, Haylor picked up propeller screws on sonar. Two ships were emerging from Dasol Bay, a destroyer and a minesweeper. The destroyer was an old tub, *Phra Ruang*, which belonged to the Thailand navy. Haylor maneuvered to attack, but the Thai destroyer turned off and went back inside the bay. The minesweeper continued on, pinging. Haylor did not like the setup, so he broke off the attack and began evading. At 6:47, he saw *Harder*'s periscope.

Later he wrote, "I believe that at 0710, the minesweeper actually had two targets, Sam and myself, and was probably somewhat confused. But at any rate, at 0728, we heard a string of fifteen depth charge explosions. . . . We remained in the vicinity the rest of the day. . . . We surfaced at 2010 and attempted to contact *Harder*, as previously arranged, with no success."

For the next two weeks, Haylor continued to try to contact Dealey. There was no reply. Gradually, Haylor let himself think the unthinkable: Sam Dealey, destroyer killer, had been killed by the minesweeper attack on the morning of August 24.

On September 10, Chester Nimitz returned for rendezvous. Haylor still hoped that Dealey had been forced to return to base and that Nimitz had word of him, but after talking it over by megaphone Nimitz concluded that Dealey had been lost. He sent a shattering message to Christie: I MUST HAVE TO THINK HE IS GONE.

When Christie received Nimitz's radio dispatch reporting the certain loss of Sam Dealey and *Harder*, he noted in his diary, "The most ghastly, tragic news we could possibly receive. . . . We can't bear this one." In just over five patrols in *Harder*, Dealey—her only skipper—had sunk sixteen ships for 54,000 tons, including four destroyers and two frigates.

The loss of the revered and seemingly indestructible Sam Dealey caused profound shock and grief all through the submarine force. It also contributed to the growing gulf between Lockwood and Christie. Lockwood and his staff took the view that Christie had pushed Dealey too hard with the luckless Patrol Number 5B and had made an error in judgment in permitting him to take *Harder* on Patrol Number 6. Thirty years and more after the event, submariners still argued as to whether Dealey was overly fatigued, Frank

Lynch, for example, insisting that he was, Ralph Christie that he wasn't.

The death of Dealey also indirectly intensified the dispute about awards and worsened relations between Christie and Admiral Kinkaid. By the time the bad news came, General MacArthur had approved the Army Distinguished Service Cross for Dealey for his fifth patrol. Upon learning of his loss, Christie decided that Dealey should receive a posthumous Medal of Honor. Accordingly, he drew up the recommendation and forwarded it to Admiral Kinkaid for approval. Kinkaid turned it down, stating that since Dealey had already received an Army Distinguished Service Cross for that patrol he should not get a navy award.

Christie was furious. He wrote angrily in his diary that Kinkaid's decision was

a bad blow to submarines. Admiral Kinkaid personally assured me before General MacArthur made the award that he offered no objection. This is a result of a personal difference of opinion between the General and the Vice Admiral [with] our very most distinguished submariner in between. . . . If Sam Dealey doesn't rate the Medal of Honor, no one ever did. I feel like turning in my suit.

Instead of that, Christie undertook a frontal assault on Kinkaid. He wrote Admiral Edwards asking his help. Then he wrote General MacArthur, outlining the problem, requesting that MacArthur consider withdrawing the Distinguished Service Cross so that the Medal of Honor might be substituted. MacArthur replied, "I most heartily recommend approval of the award of the Naval Medal of Honor to this gallant officer. If he is not entitled to it, no man ever was. I do not believe the award of the Army Distinguished Service Cross conflicts with Naval recognition. If necessary, however, I will withdraw the lesser decoration."

Then Christie sent Kinkaid a radio dispatch in a low-order code which almost everybody in the theater could read:

YOUR ENDORSEMENT THAT NO NAVY AWARD BE GIVEN DEALEY IS A VERY SERIOUS BLOW TO THE SUBMARINE SERVICE PARTICULARLY IN VIEW OF HARDER'S LOSS. IT WAS MY UNDERSTANDING THAT YOU APPROVED THE ARMY AWARD AND THAT IT WOULD NOT RESTRICT NAVY ACTION. EARNESTLY REQUEST RECONSIDERATION.

To many who still recalled the episode years later, Christie's message to Kinkaid was so public as to amount to insubordination. Kinkaid evidently saw it in that light. He responded angrily, I CONSIDER YOUR [dispatch] INAPPROPRIATE AND UNNECESSARY. Upon receiving this, Christie wrote in his diary, "Submarines . . . have received a double blow from one who should give them all his support."

In time, thanks largely to Christie's push, Sam Dealey was awarded the Medal of Honor, the fourth submariner so honored. But those on Christie's staff who were privy to his feud with Kinkaid were uneasy. It seemed to them that Christie, in his grief and frustration over Dealey's loss and the loss of *Robalo* and *Flier*, was pushing Kinkaid too hard.

The most noteworthy activity in the summer of 1944 between the Marianas operation and Palau-Morotai operations was the unqualified success of the wolf packs operating in Luzon Strait. In all, Lockwood sent eight packs to the area, composed of about twenty-five submarines. The eight packs sank fifty-six ships for 250,000 tons, not including contributions from Christie's submarines (notably Munson in *Rasher*) operating near the boundary. The bag included two escort carriers assigned to protect the convoys. In spite of fierce antisubmarine activity—particularly from land-based aircraft—no Pearl Harbor submarine had been lost. To be sure, the advance bases at Majuro and Saipan had helped furnish these high scores (enabling some boats to make double-barreled patrols), but it was clear that submarines operating in Luzon Strait in number—and in packs—in the early years of the war, and with a reliable torpedo, could have shut off the flow of oil and strategic materials to Japan much earlier.

33

Pearl Harbor and Australia, September to October 1944

The U.S. Invasions of the Palaus and Morotai

In September 1944, Nimitz's forces prepared to invade the Palaus; MacArthur made ready to invade Morotai. Admiral Bull Halsey, commanding the Third Fleet (and the fast carrier Task Force 38, now composed of sixteen carriers), supported both operations, which were only 500 miles apart.

As a preliminary, Halsey took Task Force 38 to the Palaus for pre-invasion softening up. After that, he swept toward the coast of Mindanao, launching air strikes there and then against the central Philippines and Manila. To Halsey's amazement, his carrier planes met little or no resistance. He concluded that the central Philippines were a "hollow shell with weak defenses and skimpy facilities." Halsey's pilots claimed to have destroyed 1,000 Japanese aircraft (mostly on the ground) and sunk about 150 ships.

The weakness of the opposition led Halsey to a bold idea. On September 13, following the strike in the central Philippines, he sent off a dispatch to Nimitz urging the Joint Chiefs to change the whole battle plan. He proposed that Allied forces skip the invasions of the Palaus, Morotai, and Mindanao and leap directly at Leyte in the heart of the Philippines.

Nimitz and MacArthur agreed—in part. It was almost too late to cancel the landings on the Palaus and Morotai; moreover, Nimitz was not keen on skipping the Palaus, just why has never been made clear. MacArthur held to invading Morotai but readily agreed to skipping Mindanao and reported that if this were done he could advance the timetable for invading Leyte by two months, from December 20 to October 20.

When Halsey sent off his proposal, President Roosevelt, Prime Minister Churchill, and the Combined Chiefs of Staff were meeting in Quebec at the Octogon conference.* Within ninety minutes, those assembled agreed to a wholly new plan. The invasions of the Palaus and Morotai would continue as scheduled, but Mindanao would be skipped and the timetable for Leyte moved ahead to October 20.

On September 15 MacArthur's forces, supported by his naval forces under Admiral Kinkaid, landed virtually unopposed on Morotai. The island was captured with little difficulty and few casualties. In subsequent mopping up, thirteen Americans were killed and eighty-five wounded. The biggest hurdles were rain and mud; because of mud, construction of the airfields was delayed.

The Palau Islands—Operation Stalemate II—were a different story. The Palaus are made up of three major islands: Peleliu, Angaur, and Babelthuap, the largest. Nimitz knew from codebreaking and other intelligence sources (including aerial reconnaissance) that Babelthuap was the most heavily defended (25,000 troops), Peleliu next (10,000 Japanese, 5,000 of them troops), and Angaur least (about 1,600 troops). Accordingly, Nimitz bypassed Babelthuap and landed on Peleliu and Angaur.

From the outset, Peleliu was a disaster. The Japanese had prepared strong defenses, including pillboxes and an interlocking labyrinth of caves. The marines were pinned down on the beach; some landing parties became lost and didn't know where to go. In spite of all the prelanding intelligence, the invaders found the terrain tough and forbidding.

Angaur was much easier. It was captured in a matter of a few days after the 1,600-man Japanese garrison had been wiped out. (There were only 45 prisoners.) The troops committed to Angaur were pulled out and shifted to Peleliu to make up for the massive casualties. Other troops went about 300 miles northeast and took Ulithi, which was undefended.

After a bloody week, the major objectives on Peleliu were attained. For weeks thereafter, however, the marines were busy rooting sui-

---

* Jimmy Fife was at the Quebec conference as a war planner.

cidal Japanese out of caves; they were still at it when Allied forces leapfrogged to Leyte. The whole operation cost the United States 10,000 casualties—2,000 killed and 8,000 wounded. Later, Admiral Morison wrote, "It would take more arguments than this writer can muster to prove that Operation STALEMATE II was necessary, or that the advantages were worth the cost. Admiral Halsey had the right idea: they should have been by-passed."

Pearl Harbor Support of the Landings

While these operations were in progress, the codebreakers kept close watch on the remaining units of the Japanese fleet. Most of the cruisers and battleships, including *Musashi* and *Yamato,* moved from Japan to Singapore to be closer to the oil sources and to discourage British attempts to recapture that place. The six remaining aircraft carriers and their supporting units remained in home waters training new air wings.

Although the disposition of Japanese fleet units was well known to both Nimitz and Halsey, no one could be sure of the Japanese intentions. Conceivably, Admiral Toyoda might order Admiral Ozawa to sail under radio silence and make a suicidal thrust at the forces landing in the Palaus. For this reason and others, Halsey requested that Lockwood and Christie lend heavy submarine support to the operation. Lockwood protested, wishing to intensify the blockade in Luzon Strait and tighten the pressure on the home islands, but Nimitz overruled him.

In all, Lockwood diverted over a dozen fleet boats to support Operation Stalemate II. A new boat, *Barbero,* commanded by Irvin Hartman (ex-*S-41*), took station in the east end of San Bernardino Strait, watching for Japanese fleet units that might come out. During the softening-up air strikes, *Gar,* with a new skipper, Maurice Ferrara (the first from the class of 1937 to command a fleet boat), lifeguarded off Yap, and *Grouper,* commanded by Frederick Henry Wahlig, lifeguarded off Peleliu. Ferrara picked up no airmen, but Wahlig rescued seven.

In addition to the boats initially deployed, Halsey requested that Lockwood provide a sizable force of submarines to form a scouting line between the Palaus and the Philippines. According to Halsey's plan, these boats were dispersed in two parallel lines, 100 miles apart, the submarines on each line 50 miles apart.

This unhappy flotilla consisted of nine submarines, organized into three wolf packs, all commanded by Weary Wilkins in *Seahorse*. The other two boats in his pack, known as Wilkins' Bears, were James Bizzell Grady's *Whale* and a new boat, *Segundo*, commanded by James Douglas Fulp, Jr. The second pack, Benson's Dogs, commanded by Roy Benson (ex-*Trigger*), returning with a new boat, *Razorback*,* and joined by Herm Kossler's *Cavalla* and Harold Ruble's *Piranha*. The third pack was commanded by Ike Holtz, ex-*Tuna*, returning with a new boat, *Baya*. The other two boats in his pack, known as Holtz's Cats, were also new: *Becuna*, commanded by Henry Dixon Sturr, and *Hawkbill*, commanded by Francis Worth Scanland, Jr.

These nine boats, known collectively as "Zoo," got under way from Pearl Harbor and other bases in late August. They deployed on station (joined by *Grouper* after her lifeguard duty) during the invasion of the Palaus. Since the Japanese fleet units did not oppose the landings, Wilkins' Zoo had nothing to report or shoot at. For days, they patrolled the area between Mindanao and the Palaus, killing time.

After the September 22 strike on Manila, Halsey released the Zoo submarines for normal patrol, and all three packs entered Luzon Strait to resume the assault on Japanese convoys. However, the air strikes on Manila had apparently caused a temporary cessation of convoys. The three Zoo packs found only a few targets during the last week in September and the first few days of October. One boat, Holtz's *Baya*, was pooped on September 25 and three men washed overboard. The crew caught the boat at 45 feet, resurfaced to rescue the three men, and remained on station.

On October 6 Wilkins' Bears—*Seahorse*, *Whale*, and *Segundo*—found a convoy in Luzon Strait. Wilkins in *Seahorse* sank an 800-ton frigate which was serving as escort. Grady in *Whale* sank a 1,200-ton tanker. The pack then returned to Pearl Harbor and other bases. Wilkins stepped down as skipper of *Seahorse* after this one

---

* *Razorback* had been commissioned by Albert Marion Bontier, who served on *Spearfish*, *Sculpin*, and *Snapper*. His exec was John Lyman Haines. While coming into New London, they ran *Razorback* aground and were relieved because of the error. Benson, beginning a tour at the New London PCO school, asked for and was given *Razorback*. Bontier later wound up commanding the old *Seawolf*, consigned to special missions from Australia.

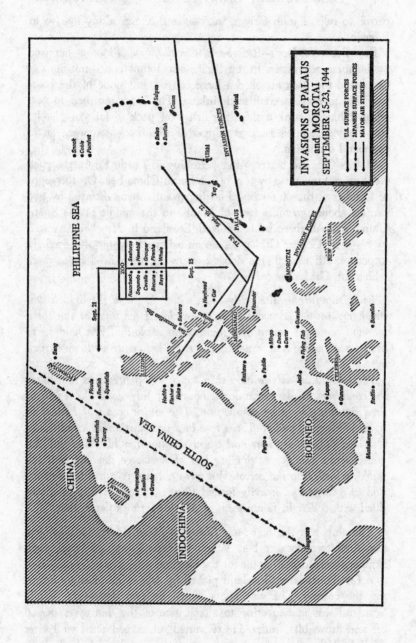

INVASIONS of PALAUS
and MOROTAI
SEPTEMBER 15-23, 1944

U.S. SURFACE FORCES
JAPANESE SURFACE FORCES
MAJOR AIR STRIKES

PHILIPPINE SEA

SOUTH CHINA SEA

CHINA

INDOCHINA

BORNEO

CELEBES

NEW GUINEA

MINDANAO

LUZON

HAINAN

Singapore

INVASION FORCES

INVASION FORCES

PALAUS

MOROTAI

ZOO

Razorback • Seahorse
Segundo • Hawkbill
Cavalla • Grouper
Becuna • Piranha
Baya • Whale

Sept. 15

Sept. 21

Snook
Cobia
Pomfret

Balao
Burrfish

Guam

Saipan

Ulithi

Yap

Wolai

San Bernardino Str.

Surigao Str.

Hawkhead
Gar

Flounder

Mingo
Dace
Darter

Flying Fish

Jack

Lapon

Gunnel

Redfin

Bonefish

Growdin

Mashalungo

Perga

Paddle

Bashaw

Haddo
Fischer
Hake

Bang

Picuda
Redfish
Spadefish

Barb
Queenfish
Tunny

Pampanito
Sealion
Growler

patrol, to relieve John Griggs, in command of Squadron Twelve in Fremantle.

Roy Benson's Dogs—*Razorback, Cavalla,* and *Piranha*—harassed by Japanese aircraft in Luzon Strait, also found poor hunting. On October 9 the pack attacked a large convoy, but none of the boats was able to make a confirmed sinking. The Dogs returned to port without having sunk a ship—the first wolf pack to fail completely. Roy Benson stepped aside as skipper of *Razorback* and went on to command a division.

Holtz's Cats did better. After patrolling in Luzon Strait, the pack went on to Fremantle by way of the South China Sea. On the night of October 7, they intercepted an important convoy escorted by two carriers about 250 miles west of Manila in the middle of the South China Sea. All three boats attacked. Scanland in *Hawkbill,* assisted by his exec, George Grider, set up on a large freighter and fired six torpedoes. All missed. He dodged an escort, then fired three more which hit. Grider wrote:

I was standing on the bridge . . . when . . . a mighty concussion shook my insides. A wave of heat enveloped me, and at the same moment came the sound of a tremendous explosion. We held on to keep from falling and watched the sight before us with awestruck eyes.

We had hit an ammunition ship, touching off fireworks that made the combined displays of a dozen Fourth of Julys look like a pair of tired lightning bugs by comparison. The entire area was bathed in light. White and yellow flames rose in a vast mushroom hundreds of feet into the air. Rockets and tracer ammunition blazed weird diagrams across the sky as flaming bits of wreckage flew up and fell smoking back into the ocean. We were witnessing the utter destruction of a large and heavily loaded ship. . . . Worth Scanland was filled with a delight reminiscent of Mush Morton's fierce glee.

The ship was the 8,400-ton *Kinugasa Maru.* Holtz in *Baya* had also fired torpedoes at her. When the attack was analyzed, each skipper received half credit for the sinking.

A few hours later, Scanland picked up one of the carriers escorting the convoy. She was accompanied by two destroyers. While Scanland was maneuvering to attack, one of the destroyers peeled off and drove him under. He remained submerged until well after daylight. When he came up, he saw a carrier and dived for a daylight periscope attack. Scanland spent eight hours trying to maneuver into position, but it was all wasted effort.

On the afternoon of October 9, near Mindoro Strait, Hank Sturr in *Becuna* picked up a convoy and flashed an alert to the other boats. As Sturr surface-attacked, Grider reported that "hell broke loose in the convoy," for at the same time Scanland in *Hawkbill* attacked submerged, firing four torpedoes at one freighter and two at another. Then an escort dropped a close depth charge on *Hawkbill*, knocking people off their feet, and Scanland went deep. Although both skippers claimed sinkings, in the postwar accounting only one ship was reported sunk: *Tokuwa Maru*, 2,000 tons. Since the attack analysis indicated it had been torpedoed by both submarines, each skipper received half credit.

At about the same time that Ike Holtz in *Baya*, patrolling to the south of *Hawkbill* and *Becuna*, received Sturr's contact report, he suffered an engine breakdown so severe he thought he might have to scuttle the boat and ordered the coding machines destroyed. But his enginemen repaired the engines and *Baya* continued on to Fremantle without further mishap.

Wolf Packs from Pearl Harbor

Following the Zoo boats, Lockwood flooded Luzon Strait and the Formosa area with wolf packs to impede the flow of reinforcements to the Philippines. Most of them were lashed by typhoons that swept the strait in early October, greatly hampering combat operations.

The first pack was a threesome, led by Frank Acker in *Pomfret*, the other two boats being *Snook*, commanded by George Henry Browne, and *Cobia*, commanded by Albert Lilly Becker. The pack departed Pearl Harbor in early September, arriving in Luzon Strait shortly after the Palau-Morotai invasions.

Acker's back, which had given trouble in Portsmouth, seemed fine —for a while. Then one day the watch reported a contact (false, as it turned out). Acker jumped up to run to the bridge but was brought to his knees by overwhelming pain. His exec, Fredric Clarke, found him sitting at the wardroom table, face buried in his arms, and carried him to his cabin. He was paralyzed from the waist down.

The next day, while running submerged, the periscope watch picked up the masts of *two* battleships, range 15 miles. Clarke (acting for Acker) went within 8 miles but could get no closer. Not seeing any aircraft cover, he surfaced *Pomfret* in broad daylight to chase, tried unsuccessfully to get off a contact report (nobody answered), and continued the chase, regaining contact at 20 miles. Both *Pomfret* and the battleships were making 20 knots. Since the battleships were zigzagging, Clarke figured *Pomfret* might overtake during the night on a straight course.

That plan was soon upended by a chilling sight: a Japanese periscope close on the port bow, an ideal firing position for the Japanese. The officer of the deck dived *Pomfret* instantly (the standard procedure) and went deep, all hands holding their breath. No torpedoes came. Was it friendly? Clarke tried to exchange recognition signals by sonar. No response. The battleships got away.

As the days passed, Acker's illness became worse. Clarke recalled, "He ate absolutely nothing and each day he seemed more gray and lined with pain . . . if something didn't change he was going to die."

On the morning of September 30, Acker called Clarke to his cabin. Clarke said later, "He told me he felt that he had taken so much medication that his judgment was temporarily impaired and he considered that he couldn't morally retain command. I relieved him of command and so informed the ship's company." That night, Clarke reported the situation to Lockwood, adding that if Lockwood did not order *Pomfret* home so Acker could get medical attention, he, Clarke, would come home anyway. Just before dawn came a message from Lockwood to return *Pomfret* to Saipan.

On the night of October 2, while on the way to Saipan, *Pomfret* made contact with a convoy: five freighters and five escorts. Clarke ordered an end around and dived ahead. The problem was "developing beautifully" when Clarke heard a noise on the conning tower ladder. He looked down and there was Acker, pulling himself up hand over hand from the control room, legs dangling in space.

"This is probably going to be my last chance to make an attack on a Japanese ship," Acker said, "and I would like to take command back from you for a while."

Clarke readily gave way. Later he said, "Frank's legs couldn't support his weight so he would support himself by his elbows hooked over the periscope handles; I would train the periscope for him while he took the bearings. When the periscope was lowered through the well in the deck, Frank would just lie on the deck until the periscope was raised for the next observation. He would grab hold of the periscope handles as the scope was being raised and let it haul him to an upright position for the next observation."

When the ships came close, Acker fired two salvos of three torpedoes at two ships. The first salvo hit the target with a resounding explosion. The ship broke in the middle and sank. It was a big transport, *Tsuyama Maru*, 6,962 tons. Some torpedoes in the second salvo hit the second target, but she didn't sink. Escorts charged and *Pomfret* went deep. Said Clarke, "Frank was so exhausted after the attack that he lay on the conning tower deck for an hour or so until he regained strength enough to haul himself below."

Clarke reassumed command and brought *Pomfret* into Saipan through the typhoon. Acker took a turn for the better, but when he reached Saipan he was relieved of command and flown to Pearl Harbor for medical treatment. The doctors thought it might have been a polio attack or a recurrence of the old disc problem. They kept Acker on light duty for a week or so; then he went to staff duty. Later he received a Bronze Star for the patrol. Clarke thought it should have been more.

Four other wolf packs followed Acker's into Luzon Strait. Alan Banister in *Sawfish* led *Icefish*, a new boat commanded by Dick Peterson, and *Drum*, commanded by Maurice Herbert Rindskopf (the first from the class of 1938 to command a fleet boat); Edward Blakely took *Shark II*, with *Blackfish*, commanded by Robert Sellars, and *Seadragon*, back from overhaul, commanded by James Henry Ashley, Jr.; Beetle Roach in *Haddock* directed *Tuna*, under a new skipper, Edward Frank Steffanides, Jr., and Pete Galantin in *Halibut*; and Chick Clarey in *Pintado*, going on his third patrol, led John Maurer (who had been exec to Sam Dealey on his early patrols in *Harder*), now commanding the new *Atule*, and another new skipper, Joseph Bryan Icenhower, commanding another new boat, *Jallao*. Tom Wogan (ex-*Tarpon*), in a new boat, *Besugo*, led Karl Raymond Wheland's *Gabilan* and Henry Stone Monroe's *Ronquil* to Bungo Suido. Three older boats returning from overhaul went to the north end of Formosa Strait, led by John Coye in *Silversides: Trigger*, still commanded by Fritz Harlfinger, and the aging *Salmon*, commanded by Harley Kent Nauman.

Dick O'Kane in *Tang*, going out on his fifth patrol, was given a choice of joining this pack or patrolling alone. He chose to patrol alone in the south end of Formosa Strait. On this trip O'Kane had a new exec, F. H. Springer, a reservist who replaced Murray Frazee. O'Kane got under way in a hurry on September 24, topped off his fuel tanks in Midway, and proceeded onward.

On October 6, while nearing Formosa, O'Kane ran into a typhoon. Hoping to sight an enemy ship, he remained on the surface, buttoned up, running on his battery. The sea, O'Kane wrote later, "was a sight such as none of us had witnessed before." The storm put *Tang* 60 miles off course.

On October 10 O'Kane rounded the northern tip of Formosa and turned south into Formosa Strait. That night he picked up a freighter steaming alone. He fired three electrics and sank *Joshu Maru*, 1,700 tons, loaded with supplies for the Philippines. The next day O'Kane sank another small freighter, *Oita Maru*, 700 tons, with a single torpedo. Afterward he returned to the northern coast of Formosa and patrolled off Kirun, adjacent to the area being patrolled by John Coye's pack.

In addition to all these boats, Lockwood sent a pack to the East China Sea led by the aggressive Moke Millican, ex-*Thresher*, bringing out a new boat, *Escolar*,* with Blish Hills in *Perch II* and John Lee in *Croaker* as packmates. The pack got under way in late September. On September 30, passing through the Bonins, Millican attacked a small gunboat with his deck gun. On October 9 Lee in *Croaker* sank a 2,200-ton freighter, *Shinki Maru*, in the East China Sea. On October 17 Millican reported to Hills in *Perch* that he was proceeding to the mouth of Tsushima Strait. Nothing was ever heard from Millican again. Although the location of the minefields in Tsushima Strait was known to Millican, Lockwood and Voge presumed that *Escolar* hit a mine and sank instantly.

Single Patrols from Pearl Harbor

Apart from all these packs, Lockwood sent many individual boats on patrol. *Scamp, Pogy, Pilotfish, Sargo, Kingfish,* and *Snapper*

---

* *Escolar* was the first product of the Cramp Shipbuilding Company in Philadelphia. The Cramp experiment did not turn out well. The company was saddled with poor management; there were continuous labor difficulties. Cramp only finished seven submarines during the war (another four on order had to be finished by other shipyards), and those boats that were finished, including *Escolar*, were not well built and had a poor reputation in the submarine force.

Charles Herbert Andrews

Raymond Henry Bass

Edward Latimer Beach

Roy Stanley Benson   Carter Lowe Bennett

James William Blanchard

William Herman Brockman   Creed Cardwell Burlingame

Admiral Carpender presenting award to Greenling wardroom; Henry Chester Bruton and James Dorr Grant are first and second from left

Bernard Ambrose Clarey

Wreford Goss Chapple

Slade Deville Cutter
(foreground) in torpedo room

John Starr Coye, Jr.

Roy Milton Davenport

Samuel David Dealey

Admiral Nimitz and Glynn Robert Donaho

Thomas Michael Dykers

Robert Edson Dornin

Frank Wesley Fenno

Joseph Francis Enright

William Joseph Germershausen (left) and R. M. Wright on Spadefish

Howard Walter Gilmore

Eugene Bennett Fluckey

George William Grider

Walter Thomas Griffith   Thomas Wesley Hogan

William Thomas Kinsella (left) and Brooks Jared Harral

Herman Joseph Kossler

Charles Elliott Loughlin

Jack Hayden Lewis (left) and Thomas Burton Klakring

Eugene Bradley McKinney

John Howard Maurer

Admiral John Sidney McCain (left) and his son, John Sidney McCain, Jr., in Tokyo Bay

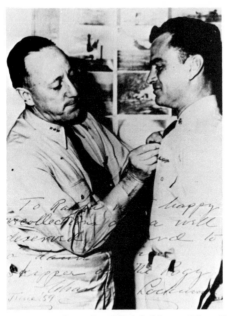

Admiral Lockwood and Ralph Marion Metcalf   *Dudley Walker Morton on the bridge of* Wahoo

Stanley Page Moseley, Lewis Smith Parks, Elton Watters Grenfell, and David Charles White (left to right)

*Admiral Nimitz pins
silver star on his son,
Chester William Nimitz, Jr.*

Henry Glass Munson

Richard Hetherington O'Kane

Admiral Nimitz and William Schuyler Post, Jr.

George Egbert Porter, Jr. Lawson Paterson Ramage

Robert Henry Rice (center) and officers of Drum, Manning Kimmel at far right

Frank Gordon Selby

Harry Clinton Stevenson (left)
and William Alfred Stevenson

Edward Dean Spruance (left) and his father, Admiral Raymond Ames
Spruance, on board a captured Japanese submarine in Tokyo Bay

George Levick Street III

Gordon Waite Underwood

Charles Otto Triebel

John Augustine Tyree, Jr.

Frederick Burdett Warder

Reuben Thornton Whitaker (left)
and Murray Jones Tichenor

Merrill Comstock (left) and Charles Warren Wilkins

patrolled the Bonins. *Sterlet, Barbel, Burrfish, Sea Dog, Skate, Saury, Billfish,* and *Sea Fox* patrolled the area between Formosa and Okinawa. *Trepang, Tambor,* and *Greenling* patrolled off Tokyo Bay. Others made the polar circuit. Two of these boats, *Sterlet* and *Trepang,* had unhappy wardrooms.

Sterlet, going on her second patrol, was commanded by Orme Campbell ("Butch") Robbins. Paul Schratz, class of 1939, who had made the two miserable patrols on *Scorpion* when Reggie Raymond was killed, was Robbins's exec.

On the first patrol from Pearl Harbor in July, Robbins and Schratz had a falling out. It was the usual problem: a young, eager exec believing the boat should do more; Robbins, the senior man, having his own way. On that patrol, Robbins made five attacks and was credited with sinking four ships for 14,200 tons, but none was confirmed in the postwar accounting. When *Sterlet* returned to Midway, Schratz began looking for a way off the boat.

The other unhappy exec was on *Trepang,* a new boat commanded by Roy Davenport. The exec was reservist Dick Garvey, who began the war on *Trigger.* Garvey, a close friend of Dusty Dornin and the hard-playing "*Trigger* crowd," did not cotton to Davenport. "I put him down as a glory seeker," Garvey said later. "He kept telling us that God would protect *Trepang;* that He had a protective shield around the boat."

Garvey was not so sure about that shield. During shakedown, *Trepang* had had two close calls. On the first trip to sea, she collided with a ferryboat near San Francisco. The Court of Inquiry exonerated—indeed, commended—Davenport, but Garvey thought that *Trepang* had not been handled well in the incident. Later, during training, three men were left topside during a dive and the conning tower was partly flooded. "This episode went unreported," Garvey said later.

Off Honshu, Davenport reported, on the night of September 30, he picked up a convoy consisting of two large tankers and one large freighter, with one escort, and fired six torpedoes, one at the escort, five at the two tankers which were "overlapping." The torpedo missed the escort, Davenport reported, but hit a tanker. "He immediately started smoking badly and I later saw him go down," Davenport wrote. "We were very happy on our first attack to have sunk one large tanker." Postwar records showed no tanker sinking at this time and place but gave Davenport credit for sinking the 750-ton freighter *Takunan Maru*.

After weathering the typhoon, Davenport reported picking up a second convoy on the night of October 10, consisting of two tankers with one escort. Davenport fired four stern tubes, reported three hits, and claimed credit for another tanker sinking. "We did not actually see it go down but heard it break up on the sound gear," Davenport said later. The Japanese records did not confirm this sinking either.

On the following day, October 11, the periscope watch picked up a Japanese landing craft. Davenport set up and fired four torpedoes. He believed all four missed, but postwar records credited him with sinking *Transport No. 5* on this day, estimated to be 1,000 tons.

The next day, October 12, Davenport took up station twelve miles southwest of Iro Zaki, a point southwest of the entrance to Tokyo Bay. That night, after he surfaced, Davenport made radar contact "on two very large ships and two escorts" moving at very high speed: 23 knots. Davenport tentatively identified the big pips as two aircraft carriers and two destroyers. He discussed the situation with a PCO on board, William Bismarck Thomas. They agreed, according to Davenport, that a night surface attack would be hopeless. The water was extremely phosphorescent; they would be blown out of the water before they could fire torpedoes. Davenport reported later:

I returned to the bridge and while watching the scene develop something came over me to tell me what to do and how to do it. If I hadn't already been a religious man I soon would have been as I saw the events of this attack take place. With the aid of a power far beyond our own we started in for the attack. I passed the word over the loudspeaker system, "We're going in on the surface, gang," and ordered left 15 degrees rudder. Only by Divine Guidance and protection could his attack be successful and the submarine escape undamaged.

Davenport rang up flank speed and started in. As he came closer, he decided the targets were not carriers but two battleships escorted by two destroyers. Davenport closed in to point-blank range and fired six bow tubes at the "battleship."

One torpedo hit in the bow of the far destroyer and the second torpedo hit in the middle of the leading battleship. Radar reported that the destroyer sank immediately and the explosion from the torpedo hit in the battleship sent flame far out over the water and this was followed by several explosions during the next ten minutes. One explosion sent flames high above the foremast. It appeared like the torpedo had hit at their number three turret.

Davenport then swung around, he reported, and fired his last torpedoes—four stern tubes—at the second "battleship." It zigged and these four missed.

The second battleship about this time turned on a searchlight, directing it forward, apparently looking for the destroyer that had been sunk to see what was happening ahead of him and then made a sweep with his light in our direction and came within 30 or 40 degrees of our position. At this time I cleared the bridge of all but the Officer personnel and made ready to dive if we actually were illuminated. They turned the searchlight off, turned it on again in a few seconds and this time turned it directly on the damaged battleship and we were able to make out clearly the pagoda-type foremast and could see again his stack midway between his fore and mainmast and were certain of our identification that it was a battleship. He turned the light out again and we could detect no countermeasures.

Davenport opened out at flank speed. When he received no gunfire, he turned back again to close the target for a look-see. The ships were now tracked at only 16 knots. Said Davenport, "It was evident that we may have gotten one of his fire rooms, he had lost some of his boiler power, he undoubtedly was drawing more water."

When Davenport returned to Majuro, he was credited with sinking three ships for 22,300 tons and damaging a battleship for 29,300 tons. The endorsements congratulated Davenport for a "splendid" attack on a "*Yamashiro*-class battleship," stating, "This will keep this formidable ship out of the enemy battle line for some time to come." Davenport received another Navy Cross, his fourth. Postwar records credited only the 750-ton freighter plus the 1,000-ton landing craft which Davenport did not claim. Total: two ships for 1,750 tons.

The exec, Dick Garvey, said later he doubted that Davenport had seen battleships.

Australian Support of the Landings

Ralph Christie diverted many submarines from regular patrol to support the Palau-Morotai invasions. *Flounder* lifeguarded in Davao Gulf during Halsey's air strikes on Mindanao. *Mingo, Dace, Darter, Guavina, Flying Fish, Jack, Paddle,* and *Bashaw* formed a scouting line in the Celebes south of Mindanao, to intercept Japanese fleet units should they sortie from Singapore. *Pargo* patrolled off northwest Borneo with the same mission. *Haddo* and *Flasher* lifeguarded off Manila during the air strike.

Crevalle, commanded by Frank Walker, was scheduled to join this formation, but she never made it. On the morning of September 11, just after passing through Lombok Strait northbound, Walker ordered a routine early morning dive. All went well. Walker then ordered the boat to the surface.

The officer of the deck, reservist Howard J. Blind, rushed to the bridge, followed by his lookouts. Someone in the control room evidently forgot to close the main ballast tank vents. After *Crevalle* surfaced normally, the air rushed out of the tanks through the open vents and *Crevalle* suddenly went down again, making standard speed. The upper and lower conning tower hatches were still open. *Crevalle* plunged like a stone with a tremendous down-angle, 42 degrees, with Blind and his lookouts still on the bridge. Tons of seawater flooded through the open conning tower hatches and down into the conning tower, control room, and pump room, until the lower hatch was shut.

The men in the conning tower could not get through the torrent of water to close the upper conning tower hatch. At 150 feet, when the water in the conning tower had reached armpit level, the hatch closed of its own accord. Evidently Howard Blind had freed it while *Crevalle* was going under.

All the while, *Crevalle* was plunging toward the bottom with the fatal down-angle. One of her crew, Robert Yeager, noticed that *Crevalle* was still making standard speed. He telephoned the maneuvering room on his own and ordered, "All back full." On his orders, the props were reversed and turned up full power. At 190 feet, *Crevalle* stopped plunging downward. The men in the control room blew main ballast, and the boat returned to the surface, backing full. *Crevalle* lay on the surface in broad daylight, disabled. All the gear in the conning tower, control room, and pump room was flooded out, including the radio transmitters. Frank Walker hurried to the bridge, ordering machine guns manned. They found one of Blind's lookouts—gunner's mate W. L. Fritchen—and hauled him on board. They saw Blind's head momentarily, but then he disappeared from sight.

Luckily for Walker, there were no Japanese planes in the vicinity. The crew patched up *Crevalle* and the boat limped back to Darwin, arriving September 15. For freeing the conning tower hatch, Howard Blind was awarded a posthumous Navy Cross, given to the Australian girl he had married just before sailing. Robert Yeager, whose orders had undoubtedly saved the boat, was awarded a Silver Star. Walker, who was not blamed for the accident, returned *Crevalle* to Mare Island for complete overhaul and then stepped down as skipper, going to new construction.

During the invasion of Morotai, there was a partial breakdown in communications between the U.S. surface forces involved in the invasion and Christie's submarines. The breakdown caused the loss of one submarine and nearly a second.

The Japanese sent five RO-class submarines to attack the Morotai invasion forces. On October 3, one of these, *RO-41*, fired torpedoes at the jeep carrier *Midway* (later renamed *St. Lo*). The torpedoes missed *Midway* but hit a destroyer escort, *Shelton*, which later capsized under tow. A companion destroyer, *Richard M. Rowell*, drove off the Japanese submarine with a few depth charges and took off *Shelton*'s crew. Aircraft from *Midway*, meanwhile, hunted Japanese submarines with a vengeance.

Later that morning Sam Loomis in *Stingray*, returning to the Admiralties submerged in the submarine safety lane from a special mission off Samar, arrived on the scene and was immediately attacked by two torpedo bombers from *Midway*, who believed *Stingray* to be the submarine that fired at *Midway* and sank *Shelton*. One of the planes dropped a bomb; the other accidentally crashed into the sea while making a run on *Stingray*. Fortunately, the bomb missed.

That same morning, *Seawolf* was en route from the Admiralties to Samar with seventeen U.S. Army agents and about ten tons of supplies. She was commanded by Al Bontier, who had been relieved on

Razorback after he put her aground off New London. *Seawolf* also passed close to the scene. She had been bucking heavy seas and had fallen a day behind in her schedule, but she was also in a safety lane. At eleven, a navy airplane spotted *Seawolf*. Wrongly assuming *Seawolf* to be the Japanese submarine that torpedoed *Shelton*, the pilot dropped two bombs and a dye marker. *Seawolf* dived. The U.S. destroyer *Rowell* hurried over. At 1:10 P.M. *Rowell's* skipper, Harry Allan Barnard, Jr., picked up a submarine on his sonar gear.

Barnard knew that he was in a submarine safety lane, but all his information indicated there was no U.S. submarine within 70 miles. *Seawolf* had reported her one-day delay in schedule to Christie, who relayed it to Kinkaid's headquarters, but the word never got to Barnard. He attacked with depth charges. The sub made no effort to evade and sent signals on her sonar—long dashes and dots. However, Barnard later reported, "the stuttering transmission bore no resemblance to the proper recognition signal." Believing the Japanese sub skipper was trying to jam his sonar, Barnard attacked again. Although the evidence was circumstantial, and Barnard stoutly insisted his target was a Jap, Jasper Holmes and other submarine authorities concluded "with little doubt" that this attack sank *Seawolf*. A large bubble came to the surface, then debris. *Seawolf* went down with all hands, plus the agents Bontier had intended to land on Samar.

That night in Fremantle, Christie made repeated attempts to call *Seawolf*. There was no answer. The famous old boat that had carried Fearless Freddy Warder, Roy Gross, and many others into battle was the first—and only—U.S. submarine lost to Allied forces in the Pacific. After *Robalo*, *Flier*, and *Harder*, *Seawolf* was the fourth submarine Christie had lost in slightly over two months.

While patrolling a lifeguard station on the southwest tip of Mindoro, Byron Nowell in *Paddle* found a small convoy. He sank one confirmed ship, *Shiniyo Maru*, 2,500 tons. By happenstance, *Shiniyo* was transporting hundreds of Allied POWs being evacuated from Mindanao to Manila or the Empire. They had been herded into the holds and told by prison guards that if an American submarine attacked the ship they would kill them all. When Nowell's torpedoes struck home and the ship started down, the guards opened fire on the POWs with tommy guns. However, a hundred or more fought up through the hatches with clubs and improvised weapons and jumped over the side. About fifteen or twenty were picked up by

Japanese boats engaged in rescuing *Shiniyo* survivors and were immediately shot. Eighty-one reached shore on Mindanao and made contact with friendly guerrillas, who sent word for a submarine to evacuate them.

Christie ordered *Narwhal,* now commanded by Jack Clarence Titus, to rescue the POWs; he picked them up on the night of September 29 and proceeded toward the Admiralties. They were in pitiful condition and grateful for their escape. However, they were almost shipwrecked a second time. The very next day, *Narwhal* was caught on the surface by a Japanese plane. During the hasty dive *Narwhal*'s stern planes jammed on hard dive, and before Titus could catch the boat she plunged at a terrifying angle. Titus backed emergency and blew all ballast tanks, catching the boat at 170 feet. *Narwhal* broached—stern first—with the Japanese plane showing on her radar. Titus dived again immediately, this time without a problem. The plane dropped no bombs.

On the way to port *Narwhal* passed through the scene of the *Shelton* sinking early on the morning of October 3 (exchanging signals with *Seawolf*) but was spared an attack by *Midway*'s eager-beaver pilots.

Big Ian Eddy, commanding *Pargo,* had made four long, aggressive patrols that had resulted in a credited total of nine ships sunk (four confirmed by JANAC). He was scheduled to make one more, but when he came off the fourth, he was in bad physical shape and feeling depressed because he thought he hadn't done enough! Deciding he needed a good long rest, Christie relieved him and sent him back to the Atlantic. *Pargo* went to David Bonar Bell, the second man in the class of 1937 to get command of a fleet boat. Bell had commissioned *Pargo* with Eddy and made all her patrols, gradually moving up the ladder to command.

Christie assigned Bell to lay a minefield off Brunei Bay, northwest Borneo, an oil port where important ships, including Japanese fleet units, frequently called and might call again in the future. Bell carried out this mission with skill and courage and afterward made repeated attacks on Japanese vessels going and coming through his area. He sank two ships, both small, a minelayer of 1,600 tons and a former net tender of 600 tons. In addition, he inflicted damage on several freighters and an escort carrier, at which he fired eight torpedoes for three hits.

Bell was relieved in that area by Hammerhead Martin in *Hammerhead*. Martin had no sooner arrived than he ran into a large convoy on October 1. In a brilliant series of attacks, Martin sank three big ships, each over 5,000 tons. On October 20 he found another convoy and in a no less brilliant attack sank two big transports. His total for the patrol: five confirmed ships for 25,200 tons. Having shot all his torpedoes, Martin was ordered to Fremantle, where he received high praise for this—one of the best patrols on record.

Martin was relieved on station by *Gurnard*, now commanded by Norman Dwight Gage, who began the war on *Tautog* and later commanded *R-1* in the Atlantic. Gage also carried a load of mines. Shortly after arriving in the area, Gage picked up a large convoy (fifteen ships, two large tankers) headed for Singapore to join Japanese fleet units. Gage, with two stern tubes filled with mines, attacked, firing six bow torpedoes, but he was unable to sink any ships. He took position off Brunei Bay, keeping a sharp lookout for Japanese fleet units.

Both Reuben Whitaker and his exec, Ray DuBois, returned from *Flasher*'s third patrol physically and mentally drained. There had been a serious question in Whitaker's mind about making another patrol. He had reached the point, he said later, where he hated to make contact with the enemy. However, while DuBois stayed in port for a "blow," replaced by one of the junior officers, Philip Thompson Glennon, Whitaker took *Flasher* out for a fourth time. "DuBois goofed," Whitaker said later. "That rest cost him command. Instead of getting *Flasher*, he was sent back to New London to command a little school boat."

Whitaker led a pack consisting of *Flasher*, *Lapon*, and *Bonefish*. *Lapon* was commanded by a new skipper, Donald G. Baer. *Bonefish* was commanded by Lawrence Lott Edge, making his second patrol.

Flasher departed Fremantle first and went up through Lombok and Mindoro straits to the Manila area. On September 18, Whitaker arrived on station and almost immediately picked up a big transport, loaded with troops, heading into Manila with four destroyers for escorts. He maneuvered in for a daylight periscope attack and fired five torpedoes, sinking *Saigon Maru*, 5,350 tons, formerly a light cruiser. The destroyers delivered a severe depth charge-attack, which drove Whitaker deep and knocked out the SJ radar.

During the next several days, Whitaker was assigned to lifeguard duties during Halsey's air strikes on Manila. Donald Baer in *Lapon* arrived off Manila on September 19. On the afternoon of September 21, Halsey's planes attacked a nearby convoy. Baer pursued the remnants of the convoy that night and sank one ship, *Shun Yuan,* 1,600 tons, but because of his lifeguard assignment Whitaker was not able to join in the attack.

Early on the morning of September 27, Whitaker sighted two battleships. He bent on four engines to make an end around and notified Baer in *Lapon,* but neither boat was able to get into position to attack. However, at about daylight, Whitaker picked up a convoy and alerted Baer. Both attacked. Baer sank a tanker, *Hokki Maru,* 5,600 tons; Whitaker sank another big transport, *Ural Maru,* 6,400 tons. The other ships of the convoy fled into Lingayen Gulf.

Meanwhile, the third boat of the pack, Edge's *Bonefish,* was on the way, pausing on September 28 near Mindoro to sink *Anjo Maru,* a 2,000-ton tanker. She joined up with the pack on September 30 off Lingayen Gulf. On October 4 Whitaker found another convoy and sank one ship, *Taihin Maru,* 6,900 tons. *Bonefish* intercepted and attacked the convoy later that night, but her torpedoes missed. On October 10 Baer in *Lapon* sank another ship, *Ejiri Maru,* 7,000 tons. On October 14 Edge in *Bonefish* sank a 2,500-ton freighter.

Whitaker, who had arrived first, departed first, going home by the usual route. Baer and Edge remained on station. On return to Fremantle, Whitaker stepped down as skipper of *Flasher,* going to the Submarine School as an instructor. In his five patrols as skipper—one on *S-44,* four on *Flasher*—he had sunk a total of fourteen confirmed ships for 56,513 tons, making him one of the leading scorers of the war.

Bluegill, commanded by Eric Barr, made up a pack with *Angler,* commanded by Frank Hess. On October 12 the relentlessly aggressive Barr battle-surfaced on some barges, for which he was later criticized by Christie; one fired back, wounding five of Barr's men. On October 14, in the Sulu Sea, Hess sank a 2,400-ton freighter. In the early morning hours four days later, Barr tore into a large southbound convoy off Manila and sank three ships for 19,630 tons. These included two big transports, *Arabia Maru,* 9,500 tons, and *Hakushika Maru,* 8,000 tons. After this attack, escorts delivered forty-seven punishing depth charges that fell so close men in the forward torpedo room reported seeing fire at the edge of the torpedo loading hatch.

Barr returned to Mios Woendi to reload and refuel, leaving *Angler* on station.

Mike Shea in *Raton*, making his second patrol, was slightly to the south of these boats. Picking up Barr's contact report on the convoy, he moved to intercept, making contact in a torrential downpour about five o'clock in the afternoon on October 18. Shea tracked and attacked in the blinding rain, obtaining position in the middle of the convoy. He fired ten torpedoes and sank two ships, a 4,700-ton freighter and a 3,800-ton transport. With seas rising and winds blowing at 40 knots, Shea bored in for a second attack, firing ten more torpedoes. Eight of them missed, probably thrown into erratic runs by the heavy seas; the other two hit for damage. Believing any further attacks would be futile, Shea hauled clear and returned to Mios Woendi to reload torpedoes and refuel.

The sister ships *Dace*, commanded by Bladen Claggett, and *Darter*, commanded by Dave McClintock, left Mios Woendi as a wolf pack off Palawan. On October 12 McClintock picked up a seven-ship southbound convoy, escorted by two destroyers. He attacked, firing four torpedoes, believing he obtained two hits but no sinkings. He flashed word to Claggett in *Dace*, patrolling to the south. Shortly after midnight on October 14, Claggett made contact and fired a ten-torpedo salvo at overlapping targets. One bow torpedo made a circular run, forcing Claggett to maneuver wildly to avoid; the other torpedoes hit hard and sank two big freighters: *Nittetsu Maru*, 6,000 tons, and *Eikyo Maru*, 7,000 tons. Claggett tried to attack again, but the convoy eluded him.

McClintock and Claggett picked up Eric Barr's convoy contact on October 18 and moved to intercept. They did not find the convoy but ran into two northbound destroyers. Both McClintock and Claggett fired four torpedoes each at the destroyers. All missed. They remained on station at the south end of Palawan Passage.

Aspro, *Cabrilla*, and *Hoe* patrolled as a pack near Manila. William Thompson in *Cabrilla* turned in a fine performance. On the night of October 1–2, he teamed with William Stevenson in *Aspro* to attack a large convoy. Thompson sank two tankers, *Zuiyo Maru*, 7,400 tons, and *Kyokuho Maru*, 10,000 tons; Stevenson sank a 6,900-ton freighter. Five nights later the two boats again teamed to attack a convoy. Thompson sank two freighters, one for 5,000 tons, one for

2,000 tons; Stevenson sank a 4,000-ton transport. During these attacks, Victor McCrea in *Hoe* sank one confirmed ship for 2,500 tons and damaged others.

Upon completion of these attacks, Thompson and Stevenson returned *Cabrilla* and *Aspro* to Pearl Harbor. McCrea returned *Hoe* to Fremantle. In this fine patrol, Thompson had sunk four ships for over 24,000 tons.

Cod, commanded by Caddy Adkins making his second patrol, and *Ray*, commanded by Bill Kinsella, patrolled as a pack near Manila. For Kinsella, who had sunk five ships on his first patrol, the second was a frustrating experience. On October 3, he saw what he believed to be a light cruiser but was unable to gain attack position. He had four battery explosions in his electric torpedoes, which ruined the warheads on three and forced him to eject one. On October 5, after rendezvousing with Adkins in *Cod*, a convoy slipped by Kinsella in a rainsquall. Adkins attacked and sank a 7,000-ton freighter, but *Ray* was too far away to join in. On October 6 Kinsella attacked a big tanker escorted by two destroyers. He fired six torpedoes and missed. Escorts drove him down, but later he resurfaced and fired six more, achieving, he believed, only damage. He wrote, "All in all, it was a very discouraging night."

His luck changed—momentarily—on October 12. During the afternoon he found a transport escorted by two destroyers. He fired four torpedoes and sank *Toko Maru*, 4,100 tons.

Two days later, October 14, the bad luck returned. While diving from a Japanese plane, *Ray* suffered a near-fatal accident: the upper conning tower hatch jammed, and a "terrific" rush of water flooded the conning tower. Kinsella, who had dropped to the control room, ordered the lower conning tower hatch shut. He then resurfaced, plane or no plane, to save the men in the conning tower. By the time *Ray* got back to the surface, the conning tower was two thirds flooded, but no one drowned.

After this, Kinsella returned to Mios Woendi for repairs. Adkins in *Cod* remained on station.

About this time, Christie's force was augmented by a squadron of ten British and Dutch submarines, some released from combat duty in Europe where they were no longer needed. They were smaller boats, comparable to the older S-boats. The squadron was commanded by Captain L. M. Shadwell, R.N. The first boat of this squadron to arrive was H.M.S. *Clyde*. Christie noted in his diary, "*Clyde*, the dirtiest submarine that ever made a dive, now in port after several false starts. I hope this isn't a sample of what we are to experience with the Limeys." And later, "*Clyde* now must remove battery for repair. Looks as if she'd have to be generally refitted and then *blasted* out of port. H.M.S. *Porpoise* in today. She too arrives unready for her job." On September 2 he noted, "The submarines of the Royal Navy arriving here are in the most horrible condition. Looks as though we'll have to rebuild [them] before they are able to do any work in enemy areas—if they have that in mind."

Christie deployed these short-legged boats to the Java Sea for patrol near Surabaya and Singapore. One of the boats turned in a good patrol. It was a British-built submarine, *Zwaardvisch* (*Swordfish*) manned by a Dutch crew commanded by H. A. W. Goossens, R.N.N. When Christie asked him where he wanted to patrol, he replied Surabaya. The Japanese had interned some relatives of his, and he wanted revenge.

While Goossens was patrolling off Surabaya, Christie received important information from the codebreakers. A German submarine, *U-168*, was en route from Germany to Japan with important technical information on radar and plans for a new submarine. The boat had put into Surabaya and was scheduled to leave on the morning of October 6.

Christie alerted Goossens, who moved into position to intercept. "The German sub was five minutes late," Christie said later. As the boat approached on the surface, Goossens fired four torpedoes. *U-168* blew up and went to the bottom in 120 feet of water. Twenty men, including the sub skipper, Commander Pich, the doctor, and eighteen ratings made it to the surface. Goossens kept Pich and the doctor and two technicians and put the other sixteen on a native boat.

Goossens was not yet finished. On October 17, he found and torpedoed the Japanese minelayer *Itsutshima*. Christie and the British squadron commander, Shadwell, met Goossens on his return to Fremantle. Christie was struck by the international flavor of the event. He later wrote, "A Dutch sailor in a British submarine under American task force command returning to an Australian port after sinking a German submarine in waters the Japanese thought were theirs. Canada was represented, too, when I presented Goossens a bottle of Canadian Club."

34

Pearl Harbor and Australia, October to November 1944

Air Strikes on Formosa and the Philippines

Admiral Bull Halsey, commanding the Third Fleet (and Task Force 38), joined forces with General MacArthur and made preparations for the invasion of Leyte. The operation was code-named King Two. On the opposite side of the fence, Admiral Toyoda drew up a counterattack, known as Sho 1. Although the Japanese fleet had been severely mauled in the Battle of the Philippine Sea, Toyoda intended to make an all-out last-ditch fight. His plan was simple. After U.S. troops landed in the Philippines (Mindanao? Leyte?), Admiral Ozawa would steam down from Japan with his four remaining "fast" aircraft carriers (*Zuikaku, Zuiho, Chitose,* and *Chiyoda*) and three jeep carriers (*Junyo, Ryuho,* and *Jinyo,* also known as *Shinyo*) and lure Admiral Halsey's Task Force 38 away from the landing area. After this had been achieved, the more powerful battleship force from Singapore would steam up and annihilate the U.S. landing force. Japanese land-based aircraft in the Philippines, Formosa, and Okinawa would support these attacks, helping to make up for Ozawa's overwhelming disparity in aircraft carriers. This time, Japanese kamikaze pilots would lend extra punch to the Japanese counterattack. Conceivably, great damage could be inflicted on Halsey's force and the invasion of the Philippines could be thwarted.

As a preliminary to the Leyte landings, Admiral Halsey employed Task Force 38 in a series of strikes aimed at softening up the area and reducing Japanese air power in the Philippines, Formosa, and Okinawa. On October 6 this force steamed out of the newly acquired Ulithi anchorage right into a typhoon. On October 8, Halsey refueled his ships at sea in heavy weather. On October 10, he struck Okinawa and the Ryukyus.

Many of Lockwood's submarines lifeguarded these air strikes. One was *Sterlet*, commanded by Butch Robbins, off Okinawa. When some naval aviators went into the water, *Sterlet* picked up six. *Saury*, commanded by Richard Albert Waugh, picked up one.

The October 10 strikes alerted Admiral Toyoda, then on Formosa, to the fact that something important was in the wind. He sent out a general warning for all bases to gear for more attacks. In addition, he ordered the carrier force in the Inland Sea to transfer its operational aircraft to land bases. This was a controversial order that would have considerable bearing on operations in the near future.

Halsey again refueled and then considered where to strike next, Luzon or Formosa. The plan called for a strike at Aparri on northeast Luzon. Following the plan, Halsey carried out that strike on October 11. It accomplished nothing worthwhile and Halsey later said, "I should have struck Formosa first." The strike on Aparri gave Toyoda an additional day to prepare his defenses and gather more planes at Formosa.

On Columbus Day, October 12, Halsey wheeled north and hit Formosa. Toyoda sent about 600 planes in counterattack. This first great fight between land- and carrier-based aircraft stretched over three brutal days—October 12, 13, and 14—with catastrophic consequences for the Japanese. Halsey destroyed most of Toyoda's aircraft, while losing only about 76. The Japanese claimed a smashing victory, stating that Japanese planes had eliminated eleven carriers, two battleships, and three cruisers and damaged eight carriers, two battleships, and four cruisers. In fact, Japanese planes had sunk no ships and seriously damaged only two, the cruisers *Canberra* and *Houston*, which were towed home.

During the strike on Formosa, Bob Ward in *Sailfish*, Fritz Harlfinger in *Trigger*, and George Browne in *Snook* were on lifeguard duty. On the first day of the strike, October 12, Ward remained on the surface in full view of Japanese air- and shore-based units and penetrated minefields to rescue twelve navy airmen. During one rescue, a Japanese patrol boat tried to get at the aviator on his raft, but Ward sank the Japanese with his deck gun. Not far away, Fritz Harlfinger in *Trigger* picked up one aviator. On October 16 Banister in *Sawfish* picked up a navy pilot who had been in the water four and a half days.

After Ward had rescued the airmen, his radio transmitter went out of commission. Red Ramage, who was nearby in *Parche,* following a couple of weeks of barren patrolling off San Bernardino Strait, moved in and escorted *Sailfish* back to Saipan. After the transmitter had been fixed, Ward and Ramage, joined by John Hess in *Pomfret,* returned to Luzon Strait as a newly created wolf pack. Hess had good luck on his maiden patrol, sinking three ships for 14,000 tons.

During the Formosa strike, October 12, Lockwood alerted all his packs and individual submarines patrolling from Luzon Strait to Tokyo Bay to be on the alert for major Japanese fleet movements. In subsequent days, his packs were disposed as follows: two in Luzon Strait (*Sawfish, Icefish,* and *Drum,* plus *Snook,* which joined them; and *Shark, Blackfish,* and *Seadragon*); one moving north toward southern Kyushu (*Silversides, Trigger, Salmon,* and *Sterlet,* which joined them); one guarding Bungo Suido, the southern outlet from the Inland Sea (*Besugo, Gabilan,* and *Ronquil*); and one in the East China Sea near Nagasaki (*Perch* and *Croaker,* less *Escolar,* which had been lost). In addition, there were many individual boats disposed along probable routes to the south: *Sea Dog, Skate, Saury, Barbel, Burrfish, Sea Fox,* and *Billfish*; and Dick O'Kane in *Tang,* patrolling inside the Formosa Strait.

The heaviest responsibility fell on the shoulders of Tom Wogan in *Besugo,* leading the pack guarding Bungo Suido. If Admiral Toyoda ordered Admiral Ozawa to sortie his depleted carrier force, Wogan's pack would be first to sight it and give the alarm. His orders were to maintain a close, observant patrol and, if he saw anything, report first and then attack.

Admiral Toyoda, meanwhile, evidently believed his pilots' reports to the effect that they caused tremendous damage to Admiral Halsey's force during the strike on Formosa. On October 15, he ordered a force of two heavy cruisers, *Nachi* and *Ashigara,* and one light cruiser, *Abukuma,* plus supporting destroyers, to leave the Inland Sea and pursue the "crippled" U.S. carriers. This force, commanded by Vice Admiral Kiyohide Shima, passed through Bungo Suido between 8 and 9 A.M., range 7,500 yards. Tom Wogan in *Besugo* saw it and reported to Lockwood. The next night, Wogan saw what he believed to be more cruisers coming out and fired six torpedoes at one. It turned out to be the destroyer *Suzutzuki*. Wogan had blown off her bow, but she made it back to Kobe.*

When Wogan flashed the initial alert, Ozzie Lynch in *Skate*, patrolling the northern Ryukyus, moved to intercept Shima's force. He found it at 10:24 that evening and attacked one cruiser, firing three electric torpedoes. He thought he got one hit, but according to Japanese records no cruiser was hit. The Shima force continued south toward Okinawa, refueled, and then retired when it received a message that "more than six carriers" were still operating east of Formosa.

By that time, Admiral Halsey was pounding the Philippines. It was now clear to Toyoda that Leyte was the invasion target. He ordered his forces to execute Sho 1. Shima was to proceed south in Formosa Strait to the Pescadores Islands (in the middle of Formosa Strait) and then cross Luzon Strait and join with the battleship forces coming from Singapore.

At about 10:30 on the morning of October 18, Butch Robbins in *Sterlet*, patrolling west of Okinawa, picked up the Shima force shortly after it left Okinawa. He reported two heavy cruisers, one light cruiser, and six destroyers, which was a near-accurate picture of the formation. The range was 15 miles. Robbins closed to 4 miles, but because it was daylight he could not overtake and gain position ahead for a submerged attack. He got off a contact report.

Farther south, John Coye's wolf pack (*Silversides, Salmon,* and *Trigger*) moved to intercept. Fritz Harlfinger in *Trigger* picked up the force, range 9 miles. He closed to 5 miles, preparing to make a night surface attack, but a Japanese aircraft and submarine (which fired a torpedo at *Trigger*) drove him off. Coye in *Silversides* did not make contact. Harley Nauman in *Salmon* was temporarily absent; one of his officers, Lieutenant J. M. McNeal, had come down with an illness—diagnosed as gallstones—and Nauman was rendezvousing with Saipan-bound *Barbel* to transfer McNeal to that boat.

Farther south still, in Formosa Strait, Dick O'Kane on *Tang* was alerted and, at 4 A.M. on October 20, made contact with the Shima force. By this time, the force was zigzagging "erratically" at 19 knots. O'Kane, who had no steam torpedoes left forward, made five at-

---

* On January 16, 1944, Charlton Lewis Murphy, Jr., in *Sturgeon*, had blown off *Suzutzuki*'s bow in almost the same location.

tempts to guess the zigzag pattern, but each time he "guessed wrong." He trailed—or tried—until dawn, but was not able to get off a shot.

After a one-night stop in the Pescadores, the Shima force got under way again to cross Luzon Strait and join the force from Singapore. A few hours after leaving port, Shima encountered the wolf pack commanded by Edward Blakely, consisting of his *Shark*, James Ashley's *Seadragon*, and Robert Sellars's *Blackfish*. Ashley picked the force up first, incorrectly identifying it as a carrier, two cruisers, and six destroyers. He notified Blakely in *Shark* and Sellars in *Blackfish* and then maneuvered in on the surface from 30,000 yards to 3,000 yards. He fired four stern tubes at the "carrier" and a cruiser which were overlapping, then went deep. He claimed hits in both ships, but the Japanese had no record of it. Blakely and Sellars made contact but were unable to get close enough to shoot.

Shima next ran into the pack commanded by Alan Banister, consisting of his *Sawfish*, Mike Rindskopf's *Drum*, and Dick Peterson's *Icefish*. At 8 A.M. the morning of October 22, while submerged, Peterson got a good look at the force and more accurately described it as two heavy cruisers and destroyer escorts. Peterson was unable to gain attack position, so two hours later he surfaced in heavy seas to get off a contact report, but Japanese planes forced him under before he could deliver the message. That night, Peterson finally managed to raise a station in Australia which took the message.

While Shima had been going south, Admiral Ozawa had been feverishly preparing his carrier force, designed to lure Halsey from the Philippines. His worst problem was trying to find aircraft. Admiral Toyoda had stripped the carriers to help defend Formosa; all Ozawa could get together were about 110 planes. For this reason, he left the jeep carriers *Junyo*, *Ryuho*, and *Jinyo* (*Shinyo*) behind. Instead of them, he had two curiosities: *Ise* and *Hyuga*, old battleships that had been fitted with a small hangar and flight deck on the after portion of the hull, making each vessel half aircraft carrier, half battleship, accommodating about twenty-four planes. However, there were not enough planes for *Ise* and *Hyuga*, and they had to go as quasi-battleships. In addition to *Ise* and *Hyuga*, Ozawa had three light cruisers, *Isuzu*, *Oyodo* and *Tama*, plus about eight destroyers.

All this time Tom Wogan in *Besugo*, lying outside Bungo Suido, had been growing restless. It seemed to him that the carriers were not going to come out. On the evening of October 18, he asked if he could attack first and then report. Lockwood granted permission. Wogan deployed *Besugo* and Henry Monroe's *Ronquil* in the westward exit of Bungo Suido and ordered Karl Wheland in *Gabilan* to watch the eastern exit.

Meanwhile, Lockwood was worried about the northern exit from the Inland Sea, Kii Suido. He reasoned that since Wogan had attacked the destroyer on the night of October 16, Admiral Ozawa knew submarines guarded Bungo Suido and might attempt to avoid them by going out Kii Suido. On October 19, Lockwood ordered Wheland in *Gabilan* to detach from the pack and shift to Kii Suido. Since Wogan kept both *Besugo* and *Ronquil* at the western exit, Lockwood's order left the eastern exit of Bungo Suido unguarded.

On the night of October 20, Ozawa gathered his force together and steamed through the eastern exit. Since Wogan and Wheland were busy looking the wrong way, Ozawa was not detected. In one sense, this was a disappointment for Ozawa because, as a decoy, he *wanted* to be seen. On the other hand, Wogan's impatience and failure to shift Monroe in *Ronquil* to guard the east exit, together with Lockwood's decision to move Wheland in *Gabilan* to Kii Suido, cost Pearl Harbor submarines a chance to deliver attacks on Ozawa's four carriers prior to the battle.

The U.S. Invasion of Leyte

Far to the south, the main Japanese surface force at Singapore executed Sho 1. Admiral Toyoda divided this force into three units. The First Force was commanded by Vice Admiral Takao Kurita. It consisted of *Yamato, Musashi,* and other newer battleships and support units. It would go through San Bernardino Strait, circle south, and attack the landing ships at Leyte. The Second Force, commanded by Vice Admiral Shoji Nishimura, was composed of older, slower battleships and support units. It would go through Surigao Strait and attack the landing ships at Leyte from the south. The Third Force consisted of the heavy cruiser *Aoba,* the light cruiser *Kinu,* a destroyer, and five troop carriers, similar to destroyer transports. The purpose of this last group was to pick up troops from the north coast of Mindanao and shuttle them over to the west coast of Leyte.

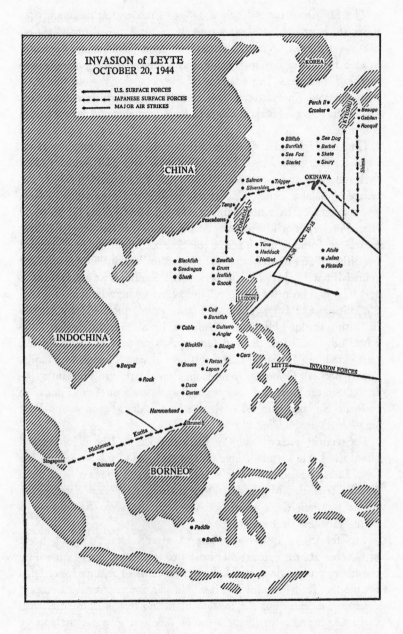

INVASION of LEYTE
OCTOBER 20, 1944

→ U.S. SURFACE FORCES
⇢ JAPANESE SURFACE FORCES
↔ MAJOR AIR STRIKES

KOREA

CHINA

Perch II ●
Croaker ●

KYUSHU

● Besugo
● Gabilan
● Ronquil

Shima

● Billfish   ● Sea Dog
● Burrfish   ● Barbel
● Sea Fox   ● Skate
● Sterlet   ● Saury

● Salmon   ● Trigger   OKINAWA
● Silversides

Tang ●

FORMOSA

Pescadores ●

Oct. 10-16

TF-38

● Tuna
● Haddock
● Halibut

● Atule
● Jallao
● Pintado

● Blackfish   ● Sawfish
● Seadragon ● Drum
● Shark   ● Icefish
                      ● Snook

LUZON

● Cod
● Bonefish

● Cobia   ● Guitarro
                   ● Angler
● Blackfin   ● Bluegill

INDOCHINA

● Cero

● Bergall   ● Bream   ● Raton
                               ● Lapon
● Rock   LEYTE ←   INVASION FORCES

● Dace
● Darter

Hammerhead ●
                        ● Brunei
        Kurita

Nishimura

Singapore ●
          ● Gurnard

BORNEO

● Paddle

● Batfish

The Singapore force departed Lingga shortly after midnight, October 18. It proceeded northeast about 700 miles to Brunei Bay, on northwest Borneo, to refuel, arriving at noon, October 20. *Gurnard*, headed to Brunei Bay to lay mines and relieve the departing *Hammerhead*, had paused to attack a convoy. For that reason, the Japanese fleet got into Brunei Bay unseen by Christie's submarines. However, the codebreakers followed its movements and kept Christie informed.

Christie deployed a dozen submarines to intercept and report on Japanese fleet movements. Claggett's *Darter* and McClintock's *Dace* took station at the south end of Palawan Passage and the west entrance of Balabac Strait. Flachsenhar's *Rock* and a new boat, *Blackfin*, commanded by a new skipper, George Hays Laird, Jr., en route from Pearl Harbor to Fremantle, took stations to the west of *Darter* and *Dace*, forming a line across the South China Sea. Another new boat, *Bergall*, en route from Pearl Harbor to Fremantle under skipper John Milton Hyde, who had been Chet Smith's exec on *Swordfish* and who had been patrolling off Indochina (where he sank a 4,200-ton ship on October 13), joined *Blackfin* and *Rock*. Moon Chapple in *Bream*, Enrique Haskins in *Guitarro*, Frank Hess in *Angler*, Lawrence Edge in *Bonefish*, and Caddy Adkins in *Cod* patrolled the area extending from the north end of Palawan Passage to Manila. Albert Becker's *Cobia*, en route from Pearl Harbor to Fremantle, patrolled Sibutu Passage. Jake Fyfe in *Batfish,* en route from Fremantle to Pearl Harbor, patrolled Makassar Strait, along with Joseph Paul Fitz-Patrick in *Paddle.*

For security reasons, none of these skippers had been forewarned about the Leyte invasion. Late on the night of October 20, after the first U.S. troops started going ashore, they heard about it from news broadcasts on the ships' radios. After that, all skippers understood the reason for their deployment and went on the alert for movements of the Japanese fleet toward Leyte.

McClintock in *Darter* was first to make contact. On the night of October 20, the Japanese Third Force—the troop ferry unit led by the heavy cruiser *Aoba* and light cruiser *Kinu*—got under way from Brunei Bay for Manila, where it would join forces with the transport destroyers to carry out the mission of lifting troops from Mindanao to Leyte. It came up to the west of Palawan Passage, making 23 knots. Shortly before midnight, McClintock intercepted. He chased at flank speed, sending off contact reports to Christie and to Claggett in *Dace*, trying to coach Claggett into intercept position. Neither *Dace* nor *Darter* could get close enough to attack, but the boats up the line near Mindoro picked up the contact report, or received it by relay from Christie, and set a sharp watch.

The Japanese force was lucky—for a while. It got by Hess in *Angler* near the north end of Palawan Passage and Haskins in *Guitarro* in the southern region of Mindoro Strait. However, at 2:40 A.M. on the morning of October 23, Moon Chapple, who was slightly north of Haskins, picked it up on radar. Chapple chased the force for forty minutes, identifying it as two cruisers, "very large." At 3:24, he commenced firing six torpedoes at one of the cruisers. The escorts charged and Chapple went deep. Chapple hit *Aoba**** with two torpedoes. She did not sink, but she was so badly damaged she had to be towed into Manila.

Early that same morning, Claggett and McClintock picked up the main Japanese fleet coming north through Palawan Passage. It was moving slowly, seemingly oblivious to submarines, the destroyers not even pinging. McClintock in *Darter,* the pack commander, sent off a contact report to Christie. Claggett kept radio silence. McClintock maneuvered the two boats into a favorable attack position. At 5:09, McClintock in *Darter* submerged. Seven minutes later, Claggett in *Dace* submerged. By the dawn light, both skippers examined this awesome sight, preparing to fire.

McClintock let the ships come within 1,000 yards. The tension in *Darter*'s conning tower was almost unbearable. The TDC operator, Eugene ("Dennis") Wilkinson, a reservist, who would later be the first skipper of the nuclear-powered submarine, *Nautilus,* kept shouting, "Give me a range! Give me a range! I want you to shoot. You can't shoot without a range!"

Each time McClintock shifted his cross hairs from ship to ship, his exec, Ernest Louis ("Ernie") Schwab, Jr., 1939, would ask, "What's there?" McClintock replied calmly, "Battleship. . . . Cruiser. . . . Battleships. . . . Cruisers."

At 5:32 A.M., McClintock fired six torpedoes at one of the cruisers. Then he swung around and fired all four stern tubes at another

---

* Admiral Samuel Eliot Morison, *History of United States Naval Operations in World War II*, volume XII, page 164, in a small oversight in an otherwise magnificent account of the battle, incorrectly states that *Aoba* and *Kinu* "split off" from Shima's force, coming down from the Inland Sea.

cruiser. While he was firing his stern tubes, the bow tubes hit the first cruiser. Later, McClintock wrote:

Whipped periscope back to the first target to see the sight of a lifetime: (Cruiser was so close that all of her could not be seen at once with periscope in high power). She was a mass of billowing black smoke from number one turret to the stern. No superstructure could be seen. Bright orange flames shot out from the side along the main deck from the bow to the after turret. Cruiser was already going down by the bow, which was dipping under. #1 turret was at water level. She was definitely finished. Five hits had her sinking and in flames. It is estimated that there were few if any survivors.

A few minutes later McClintock heard four hits in his second target. Then he went deep. He could hear breaking-up noises and depth charges and many ships roaring overhead. Curiously, the destroyers dropped no depth charges. Over on *Dace*, Claggett, awaiting his chance, wrote:

0532 *Heard five torpedo explosions. DARTER must be getting in.*

0534 *Four more torpedo hits. DARTER is really having a field day. Can see great pall of smoke completely enveloping spot where ship was at last look. Do not know whether he has sunk but it looks good. Ship to left is also smoking badly. Looks like a great day for the DARTER. Can see two destroyers making smoke headed for scene. There is much signalling, shooting of Very stars, etc. It is a great show. The big ships seem to be milling around; I hope they don't scatter too far for me to get in. Light is still pretty bad but I have counted eight large ships, battleships or cruisers, plus two destroyers. Two of these large ships have been hit so far.*

Claggett was low on torpedoes. He had none aft. As the fleet bore down on him, he picked his targets carefully. The tension in his conning tower was no less than McClintock's. His exec, Rafael Celestino ("Ralph") Benitez, 1939, read off the ranges and bearings. Two heavy cruisers came into his crosshairs, but Claggett saw something bigger behind them, probably a battleship. Later he wrote, "Famous statement: 'Will let them go by—they're only heavy cruisers.'" Then:

0552 *The two cruisers passed ahead at about 1,500 yards. They were overlapping; appeared to be running screen for my target, pre-*

senting a beautiful target—a submarine should have 24 torpedo tubes. Had a beautiful view of them and identified them positively as ATAGO or NACHI class. My target can be seen better now, and appears to be a KONGO class battleship. He looks larger than the two cruisers that have just passed ahead—he has two stacks, and superstructure appears much heavier. Have not checked the identification as well as I should as I have been busy getting complete composition of force which I consider essential for contact report. Sound also reports target screws as heavier and slower than those of cruisers.

Two minutes later, Claggett fired all six bow tubes at his "battleship." He heard four solid hits. Then:

0601 *Heard two tremendous explosions both on sound and through the hull. These explosions were apparently magazines as I have never heard anything like it. The soundmen reported that it sounded as if the bottom of the ocean was blowing up. They were obviously shallow as there was neither any shaking of the boat nor water swishing through the superstructure. Nothing could cause this much noise except magazines exploding.*

0603 *Heard tremendous breaking up noises. This was the most gruesome sound I have ever heard. I was at first convinced that it was being furnished by the DACE, and called for a check of all compartments and was much relieved to receive reports that everything was all right. Noise was coming from northeast—the direction of the target, and it sounded as if she was coming down on top of us. I have never heard anything like it. Comment from Diving officer: 'We better get the hell out of here.' After about five minutes of these tremendous breaking up noises, continued to have smaller ones and much crackling noises for next twenty minutes. These noises could be heard on sound and throughout boat. I am convinced that this ship sank; nothing else can explain these noises.*

Since both boats remained submerged for several hours, neither skipper was certain what damage he had inflicted on the Japanese force. Postwar records cleared it up. In his ten-torpedo salvo, McClintock had hit and sunk Vice Admiral Kurita's flagship, the heavy cruiser *Atago,* and severely damaged a second cruiser, *Takao.* Claggett had not hit a battleship but rather the heavy cruiser *Maya*. *Atago* sank in nineteen minutes, *Maya* in four.

The loss of the flagship *Atago* caused much confusion in the Japanese high command. The destroyer *Kishinami* came close aboard to take off Kurita, but the admiral had to jump in the water and swim for his life. While he was being rescued and dried out, Rear Admiral Matome Ugaki in *Yamato* took tactical command. Three hundred and sixty officers and men were lost on *Atago*.

Counting Chapple's *Aoba*, U.S. submarines had sunk or knocked out four heavy Japanese cruisers, all within the space of about two and a half hours.

A couple of hours later, McClintock returned to periscope depth and saw the damaged cruiser *Takao* lying motionless in the water. For most of the day, McClintock tried to get in for another shot, but Japanese destroyers hovered close by, blocking him, and aircraft circled over the cruiser. Claggett found *Takao* at about three o'clock that afternoon but decided his chances of getting in were "slim." McClintock decided to wait until nightfall and then coordinate with Claggett in a night surface attack. Meanwhile, *Takao* got her damage under control and set off for Brunei Bay, making 6 to 10 knots.

Later, Kinkaid's chief of staff, Rear Admiral Clifford Evans Van Hook, was critical of McClintock and Claggett for failing to exploit this opportunity. In part of the endorsement to the patrol report of *Dace*, Van Hook wrote, "It is regrettable that with two submarines in the vicinity, the damaged cruiser remained helpless for over twelve hours and finally escaped at creeping speed." This comment in an otherwise glowing endorsement made Christie furious—his submarines had knocked four heavy cruisers out of action in one morning—and led to the widening of the already large gap between himself and Kinkaid.*

After dark, McClintock rendezvoused with Claggett and laid out a plan of attack on *Takao*. It would take McClintock near an area of water filled with rocks and shoals, appropriately named Dangerous Ground. McClintock had not been able to get an accurate navigational fix for about twenty-four hours and during that day had been pushed along by uncertain currents in Palawan Passage. However, his mind was more intent on getting *Takao* than precise navigational

---

* Van Hook was an old friend of Lockwood's. They served together in the Naval Mission to Brazil in 1930.

fixes. He gave Claggett his orders and both boats commenced an end around at 17 knots.

The main force, meanwhile, was steaming north. Hess in *Angler*, Haskins in *Guitarro*, and Moon Chapple in *Bream* were in position to intercept. Chapple somehow failed to get the word, but Hess and Haskins picked up the main force about 8:30 P.M. Hess was closer. He bent on all possible speed and got off contact reports to Christie and Haskins. During the stern chase, Hess ran across a convoy and was tempted to break off and attack it. However, he wisely decided it was more important to trail the main body of the Japanese fleet and see exactly where it was going. By this time, Haskins in *Guitarro* was on the trail, too. Both boats tracked the fleet as it turned eastward toward Leyte. The Japanese jammed Hess's radio, but Haskins got off an accurate report to an Australian radio station, which rebroadcast it to Halsey and Kinkaid in the early morning hours of October 24. Unable to overtake and attack, Hess and Haskins returned to patrol stations off Mindoro and the northern end of Palawan Passage. U.S. carrier planes picked up the trail of the fleet the following morning.

Back at the south end of Palawan Passage, meanwhile, McClintock and Claggett were wolf-packing the damaged *Takao*. At five minutes past midnight, October 25, *Darter* ran aground with such a crash that for a moment McClintock, who was on the bridge, believed he had been torpedoed.

The exec, Ernie Schwab, who was navigating in the conning tower, rushed to the bridge. "What was that?" he said.

"We're aground," McClintock said grimly.

Schwab disappeared back in the conning tower to consult a chart. He returned to the bridge a moment later and said, "Captain, we can't be aground. The nearest land is nineteen miles away."

Darter stayed aground while McClintock tried every way possible to get his ship off the reef. He ordered all excess weight jettisoned: ammunition, food, fuel oil, fresh water. Then at high tide, 1:40 A.M., he backed the engines full and sallied ship—had the crew run back and forth to set up a rocking motion. Nothing worked. *Darter* was stuck high and dry.

When he saw it was hopeless, McClintock reluctantly radioed Claggett in *Dace*. He was reluctant, he said later, because he knew Claggett would give up trying to sink *Takao* and come to his rescue. After that, McClintock gave orders for his crew to destroy the sonar and TDC and begin destruction of classified papers and other gear.

One of the Japanese destroyers escorting *Takao*, apparently having heard *Darter* crunch aground, came close but then turned away. Belowdecks, as crewmen fed the mountain of confidential papers on the fires, *Darter* filled with smoke, causing much gagging and temporary discomfort.

Hearing the news of *Dace*'s sister ship, Claggett immediately broke off his attack on *Takao* to rescue the crew of *Darter*. Kinkaid's deputy, Van Hook, may not have believed this decision to be the wisest either. Claggett still had four torpedoes. He could have shot them at *Takao* and then rescued the *Darter* crew later in the night. But Christie approved of Claggett's decision. Had Claggett attacked *Takao*, he might have been held down by the destroyers until daylight. McClintock and his crew would have been picked up by the Japanese and probably executed for the damage they had inflicted on the fleet.

McClintock continued destroying papers and machinery and then transferred his crew to *Dace* by rubber boat, a slow, tricky operation that went on for two and a half hours. He then set demolition charges and left the ship, carrying a wardroom ashtray for a souvenir. Claggett hauled clear at full speed. The charges exploded. But in place of a deafening explosion, there was only a dull pop. Something had gone wrong.

What to do? McClintock and Claggett decided there was only one answer: torpedo *Darter*. During the next hour or so, Claggett fired four torpedoes, one at a time. All hit the reef on which *Darter* had grounded and blew up without inflicting any damage on *Darter*. The two skippers then decided to destroy *Darter* with *Dace*'s deck gun. The crew pumped twenty-one shells into *Darter*, doing some damage but not destroying her; then a Japanese plane came over and forced Claggett to break off this effort. Fortunately, the Japanese plane attempted to bomb *Darter*, not *Dace*, though unsuccessfully.

During the day, Claggett hung around, intending to put another demolition party on board *Darter* that night. A Japanese destroyer came alongside *Darter* and probably sent a boarding party on her. That night, when Claggett got within 2,000 yards of *Darter*, his sonarman picked up echo ranging. Since there was nothing on radar, Claggett and McClintock assumed the ranging to be a Japanese submarine and hauled clear again, this time setting course for Fremantle. It took eleven days to get there. With eighty-five officers and men from *Darter* on board, plus her own eighty, *Dace* soon ran low

on food. By the time the boat reached Fremantle, the men were sub-
sisting on nothing but mushroom soup and peanut butter sandwiches.

Christie made two more efforts to destroy *Darter*. He ordered John
Flachsenhar in *Rock* to try torpedoes again. Flachsenhar came
down and fired ten torpedoes at *Darter*, but these too apparently blew
up on the reef without inflicting serious damage. Finally, Christie
called in George Sharp in *Nautilus*, then in the Philippines on another special mission. With her big six-inch guns, *Nautilus* pumped
fifty-five shells into *Darter*. She didn't blow up as hoped, but she was
so badly holed that she was not worth trying to salvage and remained
on that reef for years afterward. Her crew was transferred as a unit
to new construction: *Menhaden*, in Manitowoc.

Takao limped into Brunei Bay. From there she made Singapore,
where she remained for the rest of the war, unable to find parts to
repair a smashed engine.

The Battle of Leyte Gulf

The main Japanese fleet, as planned, split into two groups. Kurita's
First Force steamed eastward from Mindoro for San Bernardino
Strait; Nishimura's Second Force steamed through Balabac Strait
eastward for Surigao Strait. Meanwhile, Admiral Ozawa was approaching Luzon from the northeast with his carrier force to "lure"
Halsey away from the landing beaches. Admiral Shima's small
cruiser force had been lost in the vast shuffle of Japanese forces. More
or less on his own, he decided to follow Admiral Nishimura through
Surigao Strait.

What took place over the next forty-eight hours—to be known as
the Battle of Leyte Gulf—was the greatest naval engagement in the
history of the world. In the first exchange, October 24, U.S. aircraft hit both Kurita's First Force and Nishimura's Second Force
while Japanese land-based planes struck at the conglomeration of
ships near the Leyte beaches. The United States sank the super-
battleship *Musashi*, damaged two battleships and two cruisers from
Kurita's force, and damaged a battleship and destroyer from Nishimura's force. The badly mauled Kurita First Force reversed course,
requesting land-based air support, then came about and charged
again for San Bernardino Strait. Nishimura's Second Force continued on, reducing speed to allow for Kurita's double turnabout.

Admiral Shima's cruiser force, not yet integrated into the battle plan, followed behind Nishimura's force.

Meanwhile, Admiral Ozawa was approaching from the north. On the afternoon of October 24, about the time Kurita was doubling back, planes from Halsey's carrier force found Ozawa. Halsey then made a decision that would keep naval strategists busy arguing for decades. Concluding that Kurita and Nishimura had been decisively attacked and presented no real threat to the landing forces, Halsey turned his carrier force north to attack Ozawa. He took the bait, just as the Japanese had hoped. San Bernardino Strait was unguarded; there was not even a submarine there.

Left by Halsey to his own resources, Admiral Kinkaid deployed his forces to stop the pincers aimed at him. To oppose Nishimura's Second Force, followed by Shima's cruiser force, Kinkaid deployed PT boats, six old battleships (some of which had been raised from the Pearl Harbor mud), six cruisers, and thirty-odd destroyers. These met and annihilated Nishimura's force, sinking everything except one destroyer, *Shigure*. Shima came up after this battle, wondering what was going on. His light cruiser, *Abukuma*, was damaged by torpedo boats and later abandoned. His heavy cruiser, *Nachi*, collided with one of Nishimura's crippled heavy cruisers, *Mogami*.* Shima then withdrew with all he had left.

Kurita's First Force, meanwhile, pushed eastward through San Bernardino Strait. To oppose this mighty fleet, Kinkaid had little more than his dozen jeep carriers, which were slow and thin-skinned. These naval forces met on the morning of October 25. The jeep carrier pilots fought gallantly, sinking three heavy cruisers, all the while sending urgent calls for help to Halsey. Kurita badly damaged the light carrier *Princeton* (later abandoned and sunk by U.S. forces), and sank the jeep carrier *Gambier Bay*, two destroyers, and a destroyer escort. With victory almost in his grasp, Kurita made a decision as controversial as Halsey's: he ordered his fleet to withdraw. This decision, he explained later, was based on misinformation and an incomplete grasp of the situation. Kurita believed that Halsey was coming up with a powerful carrier force, that land-based U.S. aircraft were gathering to assault his fleet, and that even if he did proceed to the landing beaches the landing ships would have fled by the time he got there. He retired through San Bernardino Strait,

* Poetic justice, perhaps. *Mogami* had rammed *Mikuma* in the withdrawal from the Battle of Midway after sighting *Tambor*.

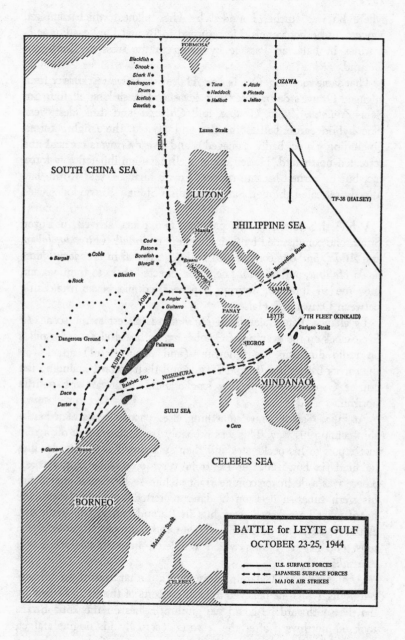

BATTLE for LEYTE GULF
OCTOBER 23-25, 1944

U.S. SURFACE FORCES
JAPANESE SURFACE FORCES
MAJOR AIR STRIKES

where he was further hounded by U.S. planes, which damaged *Yamato* and other vessels. He returned to Brunei Bay, evading submarines in Palawan Passage by going to the west of Dangerous Ground.

That same morning, October 25, Halsey's massive fast carrier force engaged Ozawa's decoy force and devastated it, sinking all four carriers—*Zuikaku, Zuiho, Chitose,* and *Chiyoda*—and three destroyers. The hybrid carrier-battleships, *Ise* and *Hyuga,* three light cruisers (including *Tama,* badly damaged), and five destroyers escaped and retreated northward. Halsey might well have annihilated this force, too, but he turned back to support Leyte, unaware that Kurita had already retreated through San Bernardino Strait.

While this battle was in progress, two packs arrived in Luzon Strait, one commanded by Chick Clarey in *Pintado* (*Pintado, Jallao,* and *Atule*) and one commanded by Beetle Roach in *Haddock* (*Haddock, Halibut,* and *Tuna*). Lockwood directed them to form a scouting line to intercept retiring Japanese cripples from the battle between Ozawa and Halsey.

By chance, Pete Galantin in *Halibut* was closest to the scene. At five o'clock on the evening of October 25, he heard U.S. carrier pilots on radio directing the follow-up (and unsuccessful) attacks on the carrier-battleships *Ise* and *Hyuga* and their escorts, including the cruiser *Oyodo.* Then he saw smoke and antiaircraft fire on the horizon.

At 5:42, Galantin saw something else: pagoda masts of a battleship coming his way. This was probably *Ise.* Galantin got off a contact report to his packmates and then submerged to attack. At 6:43 he fired six bow tubes at *Ise* from very long range, 3,400 yards. There was a destroyer coming right at him so he elected not to fire his stern tubes—a decision he later regretted—and went deep. He heard what he believed were hits in *Ise* and believed he sank her. Actually, however, he hit not *Ise* but the destroyer *Akitsuki,* 2,000 tons, one of the escorts which wandered into the torpedo track. *Akitsuki* sank.

At about 8 P.M., Galantin surfaced. To the northward, he saw signal lights, which he believed to be the escorts of the "late" battleship. To the southward he could see gunfire flashes on the horizon. He took off northward after the "escorts" (actually his original target, *Ise*). While pursuing, he received a contact report from a packmate,

Edward Steffanides in *Tuna*. Thinking *Tuna's* targets better than the "escorts" he was chasing, Galantin broke off the chase and headed for *Tuna's* position.

Actually *Tuna* had probably sighted *Ise* and *Hyuga*; Beetle Roach in *Haddock* also picked them up and chased. At about 11 P.M., Galantin found them again. The Japanese force was making 19 knots. There was no way any of the three boats could overtake and gain a firing position, so they flashed word to Clarey's pack, which had taken position farther north.

Clarey was then busy with another target. At about 8 P.M., one of his boats, *Jallao*, commanded by Joseph Icenhower making his maiden patrol as skipper, had picked up the damaged light cruiser *Tama* and flashed word to Clarey. Clarey directed his own boat, *Pintado*, and the third boat of the pack, John Maurer's *Atule*, into intercept position and gave the honors to Icenhower. Shortly after eleven o'clock, Icenhower fired seven torpedoes at *Tama*, obtaining three hits. *Tama* sank almost instantly, while Clarey, who was 15,000 yards away, watched on his bridge. When Icenhower surfaced, he learned that on his first shots of the war he had sunk a light cruiser.

During this time, John Coye's pack (*Silversides, Trigger*, and *Salmon*) had been moving down to backstop the scouting line. On the morning of October 26, Harlfinger in *Trigger* intercepted *Ise, Hyuga*, and escorts. He was slightly out of position to attack, blaming this on Galantin's contact report, which had not, Harlfinger noted, contained *Halibut's* position. Coye in *Silversides* chased on the surface in broad daylight, with land in sight 15 miles away. Nauman in *Salmon* joined the chase, but he sighted a Japanese periscope and turned away. Lockwood ordered all three boats of this pack to pursue the force northward at high speed.

Rebel Lowrance in *Sea Dog* lay along the track. On the evening of October 28, at about 9:20, he picked up the force at 10 miles. He submerged ahead to radar depth and fired six electrics at *Ise*, but at the last minute the ship zigzagged and all the torpedoes missed. By that time, the Japanese force was making 22 knots. There was no way Lowrance could end-around. He chased—making a contact report—but lost the force at 15 miles. "It was a heartbreaker," he said.

Butch Robbins in *Sterlet* lay to the north of *Sea Dog*. Robbins had sunk a big 10,000-ton tanker on the day of the battle and then joined forces with John Lee in *Croaker*, returning from the East China Sea. Robbins received Lowrance's contact report, then "went

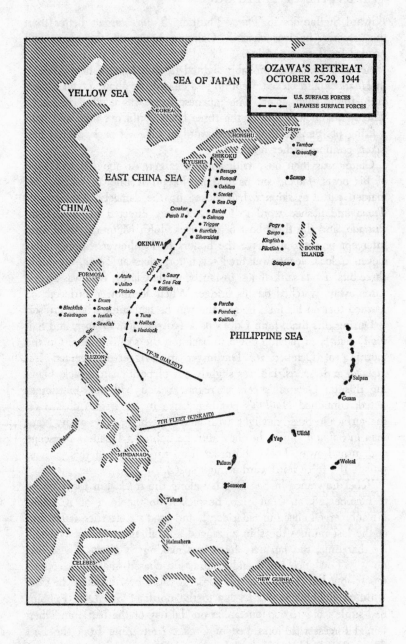

to full power to intercept." Wogan in *Besugo* and *Ronquil* dropped down from Bungo and Kii Suido to intercept. The three boats—*Sterlet, Besugo,* and *Ronquil*—formed an informal pack, Wogan leading.

At 4:15 on the morning of October 29, Robbins made contact with the two ships and destroyer escorts, range 12 miles. Robbins reported later he went to "full emergency power," meanwhile alerting the other boats. He closed to 6 miles but then, as dawn began to break, gave up the chase.* *Besugo* and *Ronquil* also made radar and visual contact with the force, but they were not able to gain firing position either.

The chase after *Ise* and *Hyuga* had taken Coye's pack northward toward Empire waters. On October 30, Fritz Harlfinger in *Trigger* picked up a large tanker with four escorts and attacked. One torpedo broached, alerting the tanker, which turned to avoid the others. Harlfinger fired again. This time his torpedoes hit, blowing off the tanker's stern. Escorts forced *Trigger* deep. Later, Harlfinger surfaced and notified his packmates, who hurried over. Harley Nauman, commanding *Salmon,* was next on the scene. That night he found the tanker, unmoving and guarded by the four alert escorts. Nauman set up, fired four torpedoes, and got two hits. The escorts charged angrily. Nauman went to 300 feet and received a severe depth-charging that drove the old thin-skinned boat to 500 feet. *Salmon* was badly damaged and leaking heavily. Nauman and his exec, Richard Boyer Laning, decided the only hope lay in returning to the surface and fighting it out with their deck guns.

Salmon came up and lay on the surface, almost helpless. The near escort was only 7,000 yards away, but he appeared to be waiting for his cohorts to join him before he attacked. This gave Nauman a few precious minutes to correct a 15-degree list, get his engines on the line, and plug some leaks. Finally, the escort charged, apparently intent on ramming. Nauman, believing the best defense to be a good offense, charged at the escort, firing everything he had, and the two vessels passed each other only 50 yards apart, like two frigates of old. As *Salmon* raked the escort from stem to stern, she apparently killed all the Japanese who were topside. The escort stopped dead in the water.

* This incident led to further friction on *Sterlet.* While the eager Schratz would probably have chased the ships right into the Inland Sea, Robbins felt he had done all that was reasonably possible.

Nauman could scarcely believe his good luck. Emboldened, he fought off a charge by a second escort and ducked into a rainsquall to hide and call his packmates for help. *Silversides* and *Trigger* answered the call at flank speed, as did *Sterlet, Besugo, Ronquil* and *Burrfish. Salmon* dived again to await their arrival.

The next night, the boats congregated near *Salmon*. Robbins in *Sterlet* took time out to polish off the tanker, *Korei Maru*, 10,000 tons (for which *Trigger, Salmon,* and *Sterlet* split credit, one third each); then he helped Coye and Harlfinger with *Salmon*. *Sterlet* escorted *Salmon* back to Saipan, arriving on November 3. When the engineers got a look at *Salmon*, they decided she was so badly damaged and so old there was no point in trying to fix her up again for combat. She went back to Portsmouth, where she was repaired and became a training vessel for the Atlantic Fleet. Nauman and her crew were transferred intact to a new boat, *Stickleback*, under construction at Mare Island.

The unhappiness on *Sterlet* was resolved by transferring both the skipper and the exec. Robbins went to a job in operations in Squadron 10; Schratz went into the exec pool and wound up on Maurer's *Atule*. Command of *Sterlet* went to Hugh Howard Lewis, formerly exec of *Seal*, who became the first reservist to command a fleet boat.*

Allied troops continued to storm the beaches on Leyte. For a while it looked easy. On the first day, in a carefully staged ceremony, General MacArthur waded ashore from a landing craft in knee-deep water and said, "People of the Philippines, *I have returned.*" After that, the fighting—and the weather—grew worse. In spite of repeated carrier strikes against the Visayas and Luzon, the Japanese managed to reinforce the 22,000 troops on Leyte with another 45,000. The land fighting dragged on for weeks. Before it was done, 68,000 Japanese were killed. The U.S. sustained 15,500 casualties, about 3,500 killed.

The Japanese sent submarines and kamikaze pilots to attack the invasion ships and carrier forces. Five RO-class and eight I-class were moved into position. The ROs found no targets and returned to port unharmed. The I-class torpedoed the jeep carrier *Santee* and the light cruiser *Reno* for damage and sank a destroyer escort, *Eversole*. U.S. forces sank six of the eight I-class boats—and sank others later.

---

* Lewis was actually a Naval Academy man who graduated second from the bottom in the class of 1934, resigned from the navy, but maintained a standing in the reserves and was called to duty when war came.

The pioneering kamikaze pilots hit the fast carriers *Franklin, Belleau Wood, Intrepid, Cabot, Essex, Lexington,* and *Hancock;* the jeep carriers *Kalinin Bay, Kitkun Bay,* and *St. Lo* (formerly *Midway*); plus many other U.S. ships. *St. Lo* sank. Many were severely damaged and sustained high casualties.

During the invasion of Leyte, the Japanese launched their first *kaiten* (human torpedo) attacks. Four I-class submarines were assigned to the mission: *I-36, I-37, I-38,* and *I-47. I-36, I-37,* and *I-47* were each fitted with four human torpedoes; *I-38* was to provide advance reconnaissance information. The targets were the U.S. fleet anchorage at Ulithi and Kossol Pass in the Palaus. On the way to station, both *I-37* and *I-38* were sunk with help from codebreakers. *I-36* and *I-47* reached Ulithi as planned. *I-36* fired one *kaiten;* the other three were defective and had to be thrown away. *I-47* fired four. At least one *kaiten* hit a fully loaded fleet tanker, *Mississinewa.* It blew up in spectacular fashion, caught fire, and sank, killing about sixty men as the salvage vessel *Extractor,* recently arrived from the States, lent assistance. The Japanese, who believed they had sunk an aircraft carrier at Ulithi, celebrated this first success and planned other forays. But the *kaiten* project was hobbled by a shortage of everything except volunteer operators: submarines for conversion to mother ships, torpedo experts (lost on Japanese submarines), and torpedoes (whose production had all but stopped because of the shortage of steel and fuel).

From a naval standpoint, the real significance of Leyte was not the land fighting and what was gained there but the four sea battles fought in support of the landings. The U.S. Navy had demolished much of the remaining striking seapower of the Japanese: the super-battleship *Musashi,* four aircraft carriers (*Zuikaku, Zuiho, Chitose,* and *Chiyoda*), and numerous other vessels. U.S. submarines had made a substantial contribution during the fight, sinking two heavy cruisers (*Atago* and *Maya*), one previously damaged light cruiser (*Tama*), and a destroyer (*Akitsuki*) and inflicting serious damage to the heavy cruisers *Aoba* and *Takao.*

After Leyte, the Japanese navy was reduced to a few major units that never again fought as an integrated force: the super-battleship *Yamato,* several other battleships and heavy cruisers—many damaged —including *Ise* and *Hyuga,* and the jeep carriers *Junyo, Ryuho,* and *Jinyo* (*Shinyo*), which were pressed into service escorting convoys.

In Japan, two other Japanese carriers were nearing completion: *Unryu* and the gigantic 60,000-ton *Shinano*, sister ship of *Musashi* and *Yamato*, converted to a carrier.

Patrols from Pearl Harbor

While the fighting was in progress on Leyte, the majority of U.S. submarines on patrol—or going on patrol—were assigned to shut off the flow of Japanese military reinforcements to the Philippines. Lockwood's boats attacked from the north—in the East China Sea, Formosa Strait, and Luzon Strait. Christie's boats attacked from the south, concentrating in the South China Sea near the approaches to Manila. Some boats operated alone, but most were organized into wolf packs.

After missing Shima's southbound cruiser force in the north end of Formosa Strait, Dick O'Kane in *Tang* shifted his effort to merchant shipping. In the early hours of October 23 he found a ten-ship convoy near the China coast, five freighters and five escorts. O'Kane maneuvered inside the escorts and joined the convoy, firing nine torpedoes from point-blank range at what he believed to be three small overlapping tankers. The convoy scattered in confusion, one freighter ramming a transport. Postwar records credit O'Kane with sinking three small freighters that night: *Toun Maru*, 2,000 tons; *Wakatake Maru*, 2,000 tons; and *Tatsuju Maru*, 2,000 tons. It is possible—even probable—that all three ships were carrying aviation gasoline for Japanese aircraft in the Philippines and that in the resulting explosions and confusion O'Kane mistook them for tankers. Counting the two ships O'Kane had sunk on October 10 and October 11, his score for the patrol now stood at five ships.

The following evening, October 24–25, as Kurita and Nishimura were charging through San Bernardino and Surigao straits, O'Kane found another convoy. He again maneuvered *Tang* inside the escorts to point-blank range and fired ten torpedoes, sinking two big, heavily laden freighters, *Kogen Maru*, 6,600 tons, and *Matsumoto Maru*, 7,000 tons, and damaging at least one other. With only two torpedoes remaining, O'Kane hauled out to catch his breath and check the torpedoes. Then he bored in again to polish off the cripple.

O'Kane set up and fired these last two torpedoes. The first ran true; the second broached and began a circular run, turning back toward *Tang*. Later, O'Kane wrote:

Rang up emergency speed. Completed part of a fishtail maneuver in a futile attempt to clear the turning circle of this erratic circular run. The torpedo was observed through about 180° of its turn due to the phosphorescence of its wake. It struck abreast the after torpedo room with a violent explosion about 20 seconds after firing. The tops were blown off the only regular ballast tanks aft and the after three compartments flooded instantly. The TANG sank by the stern much as you would drop a pendulum suspended in a horizontal position. There was insufficient time even to carry out the last order to close the hatch.

O'Kane and eight other men on the bridge were hurled into the water. One other officer in the conning tower escaped to join them. During the night these ten men tried to hang together, but one by one they slipped away and drowned. By dawn, only O'Kane and three others were left.

Belowdecks, *Tang* was a shambles. Thirty men survived the blast, many with serious injuries. Some in the control room flooded the forward ballast tanks, bringing *Tang* to rest, more or less level, at 180 feet. The thirty survivors gathered in the forward torpedo room with the intent of getting out through the escape trunk. An attempt was made to burn the confidential papers, but the smoke drove the men forward. Fire broke out in the forward battery compartment, further complicating the problem.

Commencing at about 6 A.M., four parties, comprising a total of about thirteen men, began the escape procedure they had learned in sub school, using the escape trunk and Momsen Lungs—the only known case in the war where the Momsen Lung provided escape.*
Only five men survived the ascent or subsequent exposure in the water. In all, eight men, including O'Kane, his chief boatswain, W. R. Leibold, two officers, H. J. Flanagan and L. Savadkin, and

---

* Actually, all the emphasis on the Momsen Lung, including training ascents in the sub school's 100-foot water tower, was an unfortunate error, born of ignorance. It made submariners think that a Momsen Lung was necessary for escape. After the war, experiments carried out by submariner Walter Frederick Schlech, Jr., and others demonstrated that trapped submariners could safely ascend from a sunken submarine without a lung or any other breathing device from depths up to 300 feet. Had this been known during the war, many more submariners might have saved themselves. Thus, in one sense, the Momsen Lung concept may have killed far more submariners than it rescued.

three other enlisted men survived. They were picked up by a Japanese patrol boat and severely beaten. O'Kane said later, "When we realized that our clubbings and kickings were being administered by the burned, mutilated survivors of our own handiwork, we found we could take it with less prejudice." O'Kane and the other seven served out the remainder of the war in a POW camp.

After the war, when O'Kane submitted a patrol report from memory, Lockwood credited him with sinking thirteen ships for 107,324 tons: five tankers, four transports, three freighters, and one destroyer. According to these figures, this was by far the best war patrol of the war, and for it O'Kane was awarded a Medal of Honor. Japanese records reduced the total to seven ships for 21,772 tons.

In just over four war patrols, Dick O'Kane sank twenty-four confirmed ships for 93,824 tons, which made him the leading skipper of the submarine war in terms of ships sunk. (Slade Cutter and Mush Morton tied for second place with nineteen ships each.) In addition to the Medal of Honor, O'Kane received three Navy Crosses and three Silver Stars and a Legion of Merit.

The Blakely (Shark) and Banister (Sawfish) wolf packs patrolled due south of Tang in Formosa Strait. The seven boats in these two units (Shark II, Icefish, Drum, Snook, Sawfish, Blackfish, and Seadragon) picked up several Manila-bound convoys during the period October 23–26. Some of these ships were northbound, some southbound. Some may have been the same ships attacked by O'Kane.

During the nights of October 23 and 24, the two packs sank a total of ten confirmed ships. Banister in Sawfish got the first, Kimikawa Maru, a 6,900-ton converted seaplane tender. Browne in Snook got the next, a 5,900-ton transport. Before the day was over, Browne sank two more, a 3,900-ton tanker and a 6,900-ton freighter. Rindskopf in Drum got a 4,700-ton freighter. Ashley in old Seadragon got three: a 6,500-ton transport, a 7,400-ton transport, and a 1,900-ton freighter.

Unknown to any skipper in either pack, one of the ships in the vicinity of the combined attack that day was an old freighter transporting 1,800 U.S. POWs from Manila to Japan. It is believed that Ed Blakely in Shark made contact with this vessel and then attacked. The ship was torpedoed, and all but five of the POWs were lost. These five somehow got to China and made contact with friendly forces, reporting the tragedy. Counting the work of *Paddle* on September 7 and *Sealion, Growler,* and *Pampanito* on September 12, this new loss meant that U.S. submarines had accidentally killed or drowned well over 4,000 Allied POWs within a period of six weeks. Perhaps more went unrecorded.

Blakely reported to Ashley in *Seadragon* that he was making this attack. That was the last word ever heard from Blakely. Japanese records revealed that on October 24 a submarine was attacked in Blakely's vicinity and that "bubbles, and heavy oil, clothes, cork, etc." came to the surface. Lockwood and Voge believed this was *Shark.* Since Lockwood's boats had been ordered to search for POWs after sinking an Empire-bound ship, Blakely may have been engaged in a rescue mission when he was attacked.*

One officer who was particularly shocked by the loss of *Shark II* was young John Griggs, who had left the boat just before she sailed. (Griggs had also left *Wahoo* just before she sailed to her tragic end.) When Griggs reported to *Picuda* for duty, her new skipper, Evan Tyler ("Ty") Shepard, told him, "You are not leaving this boat before I do."

Two days after *Shark* was lost, Banister's pack got into another convoy. Rindskopf in *Drum* sank two ships, both large freighters of 6,900 tons. Dick Peterson in *Icefish* sank a freighter of 4,200 tons. After that, the Banister pack withdrew from the strait and returned to port.

In the seventy-two-hour period from October 23 to October 26, O'Kane and the Blakely-Banister wolf packs sank a total of seventeen Japanese ships. Many of these had been transporting reinforcements to the Philippines.

The packs led by Chick Clarey (*Pintado, Jallao,* and *Atule*) and Beetle Roach (*Haddock, Halibut,* and *Tuna*) picked up where the Blakely-Banister packs left off. On November 1, Icenhower in *Jallao* got a contact and flashed word to his packmate, Clarey. Clarey and Icenhower chased hard but were unable to gain attack position. That same night, Jack Maurer in *Atule* found a large northbound freighter with three escorts. Poor visibility helped the attack—his first of the war—and he fired off a salvo of torpedoes, claiming two hits

---

* October 24 was a black-letter day for the submarine force; *Darter, Shark II,* and *Tang* were all lost. Including *Seawolf* and *Escolar,* five boats were lost in October in both commands.

had sunk a 10,000-ton ship. In fact, Maurer had hit and sunk the huge ex-ocean liner *Asama Maru*, 16,975 tons.

On November 2, Lockwood sent Clarey and Roach an important Ultra: a task force consisting of a carrier, battleship or cruiser, and three destroyers was southbound in Formosa Strait. Clarey's three boats and Roach's three boats formed a scouting line to intercept. At 8 P.M., just after moonrise, Clarey in *Pintado* made contact. He flashed word to Maurer in *Atule* and Icenhower in *Jallao*, then dived ahead to attack. According to Clarey's log:

As the horizon cleared with moonrise, sighted the largest enemy ship any of us have ever seen. . . . The moon was quite bright—about one and one half hours high in the east. The carrier was plainly visible as were the masts of two ships on either side of the carrier. . . . Identified the carrier as a large one with a small island forward of amidships similar to SHOKAKU *class, with one destroyer ahead, one on either beam and a light cruiser astern. The port DD was identified as a single stack modern streamlined ship.*

Clarey planned to fire six torpedoes at the carrier and four at the nearest destroyer. He fired the six bow tubes. Immediately after firing, one of the destroyers cruised into the line of fire. Four of the torpedoes smashed into *Akikaze*, 1,300 tons. She blew up and sank in four minutes. Clarey believed that at least one of his torpedoes hit the carrier (the new one, *Unryu?*), but postwar records did not bear him out. Neither Maurer nor Icenhower was able to gain attack position. The carrier—whatever it was—got away.

Ten days later, Clarey received another important Ultra: a Japanese battleship, probably *Yamato* with a heavy cruiser escort, was coming up from the south. Clarey ordered his boats into intercept position, but Icenhower in *Jallao* stumbled across a carrier, a cruiser, and four destroyer escorts, northbound, probably the same carrier Clarey had fired at on November 3. Icenhower gained attack position and got off six torpedoes, with no results. None of the boats found *Yamato*.

On November 14, Pete Galantin in *Halibut*, one of Roach's pack, picked up a four-ship convoy with three escorts. He fired four torpedoes at the largest ship from 3,100 yards, which was as close as he could get. He may have got two hits, but he couldn't stick around to find out because several aircraft pounced on *Halibut* and delivered one of the most devastating depth-charge attacks of the war. *Halibut* was almost destroyed.

Chick Clarey, close by in *Pintado*, had made an unsuccessful effort to close this same convoy and came over to lend Galantin a hand. When Lockwood was informed of the extent of *Halibut's* damage, he ordered Clarey to escort her to Saipan. Clarey left Maurer in charge of the pack. At Saipan and later in Pearl Harbor, the engineers who examined *Halibut* decided that, like *Salmon*, she was so badly wrecked she was not worth repairing. Lockwood wrote, "The stellar performance of duty by the officers and men of the *Halibut* undoubtedly saved this ship from destruction."

The other four boats—*Haddock, Tuna, Atule,* and *Jallao*—remained in the strait for two more weeks, but only Jack Maurer in *Atule* sank more ships: a 630-ton minesweeper, an 820-ton escort (classed as an old destroyer), and a 7,300-ton freighter. Total score for Maurer: four confirmed ships for almost 26,000 tons, one of the best maiden patrols on record.

When the packs returned to Saipan, Beetle Roach was severely injured in a jeep accident and spent the next six months in various navy hospitals. Command of *Haddock* was assumed by Roach's division commander, Bill Brockman, ex-*Nautilus*.

Two Lockwood packs patrolled the shallow waters of the Yellow Sea. The first was commanded by Gordon Underwood in *Spadefish*, leading Ed Shelby in *Sunfish* and a new skipper, Robert Hugh Caldwell, Jr., in *Peto*. The second was commanded by Elliott Loughlin in *Queenfish*, leading Gene Fluckey in *Barb* and Ty Shepard in *Picuda*. These two packs, operating mostly between Shanghai and southwest Korea, exchanged information and attacked the same convoys.

First contact was made by Elliott Loughlin in *Queenfish* on the night of November 8: two ships, three escorts. Loughlin fired six torpedoes at the two ships—freighters of 1,000 and 2,000 tons—and sank both. In the early hours of the morning, he found another three-ship convoy and fired another six torpedoes at a tanker and freighter, sinking the freighter, 2,100 tons, following which he was forced down by escorts.

While this was going on, his packmate Gene Fluckey in *Barb* happened on a large unescorted ship and attacked, firing three torpedoes and obtaining two hits. The ship did not sink. Fluckey came in for another attack, firing a single torpedo which broached and "ran off into the night." He fired another; it, too, missed. Fluckey then submerged and closed to point-blank range of 500 yards and fired one more. This torpedo hit. *Gokoku Maru*, a fine ship of 10,400 tons, rolled over and sank stern first.

On Armistice Day, November 11, Loughlin picked up a large convoy of a dozen freighters with six escorts. He fired four torpedoes from an unfavorable position, obtaining one hit on one freighter before escorts drove him deep and delivered an expert working-over with fifty depth charges. Later, Loughlin surfaced and flashed news of the convoy to his packmates. Fluckey in *Barb* got the word and shortly after midnight, in heavy seas, fired eight torpedoes at four ships. Some of these hit, but many of the torpedoes were thrown off course. Fluckey's crew conducted a difficult reload; then he attacked submerged, firing three torpedoes at a freighter from about 500 yards. He hit *Naruo Maru*, 4,800 tons. Later, Fluckey wrote, "First torpedo hit in forward hold and target blew up in my face, literally disintegrating. This explosion was terrific. . . . Parts of the target commenced falling on top of us, drumming on the superstructure."

Underwood's pack, patrolling to the east of the convoy, picked up Loughlin's original contact. Underwood was at that moment engaged in a lifeguard mission, but he directed Caldwell in *Peto* to intercept the convoy. Caldwell saw Fluckey's target blow up and then he attacked, firing ten torpedoes at three targets. He heard hits in all three ships, but postwar records credited only one sunk, *Tatsuaki Maru*, 2,700 tons.

About the same time, an important convoy left Manchuria, transporting the Japanese 23rd Infantry Division to the Philippines; it was the jeep carrier *Jinyo* (*Shinyo*), carrying a load of aircraft to Manila, plus freighters and tankers, all heavily escorted by about six destroyers. Lockwood received word of this convoy from the codebreakers and flashed Ultras to his two packs. All six submarines went on sharp alert for this prize.

Loughlin in *Queenfish* made the first contact on November 15. The convoy was swarming with aircraft and escorts. Submerged, Loughlin closed what he believed to be the carrier to 1,500 yards and fired four stern tubes. As destroyers drove him deep, he believed he heard two hits in the carrier, but what Loughlin had hit—and sunk—was an aircraft ferry, *Akitsu Maru*, 9,200 tons.

That night, 30 miles away, Fluckey in *Barb* found *Jinyo* (*Shinyo*) and her destroyer escorts. She looked huge to Fluckey, who identified her as a *Shokaku*-class carrier. He got as close as he could on the surface—3,500 yards—and fired five torpedoes. He believed he got one hit but there was no record of it. Fluckey chased but could not catch up. He found a freighter, fired his last two torpedoes, and then headed for home.

The other two boats of the pack, Loughlin's *Queenfish* and Shepard's *Picuda*, pursued the convoy, edging down into Underwood's territory, where the two packs merged. On the evening of November 17, Shepard attacked, sinking a troop transport, *Mayasan Maru*, 9,400 tons, and damaging a tanker. That same night, one of Underwood's boats, Shelby's *Sunfish*, found *Jinyo* (*Shinyo*) and chased, giving contact reports. Shelby could not get into position to fire, and he broke off to go after the freighters. That evening and the next morning, he sank a 7,000-ton freighter and the 5,400-ton troop transport *Seisho Maru*. Another of Underwood's boats, Caldwell's *Peto*, attacked the convoy and sank two freighters, one 7,000 tons and one 2,800 tons.

The big prize fell to Gordon Underwood in *Spadefish*, who on November 14 had sunk a 5,400-ton freighter independently of all this. Hearing Shelby's contact report on the night of November 17, Underwood moved into the probable course of *Jinyo* (*Shinyo*). He picked her up about 9 P.M., went in, and fired six torpedoes at her and four at a tanker. Later he wrote:

The carrier burst into flames and started settling by the stern. The fire could be seen spreading the length of the ship below the flight deck. . . . The carrier was loaded with planes that could be seen rolling off the deck as the ship settled aft and took a starboard list. When last seen, the bow was sticking up in the air, still burning. The stern was on the bottom in 23 fathoms of water.

Underwood had evidently missed the tanker. After reloading, he came in for a second attack. His helmsman misinterpreted an order and slowed *Spadefish* to 8 knots. An escort 1,000 yards away turned toward *Spadefish*, firing 20- and 40-mm. guns. Underwood avoided these shells, lined up on another escort, and fired four torpedoes, sinking a subchaser.

In all, these two packs sank eight ships of this convoy, including

Underwood's *Jinyo* (*Shinyo*); Loughlin's aircraft ferry, *Akitsu Maru*; and Shepard's large troop transport, *Mayasan Maru*. There are no precise records as to how many Japanese troops of the 23rd Division were drowned or knocked out of action, but the figure must have been high. In addition, ammunition, supplies, field guns, and other equipment, including many airplanes, failed to reach the Philippines. All this made MacArthur's job in the coming weeks easier.

The packs sank four more ships. On November 23, Shepard in *Picuda* got a 7,000-ton freighter and a 5,300-ton transport. On November 29, Underwood sank a 4,000-ton freighter. The next day, Shelby in *Sunfish* sank a 3,700-ton transport. All boats except *Sunfish* then returned to port.

In terms of confirmed sinkings these two packs, Underwood's and Loughlin's, were among the most successful of the war. Their grand total: nineteen ships for about 110,000 tons.

Four Pearl Harbor boats patrolled the southern waters of the East China Sea. These were a three-boat pack commanded by Sandy McGregor in *Redfish*, leading Anton Gallaher in *Bang* and Lawrence Virginius Julihn in *Shad*, and a fourth boat patrolling alone, *Sealion II*, commanded by Eli Reich.

Reich entered the East China Sea via Tokara Strait and proceeded more or less toward Shanghai. On November 15 he picked up Loughlin's report of the Shanghai-bound convoy but decided that *Sealion* was "out in left field" and broke off the chase. Off Shanghai, Reich had two torpedo malfunctions. First, during a drill, his men accidentally fired one tube with the outer door closed; the torpedo smashed through, breaking the outer door and putting the tube out of commission. A day or so later, he had a battery explosion in another tube and was forced to surface in a fleet of junks in order to back down at flank speed and eject the damaged torpedo. After that, Reich left the Shanghai area and went south toward Formosa Strait.

On November 21, Reich was at the northern mouth of Formosa Strait. Shortly after midnight he picked up three huge pips at a range of 20 miles. It was a dark moonless night, with bad visibility. Closing at flank speed, Reich saw that he had two battleships escorted by two destroyers, one ahead of the battleships, one astern. The battleships were *Kongo* and *Haruna*, en route from Brunei Bay to

Japan. (*Kongo* had supported the carrier attack on Pearl Harbor and then fought in many Pacific engagements, most recently as a part of Kurita's fleet at Leyte.) Reich decided to attack on the surface. He got off a contact report and then bent on flank speed to overtake.

Three hours went by before Reich could turn in to attack. From the long range of 3,000 yards, he fired six slow electric torpedoes at the first battleship, then three stern tubes at the second. Reich saw and heard three hits on the first battleship; his stern tubes were intercepted by one of the destroyer escorts, *Urakaze,* which blew up and sank. When Reich realized what had happened, he was "chagrined," he reported.

The battleships continued on at 16 knots. Reich again bent on flank speed, trying to catch up and turn in. During the long tedious chase, the torpedomen reloaded the nine usable tubes. Green water crashed over *Sealion*'s bridge as Reich ordered maximum power and more. Then, luck! One battleship with two destroyers began dropping astern, making only 11 knots. This was *Kongo,* badly damaged by Reich's first salvo. Reich easily overtook this group and got ready to attack *Kongo* again. But before he could fire another shot, as he wrote in his report:

0524 *Tremendous explosion dead ahead—sky brilliantly illuminated, it looked like a sunset at midnight. Radar reports battleship pip getting smaller—that it has disappeared—leaving only the two smaller pips of the destroyers. Destroyers seen to be milling around vicinity of target. Battleship sunk—the sun set.*
0525 *Total darkness again.*

Reich was stunned. He had done what no other submarine skipper had done, sunk a battleship—and he had done it with three electric torpedoes, fired from extreme range.

Reich tried to chase the other battleship, *Haruna,* but the seas were too heavy. He sent out another contact report and then turned off, returning to the scene of his battle for evidence of the kill or a prisoner. He found a large oil slick and circling planes.

McGregor's pack—*Redfish, Bang,* and *Shad*—had entered the East China Sea near northern Formosa and spent the next two weeks coping with a series of problems: a huge storm that battered the boats for five days, appendicitis attacks on two of the boats (though no surgery was improvised this time), and zero rewards in their efforts to find worthwhile targets. Finally, on the day after Reich—only 150 miles away—had sunk the battleship *Kongo,* the pack found a seven-ship convoy. McGregor ordered his three boats to attack.

In a furious three-hour battle, Gallaher in *Bang* fired off all twenty-four of his torpedoes. He believed he sank four ships for 18,000 tons, but postwar analysis gave him credit for sinking only two, one freighter of 2,800 tons and one of 2,400 tons. McGregor in *Redfish* fired twenty torpedoes. Thirteen missed. Seven hit, sinking, he believed, two ships; however, postwar records credited him with only one, a 2,300-ton freighter. Julihn in *Shad* fouled up his attack, firing many torpedoes (some by accident) but sinking nothing.

After this battle, McGregor ordered his pack to Saipan to reload torpedoes and conduct a second leg of the patrol. Leaving the area, Gallaher found a small fishing sampan. Later he wrote:

Surfaced. Thought perhaps sampan had picked up some survivors from the previous night's attack. Set sampan on fire with 20 mm. and a .30 cal. Crew consisted of three men, two boys and a woman. All but the woman jumped overboard. Picked up two of the men and a boy. All seemed to be unintelligent fishermen so brought them back close aboard their burning sampan, and let them go back aboard to put the fire out if they could. Continued search for convoy survivors on the surface.

The evening after the McGregor pack left station, November 23, Lockwood sent Reich an important Ultra: another Japanese battleship force was coming down Formosa Strait en route from Japan. It was probably *Ise* and *Hyuga* taking reinforcements to the Paracel Islands for transshipment to the Philippines. Reich maneuvered *Sealion* to the probable course and waited seventy-two hours. On November 26, at about 8 P.M., his radar picked up the force at the phenomenal range of 35 miles. At first, Reich believed his pip must be land, but it was a battleship (*Ise?*) and four destroyers.

Reich began maneuvering to attack. For a while, he doubted that he could gain a favorable position. However, the formation turned toward him, and he dived and set up to fire. Rechecking, Reich realized that the formation would pass at extreme range, 4,500 yards. That was the limit of the electric torpedo, but he fired six anyhow. All missed. Escorts drove him to the bottom in 270 feet of water and dropped two close charges. Then the formation went off.

Shortly after midnight, November 27, Reich came to the surface again. His radar picked up another Japanese task force, range 35 miles: another battleship (*Hyuga?*). However, *Ise* evidently warned *Hyuga*. The ships detoured around Reich, and he was not able to make an attack. After he sent off contact reports on both formations, Lockwood ordered Reich to Guam.

On November 24 and 27, over a hundred B-29 Superfortresses based at the newly completed airfield in the Marianas made their first two bombing runs over the Japanese mainland. Patrolling off Tokyo Bay, Frederick Gunn, commanding *Scabbardfish*, and Joseph Enright, commanding *Archerfish*, were ordered to lifeguard for these attacks. As it turned out, neither was called upon for rescues, and both boats were subsequently released to conduct regular antishipping patrols in the immediate area off Tokyo Bay. Gunn on *Scabbardfish* sank a Japanese submarine, *I-365*, 1,500 tons, almost immediately. For Enright there was bigger game.

It was Enright who had made the first patrol on *Dace* and then asked to be relieved because he had no confidence in himself. He had come to *Archerfish* after nearly a year of shore duty. Now, on the night of November 28, Enright made contact with *Shinano*, brand new sister ship of *Yamato* and *Musashi*, which had been converted to an aircraft carrier while still being built. Her conversion being almost finished, she had been hurriedly commissioned on November 18, with Captain Toshio Abe in command, and was getting her finishing touches in Tokyo Bay when the B-29 raids began. Though these initial raids did relatively little damage, they made the Japanese uneasy. On November 28 *Shinano* got under way under orders from Imperial Naval Headquarters that she be moved out of the bay to the relatively safer waters of the Inland Sea. Four destroyers escorted her.

Structurally, *Shinano* was finished, but many details, such as fire pumps, were not yet complete. There were 1,900 people on board, some of them crew, others yard workers who would finish the ship, which at 60,000 tons would be the largest warship in the world (slightly larger than *Yamato*). Many of the crew were green; they had never been to sea. There had been no training.

That night, Joe Enright in *Archerfish* patrolled the outer entrances to Tokyo Bay. At 8:48, his radar operator reported a pip at 24,700 yards. Fifty-two minutes later, Enright knew he had an aircraft carrier, headed south, speed 20 knots. He laid a course to intercept and called for flank speed. "From here on," Enright wrote later, "it was a mad race for a possible firing position. His speed was about one knot in excess of our best, but his zig plan allowed us to pull ahead very slowly."

Enright thought he was losing the race and sent off two contact reports to Lockwood, so that he could alert submarines to the south. But then at 3 A.M.—about six hours after the chase began—the carrier changed course and headed right for *Archerfish*. Enright submerged ahead. The huge ship came onward while Enright's crew made everything ready.

At 3:16, Enright began firing his bow tubes from a range of about 1,500 yards. Sigmund Albert ("Bobo") Bobczynski, his exec, was watching the TDC, holding his breath. After four torpedoes had left the tubes, he shouted, "Check fire! New setup. Switch to stern tubes." Then Enright fired two stern tubes.

Forty-seven seconds after the first torpedo was fired, Enright, manning the periscope, saw and heard a hit in the carrier's stern. "Large ball of fire climbed his side," Enright noted. Ten seconds later, he saw a second hit, 50 yards forward of the first.

There was a destroyer only 500 yards on *Archerfish*'s quarter. Enright went deep. On the way down, he said later, he heard four more properly timed hits, indicating all six of his torpedoes had hit *Shinano*. Sonar reported breaking-up noises. The escorts dropped fourteen depth charges, the nearest, Enright reported, 300 yards distant. When that noise died away, the sonarman reported more breaking-up noises. The heavy screw noise of the carrier could not be heard.

At 6:10, Enright returned to the surface for a look through the periscope. "Nothing in sight," he reported. He was certain that the carrier went down on the spot.

After the war, the records revealed that *Shinano* took four hits. Captain Abe was not overly concerned; the sister ship, *Musashi*, had taken nineteen torpedoes and many bombs before sinking at Leyte. He continued on his course at 18 knots. His inexperienced damage-control parties tried to stop the flow of water, but they fought a losing battle. It was discovered that *Shinano* did not have all her watertight doors, and some that were in place leaked. Captain Abe could have grounded *Shinano* in shallow water and saved her, but he continued on. By dawn, it was evident to all that she was sinking. At 10:18,

Abe ordered abandon ship. Half an hour later, the world's largest warship slid beneath the waves, taking down Abe and 500 men.

Enright remained on station another two weeks, lifeguarding B-29 raids. He received two calls for help but could never find the downed pilots. On December 9, another off day, he fired four torpedoes at two small patrol boats and missed. He returned *Archerfish* to Guam December 15, claiming to have sunk a *Hayatake*-class carrier of 28,000 tons.

Some people were naturally skeptical. The codebreakers believed they had identified all the remaining Japanese carriers and knew where they were. But Enright's division commander, Burt Klakring, submitted a drawing of the carrier composed by Enright, and Babe Brown, acting in Lockwood's absence, credited him with sinking a 28,000-ton carrier. It was not until after the war that the whole story of *Shinano*, converted in secret and unknown to the codebreakers, came out. Then the tonnage was upped to 71,000 and Enright received a Navy Cross.

The unlikely Joe Enright, a cautious and uncertain skipper, had by the luck of the draw sunk the largest warship in history and the largest ship ever sunk by a submarine. Although in the postwar accounting the tonnage was reduced to 59,000, from a tonnage standpoint Enright's first patrol on *Archerfish* was still the best of the war.

During this period, Lockwood lost two boats. Hugh Raynor Rimmer, who had served on *Rock* during her fitting out and commissioning and on *Tautog* for a year, relieved Jim Blanchard in command of *Albacore*. On this, his first patrol in command, he was ordered to patrol off northeast Honshu, the dangerously mined area where *Pickerel*, *Runner*, *Pompano*, and *Golet* had been lost. He had strict orders to beware of mines and stay outside waters less than 100 fathoms deep.

Albacore left Pearl Harbor on October 24, topped off her fuel tanks at Midway October 28, and was never heard from again. According to Japanese records recovered after the war, she struck a mine very close to shore off northeast Hokkaido on November 7. The Japanese witness was a patrol boat. Her crew testified that the submarine was submerged and that after the explosion much heavy oil, cork, bedding, and food supplies rose to the surface.

A week later, John Hollingsworth, who had nearly lost *Scamp* to a Japanese plane on his first patrol the previous April, was ordered to patrol off Tokyo Bay. Nothing more was ever heard from *Scamp* or from Hollingsworth either. On November 29 Lockwood received information that the area in which *Scamp* had been ordered to take station, Inubo Zaki, had been mined. He and Voge believed *Scamp* might have struck one of these mines and gone down with all hands, but nothing positive is known about her loss.

Patrols from Australia

After the battle of Leyte Gulf, Christie's skippers found the hunting poor. The first boat to sink a Japanese ship was *Rock*, which torpedoed an 800-ton tanker in Palawan Passage on October 26, not far from the stranded *Darter*, at which skipper John Flachsenhar had fired ten torpedoes. The following day, October 27, John Hyde in *Bergall*, slightly to the west of Palawan Passage in Dangerous Ground, sank another tanker, the 10,528-ton *Nippo Maru*, giving him a total of two ships for 14,700 tons for this patrol, which he was forced to terminate because of low fuel and torpedoes.

Off Manila, Moon Chapple in *Bream* and Enrique Haskins in *Guitarro*, coached into position by contact reports from Caddy Adkins in *Cod*, got on the trail of a convoy October 30. Chapple fired six torpedoes and probably got a hit in one transport. Haskins fired eight torpedoes and sank two freighters, 2,900 tons and 5,800 tons. One of these was a loaded ammunition ship. It blew up with a thunderous explosion that drove *Guitarro* down 50 feet. As Haskins noted in his report, "The Commanding Officer never wishes to hit an ammunition ship any closer than that one."

The next boat was *Blackfin,* commanded by the new skipper George Laird. On the morning of November 1, south of Mindoro, he found a five-ship convoy with three or four escorts and he sank a 2,700-ton freighter. Unknown to Laird, Bill Kinsella in *Ray* (who had reloaded and refueled at Mios Woendi) was approaching from the south. Kinsella saw Laird's target blow up with a "terrific explosion." As the convoy scattered, four small tankers headed Kinsella's way. He fired three torpedoes at two tankers and was certain he sank both, but postwar records credited him with only one ship, an 865-ton freighter. Escorts drove Kinsella deep and dropped depth charges.

That night Kinsella took time off for a special mission. He landed men and supplies on Mindoro and picked up two downed naval aviators and three refugees, two American POWs who had escaped from the Japanese on Corregidor and Maximo Kalaw, former Dean of Liberal Arts at the University of the Philippines, who was a guerrilla leader with a high price on his head.

On November 3, Kinsella joined Chapple in *Bream*, Haskins in *Guitarro*, and Shea in *Raton* to form a temporary four-boat wolf pack near Lingayen Gulf. On the afternoon of November 4, Shea found a convoy standing out of Manila. He fired six torpedoes at a large transport but they all missed, and Shea went deep as aircraft and escorts worked over the boat. The transport headed toward Moon Chapple; he fired four torpedoes and got a hit. Next, Haskins in *Guitarro* fired, obtaining four hits. After dark, Kinsella in *Ray* found the burning ship and fired two torpedoes, blowing off the bow and finally sinking her. Chapple, Haskins, and Kinsella were each awarded one third credit for *Kagu Maru*, 6,800 tons.

On the morning of November 6, the pack picked up a convoy escorted by the heavy cruiser *Kumano*, which had been damaged by Halsey's planes off Samar and, until then, undergoing repairs in Manila Bay. Halsey's fighters had struck Manila again on November 5 and driven these ships out. All four boats—*Bream, Guitarro, Ray*, and *Raton*—closed in to fire at *Kumano*. Haskins in *Guitarro* shot nine torpedoes and observed three hits. Chapple in *Bream* fired four more, claiming two hits. Shea in *Raton* fired six, at least two of which passed immediately over Kinsella in *Ray*, who was making an approach; Shea claimed four hits, but they were not credited. Kinsella fired four torpedoes and then went deep. Later he wrote, "Bombs dropped close aboard, observed splashes ahead of us. . . . It is impossible to describe the pandemonium that was taking place during these last six minutes. Bombs, torpedoes and depth charges were exploding constantly." In all, the four boats had fired twenty-three torpedoes at *Kumano*. Her bow was blown off, but she was still afloat.

Kinsella was in the best position for a second attack. He went deep, intending to get between the cruiser and the beach, but at 370 feet he struck an uncharted ledge and wiped off his sonar head, causing a bad leak. In order to stop the leak, he had to come up to periscope depth. Later, he wrote, "This is the most heartbreaking experience I have ever had or hope to have in my naval career. We are in perfect position for a kill on the cruiser and the tanker, but not being able to go deep it would be suicide to fire with the escorts only 800 yards away."

Kinsella plugged the hole and crept away. Later he saw the tanker take *Kumano* in tow; the Japanese beached her nearby. Still later, Halsey's planes found her and finished the destruction. Chapple and Haskins, having shot off all their torpedoes, returned to Fremantle.

Kinsella and Shea joined up with Jake Fyfe in *Batfish* to form another wolf pack with Kinsella, the senior man, in charge. On November 14, the pack picked up a convoy off Lingayen Gulf. After dark, Kinsella fired the first torpedoes—six at a big ship. He hit it with four, and it blew up with "terrific explosions." He also believed that one of his torpedoes hit an escort. Postwar records credited Kinsella with sinking only one ship that night, an 800-ton escort. Kinsella believed that the records were in error and that he had been short-changed. Shea in *Raton* sank two ships from this convoy, both freighters, one of 2,800 tons and one of 1,000 tons. Jake Fyfe believed he had sunk the last two ships of the convoy and was so credited, but postwar records did not confirm his claim.

After that, Kinsella fired two torpedoes at a beached freighter, both of which missed. Then all three boats—*Ray, Raton,* and *Batfish* —proceeded on to Pearl Harbor and the States, where *Ray* received an overhaul. If Kinsella's claims are credited, as they are not in postwar Japanese records, he sank five and one third ships for about 17,000 tons. Mike Shea sank four confirmed ships for 12,300 tons.

Ben Oakley in *Growler* led a pack consisting of Francis Albert Greenup's *Hardhead* and Frank Haylor's *Hake* in the area south of Mindoro. On the way to station, Greenup found a navy aviator in a life raft, Commander Fred Edward Bakutis, a friend then commanding Fighter Group 20 on the carrier *Enterprise*. Bakutis had been adrift for seven days. Greenup transferred Bakutis to *Angler*, which was returning to Fremantle.

On November 7 Oakley notified Christie that he was having problems with his radar and urgently needed spare parts. Christie ordered Moon Chapple in *Bream*, heading home, to rendezvous with *Growler* and transfer the spare parts. Early on the morning of November 8, Oakley (whose radar was evidently working at least part of the time) made contact with a small convoy and directed Greenup and Haylor to join him in the attack. About an hour later, Greenup heard what he believed to be one of Oakley's torpedoes exploding, followed by depth charges. Greenup set up and sank a 5,300-ton tanker. He was charged by escorts and badly worked over.

Haylor in *Hake* saw the tanker sink, but before he could mount an attack he was attacked by escorts and pinned down for sixteen "harrowing" hours, during which time he counted 150 depth charges, many close.

That night, Greenup and Haylor attempted to contact Oakley without success. Nothing more was ever heard from him. The famous *Growler*, which had taken Medal-of-Honor winner Howard Gilmore into combat, was gone. For Haylor, who had been with Sam Dealey when he was lost, it was the second patrol in a row in which his pack commander disappeared. Oakley's friend, Moon Chapple, arrived at the rendezvous point on the afternoon of November 10. He circled the point for twenty-four hours, waiting—until Christie told him to come on home.

Hardhead and *Hake* now became a two-boat pack, commanded by the senior man, Francis Greenup. On November 5 Greenup picked up a light cruiser off Manila but was not able to shoot. On November 18, in the same area, he found two light cruisers but, again, was unable to get close enough to shoot. On November 19 he found another light cruiser, closed, and fired six torpedoes. He sank a small frigate off Manila November 25. On November 30 he found a carrier escorted by three destroyers off Manila, but again he was unable to close.

Haylor went into Panay on a special mission and took off twenty-nine aviators who had been shot down during raids in the Philippines. The two boats returned to Australia.

Mingo, commanded by John Robert Madison, lifeguarded in Makassar Strait. In a spectacular series of rescues, Madison picked up six aviators from rubber rafts and another ten from the beaches of southern Celebes, once being bombed by a U.S. Air Force plane. Madison delivered his human cargo to Fremantle and received high praise from Christie.

The codebreakers were now the happy recipients of another windfall. An army paratroop commando team surprised and captured a small Japanese patrol boat off the north coast of Mindoro, obtaining many Japanese codebooks and ciphers, all current. The commando team notified MacArthur's staff, which in turn asked Christie to dispatch a submarine to rendezvous with the commandos and get the codebooks.

Christie alerted Laird in *Blackfin*, who attempted to rendezvous with the commandos on the north coast of Mindoro, failed, but made contact the following day, November 18. He received three bags of codebooks labeled top secret. Some of *Blackfin*'s crew overheard the commandos telling Laird what the bags contained. "The Commanding Officer," Laird later wrote in third person, "subsequently lectured the entire crew on the utmost secrecy of the information and enjoined them to forget they ever heard about it."

Laird withdrew from enemy territory and proceeded south to Morotai Island. There, off Point Anna, he transferred his valuable cargo to the Australian man-of-war *Kiama* and then proceeded to Fremantle. Christie's endorsement stated, "A special mission of great importance to Allied war strategy was accomplished. . . . This special mission was of tremendous importance to the United States and the skill and courage attendant to its conclusion are very gratifying."

During refit Laird became ill and lost command of *Blackfin*.

Irvin Hartman in *Barbero* led a three-boat pack composed of Cy Austin's *Redfin* and *Haddo*. When young Nimitz stepped down from command of *Haddo,* Christie gave the boat to Tiny Lynch, formerly exec to Sam Dealey on *Harder*. Although targets were scarce, the threesome patrolled aggressively, especially Lynch, whose endorsements called his attacks "brilliant."

On November 2, off Makassar City, Hartman sank a 2,000-ton freighter. On November 8–9, not far from the place *Growler* was lost, the pack attacked a convoy, Hartman sinking a 2,900-ton tanker, Lynch an 860-ton freighter, and Austin a 5,300-ton tanker. Lynch took *Haddo* on to Pearl Harbor and the States for overhaul. Hartman in *Barbero* and Austin in *Redfin* refueled and reloaded at Mios Woendi and took their boats to Indochina.

Guy O'Neil in *Gunnel* led a two-boat pack consisting of himself and Leonce Arnold Lajaunie, Jr., in *Muskallunge*. South of Mindoro on November 8, O'Neil sank a ship; then he and Lajaunie moved west to the South China Sea, where Albert Schorr Fuhrman in *Jack* was patrolling.

On the night of November 12, O'Neil found a heart-stopping sight: the super-battleship *Yamato* and a heavy cruiser northbound to Japan. O'Neil picked up these targets at 15 miles but was not able to get close enough for an attack. He got off a contact report and the

Lockwood wolf packs in Luzon Strait went on alert, but none ever found the ships and they reached Japan safely.

Continuing on patrol, the pack found more action. On the night of November 14–15, Fuhrman got into a convoy and sank two big freighters, one of 5,400 tons and another of 6,800 tons. Two days later, O'Neil in *Gunnel* sank a 5,600-ton transport and an escort of 600 tons. On November 20, O'Neil found a light cruiser but could not get close enough to attack. Upon concluding these patrols, *Gunnel*, *Jack* (which had had severe engine problems the whole time), and *Muskallunge* (which suffered a major casualty in a generator) returned to Pearl Harbor and the States for overhaul. Lajaunie in *Muskallunge* was relieved of command after the boat completed its overhaul, going to new construction.

James Edward Stevens in *Flounder* led a pack consisting of Richard Nichols in *Bashaw* and Carl Tiedeman in *Guavina*. On the way to patrol area, Christie sent an Ultra message that a German submarine, *U-537*, basing from Surabaya, was en route for operations off Perth. Christie positioned this pack to trap the German north of Lombok Strait. Stevens in *Flounder* got on the precise track and, on November 10, fired four torpedoes. Stevens saw one hit, then smoke and flame. *U-537* went down for the last time.*

Continuing northward, on November 21, when the pack found a convoy west of Palawan Passage in Dangerous Ground, Tiedeman sank a 2,000-ton freighter and he and Stevens shared credit for sinking the 5,700-ton freighter *Gyosan Maru*.

* She was the second German U-boat sunk in the same area—after *U-168*, sunk by Goossens in the Dutch submarine *Zwaardvisch*. *U-537* was part of a small force of U-boats sent to help Japan. The force operated mostly in the Indian Ocean, achieving little, inasmuch as the codebreakers kept a close eye on it and routed shipping away from the U-boats.

35

Pearl Harbor and Australia, November and December 1944

New Inventions for U.S. Boats

In the fall of 1944, scientists and technicians in the States, working hand in glove with submariners, developed several secret new devices for the fleet submarine designed to enhance its effectiveness in combat. These were: (1) a "noisemaker," a decoy device fired from a submarine undergoing depth-charge attack, to fool enemy sonar; (2) a "night" periscope (one that admitted much more light in darkness), also fitted with a radar known as the ST; (3) a new and extremely short-range sonar, QLA (but called FM because frequency modulated); and (4) a small electric acoustical torpedo, called a "Cutie," which would home on the noise of an enemy ship. Lockwood, forever fascinated by new gadgets that might improve sinkings or provide greater protection for his boats, took a deep and personal interest in each of these devices.

The most promising in many ways were the Cuties, which Spike Hottel and Harry Hull (ex-*Thresher*), Lockwood's force gunnery and torpedo officer, began receiving in the summer of 1944. They were based on a German design and manufactured by Westinghouse. Like all new torpedoes produced by the Bureau of Ordnance, they were imperfect. In tests, they repeatedly malfunctioned, and the first models were useless against a target going more than 8½ knots—a severe limitation.

In the fall, when the Cutie had been improved somewhat, Carter

Bennett arrived in Pearl Harbor in a new boat, *Sea Owl*. Since Bennett had a master's degree in torpedo ordnance and much combat experience, Lockwood selected him to make the first combat test of the Cutie. Bennett led a wolf pack consisting of *Sea Owl*, *Piranha*, commanded by Harold Ruble, and *Sea Poacher*, commanded by Francis Michael Gambacorta, to the East China and Yellow seas. Bennett carried several Cuties in his racks.

The pack, often diverted to lifeguard B-29 raids (staged from bases in China), had little opportunity to conduct coordinated attacks, but Bennett made three opportunities to test the Cutie. The first was in the shallow waters of the Yellow Sea. Bennett picked up a small patrol craft, then took position ahead and dived to 150 feet, the depth considered safe to fire a Cutie (anything less and the Cutie might turn and home on the launching submarine). The Cutie performed as designed, presumably, homing on the propeller noise of the patrol craft. Hearing an explosion, Bennett surfaced to investigate. He found the patrol craft in "sinking condition" and left, judging this first combat employment of the secret weapon an unqualified success.

The next two opportunities were not so conclusive. On the second, Bennett found what he believed to be a destroyer off Nagasaki. Employing the same tactics, Bennett fired a Cutie, heard an explosion, and surfaced. The target (not a destroyer but a patrol craft) appeared to be damaged but not severely. Bennett approached from dead ahead of the target and fired a Mark XVIII electric from 1,000 yards. The electric hit solidly and the patrol craft disintegrated; Bennett ran through the debris to make certain.

Not long afterward, Bennett saw what he believed to be a destroyer coming out of Nagasaki, presumably to aid the ship Bennett had just sunk. Bennett submerged (it was almost dawn by then), took position on the enemy track, and fired a couple of more Cuties. This time, no luck, either because the target was going much too fast or because it spotted the torpedoes and evaded. "The last time we saw him," Bennett said later, "he was going over the hill for Nagasaki."

When Bennett returned from patrol, Lockwood was pleased. Although the test had been "spotty" (as Lockwood described it), it seemed to him that the Cutie had merit, especially as a weapon to use against shallow-draft antisubmarine vessels. Even if the Cutie didn't sink them, it might damage the propellers and force them to stop, as had been the case in Bennett's first two attacks. Then, once they had been stopped, a submarine might actually sink them with another Cutie or with a regular electric set to run at shallow depth from short range, as Bennett had done in his second attack. However, follow-up combat tests of the Cutie were not so successful. Hull, Hottel, and others went on trying to debug it and waited for later models that could hit faster targets.

The other gadget that held promise was the FM sonar. This supersensitive device was conceived to detect mines, to prevent the tragedy that befell *Robalo* and *Flier* and probably three or four other boats off northeast Honshu. In tests conducted off the coast of California, the FM picked up dummy mines at a range of 450 yards—about a quarter of a mile. When a mine was detected on the machine, it gave off a peculiar and chilling gonging, which the submarine crews appropriately called "Hell's Bells."

One of the first FMs was mounted on *Tinosa* while she was undergoing refit in San Francisco. During that time, Richard Clark Latham, who had made one war patrol on *Perch* as a PCO, relieved Don Weiss as skipper. Latham found his crew hostile to the FM gear. It could have only one purpose, searching out enemy minefields, and few men were anxious to engage in that risky task.

Latham said later, "*Tinosa* had made seven consecutive successful war patrols under Dan Daspit and Don Weiss. The original crew was still intact . . . [reunited] with their families and loved ones again after a long time facing death. They had been promised—or had dreamed—that when *Tinosa* got back to the States, they would be transferred to refrigeration school or you-name-it, after which they would get new construction and spend a year building a sub— maybe they wouldn't have to go to war again if they were lucky."

After the refit, Latham took *Tinosa* to San Diego for more FM training with dummy minefields. The crew was less and less enthusiastic. The FM did not always perform, and many became convinced that this new inexperienced skipper would take them into a Japanese minefield and blow them all to hell. Many asked for transfers, but Latham denied these requests—at least until *Tinosa* reported to Pearl Harbor for duty. On the way out, Latham interviewed each man, learning that not less than half wanted off the boat. He sent a message to Pearl Harbor, reporting that he had never seen morale as low on any ship in the navy as *Tinosa,* and requested a rate-for-rate exchange for these men, which included some chiefs. At Pearl Harbor, Latham recalled, they didn't know whether to transfer Latham off or the men, but in the showdown Latham stood pat. Thirty-five of *Tinosa*'s crew went to other duty (many to *Shark*, on which, ironically, they were lost); thirty-five new men (many from *Shark*) reported on board.

Latham took *Tinosa* on her first patrol to the vicinity of Okinawa in December. He did not have specific orders to investigate minefields but kept the gear operating to see what he could find. One day the crew was galvanized by Hell's Bells gonging from the FM receiver. Later Latham said, "We had no doubt but that it was a minefield. . . . *Tinosa* reported the event. . . . Lockwood was elated by the news of the first minefield detection by his pet development."

Upon receiving the news, Lockwood ordered Latham to make a complete FM survey of Okinawa. Latham closed to two miles of the beach and began this arduous and nerve-racking chore. "I don't know anyone who liked it," Latham said later. "I had a St. Christopher's medal blessed by a priest which hung on a chain in my cabin —until somebody swiped chain, medal and all. I used to go in my cabin and hold the medal and bow and pray fervently and then figure that if I kept my wits and used my brain and did the best that I possibly could under whatever circumstances I found myself, I'd done all that could be done and the rest was in the hands of fate. Talk about alert! I could feel, see, hear, smell, and taste better than an Indian or a wolf. . . . I remember thinking that if I got through the war, I would never again worry about life's little travails." Latham received a Navy Cross and high praise from Lockwood for this first FM mission.

Burt's Brooms

After the Leyte invasion, Admiral Halsey planned to take Task Force 38 on a strike against the Japanese mainland, the first carrier attack since the Doolittle raid in April 1942. Halsey hoped to catch the remaining ships of the Japanese fleet in their anchorages and to damage portions of the aviation industry. The raid was code-named Operation Hotfoot.

Lockwood planned to support Operation Hotfoot. Seven submarines would steam ahead of Task Force 38, sweeping out Japanese picket boats between the Bonins and Japan which might warn Japanese authorities of the approaching fleet. Burt Klakring, commanding Submarine Division 101, was selected to head this group, and it was named in his honor: Burt's Brooms.

The Brooms staged from the Marianas, now growing into a full-scale submarine base. The tender *Fulton* had joined old *Holland* at Saipan. *Sperry* had arrived in Apra Harbor, Guam, October 20, with the headquarters of Squadron Ten, commanded by George Lucius Russell, who had relieved Charles Erck. Russell's men built a rest and recuperation camp on Guam and named it Camp Dealey, in honor of the Destroyer Killer.

As it turned out, because of the stiff fighting on Leyte, Halsey was forced to cancel Operation Hotfoot. Nevertheless, Lockwood ordered Burt's Brooms to conduct the sweep more or less as practice. The seven boats—*Ronquil, Burrfish, Sterlet, Silversides, Trigger, Tambor,* and *Saury*—left Saipan on November 10. Klakring flew his flag in *Silversides,* commanded by John Coye.

Through no fault of Klakring's, who in fact was later presented with a Silver Star for his "conspicuous gallantry and intrepidity" as commander, Burt's Brooms was a complete disaster. The weather was foul and the seas rough, making the use of deck guns perilous. Richard Waugh in *Saury* unsuccessfully attacked an armed trawler on November 18. Later, he fired eight torpedoes at a small tanker, achieving one hit. (On return to port, old *Saury* was retired from combat.) William Germershausen in *Tambor* fired six torpedoes at a patrol vessel, missing with all. Next day he battle-surfaced and sank the craft, which fired back and seriously wounded one of his men. (When he returned *Tambor* to port, she too was retired.) Butch Robbins in *Sterlet* sank a small subchaser with torpedoes. Henry Monroe in *Ronquil* and William Perkins in *Burrfish* teamed up to make a gun attack on a couple of trawlers. They sank these small craft—but at high cost; two men were wounded on *Burrfish,* and Monroe in *Ronquil* blew two holes in his own pressure hull. (His exec, Lincoln Marcy, 1939, led a repair crew that fixed *Ronquil* so she could dive again and for that risky job received a Navy Cross.)

The Brooms returned to the Marianas about November 25. In all, the seven boats had sunk two or three trawlers. Later Jasper Holmes wrote, "The Japanese responded to the raid by rushing additional patrol craft and air search planes into the area and there were probably more pickets in the area after the sweep than there were when it started."

The U.S. Invasions of Mindoro and Luzon

When Leyte was finally secure, MacArthur's invasion forces leaped 300 miles northwestward to the island of Mindoro. These forces were detected by the Japanese and assaulted by kamikaze pilots, one of whom hit the cruiser *Nashville*, killing 133 and wounding 190. Later, kamikazes demolished two LSTs. In spite of being detected, however, the soldiers went ashore without opposition.

During the landings, Bull Halsey's Task Force 38 provided air support. His planes ranged over Luzon, destroying many Japanese aircraft, including kamikazes. On December 17, while refueling, Task Force 38 ran into a typhoon. Three destroyers, *Hull*, *Monaghan*, and *Spence*, which had failed to take on salt-water ballast, capsized and sank. Seven other ships were badly damaged. About 186 aircraft were blown overboard or jettisoned. In all, 800 officers and men were lost.

The Japanese made a futile effort to counterattack the landing craft on Mindoro. On December 24–25, Admiral Masanori Kimura left Camranh Bay with a force of two cruisers (heavy cruiser *Ashigara* and light cruiser *Oyodo*) and six destroyers (part of Admiral Shima's original group) and proceeded across the South China Sea toward Mindoro, protected by foul weather generated by the typhoon. Kimura was spotted 200 miles west of Mindoro by an army plane. Nevertheless, he approached the beaches of Mindoro on the night of December 26–27 and conducted a brief—and ineffectual—bombardment; U.S. aircraft forced him to return hurriedly to Camranh Bay, and a PT boat sank one of his destroyers.

After Mindoro was secure, MacArthur's forces made another leap, the biggest and grandest of all. On January 9 they landed on Luzon, going ashore in Lingayen Gulf, where the Japanese had landed three years before. Kamikaze pilots mounted a furious assault on navy ships, sinking the jeep carrier *Ommaney Bay* and severely damaged the jeep carrier *Manila Bay*, the cruisers *Louisville* and *Australia*, a destroyer, and other ships in the initial attacks and hitting sixteen ships, badly damaging ten, on January 6.

But the Allied ground troops landed virtually unopposed, and in the following days and weeks other troops landed at Subic Bay, Manila Bay, and elsewhere. The Japanese were disorganized and dis-

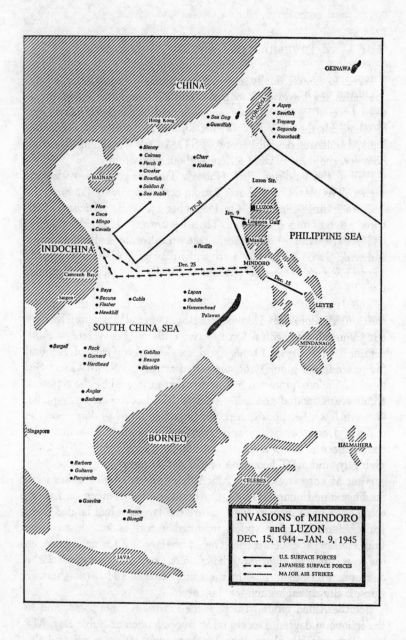

INVASIONS of MINDORO
and LUZON
DEC. 15, 1944 – JAN. 9, 1945

U.S. SURFACE FORCES
JAPANESE SURFACE FORCES
MAJOR AIR STRIKES

pirited and completely lacking in air power. General MacArthur reconquered Luzon at his leisure and with light casualties. By February 4, Manila was his. In subsequent months his troops (aided by the 100,000 guerrillas MacArthur had supplied all these years of the occupation) recaptured the rest of the Philippine Islands.

During the landings on Luzon, Halsey, having repaired his battered Task Force 38, supported the ground troops with air strikes. On the night of January 9–10, while the troops were consolidating positions in Lingayen Gulf, Halsey steamed boldly through Luzon Strait into the South China Sea. Believing the carrier-battleships *Ise* and *Hyuga* to be in Camranh Bay, he swung south and launched air strikes there on January 12. *Ise* and *Hyuga* were not in the bay— they were in Singapore loading drums of oil for shipment to Japan —but Halsey's planes sank forty-seven ships off Indochina, including seven large tankers. Withdrawing through Luzon Strait, Halsey's planes hit Formosa on January 15 and Hong Kong on January 16. On January 17 Halsey slipped back through Luzon Strait, hit Formosa again, and then conducted a photo-reconnaissance of Okinawa. During the last days of this foray, the Japanese bombed the new carrier *Langley*; kamikazes hit the carrier *Ticonderoga* and destroyer *Maddox*. On January 25 Halsey arrived back in Ulithi, where he turned the task force over to Admiral Spruance.

Patrols from Australia

During these operations, Ralph Christie's submarines—joined by half a dozen or more Pearl Harbor boats en route to Australia—were plying the South China Sea and other waters, lifeguarding, attacking enemy shipping, and watching for enemy fleet units. After the landings on Mindoro, the boats were excluded from Philippine waters. They concentrated in the areas near Singapore, Borneo, and Indochina. High priority was given to remaining enemy men-of-war and, as always nowadays, tankers.

Herman Kossler in *Cavalla*, going on his third patrol, took up station off Singapore with *Baya* and *Hoe*. On the night of November 25, Kossler came across what he thought was a cruiser or two; he set up on one and fired four torpedoes. It was a destroyer, *Shimotsuki*, 2,300 tons, which blew up and sank instantly. The other destroyer tried to find *Cavalla,* but Kossler evaded at high speed on the surface.

A week later, December 2, Kossler picked up a "task force" on radar. It was a battleship—perhaps *Ise* or *Hyuga*—escorted by three destroyers. Kossler made an end around and submerged to attack the battleship, but just as he was ready to fire, an escort came right down his track, forcing him to go deep to avoid being rammed. On the way down, Kossler fired six torpedoes at the battleship anyway. All missed.

Swede Bryant, Commander, Squadron Eighteen, led a wolf pack using Worth Scanland's *Hawkbill* for his flagship. The pack consisted of *Hawkbill;* Reuben Whitaker's famous *Flasher,* now commanded by George Grider, moving up from serving as exec in *Hawkbill;* and Hank Sturr's *Becuna.* The pack patrolled west of Mindoro during the invasion to stop the approach of Japanese fleet units, should they elect to sortie from Singapore.

On December 4, Scanland picked up a westbound convoy about 200 miles west of Mindoro. Grider in *Flasher* was 15 miles off his proper position and, by chance, right on the track of the convoy. When it came in sight, Grider was apprehensive. Later he wrote, "I stood in the quiet conning tower, feeling the rush of blood to my skin, knowing the test I had dreamed and wondered and worried about since my earliest days at the Naval Academy was upon me at last. My day of command in combat had arrived. What would I do with it?"

Assisted by his exec, Philip Glennon, who had been Whitaker's last exec on *Flasher,* Grider prepared to attack, submerging and maneuvering for favorable position. Then it began to rain. Grider felt heartsick. Glennon reported high-speed screws coming close, obviously an escort. Grider swung the periscope, searching, worrying that he would bungle his first attack. Then he saw the destroyer.

Grider fired four torpedoes and felt two hits. Later he wrote that "as I swung the scope to look, a feeling of exaltation like nothing I had ever experienced before swept over me. By heaven, I had paid my way as a skipper now, no matter what happened." The destroyer began to smoke heavily. Its screws stopped; the ship fell off to the left, settling aft and listing.

Through the mist, Grider saw a large tanker. Setting up quickly, he fired two torpedoes, then checked fire when he saw the tanker turning. He turned his attention back to the damaged destroyer.

Then he saw another destroyer or patrol boat boiling in and he went deep.

As *Flasher* was going down, Grider heard two timed hits in the tanker. Phil Glennon said, almost in disbelief, "My God. We hit him!" When *Flasher* reached 250 feet, the depth charges began to explode. In all, there were sixteen, mostly close.

About an hour and a half later, Grider returned to periscope depth. He found the tanker burning furiously and settling aft. In addition—unbelievably—he saw another destroyer motionless on the water. Grider was wary. Why was this destroyer making himself a perfect target? He fired four torpedoes: three at the stopped destroyer, one at the tanker just beyond. Three torpedoes hit the destroyer.

Grider went deep again to avoid depth charges from the other escorts. When he returned to the surface, he could see the tanker, still burning. Then he saw Sturr's *Becuna*. Grider surfaced. Both boats approached the burning tanker cautiously. It was abandoned. Sturr went on his way; Grider held back to deliver the coup de grace, one more stern torpedo. The tanker sank quickly.

In this, his first attack of the war, Grider claimed he sank two destroyers and one large tanker. Postwar records bore him out. With only eleven torpedoes he had sunk the destroyers *Kishinami* and *Iwanami*, both 2,100 tons, and *Hakko Maru*, 10,000 tons.

Bryant's pack remained on scouting line west of Mindoro during the invasion while, to the south, Hammerhead Martin in *Hammerhead* disposed another pack—*Hammerhead*, *Paddle*, *Lapon*, and *Mingo*—near Brunei Bay. On December 8, Martin in *Hammerhead* and Fitz-Patrick in *Paddle* sank a 2,800-ton tanker in a joint attack, but none of the boats on the scouting lines encountered any major units of the Japanese fleet. For the time being they were keeping to Singapore and Camranh Bay.

Bergall, under John Hyde, and *Dace*, commanded by a new skipper, Otis Robert Cole, Jr., both carried a load of mines aft to be laid off Indochina.

On the evening of December 13, while preparing to lay his mines, Hyde picked up masts on the horizon at 35,000 yards. On this patrol, he was assisted by PCO Ben Jarvis (ex-*Sailfish*), who had been serving in *Nautilus* as exec. The water was extremely shallow, about 80 feet average. Hyde and Jarvis decided to attack—and escape—on the surface.

Closing in, Hyde got radar contact at 26,000 yards. An hour later he identified the contact as two cruisers; in fact, it was the heavy cruiser *Myoko* and a destroyer escort en route from Singapore to Camranh Bay. Hyde closed to 3,300 yards and, with both targets overlapping, fired six bow tubes. Moments later he saw an awesome explosion. Flames billowed up to 750 feet. To Hyde, the cruiser seemed to break in two. However, *Myoko* was only badly damaged. She limped back to Singapore, where she stayed until the end of the war.

Hyde hauled clear to reload. The other "cruiser" did not pursue, leading Hyde and Jarvis to conclude she too had been hit. Hyde came back in for a second attack, but when he had closed to 9,000 yards the destroyer opened fire. One shell landed behind *Bergall*, the other directly on her forward torpedo loading hatch, smashing a large opening in the pressure hull. Hyde retreated at full speed.

After a thorough inspection, Hyde found himself in a serious predicament. There was no way to patch the pressure hull. *Bergall* could not dive. The ship was 2,000 miles from the closest Allied base —Exmouth Gulf—and 1,200 miles of that was controlled by the enemy. What to do?

Hyde got off a report to Christie. Christie consulted his operations board and found that *Angler*, commanded by a new skipper, H. Bissell, Jr.,* was patrolling in the Java Sea with *Bashaw*. Christie ordered *Angler*, *Bashaw*, and *Paddle* to rendezvous, remove the crew of *Bergall*, and then destroy *Bergall*. *Angler* found *Bergall* on the night of December 15. Neither *Bashaw* nor *Paddle* could find her.

Hyde was reluctant to sink his own ship and decided to disobey Christie's orders. Later he wrote:

I was convinced that, if no other boat was contacted, I could get through Karimata, the Java Sea and Lombok on the surface with a good chance of success. This was based on two previous trips over the same route in which no plane contacts were made. By adjusting speed to pass through and well clear of Karimata during darkness; to cross the Surabaya-Balikpapen route at night and to stay well north

* Bissell was the second reserve officer, after Hugh Lewis, to command a fleet boat. The third was James L. Hunnicutt (ex-*Tinosa*), who put the new boat *Carp* in commission.

of Lombok until dark, I felt sure of avoiding aircraft. Therefore I decided to head on down towards Karimata.

Splitting his crew, Hyde sent one officer and fifty-four men to *Angler* and kept eight officers and twenty-one men on *Bergall.* Then he destroyed confidential gear, set demolition charges by his torpedoes and mines, and got under way for Exmouth Gulf. *Angler* trailed behind, ready to take *Bergall's* men on board if the Japanese threatened.

Hyde got away with it, traveling 1,200 miles of enemy-controlled waters without being seen by an aircraft or surface ship. On December 20 *Bergall* and *Angler* arrived at Exmouth Gulf. *Angler* then returned to patrol. Christie said later that he was pleased that Hyde had elected to disobey his orders.

Bashaw and *Guavina,* operating as a two-boat wolf pack, patrolled south of Camranh Bay. On the morning of December 14, Nichols in *Bashaw* found what he believed to be "two *Nagato*-class battleships," a light cruiser, and several destroyers heading north. Believing a report more important than attack, Nichols waited, withheld fire, then surfaced and got off a report. Carl Tiedeman in *Guavina* saw the same ships, identifying them as two *Fuso*- or *Nagato*-class battleships. He too got off a contact report and chased, but he could not catch up. These ships might have been *Ise* and *Hyuga,* bound for Camranh Bay.

John Madison in *Mingo* replaced *Bergall* off Indochina. Otis Cole in *Dace* had arrived in the area and, on December 16, laid his minefield off Palau Gambir. The next morning, in typhoon weather, Madison saw many ships standing out of Camranh Bay, including what he reported as "two *Ise*-class battleships," one or two heavy cruisers, and several destroyers. Madison reduced the range from 6 miles to 4 miles but could get no closer. Later he sent off a contact report.

After receiving Madison's report, the staff at Fremantle ordered half a dozen submarines to converge on Camranh Bay, among them *Dace, Hoe, Paddle,* and two boats from Swede Bryant's pack, *Flasher* and *Becuna.* The seas were mountainous; George Grider reported "forty-foot waves."

On December 19, Cole in *Dace* picked up a five-ship convoy with three escorts coming out of Camranh Bay, headed north. He made a submerged approach in the heavy seas, but the weather defeated him. A Japanese plane or escort detected *Dace* and dropped bombs or depth charges, forcing Cole to break off the attack. In her evasion, *Dace* hit bottom, and the strong current carried her bumping, scraping, and clanking along the seabed. (During this busy patrol for *Dace*, Cole later picked up a large convoy escorted by a jeep carrier and fired three torpedoes at the carrier, but they all missed.)

Grider picked up Cole's contact report and tried to move north to intercept. "It was impossible to make over seven knots into the sea," Grider reported, "and the current was setting south at four knots." Making northward progress of only 3 knots, *Flasher* gave up the chase after half an hour. That night, she exchanged places with *Dace*, guarding the Camranh Bay entrance.

On December 21 the weather moderated slightly. Shortly after 9 A.M., Grider spotted a convoy: five fat tankers, three small escorts, and a destroyer bringing up the rear. The destroyer passed by at 2,000 yards but Grider withheld fire, believing that his torpedoes would broach in the heavy seas. After the convoy passed by, Grider surfaced and headed north in pursuit. The best speed Grider could make in the heavy seas was 12½ knots. He was fighting a 3-knot southerly current, so his true speed was 9½ knots. The convoy was making 8½ knots. Grider's speed advantage: 1 knot.

Grider chased north all day and into the night. The convoy pulled out of reach, Grider reported; "Our spirits began to droop." But he decided to go on another three hours, hoping he would regain contact; the seas had calmed down and he could make better speed. At 1 A.M. on December 22, as Grider was preparing to break off and return to Camranh Bay, Phil Glennon saw the convoy on radar.

In one of the most daring attacks of the war, Grider eased *Flasher* into shallow water between the convoy and shore. He fired three bow tubes that hit two tankers. One blew up and "illuminated the area like a night football game." Grider swung and fired four stern tubes at a third tanker. All hit and the tanker blew up. "The flames from the second and third targets flowed together," Grider wrote in his report, "and made a really impressive fire." Moments later the first target blew up and "added his light to the flames. The entire sea aft was covered with billowing red fire which burned for about forty minutes." None of the escorts attacked *Flasher*. The tankers sunk by Grider in this brilliant attack were *Omurosan Maru*, 9,200 tons; *Otowasan Maru*, 9,200 tons; and *Arita Maru*, 10,238 tons.

When Grider reported the results to Christie, the latter replied: WONDERFUL CHRISTMAS PRESENT GRIDER. CONGRATULATIONS TO YOU ALL. COME ON HOME. REUBEN IS GOING TO BE PROUD OF HIS OLD SHIP.

There was every reason to be. On this, Grider's first patrol, he had sunk a total of six ships, two destroyers and four large tankers. He was credited with six ships for 41,700 tons, upped postwar to 42,800 tons. In terms of confirmed tonnage sunk, it was the third best patrol of the war, after Enright in *Archerfish*'s fifth patrol and Hank Munson in *Rasher*'s fifth. In terms of tanker tonnage, it was the best of the war.

After *Flasher* left, Christie directed Norman Gage in *Gurnard* to take his place. On Christmas Eve, then, there were many submarines lying in wait off Camranh Bay, including *Gurnard*, *Guitarro*, *Hoe*, *Dace*, *Paddle*, and *Becuna*. Others, including *Hawkbill*, *Baya*, *Cavalla*, *Redfin*, *Hammerhead*, and *Lapon*, lay to the eastward between Camranh Bay and Mindoro.

On December 22, Joseph Fitz-Patrick in *Paddle*, making his seventeenth patrol of the war—a record—reported "two very large ships." These, undoubtedly, were Admiral Kimura's heavy cruiser *Ashigara* and the light cruiser *Oyodo*, preparing for the dash to bombard the beaches of Mindoro. The next day, Hank Sturr in *Becuna* saw the force go into Camranh Bay. (Sturr mistakenly identified *Ashigara* as a "*Yamato*-class battleship.") But when Admiral Kimura left Camranh Bay on Christmas Eve, none of the boats off Camranh Bay saw him; nor did any of the boats lying to the east toward Mindoro.

On Kimura's return trip to Camranh Bay, Thomas Bullard Dabney in *Guitarro* and Gage in *Gurnard* saw the force barreling in at 25 knots. It passed within 5,000 yards of *Guitarro*, but so fast that Dabney had no chance to set up and shoot. Neither did Gage in *Gurnard*. In all, going and coming, Admiral Kimura had eluded about a dozen submarines.

In the days following, the boats off Camranh Bay made other contacts, but heavy antisubmarine measures drove them off and prevented many attacks. Irvin Hartman in *Barbero*, returning to Fremantle by way of Karimata Strait, was nearly lost. While attacking a Japanese vessel on December 27, Hartman was caught by a Japanese aircraft whose bombs hit *Barbero*. Going deep to evade and assess damage, Hartman found the boat to be badly wrecked. He surfaced and limped back to Fremantle, where, after a close inspection, *Barbero* was ordered back to the States for a navy yard overhaul. She did not make another war patrol.

Patrols from Pearl Harbor

After the Burt's Brooms fiasco, Lockwood resumed his normal patrol cycles, sending boats in packs or singly to Luzon Strait, the East China Sea, and elsewhere.

On December 2 Ralph Emerson Styles in *Sea Devil* found a seven-ship convoy off southwest Kyushu. Maneuvering around four escorts, Styles sank two large ships: a 6,900-ton freighter, *Akigawa Maru,* and a 9,500-ton transport, *Hawaii Maru.*

About December 7 Lockwood received word from the codebreakers that an important task force would arrive in the Nagasaki area. By then Carter Bennett had tested his Cuties, so Lockwood concentrated Bennett's pack—*Sea Owl, Piranha,* and *Sea Poacher*—plus Sandy McGregor in *Redfish,* Shelby in *Sunfish,* Clyde Stevens in *Plaice,* and Styles in *Sea Devil,* near the island of Danjo Gunto.

On the night of December 8, Sandy McGregor made contact with the enemy force on radar at 15 miles. It consisted of the light carrier *Junyo* and several destroyers. He sent off a contact report to all submarines and began tracking.

About 9:30 that night, Styles in *Sea Devil* made contact with the task force, range 8 miles. Styles approached submerged to radar depth and fired four torpedoes at the largest target—*Junyo,* range 4,300 yards. He was lucky. Two torpedoes hit the carrier. He raised his radio antenna and got off a contact report.

Clyde Stevens in *Plaice* picked up the task force shortly after midnight, range 12 miles. As he was closing to attack, he heard torpedo explosions—*Sea Devil*'s attack. Stevens picked the closest target, a destroyer, and fired three torpedoes. Then "the big boy" popped out of the mist. Stevens had no chance to fire at the carrier, but he shot another three torpedoes at another destroyer. He heard hits in the first destroyer and believed it sank, but postwar records did not bear out the claim.

On the other side of the formation, Sandy McGregor in *Redfish* moved in close to the carrier and fired six steam torpedoes at a range of 2,900 yards. One made an erratic circular run, forcing McGregor to maneuver wildly to avoid it, but the other five ran true. McGregor "heard and saw one terrific hit in carrier." He reloaded his forward tubes, came in for another attack, and fired six more torpedoes. One prematured, but others hit. *Junyo* limped into Nagasaki so badly damaged she was out of the war for the duration.

McGregor in *Redfish* rendezvoused with Lawrence Julihn in *Shad* about December 12, and the two boats snooped around Shanghai and then dropped down toward the mouth of Formosa Strait. On about December 16, McGregor received an Ultra from Lockwood stating that "an important enemy task force" was proceeding south.

McGregor took up position "along track that Jap task forces use between Empire and Formosa and/or Philippines." He was not altogether confident of his location; the weather had been bad for several days. A day passed, and then another, with no sign of the Japanese task force. (Later McGregor said, "They were late because they had trouble getting out of the shipyard.")

At 4:27 on the afternoon of December 19, while submerged, McGregor picked up the enemy force. It was a brand-new carrier, *Unryu*, with three destroyer escorts, one ahead and one on either beam. McGregor closed to point-blank range (1,470 yards) and fired four torpedoes. One hit, causing *Unryu* to stop. She took a strong starboard list and McGregor saw a fire break out aft. When *Unryu* trained her guns on *Redfish*'s periscope and commenced firing, McGregor responded by firing his four stern tubes, which missed.

While his torpedo crews reloaded one torpedo aft, McGregor fearlessly kept his periscope eye on the damaged carrier. The destroyers zipped about wildly, dropping depth charges. When the torpedo was in the tube, McGregor closed to 1,100 yards and fired. As he wrote later, "Torpedo hit carrier at point of aim. The sharp crack of the torpedo explosion was followed instantly by thundering explosions apparently from magazine or gasoline stowage, probably the latter. Huge clouds of smoke, flame, and debris burst into the air completely enveloping the carrier. . . . He has sunk!" The escorts came after *Redfish* in a fury, and McGregor hastily ordered 200 feet. As he recorded the results of their attack:

On passing 150 feet all Hell broke loose when seven well placed depth charges exploded alongside starboard bow. The closest one of these charges is believed to have exploded a little above keel depth and gave the sensation of pushing the bow sideways to port. At this time the following casualties were reported: Steering gear jammed on hard left and hydraulic leak in after room manifold, bow planes jammed on 20 degrees rise, and hydraulic oil leak in pump room and loss of all hydraulic power, all sound gear out of commission, pressure hull cracked in forward torpedo room with gear out of commission, pressure hull cracked in forward torpedo room with water leaking through #1 M.B.T. riser [main ballast tank pipe] and #1 Sanitary Tank discharge valve numerous air leaks throughout boat and a torpedo making a hot run in #8 torpedo tube. One man was injured when a W.T. [watertight] door jolted loose and hit him in the head practically severing one ear.

McGregor crept away from the scene of the battle as quietly as he could. Then he limped to Midway, where he received full credit for dispatching *Unryu* and relinquished command of the battered boat to his exec, Robert Lakin Gurnee, going on to command a division. In his four war patrols—two on *Pike*, two on *Redfish*—he had fired at three aircraft carriers, severely damaging two and sinking one.

Gurnee returned *Redfish* to Portsmouth Navy Yard, where she had been built. Later he described his arrival:

A large crowd waited on the dock for the ship to tie up. This crowd was composed mainly of the same yard workmen who had helped build the Redfish. They swarmed aboard and sped immediately to the areas on the ship that they had built to see if their portion had held together. I overheard more than one as he left the ship telling his buddy proudly, "Yes, sir, my welds held together even though the steel hull was dimpled and the whole bow knocked off center." Needless to say, many of us who had been aboard during the depth charging were emotionally moved by this incident and more than one of the brave Redfish sailors dried damp eyes.

Roy Davenport in *Trepang* led a pack to Luzon Strait, the other boats being James Fulp's *Segundo* and *Razorback*, with a new skipper, Charles Donald Brown, 1938. On December 6, bedeviled by heavy seas, the pack picked up a seven-ship convoy with three escorts. Davenport fired twenty-two torpedoes, claiming four ships sunk for 35,000 tons, postwar records credited three ships for about 13,000 tons. Brown on *Razorback* and Fulp on *Segundo* shared credit for sinking a 7,000-ton freighter from the convoy. Davenport, who had only two torpedoes remaining, left the strait, returning to Pearl Harbor three days before Christmas. *Segundo* and *Razorback* remained on station during the month of December. Brown in *Razorback* sank an old destroyer, *Kuretake,* December 30. Total for the pack: five confirmed ships for about 21,000 tons.

After this patrol, Davenport, who felt that he no longer had "quite the punch" that he used to have, asked for shore duty and returned to the Naval Academy as an instructor in marine engineering. In all, he had made ten war patrols, four on Burlingame's *Silversides,* four as skipper of *Haddock,* and two as skipper of *Trepang.* In his six patrols as commanding officer, Davenport had been credited with sinking seventeen ships for 151,900 tons, ranking him third behind Dick O'Kane (227,800 tons) and Gene Fluckey (179,000 tons) in tonnage. Postwar accounting reduced Davenport's claims to eight ships for only about 30,000 tons.

Davenport had earned five Navy Crosses during his six patrols in command of *Haddock* and *Trepang,* more than any other skipper. Except for the men who won Medals of Honor, he was the most-decorated submariner of the war.

Another pack followed Davenport into Luzon Strait, remaining there during the invasion of Luzon. It was commanded by Rebel Lowrance in *Sea Dog.* The other two boats were *Sea Robin,* commanded by Paul Cecil Stimson, and the famous *Guardfish,* now commanded by Douglas Hammond, whom Christie had relieved from command of *Cabrilla* after two luckless patrols but to whom Lockwood had decided to give a second chance.

By the time this pack reached Luzon Strait, the area was barren of shipping. It was raked by Halsey in early January when Task Force 38 entered the South China Sea to strike Camranh Bay. Lowrance went far west—toward Hainan. Stimson in *Sea Robin* was lucky to find a small convoy and sink a tanker off Hainan January 6. That same day, Hammond fired three torpedoes from long range at what he believed to be a decoy or Q-ship but may have been Stimson's convoy. Hammond, conducting an extremely cautious patrol, did not follow up the attack.

On January 23, when *Guardfish* was returning to Guam, Hammond picked up a radar contact in the middle of the Philippine Sea. Believing this might be a Japanese I-class submarine, he began tracking by radar and sent off two messages to Lowrance and Lockwood, reporting the contact and asking if any U.S. submarines or surface ships might be in the area. Lockwood replied that there were no U.S. submarines in the area and stated that if it turned out to be a surface ship it was probably friendly. Lockwood reminded Hammond that he was in a "joint area," where friendly surface ships might be operating, and that positive evidence that the ship was enemy had to be obtained before firing.

The ship was indeed friendly. She was the salvage vessel *Extractor*, commanded by H. M. Babcock, which had helped the stricken tanker *Mississinewa* at Ulithi. *Extractor* was en route from Guam to the Philippines, unescorted. The day before, she had been sent a message ordering her back to Guam, but the message arrived "badly garbled." Later, Babcock reported, "Numerous attempts were made to decipher the message using all available effective codes with no results. I did not consider it advisable to break radio silence to request a repeat." The people at Guam who kept track of U.S. vessels assumed *Extractor* had received this message and was on her way back.

Hammond continued tracking. At 5:42, he submerged ahead to inspect his target through the periscope. It was almost sunrise. The sky was overcast. There were passing light rainsqualls. Hammond and his exec made six separate observations, ranges 6,800 yards to 1,800 yards. These looks convinced them absolutely that *Extractor* was an I-class Japanese submarine, running on the surface. At 6:20, Hammond fired four electric torpedoes from his bow tubes, range 1,200 yards.

Two torpedoes hit and *Extractor* blew up and sank. Four men in the bow were killed instantly; two others drowned. But seventy-three, including Babcock, survived. Twenty minutes after the firing, Hammond surfaced to run through the wreckage. Later, he wrote, "Upon drawing close aboard the first life raft realized the full extent of our mistake. The survivors were American."

With a heavy heart, Hammond picked up the seventy-three men in the water and sent them below—to an awkward confrontation with *Guardfish*'s crew. Hammond spent three hours futilely looking for the missing six men. Then he sent a dispatch to Lockwood reporting the tragic mistake and set course for Guam. Forty-eight hours later, he rendezvoused with the destroyer escort *George*, which took off the *Extractor* crew.

Once-proud *Guardfish* moored alongside *Sperry* in Apra Harbor,

Guam, and her crew went to the rest area, Camp Dealey. Ironically, it fell to Burt Klakring, the man who made *Guardfish* famous, to write the patrol report endorsement. During the refit, a Court of Inquiry was conducted. Hammond and Babcock more or less shared blame for the incident, Babcock for not requesting a rebroadcast of the message that would have removed him from danger, Hammond for mistakenly identifying *Extractor*. Babcock and the *Extractor* crew returned to the States for survivor's leave. Hammond retained command of *Guardfish* and her fine—but hangdog—crew.

Extractor was the only U.S. ship sunk by U.S. submarines in the war.

Dragonet, the second Cramp Shipyard boat to reach combat (after *Escolar*), went on the polar circuit. She was commanded by Jack Lewis, who commanded *Trigger* on her first patrol and *Swordfish* on her seventh. Lewis had so much trouble getting *Dragonet* mechanically ready for patrol that wags dubbed the boat "The Reluctant Dragonet."

Off Matsuwa To on December 15, Lewis submerged for routine patrol. At 7:17 A.M., while at 70 feet, Lewis felt a jar he thought might have been a Japanese bomb. In fact, he had run aground. In the mishap, the whole forward torpedo room flooded, giving *Dragonet* a terrific down-angle. The men in the torpedo room escaped aft and slammed the watertight doors. Lewis put "salvage air" into the forward room, and *Dragonet* settled on the bottom—making ominous noises.

In a fine piece of seamanship, Lewis finally emptied the forward torpedo room of water, but *Dragonet* was badly damaged. Lewis surfaced in sight of Matsuwa, later writing, "Exchanged feel of temporary relief for one of shameful nakedness." He put all four engines on the line and ran out to sea.

Lewis headed for Midway. On the way, he ran into a bad storm; one time, *Dragonet* rolled 63 degrees to port—and hung there. She finally arrived at Midway on December 20 with a heavy port list and was sent back to the States for a navy yard overhaul. *Dragonet* was the only submarine in the war to completely flood her forward torpedo room and survive.

Spearfish, commanded by Cy Cole, made a photographic reconnaissance of Iwo Jima and then lifeguarded during a B-29 strike against Japan. On December 19 a B-29 ditched and Cole rescued seven members of the crew, the first of many B-29 crews rescued by U.S. submarines.

During the course of this patrol (as Cole later officially reported), he was caught on the surface by a friendly bomber. Cole had his radio tuned to the aircraft circuit and heard the following exchange:

"Looks like a sub."

"May be a ship."

"Let's bomb the bastard anyway."

Cole dived quickly. His officer of the deck saw bombs hit close aboard and heard bullets whine. Cole radioed Lockwood, LIBERATOR FAILED TO SCORE. . . . DAMAGE TO PRIDE AND TEMPER ONLY.

On return to port, Cole was praised for his patrol, but old *Spearfish* was retired from combat, and Cole went to a staff job at Pearl Harbor.

Jack Gerwick, commanding *Greenling* for a third time out, patrolled to the north of Okinawa. On January 25 he found a well-escorted convoy and attacked. The escorts counterattacked with awesome speed and persistence, four of them boxing *Greenling* at 300 feet and dropping about a hundred depth charges. "Those boys were experts," Gerwick reported later. *Greenling* was knocked down 60 feet—to 360 feet—by one of the charges, which started five hot runs in the tubes. Finally, *Greenling* shook loose and limped into Saipan. She was considered to be so badly damaged she was retired from combat and sent to New London.

The famous old *Swordfish,* commanded by Keats Montross, went to Okinawa to conduct a photographic reconnaissance. Two other boats were in the same area: a new one, *Kete,* commanded by Royal Rutter, and *Puffer,* commanded by Carl Redmond Dwyer. Dwyer sank a small ship on January 10.

Early on the morning of January 12, *Swordfish* and *Kete* exchanged calls. Four hours later, Rutter heard heavy depth-charging. After that, nothing further was heard from Montross. *Swordfish* was lost either by this depth-charging or by striking a new minefield that had been planted at Okinawa. John Briscoe Pye, son of the admiral, perished with her.

*   *   *

Tautog, commanded by Tom Baskett, made her final combat patrol of the war in the East China Sea as half of a two-boat wolf pack. Her packmate *Silversides,* now commanded by John Culver Nichols (the only *Squalus* officer to command a boat during the war), had little luck, but Baskett made five attacks and sank two confirmed ships—a 1,500-ton transport and a PT-boat tender of 1,800 tons. Nichols in *Silversides* wound up the patrol by finally sinking a freighter, and the two boats then returned to base. *Tautog,* which had made thirteen war patrols, was also retired from combat, and Baskett went to the PCO pool.

When all the Japanese records had been compiled and studied, it was discovered that *Tautog* sank more confirmed ships than any other submarine: twenty-six. Joe Willingham had gotten five ships (including two submarines); Barney Sieglaff thirteen ships (including two destroyers but not including a third destroyer, *Amagiri,* sunk by a minefield laid by Sieglaff); and Baskett, eight ships.

Two new boats patrolled from Pearl Harbor to Australia. These were *Boarfish,* commanded by Roy Gross (ex-*Seawolf*), and *Blenny,* commanded by William Hazzard. Both patrols were among the most aggressive on record; Gross and Hazzard made eight attacks each, firing most of their torpedoes into convoys. The confirmed results, however, were thin. Hazzard was credited with an 800-ton frigate and a 4,000-ton freighter, Gross with sinking one 7,000-ton freighter plus half credit for a 6,900-ton ship shared with land-based army aircraft.

Gene Fluckey in *Barb,* Elliott Loughlin in *Queenfish,* and Ty Sheppard in *Picuda* teamed up again to make a three-boat pack. They were assigned to Formosa Strait with the mission of stopping any reinforcements the Japanese might send to the Philippines.

The pack left from Guam, sweeping northward toward the Bonins before turning west. On January 1, Shepard and Loughlin came across a patrol craft and attacked with their deck guns. Then Fluckey came up behind and sent a boarding party on the riddled craft to pick up charts and codebooks. Unknown to Fluckey, there were some Japanese hiding belowdecks. After the boarding party returned to *Barb,* Fluckey ordered his gun crew to sink the boat. Later Fluckey wrote, "When the diesel tanks caught fire, the eight or nine Japs came running out . . . on deck. They stopped for a minute and our 4-inch crew, being very blood-thirsty at that time, landed a shot right in their midst which blew them all apart."

The pack took station in Formosa Strait in shallow water, close to the spot where Dick O'Kane in *Tang* had gone down. Early on the morning of January 7, Fluckey picked up a seven-ship convoy and broadcast a contact report. Then he made an end around in broad daylight, submerging ahead of the convoy. When the convoy came along an hour later, visibility was bad and Fluckey had a hard time getting set on a target. He picked a big tanker, but it zigged away just as he got ready to fire. A destroyer came by but Fluckey withheld his fire, writing later, "I have now developed enough self-control to resist the temptation to let three torpedoes fly at an escort unless conditions are right. The latter the result of twelve torpedoes I have wasted in the last three patrols."

The convoy got by Fluckey. At 9:41 A.M. he surfaced to make another end around. While this was in progress, Shepard in *Picuda*, who had received Fluckey's contact report and submerged in good position, fired four torpedoes at a 10,000-ton tanker, *Munakata Maru*. Some hit and the tanker was severely damaged, but the attack alerted the convoy, which scattered and scurried into Formosa before Fluckey or Loughlin in *Queenfish* (too far away) could attack. All in all, it was a less than satisfactory beginning. "Some consolation in *Picuda* making the grade," Fluckey wrote.

The pack regrouped close to the China coast. The next day, January 8, at about one in the afternoon, Fluckey picked up another big convoy and flashed the word. Again he made an end around on the surface, submerging ahead of the convoy. It came along on track and Fluckey planned his attack to drive the ships away from the coast and toward his packmates. He began to fire, shooting three torpedoes at one freighter and three at another. While swinging around for a stern shot, there was an awesome explosion that forced *Barb* down sideways. Fluckey had hit an ammunition ship. Loughlin saw it blow up and "completely disintegrate in a sheet of fire, explosions and bursting shells." Fluckey went "deep" to 140 feet to reload. After dark, he surfaced.

About that time, Loughlin in *Queenfish* attacked, firing ten torpedoes: four at one ship, three each at two others. All torpedoes missed. "It seemed incredible," Loughlin wrote in his report, "but no explosions were seen or heard." Loughlin pulled off to reload.

Then it was Shepard's turn. Like Loughlin, he fired ten torpedoes in one great salvo: four at a tanker, three each at two freighters. Shepard got hits in at least two of his targets, maybe three. He pulled off to reload and Fluckey moved in for his second attack.

Fluckey fired six more torpedoes, three each at two targets. One blew up with another awesome explosion. Fluckey wrote later, "Three hits timed and observed followed by a stupendous earth-shaking eruption. This far surpassed Hollywood and is one of the biggest explosions of the war. . . . A high vacuum resulted in the boat. Personnel in the control room said they felt as if they were being sucked up the hatch." Loughlin saw this explosion, too.

Queenfish moved in for another attack. Loughlin picked out a tanker and fired four bow tubes. Two hit. A destroyer charged *Queenfish* and Loughlin fired two stern torpedoes down the throat. Both missed, forcing him to make evasion maneuvers. Meanwhile, Shepard in *Picuda* conducted a second attack.

No one is really certain who sank what in these series of attacks, but in the postwar accounting Fluckey was credited with sinking three ships: *Shinyo Maru*, a 5,892-ton freighter; *Anyo Maru*, a 9,256-ton transport; and *Sanyo Maru*, a 2,854-ton tanker. In addition, he shared one third credit with Loughlin and Shepard for sinking *Hokishima Maru*, another 2,854-ton tanker. The pack also inflicted severe damage on two freighters, *Meiho Maru* and *Hisagawa Maru*, and a 6,516-ton tanker, *Manju Maru*. Whatever the convoy was carrying never reached the Philippines.

In subsequent days, the boats of the pack operated more or less independently. On January 18, Loughlin picked up a small convoy near the China coast and fired eight torpedoes at several ships, but all of them missed. He returned to Pearl Harbor. Shepard in *Picuda* attacked a small convoy on January 29, firing his last torpedoes at a transport and freighter. He hit both, and the transport *Clyde Maru*, 5,500 tons, sank.

Gene Fluckey still had twelve torpedoes left. Although he hunted relentlessly, he could find no targets. Based on information from coast watchers in China and the China Air Force, he reasoned that the convoys were hugging the coast very close and holing up in harbors at night. When he received word on a northbound convoy, Fluckey closed the coast, mingled with some fishing craft, and confirmed his belief: radar showed a mass of ships anchored in Namkwan Harbor.

Fluckey decided the best way to get at these ships was simply to proceed up the long, ill-charted, and perhaps mine-infested channel into the harbor and shoot. He put his exec on the bridge to conn the ship and took station in the conning tower at the radar set. On the long and scary trip in, the fathometer registered 36 feet of water, sometimes less.

Once inside the harbor, Fluckey decided he would fire eight torpedoes, leaving four in case he had to shoot his way out through the escorts. He fired four bow tubes, range to targets 3,200 yards, swung around, and fired four stern tubes, range 3,000 yards. Ordering flank speed, he took station on the bridge. All over the harbor, he saw ships blowing up and firing guns. He believed he had sunk at least four, but postwar records credited him only one, *Taikyo Maru*, 5,244 tons. Threading her way through the junks and sampans to deep open water, *Barb* was not even scratched.

Fluckey fired his last four torpedoes at a freighter, but they all missed. After that he returned to Pearl Harbor, where he was received with a red carpet. His endorsements were ecstatic. One stated, "*Barb* is one of the finest fighting submarines this war has ever known." Fluckey was credited with sinking eight big ships for 60,000 tons and damaging four for 25,000 tons, making his total bag (sunk and damaged) 85,000 tons. The sinkings were reduced in postwar records to a total of four and one third for 24,197 tons.

For this outstanding performance, Gene Fluckey was awarded the Medal of Honor.

36

Submarine Command, December 1944

All during the fall of 1944, Lockwood was involved in a bitter feud with Louis Denfeld and Bob Rice in the Bureau of Personnel. Angry letters and radio dispatches flowed from Pearl Harbor almost daily. Lockwood objected strenuously to Admiral King's edict to trim his "overhead" of older men. He also accused Denfeld and Rice of raiding his staff of fine younger men to fill nonsubmarine jobs. He complained—repeatedly—about the shortage of qualified Naval Academy graduates available to command fleet boats. The shortage had forced him and Christie to reach down to the class of 1938 for skippers and even to appoint two reservists—Lewis (*Sterlet*) and Bissell (*Angler*)—to command. He accused Freeland Daubin of keeping too many qualified people in his outfit and complained that most submarine wardrooms were composed of "mere children."

In the end, Lockwood lost all these personnel battles. The skippers became younger and younger; more execs came from the reserve ranks. There was another game of musical chairs.

Gin Styer, commanding the Submarine School in New London, was slated to command a battleship. However, Freeland Daubin was relieved as Commander Submarines Atlantic, and sent to be commandant of the New York Navy Yard; Styer, promoted to rear admiral, took Daubin's job. Lockwood, still looking for a good job for Babe Brown (finally promoted to rear admiral), was disappointed, believing Brown should have had the Daubin job. As a consolation, Brown was named "Deputy Commander," Submarines Pacific Fleet.

Merrill Comstock, promoted to the honorary rank of commodore, remained as Lockwood's chief of staff. The "genius," Dick Voge, remained as Lockwood's operations officer. Tex McLean, commanding Squadron Sixteen, relieved Gin Styer in command of the sub school. McLean was relieved in Squadron Sixteen by Pilly Lent.

Swede Momsen, who had been relieved as commander of Squadron Four (and Two), worked briefly in the Navy Department's postal service and then was sent to command the battleship *South Dakota*. William Vincent O'Regan took over as commander of Squadron Four.

John Haines, who had been commanding the Brisbane submarines, was sent to command the battleship *New Mexico*.

Christie's chief of staff, P. G. Nichols, was relieved by Swede Bryant, commanding Squadron Eighteen. Dutch Will, who hoped to get Nichols's job, went back to the States to command a new squadron, Twenty-eight. Nichols, after making a war patrol on John Hyde's *Bergall*, went to be Deputy Chief of Staff (Personnel), 13th Naval District, Seattle, Washington. Swede Bryant was relieved as commander of Squadron Eighteen by Stan Moseley. Bull Wright replaced Murray Tichenor as operations officer.

John Griggs, commanding Squadron Twelve, was sent to command the cruiser *St. Louis*, and Weary Wilkins was appointed to command Squadron Twelve.

Willard Downes, commanding Squadron Eight, was sent to command the light cruiser *Boise*. He was relieved by George Edmund Peterson.

John Bailey Longstaff, commanding Squadron Fourteen, was sent to be chief of staff to the commandant of the 8th Naval District. He was replaced by Warren Dudley Wilkin.

Leo Leander Pace, commanding Squadron Twenty, left to relieve Swede Momsen in the navy's postal service. Lew Parks replaced Pace as commander of Squadron Twenty.

Charles Erck, commanding Squadron Ten, who was replaced by George Russell, was sent to command the navy's amphibious training base in Norfolk.

Shorty Edmunds, commanding Squadron Six, was sent to command the U.S. Naval Reserve Midshipman's School at Columbia University. His job was not filled. Squadron Six was more or less disbanded and moved to New London.

Joe Connolly, who began the war in Manila commanding a division, took command of a new squadron, Twenty-two. Turkey Neck Crawford, relieved as chief of staff to Commander Submarines Atlantic, took command of another new squadron, Twenty-four. Savvy Huffman got command of Squadron Twenty-six. Karl Hensel took command of Squadron Thirty and Kenneth Hurd (ex-*Seal*), Squadron Thirty-two. Freddy Warder became officer in charge of the Submarine School.

The biggest job change—and biggest shock—came to Ralph Christie: Admiral Kinkaid asked that Christie be relieved. Kinkaid gave no reasons for this decision. However, Christie and those close to him believed Kinkaid was upset with Christie because of his push for Sam Dealey's Medal of Honor and for his habit of presenting medals to some skippers at dockside. Kinkaid may also have been upset over the loss of his nephew, Manning Kimmel, on *Robalo* (and other Christie losses).

The dispatch pronouncing this change arrived in late November. It named Jimmy Fife, recently promoted to rear admiral, as Christie's relief. Christie noted in his diary, "Received about the same news I got two years ago and I don't like it any better: detachment and same relief, Fife. It disturbed my sleep."

As he had two years before in Brisbane, Christie took immediate steps to have the orders revoked. He flew up to Hollandia to see Kinkaid and Van Hook. Both men were away. Christie took the matter up with Kinkaid's staff. There was then a plan afoot to shift the Brisbane submarine unit to Subic Bay, Luzon, after that place had been recaptured. Christie suggested that he stay on until this shift had been made—perhaps another six months.

It was no use. Jimmy Fife, who had been in Washington close to Admirals King and Edwards, was on his way to Perth, via Pearl Harbor, and was determined to get the job. He arrived in Pearl Harbor December 13, where he found Nimitz and Lockwood preparing to move their headquarters forward to Guam. Lockwood was disappointed that Babe Brown had not been selected to replace Christie, but he wrote Fife that he was "delighted" at Fife's appointment. The two men conferred for two days, planning future operations and discussing Fife's move forward to Subic Bay. Fife left for Australia on December 15.

While Fife was en route to his new post, Kinkaid sent a message to the Secretary of the Navy which seemed to Lockwood to imply that

Kinkaid might want to delay the change of command, as Christie had proposed. Lockwood radioed Fife in the Admiralties to detour via Leyte, where Kinkaid and Van Hook were then basing, to clear the matter up.

Fife found Kinkaid in his flagship, *Wasatch*. When Fife inquired what was going on—whether Christie would stay—Kinkaid said Christie had "given him the impression Daubin was coming out" to relieve Christie. Fife later wrote Lockwood, "Admiral Kinkaid said had he known I was lined up he would not have agreed to sending any messages . . . he seemed to me genuinely pleased that I was out here and was familiar with the geography."

Fife went on to Perth, where he arrived Christmas Eve. Kinkaid had told him to take over in a "day or two," but Christie dragged his heels. The official relieving ceremony did not take place until December 30. After it, Christie stayed on for a few days of leave and recreation and then returned to the States, having been informed by Kinkaid that he would be recommended for a Distinguished Service Medal.

Christie went to Washington to confer with the navy high command. His next job was to be commandant of the Puget Sound Navy Yard, Bremerton, Washington. This assignment, Christie noted in his diary, "doesn't thrill me." He asked Admiral Edwards why he had been relieved and sent to this shore job. Later Christie said, "Admiral Edwards evaded my question . . . saying only that I had done a very super job and since our submarine war was about over, he was mighty glad to have me to help with a very bad situation in Bremerton."

While in Washington, Christie ran into the chairman of the U.S. Navy's Board of Awards and Decorations. Before Christie could even say hello, the chairman said, "Christie, every member of my board wanted to give Dealey the Medal of Honor but we couldn't because of Kinkaid's endorsement. Why don't you put in a request for reconsideration now that you are out from under Kinkaid? The routing now will go through MacArthur first, then Kinkaid."

After Christie arrived at Bremerton, he followed the chairman's advice. MacArthur promptly approved the award and, as Christie later said, "Kinkaid hardly had the nerve to stand in the way." The Medal of Honor was awarded posthumously to Dealey's widow—a tardy consolation for Edwina Dealey and at best a Pyrrhic victory for Ralph Christie.

37

Summary, 1944

The third year of the submarine war against Japan was devastatingly effective. During the year, and allowing for losses, the force level increased another thirty-three boats. These additions, plus the use of advance bases in Milne Bay, Manus, Mios Woendi, Majuro, Saipan, and Guam, enabled the three commanders to mount a total of 520 war patrols (some double-barreled), compared to about 350 in 1941–42 and 1943. The commands claimed sinking 849½ men-of-war and merchant ships for about 5.1 million tons. The postwar records credited 603 ships for about 2.7 million tons. This was more shipping and tonnage than in 1941, 1942, and 1943 combined (515 ships for 2.2 million tons).

The 1944 sinkings drastically impeded Japanese shipping services. Imports of bulk commodities fell from 16.4 million tons in 1943 to a disastrous 10 million tons. At the beginning of 1944 the Japanese had 4.1 million tons of merchant shipping afloat, excluding tankers. At the end of 1944 this figure had declined to about 2 million tons, excluding tankers. As for tanker tonnage, the Japanese began the year with 863,000 tons, built 204 tankers for 624,000 tons, and ended the year with 869,000 tons. Including tankers and merchant ships, the net loss in 1944 was over 2 million tons.

The flow of oil from the southern regions to Japan was almost completely stopped after the invasion of Mindoro. In September 1944 (in spite of all the losses), about 700,000 tons of Japanese tanker tonnage was engaged in transporting oil from the south to the home islands. By the end of the year this figure had been reduced to about 200,000 tons. Reserve stocks were so low that Japanese leaders launched experiments in making oil from potatoes.

U.S. submarines took a heavy toll of Japanese men-of-war. During the year there were about one hundred contacts on major Japanese fleet units. These developed roughly into ten attacks against battleships, twenty-five attacks against aircraft carriers, fifteen attacks against heavy cruisers, and twenty attacks against light cruisers. U.S. submarines sank one battleship, seven aircraft carriers, two heavy cruisers, seven light cruisers, about thirty destroyers, and seven submarines. In addition, they severely damaged the carrier *Junyo* and four heavy cruisers: *Myoko, Aoba, Takao,* and *Kumano.*

The major sinkings were:

Carriers and Battleships

Shokaku (30,000 tons)	June 19	*Cavalla* (Kossler)
Taiho (31,000 tons)	June 19	*Albacore* (Blanchard)
Taiyo (Otaka) (20,000 tons)	August 18	*Rasher* (Munson)
Unyo (20,000 tons)	September 16	*Barb* (Fluckey)
Jinyo (Shinyo) (21,000 tons)	November 17	*Spadefish* (Underwood)
Kongo (31,000 tons)	November 21	*Sealion II* (Reich)
Shinano (59,000 tons)	November 29	*Archerfish* (Enright)
Unryu (18,500 tons)	December 19	*Redfish* (McGregor)

Cruisers

Agano (7,000 tons)	February 16	*Skate* (Gruner)
Tatsuta (3,300 tons)	March 13	*Sandlance* (Garrison)
Yubari (3,500 tons)	April 27	*Bluegill* (Barr)
Oi (5,700 tons)	July 19	*Flasher* (Whitaker)
Nagara (5,700 tons)	August 7	*Croaker* (Lee)
Natori (5,700 tons)	August 18	*Hardhead* (McMaster)
Maya (12,200 tons)	October 23	*Dace* (Claggett)
Atago (12,000 tons)	October 23	*Darter* (McClintock)
Tama (5,200 tons)*	October 25	*Jallao* (Icenhower)

U.S. submarine losses continued to mount. Lockwood lost thirteen fleet boats† and Christie lost six,‡ for a total of nineteen, compared to seven in 1942 (excluding S-26, lost in the Gulf of Panama) and fifteen in 1943 (excluding *Dorado* and *R-12,* lost in the Atlantic). In addition, S-28, commanded by a reservist, J. G. Campbell, was

* Previously damaged by naval aircraft.
† *Scorpion, Grayback, Trout, Tullibee, Gudgeon, Herring, Golet, Shark II, Tang, Escolar, Albacore, Scamp,* and *Swordfish.*
‡ *Robalo, Flier, Harder, Seawolf, Darter,* and *Growler.*

lost in a training accident at Pearl Harbor. Forty-nine men died on S-28.

During 1944 lifeguarding became big business for the submarine force; Pacific submarines rescued 117 navy and air corps airmen. Dick O'Kane in *Tang* was the leading rescuer, having picked up 22 airmen in his daring cruise off Truk.

During the year, twenty-three older submarines were retired from combat or readied for retirement* and three (*Barbero, Halibut,* and *Redfish*) were retired because of battle damage. Most of the famous old boats went to training duties.

Japanese submarines, many detailed to resupply missions, continued to be ineffective and to suffer heavy losses. Japanese submarines deployed to stop the invasions of the Marshalls, Marianas, Palaus, and Philippines achieved almost nothing. During the year, the Japanese submarine force lost fifty-six boats—seven to U.S. submarines.

The "skipper problem" in the U.S. submarine force remained constant. There was always a shortage and always nonproductivity. During the year, perhaps 35 of about 250 skippers were relieved for nonproductivity. This was 14 percent, compared to 30 percent in 1942 and about 14 percent in 1943. Both Lockwood and Christie were forced to dip down to the class of 1938 for new skippers and even to use a few reserve officers, who had been steadfastly denied command during three years of war. The impetus came from Admiral Nimitz: foreseeing a large postwar navy which would have to be manned for the most part by reservists, Nimitz encouraged Lockwood (and others) to give them credit and command. After Lewis (*Sterlet*), Bissell (*Angler*), and Hunnicutt (*Carp*), four more reservists were named in 1945, making a total of seven reserve officers who commanded fleet boats on war patrol in World War II.

During the 520 war patrols in 1944, Pacific submarines fired a total of 6,092 torpedoes. This was more than all the boats had fired in 1942 and 1943 put together (5,379). In spite of improved torpedo performance on both the Mark XIV steam and Mark XVIII electric, statistically it took an average 10 torpedoes to sink a ship—compared to 8 in 1942 and 11.7 in 1943. One reason was that many skippers, no longer under orders to conserve torpedoes, fired full salvos. Another was that submarines, generally, encountered many more big

---

* *Gar, Greenling, Narwhal, Nautilus, Permit, Plunger, Pollack, Sailfish, Salmon, Sargo, Saury, Seadragon, Seal, Searaven, Skipjack, Snapper, Spearfish, Stingray, Sturgeon, Tambor, Tarpon, Tautog,* and *Tuna.*

targets (and convoys) deserving of full salvos. Again, skippers reported many more hits for damage. Had the torpedo warheads been larger—as large as Japanese submarine torpedo warheads—many more ships would have gone to the bottom.

For all practical purposes, the U.S. submarine war against Japanese shipping ended in December 1944. The enemy ships that were left were forced to operate in the confined waters of the Sea of Japan or the Yellow Sea, running very close to shore and holing up in harbors at night, making it almost impossible for submarines to get at them.

Part VI

38

Pearl Harbor and Guam,
January through March 1945

The U.S. Invasions of Iwo Jima and Okinawa

By January 1945 the war that had involved most of the world since 1939 was drawing to a close. In Europe, General Eisenhower's troops were poised to drive for the Rhine River. The Russian army crossed the Vistula and swept toward Germany from the east. In four months Hitler would be crushed, Germany defeated.

In the Pacific, Japan was almost beaten. Her navy had been reduced to a few remaining units, notably the carrier-battleships *Ise* and *Hyuga* in Singapore and the super-battleship *Yamato* in the Inland Sea. The merchant marine had been riddled by U.S. submarines and carrier aviation. In the homeland, there was almost no oil for the fleet or aviation gasoline for the aircraft. Production of new weapons had fallen off drastically for want of raw materials and electricity.

President Roosevelt and Prime Minister Churchill had agreed—and let it be known—that Japan would not be permitted to surrender except unconditionally. There would be no deals. Japan must lay down all her arms, give up all conquered territory, and face total occupation by Allied troops. Her leaders (except perhaps the Emperor) would be tried for war crimes.

Few militarists believed Japanese leaders would accept these terms. Almost everywhere that Allied troops had met Japanese troops, they had encountered fanatical, suicidal resistance. Kamikazes (and their submarine counterparts, the *kaitens*) were still being trained by the hundreds. Nimitz and MacArthur concluded that Japan could only finally and totally be brought to her knees by an invasion of the homeland, an immense enterprise that would probably cost many hundreds of thousands of Allied casualties.

Most of the military planning was now dominated by this objective. The initial plan, Operation Olympic, called for an invasion of Kyushu, the southernmost Japanese home island, on November 1. To support it, Allied navies, armies, and air forces from all over the world would converge in the Pacific. The troops would stage from the Marianas, the Philippines, and Okinawa, scheduled to be seized in April.

Part of the overall plan for crushing Japan was to subject the homeland to massive bomber attack by B-29 Superfortresses basing from the Marianas. During late 1944, the U.S. Air Force built airstrips and supply depots on Saipan, Guam, and Tinian. The strikes, begun in November, continued regularly thereafter. The bombers did not do as well as expected. It was a 3,000-mile round trip from the Marianas to Tokyo. In order to make it, the bombers had to reduce their pay load from ten to three tons of bombs. Since fighter planes had nowhere near that range, the bombers had to fly unescorted. To protect themselves, they flew—and bombed—from high altitude (28,000 feet) where precision was impossible. Going and coming to Japan, they were attacked by Japanese fighters based in the Volcano and Bonin islands.

The logical solution to the bomber problem was to seize a way station in the Bonins: Iwo Jima. With Iwo Jima in Allied hands, Japanese interdiction would cease. U.S. fighters basing on Iwo Jima could escort the bombers to and from Tokyo. Iwo Jima could also provide a base for air rescue teams to hunt for downed pilots and an emergency strip for damaged B-29s returning from Japan.

This plan—code-named Operation Detachment—was approved and the job handed to Admiral Nimitz, who designated Admiral Spruance overall naval commander. Halsey stepped down to plan the follow-on invasion of Okinawa. In accordance with custom, the Fleet designation was changed from Third to Fifth and the Fast Carrier Task Force from 38 to 58. The invasion date was set for February 19.

As a preliminary to the invasion, Spruance decided to conduct a carrier strike on Tokyo on February 16–17. The main objective of this strike was to find and destroy Japanese air and sea power that might be thrown against the Iwo Jima invasion forces—in short, to "isolate" Iwo Jima. Spruance knew that *Yamato* and some other old battleships, heavy cruisers, and one or two new carriers were basing in Japanese waters. Perhaps he hoped they might make a suicidal dash at his mighty fleet and be destroyed.

In a reincarnation of Burt's Brooms, Lockwood provided eight submarines to conduct an antipicket sweep for Task Force 58. This time the plan was more sophisticated. Three of the boats were ordered to conduct a noisy, blatant diversionary sweep aimed toward the Inland Sea. The other five were ordered to proceed ahead of Task Force 58, blasting pickets from the seas by making undetected attacks with the homing torpedoes, or Cuties. The hope was that a picket hit by a Cutie would blow up and sink before it could get off a radio warning.

The five submarines leading the real cleanup toward Honshu were *Sterlet, Pomfret, Piper, Trepang,* and *Bowfin.* This unit, known as "Mac's Mops," was commanded by Barney McMahon, skipper of the new boat *Piper.* Mac's Mops went to work about February 10. None of the boats found any pickets and thus had no chance to experiment further with the Cuties. Afterward, the five boats deployed off Tokyo as lifeguard submarines.

The three boats assigned to the diversionary sweep—toward Shikoku and access to the Inland Sea—were *Haddock, Lagarto,* and *Sennet.* This unit, known as "Latta's Lances," was commanded by Frank Latta (ex-*Narwhal*) in the new boat *Lagarto.* Bill Brockman, now a division commander, took command of *Haddock* for this one patrol, replacing Beetle Roach, who had been injured in a jeep accident on Saipan. The Lances carried out their job well, making a lot of noise and even turning on searchlights at night. The group destroyed three pickets. Afterward, Latta in *Lagarto* sank a small freighter and a submarine, *RO-49,* off Bungo Suido. George Porter, commanding *Sennet,* sank a small coastal minelayer.

Task Force 58, helped by foul overcast weather, reached launch position off Japan without being detected and Spruance sent his planes over Tokyo. Hampered by the same foul weather, they did little damage.

Pomfret, commanded by John Hess, made a spectacular rescue. A pilot from the carrier *Cabot* was forced to ditch in the outer waters

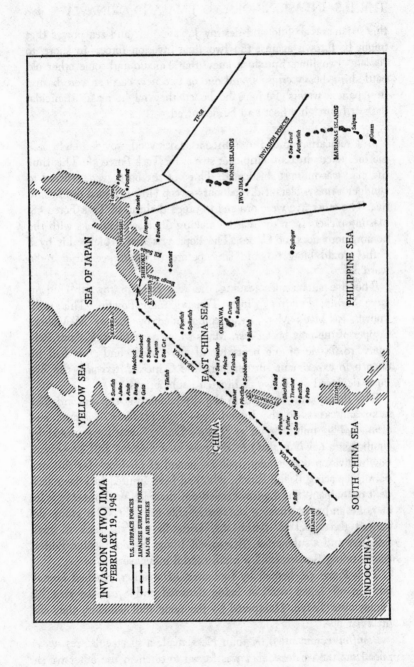

INVASION of IWO JIMA
FEBRUARY 19, 1945

U.S. SURFACE FORCES
JAPANESE SURFACE FORCES
MAJOR AIR STRIKES

SEA OF JAPAN

YELLOW SEA

KOREA

HONSHU

SHIKOKU

KYUSHU

KII Suido

Bungo Suido

Osumi Gunto

TF 58

Tokyo

Piper
Pipefish
Pomfret
Sterlet
Trepang
Bowfin
Sennet
Sea Cat
Tilefish

Plaice
Spikefish

EAST CHINA SEA

OKINAWA
Drum
Billfish

Sea Panther
Plaice
Finback
Scabbardfish
Bluefish

Balao
Atule
Bang
Gato
Sunfish
Haddock
Razorback
Segundo
Lagarto

FORMOSA

BONIN ISLANDS

IWO JIMA

INVASION FORCES

Sea Devil
Archerfish

MARIANAS ISLANDS
Saipan
Guam

PHILIPPINE SEA

Springer

Rasher
Blackfish
Shad
Bluefish
Thresher
Batfish
Peto

Piranha
Puffer
Sea Owl

LUZON

CHINA

Bullhead

HAINAN

SOUTH CHINA SEA

INDOCHINA

of Tokyo Bay. Fighters circled over *Pomfret*, guiding Hess to the rubber life raft. Hess fearlessly took *Pomfret* into these restricted waters and rescued the pilot, Ensign R. L. Buchanan. During this same bold operation, Hess picked up another pilot, Lieutenant Joseph P. Farrell from *Hornet*, and a Japanese pilot. War correspondent Ernie Pyle devoted a column to the rescue entitled "Even If You Was Shot Down in Tokyo Harbor, the Navy Would Be In to Get You."

The Mops had other adventures. *Bowfin*'s skipper, Alexander Kelly Tyree, younger brother of John Tyree, rescued two more aviators and sank what was believed to be a destroyer but which postwar records identified as an 800-ton frigate. Reservist Hugh Lewis, in *Sterlet*, sank a 1,150-ton freighter. Allen Russell Faust, commanding *Trepang*, sank two small freighters for 2,261 tons.

After this swipe at Japan, Spruance took Task Force 58 southward to hit Iwo Jima. On February 19, the invasion forces went ashore as planned. They met fierce resistance, and the fighting went on for three bloody weeks. Kamikaze pilots hit the old carrier *Saratoga*, causing 300 casualties, and sank the jeep carrier *Bismarck Sea*, with the loss of 350 men. Before the island was secure, U.S. casualties totaled 17,000—7,000 dead. Soon after the island was secure, air force fighters moved there and began assisting the B-29s in raiding Japan.

After lending support to the Iwo Jima invasion, Task Force 58 wheeled around and hit Tokyo again, coordinating the assault with a massive B-29 raid. The 200 B-29s were carrying new incendiary bombs to test their efficiency against what were believed to be the highly inflammable residential districts of Tokyo. In this "test," the B-29s burned out 2 square miles of the city. The carrier planes, attacking military targets, destroyed about 150 Japanese planes. After that, Task Force 58 swung south to Ulithi to rest and replenish for the next mission: the invasion of Okinawa.

In early March, the air force launched an all-out B-29 fire raid against major Japanese cities. On the night of March 9–10, about 334 B-29s left bases in the Marianas and bombed Tokyo from low level. The bombs burned out 15 square miles of the city, destroying 267,000 buildings. About 84,000 people were killed and 40,000 wounded during that one night, and over a million were left homeless. In subsequent raids, the air force hit Nagoya, Kobe, Osaka, Yokohama, and Kawasaki, killing and wounding tens of thousands

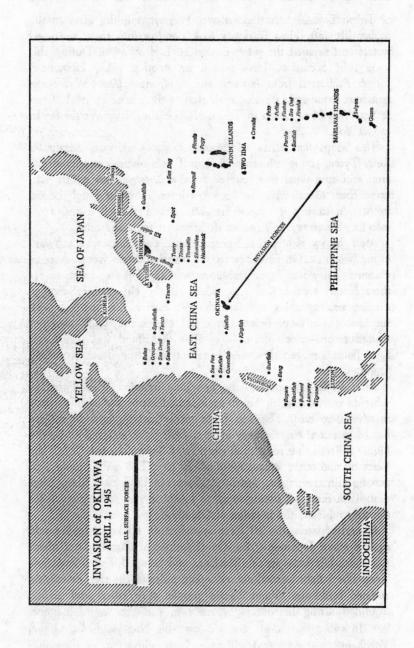

INVASION of OKINAWA
APRIL 1, 1945

— U.S. SURFACE FORCES

SEA OF JAPAN

YELLOW SEA

KOREA

HONSHU

Tokyo

• Guardfish

SHIKOKU

Kii Suido

KYUSHU

Bungo Suido

CHINA

• Babo
• Grouper
• Spadefish
• Sea Devil
• Tench
• Seahorse

• Sea Fox
• Swiftish
• Queenfish

• Tirante

• Tunny
• Tinosa
• Threadfin
• Silversides
• Hackleback

• Spot

• Sea Dog

EAST CHINA SEA

OKINAWA

• Icefish

• Kingfish

FORMOSA

• Sunfish

• Bang

• Bugara
• Blackfish
• Bullhead
• Lamprey
• Tigrone

LUZON

• Ronquil

BONIN ISLANDS

• Picuda
• Pogy

IWO JIMA

• Crevalle

INVASION FORCES

PHILIPPINE SEA

• Peto
• Puffer
• Finback
• Sea Owl
• Piranha

• Parche
• Sunfish

MARIANAS ISLANDS

Saipan

Guam

SOUTH CHINA SEA

HAINAN

INDOCHINA

more. In all, these bombers destroyed 105 square miles of Japanese cities—including half of Tokyo. Still there was no sign that Japanese leaders were ready to surrender.

The navy, meanwhile, continued plans for the invasion of Okinawa, code-named Operation Iceberg. Lockwood's submarines played a small role in the preliminaries. *Swordfish* had already been lost while conducting a reconnaissance mission there, photographing the beaches. Dick Latham had charted minefields with the new FM sonar. George Pierce in *Tunny*, using the FM gear (plus plenty of nerve), plotted the location of 222 mines, later swept up by U.S. forces. The information on mines proved useful to the amphibious forces.

As a preliminary to the invasion, Spruance again attacked the Japanese home islands with Task Force 58. This time the targets were Kyushu and the fleet unit in the Inland Sea. U.S. aircraft destroyed dozens of Japanese planes on the ground and in the air but inflicted only light damage on targets inside the Inland Sea. They missed several prizes: the super-battleship *Yamato* and two new carriers, *Amagi* and *Katsuragi*.

During this action, March 18–19, the Japanese counterattacked Task Force 58. Japanese planes bombed the carriers *Enterprise*, *Yorktown*, *Franklin*, and *Wasp*. *Franklin* was severely damaged, and more than 700 crewmen were killed, but the ship, racked by fire and exploding stores, was saved by a brave and efficient damage-control party. Later, she headed for the United States under her own steam, to finish out the war in a navy yard.

During the strikes on Kyushu, many of Lockwood's submarines served as lifeguards and lookouts, should *Yamato* steam out of the Inland Sea. Douglas Hammond in *Guardfish* joined two boats left over from Mac's Mops, *Sterlet* and *Bowfin*, to guard Kii Suido. *Guardfish* began one day by dodging a torpedo from a Japanese submarine and then surfacing in sight of land to pick up two airmen from the carrier *Hancock*. Alex Tyree in *Bowfin* picked up two more.

Two submarines in this concentration between Japan and Okinawa were lost. The first was *Kete*, making her second patrol under Edward Ackerman, one of the first officers from the class of 1939 to command a fleet boat. On March 10, Ackerman attacked a convoy, sinking three small freighters for 6,881 tons. On March 20, he broadcast a special report for Spruance. Nothing further was heard from *Kete*. Jasper Holmes thought she may have been sunk by a Japanese submarine en route to Okinawa, but he could never confirm his belief.

The second boat lost was the famous old *Trigger*, commanded by David Rikart Connole. On March 18 and March 27, Connole sank two small ships for 2,500 tons. Nothing further was heard from him either.

Lockwood organized some of the boats into combinations of wolf packs. In late March, he ordered Earl Twining Hydeman to form a pack consisting of Hydeman's *Sea Dog*, *Trigger*, and *Threadfin*, commanded by John Joseph Foote. When the response from *Trigger* was only silence, Lockwood gave up forming that pack. He ordered *Sea Dog* to carry out an individual patrol and *Threadfin* to join a new pack consisting of John Nichols in *Silversides* and Frederick Emery Janney, commanding a new Cramp boat, *Hackleback*. This pack moved north to cover Bungo Suido.

A second pack moved up to take position south of Nichols's pack. The threesome, commanded by Arthur Chester Smith in a new boat, *Trutta*, included another new one, *Lionfish*, commanded by the son of Admiral Spruance, Edward Spruance, and *Parche*, commanded by Woodrow Wilson McCrory, Ramage's old exec. On leaving Saipan, *Trutta* struck a submerged cable and damaged a propeller, so while *Parche* and *Lionfish* proceeded on patrol, *Trutta* followed a few days behind. Another boat, *Crevalle*, commanded by Everett Hartwell Steinmetz, patrolled in the same area.

The landings on Okinawa, supported by Task Force 58, proceeded as scheduled on April 1. Within the first five days, Japanese kamikazes hit thirty-nine naval vessels, including Spruance's flagship *Indianapolis*, two old battleships, three cruisers, and a jeep carrier. On April 6, 355 kamikaze planes attacked Task Force 58 and the landing beaches, sinking two destroyers, *Bush* and *Calhoun*, and damaging many others.

On about April 5, Admiral Toyoda ordered the super-battleship *Yamato*, the light cruiser *Yahagi*, and eight destroyers to get under way for Okinawa, their mission to damage further the landing craft and support vessels he hoped were already badly smashed up by the kamikaze raids. The commander of this unit, Vice Admiral Seiichi Ito, could find no more than 2,500 barrels of oil, not enough for a round trip. Clearly it had to be a one-way suicidal voyage. Toyoda

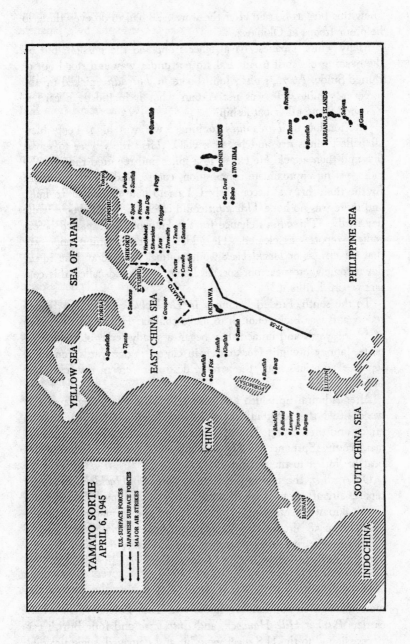

YAMATO SORTIE
APRIL 6, 1945

———— U.S. SURFACE FORCES
- - - - JAPANESE SURFACE FORCES
====▷ MAJOR AIR STRIKES

SEA OF JAPAN

YELLOW SEA

KOREA

HONSHU

Tokyo

Parche
Sunfish

Spot
Picuda
Sea Dog
Trigger

SHIKOKU

Seahorse
Hackleback
Silversides
Kete
Tench
Threadfin
Sennet

KYUSHU

Tjunta
Spadefish

EAST CHINA SEA

Grouper

Trutta
Crevalle
Lionfish

YAMATO

OKINAWA

TF-58

Queenfish
Sea Fox
Icefish
Kingfish

Sawfish

Burrfish
Baya

FORMOSA

Blackfish
Bullhead
Lamprey
Tigrone
Bugara

CHINA

SOUTH CHINA SEA

HAINAN

INDOCHINA

LUZON

PHILIPPINE SEA

BONIN ISLANDS

IWO JIMA

Sea Devil
Bebo

Tinos
Bowfish

Ronquil

MARIANAS ISLANDS

Saipan

Guam

knew this but, as he said after the war, "We had to do everything to help our troops at Okinawa."

Many senior Japanese naval officers opposed the mission, but on the evening of April 6 Admiral Ito got under way and stood out of Bungo Suido. At 7:44 P.M., John Foote in *Threadfin* picked up the force at 5 miles. He was not certain what it included: a carrier? *Yamato?* Some other battleship?

The tension in *Threadfin's* conning tower was high. Foote blew all ballast tanks dry and began a chase. His orders were to report first and then attack. He closed to 4 miles and reported the force by radio, giving approximate composition, course, and speed—22 knots. By the time this was accomplished, *Yamato* had opened to 10 miles and there was no hope *Threadfin* could catch up. Later, Foote wrote dejectedly, "*Threadfin's* chance for the Hall of Fame passed before contact report was cleared." He added, "Our remaining hope was that *Silversides* or *Hackleback* would [attack and] slow [the force] down somewhere near our speed." Later, Lockwood called this contact report "brilliant."

To the south, Frederick Janney in *Hackleback* picked up Foote's report and was lucky enough to make contact. He found the group at 25,000 yards and immediately began a steady series of contact reports. Janney brought *Hackleback* in close (13,000 yards) on three separate occasions, but the strong destroyer screen thwarted any hope of attack.

After Admiral Spruance had been told what was going on, Lockwood lifted the report-attack restriction, freeing all submarines to attack and then report. However, none of the other boats made contact. Young Spruance in *Lionfish* missed a golden opportunity to beat his father to the punch.

On April 7, the morning after the *Threadfin-Hackleback* contact report, aircraft from Task Force 58, which had moved northward from Okinawa to intercept *Yamato,* found the formation. At noon, Task Force 58 aircraft struck, sinking *Yamato, Yahagi,* and two of the destroyers; two other destroyers were so badly damaged the Japanese sank them before fleeing to the nearest friendly port.

During the days and weeks that followed, kamikaze pilots inflicted more damage on the landing forces and Task Force 58. The U.S. carriers *Bunker Hill, Hancock,* and *Enterprise* and four British carriers assigned to the U.S. fleet were hit and damaged, some severely.

In all, a dozen destroyers were sunk, including *Mannert L. Abele,* named for the skipper of *Grunion,* lost on her first patrol.

The fighting on Okinawa dragged on for weeks. When the island was finally secure, the United States counted 13,000 dead, nearly 5,000 of them navy. Many B-29s had been diverted to support the U.S. Navy, carrying out strikes on airfields on the Ryukyus and elsewhere and planting mines in Japanese seaports. On May 11 they were released to resume their main objective of destroying Japanese cities, aircraft factories, shipyards, and other industrial targets. Day after day they flew over Japan by the score, dropping tens of thousands of tons of bombs, but Japan hung on stubbornly.

Patrols from Guam

Throughout this period, Lockwood, who had established his main headquarters in Guam on the tender *Holland,* continued to send submarines on patrol, singly or in wolf packs. A number of these were assigned to lifeguard duty and rescued many downed pilots. Others cruised Luzon Strait and the East China and Yellow seas. Lockwood was running out of sea room—and targets.

A wolf pack led by Joe Enright in *Archerfish* took station in Luzon Strait. The other boats were *Batfish,* commanded by Jake Fyfe, and *Blackfish,* commanded by Robert Sellars.

About the time this pack reached Luzon Strait, the codebreakers picked up information that the Japanese intended to evacuate some pilots from Luzon to Formosa by submarine. The four boats detailed to this mission were *RO-46, RO-112, RO-113,* and *RO-115.* The routes and sailing dates were relayed to Enright, who deployed his pack in a probable intercept position in the strait. The pack was joined by another made up of *Plaice, Scabbardfish,* and *Sea Poacher.*

The scouting line waited patiently. On the night of February 9, at about 10:15, Jake Fyfe in *Batfish* picked up radar emissions on a device known as the APR. A little later, he got radar contact at 6 miles. Believing this to be one of the Japanese submarines southbound from Formosa, he closed to 1,850 yards and fired three torpedoes. All missed. The Japanese skipper evidently did not see the torpedoes; he continued on course. When only 1,000 yards away, Fyfe fired three more torpedoes. One ran hot in the tube, but the second hit the sub, causing a "brilliant red explosion that lit up the whole sky." This was RO-115.

The following morning Fyfe intended to remain on the surface for a daylight search, but friendly aircraft (perhaps also looking for the Japanese submarines) drove him under. At about 10 A.M., when Fyfe came up to have a look through his periscope, the friendly planes attacked Batfish, firing an aerial torpedo. Fyfe went deep in a hurry. The torpedo passed over Batfish. "A tender moment," Fyfe wrote later, "and a very unfriendly act."

Plaice, Scabbardfish, and Sea Poacher left the scouting line to patrol elsewhere. Batfish, Archerfish, and Blackfish remained in position. On the evening of February 11, shortly after surfacing to charge batteries, Fyfe again picked up radar emissions on his APR. Then he saw a Japanese submarine, range 1,200 yards. As Fyfe was setting up to fire, the submarine dived. Fyfe thought that was that, but the sub surfaced again half an hour later, giving off radar emissions. Fyfe made an end around and at about ten o'clock fired four torpedoes from the point-blank range of 880 yards. Fyfe later wrote, "The target literally blew apart and sank almost immediately." This was RO-112, southbound from Formosa.

The next night, shortly after midnight, Fyfe again picked up Japanese radar emissions on APR. At 2:15, he made contact on his own radar, range 5 miles. Fyfe moved in but the sub dived. An hour later, Fyfe picked the target up on radar again and attacked, firing three torpedoes from 1,500 yards. One hit, and the submarine blew up in a "large yellow ball of fire." This was RO-113, southbound from Formosa.

On the following evening, February 14, Joe Enright in Archerfish believed he picked up yet another Japanese submarine. Firing two salvos of four torpedoes, he saw a "large white flash" that illuminated the target and believed he sank a submarine. Lockwood credited him with the sinking, but postwar records did not bear it out. After this attack, the pack returned to Saipan and Guam.

Joe Willingham, on the first patrol of Tautog, had sunk two Japanese submarines and nearly sunk two or three more, but no other skipper had ever actually sunk three on one patrol, let alone three in three days. Lockwood, sparing no praise, called Fyfe's performance "brilliant." The Japanese gave up trying to evacuate the aviators by submarine. Counting RO-49, sunk by Frank Latta in Lagarto on

February 24, the Japanese lost four boats to U.S. submarines in February.

In April the Japanese lost another. Carter Bennett, returning to Pearl Harbor in *Sea Owl* at the end of a long unrewarding wolf-pack patrol in Luzon Strait and the South China Sea, received an Ultra reporting a Japanese submarine en route from Japan to Wake Island on a resupply mission. "It was very specific information," Bennett said later. Bennett had a tough time finding the sub, but on the morning of April 16 he picked it up 7 miles northwest of the island. Taking his time to be sure of a kill, Bennett tracked the boat "playing hide and seek," but it slipped into the Wake anchorage before he could shoot. Seeing the sub anchored at the boat landing, Bennett crept into shallow water submerged and fired his torpedoes. *RO-56* blew up and sank.

The U.S. submarine *Snook*, commanded by John Walling, was lost in April. After patrolling in Luzon Strait with a pack led by Hiram Cassedy in *Tigrone*, Walling was assigned on April 12 to lifeguard east of Formosa for a British carrier strike. On April 20, the British officer commanding the force reported a plane down in *Snook*'s vicinity and requested Walling to rescue. Walling did not reply. Nothing more was ever heard from him. *Snook* disappeared with all hands. There was no clue in Japanese records as to her loss.

Bill Post, ex-*Gudgeon*, brought out a new boat, *Spot*. On his first patrol, he led a pack called "Post's Panzers" (*Spot, Icefish,* and *Balao*) to the coast of China, firing off all his torpedoes. He believed he had sunk four ships and was so credited, but postwar records failed to confirm any. During the patrol, Post emulated his feats on *Gudgeon* by conducting a gun attack on a fairly large auxiliary. After he had disabled it, he sent over a boarding party, which gathered intelligence data and got a prisoner. During the boarding, the ship sank. Four of Post's men jumped on *Spot*, but three others had to be fished from the water.

On his second patrol, commencing in March, Post led another threesome, "Post's Panzers II." The other boats were *Sea Fox*, commanded by Roy Craig Klinker, and *Queenfish*, commanded by Elliott Loughlin. *Sea Fox* had recently suffered a senseless tragedy. While the crew was resting at Camp Dealey on Guam, seven enlisted men persuaded a native Guamanian to take them on a strictly forbidden souvenir hunt in the jungles. A group of about thirty Japanese holdouts ambushed the sightseers, shooting them with carbines. Six, including the guide, died instantly. Two of *Sea Fox's* crewmen, badly wounded, managed to crawl off and survive.

Post took the pack to northern Formosa Strait, patrolling close off the coast of China. He found action right away, again firing all his torpedoes. He sank *Nanking Maru*, a 3,000-ton freighter, and shared half credit with navy aircraft for sinking *Ikomasaw Maru*, a 3,173-ton transport. He again engaged in a running gun battle with a fairly large vessel, a minelayer which came within 100 yards of ramming *Spot*. After this, Post requested permission to return to Guam for more torpedoes.

On the way to Guam, Post had a harrowing experience. After sunset on the evening of March 31, *Spot* encountered a friendly destroyer of Task Force 58, supporting the Okinawa invasion, U.S.S. *Case*. *Case* was in a "safe" submarine zone and was prohibited from attacking any submarine unless it had been identified as enemy "beyond possibility of doubt." *Case* made some attempt at exchanging recognition signals but then opened fire with her guns from 3,000 to 4,000 yards. After *Case* had fired three shots, Post fired a red flare and dived. The skipper of *Case* then realized his error and ceased firing. Post made it into Guam without further incident. After this, he stepped down as skipper of *Spot* and was promoted to command a division.

With Post gone, command of the pack, now reduced to *Queenfish* and *Sea Fox*, devolved upon the senior man, Elliott Loughlin in *Queenfish*. While they were patrolling, a curious drama was coming to its climax which would directly involve Loughlin. It had begun in mid-1944. The U.S. government, concerned over the brutal treatment given U.S. prisoners of war in the southern territories, had asked Japan (through neutral Switzerland) if she would transport Red Cross packages provided by the United States from Japan to the southern regions. The Japanese were initially cold to the idea. But after the sea lanes to the south had been cut, they seized on the request as a way of surreptitiously shipping some ammunition and supplies to cut-off troops and returning hundreds of stranded sea captains and crewmen to Japan.

Accordingly, in February 1945, the U.S. request was granted. The Japanese picked huge *Awa Maru* and loaded her with tons upon tons of spare aircraft parts and ammunition, along with a mere 2,000 tons of relief supplies. The Japanese broadcast her routing: she would leave Meji, Japan, February 17, go to Singapore and Indonesian ports, return via Hong Kong and Takao, Formosa, and thence up the Formosa Strait to Japan. She would have special markings: a white cross on each side of her funnel and lighted white crosses at night. She would also run with navigation lights at night.

Lockwood and Fife were among those who were skeptical about this voyage. They (and other naval officers) had long been suspicious of the excessive number of Japanese hospital ships which plied the waters to and from Japan. However, they raised no protest. It was State Department business, and it would be futile—and seemingly cold-blooded—to question the matter. In early February, both men sent out plain-language dispatches notifying all submarines in detail of *Awa Maru*'s routing with instructions to let her pass. Lockwood sent his message three times each for three nights, nine times in all.

Awa Maru passed safely to the south and made her rounds, observed closely by submarines on patrol. While making these rounds, she loaded her holds with thousands upon thousands of bales of raw rubber and other critically needed strategic materials. In addition, she rounded up about 1,700 passengers, mostly stranded merchant ship captains, mates, engineers, and seamen, plus some government officials.

A further item in this bizarre drama that made Lockwood still more suspicious was the return route of *Awa Maru*, as provided by the Japanese. He and Dick Voge noticed that it would take her through a big minefield lying between the west coast of the Ryukyus and the China coast. Lockwood and Voge knew from intelligence sources that the field was there but wondered if the Japanese were trying to deceive the U.S. Navy into believing the area was clear, hoping to lure U.S. submarines into the field.

But before setting off on the return voyage, *Awa Maru* broadcast a corrected return route that would take her outside the minefield. In early March, Lockwood sent a message to "all submarines" concerning the return route of *Awa Maru*. Again, he sent the message in plain language, three times a night for three nights. On March 28, Lockwood sent an additional message, this one encoded, to "all submarines" which stated, in effect, LET PASS SAFELY THE AWA MARU CARRYING PRISONER OF WAR SUPPLIES. SHE WILL BE PASSING THROUGH

YOUR AREAS BETWEEN MARCH 30 AND APRIL 4. SHE IS LIGHTED AT
NIGHT AND PLASTERED WITH WHITE CROSSES.

Loughlin received this encoded message, but he had not previously
been briefed on *Awa Maru*, nor had his communications officer
bothered to show him any of the many plain-language broadcasts
regarding her that had been received on *Queenfish*. When Loughlin
saw Lockwood's decoded message of March 28, he thought it (as he
recalled later) "the stupidest message" he'd ever seen. It was not
directed to any specific submarine and gave no details of course,
speed, or routing.

On April 1, Loughlin's packmate, Roy Klinker in *Sea Fox*, got into
a small convoy and attacked, damaging a freighter. That night at
7:40, Klinker broadcast a contact report to Loughlin. Two hours and
twenty minutes later, *Queenfish* made radar contact on a single ship,
range 17,000 yards. Loughlin judged from the radar pip that it was
a Japanese destroyer, hunting the submarine that had attacked the
convoy.

A dense fog reduced visibility to 200 yards. Loughlin could see
nothing from the bridge. Watching his radar, he closed to 1,200
yards, swung around, and fired four stern tubes set on 3 feet with
a 300-foot spread. He heard and saw four hits, properly timed. The
radar pip disappeared quickly. Loughlin must have privately mar-
veled at his accuracy: four hits in a 300-foot destroyer!

Easing *Queenfish* to the scene of the sinking to pick up a survivor,
Loughlin found a large oil slick and fifteen or twenty men clinging
to wreckage. One agreed to come aboard. He was in bad shape and
"no coherent information was immediately forthcoming," Loughlin
wrote later. However, within a few hours Loughlin learned the
dreadful truth: he had sunk *Awa Maru*.

Loughlin immediately reported his error to Lockwood. When the
duty officer woke Lockwood with the news, the admiral was gravely
concerned on at least three counts: (1) that the incident would cause
an international furor (similar to *Lusitania*), embarrassing to the
United States; (2) that the Japanese might "wreak barbarous re-
prisals" upon U.S. prisoners of war, especially submariners; and (3)
that Loughlin, one of his best skippers, would be crucified. Lockwood
notified Nimitz and Admiral King and then ordered Loughlin
and Klinker to search the area for additional survivors.

When Admiral King received the news, his response was typically
cold and curt. He radioed Lockwood: ORDER QUEENFISH INTO PORT

IMMEDIATELY . . . DETACH LOUGHLIN FROM HIS COMMAND AND HAVE HIM TRIED BY A GENERAL COURT-MARTIAL.

At the scene of the sinking, neither Loughlin nor Klinker could find any more survivors. The crew and the 1,700 passengers had evidently drowned. As the two boats steamed around hunting through the debris, they saw an estimated four thousand bales of raw rubber floating on the sea. Loughlin recovered four of the bales and stored them below. Then, with heavy heart, he set course for Saipan.

Along the way, Loughlin received word that some airmen were down in his vicinity. Detouring to search, he found thirteen men—the crew of a big navy patrol plane—in rubber rafts. They had been in the water almost four days. He took them on board and proceeded to Guam, arriving on April 12, the day President Roosevelt died.

Once in Guam, Loughlin was somewhat startled—and relieved—to find his boss 100 percent on his side. Lockwood had already fired off half a dozen memos to Nimitz and others, partly blaming himself for the disaster because he had not been more specific in his March 29 encoded dispatch. He had lined up lawyer Chester Bruton and a marine assistant to defend Loughlin. When the court-martial convened, Lockwood, in absentia (he had returned briefly to the States for an FM sonar conference), submitted depositions in Loughlin's behalf.

At the court-martial, Chester Bruton and his assistant tried everything they could think of. The chief line of defense was that by carrying munitions and contraband *Awa Maru* had sacrificed her right to safe conduct. To prove this, Loughlin's lawyers produced the lone survivor rescued by Loughlin, Kantora Shimoda, a steward. However, the court* dismissed this as irrelevant on the grounds that Loughlin had no way of knowing what the ship carried, and even if he did he had no right to disregard the safe-conduct granted by the State Department.

Loughlin's lawyers then shifted to another defense, lack of intent. This was easily proved by the way Loughlin had attacked. Had he been trying to sink a big ship like *Awa Maru* instead of the destroyer he believed it to be, he would have set his torpedoes to run deeper and used a much broader spread. (As Dick Voge later pointed out, they might have raised another point in Loughlin's behalf: if he had

---

* The president of the board was Vice Admiral John Howard Hoover, known ironically as "Genial John"; the youngest and least senior member, representing the submarine force, was Lew Parks.

deliberately sunk *Awa Maru,* why rescue and bring home a survivor who could convict him of the crime?)

The way Bruton handled the defense enabled him to introduce Loughlin's superior war record—not normally allowed in a court-martial. This impressed the court favorably. Another point in Lough-lin's favor was the fact that he steadfastly refused to put any blame on the communications officer or on others who had failed to bring all the messages regarding *Awa Maru* to his attention. This display of loyalty "down" also impressed the court.

After hearing the evidence, the court returned a murky verdict. It dismissed charges against Loughlin of culpable inefficiency in the performance of duty and disobeying the lawful order of a superior but found him guilty of negligence in obeying orders and sentenced him to receive a Letter of Admonition from the Secretary of the Navy. Nimitz, who believed the punishment should have been sterner, was furious. He gave the members of the court a Letter of Reprimand—a more serious punishment than the court gave Lough-lin—but apparently did not put it in their records, at least not in that of Lew Parks.

But temporarily, at least, Loughlin was hurt professionally. "By edict of Admiral King," he said later, "I could not have another command." Lockwood transferred Loughlin to his staff and assigned him to the training command. Later, he became operations officer to Gin Styer in the Atlantic Fleet.

A similar tragedy was only narrowly avoided. *Razorback,* commanded by Charles Brown, picked up a solitary vessel in the East China Sea. Bedeviled by fogging periscopes, Brown believed it to be a transport, even though it was steering a steady course without escort. Brown closed to 3,200 yards and fired five steam torpedoes. After they left the tube, Brown saw a red cross on the side of the hull, indicating a hospital ship, which all submarines were to give free passage. Brown held his breath while the torpedoes streaked toward the hull. All missed; luckily, Brown had overestimated the range. An endorser, in one of the great understatements of the war, wrote, "It is fortunate the attack was not successful."

Boats that patrolled to the East China and Yellow seas also found that targets were increasingly scarce and hard to find. A pack led by Ben Adams (who had been fired from *Flier*), in the famous *Rasher,* with *Pilotfish* and *Finback*, made only two attacks for zero results, and Adams was relieved after this, his only patrol as skipper. Ed Shelby in *Sunfish*, Dixie Farrell in *Gato*, and Joseph Icenhower in *Jallao* all conducted extremely aggressive patrols as a pack, but the only confirmed sinkings were Farrell's: two small ships for 3,125 tons. The combination of Barney Sieglaff in the new *Tench*, Robert Worthington in *Balao*, Ralph Styles in *Sea Devil*, and Frederick Wahlig in *Grouper* was most successful; Worthington sank two confirmed ships for 11,293 tons and Styles three for about 10,000 tons. Afterward, old *Grouper* was retired and Sieglaff turned *Tench* over to Tom Baskett and went to work on Lockwood's staff.

Caddy Adkins, returning *Cod* from a long overhaul in the States, also patrolled the East China Sea, sinking a tugboat and a minesweeper. A day after *Cod* received "the most severe depth-charging of her career," fire broke out in the after torpedo room, caused by a short circuit in one of the electric torpedoes. The compartment instantly filled with smoke and had to be evacuated. A party of volunteers donned breathing apparatus to enter the compartment, load the burning torpedo into a tube, and fire it to sea. Quartermaster Lawrence E. Foley and another man, going aft topside to open the torpedo room deck hatch to help, were caught by a wave and knocked overboard. Foley had a life jacket; his helper did not. They drifted off into the darkness. Adkins launched a search that went on for eight hours. Near dawn—by what seemed to be a miracle—he found the two men and recovered them. All that time, Adkins reported later, Quartermaster Foley had kept his shipmate afloat.

Attacks from the Air

With the skies now black with Allied aircraft, the number of accidental bombings increased—in spite of all precautions. U.S. submariners came to fear the sight of any aircraft.

Bullhead, a new boat commanded by Walt Griffith (ex-*Bowfin*), patrolled the South China Sea en route to report to Jimmy Fife. She carried a unique passenger: Martin Sheridan, a reporter for the *Boston Globe*, the only war correspondent permitted to make a submarine war patrol in World War II. Nimitz had authorized his trip—without checking with Admiral King.

Griffith found few targets. On April 8, while *Bullhead* was cruising the surface, a B-24 Liberator, flying low, popped out of the clouds. The pilot set up on *Bullhead* and dropped three bombs. They fell about 75 yards astern of the boat.

Later, Sheridan reported, "Though the boat dove rapidly, it didn't seem half fast enough. . . . Men in the maneuvering and after torpedo rooms were shaken up a bit by the underwater blasts. . . . One serious case of constipation was known to be cured by the attack."

Griffith picked up three airmen and returned to base, stepping down to join Lockwood's staff after one more patrol. When King learned Sheridan had been on board *Bullhead*, he sent a dispatch to all submarine commands: WAR CORRESPONDENTS MAY NOT REPEAT NOT GO ON SUBMARINE WAR PATROLS.

Pogy, commanded by John Michael Bowers, was strafed by a U.S. Army Liberator while lifeguarding near Tokyo Bay, and a flight of navy aircraft attacked Gordon Underwood in *Spadefish* as he led *Pompon* (commanded by Stephen Gimber), *Bang* (commanded by Anton Gallaher), and *Atule* (commanded by John Maurer) to the Yellow Sea. The navy planes dropped two bombs before Underwood could dive, as Maurer in *Atule* witnessed this senseless performance. (Fortunately, the bombs did only slight damage.) When the planes flew over *Atule*, Maurer exchanged recognition signals in time and was spared a similar fate.

Maintaining his record—he had sunk ten confirmed ships, including the carrier *Jinyo* (*Shinyo*)—Underwood sank four ships for 13,-423 tons; Maurer sank one big freighter, *Taiman Maru I*, 6,888 tons; Gallaher in *Bang*, who had eight confirmed ships to his credit, was fiercely aggressive but had bad luck; and Gimber in *Pompon* had to leave station early, after a dive with the conning tower hatch open flooded the pump room and damaged the machinery there. (Gimber and Underwood asked for transfers, Gimber going to new construction and Underwood to the Bureau of Ships.)

Tirante's First Patrol

In March a new boat, *Tirante*, commanded by George Levick Street III, arrived at Saipan for her first war patrol. Street's exec was Ned Beach, who had made ten previous patrols on *Trigger*; Street had made nine previous war patrols on *Gar*. The two men got along famously, Street later describing Beach as "one of the outstanding young submariners of all times."

Lockwood sent *Tirante* to the East China Sea. Street began by patrolling the approaches of Nagasaki (in the area where John Lee in *Croaker* had sunk the light cruiser *Nagara*) and on March 25 sank a small tanker, *Fuji Maru*. Three days later, he sank a small freighter, *Nase Maru*. During the next few days, while U.S. troops went ashore at Okinawa, Street stood guard at the western exit of the Inland Sea in case major Japanese fleet units should come out.* During this time, he battle-surfaced and sank a lugger and missed an amphibious vessel with three electric torpedoes.

After being released from reconnaissance duty, Street moved north to patrol off the south coast of Korea. Soon after reaching these waters, Street battle-surfaced on a schooner. A boarding party captured three Koreans, one of whom escaped by diving over the side. On April 7 Street attacked a small single freighter, firing two electric torpedoes and observing the thunderous double explosion through the periscope. He surfaced immediately and surveyed the wreckage, saw two survivors clinging to debris, and by hand signals vectored a nearby native Korean craft to rescue them. This is another sinking that must have slipped through, for postwar records failed to confirm it.

Tirante had an extraordinarily powerful SJ radar, and her engineers had fixed the speed governors on her Fairbanks-Morse diesels so as to increase her maximum speed by about a knot. When Street learned from the *Threadfin* and *Hackleback* reports that *Yamato* had sortied from the Inland Sea, it seemed logical to him and Beach that she might round Kyushu, perhaps heading for the naval base at Sasebo, in *Tirante*'s area (since the only other way to get there, through Shimonoseki Strait, was now blocked by aircraft-laid mines). With her speed and radar both operating at maximum, *Tirante* ran a "retiring search curve" which completely blanketed all *Yamato*'s possible positions, had Sasebo been her destination. To Street and his eager crew, it seemed certain they would have a shot

---

* It was during this period that Voge ordered *Trigger* to form up with *Sea Dog* and *Threadfin*. When *Trigger* wasn't heard from, Voge directed her to rendezvous with *Tirante*. Street and Beach waited three days. When Beach realized his old ship was gone forever, he was devastated. After the war he immortalized her in a book, *Submarine!*

at her. They were of course disappointed, but there was other business coming their way.

Responding to an Ultra on April 9, *Tirante* attacked a small convoy. Street fired six electric torpedoes at two different ships. He missed one but the others hit *Nikko Maru*, a 5,500-ton transport which was jammed with troops and seamen returning from Shanghai. Escorts jumped *Tirante* and delivered a close attack. Street responded by firing one Cutie. It apparently hit the mark because there was a terrific overhead explosion and breaking-up noises. The escort either was too small for the records or did not sink.

On the night of April 12 or 13 (as Beach later recalled) *Tirante* received an Ultra reporting that an important transport had holed up for the night in a small harbor on Quelpart Island (Cheju Do) about 100 miles due south of the southwestern tip of Korea. Street proceeded there, arriving the night of April 13. *Tirante* went to battle stations and, proceeding boldly on the surface past an escort, crossed into 60 feet of water. Then Street nosed *Tirante*'s bow into the harbor—à la Gene Fluckey.

Beach, manning the TBT binoculars on the bridge, picked up three targets anchored in the murk: the transport and two small frigate escorts. While Beach aimed from the bridge, Street in the conning tower made ready torpedo tubes and fired three steam torpedoes at the transport. Moments later, it blew up with an awesome explosion. Street ordered *Tirante* to head for deep water, changed his mind, paused, and fired three torpedoes at the two frigates. Both blew up and sank while *Tirante* was making flank speed out of the harbor. Confirmed result: with six torpedoes, Street and Beach had sunk *Juzan Maru*, 4,000 tons, and two frigates of about 900 tons each.

With only one torpedo remaining, Street headed for the barn. On the way home, he found three Japanese airmen sitting on the overturned float of a seaplane. He captured two, but the third drowned himself. For all these exploits—including the sinking of six confirmed ships for 12,621 tons—George Street received the Medal of Honor and Ned Beach, one of a few execs so honored, a Navy Cross. Following this, Beach received orders to command his own boat.

Generally, targets were now scarce. Of the eighty-seven war patrols mounted from Pearl Harbor and Guam from January to March, sixty

—almost 70 percent—were without sinkings. The other twenty-seven produced 51½ sinkings. The high scorer was George Street. Next was John Ward Reed in *Sunfish*, who was lucky to find—and sink— four ships for 5,461 tons off the east coast of Honshu.

39

Fremantle and Subic Bay, January through August 1945

The Move to Subic Bay

When Jimmy Fife relieved Ralph Christie in Fremantle, he found the staff busy with plans to move the Brisbane repair base forward to Subic Bay, Philippines—a monumental operation. After the Subic Bay area had been recaptured by MacArthur's troops, Fife flew there for an inspection, chose a site for the base, and set work crews in motion. The tender *Fulton* arrived in Subic Bay on February 11 with the advance contingent.

This move reminded many old hands on the staff of the abortive move to Exmouth Gulf in 1943. Subic Bay was a humid, unhealthy, desolate Siberia. "And," said Chester Smith, who moved there commanding Squadron Thirty, "it was too far from everything." Few (except Fife) wanted to move there, let alone build the big submarine base the plans called for.

Unmoved by these objections, Fife pushed ahead, believing that submarines would be based there after the war had been won. The Seabees who did the construction were in a race with time, hoping to finish the base before the heavy seasonal rains began in mid-May. They made one grave error: they built the staff headquarters and communications building before they built the roads. Everything fell behind schedule, and the rains came before the roads were finished. The result was a vast quagmire of mud. The heavy equipment brought up from Brisbane on the Liberty ship *Ganymede* had to be stored on the beach, and much of it was damaged or lost.

By March, most of the staff had moved. Two other tenders joined *Fulton, Anthedon,* and *Gilmore,* arriving March 13. A rest camp—named for James Wiggins Coe, lost on *Cisco*—was hacked out of the jungle. But all this was primitive, a far cry from the pleasant climate, facilities, and girls of Australia.

Pursuit of *Ise* and *Hyuga*

Meanwhile, Fife directed his submarines against the shrinking list of Japanese vessels stationed in southern waters. The most important of these were basing in Singapore: the carrier-battleships *Ise* and *Hyuga,* the heavy cruisers *Tone, Haguro,* and *Ashigara,* two damaged heavy cruisers, *Takao* (hit by *Darter*) and *Myoko* (by *Bergall*), the light cruiser *Isuzu,* several destroyers, and a number of tankers and freighters converted to tankers.

Fife's skippers performed remarkably well against the tankers and small men-of-war. The reservist H. S. Simpson, commanding *Bashaw,* sank the 10,000-ton tanker *Ryoei Maru.* Bill Hazzard, making a spectacular second patrol in *Blenny,* sank the 10,000-ton tanker *Amato Maru,* a smaller tanker, and two freighters. Ben Jarvis, commanding *Baya,* sank the 5,236-ton tanker *Palembang Maru.* Hank Sturr in *Becuna* sank a 2,000-ton tanker. Paul Stimson, making an aggressive second patrol in *Sea Robin,* sank four freighters. Ralph Huntington Lockwood (no kin to the admiral) in *Guavina* sank the 8,673-ton tanker *Eiyo Maru.* Eric Barr in *Bluegill* damaged and beached the 5,542-ton tanker *Honan Maru* and then sent a demolition party ashore to finish her off. Dave Bell in *Pargo* sank the destroyer *Nokaze,* and William Lawrence Kitch in *Blackfin* sank the destroyer *Shigure.* Other skippers picked off a freighter here and there.

The two targets that fascinated Fife most were *Ise* and *Hyuga,* arrived in Singapore to load drums of oil for the homeland. The codebreakers watched their movements closely. Fife was determined to do all in his power to prevent these ships—and the oil—from reaching Japan.

Ise and *Hyuga* left Singapore on February 11, with thousands of drums of oil aboard. On that day, one of Fife's British submarines,

Tantalus, was patrolling off Singapore. *Tantalus*, commanded by Rufus MacKenzie, saw the ships come out. MacKenzie tried to attack, but Japanese aircraft screening the force drove him away. He sent off a contact report. Fife had already laid an ambush of fourteen fleet boats along the projected route north.

The next day at about 1:45 P.M., *Charr*, commanded by Francis Dennis Boyle, patrolling down from Pearl Harbor to Fremantle, picked up the force on radar at 9 miles. *Flounder*, *Blackfin*, *Tuna*, *Pintado*, and *Pargo* were nearby. Boyle surfaced and got off a contact report. An hour later, Kitch in *Blackfin* picked up the force on radar at 15 miles. *Charr*, *Blackfin*, *Flounder*, *Pargo*, and *Tuna* chased after *Ise* and *Hyuga* for the next fourteen hours, trying to make an end around, but they never could do it. Said James Edward Stevens in *Flounder*, "It was heartbreaking, to say the least."

Three more boats lay to the north, waiting: *Hake*, commanded by Frank Haylor; *Pampanito*, commanded by Paul Summers; and Ralph Lockwood's *Guavina*. None of these three managed to attain firing position.

Three more lay north of these: *Bergall*, commanded by John Hyde; *Blower*, a new boat patrolling down from Pearl Harbor, commanded by James Harry ("Soupy") Campbell; and *Guitarro*, commanded by Thomas Dabney. On February 13 Hyde picked up the force at 12:13 P.M. Being submerged right on the track, he saw *Ise* and *Hyuga*, a heavy cruiser, and several destroyers. Hyde rang up full speed to get into position. He could not decrease the range below 4,800 yards, but he fired six torpedoes. Hyde heard one explosion and was later credited with a hit, but it was not confirmed in postwar records.

Campbell, on *Blower*, was in the best position. He closed for a daylight periscope attack and fired five torpedoes at one of the battleships and one at the heavy cruiser. Campbell claimed two hits on the battleship but Fife did not credit it, nor did postwar Japanese records. Campbell missed the cruiser, too. Fife was exasperated by this failure. After Campbell made one more war patrol he went to staff duty.

The last two of Fife's fifteen submarines deployed to sink *Ise* and *Hyuga* lay to the north. They were *Flasher*, commanded by George Grider, and *Bashaw*, commanded by H. S. Simpson. The task force came out of a rainsquall at 3:15. Before Simpson could set up, one of the battleships saw *Bashaw*, launched a plane, and opened fire

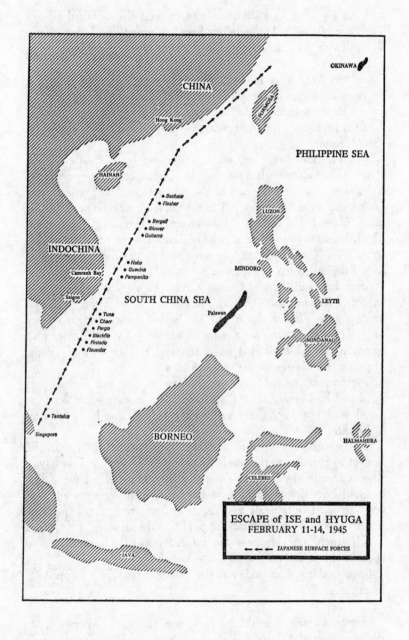

ESCAPE of ISE and HYUGA
FEBRUARY 11-14, 1945

←·←·← JAPANESE SURFACE FORCES

with her big guns. One shell landed a mile off the starboard quarter "with a loud roar and tremendous flash." Simpson dived. After dark, he and Grider in *Flasher* joined in the mass chase. None could overtake.

Lockwood and Voge followed all this by radio and, after projecting the probable course of *Ise* and *Hyuga* from Luzon Strait to Japan, deployed eleven submarines to intercept. None made contact. On this, the final voyage of *Ise* and *Hyuga*, the ships eluded a total of twenty-six submarines.

Both Fife and Lockwood were nonplussed by this failure. Fife, blaming the failure on bad weather, the high speed of the task force, and a new ability on the part of the Japanese to detect radar, wrote Lockwood, "It was a bitter pill to take and I make no alibi." Lockwood blamed his failure on incorrect codebreaking information which led him to position his eleven boats too far to the west. He wrote Fife, "Our dope certainly went sour at the last moment. Perhaps I depended too much on it."

After his futile chase, George Grider in *Flasher* sank a small freighter, *Koho Maru*, 850 tons. He did not know it then, but that sinking gave *Flasher* the record for Japanese tonnage sunk by a single U.S. submarine: 100,231 tons. (Second place was *Rasher* with 99,901 tons.) *Flasher's* total was a result of Reuben Whitaker's 56,-513 tons and George Grider's 43,718 tons.

One boat not available for the *Ise-Hyuga* chase was *Barbel*, commissioned by Conde LeRoy Raguet. Raguet, another youngster from the class of 1938, was the son of a navy captain, and had been exec of *Blackfin*.

On February 1, Edward Steffanides, commanding *Tuna*, told Raguet to patrol near the southern end of Palawan. On February 3, Raguet reported by radio to *Tuna* that he was patrolling the station but had been driven down by numerous aircraft contacts and had been attacked by aircraft and depth charges three times. Japanese records reported an air attack of a U.S. submarine on February 4 which scored one hit near the bridge. Jasper Holmes wrote, "It appears almost certain that this attack sank *Barbel*."

Raguet, thirty years old, was the youngest fleet boat skipper lost in the war.

One boat involved in the *Ise* chase was almost lost afterward. On the afternoon of February 23, James Stevens in *Flounder* was cruis-

ing submerged off Indochina. There was no traffic visible in the periscope and no enemy on sonar. At about 5 P.M., *Flounder* was
suddenly shaken by a terrifying jolt and started down, out of control. Then came another jolt. The sonar operator reported screws and
then the sound of a submarine blowing ballast tanks.

Stevens realized at once what had happened: *Flounder* had been
hit by a submerged submarine. He believed it must be Japanese.
He came back to periscope depth for a cautious look but saw
nothing.

Later in the afternoon, Stevens saw a U.S. submarine through his
periscope and realized it was the boat that had hit *Flounder*. It was
Hoe, commanded by Miles Refo. When Stevens surfaced, he found
that *Hoe*'s keel had sliced a 25-foot gash in *Flounder*'s superstructure
on the starboard side. Stevens broke off his patrol and returned to
Subic Bay for repairs.

This was the only submerged collision of two submarines in the
war. Both Stevens and Refo were lucky that it was not more serious.

The Remaining Targets: *Isuzu, Haguro, Ashigara,* and *Takao*

After the *Ise-Hyuga* fiasco, Fife was ready to move his own bag
and baggage from Fremantle to Subic Bay. He decided to return to
the Philippines by the same means he had left there three years
earlier: submarine. Along the way, the boat would conduct a regular
patrol. Thus Fife, after Christie, became the second and last admiral
to go on patrol.

Fife chose *Hardhead,* commanded by Francis Greenup, for his
transportation. The boat departed March 20, going to Indochina
by way of Lombok and Karimata straits. On April 2, Greenup laid a
small minefield off Indochina and then conducted a regular war patrol in the Gulf of Siam, an area believed to be heavily mined and
not hitherto exploited.

Hardhead had a busy time. On the night of April 5, Greenup
picked up a small convoy consisting of a big tanker, a freighter, and
a trawler. Greenup chose the tanker, which was empty, as his target.
He made a night surface attack, firing six torpedoes. One hit forward
of the bridge. The men in the tanker fired at *Hardhead* with a gun

of "medium" caliber. Greenup responded by firing another three torpedoes. All missed. Greenup fired another two. Both missed.

Somewhat chagrined by all this missing with his boss on board, Greenup submerged to avoid the gunfire and made another approach at radar depth, closing to point-blank range of 400 yards. He fired another torpedo. It missed. Greenup surfaced and fired another two bow tubes. The first of these hit below the tanker's funnel amidships, the second hit below the bridge. Greenup saw "satisfactory explosions with flames." The ship, identified in postwar records as *Araosan Maru*, 6,886 tons, sank.

Having expended sixteen torpedoes in this effort, Greenup had none left for the freighter. He battle-surfaced on the trawler escort, firing about fourteen rounds. None hit. The trawler returned fire, so Greenup broke off the attack and lobbed four shells at the freighter from 3,000 yards. None of these hit either.

Following this, Greenup took *Hardhead* to Subic Bay, arriving on April 11 after a voyage of twenty-two days. Fife declared the patrol successful, so he received a submarine combat pin. He wrote Lockwood, "My jaunt in *Hardhead* was the best vacation I have had since the war started. . . . We have now covered the entire Gulf [of Siam] without getting trouble." He expressed the hope that one of the minefields in the Gulf of Siam would "legally catch a playmate of *Awa Maru.*"

After this ice-breaking voyage, Fife sent many submarines into the Gulf of Siam. Generally, they found poor hunting, since Allied aircraft had sunk those ships the submarine force had not already eliminated. One boat, John Hyde's *Bergall*, ran into a minefield planted by the Allies, and one of the mines exploded. *Bergall* was lucky; she received only minor damage in her stern. She made it back to Subic Bay for temporary repairs and then returned to the States for permanent repairs.

Another boat, *Lagarto*, commanded by the immensely capable—and popular—Frank Latta, was lost in the Gulf of Siam. On May 2, Latta rendezvoused with Ben Jarvis in *Baya* to conduct a joint patrol. Later in the day, Jarvis found a small convoy and alerted Latta. They made a joint approach but were driven off by radar-equipped escorts. The two skippers met again and drew up a new plan for an attack the following day. This attack, too, was repulsed. After this, when Jarvis tried to raise Latta, he got no answer. Japanese records showed that *Hatsutaka,* a minelayer (and believed to be one of the radar-equipped escorts) attacked a submarine at this time and place. Jasper Holmes believed *Hatsutaka* sank *Lagarto.* She went down with all hands.

Hatsutaka did not long celebrate her victory. About two weeks later—May 16—Worth Scanland in *Hawkbill* found her inside the gulf and torpedoed her. She blew up and sank immediately.

After Fife moved to Subic Bay, he became ill with a mild case of malaria. Even so, he kept on the job, determined to sink everything Japanese that floated in southern waters. One target that intrigued him was the light cruiser *Isuzu,* then engaged in shifting Japanese troops from base to base.

In early April, intelligence reported *Isuzu* was in Surabaya. A three-boat wolf pack, led by Francis Boyle in *Charr,* patrolled the Java Sea off Surabaya. The other boats were *Besugo,* commanded by Herman Edward Miller, and *Gabilan,* commanded by William Brownlee Parham. They lay in wait along the probable track of the cruiser.

On the morning of April 4, Herman Miller in *Besugo* made contact with *Isuzu* and an escort of four small vessels. Miller was too far off the track to shoot, so he surfaced to trail. About that time, William Parham in *Gabilan* picked up the force through his periscope at 10 miles. Parham saw *Besugo* trailing. After waiting for *Besugo* to pass, he surfaced to join the chase. Francis Boyle in *Charr* saw smoke at 13 miles. He too joined the chase. However, aircraft forced all three boats down and *Isuzu* got away.

Intelligence reported the next stop for *Isuzu* was Bima Bay on the north coast of the island of Soembawa. The pack took up station there on April 6, joined by one of Fife's British submarines, *Spark.*

On the morning of April 6, *Isuzu* showed up on schedule. All four boats, waiting submerged, saw her. Parham in *Gabilan* picked her up at 6,500 yards, running close to the beach. He prepared to attack, but *Isuzu* opened out to 7,500 yards—beyond reach. Miller in *Besugo* had a better chance. The cruiser, "loaded with troops," came close. Miller fired three stern tubes from 500 yards, then six bow tubes. All nine torpedoes missed the cruiser, but one or more hit one of the escorts, *Minesweeper No. 12,* 630 tons. It sank.

Isuzu went into Bima Bay unharmed, while the pack waited for her to come out again. The following morning at about 3 A.M., Boyle in *Charr* made radar contact at 7 miles and alerted Parham in *Gabilan*. Almost immediately, Parham got contact. He closed and fired six bow tubes. One tube failed to fire, but the other five torpedoes streaked toward *Isuzu* and at least one torpedo hit. The sonarman reported *Isuzu*'s screws had stopped. Escorts drove Parham under and dropped depth charges.

Boyle in *Charr* now closed in. At 5:20—when it was getting light —he submerged and prepared to attack. Parham, he saw, had done good work; *Isuzu* was down by the bow and listing, but she was still making 10 knots. At 1,200 yards, Boyle fired four torpedoes. Two hit. Boyle fired two more torpedoes. Another hit. Boyle's TDC operator jumped up and down excitedly, exclaiming, "Jeezie beezie! We hit him. We hit him!" Escorts charged *Charr* and Boyle went to 420 feet. Boyle heard "loud breaking-up noises."

All this time, the British submarine *Spark* stood off to one side, watching. The skipper saw the hits on *Isuzu*, then smoke and flame, then Japanese leaping over the side. That night when *Charr* and *Gabilan* surfaced, he reported that the cruiser had sunk. Parham and Boyle shared equal credit for her sinking.

Later, Miller in *Besugo*, who was too far off the track to see the final battle, sank another man-of-war. On April 23, off Surabaya, he picked up a submarine flying a Japanese flag. He closed and fired six torpedoes. At least one hit. The submarine sank instantly, leaving one man—the officer of the deck—in the water. Miller picked him up. He identified the submarine as the German *U-183*. She was the third U-boat sunk in the Pacific by Allied submarines (two of them by U.S. boats). In all, U.S. submarines sank four German vessels in the Pacific: the two U-boats, Herb Andrews's freighter, and Tom Wogan's merchant raider, *Michel*.

Once *Isuzu* went down there were only two important Japanese men-of-war left in Singapore, the heavy cruisers *Haguro* and *Ashigara*. Fife kept close watch on both.

In early May, *Haguro*, escorted by one destroyer, sortied from Singapore to carry supplies to the Japanese army in Burma. She swung northwest and went up Malacca Strait, where British submarines basing from India were patrolling. Two of these, *Statesman* and *Subtle*, sighted *Haguro* and were able to fire torpedoes at her. Both missed.

The two boats got off contact reports, alerting British surface forces operating in the Indian Ocean. None could get into position in time, but when *Haguro* got ready to return to Singapore, the ambush had been laid. On May 16, a British aircraft from a jeep carrier found *Haguro* and attacked, achieving damage. That same night, four British destroyers closed on her like a pack of wolves. The destroyers boldly attacked, firing guns and torpedoes. *Haguro* went down.

After that, there remained only *Ashigara*. On June 5, Merrill Clementson in *Blueback* and Doug Rhymes in *Chub,* alerted by an Ultra, picked her up coming into Djakarta, on the northwest tip of Java, but neither boat had an opportunity to shoot.

Fife's staff calculated that *Ashigara* would soon return to Singapore. *Blueback* and *Chub*—joined by other fleet boats—lay in wait off Djakarta. Meanwhile, Fife, believing that *Ashigara* would return to Singapore via the narrow mined waters of Bangka Strait, positioned two of his British submarines in the strait close to the minefields. These were *Trenchant,* commanded by Arthur Richard Hezlet, and *Stygian,* commanded by Commander Clarabut.

On June 7, Clementson picked up *Ashigara* leaving Djakarta. Neither Clementson nor Rhymes was able to reach attack position in time, but Clementson got off a contact report and Fife alerted Hezlet and Clarabut in Bangka Strait.

Ashigara was escorted by a destroyer—leading. Early on the morning of June 8, Hezlet in *Trenchant* picked up the destroyer in Bangka Strait, boldly remaining on the surface. Hezlet did not fire at the destroyer, not wishing to alert *Ashigara* to the ambush. The destroyer saw *Trenchant* and opened fire. Hezlet avoided this fire and submerged to await the oncoming *Ashigara*.

Later that morning, Hezlet's tactics paid off. While lying submerged in the strait, he saw *Ashigara* coming north, hugging the coast of Sumatra. He set up and fired his bow tubes at the extreme range of 4,700 yards. The Japanese on *Ashigara* saw the torpedoes coming and tried to avoid, but the ship was too close to shore for radical maneuvers. Five of Hezlet's torpedoes slammed into the ship, leaving it, according to Jasper Holmes, "a broken wreck." Hezlet swung around and fired his stern tubes—while *Ashigara* shot at his periscope. The stern tubes missed, but *Ashigara* was mortally holed nevertheless and sank later in the day.

The British proposed that some of their midget submarines be brought from Europe to make raids on the Japanese men-of-war in Singapore. Two of these little 35-ton craft had succeeded in damaging the German battleship *Tirpitz* on September 22, 1943, putting her out of action for about six months.

Both Lockwood and Fife were opposed to this scheme. They doubted that the midgets could do the job, and the risks involved did not appear to justify the possible rewards. *Tirpitz*, Germany's largest battleship, had been a definite threat to Allied naval forces in European waters. But the Japanese had no comparable prize in Singapore after *Ise* and *Hyuga* left. However, the British persisted. Singapore had been a British base; they wanted to strike a blow.

In July the British tender *Bonaventure* arrived at Subic Bay with several midgets on board. By that time there were only two worthwhile targets left in Singapore, the heavy cruisers *Takao* and *Myoko*, both damaged by U.S. submarines. Allied reconnaissance showed them to be anchored in shallow water behind torpedo nets, safe from attack by conventional submarines.

In late July the British set off to get these ships. The midgets were towed to a launch point off Singapore by British submarines. *Spark* towed *XE-1*, commanded by Lieutenant J. E. Smart, and *Stygian* towed *XE-3*, commanded by Lieutenant I. E. Fraser. On midnight, July 30, the midgets were launched off Horsburg Light.

The two little boats crept 25 miles up the channel toward Singapore in bright moonlight. About 10:30 A.M., *XE-3* went into Singapore Harbor. *XE-1* followed her through a little later. *XE-3* found *Takao*, attached limpet mines and saddle charges (with delayed fuses) to her, and withdrew. *XE-1*, unable to reach *Myoko*, shifted to *Takao* and added her explosives to *XE-3*'s. Both boats then withdrew to sea and rendezvoused with *Spark* and *Stygian* as planned.

The explosives detonated on schedule. They blew the bottom out of *Takao*, which settled in the mud and remained there for the duration. Lockwood and Fife were amazed—and relieved—when all this was finished.

Fife's boats finally ran out of targets. During the waning days of the war, they roved the seas on the surface like destroyers, blasting away with deck guns at trawlers, sampans, and other small craft, most of them manned by natives, not Japanese. When the boats ran out of ammunition, they boarded the craft and blew them up with grenades and demolition charges. On one patrol, Bill Hazzard in

Blenny sank sixty-three such vessels. On another, Arnold Schade in a new boat, *Bugara*, sank fifty-seven. Edwin Monroe Westbrook, Jr., commanding *Cod*, temporarily lost one of his boarding parties when a Japanese plane drove him under and an escort came along. Later, Hazzard in *Blenny* found the party and took them aboard. Eric Barr in *Bluegill*, looking for something colorful to do, sent a commando party ashore on the deserted island of Pratas (160 miles southeast of Hong Kong) and "captured" it. Roy Gross in *Boarfish* landed a commando party on the coast of Indochina near Hue and set a demolition charge on a railroad track, receiving credit for "derailing and/or damaging" a train.

One skipper who missed this sport was Edward Rowell Holt, Jr., who had relieved Walt Griffith in *Bullhead*. Holt, the eighteenth—and last—officer from the class of 1939 to command a fleet boat in combat, was caught by a Japanese army plane in Lombok Strait. The pilot claimed two direct hits and said thereafter he saw a "great amount of gushing water and air bubbles rising in the water." *Bullhead* went down with all hands.

40

Pearl Harbor and Guam, April through August 1945

New Forays in the Sea of Japan

In their endless search to find targets, Lockwood and Voge once again cast covetous eyes on the Sea of Japan. It had not been exploited since September 1943, when Mush Morton was lost in *Wahoo* trying to exit through La Pérouse Strait. Now, Lockwood and Voge believed, the Sea of Japan must be thick with ships, forced there by U.S. submarines and carrier task forces.

The big problem still was how to get in and out. The east and west straits (separated by the island of Tsushima) were heavily mined. The narrow center exit, Tsugaru Strait, was also mined. The northern exit, La Pérouse, where Morton was lost, was believed to be heavily patrolled by aircraft and surface vessels. Lockwood doubted that a submarine could enter from La Pérouse (as the eight boats had done in the summer and fall of 1943) without being detected.

By now, Lockwood believed, the FM sonar gear was sensitive enough to pick up mines—as *Tinosa* and *Tunny* had demonstrated at Okinawa. If the sets proved reliable enough, if a group of operators could be trained to use them properly, they might serve to guide a submarine through the minefields of Tsushima Strait into the Sea of Japan, and the boats could get out by making a dash through La Pérouse.

This scheme dominated Lockwood's waking hours for weeks. He appointed Barney Sieglaff to work on it full time; hence the plan was called Operation Barney. Lockwood himself worked on the FM sonar problems, urging the manufacturers who were hand-building the sets to hurry up and to make improvements. When boats arrived at Guam equipped with FM sonar, Lockwood took them to a dummy minefield and personally trained both operators and skippers in the use of the gear. He was an exacting taskmaster.

As a preliminary, Lockwood sent out two boats to probe minefields —that is, to check the FM against the real thing. The boats were *Tinosa*, commanded by Dick Latham, and *Spadefish*, now commanded by William Germershausen. Latham was ordered to minefields in the East China Sea, Germershausen to the field at Tsushima Strait.

On the way out, Lockwood sent the two boats an Ultra to intercept a convoy southbound from Japan. Germershausen found it and sank a 2,300-ton freighter. Latham, trying to intercept, was driven down by a Japanese plane. On the way down, the bow planes failed to rig out. Latham went to 180 feet and remained there, trying to fix them. During that time, *Tinosa* was swept along by strong currents and grounded lightly on an island, damaging one of the outer torpedo doors. With all this trouble, *Tinosa* missed an opportunity to attack the convoy.

Latham then proceeded to his minefield plotting mission, determined to do it on the surface if necessary. The FM gear was operating "beautifully" at first, and Latham was getting a good minefield plot. But in the middle of the operation, the FM broke down—with mines all around. *Tinosa* was then in about 100 fathoms of water. Latham decided the best thing he could do until the FM gear was repaired was anchor, so he began walking the anchor out. He had 120 fathoms of anchor chain. At 89 fathoms, the chain broke—from the weight of the anchor and chain. However, the FM gear was repaired and Latham slipped out to sea, finishing out the patrol with a cruise along the China coast.

Germershausen took *Spadefish* to the edge of the minefields at Tsushima Strait. His FM gear was not working properly either. He made three separate attempts to close—and chart mines—but all failed. Later, he wrote, "I must say mine-hunting was dull, unrewarding work that could not compare with the thrill of coming to grips with a big, fat enemy ship." Germershausen returned to regular patrol in the Yellow Sea, where he sank another freighter.

Next, Lockwood sent a pack of four FM-equipped boats to probe the minefields: *Bowfin*, commanded by Alexander Tyree; *Seahorse*, commanded by Harry Holt Greer, Jr.; *Bonefish*, commanded by Lawrence Edge; and *Crevalle*, commanded by Everett Steinmetz. (On the way to her job, *Seahorse* was bombed and strafed by a B-24 Liberator, which fortunately did little damage.) At the Tsushima minefields, these boats did good work. The FM gear was more reliable, and the operators obtained more information on mine locations.

After completing these special tasks, the boats went on to normal patrol. Tyree in *Bowfin* sank two ships off northeast Honshu, one a transport and one a freighter. Greer in *Seahorse* sank a junk. Later the boat was attacked by two patrol boats that delivered a punishing depth-charge attack. The boat survived, but, her historian reported, "*Seahorse* was a shambles of broken glass, smashed instruments, cork and dirt, with hydraulic oil spilled over everything," and she was returned to Pearl Harbor for a complete overhaul. Her FM gear (still intact) was shifted to *Sea Dog*.

By May, Lockwood felt he had enough information—and the FM gear worked well enough—to send a submarine task group into the Sea of Japan. He asked Nimitz's permission to lead the group in person—his sixth request to make a war patrol. Nimitz, of course, denied the request.

To lead the expedition, Lockwood picked Earl Hydeman, an older officer from the class of 1932 who had had relatively little combat experience. Hydeman had spent most of the war in New London and Washington. He had made his first war patrol as a PCO on *Pampanito*, October 1944, when that boat was commanded by Mike Fenno. After Fenno's OK, Hydeman was ordered to relieve Rebel Lowrance in *Sea Dog*. On his first patrol off Tokyo Bay, Hydeman had sunk a 6,850-ton freighter and rescued a fighter pilot from the carrier *Intrepid*.

In all, Lockwood assigned nine FM-equipped boats to make the foray. The group, code-named "Hell Cats," was divided into three wolf packs, as follows:

Hydeman's Hep Cats
Sea Dog (Earl T. Hydeman)
Crevalle (Everett H. Steinmetz)
Spadefish (William J. Germershausen)

Pierce's Pole Cats

Tunny (George E. Pierce)
Skate (Richard B. Lynch)
Bonefish (Lawrence L. Edge)

Risser's Bob Cats

Flying Fish (Robert D. Risser)
Bowfin (Alexander K. Tyree)
Tinosa (Richard C. Latham)

Before departure, each of the nine boats was equipped with external "clearing wires." These were steel cables strung from the bow to the tips of the bow planes and from the stern deck to the tips of the stern planes. The wires—in theory—would prevent a mine cable from hooking on bow or stern planes.

Hydeman and five other skippers left from Pearl Harbor on May 27 and May 29. *Tunny*, *Skate*, and *Bonefish* received last-minute additional FM training under Lockwood's supervision at Guam and then left from there on May 28.

On the way to the rendezvous at the south end of the strait, Dick Latham in *Tinosa* picked up ten airmen from a B-29. Later Jasper Holmes wrote, "When the aviators learned of *Tinosa's* destination they were unanimous in their desire to be put safely back in their rubber boats." Lockwood arranged a rendezvous with *Scabbardfish*, returning from patrol, and Latham turned the pilots over to her.

South of Kyushu, the expedition commander, Earl Hydeman in *Sea Dog*, had a severe casualty: his radar went out of commission. He joined up with Steinmetz in *Crevalle* and Steinmetz provided "Seeing-Eye" services, leading *Sea Dog* toward the strait in bad weather by short-range radio.

The boats went through the field by packs. *Sea Dog*, *Crevalle*, and *Spadefish* went first on June 4. All stayed deep—below 150 feet—to avoid the mines. Some of the boats had the FM sound head mounted near the keel. These went through with a 6-degree up-angle, so the FM gear could "look" forward and pick up mines. Hydeman reported, "During this passage, no FM contacts were made which could possibly have been mines."

There were, however, many disquieting moments. A few hours after submerging, Hydeman heard "several distant explosions." An hour later he heard "nine distant explosions, heavy enough to shake us a bit," followed by six more. Germershausen in *Spadefish* and

Steinmetz in *Crevalle* also heard these explosions. Germershausen later described them as "loud." He wrote, "From then on our spirits were considerably depressed. Had *Sea Dog* or *Crevalle* come to grief?" They had not. All three boats made it safely. The explosions remained a mystery.

After *Sea Dog* reached the Sea of Japan, as Hydeman wrote, "All hands breathed a little easier. The emotional strain, especially on the officers, was very heavy and its effects were now quite evident. Everybody was on their toes at all times however; officers and men performed their duties in a manner deserving of the highest praise."

The next day, June 5, Pierce took his pack through (*Tunny, Skate,* and *Bonefish*). Ozzie Lynch on *Skate* had a spine-chilling experience. At about 9 A.M., his FM operator picked up the unmistakable bell-like tone of a mine line 400 yards ahead. The mines were closely set. Lynch dropped to 175 feet and proceeded. Then every man on the boat heard a noise none ever forgot: a mine cable scraped down the entire length of the boat. Lynch and his crew held their collective breath, praying that the cable would not snag and drag the mine down to *Skate*. The clearing lines evidently worked.

After passing the second of four mine lines (that is, while in the middle of the field), Lynch, perhaps feeling *Skate* had developed some kind of mine immunity, decided to come up to periscope depth and get a fix on the location of the field. He rose slowly to 60 feet, poked up "the pole," and took bearings on landmarks on the shoreline. Then—having obtained this valuable information—Lynch went deep again and proceeded to underrun the last two lines.

The next day, June 6, Bob Risser led the Bob Cats (*Flying Fish, Bowfin,* and *Tinosa*) through the fields. *Tinosa,* too, had a close call. Latham ran right up on a mine, maneuvered to avoid it, and then stopped his screws. Later he wrote:

Tinosa stopped swinging right and started left again, but that mine was coming closer and closer abeam until it was too close any longer to show on the [FM] scope. Then there was a scraping, grinding noise as the mine cable slid down the starboard side. No one moved or spoke. Would it snag and drag the mine into us? We were at 120 feet keel depth and the mine was hopefully clear of us. God bless the fairing cables leading from the hull to the outboard forward edge of our stern planes! That mine cable slid on aft past the stern planes and our silent screw and off the end. How much it

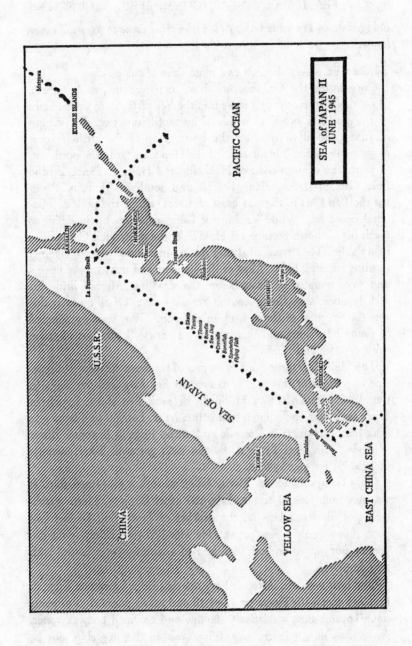

SEA of JAPAN II
JUNE 1945

PACIFIC OCEAN

Matuwa

KURILE ISLANDS

SAKHALIN

HOKKAIDO

Otaru

La Perouse Strait

Tsugaru Strait

Hakhim

U.S.S.R.

SEA OF JAPAN

HONSHU

Tokyo

Skate
Tunny
Tinosa
Bowfin
Sea Dog
Crevalle
Bonefish
Spadefish
Flying Fish

SHIKOKU

Tsushima Strait

Tsushima

KOREA

CHINA

YELLOW SEA

EAST CHINA SEA

dragged down the mine or how close the mine came to us, we'll never know.

Tinosa went safely through two more lines of mines.

Once inside the sea, the nine boats deployed to patrol stations. (Like the boats on the first foray into the Sea of Japan in the summer of 1943, all had orders to withhold fire until sunset on the evening of June 9—to allow time for the boats going to the farthest point to get into position.) Hydeman led the Hep Cats far to the northeast, to patrol the western coast of Hokkaido and Honshu. Pierce led the Pole Cats to station along central and southern Honshu. Risser led the Bob Cats to the east coast of Korea, where the pack encountered dense fog. While waiting for Germershausen in *Spadefish* to reach his far north position off Hokkaido, the other Hell Cats passed many ships. They were all sitting ducks—unescorted, not zigzagging, burning running lights. Most of the skippers had itchy trigger fingers and were tempted to shoot before the deadline. After sighting his fifth Japanese ship, Steinmetz in *Crevalle* wrote, "Of all contacts this was the toughest to throw back in the pond. Was strongly tempted to swing left, shoot and then use as an excuse 'I was just cleaning my torpedoes and . . . !'"

The Hell Cats turned out to be one of the most successful submarine operations of the war. Hydeman in *Sea Dog* sank six ships in ten days. Germershausen in *Spadefish* sank five ships. Lynch in *Skate* sank four, including a submarine, *I-122*. Latham in *Tinosa* also sank four. Steinmetz in *Crevalle* sank three. Edge in *Bonefish*, Risser in *Flying Fish*, and Tyree in *Bowfin* each got two. Total: twenty-eight ships for 54,784 tons.

Only George Pierce in *Tunny* failed to sink a confirmed ship. It was not from lack of trying. Like the other skippers, Pierce practically put his boat's bow on the beaches of Japan, but he had bad luck; he saw only a few targets. He attacked two, firing seven torpedoes, but missed on both, and he had a "running gun battle" with two destroyers.

One boat was lost. After sinking one big ship, Lawrence Edge in *Bonefish* met with Pierce on June 18 and asked permission to penetrate Toyama Bay, a relatively shallow and confined body of water. As soon as he got in the bay, Edge sank another big ship, but he was spotted and pounced on by Japanese antisubmarine forces. They delivered a depth-charge attack which fatally holed the famous *Bonefish*. She was lost with all hands.

The pack made one serious error. On the night of June 13, Germershausen in *Spadefish*, patrolling to the northwest of La Pérouse Strait, picked up a freighter on radar. This was an area where Russian ships passed en route to and from Vladivostok, so Germershausen closed to 1,100 yards to look over his quarry. The ship had no lights burning and "was not following a designated Russian route." Germershausen fired two torpedoes and sank it. It was the Russian ship *Transbalt*, 11,000 tons.*

The Russians protested almost immediately. Lockwood radioed the Hell Cats, DID ANYBODY SHOOT NORTHWEST OF LA PEROUSE STRAIT? Germershausen, who by then suspected he had made a mistake, replied GUILTY.

Not wishing to disclose that U.S. submarines were again operating in the Sea of Japan, Nimitz or King blamed the incident on a Japanese submarine. But the Russians weren't fooled. Germershausen joked later, "They blamed it on a reactionary U.S. submarine skipper."

With this sinking (actually giving *Spadefish* a total of six ships sunk), Germershausen swelled the Russian-ship-sinking club membership to four, joining Eugene Sands (two Russian ships), Moon Chapple (one), and Malcolm Garrison (one).

After two weeks inside the Sea of Japan, the Hell Cats prepared to leave. This, they feared, would be the hardest part of all; surely the Japanese would be guarding the exits with everything they had. Hydeman decided the best way out was to exit through La Pérouse Strait at night on the surface, gun crews standing by. Should the group be attacked by Japanese destroyers, they could fight back with the combined firepower of nine 5-inch deck guns—a considerable array of armament.

In addition, Lockwood provided a diversionary act to trick the Japanese into believing the boats were going out through Tsushima Strait. Early on the morning of June 24, *Trutta*, now commanded by a reserve officer, Frank P. Hoskins, shelled the island of Hirado Shima on the east channel of Tsushima Strait in a "purposely conspicuous manner."

On the night of June 24, the boats rendezvoused just inside La

---

* It was the second time Germershausen had shot at a Soviet ship. The first time—on *Tambor*—he missed.

Pérouse Strait—all but *Bonefish*. With eight submarines bunched together, Hydeman could not wait. He ordered the pack to enter the strait at 18 knots. Hydeman in *Sea Dog* led one column, but his radar failed again and *Crevalle* resumed her role as Seeing-Eye dog. A dense fog shrouded the boats as they barreled through the strait. There were two contacts—a lighted ship, probably Russian, and a Japanese minelayer that did not see them. By 5:20 A.M. on June 25, all eight boats had made it out without a shot being fired at them. No one could understand why it had been so easy.

Pierce in *Tunny* received permission from Hydeman to go into the Sea of Okhotsk to wait for—and radio—*Bonefish*. On the night of June 25, Pierce sent two messages to *Bonefish*. When no reply was received, Pierce set course for Midway. He arrived on July 2, a day or two after the other boats. Then all went to Pearl Harbor for an epic party—and medals and praise from Lockwood.

Germershausen had some unfinished business regarding the Russian ship he sank. As he recalled it later, when he got into port, Lockwood said, "Go see Nimitz." Germershausen reported as ordered, expecting a royal chewing out or worse. "He asked what happened," Germershausen recalled. "I told him I didn't see any markings. All he said was, 'Glad you made it back safely, son.'"

After this "first wave," Lockwood sent seven other boats singly into the Sea of Japan: *Sennet*, *Piper*, *Pargo*, *Pogy*, *Jallao*, *Stickleback*, and *Torsk*. Charles Robert Clark, Jr., in *Sennet*, another young officer from the class of 1939, went first and sank the most ships: four for 13,105 tons, thereby establishing himself as the top skipper of that class. He returned via La Pérouse Strait with no difficulty.

Rescues and Targets

While this submarine spectacular was in progress, other Lockwood boats roamed familiar hunting grounds, picking up aviators and looking for ships to attack.

Gato—the boat that was famous for having fought it out with a Japanese plane on the surface in the Solomons—lifeguarded off Kyushu. Now commanded by Richard Holden, *Gato* rescued ten airmen from ditched B-29s, some very close to the coast. On April 29, about to make one of these rescues, *Gato* was again caught on the surface by a Japanese fighter. Holden, anxious to save the airman, manned his deck guns and fired back at the aircraft, emulating *Gato*'s former skipper, Bob Foley. The Japanese fighter dropped two bombs—fortunately near misses—and wheeled around for a strafing run. Holden submerged. Later, when the plane was gone, he surfaced and picked up the airman.

Hiram Cassedy, lifeguarding off Honshu in his new boat *Tigrone*, received a call for help on May 26; a navy bomber had two engines out and had to ditch. The pilot put the plane down near *Tigrone*. Cassedy's efficient rescue crew pulled five men on board.

Four days later, Cassedy got another call for help. An army seaplane which had landed to pick up the crew of a ditched B-29 had itself crashed on takeoff. Cassedy responded to the call and took off the B-29 crew and the seaplane crew, sixteen men in one swoop. One died, leaving *Tigrone*'s airman population at twenty.

In the days following, Cassedy picked up ten more airmen, bringing his total to thirty-one, a record for a single patrol.

Off northeast Honshu, Tom Baskett in *Tench* sank four confirmed ships in June—one of them just a half mile offshore. George Street, with six confirmed ships to his credit for his first patrol (plus a Medal of Honor), returned *Tirante* to Nagasaki for his second patrol and added two more.

Another Medal-of-Honor skipper waged a land as well as a sea campaign on his next patrol. Gene Fluckey, who had fourteen confirmed ships to his credit, took *Barb* to Hokkaido and the Kuriles. On this trip *Barb* was fitted with an experimental gadget, a 5-inch rocket launcher for shore bombardment.

Arriving June 21 on station off the northeast coast of Hokkaido, Fluckey saw two trawlers. He battle-surfaced and sank both with his deck gun, then was driven under by a Japanese plane. Fluckey surfaced after dark and shortly after midnight, June 22, fired twelve small rockets on shore. The next day, Fluckey sank another trawler, taking one prisoner.

Going northward, Fluckey found a small convoy and attacked. He expended many torpedoes but achieved no sinkings; the escorts drove him off. On July 2, he closed Kaiyo on the eastern extremity of the Karafuto Peninsula (the lower half of Sakhalin Island) and bombarded the town with his deck gun, setting fires, damaging a seal rookery, and destroying three sampans at dockside. The next day he launched a rocket attack on the town of Shikuka, and the day after, in another area, he sank a 2,800-ton freighter with torpedoes.

Shifting areas again, Fluckey battle-surfaced and sank a lugger and a sampan and then torpedoed a frigate with his last torpedoes.

While cruising off Otasamu, on the east coast of Karafuto, Fluckey noted a railroad running along the coast and sent a commando party ashore to set demolition charges on the tracks. As they were pulling away from shore in their rubber boats, a train came along and set off the charges. The engine blew up with a terrific explosion, and about twelve freight cars, two passenger cars, and a mail car rolled over the tracks. "Wreckage flew two hundred feet in the air . . . cars piled up and rolled off the tracks in a writhing, twisting mass of wreckage. Cheers!" Fluckey wrote. Later reports from a prisoner of war stated that 150 passengers—including women and children—had been killed in the wreckage.

Again shifting locations, Fluckey fired thirty-two 5-inch rockets into the town of Shiritori and twelve rockets into the town of Kashiho. Withdrawing, Fluckey bombarded Shibertoro and Chiri, destroying a lumberyard and a nest of sampans.

Returning to port, Fluckey was praised for his ingenuity and resourcefulness. He stepped down from command of *Barb*, having earned, in addition to his Medal of Honor, four Navy Crosses. Fluckey went to new construction and eventually wound up as aide to Admiral Nimitz.

Tiny Lynch, returning *Haddo* from a long overhaul, patrolled in the Yellow Sea. On July 1, off Inchon, Korea, in a dense fog, Lynch picked up a four-ship convoy with two escorts. Maneuvering in water only 65 feet deep, Lynch set up and fired eight torpedoes—two at each freighter in the convoy. Two of these blew up and sank.

At that point, the fog, which had afforded Lynch good protection, lifted and Lynch saw one of the escorts—a frigate—charging in. He sent his lookouts below and ordered flank speed. The frigate and *Haddo* passed on opposite courses, like *Salmon* and her attacker, the frigate firing all its guns. Lynch and the officer of the deck, J. H. M. Nason, crouched behind the shears, laughing hysterically—from fear.

When Lynch reached "deep water"—that is, 80 feet—he dived. The two escorts followed. At that point, Lynch fired two Cuties (which were not supposed to be fired from a depth less than 150 feet) and prayed. One hit one of the escorts, *Coast Defense Vessel No. 72,* an 800-ton frigate. It blew up and sank. The other escort broke off to go collect survivors.

In the space of fifteen minutes, Tiny Lynch had sunk two ships of a four-ship convoy, damaged two others, and sunk one of two escorts.

The Japanese Surrender

In early July, Admiral Halsey, commanding the Third Fleet, left from Leyte Gulf for another series of strikes on the Japanese home-land. Most of these were to be air strikes, but this time he planned to bring some of his battleships close to shore and conduct a bombardment. Lockwood provided submarines to conduct an antipicket sweep in front of the carriers and to lifeguard. Two FM-equipped boats, *Runner II,* commanded by Benny Bass, and *Redfin,* commanded by Charles Kilday Miller, conducted mine location probes along the coast where the bombardment was to be conducted.

Task Force 38, joined by twenty-eight British warships, reached Japanese home waters without incident. On July 10, Halsey's planes struck Tokyo. Four days later they raked Hokkaido, and the battle-ships blasted coastal cities, including the steel mills bombarded by Dave Whelchel in *Steelhead* in May 1943. Wheeling south, Halsey struck Tokyo again, then Kure and the ships in the Inland Sea. In the following days, he struck Hokkaido again and returned to Tokyo. In all, the air raids went on for well over a month.

The strikes against ships in the Inland Sea July 24 and July 28 destroyed what was left of the Japanese navy. The carrier-battleships *Ise* and *Hyuga,* the battleship *Hurana,* two new aircraft carriers, *Amagi* and *Katsurage,* and the cruisers *Tone, Aoba, Oyodo, Twatem, Izume,* and *Settsu* were ruined beyond repair. Only the carrier *Ryuho* (severely damaged in the March raids) survived afloat. She had been skillfully camouflaged and moored next to a secluded beach.

During these activities, Lockwood's submarines lifeguarded, picking up dozens of pilots. And, in spite of all precautions, on four occasions his boats were attacked by friendly air and surface forces.

Sea Robin, commanded by Paul Stimson and returned from Fife's command, patrolled on lifeguard station off Honshu. On June 26, a B-29 attacked her, dropping a "full load of bombs" through a heavy overcast. Fortunately for *Sea Robin*, the bombs all missed by half a mile. *Sea Robin* rescued one airman during her lifeguarding.

Gabilan, commanded by William Parham, picked up fifteen airmen in a remarkably bold series of rescues—three at the entrance of the bay. Then she was told on July 18 to vacate the area because U.S. surface forces were approaching for a strike. This word came a little late. Parham rang up flank speed and pushed northeastward through heavy seas.

Three hours later, Parham picked up the U.S. force on radar and turned on electronic identification signals. Two destroyers peeled out of the formation and began shooting. After they had fired six salvos at *Gabilan*, Parham fired a green star rocket—the proper recognition signal for that hour. This move brought a "rain" of shells from the U.S. task force. Parham dived and went to 300 feet, remembering the fate of *Seawolf*. He gave orders to rig for depth charge and ran silently, evading at deep depth. He outwitted the two U.S. destroyers and got away, writing in his log, "It is an act of God that we are still here."

Toro, a new boat commanded by James Dorr Grant (ex-*Greenling*), lifeguarding off Shikoku on July 24, had an encounter with a destroyer similar to the *Spot-Case* incident. After a mix-up in recognition signals, the destroyer *Colahan* opened fire on *Toro*, firing fifty-two rounds. Grant fired a flare and smoke bomb and dived and saved his ship.

Batfish, commanded by Walter Small (ex-*Flying Fish*), was caught south of Kyushu. On August 1, while *Batfish* cruised the surface lifeguarding, an army B-25 turned and challenged her with a signal light. Small replied with the correct recognition signal and called the plane on his radio. In spite of all this, the B-25 came in and dropped five bombs on *Batfish*'s port beam. All missed.

While the July carrier strikes were in progress, a group of nuclear physicists led by Dr. J. Robert Oppenheimer set off the first atomic bomb in the desert of Alamagordo, New Mexico. After this test, two atomic bombs were completed and shipped to a special Air Force B-29 unit on Tinian. Parts of the bombs were delivered by the cruiser *Indianapolis*, which continued on to the Philippines. On July 30, west of the Marianas, she was torpedoed and sunk either by regular torpedoes or by *kaitens* launched from *I-58*. Although the codebreakers picked up and decoded *I-58*'s report of the sinking, no search efforts were launched until a navy plane from the Palaus, on a routine mission, found some survivors. Of *Indianapolis*'s 1,199 men, 883 died.

The first atomic bomb was loaded on a B-29 named *Enola Gay*, piloted by Colonel Paul W. Tibbets, Jr. He took off from Tinian at 2:45 on the morning of August 6. At 8:15 Hiroshima time, he released the bomb over the city. It exploded at about 2,000 feet, destroying 4.7 square miles of Hiroshima and killing an estimated 72,-000 men, women, and children. Another 68,000 were wounded, and thousands were inflicted with radiation sickness. Tibbets returned to Tinian, landing at 2:58 P.M. Sixteen hours after the bomb fell, President Harry Truman gave the news to the rest of the world.

Two days later, Russia, which had steadfastly maintained a neutral attitude toward Japan, declared war. Russian troops immediately invaded Manchuria and northern Korea.

On August 9, the second atomic bomb was loaded into a B-29 named *Bock's Car*, piloted by Major Charles W. Sweeney. Sweeney's drop was more difficult. His primary target was Kokura, but there he ran into cloudy weather and switched to the secondary target, Nagasaki. At 10:58 A.M. (Nagasaki time) he found an opening in the clouds. This bomb killed about 40,000 people and injured 60,-000. Because he was low on fuel, Sweeney had to make a stop at Okinawa. Later that night, he returned to Tinian.

On the following day, while Task Force 38 roamed up and down the Japanese coast with impunity, Emperor Hirohito advised his cabinet to accept the unconditional surrender terms demanded by the Allies. Hirohito's advisers agreed to do this—provided the Allies would not dethrone or charge the Emperor with war crimes. The message was relayed through Swiss and Swedish channels. The Allies replied that these terms were acceptable, provided the Emperor submit to the authority of a Supreme Allied Commander and give the Japanese people the right to decide his ultimate status through free elections.

While these messages were going back and forth, Lockwood's submarines continued to fire away at Japanese shipping. On August 11, Joseph Icenhower in *Jallao,* patrolling the Sea of Japan, sank a big transport, *Teihoku Maru,* 5,795 tons. On August 13, Robert Raymond Managhan in *Spikefish* sank *I-373* off Okinawa. On that same day, Bafford Lewellen in *Torsk,* patrolling the Sea of Japan, sank a small freighter, *Kaiho Maru,* 873 tons. The following day, August 14, Lewellen sank two frigates, *Coast Defense Vessels Nos.* 13 and 47, each about 800 tons. These were the last torpedoes fired by any naval vessel in World War II and the last Japanese ships sunk.

Emperor Hirohito accepted the terms imposed by the Allies and notified them. At fifty-six minutes to midnight, August 14, Admiral Nimitz sent a message to all naval units:

CEASE OFFENSIVE OPERATIONS AGAINST JAPANESE FORCES. CONTINUE SEARCH AND PATROLS. MAINTAIN DEFENSIVE AND INTERNAL SECURITY MEASURES AT HIGHEST LEVEL AND BEWARE OF TREACHERY OR LAST MOMENT ATTACKS BY ENEMY FORCES OR INDIVIDUALS.

Lockwood relayed this message to his submarines. Privately, he was not happy with the surrender terms. Later he wrote, "Why we ever acceded to [the terms] I will never understand, for certainly in the opinion of everyone I talked to among the fighting forces, he [Hirohito] had earned a place right alongside Hitler and Mussolini."

When the cease-fire message was received on board U.S. submarines on war patrol, most skippers and men cheered wildly. Some did not. One was Ned Beach, commanding *Piper,* who had just penetrated the minefield into the Sea of Japan. After having helped Roy Benson, Dusty Dornin, Fritz Harlfinger, and George Street sink twenty-two confirmed ships for 88,000 tons, Beach wanted to sink at least one for himself. When the cease-fire came, Beach later wrote, "Instead of wild exultation, a fit of the deepest despondency descended upon me."

Herman Kossler in *Cavalla* was lifeguarding off the coast of Honshu near Tokyo Bay when he got the word. He remained on the surface in broad daylight 25 miles from land. It occurred to Kossler that he should celebrate by passing out a ration of medicinal brandy. He asked his exec to break it out, mix it with pineapple juice, and give every man one drink.

While the exec was attending to this, Kossler remained on the bridge, planning to run in and look at the coast close up. Two minutes after noon, August 15, Kossler's radar operator picked up an aircraft contact dead ahead. "He was coming right at us," Kossler said later. "So, just in case, I rang up full power."

The plane roared in. Kossler watched, half hypnotized. Then he saw a bomb falling toward *Cavalla* and swung ship to avoid; the bomb landed 100 yards off the starboard quarter. Seeing the plane climb for another run, Kossler cleared the bridge and dived.

When *Cavalla* was safely at deep depth, Kossler remembered the brandy ration and asked where it was. His exec replied, "Captain, I talked it over with the boys and they decided to wait until the treaty was signed."

Half an hour later, Kossler surfaced and reported the incident to Admiral Halsey in Task Force 38. Several hours later, Halsey sent a message to his fleet units. "He said," Kossler remembered, "that if you saw an enemy plane approaching you directly, shoot it down—but do it in a gentlemanly fashion."

Admiral Nimitz invited Lockwood to attend the surrender ceremonies which would take place September 2 on the deck of Halsey's flagship, the battleship *Missouri,* in Tokyo Bay. Lockwood received permission to have a dozen submarines and a tender, *Proteus,* present for the ceremony, and *Proteus,* with Lew Parks, commanding Squadron Twenty, got under way for Japan immediately.

Lockwood flew from Guam to Yokosuka Naval Base in a seaplane. Lew Parks, meanwhile, having arrived in Japan, moved boldly ashore, taking possession of the submarine base at Yokosuka. He found several old Japanese submarines moored there, as well as dozens of midget submarines and *kaitens* being assembled for use against U.S. invasion forces. Parks and two of his division commanders, Rob Roy McGregor and Barney McMahon, then slipped into Tokyo to visit the Emperor's palace—before General MacArthur arrived. Said Parks later, "We were the first U.S. military forces to set foot inside Tokyo."

The Japanese surrendered three submarines to U.S. forces at sea. These were amazing craft, huge I-class submarines with hangars capable of storing four planes. They had been built for a special mission: to bomb the Panama Canal.* Hi Cassedy and Barney Sieglaff were assigned to head prize crews for two of these submarines. Cassedy violated strict orders not to take souvenirs (he passed out some swords). When Halsey heard about it, he was furious and ordered Cassedy relieved of command. Cassedy thus had the distinction of

---

* Why the Japanese had not bombed the Panama Canal long ago with earlier-model I-class submarines carrying aircraft remained a mystery to the U.S. Navy. Had they done so, they would have severely retarded movement of U.S. warships and supply vessels to the Pacific.

being the only U.S. submarine skipper relieved of command of a Japanese submarine for cause.

Missouri steamed into Tokyo Bay early on the morning of August 29. Her skipper was Lockwood's old chief of staff, Sunshine Murray, and it fell to Murray to make all the incredibly complex arrangements for the ceremony.

The British, who wanted to contribute something to the surrender, sent over a table and chairs to be used for signing the papers. Murray said later, "It was a small thing. There wasn't room for one copy of the surrender documents on it, much less two." Murray rushed around, finally got a table and chairs from the crew's mess, and covered the stainless steel tabletop with a green felt cloth that had covered a table in the officers' wardroom.

On September 2 Murray's boatswain piped Nimitz and Mac-Arthur on board at 8:05. After them came legions of Allied admirals and generals, including Lockwood, who, Murray recalled, "got a place in the front rank." The Japanese contingent, led by the new foreign minister, Mamoru Shigemitsu, and including Admiral Toyoda's operations officer, Rear Admiral Sadatoshi Tomioka, arrived at 8:55. The principals gathered at the mess table. After the last signature had been put to the papers, General MacArthur turned and addressed the huge assemblage on *Missouri*'s deck:

"Let us pray that peace be now restored to the world, and that God will preserve it always. These proceedings are closed."

Part VII

41

After the War

After the surrender ceremonies, most of the submarines in the Pacific returned almost immediately to the United States. They nested in seaports and were opened to the public. The skippers and crews were permitted—for the first time—to discuss their exploits freely with friends and newsmen. The books on submarine operations written during the war but held up by Admiral Edwards were released. But in the flood of postwar news, the submarine service failed to get its story across—it remained a silent victory.

Meanwhile, Lockwood and his staff tabulated the final results for all submarine commands and submitted the figures to the Navy Department. Lockwood claimed that U.S. submarines had sunk about 4,000 Japanese vessels for about 10 million tons. His figures included one battleship, eight heavy and light aircraft carriers, and twenty heavy and light cruisers. Fifty-two submarines had been lost from all causes (including training) during the war, including forty-five fleet boats. About 375 officers and 3,131 enlisted men had died out of about 16,000 who actually made war patrols. This was a casualty rate of almost 22 percent, the highest for any branch of the military.*

The Joint Army-Navy Assessment Committee (JANAC) drastically trimmed Lockwood's sinking figures. By the (imperfect) reckoning of this group, the U.S. submarine force actually sank 1,314

---

* But small compared to other submarine forces. The Germans lost 781 U-boats (including two captured); of a total enlistment of 39,000 men, 28,000 were killed and 5,000 taken prisoner. The Japanese lost 130 submarines; the Italians 85.

enemy vessels for 5.3 million tons.* The figures included one battle-ship, eight heavy and light carriers, and three heavy and eight light cruisers. The tonnage figure, 5.3 million, represented 55 percent of all Japanese vessels lost. The other 45 percent were lost to army and navy aircraft, mines, and other causes. (In addition, JANAC gave submarines "probable" credit for another 78 vessels of 263,306 tons.)

The JANAC figures significantly altered the scores of many lead-ing skippers. Medal-of-Honor winner Dick O'Kane, for example, had been credited with sinking thirty-one ships for 227,800 tons; JANAC reduced him to twenty-four ships for 93,824 but still left him the leading submarine ace of the war, in terms of ships sunk. By JANAC figures, Slade Cutter and Mush Morton tied for second place with nineteen confirmed ships each. Medal-of-Honor winner Gene Fluckey came in fourth with sixteen and a third ships for 95,360 tons. This was the highest tonnage sunk by any skipper. The most spectacular drop in standing was Roy Davenport's. Credited with seventeen ships sunk for 151,900 tons during the war, his score as confirmed by JANAC was only eight ships for 29,662 tons.†

This downward readjustment caused an awkward moment for the navy. Most of the medals awarded submarine skippers during the war had been given out on the basis of ships or tonnage scores. Should they now be withdrawn? There was no way, and nobody was inclined to do it. Roy Davenport, for example, kept his five Navy Crosses, just as many air force and naval aviators kept medals awarded for claims that were undoubtedly exaggerated or were dis-claimed by postwar accounting. The only complaint raised about medals was that there should have been more Medals of Honor awarded. Only six skippers had received them; many more were de-serving.

The loss of men in the Japanese merchant marine was heavy. Japan began the war with about 122,000 merchant marine personnel. About 116,000 of these became casualties: 27,000 killed, 89,000 wounded or "otherwise incapacitated." Of this total, the majority of the casualties—16,200 killed and about 53,400 wounded or "other-wise incapacitated"—were inflicted by submarine attack.

* In World War I, primitive German submarines sank 5,078 merchant ships for about 11 million tons and ten battleships and eighteen cruisers, losing 178 submarines and about 5,000 officers and men. In World War II, Nazi U-boats sank 2,882 Allied merchant vessels, for 14.4 million tons, plus 175 men-of-war.

† For a listing of most skippers and Medal-of-Honor winners, see Appendix G.

When confronted with the revised sinking figures according to JANAC, Lockwood laid most of the blame for the large discrepancy between claims and actuality on defective torpedoes. A total of 14,-748 torpedoes had been fired. Had all these run, hit, and detonated as designed, the claims might well have been closer to the actuality, he maintained. Few could disagree. The torpedo scandal of the U.S. submarine force in World War II was one of the worst in the history of any kind of warfare.

Lockwood took pains to point out that the actual damage inflicted on the Japanese navy and merchant marine by U.S. submarines was, in reality, large compared with the effort expended. The U.S. submarine force, composed in total of about 50,000 officers and men (including back-up personnel and staffs), represented only about 1.6 percent of the total navy complement. In other words, a force representing less than 2 percent of the U.S. Navy accounted for 55 percent of Japan's maritime losses.

No matter how the figures were looked at, the damage inflicted by the U.S. submarine force on Japan was severe and contributed substantially to winning the war in the Pacific. As the report of the United States Strategic Bombing Survey stated, "The war against shipping was perhaps the most decisive single factor in the collapse of the Japanese economy and logistic support of Japanese military and naval power. Submarines accounted for the majority of vessel sinkings and the greater part of the reduction in tonnage."

After the cessation of hostilities, Lockwood looked forward to a peacetime in which the navy—and the submarine force—would remain large and strong. In the back of his mind he had created a job for himself: Deputy Chief of Naval Operations for Submarines, the "czar" concept that Daubin had proposed during the war and Lockwood strenuously opposed.

But none of this was to be. There was a strong national sentiment to "bring the boys home." President Truman ordered a general demobilization of the armed forces. Most of the fleet submarines in commission were mothballed and moored upriver from the New London Submarine Base and at other places. When Admiral Nimitz replaced Admiral King as Chief of Naval Operations in January 1946, he ordered Lockwood to become the Navy's Inspector General—in short, chief of what Lockwood called the "Gestapo." For Lockwood, who prized friendships and loyalty above all else, the job was reprehensible.

He worked at this job halfheartedly for a little over a year. One task assigned to him was to investigate the Green Bowl Society, a secret Naval Academy drinking club. It had been alleged in Congress that members of the Green Bowl had an inside track on promotions; that its members looked after one another on selection boards. Lockwood's best friend, Gin Styer, was a Green Bowler.

Seeking a way out of the "Gestapo," Lockwood proposed to Nimitz that he create a Deputy Chief of Naval Operations for Submarines. The Secretary of the Navy, James Forrestal, approved the idea, but Nimitz did not and would not create the job. When it became known that Lockwood's friend Louis Denfeld would succeed Nimitz as Chief of Naval Operations in the fall of 1947, Lockwood approached Denfeld with the idea. Denfeld didn't like it either and countered by offering Lockwood four stars and a fleet, Atlantic or Pacific. Lockwood declined the offer and asked for retirement. It was granted and took effect September 1, 1947.

Gin Styer, commanding Submarines Atlantic, soon followed in Lockwood's steps. He was replaced by John Wilkes and transferred to the Navy Department. There he got into a squabble with the new Secretary of the Navy, John Sullivan, about the extent of the Soviet submarine threat. Sullivan, not a popular Secretary of the Navy, told the press it was serious. Styer told the press the truth: it was not. On July 1, 1948, Styer voluntarily retired.

During the war, Lockwood and Styer had bought a ten-acre tract on a beautiful hillside in Los Gatos, California, south of San Francisco. After retirement, both men moved there. Styer went into the real estate business; Lockwood busied himself with civic affairs, hunting, and writing books about his peacetime years in submarines, submarine disasters, and the wartime submarine years.

When Wilkes was ready to retire, Ralph Christie, winding up two years at the Bremerton Navy Yard, sought the Atlantic submarine command. Denfeld gave it to Jimmy Fife, who was in the Navy Department working for the General Board and Joint Chiefs of Staff. Christie was sent to command U.S. naval forces in the Philippines; he retired after a year as of August 1, 1949, lived on the West Coast selling life insurance and dabbling in other ventures, and then gave it all up and moved to Hawaii, where in 1973, hale and hearty, he celebrated his eightieth birthday.

Dick Voge spent the last half year of the war and the following year writing a massive, classified operational and administrative history of the submarine war. After that was done, he decided to take a fling at the business world. Retiring from the navy in August 1946, he had a heart attack two years later and died.

Others who had served Lockwood in a staff capacity had long and distinguished careers. Sunshine Murray climbed the ranks to three stars and then retired. So did Swede Momsen, Dutch Will, Al McCann, Swede Bryant, and George Russell. Cliff Crawford, Savvy Huffman, Tex McLean, and others made two stars.*

After the war, the codebreakers stood temporarily, and uneasily, in the limelight; many were called to testify in the Pearl Harbor hearings conducted by Congress. They talked about their work up to and including the attack on Pearl Harbor but not about their work during the war itself. Generally, most supported the Roosevelt Administration thesis that the codebreaking information had not pinpointed a Japanese attack on Pearl Harbor. Admiral Kimmel and his supporters testified to the contrary.

After that, the codebreakers retired to obscurity, reluctant to talk further about their contribution to the war. They received small reward for their work. The Navy handed out only five important decorations—Distinguished Service Crosses; these went to Thomas Dyer, Jasper Holmes, Joseph Wenger, Rosey Mason, and Howard T. Engstrom, who was in charge of breaking U-boat codes. Joe Rochefort, Tom Mackie, and others who decoded key messages during the war received no official recognition. Few involved in codebreaking made flag rank. One notable exception was linguist Rufus Taylor, who rose to vice admiral and to the post of deputy director of the Central Intelligence Agency.

All submariners, Lockwood included, were astonished when they finally had an opportunity to look over captured German and Japanese submarines and torpedoes. German submarine technology was superior in almost every respect to U.S. submarine technology. German submarines had better surface and submerged speed and superior sonar, optics, diesel engines, and batteries. They could dive deeper and faster. The Japanese submarine torpedo was far superior

* A complete list of submarine skippers selected to flag rank appears in Appendix B.

to anything the Bureau of Ordnance had turned out. Both the Germans and the Japanese had built submarines with snorkels—breathing pipes that enabled the submarine to run submerged on diesel engines, thereby obviating the need to surface at night to charge batteries.

During the postwar years, American submariners grafted some of the best features of the German boats—snorkels and streamlining—onto the U.S. fleet boat. These modified boats were called Guppies, an acronym for Greater Underwater Propulsion. In addition, the submarine force drew up plans for an improved fleet boat, designed from scratch, incorporating the best features of the German boats. These submarines, known as the *Tang* class (in honor of Dick O'Kane's famous old boat), were launched in 1951 and included *Tang, Trigger, Wahoo, Trout, Gudgeon,* and *Harder*. They were powered by a radically new "pancake" diesel engine, produced by General Motors. They were supposed to have a new homing torpedo based on the superior German acoustical torpedoes. The engines were a complete failure, reminiscent of the H.O.R.s. The torpedo fell years behind schedule.*

While these abortive projects were in progress, a senior captain in the Bureau of Ships named Hyman George Rickover became fascinated with the concept of adapting nuclear power to submarines.† He took a course in nuclear physics at the atomic energy facility at Oak Ridge, Tennessee and, after deft bureaucratic maneuvering, got plans approved for the first nuclear-powered submarine, *Nautilus*. It was contracted for in 1950 and launched in 1954.

Nautilus was crude but successful. With the publicity attendant on its launching, Rickover rose to be the new Mr. Submarine, displacing Lockwood and Fife and the other wartime submarine leaders. He not only turned out submarines, he also insisted on the right to pick the men to command and man them. Thus the new nuclear submarine navy bore Rickover's personal stamp, and the new age

---

* So did all the follow-on models. For example, the most recent torpedo, the Mark 48, is years behind schedule and cost hundreds of millions more than estimated.

† Rickover had served on S-48 (the worst of the S-boats), in the late 1920s and early 1930s, rising to exec. However, he was a man of difficult temperament and was judged not qualified for command. He left submarines and became an engineering specialist. During the war, he specialized in electrical machinery and held down a desk in the Bureau of Ships in Washington.

was his alone. Lockwood died in June 1967, holding bitter feelings toward Rickover.

Rickover worked diligently, if not fanatically, to improve the nuclear-powered submarine. The next models launched at Electric Boat (among them *Swordfish*, *Sargo*, *Seadragon*, and *Skate*) were significant improvements over the prototype *Nautilus*. In 1960, after the navy had perfected the solid-propellant, long-range ballistic missile Polaris, it was "married" to the nuclear-powered submarine to form the Polaris weapons system.* In the late 1960s, the Polaris boats were equipped with a new missile, Poseidon, with a longer range and more warheads. In 1970, the navy embarked on a super-Polaris system called Trident, whose missiles would have a range of 5,000 miles.

In the immediate postwar years, the younger submariners did not fare exceptionally well in the navy. There were only two flag-rank billets: Commander Submarines Atlantic and Commander Submarines Pacific.† To get ahead, most men had to branch out into other parts of the navy. Even so, they found it difficult. Herman Kossler (a rear admiral) maintained that aviators and destroyer men dominated the navy and were able to "divide up the flag rank vacancies as they saw fit," that there was a "general feeling, particularly by destroyer officers, that submariners were not qualified to man surface flag billets," and that there was "jealousy between destroyer men and submariners."

When Polaris came on the scene as a major weapons system, the situation changed. By 1970 the submarine force began to dominate the navy, spending 25 percent of the navy's entire budget on new weapons and personnel. The commanders of Atlantic and Pacific submarine forces were elevated to vice admirals, thereby opening up many more submarine flag billets. In addition, the navy finally adopted the Lockwood plan for a Deputy Chief of Naval Operations for Submarines.

There were 465 skippers who commanded submarines in combat in World War II. Almost all made it to the rank of captain. About sixty—13 percent—became rear admirals, some of the first being Lew Parks, C. C. Kirkpatrick, Freddy Warder, Gene McKinney, Chester

* The Polaris boats, big 6,000-ton submarines, were named not for fish but historical figures such as *George Washington*, *Patrick Henry*, and *Robert E. Lee*.
† For a listing of men who held those commands, see Appendixes C and D.

Bruton, Chuck Triebel, Roy Benson, Mike Fenno, Pete Ferrall, Barney Sieglaff, Bill Post, Reuben Whitaker, and Weary Wilkins.

One of the younger skippers who later made rear admiral (in 1961) was Elliott Loughlin, who had received a general court-martial for sinking the safe-conduct ship *Awa Maru*. His selection astounded many fellow officers; he had been found guilty of negligence in obeying orders and that damning note had gone in his record, seemingly denying him flag rank forever. However, after the dust of the war settled, Loughlin went on to a splendid professional career: command of a submarine division, director of athletics at the Naval Academy, command of the cruiser *Toledo*, and command of a cruiser-destroyer flotilla.

Said Roy Benson, "I think submariners fared very well indeed in the peacetime years; not because they were submariners, nor in spite of it. They simply did a good job in other assignments."

Twelve of the 465 skippers—those who branched out—went a notch farther, to vice admiral: Chick Clarey, Pete Galantin, Fritz Harlfinger, Junior McCain, Donc Donaho, Joe Grenfell, Rebel Lowrance, Red Ramage, Eli Reich, Arnold Schade, John Tyree, and Frank Watkins. Three of these—Junior McCain, Chick Clarey, and Pete Galantin—went all the way to full admiral. In terms of power and prestige, McCain held down the biggest job: Commander in Chief, Pacific. As such, he commanded all U.S. Navy, Air Force, and Army units in the Pacific Theater, including those who fought the Vietnam war. Chick Clarey was next; he became Commander in Chief, Pacific Fleet, working under McCain, and later Vice Chief of Naval Operations, the second highest job in the U.S. Navy. Pete Galantin rose to four stars commanding the navy's Matériel Command.

About 25 percent of all World War II submarine skippers retired from the navy under the tombstone promotion law.* Most of them retired in 1957, 1958, and 1959, when the tombstone law was finally abolished. For this reason, there were many "rear admirals" among the retired submarine skippers.

Some outstanding skippers left the navy to follow other pursuits. George Grider retired in 1947, returned to college for a law degree, and ran successfully for Congress from Memphis. He served one

---

* In 1949, the Congress repealed that section of the law which gave added retirement pay. After that, the only additional benefit was the honorary increase in rank.

term and was then unseated.* Chester Nimitz, Jr., retired in 1957 to take a job in industry, with the tombstone rank of rear admiral. Tommy Dykers took a tombstone retirement in 1949 and went on to produce a popular weekly television series, *The Silent Service*. Murray Tichenor took a tombstone retirement to rear admiral to enter business.

By 1965, all but a few World War II skippers were retired. Only a small handful had died. (Three committed suicide.) The retirees clustered in groups near navy hospitals and base exchanges—San Francisco, Washington, D.C., San Diego, Norfolk, Charleston, South Carolina, Boston, New London—in fine houses, elegantly furnished. They were, as a whole, among the most affluent of the senior citizens. Almost every home had a single room in common, a den decorated with nautical gewgaws and photographs of Lockwood, Christie, Fife, submarines, Japanese ships sinking, and shipmates, living or dead.†

Over the years, some of the old shipmates slipped away, and there were funerals to attend. The most unusual farewell took place at the small submarine base in Key West, Florida, for Hiram Cassedy (*Searaven/Tigrone*). Friends and fellow submariners placed his ashes in a flare box covered by canvas and took them aboard a new, small experimental submarine, *Barracuda*. The submarine got under way and put to sea. When the appointed place had been reached, the crew gently placed Cassedy's remains in a forward torpedo tube. On command, the tube was fired, and Hi Cassedy joined Howard Gilmore, Mush Morton, Sam Dealey, and many others who had gone long before.

---

* Another submariner elected to Congress was William R. Anderson, who served on *Tarpon, Narwhal,* and *Trutta*. After the war, Anderson became the second skipper of the nuclear-powered *Nautilus,* took her on a famous voyage beneath the ice cap, later retired from the navy, and, like Grider, ran for Congress in Tennessee. He served four terms before being unseated in 1972.

† Many had pictures, too, of sons who were Naval Academy graduates, carrying on the family tradition. Two skippers, Junior McCain and Chuck Triebel, had sons who were POWs in North Vietnam. Both returned in 1973.

Appendixes

Appendix A
World War II Submarine
Squadron Commanders, Pacific

(Odd-numbered squadrons, far fewer in number, were stationed in the Atlantic)

Squadron Two
(merged with Four)
James Fife, class of 1918
Charles Bowers Momsen, 1919

Squadron Four
John Herbert Brown, 1914
William Vincent O'Regan, 1923
Edward S. Hutchinson, 1926

Squadron Six
(returned to New London)
Allan Rockwell McCann, 1917
Charles Dixon Edmunds, 1920

Squadron Eight
(merged with Ten)
Clifford Harris Roper, 1916
Willard Merrill Downes, 1920
George Edmund Peterson, 1924

Squadron Ten
Charles Wilkes Styer, 1917
Charles Frederick Erck, 1921
George Lucius Russell, 1921
George Edmund Peterson, 1924

Squadron Twelve
John Bradford Griggs, 1918
Charles Warren Wilkins, 1924

Squadron Fourteen
John Bailey Longstaff, 1920
Warren Dudley Wilkin, 1924

Squadron Sixteen
John Meade Haines, 1917
Willis Ashford Lent, 1925

Squadron Eighteen
Eliot Hinman Bryant, 1918
Stanley Page Moseley, 1925

Squadron Twenty
Leo Leander Pace, 1921
Lewis Smith Parks, 1925

Squadron Twenty-two
Joseph Anthony Connolly, 1921
Edward S. Hutchinson, 1926

Squadron Twenty-four
George Clifford Crawford, 1921
Frank Wesley Fenno, 1925

Squadron Twenty-six
Leon Joseph Huffman, 1922
Barton Elijah Bacon, Jr., 1925

Squadron Twenty-eight
John Mylin Will, 1923
Joseph Harris Willingham, 1926

Squadron Thirty
Karl Goldsmith Hensel, 1923
Chester Carl Smith, 1925

Squadron Thirty-two
Kenneth Charles Hurd, 1925

Squadron Thirty-four
Elton Watters Grenfell, 1926

Squadron Thirty-six
Jesse Lyle Hull, 1926

Appendix B
World War II
Submarine Skippers
Selected to Flag Rank

ADMIRAL

Bernard Ambrose Clarey (*Pintado*)	1934
Ignatius Joseph Galantin (*Halibut*)	1933
John Sidney McCain, Jr. (*Gunnel, Dentuda*)	1931

VICE ADMIRAL

Glynn Robert Donaho (*Flying Fish, Picuda*)	1927
Elton Watters Grenfell (*Gudgeon*)	1926
Frederick Joseph Harlfinger II (*S-32, Trigger*)	1935
Vernon Long Lowrance (*Kingfish, Sea Dog*)	1930
Lawson Paterson Ramage (*Trout, Parche*)	1931
Eli Thomas Reich (*Sealion II*)	1935
Arnold Frederic Schade (*Growler, Bugara*)	1933
John Augustine Tyree, Jr. (*Finback*)	1933
Frank Thomas Watkins (*Flying Fish*)	1922

REAR ADMIRAL

Donald G. Baer (*Lapon*)	1937
David Bonar Bell (*Pargo*)	1937
Roy Stanley Benson (*Trigger, Razorback*)	1929
Francis Dennis Boyle (*Charr*)	1934
Henry Chester Bruton (*Greenling*)	1926
John Starr Coye, Jr. (*Silversides*)	1933
Earl Russell Crawford (*S-46*)	1936
Lawrence Randall Daspit (*Tinosa*)	1927
John Frederick Davidson (*Mackerel, Blackfish*)	1929
James White Davis (*S-47, Raton*)	1930
James Charles Dempsey (*S-37, Spearfish, Cod*)	1931

Edward Joseph Fahy (*Plunger*)   1934
Frank Wesley Fenno (*Trout, Runner I, Pampanito*)   1925
William Edward Ferrall (*Seadragon*)   1927
Eugene Bennett Fluckey (*Barb*)   1935
Harry Hull (*Thresher*)   1932
William Davis Irvin (*Nautilus*)   1927
Donald Greer Irvine (*Piranha*)   1934
Frederick Emery Janney (*Hackleback*)   1937
Russell Kefauver (*Tambor, Springer*)   1933
Charles Cochran Kirkpatrick (*Triton*)   1931
Herman Joseph Kossler (*Cavalla*)   1934
Charles Elliott Loughlin (*S-14, Queenfish*)   1933
Richard Barr Lynch (*Seawolf, Skate*)   1935
John Howard Maurer (*Atule*)   1935
Woodrow Wilson McCrory (*Parche*)   1938
Lucien Berry McDonald (*Lamprey*)   1938
Eugene Bradley McKinney (*Salmon, Skate*)   1927
Henry Stone Monroe (*S-35, Ronquil*)   1933
Charles Derick Nace (*Rasher*)   1939
William Thackeray Nelson (*R-7, Peto, Lamprey*)   1930
Lewis Smith Parks (*Pompano*)   1925
William Schuyler Post, Jr. (*Gudgeon, Spot*)   1930
Robert Henry Rice (*Drum, Paddle*)   1927
Maurice Herbert Rindskopf (*Drum*)   1938
Walter Frederick Schlech, Jr. (*Tilefish*)   1936
William Bernard Sieglaff (*Tautog, Tench*)   1931
Walter Lowry Small (*Batfish*)   1938
Chester Carl Smith (*Swordfish*)   1925
Edward Clark Stephan (*Grayback, Devilfish*)   1929
Arthur Howard Taylor (*Haddock*)   1927
Charles Otto Triebel (*S-15, Snook*)   1929
George Herrick Wales (*S-22, Pogy*)   1929
Norvell Gardiner Ward (*Guardfish*)   1935
Robert Elwin McCramer Ward (*Sailfish*)   1935
Frederick Burdett Warder (*Seawolf*)   1925
Reuben Thornton Whitaker (*S-44, Flasher*)   1934
Charles Warren Wilkins (*Narwhal, Seahorse*)   1924
Joseph Warford Williams, Jr. (*Spearfish, Bumper*)   1933

Appendix C
Postwar Commanders of Submarines
Atlantic Fleet

RAdm. John Wilkes	1946 to 1947
RAdm. James Fife	1947 to 1950
RAdm. Stuart S. Murray	1950 to 1952
RAdm. George C. Crawford	1952 to 1954
RAdm. Frank T. Watkins	1954 to 1957
RAdm. Charles W. Wilkins	March 1957 to September 1957
RAdm. Frederick B. Warder	September 1957 to 1960
RAdm. Lawrence R. Daspit	January 1960 to September 1960
VAdm. Elton W. Grenfell	September 1960 to 1964
VAdm. Vernon L. Lowrance	1964 to 1966
VAdm. Arnold F. Schade	1966 to 1970
VAdm. Eugene P. Wilkinson*	1970 to 1972
VAdm. Robert L. J. Long	1972 to ———

* Last World War II submariner to hold the command

Appendix D
Postwar Commanders of Submarines
Pacific Fleet

RAdm. Allan R. McCann	1946 to 1948
RAdm. Oswald S. Colclough	1948 to 1949
RAdm. John H. Brown	1949 to 1951
RAdm. Charles B. Momsen	1951 to 1953
RAdm. George L. Russell	1953 to 1955
RAdm. Leon J. Huffman	1955 to 1956
RAdm. Elton W. Grenfell	1956 to 1959
RAdm. William E. Ferrall	1959 to 1960
RAdm. Roy S. Benson	1960 to 1962
RAdm. Bernard A. Clarey	1962 to 1964
RAdm. Eugene B. Fluckey	1964 to 1966
RAdm. John H. Maurer	1966 to 1968
RAdm. Walter L. Small	1968 to 1970
RAdm. Paul L. Lacy, Jr.*	1970 to 1972
RAdm. Frank D. McMullen	1972 to ———

* Last World War II submariner to hold the command

After the United States declared war on Nazi Germany, Admiral Doenitz decided to launch U-boats against the East Coast of the United States, choosing eleven ace skippers whose boats had been equipped with electric torpedoes. The results were gratifying—for Doenitz. From January to March 1942, while Withers's fifteen Pearl Harbor boats sank 15 ships in Japanese waters, Doenitz's eleven boats sank 204 ships in U.S. waters—over one million tons of shipping.

The U.S. Navy, which had put the bulk of its resources into building big ships, was utterly unprepared for the U-boat onslaught. Lacking other antisubmarine forces, it ordered every available submarine into the winter battle: about twenty S-boats Ralph Christie was preparing for the European submarine force, some demothballed R-class, the demothballed *Barracuda*, *Bass*, and *Bonita*, and the new experimental boats *Mackerel* and *Marlin*.

These boats stood out to sea from bases along the U.S. East Coast, Bermuda, and Panama. Several encountered U-boats. One was *R-1*, commanded by James Dorr Grant. On April 18, while 300 miles northeast of Bermuda, he made contact with a U-boat and fired four torpedoes. Grant believed the torpedoes had hit and the U-boat sank. His superiors gave him credit for the sinking—the only credited U-boat sinking by U.S. submarines in the Atlantic—and awarded Grant a Navy Cross. However, in postwar accounting the credit was reduced to damage.

Because the United States feared at first that the Japanese might bomb the Panama Canal, some submarines basing in Panama made limited patrols on the Pacific approaches to the canal. The Japanese mounted no such attack, so the submarines saw no action. One, *Bass*, suffered a battery fire which killed twenty-five men, but the boat was saved.

In all, these submarines conducted eighty-six patrols in 1942. *Mackerel* made two, *Marlin* two, *Barracuda* six, *Bass* four, *Bonita* seven, the R-boats six, and the S-boats fifty-nine. Confirmed sinkings: zero. Many boats were mistakenly bombed by U.S. aircraft. One, *S-26*, was rammed by its escort and sank with loss of forty-six lives.

Afterward, *Mackerel*, *Marlin*, *Barracuda*, *Bass*, *Bonita*, and the Rs were sent to noncombatant duty. Said one S-boat skipper, "I think we probably made a lot of U-boat skippers nervous and caused them to lose sleep. The real miracle is that we didn't lose one of our own boats to friendly aircraft."

The anti-U-boat patrols and the Panama Canal pickets are lumped together on the following chart. The area is labeled simply "Atlantic," but some Panama Canal patrols were conducted in the Pacific.

SUBMARINE WAR PATROLS DEPARTING ATLANTIC AND PANAMANIAN BASES, 1942

BOAT, PATROL NUMBER	SKIPPER AND CLASS	DAYS	SHIPS/TONNAGE Wartime Credit	SHIPS/TONNAGE Postwar Credit	AREA
Barracuda-1	James M. Hicks	16	zero	zero	Atlantic
Barracuda-2	James M. Hicks	15	zero	zero	Atlantic
Barracuda-3	?	16	zero	zero	Atlantic
Barracuda-4	?	20	zero	zero	Atlantic
Barracuda-5	Mason J. Hamilton	25	zero	zero	Atlantic
Barracuda-6	Mason J. Hamilton	19	zero	zero	Atlantic
Bass-1	Gordon Campbell	20	zero	zero	Atlantic
Bass-2	Gordon Campbell	?	zero	zero	Atlantic
Bass-3	Anthony H. Dropp	26	zero	zero	Atlantic
Bass-4	Anthony H. Dropp	23	zero	zero	Atlantic
Bonita-1	Stanley G. Nichols	22	zero	zero	Atlantic
Bonita-2	Stanley G. Nichols	15	zero	zero	Atlantic
Bonita-3	Stanley G. Nichols	?	zero	zero	Atlantic
Bonita-4	Stanley G. Nichols	?	zero	zero	Atlantic
Bonita-5	Stanley G. Nichols	12	zero	zero	Atlantic
Bonita-6	Stanley G. Nichols	25	zero	zero	Atlantic
Bonita-7	Charles F. Brindupke	20	zero	zero	Atlantic
Mackerel-1	John F. Davidson	?	zero	zero	Atlantic
Mackerel-2	John F. Davidson	?	zero	zero	Atlantic
Marlin-1	George A. Sharp	?	zero	zero	Atlantic
Marlin-2	Paul H. Grouleff	?	zero	zero	Atlantic

R-1-1	James D. Grant	'30	?	zero		zero	Atlantic
R-1-2	James D. Grant	'30	12	zero*		zero	Atlantic
R-5-1	Dudley W. Morton	'30	?	zero		zero	Atlantic
R-7-1	William T. Nelson	'30	?	zero		zero	Atlantic
R-7-2	William T. Nelson	'30	?	zero		zero	Atlantic
R-7-3	William T. Nelson	'30	?	zero		zero	Atlantic
S-11-1	William B. Perkins, Jr.	'32	20	zero		zero	Atlantic
S-11-2	William B. Perkins, Jr.	'32	15	zero		zero	Atlantic
S-11-3	William B. Perkins, Jr.	'32	17	zero		zero	Atlantic
S-11-4	William B. Perkins, Jr.	'32	?	zero		zero	Atlantic
S-11-5	William B. Perkins, Jr.	'32	19	zero		zero	Atlantic
S-11-6	William B. Perkins, Jr.	'32	17	zero		zero	Atlantic
S-12-1	John E. Lee	'30	?	zero		zero	Atlantic
S-12-2	John E. Lee	'30	?	zero		zero	Atlantic
S-12-3	John E. Lee	'30	?	zero		zero	Atlantic
S-12-4	John E. Lee	'30	?	zero		zero	Atlantic
S-12-5	Fitzhugh McMaster	'33	?	zero		zero	Atlantic
S-12-6	Fitzhugh McMaster	33	16	zero		zero	Atlantic
S-13-1	David L. Whelchel	'30	20	zero		zero	Atlantic
S-13-2	David L. Whelchel	'30	5	zero		zero	Atlantic
S-13-3	David L. Whelchel	'30	25	zero		zero	Atlantic
S-13-4	Karl R. Wheland	31	17	zero		zero	Atlantic

* Credited with damaging a U-boat for 700 tons

SUBMARINE WAR PATROLS DEPARTING ATLANTIC AND PANAMANIAN BASES, 1942 (*Cont.*)

Boat, Patrol Number	Skipper and Class	Days	Ships/Tonnage Wartime Credit	Ships/Tonnage Postwar Credit	Area
S-14-1	Charles E. Loughlin '33	32	zero	zero	Atlantic
S-14-2	Charles E. Loughlin '33	10	zero	zero	Atlantic
S-14-3	Charles E. Loughlin '33	17	zero	zero	Atlantic
S-14-4	Charles E. Loughlin '33	24	zero	zero	Atlantic
S-15-1	Charles O. Triebel '29	?	zero	zero	Atlantic
S-15-2	Charles O. Triebel '29	20	zero	zero	Atlantic
S-15-3	Charles O. Triebel '29	6	zero	zero	Atlantic
S-16-1	Oscar E. Hagberg '31	?	zero	zero	Atlantic
S-16-2	Oscar E. Hagberg '31	8	zero	zero	Atlantic
S-16-3	Oscar E. Hagberg '31	?	zero	zero	Atlantic
S-16-4	Oscar E. Hagberg '31	20	zero	zero	Atlantic
S-16-5	Oscar E. Hagberg '31	16	zero	zero	Atlantic
S-16-6	Oscar E. Hagberg '31	5	zero	zero	Atlantic
S-17-1	Thomas B. Klakring '27	?	zero	zero	Atlantic
S-17-2	Brooks J. Harral '32	6	zero	zero	Atlantic
S-17-3	Brooks J. Harral '32	?	zero	zero	Atlantic
S-17-4	Brooks J. Harral '32	20	zero	zero	Atlantic
S-17-5	Brooks J. Harral '32	11	zero	zero	Atlantic
S-17-6	Brooks J. Harral '32	5	zero	zero	Atlantic
S-17-7	Brooks J. Harral '32	5	zero	zero	Atlantic
S-18-1	William J. Millican '28	?	zero	zero	Atlantic

S-21-1	John A. Bole, Jr.	'28	17	zero	zero	zero	Atlantic
S-21-2	John A. Bole, Jr.	'28	14	zero	zero	zero	Atlantic
S-21-3	John A. Bole, Jr.	'28	19	zero	zero	zero	Atlantic
S-22-1	George H. Wales	'29	16	zero	zero	zero	Atlantic
S-22-2	?		?	zero	zero	zero	Atlantic
S-22-3	?		20	zero	zero	zero	Atlantic
S-24-1	John Corbus	'30	16	zero	zero	zero	Atlantic
S-24-2	John Corbus	'30	?	zero	zero	zero	Atlantic
S-24-3	John Corbus	'30	20	zero	zero	zero	Atlantic
S-24-4	John Corbus	'30	21	zero	zero	zero	Atlantic
S-26-1	Earle C. Hawk	'28	17	zero	zero	zero	Atlantic
S-26-2	Earle C. Hawk	'28	lost	zero	zero	zero	Atlantic
S-29-1	Eugene T. Sands	'30	17	zero	zero	zero	Atlantic
S-29-2	Eugene T. Sands	'30	16	zero	zero	zero	Atlantic
S-29-3	Eugene T. Sands	'30	19	zero	zero	zero	Atlantic
S-30-1	Frederick W. Laing	'30	?	zero	zero	zero	Atlantic
S-30-2	Frederick W. Laing	'30	?	zero	zero	zero	Atlantic
S-30-3	Frederick W. Laing	'30	?	zero	zero	zero	Atlantic
S-31-1	Thomas F. Williamson	'32	?	zero	zero	zero	Atlantic
S-31-2	Thomas F. Williamson	'32	?	zero	zero	zero	Atlantic
S-32-1	Maximilian G. Schmidt	'32	?	zero	zero	zero	Atlantic
S-32-2	Maximilian G. Schmidt	'32	?	zero	zero	zero	Atlantic
S-33-1	Walter P. Schoeni	'31	?	zero	zero	zero	Atlantic

Later in the year 1942, the United States sent a small force of fleet boats to the British Isles, as described on page 239. The boats conducted twenty-seven war patrols in 1942–43, claiming the sinking of four Nazi ships or submarines for 8,100 tons. None of the four sinkings was confirmed in postwar German records.

The European patrols are shown on the following chart.

SUBMARINE WAR PATROLS DEPARTING EUROPEAN BASES, 1942–1943

Boat, Patrol Number	Skipper and Class	Days	Ships/Tonnage		Area
			Wartime Credit	Postwar Credit	
OCTOBER 1942					
Barb-1	John R. Waterman '27	36	zero	zero	North Africa
Blackfish-1	John F. Davidson '29	37	zero	zero	North Africa
Gunnel-1	John S. McCain, Jr. '31	49	zero	zero	North Africa
Herring-1	Raymond W. Johnson '30	35	1/7,000	zero	North Africa
Shad-1	Edgar J. MacGregor III '30	35	zero	zero	North Africa
NOVEMBER					
Gurnard-1	Charles H. Andrews '30	30	zero	zero	Europe
DECEMBER					
Barb-2	John R. Waterman '27	31	zero	zero	Europe
Blackfish-2	John F. Davidson '29	29	zero	zero	Europe
Herring-2	Raymond W. Johnson '30	58	2/600	zero	Europe
Shad-2	Edgar J. MacGregor III '30	44		zero	Europe

872

FEBRUARY 1943						
Barb-3	John R. Waterman	'27	37	zero	zero	Europe
Blackfish-3	John F. Davidson	'29	22	zero	zero	Europe
MARCH						
Herring-3	John Corbus	'30	37	1/500	zero	Europe
Shad-3	Edgar J. MacGregor III	'30	37	zero	zero	Europe
APRIL						
Barb-4	Nicholas Lucker, Jr.	'30	44	zero	zero	Europe
Blackfish-4	John F. Davidson	'29	39	zero	zero	Europe
Haddo-1	Willis A. Lent	'25	21	zero	zero	Europe
Hake-1	John C. Broach	'27	23	zero	zero	Europe
MAY						
Haddo-2	Willis A. Lent	'25	37	zero	zero	Europe
Hake-2	John C. Broach	'27	51	zero	zero	Europe
Herring-4	Raymond W. Johnson	'30	35	zero	zero	Europe
Shad-4	Roland F. Pryce	'27	43	zero	zero	Europe
JUNE						
Barb-5	John R. Waterman	'27	41	zero	zero	Europe
Blackfish-5	Eliot Olsen	'27	48	zero	zero	Europe
JULY						
Haddo-3	John Corbus	'30	19	zero	zero	Europe
Herring-5	Raymond W. Johnson	'30	19	zero	zero	Europe
Shad-5	Edgar J. MacGregor III	'30	19	zero	zero	Europe
		TOTALS:		4/8,100		

In January 1943 the Chief of Staff, U.S. Army, and the Commander in Chief, U.S. Navy, ordered the formation of a committee to assess Japanese naval and merchant-ship losses to submarines, carrier-based aircraft, land-based aircraft, mines, and other causes. During and after the war the committee, known as the Joint Army-Navy Assessment Committee (JANAC), tried to determine just who had sunk what Japanese ship of more than 500 gross tons. It made use of many sources: codebreaking, POW reports, captured documents, photographic intelligence, action reports of submarines, aircraft, and surface vessels, and lists of losses prepared by the Japanese after hostilities ceased. In February 1947 the final reports were issued. Japanese shipping losses to submarines were itemized by the name of the submarine and included name of the Japanese ship, its approximate tonnage, date and position lost.

The JANAC task was not easy. Japanese records were not complete or precise. Some vessels, sailing alone, had disappeared without trace and there was no way to determine why. Some sinkings were attributed to submarines that could not have taken place. Other positive sinkings by submarines were denied because no record could be found. Most U.S. submarine skippers found fault with the JANAC list. Recently, many conveyed to the author specific examples of inconsistencies and inaccuracies.

In the belief that JANAC did the best possible job with the tools at hand, the author has not attempted to revise or correct the submarine sinkings as reported, except in one or two flagrant instances. To revise JANAC's list would require years of work in the United States and Japan, and even after that no one could be certain that the revised list was any better. Thus JANAC's figures should be viewed more or less as an approximation—a fairly reliable yardstick—rather than as a precise accounting.

According to JANAC, U.S. submarines sank 540,192 tons of Japanese naval vessels and 4,779,902 tons of merchant shipping. Taken together the figures—5,320,094 tons—represent 54.6 percent of all Japanese naval and shipping losses to all causes. The three submarine commands credited the skippers with sinking a total of 10,689,800 tons and damage to 5,785,500 tons. The sinking credits, from a tonnage standpoint, were overclaimed, according to JANAC, by almost precisely 100 percent.

In the following charts, compiled from patrol reports, command war diaries, ships' histories, interviews with skippers, reports of the Submarine Operations Group (SORG) at Pearl Harbor, biographies, and JANAC, the submarine war patrols are broken down by place of departure, skipper (and Naval Academy class), days at sea, area patrolled, credited results during wartime, and results according to JANAC. In some instances, both wartime credits and postwar credits are rounded off to the nearest 100 tons.

SUBMARINE WAR PATROLS DEPARTING PEARL HARBOR, DECEMBER 1941

BOAT, PATROL NUMBER	SKIPPER AND CLASS		DAYS	SHIPS/TONNAGE Wartime Credit	JANAC Credit	AREA
Gudgeon-1	Elton W. Grenfell	'26	50	2/6,500	1/1,800	Empire
Pollack-1	Stanley P. Moseley	'25	39	2/16,000	2/7,600	Empire
Plunger-1	David C. White	'27	52	1/7,200	1/4,700	Empire
Pompano-1	Lewis S. Parks	'25	43	1/16,000	zero	Marshalls
Dolphin-1	Gordon B. Rainer	'25	42	zero	zero	Marshalls
Tautog-1	Joseph H. Willingham	'26	41	zero	zero	Marshalls
Thresher-2*	William L. Anderson	'26	58	1/4,500	zero	Marshalls
On patrol at Midway						
Argonaut-1	Stephen G. Barchet	'24	59	zero	zero	
Trout-1	Frank W. Fenno	'25	22	zero	zero	
On patrol at Wake						
Tambor-1	John W. Murphy, Jr.	'25	35	zero	zero	
Triton-1	Willis A. Lent	'25	42	zero	zero	
		TOTALS:		7/50,200	4/14,100	

* Prewar patrol to Wake counted as #1

875

SUBMARINE WAR PATROLS DEPARTING MANILA, DECEMBER 1941

Boat, Patrol Number	Skipper and Class		Days	Ships/Tonnage		Area
				Wartime Credit	JANAC Credit	
First Patrol						
Seawolf-1	Frederick B. Warder	'25	18	zero	zero	East Luzon[1]
Sculpin-1	Lucius H. Chappell	'27	45	1/5,000	zero	East Luzon[2]
Skipjack-1	Charles L. Freeman	'27	36	zero	zero	East Luzon[3]
S-39-1	James W. Coe	'30	18	1/5,000	zero	East Luzon[1]
Tarpon-1	Lewis Wallace	'25	33	zero	zero	East Luzon[3]
S-36-1	John R. McKnight	'30	18	zero	zero	West Luzon[1]
Sailfish-1	Morton C. Mumma, Jr.	'25	9	1/1,500	zero	West Luzon[1]
Saury-1	John L. Burnside, Jr.	'26	53	zero	zero	West Luzon[2]
Perch-1	David A. Hurt	'25	38	1/5,000	zero	Formosa[3]
Permit-1	Adrian M. Hurst	'24	9	zero	zero	West Luzon[1]
Stingray-1	Raymond S. Lamb	'26	13	zero	1/856	West Luzon[1]
Seal-1	Kenneth C. Hurd	'25	53	1/5,000	zero	West Luzon[2]
Salmon-1	Eugene B. McKinney	'27	55	1/1,500	zero	West Luzon[2]
Porpoise-1	Joseph A. Callaghan	'24	39	zero	zero	West Luzon[2]
Shark-1	Louis Shane, Jr.	'26	12	zero	zero	South Luzon[1]
S-37-1	James C. Dempsey	'31	10	zero	zero	South Luzon[1]
S-38-1	Wreford G. Chapple	'30	18	2/10,000	1/5,445	South Luzon[1]
S-40-1	Nicholas Lucker, Jr.	'30	9	zero	zero	South Luzon[1]
S-41-1	George M. Holley, Jr.	'30	31	zero	zero	South Luzon[2]
Sturgeon-1	William L. Wright	'25	17	zero	zero	Formosa[1]
Searaven-1	Theodore C. Aylward	'26	41	zero	zero	Formosa[3]
Pike-1	William A. New	'25	21	zero	zero	Hong Kong[1]

Submarine	Commander	Yr	No.			Area
Snapper-1	Hamilton L. Stone	'25	53	zero	zero	Hong Kong[2]
Swordfish-1	Chester C. Smith	'25	19	4/31,700	1/8,662	Indochina[1]
Pickerel-1	Barton E. Bacon, Jr.	'25	21	zero	zero	Indochina[1]
Spearfish-1	Roland F. Pryce	'27	51	zero	zero	Indochina[2]
Sargo-1	Tyrrell D. Jacobs	'27	48	zero	zero	Indochina[2]
Seadragon-1	William E. Ferrall	'27	45	2/10,000	1/6,441	Indochina[2]
Second Patrol						
Permit-2	Adrian M. Hurst	'24	6	zero	zero	Lingayen[1]
Pickerel-2	Barton E. Bacon, Jr.	'25	30	2/10,000	1/2,929	Celebes[2]
Pike-2	William A. New	'25	25	zero	zero	Celebes[3]
S-36-2	John R. McKnight	'30	lost	1/5,000	zero	Celebes
S-37-2	James C. Dempsey	'31	35	zero	zero	Celebes[2]
S-38-2	Wreford G. Chapple	'30	20	zero	zero	Celebes[2]
S-39-2	James W. Coe	'30	23	zero	zero	Celebes[2]
S-40-2	Nicholas Lucker, Jr.	'30	42	zero	zero	Celebes[2]
Sailfish-2	Richard G. Voge	'25	55	zero	zero	Celebes[2]
Seawolf-2	Frederick B. Warder	'25	10	zero	zero	Formosa[2]
Stingray-2	Raymond J. Moore	'27	44	zero	zero	special mission[*]
Sturgeon-2	William L. Wright	'25	46	1/10,700	1/5,167	Indochina[2]
Shark	Louis Shane, Jr.	'26	7	3/20,000	zero	special mission[†]
Swordfish	Chester C. Smith	'25	8	zero	zero	special mission[‡]
Third Patrol						
Permit-3	Adrian M. Hurst	'24	38	zero	zero	Celebes[2]
			TOTALS:	21/120,400	6/29,500	

[*] Transporting staff to Australia
[†] Transporting Admiral Hart to Surabaya
[‡] Transporting Wilkes to Surabaya

[1] Returned to Manila
[2] Returned to Java
[3] Returned to Darwin

SUBMARINE WAR PATROLS DEPARTING JAVA AND AUSTRALIA, JANUARY 1942

BOAT, PATROL NUMBER	SKIPPER AND CLASS	DAYS	Ships/Tonnage Wartime Credit	JANAC Credit	AREA
From Surabaya, Java					
S-38-3	Henry G. Munson '32	22	zero	zero	Barrier[1]
Sculpin-2	Lucius H. Chappell '27	29	1/1,500	zero	Barrier[2]
Swordfish-2*	Chester C. Smith '25	52	4/20,000	1/4,124	Celebes[2]
Shark-2	Louis Shane, Jr. '26	lost			Celebes
From Darwin, Australia					
Searaven-2	Theodore C. Aylward '26	43	1/1,500	zero	Indochina[2]
Seawolf-3	Frederick B. Warder '25	22	zero	zero	special mission[†1]
Skipjack-2	Charles L. Freeman '27	40	zero	zero	Celebes[2]
Tarpon-2	Lewis Wallace '25	40	zero	zero	Barrier[2]
		TOTALS:	6/23,000	1/4,124	

* Evacuated Quezon and Sayre parties from Corregidor
† Took ammunition to Corregidor

[1] Returned to Java
[2] Returned to Australia

SUBMARINE WAR PATROLS DEPARTING JAVA AND AUSTRALIA, FEBRUARY 1942

BOAT, PATROL NUMBER	SKIPPER AND CLASS	DAYS	Ships/Tonnage Wartime Credit	JANAC Credit	AREA
From Java					
Permit-4	Wreford G. Chapple '30	44	zero	zero	Barrier[2]
Pickerel-3	Barton E. Bacon, Jr. '25	41	zero	zero	Barrier[1]

Submarine	Commander	Year	No.			
Porpoise-2	John R. McKnight	'30	49	zero	zero	Barrier[1]
S-37-3	James C. Dempsey	'31	18	zero	1/1,900	Barrier[2]
S-37-4	James R. Reynolds	'31	21	zero	zero	Barrier[1]
S-38-4	Henry G. Munson	'32	19	zero	zero	Barrier[1]
S-39-3	James W. Coe	'30	32	1/5,000	1/6,500	Barrier[1]
S-40-3	Nicholas Lucker, Jr.	'30	26	zero	zero	Barrier[1]
S-41-2	George M. Holley, Jr.	'30	34	1/5,000	1/6,440	Barrier[1]
Sailfish-3	Richard G. Voge	'25	28	zero	zero	Barrier[1]
Salmon-2	Eugene B. McKinney	'27	31	zero	zero	special mission*[2]
Sargo-2	Tyrrell D. Jacobs	'27	25	zero	zero	Barrier[1]
Saury-2	John L. Burnside, Jr.	'26	38	zero	zero	Barrier[1]
Seal-2	Kenneth C. Hurd	'25	48	2/10,000	2/10,000	Barrier[2]
Spearfish-2	Roland F. Pryce	'27	27	zero	zero	Barrier[1]
Seawolf-4	Frederick B. Warder	'25	51	3/14,000	3/14,000	Barrier[1]
From Australia						
Perch-2	David A. Hurt	'25	lost	zero	zero	Barrier
Pike-3	William A. New	'25	51	zero	zero	Barrier[1]
		TOTALS:		7/34,000	3/14,840	

Note: The following submarines evacuated staff from Java to Australia:

Snapper	Hamilton L. Stone
Stingray	Raymond John Moore
Sargo	Tyrrell D. Jacobs
Spearfish	James C. Dempsey
Sturgeon	William L. Wright
Seadragon	William E. Ferrall

* Took ammunition to Mindanao

[1] Returned to Australia
[2] Returned to Java

SUBMARINE WAR PATROLS DEPARTING FREMANTLE, MARCH 1942

Boat, Patrol Number	Skipper and Class	Days	Ships/Tonnage		Area
			Wartime Credit	JANAC Credit	
Sargo-3	Richard V. Gregory	'32	52	zero	zero	Indochina
Sculpin-3	Lucius H. Chappell	'27	45	zero	zero	Banda Sea
Seadragon-2	William E. Ferrall	'27	39	zero	zero	special mission*
Snapper-2	Hamilton L. Stone	'25	50	1/3,000	zero	special mission*
Spearfish-3	James C. Dempsey	'31	54	2/10,000	2/10,995	special mission*
Stingray-3	Raymond J. Moore	'27	48	zero	zero	Java Sea
Sturgeon-3	William L. Wright	'25	53	2/6,500	2/1,592	Java Sea
Tarpon-3	Lewis Wallace	'25	52	zero	zero	→Pearl Harbor[1]
		TOTALS:		5/19,500	4/12,587	

* Corregidor

[1] Returned to Pearl Harbor via Palau, Marianas, Truk

SUBMARINE WAR PATROLS DEPARTING PEARL HARBOR, JANUARY–MARCH 1942

Boat, Patrol Number	Skipper and Class	Days	Ships/Tonnage		Area
			Wartime Credit	JANAC Credit	
JANUARY					
Cachalot-1	Waldeman N. Christensen	'25	66	zero	zero	Carolines
Cuttlefish-1	Martin P. Hottel	'27	54	zero	zero	Marshalls
Grayling-1	Eliot Olsen	'27	61	zero	zero	Carolines
Triton-2	Willis A. Lent	'25	52	2/12,000	2/5,982	East China Sea
Trout-2	Frank W. Fenno	'25	50	1/5,200	1/2,719	special mission*
Tuna-1	John L. DeTar	'27	54	1/6,000	1/4,000	Empire
FEBRUARY					
Gar-1	Donald McGregor	'26	54	1/10,000	1/1,520	Empire
Grampus-1	Edward S. Hutchinson	'26	48	2/20,000	1/8,636	Marshalls
Grayback-1	Willard A. Saunders	'27	54	2/11,800	1/3,291	Marianas
Grenadier-1	Allen R. Joyce	'26	48	zero	zero	Empire
Gudgeon-2	Elton W. Grenfell	'26	52	2/15,000	2/8,000	East China Sea
Narwhal-1	Charles W. Wilkins	'24	54	2/12,000	1/1,244	East China Sea
Pollack-2	Stanley P. Moseley	'25	49	1/5400	1/1,454	Formosa
MARCH					
Grayling-2	Eliot Olsen	'27	51	1/6,000	1/6,243	Empire
Tambor-2	John W. Murphy, Jr.	'25	58	1/7,000	zero	Marshalls
Thresher-3	William L. Anderson	'26	37	1/5,000	1/3,039	special mission†
Trout-3	Frank W. Fenno	'25	54	5/31,000	2/7,133	Empire
		TOTALS:	22/146,400	15/53,261	

* Corregidor
† Supported Doolittle raid on Tokyo

881

SUBMARINE WAR PATROLS DEPARTING PEARL HARBOR, APRIL–JUNE 1942

Boat, Patrol Number	Skipper and Class		Days	Ships/Tonnage Wartime Credit	JANAC Credit	Area
APRIL						
Cuttlefish-2	Martin P. Hottel	'27	56	zero	zero	Marianas*
Drum-1	Robert H. Rice	'27	56	4/24,000	4/20,000	Empire*
Gar-2	Donald McGregor	'26	50	1/4,000	zero	→Fremantle
Gato-1	William G. Myers	'26	51	zero	zero	Marshalls*
Grampus-2	Edward S. Hutchinson	'26	51	zero	zero	→Fremantle
Greenling-1	Henry C. Bruton	'26	57	1/5,800	1/3,300	Truk*
Grenadier-2	Willis A. Lent	'25	59	2/24,000	1/14,500	East China Sea*
Pompano-2	Lewis S. Parks	'25	58	2/16,400	2/8,900	East China Sea*
Silversides-1	Creed C. Burlingame	'27	52	4/25,600	1/4,000	Empire*
Tautog-2	Joseph H. Willingham	'26	47	6/19,500	3/7,500	→Fremantle
Triton-3	Charles C. Kirkpatrick	'31	52	5/24,200	5/15,843	East China Sea
Tuna-2	John L. DeTar	'27	60	1/8,000	1/800	East China Sea*
MAY						
Grayback-2	Willard A. Saunders	'27	50	zero	zero	→Fremantle
Pollack-3	Stanley P. Moseley	'25	45	1/900	zero	Empire*
Deployed for Battle of Midway						
Gudgeon-3	Hyland B. Lyon	'31	20	zero	zero	Midway
Grouper	Claren E. Duke	'27	15[1]	zero	zero	Midway
Nautilus	William H. Brockman	'27	15[1]	1/30,000†	zero	Midway
Grayling	Eliot Olsen	'27	15[1]	zero	zero	Midway
Trout-4	Frank W. Fenno	'25	26	zero	zero	Midway

Dolphin	Royal L. Rutter	'30	15[1]	zero	zero	Midway
Tambor	John W. Murphy, Jr.	'25	15[1]	zero	zero	Midway
Flying Fish	Glynn R. Donaho	'27	15[1]	zero	zero	Midway
Cachalot	George A. Lewis	'27	15[1]	zero	zero	Midway
Plunger	David C. White	'27	15[1]	zero	zero	Midway
Narwhal-2	Charles W. Wilkins	'24	15	zero	zero	Midway
Trigger	Jack H. Lewis	'27	15[1]	zero	zero	Midway
Growler	Howard W. Gilmore	'26	15[1]	zero	zero	Midway
Finback	Jesse L. Hull	'26	15[1]	zero	zero	Midway
Tarpon-4	Lewis Wallace	'25	9	zero	zero	Midway
Pike-5	William A. New	'25	11	zero	zero	Midway
Porpoise-3[2]	John R. McKnight, Jr.	'30	53	zero	zero	Midway
JUNE						
Cachalot-2	George A. Lewis	'27	47	zero	zero	Empire
Dolphin-2	Royal L. Rutter	'30	68	zero	zero	Empire
Nautilus-1	William H. Brockman	'27	48	3/13,200	1/1,600	Empire
Flying Fish-1	Glynn R. Donaho	'27	51	zero	zero	East China Sea
Grouper-1	Claren E. Duke	'27	56	zero	zero	East China Sea
Plunger-2	David C. White	'27	36	2/19,000	2/6,300	East China Sea
Thresher-4	William J. Millican	'28	50	1/6,000	1/4,800	→Fremantle
		TOTALS:		34/220,600	22/87,600	

* Participated in Battle of Midway en route home
† *Soryu,* later discredited

[1] Estimated
[2] En route from Australia

SUBMARINE WAR PATROLS DEPARTING FREMANTLE, APRIL–AUGUST 1942

Boat, Patrol Number	Skipper and Class		Days	Ships/Tonnage		Area
				Wartime Credit	JANAC Credit	
APRIL						
Pickerel-4	Barton E. Bacon, Jr.	'25	52	zero	zero	Philippines[1]
Pike-4	William A. New	'25	35	zero	zero	→Pearl Harbor
Porpoise-3	John R. McKnight, Jr.	'30	53	zero	zero	→Pearl Harbor
Sailfish-4	Richard G. Voge	'25	28	zero	zero	special mission*
Saury-3	John L. Burnside, Jr.	'26	61	zero	zero	Davao
Searaven-3	Hiram Cassedy	'31	23	zero	zero	special mission†
Skipjack-3	James W. Coe	'30	50	4/28,300	3/12,800	Camranh Bay
Swordfish-3	Chester C. Smith	'25	31	zero	zero	special mission*
MAY						
Permit-5	Wreford G. Chapple	'30	38	zero	zero	Makassar Strait
Salmon-3	Eugene B. McKinney	'27	52	2/9,800	2/15,800	Indochina
Saury-3	John L. Burnside, Jr.	'26	61	zero	zero	Manila
Sculpin-4	Lucius H. Chappell	'27	78	1/7,000	zero	South China Sea
Seal-3	Kenneth C. Hurd	'25	53	1/5,000	1/2,000	Indochina
Seawolf-5	Frederick B. Warder	'25	51	zero	1/1,200	Manila
Snapper-3	Harold E. Baker	'32	49	zero	zero	Celebes
Stingray-4	Raymond J. Moore	'27	50	zero	1/1,300	→Pearl Harbor
Swordfish-4	Chester C. Smith	'25	50	2/11,900	2/6,500	South China Sea
JUNE						
Sailfish-5	Richard G. Voge	'25	49	1/7,000	zero	Indochina
Sargo-4	Richard V. Gregory	'32	56	zero	zero	South China Sea

Seadragon-3	William E. Ferrall	'27	52	3/18,100	3/15,900	Indochina
Searaven-4	Hiram Cassedy	'31	40	zero	zero	Kendari
Spearfish-4	James C. Dempsey	'31	52	1/12,000	zero	South China Sea
Sturgeon-4	William L. Wright	'25	47	1/10,000	1/7,300	Manila
JULY						
Gar-3	Donald McGregor	'26	50	zero	zero	South China Sea
Grampus-3	Edward S. Hutchinson	'26	54	zero	zero	Manila
Grayback-3	Willard A. Saunders	'27	51	zero	zero	Indochina
Permit-6	Wreford G. Chapple	'30	50	zero	zero	→Pearl Harbor
Salmon-4	Eugene B. McKinney	'27	49	zero	zero	South China Sea
Saury-4	Leonard S. Mewhinney	'27	55	1/10,000	1/8,600	Manila
Seawolf-6	Frederick B. Warder	'25	52	2/8,100	2/4,462	Celebes
Skipjack-4	James W. Coe	'30	49	zero	zero	Java Sea
Swordfish-5	Albert C. Burrows	'28	55	zero	zero	Celebes
Tautog-3	Joseph H. Willingham	'26	57	1/7,000	1/5,900	Celebes
AUGUST						
Sargo-5	Richard V. Gregory	'32	59	1/7,000	1/4,500	Celebes
Seadragon-4	William E. Ferrall	'27	55	2/12,500	1/2,500	Indochina
Seal-4	Kenneth C. Hurd	'25	53	zero	zero	Indochina
Snapper-4	Harold E. Baker	'32	79	zero	zero	South China Sea
			TOTALS:	23/153,000	20/88,762	

* Corregidor
† Timor

1 Returned to Brisbane

SUBMARINE WAR PATROLS DEPARTING BRISBANE, APRIL–SEPTEMBER 1942

Boat, Patrol Number	Skipper and Class	Days	Ships/Tonnage		Area
			Wartime Credit	JANAC Credit	
APRIL					
S-38-5	Henry G. Munson '32	25	zero	zero	Solomons
S-42-1	Oliver G. Kirk '29	24	1/9,800	1/4,400	Solomons
S-44-1	John R. Moore '29	29	1/1,900	1/5,644	Solomons
S-47-1	James W. Davis '30	30	zero	zero	Solomons
MAY					
S-39-4	Francis E. Brown '33	27	zero	zero	Solomons
S-40-4	Nicholas Lucker, Jr. '30	30	zero	zero	Solomons
S-41-3	George M. Holley, Jr. '30	27	zero	zero	Solomons
S-43-1	Edward R. Hannon '29	28	zero	zero	Solomons
S-45-1	Ian C. Eddy '30	38	zero	zero	Solomons
S-46-1	Ralph C. Lynch, Jr. '29	35	zero	zero	Solomons
JUNE					
S-37-5	James R. Reynolds '31	29	zero	zero	Solomons
S-38-6	Henry G. Munson '32	13	zero	zero	Solomons
S-40-5	Nicholas Lucker, Jr. '30	27	zero	zero	Solomons
S-44-2	John R. Moore '29	28	1/1,100	1/2,626	Solomons
S-47-2	James W. Davis '30	25	zero	zero	Solomons
JULY					
Pickerel-5	Barton E. Bacon, Jr. '25	47	zero	zero	→Pearl Harbor
S-38-7	Henry G. Munson '32	25	1/8,000	1/5,628	Solomons*
S-39-5	Francis E. Brown '33	lost	zero	zero	Solomons
S-42-2	Oliver G. Kirk '29	25	zero	zero	Solomons
S-43-2	Edward R. Hannon '29	31	zero	zero	Solomons

S-44-3	John R. Moore	'29	30	1/7,100	1/8,800	Solomons
S-46-2	Ralph C. Lynch, Jr.	'29	26	zero	zero	Solomons
S-47-3	James W. Davis	'30	56	1/7,100	zero	Solomons
AUGUST						
S-37-6	Thomas S. Baskett	'35	27	zero	zero	Solomons
S-40-6	Francis M. Gambacorta	'35	28	zero	zero	Solomons
S-41-4	Irvin S. Hartman	'33	25	1/1,500	zero	Solomons*
S-42-3	Harley K. Nauman	'34	29	zero	zero	Solomons
S-45-2	Ian C. Eddy	'30	28	zero	zero	Solomons
Shifted from Fremantle						
Sailfish	Richard G. Voge					
Sculpin	Lucius H. Chappell					
Sturgeon	William L. Wright					
SEPTEMBER						
Sailfish-6	John R. Moore	'29	49	zero	zero	Solomons
Sculpin-5	Lucius H. Chappell	'27	54	3/24,100	2/6,652	Solomons
Sturgeon-5	Herman A. Pieczentkowski	'30	51	2/17,000	1/8,033	Solomons
S-38-8	Henry G. Munson	'32	30	zero	zero	→Pearl Harbor
S-41-5	Irvin S. Hartman	'33	42	zero	zero	→Pearl Harbor
S-43-3	Francis E. Brown	'33	35	zero	zero	Solomons*
S-44-4	Reuben T. Whitaker	'34	28	1/1,500	zero	Solomons*
S-46-3	Earl R. Crawford	'36	31	zero	zero	Solomons*
Shifted from Fremantle						
Grampus	Edward S. Hutchinson					
Grayback	Willard A. Saunders					
Gudgeon	William S. Stovall		TOTALS:	13/79,100	8/41,783	

* Then to the States

SUBMARINE WAR PATROLS DEPARTING ALASKA, 1942

Boat, Patrol Number	Skipper and Class		Days	Ships/Tonnage Wartime Credit	Ships/Tonnage JANAC Credit	Area
FEBRUARY						
S-18-2	William J. Millican	'28	20	zero	zero	Alaska
S-23-1	John R. Pierce	'28	10	zero	zero	Alaska
MARCH						
S-18-3	James H. Newsome	'30	12	zero	zero	Alaska
APRIL						
S-34-1	Thomas L. Wogan	'31	28	zero	zero	Alaska
S-35-1	James E. Stevens	'30	19	zero	zero	Alaska
MAY						
S-18-4	James H. Newsome	'30	51	zero	zero	Alaska
S-23-2	John R. Pierce	'28	43	zero	zero	Alaska
S-27-1	Herbert L. Jukes	'32	lost	zero	zero	Alaska
S-28-1	John D. Crowley	'31	40	zero	zero	Alaska
S-34-2	Thomas L. Wogan	'31	29	zero	zero	Alaska
S-35-2	James E. Stevens	'30	35	zero	zero	Alaska
JUNE						
Growler-1*	Howard W. Gilmore	'26	27	2/3,400	1/1,500	Alaska
Finback-1*	Jesse L. Hull	'26	48	zero	zero	Alaska
Trigger-1*	Jack H. Lewis	'27	51	zero	zero	Alaska
Triton-4*	Charles C. Kirkpatrick	'31	60	2/3,100	1/1,600	Alaska
Grunion-1*	Mannert L. Abele	'26	lost	3/4,500	2/600	Alaska

888

JULY						
S-18-5	James H. Newsome	'30	18	zero	zero	Alaska
S-23-3	Harold E. Duryea	'30	34	zero	zero	Alaska
S-28-2	John D. Crowley	'31	34	zero	zero	Alaska
S-31-3	Thomas F. Williamson	'32	34	zero	zero	Alaska
S-32-3	Maximilian G. Schmidt	'32	34	zero	zero	Alaska
S-33-2	Walter P. Schoeni	'31	36	zero	zero	Alaska
S-35-2	James E. Stevens	'30	29	zero	zero	Alaska
Gato-2*	William G. Myers	'26	50	1/9,300	zero	Alaska
Tuna-3*	Arnold H. Holtz	'31	42	zero	zero	Alaska
AUGUST						
S-30-4	Ferderick W. Laing	'30	32	zero	zero	Alaska
S-31-4	Robert F. Sellars	'34	33	zero	zero	Alaska
S-32-5	Maximilian G. Schmidt	'32	19	zero	zero	Alaska
S-33-3	Walter P. Schoeni	'31	33	zero	zero	Alaska
Halibut-1*	Philip H. Ross	'27	45	zero	zero	Alaska
SEPTEMBER						
S-28-3	John D. Crowley	'31	24	zero	zero	Alaska
S-30-5	Frederick W. Laing	'30	20	zero	zero	Alaska
S-34-3	Robert A. Keating, Jr.	'33	25	zero	zero	Alaska
Cachalot-3*	Harry C. Stevenson	'30	46	zero	zero	Alaska
OCTOBER						
S-18-6	George H. Browne	'34	29	zero	zero	Alaska
S-31-5	Robert F. Sellars	'34	28	1/3,000	1/2,864	Alaska
S-32-5	Maximilian G. Schmidt	'32	19	zero	zero	Alaska

* From Pearl Harbor

SUBMARINE WAR PATROLS DEPARTING ALASKA, 1942 (*Cont.*)

Boat, Patrol Number	Skipper and Class	Days	Ships/Tonnage Wartime Credit	Ships/Tonnage JANAC Credit	Area
S-33-4	Walter P. Schoeni	'31	27	zero	zero	Alaska
S-34-4	Robert A. Keating, Jr.	'33	29	zero	zero	Alaska
S-35-4	Henry S. Monroe	'33	30	zero	zero	Alaska
Halibut-2	Philip H. Ross	'27	21	zero	zero	Alaska
Dolphin-3	Royal L. Rutter	'30	51	zero	zero	Alaska
NOVEMBER					
S-18-7	George H. Browne	'34	28	zero	zero	Alaska
S-33-5	Walter P. Schoeni	'31	16	zero	zero	Alaska
DECEMBER					
S-23-5	Harold E. Ruble	'33	20	zero	zero	Alaska
S-28-4	John D. Crowley	'31	27	zero	zero	Alaska
S-34-5	Robert A. Keating, Jr.	'33	24	zero	zero	Alaska
S-35-5	Henry S. Monroe	'33	18	zero	zero	Alaska
	TOTALS:		9/22,300	5/6,564	

890

SUBMARINE WAR PATROLS DEPARTING PEARL HARBOR, JULY–DECEMBER 1942

BOAT, Patrol Number	Skipper and Class		Days	Ships/Tonnage Wartime Credit	Ships/Tonnage JANAC Credit	Area
JULY						
Cuttlefish-3	Elliott E. Marshall	'31	69	2/29,600	zero	Empire
Drum-2	Robert H. Rice	'27	54	zero	zero	Truk
Grayling-3	Eliot Olsen	'27	43	1/10,000	zero	Truk
Greenling-2	Henry C. Bruton	'26	53	2/24,000	2/17,250	Truk
Grenadier-3	Bruce L. Carr	'31	67	1/15,000	zero	→Fremantle*
Gudgeon-4	William S. Stovall	'29	53	4/35,000	1/4,900	→Fremantle*
Haddock-1	Arthur H. Taylor	'27	52	3/24,300	2/6,200	East China Sea
Narwhal-3	Charles W. Wilkins	'24	49	4/14,500	3/7,000	Empire
Pompano-3	Willis M. Thomas	'31	55	3/9,000	2/9,600	Empire
Silversides-2	Creed C. Burlingame	'27	56	3/15,000	2/9,800	Empire
Tambor-3	Stephen H. Ambruster	'28	57	2/12,000	2/5,800	→Fremantle*
AUGUST						
Albacore-1	Richard C. Lake	'29	53	zero	zero	Truk
Argonaut-2	John R. Pierce	'28	18	zero	zero	special mission†
Flying Fish-2	Glynn R. Donaho	'27	31	1/400	zero	Truk
Grouper-2	Rob Roy McGregor	'29	53	2/12,000	2/11,100	East China Sea
Growler-2	Howard W. Gilmore	'26	49	4/26,000	4/15,000	East China Sea
Guardfish-1	Thomas B. Klakring	'27	40	6/50,000	5/16,709	Empire
Nautilus-2	William H. Brockman	'27	18	zero	zero	special mission†

* Via Truk
† Makin Island raid

SUBMARINE WAR PATROLS DEPARTING PEARL HARBOR, JULY–DECEMBER 1942 (Cont.)

Boat, Patrol Number	Skipper and Class		Days	Ships/Tonnage		Area
				Wartime Credit	JANAC Credit	
Trout-5	Lawson P. Ramage	'31	47	1/8,200	1/900	→Brisbane*
Wahoo-1	Marvin G. Kennedy	'29	55	1/6,500	zero	Truk
SEPTEMBER						
Amberjack-1	John A. Bole, Jr.	'28	57	3/28,500	2/5,200	→Brisbane*
Drum-3	Robert H. Rice	'27	46	3/19,500	3/13,200	Empire
Finback-2	Jesse L. Hull	'26	58	2/14,100	3/22,000	East China Sea
Greenling-3	Henry C. Bruton	'26	41	4/32,100	4/20,400	Empire
Guardfish-2	Thomas B. Klakring	'27	59	2/15,400	2/10,400	East China Sea
Kingfish-1	Vernon L. Lowrance	'30	55	2/12,000	2/5,500	Empire
Nautilus-3	William H. Brockman	'27	56	2/10,100	3/12,000	Empire
Trigger-2	Roy S. Benson	'29	46	1/5,000	1/5,900	Empire
OCTOBER						
Flying Fish-3	Glynn R. Donaho	'27	50	2/3,000	zero	→Brisbane*
Grayling-4	John E. Lee	'30	55	1/5,300	1/4,000	→Fremantle*
Growler-3	Howard W. Gilmore	'26	49	zero	zero	→Brisbane*
Haddock-2	Arthur H. Taylor	'27	54	3/24,000	2/8,500	East China Sea
Plunger-3	David C. White	'27	27	zero	zero	→Brisbane*
Pollack-4	Robie E. Palmer	'27	49	zero	zero	Truk
Silversides-3	Creed C. Burlingame	'27	54	2/10,800	zero	→Brisbane*
Stingray-5	Raymond J. Moore	'27	55	zero	zero	Truk
Tarpon-5	Thomas L. Wogan	'30	42	zero	zero	Truk
Whale-1	John B. Azer	'30	32	1/9,400	zero	Empire‡

NOVEMBER						
Albacore-2	Richard C. Lake	'29	49	2/9,200	1/3,300	→Brisbane*
Drum-4	Bernard F. McMahon	'31	56	zero	zero	Empire‡
Gato-3	Robert J. Foley	'27	48	zero	zero	→Brisbane*
Grouper-3	Rob Roy McGregor	'29	49	1/8,400	1/4,000	→Brisbane*
Halibut-3	Philip H. Ross	'27	54	4/30,300	3/12,400	Empire
Kingfish-2	Vernon L. Lowrance	'30	58	2/14,100	2/10,000	East China Sea
Porpoise-4	John R. McKnight, Jr.	'30	47	1/5,300	1/5,000	Empire
Sunfish-1	Richard W. Peterson	'31	53	zero	zero	Empire‡
Tuna-4	Arnold H. Holtz	'31	48	zero	zero	→Brisbane*
Wahoo-2	Marvin G. Kennedy	'29	48	2/7,600	1/5,400	→Brisbane*
DECEMBER						
Argonaut-3	John R. Pierce	'28	lost	zero	zero	→Brisbane
Finback-3	Jesse L. Hull	'26	52	1/200	zero	Empire
Haddock-3	Arthur H. Taylor	'27	51	2/13,300	1/4,000	Empire
Greenling-4	Henry C. Bruton	'26	52	4/20,700	4/14,000	→Brisbane*
Guardfish-3	Thomas B. Klakring	'27	56	3/11,500	3/6,000	→Brisbane*
Nautilus-4	William H. Brockman	'27	55	1/1,000	1/1,500	→Brisbane*
Pike-6	William A. New	'25	48	zero	zero	Empire
Pollack-5	Robie E. Palmer	'27	41	zero	zero	Empire
Trigger-3	Roy S. Benson	'29	51	4/23,700	2/6,500	Empire‡
Triton-5	Charles C. Kirkpatrick	'31	40	3/17,300	2/5,300	→Brisbane*
			TOTALS:	98/643,300	71/288,750	

* Via Truk
‡ Planted minefield

SUBMARINE WAR PATROLS DEPARTING BRISBANE, OCTOBER–DECEMBER 1942

Boat, Patrol Number	Skipper and Class		Days	Ships/Tonnage		Area
				Wartime Credit	JANAC Credit	
OCTOBER						
Grampus-4	John R. Craig	'30	58	1/1,400	zero	Solomons
Grayback-4	Edward C. Stephan	'29	41	2/15,200	zero	Solomons
Gudgeon-5	William S. Stovall, Jr.	'29	54	3/22,000	zero	Solomons
Saury-5	Leonard S. Mewhinney	'27	51	zero	zero	→Pearl Harbor
Snapper-5	Augustus R. St. Angelo	'29	64	zero	zero	Solomons
Swordfish-6	Charles C. Smith	'25	50	1/4,400	zero	Solomons
Trout-6	Lawson P. Ramage	'31	28	zero	zero	Solomons*
S-37-7	Thomas S. Baskett	'35	28	zero	zero	Solomons*
S-40-7	Francis M. Gambacorta	'35	30	zero	zero	Solomons*
S-42-4	Harley K. Nauman	'34	27	zero	zero	Solomons*
S-45-3	Robert H. Caldwell, Jr.	'36	28	zero	zero	Solomons*
S-47-4	Frank E. Haylor	'36	28	zero	zero	Solomons*
Shifted from Fremantle						
Swordfish	Chester C. Smith					
Saury	Leonard S. Mewhinney					
Snapper	Augustus R. St. Angelo					
Seadragon	William E. Ferrall					
Sargo	Richard V. Gregory					
Holland	Perley E. Pendleton					
NOVEMBER						
Amberjack-2	John A. Bole, Jr.	'28	51	zero	zero	Solomons
Plunger-4	David C. White	'27	53	1/1,300	zero	→Pearl Harbor
Sailfish-7	John R. Moore	'29	53	zero	zero	→Pearl Harbor

894

Boat, Patrol Number	Skipper and Class		Days	Wartime Credit	JANAC Credit	Area
Sargo-6	Edward S. Carmick	'30	53	zero	zero	→Pearl Harbor
Sculpin-6	Lucius H. Chappell	'27	52	zero	zero	→Pearl Harbor
Seadragon-5	William E. Ferrall	'27	46	2/7,400	1/2,000	→Pearl Harbor
Sturgeon-6	Herman A. Pieczentkowski	'30	51	zero	zero	→Pearl Harbor
DECEMBER						
Grampus-5	John R. Craig	'30	37	3/24,000	zero	Solomons
Grayback-5	Edward C. Stephan	'29	47	1/2,000	1/2,000	Solomons
Gudgeon-6	William S. Stovall, Jr.	'29	53	zero	zero	Manila†
Silversides-4	Creed C. Burlingame	'27	46	1/10,000	4/27,798	→Pearl Harbor
Spearfish-6	James C. Dempsey	'31	55	zero	zero	→Pearl Harbor
			TOTALS:	15/87,700	6/31,800	

* Then to the States
† Returned to Fremantle

SUBMARINE WAR PATROLS DEPARTING FREMANTLE, SEPTEMBER–DECEMBER 1942

Boat, Patrol Number	Skipper and Class		Days	Ships/Tonnage		Area
				Wartime Credit	JANAC Credit	
SEPTEMBER						
Gar-4	Donald McGregor	'26	51	zero	zero	South China Sea*
Searaven-5	Hiram Cassedy	'31	58	2/21,900	zero	South China Sea
Skipjack-5	James W. Coe	'30	60	1/7,000	1/6,800	→Pearl Harbor
Spearfish-5	James C. Dempsey	'31	64	1/3,000	zero	Manila†
Thresher-5	William J. Millican	'28	61	1/3,000	1/3,000	South China Sea*

* Laid minefields
† Returned to Brisbane

SUBMARINE WAR PATROLS DEPARTING FREMANTLE, SEPTEMBER–DECEMBER 1942 (Cont.)

Boat, Patrol Number	Skipper and Class		Days	Ships/Tonnage		Area
				Wartime Credit	JANAC Credit	
OCTOBER						
Grenadier-4	Bruce L. Carr	'31	58	zero	zero	Indochina*
Salmon-5	Eugene B. McKinney	'27	58	1/6,100	1/5,900	→Pearl Harbor
Seal-5	Kenneth C. Hurd	'25	37	1/5,500	1/5,500	→Pearl Harbor
Seawolf-7	Frederick B. Warder	'25	55	3/16,800	3/13,000	→Pearl Harbor
Tambor-4	Stephan H. Ambruster	'28	38	1/10,000	1/2,500	Indochina*
Tautog-4	Joseph H. Willingham	'26	44	1/5,100	1/4,000	Indochina*
Shifted from Brisbane						
Trout	Lawson P. Ramage					
NOVEMBER						
Gar-5	Philip D. Quirk	'32	53	zero	1/600	Manila
DECEMBER						
Searaven-6	Hiram Cassedy	'31	55	1/5,900	1/5,700	→Pearl Harbor
Tambor-5	Stephan H. Ambruster	'28	41	zero	zero	Sunda Strait
Tautog-5	William B. Sieglaff	'31	46	2/6,900	2/2,900	Java Sea
Thresher-6	William J. Millican	'28	25	2/17,000	1/2,700	Java Sea
Trout-7	Lawson P. Ramage	'31	58	2/10,800	2/4,900	Indochina
			TOTALS:	19/118,200	16/57,500	

* Laid minefields
† Returned to Brisbane

896

SUBMARINE WAR PATROLS DEPARTING BRISBANE, JANUARY–MAY 1943

Boat, Patrol Number	Skipper and Class		Days	Ships/Tonnage		Area
				Wartime Credit	JANAC Credit	
JANUARY						
Albacore-3	Richard C. Lake	'29	50	1/1,300	2/2,500*	Solomons
Flying Fish-4	Glynn R. Donaho	'27	54	2/13,000	1½/5,000*	→Pearl Harbor
Gato-4	Robert J. Foley	'27	44	4/27,600	3½/11,500†	Solomons
Grouper-4	Rob Roy McGregor	'29	56	zero	zero	Solomons
Growler-4	Howard W. Gilmore	'26	48	2/7,900	1/5,900	Solomons
Snapper-6	Augustus R. St. Angelo	'29	46	zero	½/4,150*	→Pearl Harbor
Swordfish-7	Jack H. Lewis	'27	46	1/4,200	1/4,200	→Pearl Harbor
Tuna-5	Arnold H. Holtz	'31	31	zero	zero	Solomons
Wahoo-3	Dudley W. Morton	'30	23	5/31,900	3/11,300	→Pearl Harbor
Shifted to Pearl Harbor: *Holland, Sperry*						
FEBRUARY						
Amberjack-3	John A. Bole, Jr.	'28	lost	1/4,000	zero	Solomons
Grampus-6	John R. Craig	'30	lost	zero	zero	Solomons
Grayback-6	Edward C. Stephan	'29	47	1/6,400	zero	Solomons
Greenling-5	James D. Grant	'30	64	zero	zero	Solomons
Triton-6	George K. MacKenzie, Jr.	'31	lost	2/8,000	1/3,000	Solomons
MARCH						
Gato-5	Robert J. Foley	'27	72	zero	zero	→Pearl Harbor
Guardfish-4	Thomas B. Klakring	'27	52	zero	zero	Solomons
Tuna-6	Arnold H. Holtz	'31	47	1/8,500	1/5,000	Solomons

* *Flying Fish* and *Snapper* shared credit
† Shared credit with Navy Air

897

SUBMARINE WAR PATROLS DEPARTING BRISBANE, JANUARY–MAY 1943 (Cont.)

| Boat, Patrol Number | Skipper and Class | | Days | Ships/Tonnage | | Area |
				Wartime Credit	JANAC Credit	
Shifted to Pearl Harbor						
Nautilus	William H. Brockman					
April						
Albacore-4	Richard C. Lake	'29	50	zero	zero	Solomons
Grayback-7	Edward C. Stephan	'29	36	zero	2/12,300	→Pearl Harbor
Grouper-5	Martin P. Hottel	'27	47	zero	zero	Solomons
Peto-1	William T. Nelson	'30	48	zero	zero	Solomons
May						
Greenling-6	James D. Grant	'30	52	1/5,400	zero	Solomons
Growler-5	Arnold F. Schade	'33	48	1/4,500	1/5,200	Solomons
Guardfish-5	Norvell G. Ward	'35	70	1/4,000	1/900	Solomons
Tuna-7	Arnold H. Holtz	'31	47	zero	zero	Solomons
			TOTALS:	23/126,700	18½/70,950	

SUBMARINE WAR PATROLS DEPARTING FREMANTLE, JANUARY–JULY 1943

| Boat, Patrol Number | Skipper and Class | | Days | Ships/Tonnage | | Area |
				Wartime Credit	JANAC Credit	
January						
Grayling-5	John E. Lee	'30	49	3/14,400	1/750	Manila
Grenadier-5	John A. Fitzgerald	'31	51	2/1,300	zero	Java Sea
Thresher-7	William J. Millican	'28	45	2/14,000	2/11,000	Sunda Strait

898

FEBRUARY						
Gar-6	Philip D. Quirk	'32	53	zero	zero	South China Sea
Tambor-6	Stephen H. Ambruster	'28	55	zero	zero	Davao
Tautog-6	William B. Sieglaff	'31	53	2/6,800	2/7,000	Flores Sea*
MARCH						
Grayling-6	John E. Lee	'30	38	3/14,600	1/4,000	Manila
Grenadier-6	John A. Fitzgerald	'31	lost	zero	zero	Malacca Strait
Gudgeon-7	William S. Post, Jr.	'30	24	4/29,600	2/15,000	Java Sea
Trout-8	Lawson P. Ramage	'31	42	zero	zero	South China Sea*
APRIL						
Gar-7	Philip D. Quirk	'32	34	5/16,500	3/8,000	Manila
Gudgeon-8	William S. Post, Jr.	'30	41	3/19,600	2/23,000	→Pearl Harbor
Thresher-8	Harry Hull	'32	50	zero	zero	Java Sea
MAY						
Grayling-7	John E. Lee	'30	50	1/5,600	zero	South China Sea
Tambor-7	Russell Kefauver	'33	50	3/17,000	1/2,500	Indochina
Tautog-7	William B. Sieglaff	'31	53	2/14,300	2/5,300	→Pearl Harbor
Trout-9	Albert H. Clark	'33	59	3/17,200	2/5,800	Indochina
JUNE						
Gar-8	Philip D. Quirk	'32	34	zero	zero	Java Sea
Thresher-9	Harry Hull	'32	42	2/20,000	1/5,000	→Pearl Harbor
JULY						
Finback-6	John A. Tyree, Jr.	'33	56	3/17,100	3/11,000	→Pearl Harbor
Grayling-8	Robert M. Brinker	'34	lost	1/5,500	1/5,500	→Pearl Harbor
Tambor-8	Russell Kefauver	'33	55	1/4,400	zero	→Pearl Harbor
			TOTALS:	40/211,800	23/103,850	

* Laid minefields

899

SUBMARINE WAR PATROLS DEPARTING PEARL HARBOR, JANUARY–MARCH 1943

Boat, Patrol Number	Skipper and Class		Days	Ships/Tonnage		Area
				Wartime Credit	JANAC Credit	
JANUARY						
Pickerel-6	Augustus H. Alston, Jr.	'31	37	1/6,100	1/2,000	Empire
Pompano-4	Willis M. Thomas	'31	44	zero	zero	Marshalls
Runner-1	Frank W. Fenno, Jr.	'25	48	3/19,800	zero	Palau
Sawfish-1	Eugene T. Sands	'30	53	3/13,300	zero	Empire
Stingray-6	Otis J. Earle	'30	55	zero	zero	Truk
Tarpon-6	Thomas L. Wogan	'30	47	2/21,000	2/27,910	Empire
Tunny-1	John A. Scott	'28	43	2/16,700	1/5,300	East China Sea
Whale-2	John B. Azer	'30	30	2/19,300	3/19,000	Truk
FEBRUARY						
Finback-4	John A. Tyree, Jr.	'33	44	½/5,300	½/2,500*	Truk
Halibut-4	Philip H. Ross	'27	50	2/15,100	2/10,711	Palau
Kingfish-3	Vernon L. Lowrance	'30	52	2/13,000	1/8,000	East China Sea
Permit-7	Wreford G. Chapple	'30	38	2/10,300	1/2,700	Empire
Plunger-5	Raymond H. Bass	'31	29	1/9,000	1/1,800	Marshalls
Porpoise-5	John R. McKnight, Jr.	'30	48	1/3,000	zero	Truk
Sunfish-2	Richard W. Peterson	'31	58	2/12,200	1/3,200	East China Sea
Trigger-4	Roy S. Benson	'29	56	zero	1/3,000	Palau
Wahoo-4	Dudley W. Morton	'30	42	8/36,700	9/20,000	East China Sea
Whale-3	Albert C. Burrows	'28	42	4/33,500	1/6,500	Marianas
MARCH						
Drum-5	Bernard F. McMahon	'31	47	3/15,900	2/10,000	→Brisbane
Flying Fish-5	Glynn R. Donaho	'27	48	4/28,000	3/7,500	Empire
Haddock-4	Roy M. Davenport	'33	39	1/11,900	2/9,200	Palau

900

Pickerel-7	Augustus H. Alston, Jr.	'31	lost	zero	zero	Empire
Pike-7	Louis D. McGregor, Jr.	'30	40	zero	zero	Truk
Pollack-6	Robie E. Palmer	'27	44	zero	zero	Marshalls
Pompano-5	Willis M. Thomas	'31	52	zero	zero	Empire
Scamp-1	Walter G. Ebert	'30	26	zero	zero	Empire
Tarpon-7	Thomas L. Wogan	'30	47	zero	zero	Truk
Tunny-2	John A. Scott	'28	36	2½/18,700	2½/17,000*	→Brisbane
S-31-6	Robert F. Sellars	'34	28	zero	zero	
		TOTALS:		46/308,800	34/156,321	

* Finback and Tunny shared credit (Wake Island)

SUBMARINE WAR PATROLS DEPARTING ALASKA, 1943

Boat, Patrol Number	Skipper and Class	Days	Ships/Tonnage		Area
			Wartime Credit	JANAC Credit	
JANUARY					
S-18-8	George H. Browne	'34	23	zero	zero	Alaska
S-23-6	Harold E. Ruble	'33	28	zero	zero	Alaska
FEBRUARY					
S-28-5	John D. Crowley	'31	22	zero	zero	Alaska
S-32-6	Maximilian G. Schmidt	'32	23	3/4,300	zero	Alaska
MARCH					
S-23-7	Harold E. Ruble	'33	28	zero	zero	Alaska
S-32-7	Maximilian G. Schmidt	'32	22	1/9,000	zero	Alaska

SUBMARINE WAR PATROLS DEPARTING ALASKA, 1943 (*Cont.*)

BOAT, PATROL NUMBER	SKIPPER AND CLASS	DAYS	SHIPS/TONNAGE Wartime Credit	JANAC Credit	AREA
APRIL					
S-30-6	William A. Stevenson '34	28	zero	zero	Alaska
S-33-6	Clyde B. Stevens, Jr. '30	28	zero	zero	Alaska
S-34-6	Robert A. Keating, Jr. '33	28	1/3,000	zero	Alaska
Narwhal-4	Frank D. Latta '32	38	zero	zero	special mission*
Nautilus-5	William H. Brockman '27	36	zero	zero	special mission*
MAY					
S-30-7	William A. Stevenson '34	29	zero	1/5,228	Alaska
S-32-8	Frederick J. Harlfinger '35	19	zero	zero	Alaska
S-41-6	Irvin S. Hartman '33	31	2/6,200	1/1,036	Alaska
Shifted from States					
S-40					
S-41					
S-42					
S-44					
S-45					
S-46					
S-47					
JUNE					
S-33-7	Clyde B. Stevens, Jr. '30	27	zero	zero	Alaska
S-34-7	Robert A. Keating, Jr. '33	39	zero	zero	Alaska
S-35-6	Henry S. Monroe '33	38	1/8,200	1/5,430	Alaska
S-40-8	Francis M. Gambacorta '35	37	zero	zero	Alaska

902

S-41-7	Irvin S. Hartman	'33	36	zero	zero	Alaska
JULY						
S-28-6	Vincent A. Sisler, Jr.	'35	33	zero	zero	Alaska
S-30-8	William A. Stevenson	'34	34	zero	zero	Alaska
S-33-8	Clyde B. Stevens, Jr.	'30	23	zero	zero	Alaska
AUGUST						
S-30-9	William A. Stevenson	'34	28	zero	zero	Alaska
S-35-7	Henry S. Monroe	'33	23	zero	zero	Alaska
S-40-9	Francis M. Gambacorta	'35	30	zero	zero	Alaska
S-41-8	Irvin S. Hartman	'33	39	zero	zero	Alaska
SEPTEMBER						
S-28-7	Vincent A. Sisler, Jr.	'35	40	1/4,000	1/1,368	Alaska
S-42-5	Harley K. Nauman	'34	40	zero	zero	Alaska
S-44-5	Francis E. Brown	'33	lost	zero	zero	Alaska
S-46-4	Earl R. Crawford	'36	33	zero	zero	Alaska
OCTOBER						
S-47-5	Frank E. Haylor	'36	28	zero	zero	Alaska
NOVEMBER						
S-35-8	Robert B. Byrnes	'38	20	zero	zero	Alaska
DECEMBER						
S-45-4	Robert H. Caldwell	'36	28	zero	zero	Alaska
S-46-5	Gordon Campbell	'26	33	zero	zero	Alaska
S-47-6	Frank E. Haylor	'36	26	zero	zero	Alaska
			TOTALS:	9/34,700	4/13,062	

* From Pearl Harbor to land commandos at Attu

903

SUBMARINE WAR PATROLS DEPARTING PEARL HARBOR, APRIL–AUGUST 1943

Boat, Patrol Number	Skipper and Class	Days	Ships/Tonnage		Area
			Wartime Credit	JANAC Credit	
APRIL					
Permit-8	Wreford G. Chapple	'30 49	2/15,000	zero	Truk
Plunger-6	Raymond H. Bass	'31 29	3/24,100	2/15,000	Marshalls
Pogy-1	George H. Wales	'29 51	2/9,100	2/3,300	Empire
Runner-2	Frank W. Fenno	'25 35	zero	zero	East China Sea
Salmon-6	Nicholas J. Nicholas	'32 51	zero	zero	Empire*
Sawfish-2	Eugene T. Sands	'30 53	zero	1/3,000	Empire
Scamp-2	Walter G. Ebert	'30 46	1/15,600	1/7,000	→Brisbane
Scorpion-1	William N. Wylie	'30 33	3/13,100	2/8,300	Empire*
Seal-6	Harry B. Dodge	'30 50	1/10,200	1/7,354	Palau
Seawolf-8	Royce L. Gross	'30 30	3/13,100	2/5,300	East China Sea
Skipjack-6	Howard F. Stoner	'32 45	zero	zero	Marshalls
Snook-1	Charles O. Triebel	'29 42	3/12,000	3/8,600	East China Sea*
Steelhead-1	David L. Whelchel	'30 49	zero	zero	Empire*
Stingray-7	Otis J. Earle	'30 46	1/7,500	1/8,156	East China Sea*
Sunfish-3	Richard W. Peterson	'31 57	zero	zero	Palau
Trigger-5	Roy S. Benson	'29 53	1/8,200	1/2,000	Empire
Wahoo-5	Dudley W. Morton	'30 26	3/24,700	3/10,500	Empire†
MAY					
Finback-5	John A. Tyree, Jr.	'33 44	4/23,200	3/13,000	→Fremantle
Hoe-1	Victor B. McCrea	'32 45	1/9,500	zero	Palau
Pollack-7	Bafford E. Lewellen	'31 46	2/9,300	2/8,400	Marshalls
Runner-3	Joseph H. Bourland	'33 lost	zero	zero	Empire†
Sailfish-8	John R. Moore	'29 49	zero	2/5,800	Empire

Sargo-7	Edward S. Carmick	'30	43	1/6,600	1/5,200	Truk
Saury-6	Anthony H. Dropp	'32	38	3/24,900	4/20,000	East China Sea
Scorpion-2	William N. Wylie	'30	48	zero	2/10,000	East China Sea
Sculpin-7	Lucius H. Chappell	'27	41	zero	zero	Empire
Seadragon-6	Royal L. Rutter	'30	43	zero	zero	Truk
Seawolf-9	Royce L. Gross	'30	56	1/4,300	1/4,700	East China Sea
Silversides-5	Creed C. Burlingame	'27	44	1/10,000	1/5,200	→Brisbane*
Tinosa-1	Lawrence R. Daspit	'27	47	zero	zero	Empire
Tunny-3	John A. Scott	'28	50	1/3,100	1/2,000	Marianas
Whale-4	Albert C. Burrows	'28	47	2/13,000	1/3,500	Empire
JUNE						
Flying Fish-6	Frank T. Watkins	'22	55	1/8,700	1/2,820	East China Sea
Gunnel-2	John S. McCain, Jr.	'31	31	3/15,600	2/13,300	East China Sea
Gurnard-2	Charles H. Andrews	'30	43	3/15,600	1/2,000	Palau
Haddock-5	Roy M. Davenport	'33	41	1/10,900	1/5,500	Palau
Halibut-5	Philip H. Ross	'27	49	zero	zero	Truk
Harder-1	Samuel D. Dealey	'30	33	3/15,400	1/7,000	Empire
Jack-1	Thomas M. Dykers	'27	40	3/24,300	3/16,400	Empire†
Lapon-1	Oliver G. Kirk	'29	41	zero	zero	Empire‡
Mingo-1	Ralph C. Lynch, Jr.	'29	57	zero	zero	Palau
Narwhal-5	Frank D. Latta	'32	42	zero	zero	Empire§
Permit-9	Wreford G. Chapple	'30	37	3/16,100	2/3,000	Empire‡
Plunger-7	Raymond H. Bass	'31	32	1/5,100	1/2,500	Empire‡
Pogy-2	George H. Wales	'29	53	1/15,600	1/7,500	Truk
Pompano-6	Willis M. Thomas	'31	52	zero	zero	Empire

* Laid mines
† Polar patrol–Kuriles and Hokkaido
‡ Sea of Japan
§ Supported Sea of Japan mission

SUBMARINE WAR PATROLS DEPARTING PEARL HARBOR, APRIL–AUGUST 1943 (*Cont.*)

BOAT, Patrol Number	Skipper and Class		Days	Ships/Tonnage			Area
				Wartime Credit	JANAC Credit		
Porpoise-6	Carter L. Bennett	'33	36	2/17,300	1/3,000		Marshalls
Sawfish-3	Eugene T. Sands	'30	41	3/25,600	1/720		East China Sea
Seal-7	Harry B. Dodge	'30	30	zero	zero		Empire
Searaven-7	Hiram Cassedy	'31	43	zero	zero		Marianas
Snook-2	Charles O. Triebel	'29	40	1/17,600	2/11,000		East China Sea
Spearfish-7	George A. Sharp	'29	57	zero	zero		Truk
Steelhead-2	David L. Whelchel	'30	47	1/4,800	zero		Truk
Stingray-8	Otis J. Earle	'30	50	zero	zero		→Brisbane
Sturgeon-7	Herman A. Pieczentkowski	'30	51	zero	zero		Empire
S-38-9	Cassius D. Rhymes	'35	30	zero	zero		→Brisbane
JULY							
Paddle-1	Robert H. Rice	'27	54	1/5,500	1/5,248		Empire
Pike-8	Louis D. McGregor, Jr.	'30	50	1/5,000	1/2,000		Marianas
Sailfish-9	William R. Lefavour	'31	51	zero	zero		East China Sea
Salmon-7	Nicholas J. Nicholas	'32	40	2/11,100	1/2,500		Empire†
Saury-7	Anthony H. Dropp	'30	30	zero	zero		Empire
Sculpin-8	Lucius H. Chappell	'27	54	1/4,500	1/3,183		East China Sea
Seadragon-7	Royal L. Rutter	'30	43	zero	zero		Marshalls
Skipjack-7	Howard F. Stoner	'32	49	zero	zero		Empire
Snapper-7	Merrill K. Clementson	'33	54	2/10,400	1/860		Truk
Sunfish-4	Richard W. Peterson	'31	60	3/29,100	1/2,000		East China Sea
Tarpon-8	Thomas L. Wogan	'30	40	1/1,000	zero		Empire
Tinosa-2	Lawrence R. Daspit	'27	27	zero	zero		Truk

Tullibee-1	Charles F. Brindupke	'32	50	1/7,000	1/4,000	Truk
Whale-5	Albert C. Burrows	'28	46	1/10,000	1/7,149	East China Sea
Swordfish-8	Frank M. Parker	'32	57	1/7,000	2/6,000	Palau
Pollack-8	Bafford E. Lewellen	'31	47	zero	2/7,000	Empire
Kingfish-4	Vernon L. Lowrance	'30	56	zero	zero	→Fremantle
AUGUST						
Halibut-6	Ignatius J. Galantin	'33	28	2/9,700	2/9,800	Empire
Harder-2	Samuel D. Dealey	'30	46	4/25,300	5/15,272	Empire
Hoe-2	Victor B. McCrea	'32	59	zero	zero	Truk
Narwhal-6	Frank D. Latta	'32	31	1/4,500	1/4,200	→Fremantle
Pargo-1	Ian C. Eddy	'30	49	4/27,600	zero	East China Sea
Permit-10	Carter L. Bennett	'33	32	3/27,700	zero	Marshalls
Plunger-8	Raymond H. Bass	'31	30	2/9,000	3/10,500	Empire‡
Pompano-7	Willis M. Thomas	'31	lost	zero	2/8,500	Empire
Sargo-8	Edward S. Carmick	'30	46	zero	zero	Truk
Seahorse-1	Donald McGregor	'26	55	zero	zero	Palau
Seal-8	Harry B. Dodge	'30	50	zero	zero	Empire†
Searaven-8	Hiram Cassedy	'31	47	zero	zero	Empire
Seawolf-10	Royce L. Gross	'30	32	2/15,300	3/13,000	East China Sea
Snook-3	Charles O. Triebel	'29	52	2/12,400	2/10,000	East China Sea
Spearfish-8	Joseph W. Williams, Jr.	'33	47	2/12,600	zero	Empire
Sturgeon-8	Charlton L. Murphy, Jr.	'32	59	zero	zero	Empire
Tunny-4	John A. Scott	'28	34	zero	zero	Palau
Wahoo-6	Dudley W. Morton	'30	27	zero	zero	Empire‡
			TOTALS:	101/683,000	86/348,264	

† Polar patrol—Kuriles and Hokkaido
‡ Sea of Japan

SUBMARINE WAR PATROLS DEPARTING BRISBANE, JUNE–DECEMBER 1943

BOAT, PATROL NUMBER	SKIPPER AND CLASS		DAYS	SHIPS/TONNAGE		AREA
				Wartime Credit	JANAC Credit	
JUNE						
Albacore-5	Oscar E. Hagberg	'31	45	zero	zero	Bismarck
Drum-6	Bernard F. McMahon	'31	49	1/8,700	1/5,000	Bismarck
Grouper-6	Martin P. Hottel	'27	46	zero	zero	Bismarck
Peto-2	William T. Nelson	'30	53	1/2,000	zero	Bismarck
Scamp-3	Walter G. Ebert	'30	47	1/2,300	1/2,000	Bismarck
JULY						
Balao-1	Richard H. Crane	'31	51	zero	zero	Bismarck
Growler-6	Arnold F. Schade	'33	53	zero	zero	Bismarck
Pompon-1	Earle C. Hawk	'28	43	1/6,600	1/5,871	Bismarck
Silversides-6	John S. Coye	'33	53	zero	zero	Bismarck
Greenling-7	James D. Grant	'30	51	zero	zero	→Pearl Harbor
S-31-7	Robert F. Sellars	'34	21	zero	zero	Bismarck
AUGUST						
Albacore-6	Oscar E. Hagberg	'31	26	1/4,200	1/2,600	Bismarck
Grouper-7	Martin P. Hottel	'27	47	zero	zero	→Pearl Harbor
Guardfish-6	Norvell G. Ward	'35	70	2/13,000	1/5,460	Bismarck
Drum-7	Bernard F. McMahon	'31	51	3/12,900	1/1,334	Bismarck
Stingray-9	Otis J. Earle	'30	50	zero	zero	→Pearl Harbor
S-31-8	Robert F. Sellars	'34	27	zero	zero	Bismarck
SEPTEMBER						
Peto-3	William T. Nelson	'30	51	2/10,500	2/10,000	Bismarck
Scamp-4	Walter G. Ebert	'30	30	2/14,600	1/8,600	Bismarck

OCTOBER						
Albacore-7	Oscar E. Hagberg	'31	54	1/9,000	1/4,700	Bismarck
Balao-2	Richard H. Crane	'31	43	1/5,000	zero	Bismarck
Growler-7	Arnold F. Schade	'33	35	zero	zero	→Pearl Harbor
Scamp-5	Walter G. Ebert	'30	35	1/6,500	1/6,400	Bismarck
Silversides-7	John S. Coye	'33	36	4/22,100	4/15,000	→Pearl Harbor
Blackfish-6	John F. Davidson	'29	47	1/4,500	zero	Bismarck
NOVEMBER						
Gato-7	Robert J. Foley	'27	54	3/21,100	2/8,544	Bismarck
Peto-4	William T. Nelson	'30	54	1/8,200	1/2,345	Bismarck
Ray-1	Brooks J. Harral	'32	24	2/14,300	1/2,562	Bismarck
Raton-1	James W. Davis	'30	24	3/18,700	3/18,000	Bismarck
Drum-8	Delbert F. Williamson	'27	34	1/11,900	1/11,621	→Pearl Harbor
DECEMBER						
Albacore-8	James W. Blanchard	'27	59	2/6,800	2/4,500	→Pearl Harbor
Balao-3	Cyrus C. Cole	'35	38	zero	zero	Bismarck
Guardfish-7	Norvell G. Ward	'35	54	2/11,900	2/11,500	→Pearl Harbor
Scamp-6	Walter G. Ebert	'30	52	1/10,000	1/10,000	Bismarck
Blackfish-7	John F. Davidson	'29	50	1/6,000	1/2,000	Bismarck
	TOTALS:			38/239,800	29/138,037	

SUBMARINE WAR PATROLS DEPARTING FREMANTLE, AUGUST–DECEMBER 1943

Boat, Patrol Number	Skipper and Class		Days	Ships/Tonnage		Area
				Wartime Credit	JANAC Credit	
AUGUST						
Billfish-1*	Frederic C. Lucas, Jr.	'30	59	zero	zero	South China Sea
Bowfin-1*	Joseph H. Willingham	'26	57	3/23,900	1/8,120	South China Sea
Gar-9	George W. Lautrup, Jr.	'34	37	1/4,000	1/1,000	Celebes
Puffer-1*	Marvin J. Jensen	'31	54	1/5,300	zero	Makassar Strait
Trout-10	Albert H. Clark	'33	54	3/15,000	3/12,542	→Pearl Harbor
Tuna-8*	Arnold H. Holtz	'31	54	zero	zero	South China Sea
SEPTEMBER						
Bluefish-1*	George E. Porter	'32	25	4/16,200	2/3,822	South China Sea
Bonefish-1*	Thomas W. Hogan	'31	45	6/40,200	3/24,206	South China Sea
Cisco-1*	James W. Coe	'30	lost	zero	zero	South China Sea
Kingfish-5†	Vernon L. Lowrance	'30	52	2/19,100	1/3,365	South China Sea
Pompon-2*	Earle C. Hawk	'28	55	zero	zero	South China Sea
Rasher-1*	Edward S. Hutchinson	'26	61	4/21,300	4/8,894	Celebes
OCTOBER						
Bluefish-2	George E. Porter	'32	32	3/22,800	2/11,390	South China Sea
Cod-1*	James C. Dempsey	'31	63	1/7,100	zero	South China Sea
Crevalle-1*	Henry G. Munson	'32	49	4/29,800	1/6,783	Manila
Narwhal-7	Frank D. Latta	'32	31	zero	zero	special mission
Capelin-1*	Elliott E. Marshall	'31	lost	2/7,400	1/3,000	Makassar Strait

910

NOVEMBER						
Billfish-2	Frederic C. Lucas, Jr.	'30	53	zero	zero	South China Sea
Bonefish-2	Thomas W. Hogan	'31	27	3/16,600	2/7,367	Celebes
Bowfin-2	Walter T. Griffith	'34	39	9/70,900	5/26,458	South China Sea
Narwhal-8	Frank D. Latta	'32	23	1/4,000	1/834	special mission
Pompon-3†	Earle C. Hawk	'28	60	zero	zero	South China Sea
Puffer-2	Frank G. Selby	'33	49	1/1,500	2/7,527	South China Sea
Tuna-9	James T. Hardin	'29	56	zero	1/5,484	→Pearl Harbor
DECEMBER						
Bluefish-3†	George E. Porter	'32	27	2/20,100	2/11,000	South China Sea
Cabrilla-2†	Douglas T. Hammond	'31	52	1/4,100	1/2,700	South China Sea
Crevalle-2†	Henry G. Munson	'32	60	3/19,900	1/2,552	South China Sea
Kingfish-6	Herbert L. Jukes	'32	42	3/22,300	3/14,571	→Pearl Harbor
Rasher-2†	Willard R. Laughon	'33	36	1/7,200	1/7,251	South China Sea
*Raton-2**	James W. Davis	'30	45	2/18,000	1/5,578	Celebes
*Ray-2**	Brooks J. Harral	'32	24	2/14,300	2/8,696	Celebes
Gar-10	George W. Lautrup, Jr.	'34	55	3/21,500	2/9,000	→Pearl Harbor
			TOTALS:	65/432,500	43/192,140	

* From Brisbane via Darwin
† Laid minefield

SUBMARINE WAR PATROLS DEPARTING PEARL HARBOR, SEPTEMBER–DECEMBER 1943

Boat, Patrol Number	Skipper and Class		Days	Ships/Tonnage		Area
				Wartime Credit	JANAC Credit	
SEPTEMBER						
Barb-6	John R. Waterman	'27	53	1/8,000	zero	East China Sea
Cabrilla-1	Douglas T. Hammond	'31	54	zero	zero	→Fremantle
Cero-1	David C. White	'27	52	1/6,000	zero	East China Sea
Grayback-8‡	John A. Moore	'32	45	2½/18,700	2½/19,000	East China Sea
Gudgeon-9	William S. Post, Jr.	'30	37	2/15,000	1/3,158	Marianas
Gurnard-3	Charles H. Andrews	'30	52	2/18,000	2/11,000	East China Sea
Gato-6	Robert J. Foley	'27	50	zero	zero	→Brisbane
Haddock-6	Roy M. Davenport	'33	27	3/39,200	zero	Truk
Jack-2	Thomas M. Dykers	'27	30	zero	zero	Empire
Lapon-2	Lowell T. Stone	'29	39	1/2,900	1/2,000	Empire
Mingo-2	Ralph C. Lynch, Jr.	'29	53	zero	zero	Truk
Muskallunge-1	Willard A. Saunders	'27	48	zero	zero	Palau
*Nautilus-6**	William D. Irvin	'27	31	zero	zero	Gilberts
Pogy-3	George H. Wales	'29	49	1/6,600	1/7,000	Palau
Salmon-8	Nicholas J. Nicholas	'32	51	zero	zero	Empire
Sawfish-4	Eugene T. Sands	'30	36	zero	zero	Empire[1]
Seadragon-8	Royal L. Rutter	'30	42	1/8,200	zero	Marshalls
Shad-6‡	Edgar J. MacGregor	'30	58	1½/13,400	½/4,500	East China Sea
*Skate-1**	Eugene B. McKinney	'27	31	zero	zero	Wake
*Skipjack-8**	George G. Molumphy	'31	43	zero	zero	Marshalls
Steelhead-3‡	David L. Whelchel	'30	72	zero	½/4,000	Palau
Tinosa-3‡	Lawrence R. Daspit	'27	23	1/10,500	½/4,000	Palau

Trigger-6	Robert E. Dornin	'35	29	5/40,000	4/27,095	East China Sea
Tullibee-2	Charles F. Brindupke	'32	52	1/6,000	1/5,866	East China Sea
Wahoo-7	Dudley W. Morton	'30	lost	1/7,100	4/13,000	Empire[1]
OCTOBER						
Dace-1	Joseph F. Enright	'33	49	zero	zero	Empire
Flying Fish-7	Glynn R. Donaho	'27	34	1/7,000	1/6,500	Palau
Gudgeon-10	William S. Post, Jr.	'30	41	3/13,700	2/7,644	East China Sea
Haddock-7	Roy M. Davenport	'33	27	5/32,600	zero	Truk
Halibut-7	Ignatius J. Galantin	'33	37	1/3,500	1/4,653	Empire
Harder-3	Samuel D. Dealey	'30	31	5/24,800	3/15,273	Marianas
Paddle-2†	Robert H. Rice	'27	58	zero	zero	Marshalls
Pargo-2	Ian C. Eddy	'30	40	2/17,700	2/7,810	Marianas
Sargo-9	Philip W. Garnett	'33	55	2/15,900	2/6,419	East China Sea
Saury-8	Anthony H. Dropp	'32	53	zero	zero	Truk
Scorpion-3	Maximilian G. Schmidt	'32	53	zero	zero	Marianas
Seahorse-2	Slade D. Cutter	'35	53	6/48,700	5/27,579	East China Sea
Seawolf-11	Royce L. Gross	'30	53	2/14,000	2/6,399	East China Sea
Snapper-8	Merrill K. Clementson	'33	56	3/20,300	1/4,575	Empire
Sunfish-5	Richard W. Peterson	'31	59	zero	zero	East China Sea
Snook-4	Charles O. Triebel	'29	38	2/14,500	2/8,440	Marianas
Swordfish-9	Frank L. Barrows	'35	42	zero	zero	Empire
Tarpon-9	Thomas L. Wogan	'30	34	1/10,000	1/German	Empire
Tautog-8	William B. Sieglaff	'31	41	1/3,800	1/100	Palau
Trigger-7	Robert E. Dornin	'35	49	6/44,700	4/15,114	East China Sea
Tinosa-4	Lawrence R. Daspit	'27	49	4/18,500	4/18,000	East China Sea

→Fremantle

[1] Sea of Japan

* Special mission
† Galvanic
‡ Shared credit: *Grayback* and *Shad*, *Steelhead* and *Tinosa*

913

SUBMARINE WAR PATROLS DEPARTING PEARL HARBOR, SEPTEMBER–DECEMBER 1943 (Cont.)

BOAT, PATROL NUMBER	SKIPPER AND CLASS		DAYS	SHIPS/TONNAGE		AREA
				Wartime Credit	JANAC Credit	
NOVEMBER						
Apogon-1†	Walter P. Schoeni	'31	45	1/3,000	1/3,000	Truk
Aspro-1	Harry C. Stevenson	'31	39	3/25,600	zero	East China Sea
Corvina-1†	Roderick S. Rooney	'29	lost	1/1,600	zero	Truk
Flying Fish-8	Robert D. Risser	'34	59	2/15,800	2/18,784	East China Sea
Gunnel-3	John S. McCain, Jr.	'31	51	1/9,500	1/4,086	Empire
Gurnard-4	Charles H. Andrews	'30	40	2/11,000	3/14,000	Empire
Herring-6	Raymond W. Johnson	'30	56	4/30,000	2/10,000	East China Sea
Muskallunge-2	Michael P. Russillo	'27	56	1/8,200	zero	Palau
Nautilus-7†	William D. Irvin	'27	27	zero	zero	Gilberts
Plunger-9†	Raymond H. Bass	'31	42	zero	zero	Marshalls
Pogy-4	Ralph M. Metcalf	'35	29	3/19,500	2/9,860	Palau
Sailfish-10	Robert E. M. Ward	'35	49	3/35,700	3/29,571	Empire
Sawfish-5	Eugene T. Sands	'30	48	1/6,000	1/3,267	Bonins
Sculpin-9†	Fred Connaway	'32	lost	zero	zero	Truk
Seal-9†	Harry B. Dodge	'30	42	zero	zero	Marshalls
Searaven-9†	Melvin H. Dry	'34	49	1/10,100	1/10,000	Truk
Skate-2	Eugene B. McKinney	'27	54	1/6,400	1/6,429	Truk
Spearfish-9†	Joseph W. Williams, Jr.	'33	41	zero	zero	Marshalls
Thresher-10†	Harry Hull	'32	29	1/5,600	1/4,862	Truk
DECEMBER						
Archerfish-1	George W. Kehl	'32	53	1/9,000	zero	East China Sea
Batfish-1	Wayne R. Merrill	'34	50	2/15,700	1/5,486	Empire

Darter-1	William S. Stovall, Jr.	'29	66	zero	zero	→Brisbane
Finback-7	John A. Tyree, Jr.	'33	58	1/10,200	1/10,000	East China Sea
Grayback-9	John A. Moore	'32	33	6/24,000	4/10,000	East China Sea
Greenling-8	James D. Grant	'30	39	1/1,900	1/2,000	Truk
Haddo-4	John Corbus	'31	53	zero	zero	→Fremantle
Hake-3	John C. Broach	'27	55	3/16,500	3/19,384	→Fremantle
Halibut-8	Ignatius J. Galantin	'33	50	zero	zero	Marianas
Salmon-9	Nicholas J. Nicholas	'32	59	zero	zero	Empire
Saury-9	Anthony H. Dropp	'32	62	zero	zero	East China Sea
Seadragon-9	Royal L. Rutter	'30	46	1/7,400	zero	Truk
Seawolf-12‡	Royce L. Gross	'30	36	4/24,000	4½/25,793	East China Sea
Silversides-8	John S. Coye	'33	42	3/18,500	3/7,192	Palau
Steelhead-4	David L. Whelchel	'30	61	1/9,000	1/6,795	Empire
Sturgeon-9	Charlton L. Murphy, Jr.	'32	55	3/19,200	2/8,603	Empire
Swordfish-10	Karl G. Hensel	'23	40	2/15,200	3/12,543	Empire
Tarpon-10*	Thomas B. Oakley, Jr.	'34	39	zero	zero	Marshalls
Tautog-9	William B. Sieglaff	'31	49	2/9,700	2/6,000	Empire
Thresher-11	Duncan C. MacMillan	'26	54	4/26,300	4/14,523	East China Sea
Trullibee-3	Charles F. Brindupke	'32	58	1/2,500	1/549	Marianas
Whale-6‡	Albert C. Burrows	'28	44	2/14,000	1½/8,322	Bonins
Cero-2	Edward F. Dissette	'34	29	zero	zero	→Brisbane
Haddock-8	John P. Roach	'32	53	zero	zero	Marianas
	TOTALS:			130/900,400	99/475,981	

* Special mission
† Galvanic
‡ Seawolf and Whale shared credit

SUBMARINE WAR PATROLS DEPARTING PEARL HARBOR, JANUARY–APRIL 1944

Boat, Patrol Number	Skipper and Class		Days	Ships/Tonnage		Area
				Wartime Credit	JANAC Credit	
JANUARY						
Angler-1	Robert I. Olsen	'33	25	1/8,700	1/890	Marianas
Apogon-2	Walter P. Schoeni	'31	55	2/24,000	zero	Marianas
Dace-2	Bladen D. Claggett	'35	48	zero	zero	→Brisbane
Darter-1	William S. Stovall, Jr.	'29	66	zero	zero	→Brisbane
Flasher-1	Reuben T. Whitaker	'34	53	4/26,500	4/10,528	→Fremantle
Grayback-10	John A. Moore	'32	lost	4/20,800	3/16,689	East China Sea
Gudgeon-11	William S. Post, Jr.	'30	49	1/10,100	zero	East China Sea
Hoe-3	Victor B. McCrea	'32	38	4/29,500	1/10,526	→Fremantle
Jack-3	Thomas M. Dykers	'27	51	7/53,500	4/20,441	→Fremantle
Nautilus-8	William D. Irvin	'27	57	1/6,100	1/6,100	Marianas
Permit-11	Carter L. Bennett	'33	74	zero	zero	Truk
Plunger-10	Raymond H. Bass	'31	55	4/22,500	3/9,600	Empire
Pogy-5	Ralph M. Metcalf	'35	54	4/22,400	5/21,150	East China Sea
Robalo-1	Stephen H. Ambruster	'28	57	zero	zero	→Fremantle
Sargo-10	Philip W. Garnett	'33	46	1/7,000	2/11,800	Palau
Scorpion-4	Maximilian G. Schmidt	'32	lost	zero	zero	East China Sea
Seahorse-3	Slade D. Cutter	'35	41	5/30,900	5/20,900	Palau
Seal-10	Harry B. Dodge	'30	50	zero	zero	Truk
Searaven-10	Melvin H. Dry	'34	47	zero	zero	Truk
Skipjack-9	George G. Molumphy	'31	57	2/8,400	2/8,200	Marianas
Snook-5	Charles O. Triebel	'29	60	5/26,800	5/21,046	East China Sea
Spearfish-10	Joseph W. Williams, Jr.	'33	43	4/21,800	1/3,600	Luzon Strait
Sunfish-6	Edward E. Shelby	'33	53	2/30,400	2/9,400	Marianas
Tambor-9	Russell Kefauver	'33	60	4/30,100	4/18,400	East China Sea

Tang-1	Richard H. O'Kane	'34	41	5/42,000	5/21,400	Marianas
Trigger-8	Robert E. Dornin	'35	55	2/11,800	2/12,443	Truk
FEBRUARY						
Angler-2	Robert I. Olsen	'33	53	zero	zero	→Fremantle
Aspro-2	William A. Stevenson	'34	54	1/2,200	1/2,200	Truk
Batfish-2	Wayne R. Merrill	'34	53	zero	zero	Empire
Burrfish-1	William B. Perkins, Jr.	'32	50	zero	zero	Truk
Flying Fish-9	Robert D. Risser	'34	49	3/10,500	3/9,928	East China Sea
Growler-8	Arnold F. Schade	'33	55	zero	zero	East China Sea
Gunnel-4	John S. McCain, Jr.	'31	60	zero	zero	→Fremantle
Herring-7	David Zabriskie, Jr.	'36	54	zero	zero	Empire
Kingfish-7	Herbert L. Jukes	'32	49	zero	zero	Marianas
Lapon-3	Lowell T. Stone	'29	47	4/32,700	3/19,500	→Fremantle
Mingo-3	Joseph J. Staley	'34	73	zero	zero	→Brisbane
Picuda-1	Albert Raborn	'34	49	3/24,400	3/10,000	Truk
Pollack-9	Bafford E. Lewellen	'31	43	4/21,400	3/5,400	Empire
Rock-1	John J. Flachsenhar	'35	35	zero	zero	East China Sea
Sandlance-1	Malcolm E. Garrison	'32	44	5/28,300	4/16,056	Polar circuit
Silversides-9	John S. Coye	'33	52	2/7,500	1/1,900	→Fremantle
Skate-3	William P. Gruner	'35	42	1/7,000	1/7,000	Palau
Tautog-10	William B. Sieglaff	'31	28	5/17,700	4/11,277	Polar circuit
Trout-11	Albert H. Clark	'33	lost	1/9,200	1/7,100	East China Sea
Tunny-5	John A. Scott	'28	44	1/2,100	1/2,200	→Brisbane
MARCH						
Archerfish-2	George W. Kehl	'32	42	zero	zero	Palau
Bang-1	Anton R. Gallaher	'33	46	3/20,200	3/10,700	Luzon Strait
Barb-7	John R. Waterman	'27	55	1/2,200	1/2,200	Marianas
Finback-8	John A. Tyree, Jr.	'33	55	zero	zero	Truk
Gar-11	George W. Lautrup, Jr.	'34	49	zero	zero	Palau

SUBMARINE WAR PATROLS DEPARTING PEARL HARBOR, JANUARY–APRIL 1944 (*Cont.*)

Boat, Patrol Number	Skipper and Class		Days	Ships/Tonnage		Area
				Wartime Credit	JANAC Credit	
Golet-1	Philip H. Ross	'27	46	zero	zero	Polar circuit
Greenling-9	James D. Grant	'30	53	zero	zero	Marianas
Grouper-8	Frederick H. Wahlig	'33	59	zero	zero	Luzon Strait
Haddock-9	John P. Roach	'32	62	1/1,000	zero	Empire
Halibut-9	Ignatius J. Galantin	'33	58	2/4,800	3/5,550	Empire
Harder-4	Samuel D. Dealey	'30	47	2/5,300	2/9,000	→Fremantle
Paddle-3	Byron H. Nowell	'35	54	2/10,800	2/9,700	→Fremantle
Pampanito-1	Paul E. Summers	'36	54	zero	zero	Marianas
Parche-1	Lawson P. Ramage	'31	56	3/23,900	2/11,700	Luzon Strait
Pargo-3	Ian C. Eddy	'30	60	2/12,200	1/758	→Fremantle
Seahorse-4	Slade D. Cutter	'35	56	4/25,700	5/19,374	→Brisbane
Searaven-11	Melvin H. Dry	'34	45	2/6,500	zero	Bonins
Snapper-9	William W. Walker	'34	57	zero	zero	Bonins
Steelhead-5	David L. Whelchel	'30	62	zero	zero	East China Sea
Stingray-10	Sam C. Loomis, Jr.	'35	54	1/8,600	1/3,900	Marianas
Swordfish-11	Keats E. Montross	'35	46	zero	zero	Marianas
Tang-2	Richard H. O'Kane	'34	61	zero	zero	Palau
Thresher-12	Duncan C. MacMillan	'26	51	zero	zero	Truk
Tinosa-6	Donald F. Weiss	'29	46	4/31,200	2/12,900	Luzon Strait
Trigger-9	Frederick J. Harlfinger II	'35	58	5/33,200	1/11,700	Palau
Tullibee-4	Charles F. Brindupke	'32	lost	zero	zero	Palau
Whale-7	James B. Grady	'33	57	1/5,000	1/5,400	East China Sea
APRIL						
Apogon-3	Walter P. Schoeni	'31	49	zero	zero	Empire
Aspro-3*	William A. Stevenson	'34	54	2/11,500	1½/8,650	→Fremantle

Balao-5	M. Ramirez DeArellano	'35	48	zero	zero	Palau
Burrfish-2	William B. Perkins, Jr.	'32	52	1/5,000	1/5,900	Empire
Drum-9	Delbert F. Williamson	'27	50	zero	zero	Bonins
Gabilan-1	Karl R. Wheland	'31	46	zero	zero	Marianas
Gato-9	Richard M. Farrell	'35	48	zero	zero	Truk
Guavina-1	Carl Tiedeman	'33	52	3/19,500	1/2,300	Bonins
Gudgeon-12	Robert A. Bonin	'36	lost	zero	zero	Marianas
Gurnard-5	Charles H. Andrews	'30	56	4/26,900	4/29,700	→Fremantle
Muskallunge-3	Michael P. Russillo	'27	65	zero	zero	→Fremantle
Perch II-1	Blish C. Hills	'33	35	zero	zero	Luzon Strait
Permit-12	Donald A. Scherer	'34	42	1/2,200	zero	Truk
Peto-6	Paul Van Leunen, Jr.	'34	52	zero	zero	Luzon Strait
Pogy-6	Ralph M. Metcalf	'35	52	3/12,900	3/9,000	Empire
Rock-2	John J. Flachsenhar	'35	55	zero	zero	Empire
Salmon-10	Harley K. Nauman	'34	51	zero	zero	Palau
Sandlance-2	Malcolm E. Garrison	'32	35	4/22,300	5/18,328	→Fremantle
Sargo-11	Philip W. Garnett	'33	49	1/5,000	1/4,800	Empire
Sawfish-6	Alan B. Banister	'28	49	1/5,100	zero	Empire
Seadragon-10	James H. Ashley, Jr.	'34	54	zero	1/1,300	Empire
Skate-4	William P. Gruner, Jr.	'35	50	zero	zero	Bonins
Spearfish-11	Joseph W. Williams, Jr.	'33	58	2/14,900	1/2,500	East China Sea
Sturgeon-10	Charlton L. Murphy, Jr.	'32	50	3/15,400	1/2,000	Bonins
Tambor-10	Russell Kefauver	'33	54	1/6,700	1/650	Marianas
Tautog-11	Thomas S. Baskett	'35	35	4/20,500	4/16,100	Polar circuit
Tilefish-1	Roger M. Keithly	'35	54	zero	zero	Empire
Tuna-10	James T. Hardin	'29	56	zero	zero	Palau
Tunny-6	John A. Scott	'28	66	1/5,200	1/5,000	Marianas
Shifted to Australia						
Nautilus	—George A. Sharp					
			'29 TOTALS:	156/960,000	124½/524.477	

* Shared ½ credit with *Bowfin* coming from Fremantle

919

SUBMARINE WAR PATROLS DEPARTING AUSTRALIA, JANUARY–MARCH 1944

Boat, Patrol Number	Skipper and Class		Days	Ships/Tonnage		Area
				Wartime Credit	JANAC Credit	
JANUARY—FREMANTLE						
Billfish-3	Vernon C. Turner	'33	66	1/1,000	zero	Indochina
Bonefish-3	Thomas W. Hogan	'31	60	2/21,300	zero	South China Sea
Bowfin-3*	Walter T. Griffith	'34	28	3/12,600	1/4,408	Makassar
Cod-2	James D. Dempsey	'31	62	2/9,900	2/9,823	Halmahera
Narwhal-9	Frank D. Latta	'32	29	zero	zero	special mission
Tinosa-5	Donald F. Weiss	'29	55	3/16,900	4/15,600	→Pearl Harbor
Redfin-1†	Robert D. King	'31	45	1/1,700	zero	South China Sea
JANUARY—BRISBANE						
None						
FEBRUARY—FREMANTLE						
Bluefish-4	Charles M. Henderson	'34	58	1/7,500	1/10,500	South China Sea
Bowfin-4	Walter T. Griffith	'34	33	3/21,000	3/15,000	Celebes
Cabrilla-3	William C. Thompson, Jr.	'35	56	zero	zero	Sunda Strait
Haddo-5	Chester W. Nimitz, Jr.	'36	54	zero	zero	Makassar
Narwhal-10	Frank D. Latta	'32	33	zero	zero	special mission
Pompon-4	Stephen H. Gimber	'35	50	zero	zero	→Pearl Harbor
Puffer-3	Frank G. Selby	'33	61	1/15,100	1/15,100	South China Sea
Rasher-3	Willard R. Laughon	'33	45	5/28,600	4/20,100	Celebes
Raton-3	James W. Davis	'30	45	zero	zero	South China Sea
Ray-3*	Brooks J. Harral	'32	50	zero	zero	South China Sea
FEBRUARY—BRISBANE						
Balao-4	Cyrus C. Cole	'35	43	4/20,300	3/15,300	→Pearl Harbor
Cero-3	Edward F. Dissette	'34	23	1/6,100	zero	Bismarck

Boat, Patrol Number	Skipper		Days	Wartime Credit	JANAC Credit	Area
Gato-8	Robert J. Foley	'27	60	3/17,300	2/6,070	→Pearl Harbor
Peto-5	Paul Van Leunen, Jr.	'34	57	1/4,400	1/4,370	→Pearl Harbor
MARCH—FREMANTLE						
Hake-4	John C. Broach	'27	42	2/20,400	1/5,174	South China Sea
Redfin-2	Marshall H. Austin	'35	44	5/30,200	3/10,300	Celebes
MARCH—BRISBANE						
Bashaw-1	Richard E. Nichols	'34	60	zero	zero	Davao
Blackfish-8	Robert F. Sellars	'34	80	zero	zero	→Pearl Harbor
Dace-3	Bladen D. Claggett	'35	55	zero	zero	Davao
Darter-2	William S. Stovall	'29	63	1/6,800	1/2,800	Davao
Flounder-1	Carl A. Johnson	'29	54	zero	zero	Halmahera
Scamp-7	John C. Hollingsworth	'31	51	zero	zero	→Pearl Harbor
			TOTALS:	39/241,100	27/134,745	

* Laid minefield
† Via Darwin

SUBMARINE WAR PATROLS DEPARTING AUSTRALIA, APRIL–JUNE 1944

Boat, Patrol Number	Skipper and Class		Days	Ships/Tonnage		Area
				Wartime Credit	JANAC Credit	
APRIL—FREMANTLE						
Bonefish-4	Thomas W. Hogan	'31	48	4/27,400	2/2,756	Celebes
Bowfin-5*	John Corbus	'30	58	1/6,500	½/2,250	→Pearl Harbor
Billfish-4	Vernon C. Turner	'33	57	1/8,500	zero	→Pearl Harbor
Cod-3	James C. Dempsey	'31	56	2/10,100	2/8,076	Manila
Crevalle-3	Francis D. Walker	'35	54	2/26,400	2/17,771	South China Sea

* Shared ½ credit with *Aspro*

921

SUBMARINE WAR PATROLS DEPARTING AUSTRALIA, APRIL–JUNE 1944 (Cont.)

Boat, Patrol Number	Skipper and Class		Days	Ships/Tonnage		Area
				Wartime Credit	JANAC Credit	
Flasher-2*	Reuben T. Whitaker	'34	54	3/12,600	3/6,709	South China Sea
Hoe-4	Victor B. McCrea	'32	59	1/4,000	zero	South China Sea
Jack-4	Thomas M. Dykers	'27	35	zero	1/5,425	Manila
Lapon-4	Lowell T. Stone	'29	42	2/15,000	2/11,253	South China Sea
Puffer-4*	Frank G. Selby	'33	52	3/24,300	3/7,600	Manila
Rasher-4*	Willard R. Laughon	'33	55	4/24,400	4/10,900	Celebes
Ray-4	Brooks J. Harral	'32	53	6/42,500	1/6,000	Celebes
Robalo-2	Manning M. Kimmel	'35	51	1/7,500	zero	Indochina
Silversides-10	John S. Coye	'33	47	5/23,600	6/14,141	→Pearl Harbor
APRIL—BRISBANE						
Bluegill-1	Eric L. Barr, Jr.	'34	67	3/13,600	3/14,100	Davao
Cero-4	Edward F. Dissette	'34	60	zero	1/2,800	Davao
Tunny-6	John A. Scott	'28	66	1/5,200	1/5,000	→Pearl Harbor
MAY—FREMANTLE						
Angler-3*	Robert I. Olsen	'33	27	1/5,700	1/2,100	Sunda Strait
Bluefish-5*	Charles M. Henderson	'34	53	2/7,000	2/4,700	Celebes
Cabrilla-4	William C. Thompson, Jr.	'35	34	1/8,500	1/8,360	Celebes
Gunnel-5*	John S. McCain, Jr.	'31	63	zero	zero	South China Sea
Haddo-6	Chester W. Nimitz, Jr.	'36	59	zero	zero	Celebes
Hake-5	John C. Broach	'27	50	3/14,500	3/13,375	Celebes
Harder-5	Samuel D. Dealey	'30	45	5/8,500	3/6,500	Celebes
Narwhal-11	Jack C. Titus	'33	33	zero	zero	special mission
Nautilus-9	George A. Sharp	'29	13	zero	zero	special mission
Raton-4*	James W. Davis	'30	46	5/7,200	2/1,660	South China Sea
Redfin-3	Marshall H. Auston	'35	47	2/16,100	2/8,000	Celebes

922

MAY—BRISBANE

JUNE—FREMANTLE

JUNE—BRISBANE

Bashaw-2	Richard E. Nichols	'34	50	1/5,700	1/6,440	Halmahera
Angler-4	Franklin G. Hess	'35	54	zero	zero	South China Sea
Bonefish-5	Lawrence L. Edge	'35	49	2/12,800	1/10,000	Sulu Sea
Crevalle-4†	Francis D. Walker, Jr.	'35	50	3½/28,000	1½/10,950	South China Sea
Flasher-3†	Reuben T. Whitaker	'34	49	6½/47,900	4½/24,949	South China Sea
Hoe-5	Victor B. McCrea	'32	55	zero	zero	Manila
Jack-5	Arthur E. Krapf	'34	39	4/25,000	3/15,748	Manila
Lapon-5	Lowell T. Stone	'29	42	3/18,000	2/6,560	South China Sea
Narwhal-12	Jack C. Titus	'33	27	zero	zero	special mission
Nautilus-10	George A. Sharp	'29	15	zero	zero	special mission
Paddle-4	Byron H. Nowell	'35	54	1/1,200	1/1,300	Celebes
Pargo-4	Ian C. Eddy	'30	57	1/6,600	1/5,236	Celebes
Robalo-3	Manning M. Kimmel	'35	lost	zero	zero	South China Sea
Bream-1	Wreford G. Chapple	'30	29	zero	1/5,700	Davao
Cero-5	Edward F. Dissette	'34	56	1/8,000	1/6,500	Davao
Dace-4	Bladen D. Claggett	'35	60	2/3,200	1/1,100	Davao
Darter-3	David H. McClintock	'35	48	1/4,400	1/4,400	Davao
Flounder-2	James E. Stevens	'30	39	1/4,000	1/2,680	Davao
Mingo-4	Joseph J. Staley	'34	46	1/1,700	1/2,100	Celebes
S-47-7	Lloyd V. Young	'41	29	zero	zero	special mission
Seahorse-5	Slade D. Cutter	'35	47	6/37,000	4/11,000	→Pearl Harbor
			TOTALS:	92/522,600	70½/274,139	

* Surabaya air strike, May 17
† Crevalle and Flasher shared credit

SUBMARINE WAR PATROLS DEPARTING PEARL HARBOR, MAY–JUNE 1944

BOAT, PATROL NUMBER	SKIPPER AND CLASS	Days	SHIPS/TONNAGE Wartime Credit	JANAC Credit	AREA
MAY					
Albacore-9	James W. Blanchard '27	48	2/30,800	2/32,000	Philippine Sea
Archerfish-3	William H. Wright '36	48	1/1,400	1/800	Bonins
Barb-8	Eugene B. Fluckey '35	49	5/37,500	5/15,472	Polar circuit
Batfish-3	John K. Fyfe '36	43	4/9,500	1/1,000	Empire
Finback-9	James L. Jordan '33	50	zero	zero	Philippine Sea
Flier-1	John D. Crowley '31	44	4/19,500	1/10,400	→Fremantle
Flying Fish-10	Robert D. Risser '34	61	1/4,000	2/8,200	→Brisbane
Gar-12	George W. Lautrup, Jr. '34	47	1/900	zero	Bonins
Golet-2	James S. Clark '35	lost	zero	zero	Polar circuit
Grouper-9	Frederick H. Wahlig '33	50	1/3,500	1/2,800	Empire
Growler-9	Thomas B. Oakley, Jr. '34	64	1/10,000	1/2,000	Philippine Sea
Guitarro-1	Enrique D. Haskins '33	51	3/21,200	2/3,100	→Fremantle
Herring-8	David Zabriskie, Jr. '36	lost	3/8,200	4/9,960	Polar circuit
Kingfish-8	Herbert L. Jukes '32	50	zero	zero	Bonins
Picuda-2*	Albert Raborn '34	54	3/13,000	1½/2,786	Luzon Strait
Pilotfish-1	Robert H. Close '34	49	zero	zero	Marianas
Pintado-1	Bernard A. Clarey '34	46	4/31,000	3/13,200	Marianas
Pipefish-1	William N. Deragon '34	52	zero	zero	Philippine Sea
Plunger-11	Edward J. Fahy '34	56	zero	zero	Bonins
Pollack-10	Bafford E. Lewellen '31	32	1/1,500	1/1,300	Empire
Pompon-5	Stephen H. Gimber '35	50	1/2,300	1/742	Empire
Shark II-1	Edward N. Blakely '34	32	4/32,200	4/21,672	Marianas

924

Snapper-10	William W. Walker	'34	56	zero	zero	Truk
Stingray-11	Sam C. Loomis, Jr.	'35	45	zero	zero	Marianas
Swordfish-12	Keats E. Montross	'35	49	2/7,000	2/5,100	Bonins
Whale-8	James B. Grady	'33	50	zero	zero	Empire

JUNE

Apogon-4	Walter P. Schoeni	'31	37	zero	zero	Luzon Strait
Bang-2	Anton R. Gallaher	'33	58	3/24,000	zero	Philippine Sea
Cavalla-1	Herman J. Kossler	'34	64	1/29,900	1/30,000	Philippine Sea
Cobia-1	Albert L. Becker	'34	49	5/24,300	3/11,455	Bonins
Drum-10	Maurice H. Rindskopf	'38	51	zero	zero	Palau
Gabilan-2	Karl R. Wheland	'31	49	1/1,700	1/492	Empire
Guardfish-8	Norvell G. Ward	'35	46	8/58,200	4/20,400	Luzon Strait
Guavina-2	Carl Tiedeman	'33	42	1/5,800	1/3,000	→Brisbane
Hammerhead-1	John C. Martin	'34	65	1/8,700	zero	→Fremantle
Pampanito-2	Paul E. Summers	'36	50	zero	zero	Empire
Parche-2†	Lawson P. Ramage	'31	59	4/34,300	2½/19,200	Luzon Strait
Perch II-2	Blish C. Hills	'33	59	zero	zero	Philippine Sea
Permit-13	Donald A. Scherer	'34	45	1/800	zero	→Brisbane
Piranha-1	Harold E. Ruble	'33	52	2/17,400	2/12,300	Luzon Strait
Plaice-1	Clyde B. Stevens, Jr.	'30	52	4/18,900	3/2,150	Bonins
Pomfret-1	Frank C. Acker	'32	54	zero	zero	Empire
Rock-3	John J. Flachsenhar	'35	52	zero	zero	→Fremantle
Saury-10	Anthony H. Dropp	'32	54	zero	zero	Philippine Sea
Sawfish-7	Alan B. Banister	'28	55	1/1,900	1/2,200	Luzon Strait
Sealion II-1	Eli T. Reich	'35	42	4/19,700	4/7,800	East China Sea

* Shared ½ credit with land-based aircraft
† Shared ½ credit with Steelhead

SUBMARINE WAR PATROLS DEPARTING PEARL HARBOR, MAY–JUNE 1944 (*Cont.*)

| BOAT, PATROL NUMBER | SKIPPER AND CLASS | Days | Ships/Tonnage | | AREA |
			Wartime Credit	JANAC Credit	
Seawolf-13	Richard B. Lynch '35	32	zero	zero	Palau
Skate-5	William P. Gruner, Jr. '35	45	3/13,300	3/4,500	Polar circuit
Snook-6	George H. Browne '34	51	zero	zero	Empire
Steelhead-6*	David L. Whelchel '30	60	2/14,000	2½/20,000	Luzon Strait
Sturgeon-11	Charlton L. Murphy, Jr. '32	55	2/18,600	2/14,000	Empire
Sunfish-7	Edward E. Shelby '33	40	4/18,500	2/8,800	Polar circuit
Tang-3	Richard H. O'Kane '34	36	8/56,000	10/39,100	East China Sea
Tarpon-11	Saverio Filippone '37	41	zero	zero	Truk
Tautog-12	Thomas S. Baskett '35	48	2/4,300	2/2,787	Empire
Thresher-13	Duncan C. MacMillan '26	44	6/35,100	2/7,700	Luzon Strait
Tilefish-2	Roger M. Keithly '35	55	1/1,700	zero	Luzon Strait
Tinosa-7	Donald F. Weiss '29	54	2/19,000	2/10,700	East China Sea
		TOTALS:	107/659,600	80½/348,229	

* Shared ½ credit with *Parche*

926

SUBMARINE WAR PATROLS DEPARTING PEARL HARBOR, JULY–AUGUST 1944

Boat, Patrol Number	Skipper and Class	Days	Ships/Tonnage		Area
			Wartime Credit	JANAC Credit	
JULY					
Balao-6	Marion Ramirez DeArellano	'35	48	zero	zero	Palau
Barbel-1	Robert A. Keating, Jr.	'33	36	4/32,900	3/5,170	Empire
Billfish-5	Vernon C. Turner	'33	65	zero	zero	Empire
Bowfin-6	John Corbus	'30	59	9/26,700	1/6,754	Empire
Burrfish-3	William B. Perkins, Jr.	'32	46	zero	zero	Palau
Croaker-1	John E. Lee	'30	43	4/17,600	3/13,900	East China Sea
Gato-10	Richard M. Farrell	'35	49	zero	zero	Bonins
Greenling-10	John D. Gerwick	'35	63	zero	zero	Luzon Strait
Hardhead-1	Fitzhugh McMaster	'33	60	1/5,200	1/5,700	→Fremantle
Picuda-3	Glynn R. Donaho	'27	66	5/20,000	4/11,270	Luzon Strait
Pilotfish-2	Robert H. Close	'34	49	zero	zero	Bonins
Pintado-2	Bernard A. Clarey	'34	54	5/46,300	2/24,663	East China Sea
Plunger-12	Edward J. Fahy	'34	51	1/5,000	zero	Truk
Pollack-11	Everett H. Steinmetz	'35	60	zero	zero	→Brisbane
Pompon-6	Stephen H. Gimber	'35	46	1/4,300	1/2,200	Polar circuit
Redfish-1	Louis D. McGregor, Jr.	'30	65	5/33,500	3/21,800	Luzon Strait
Ronquil-1	Henry S. Monroe	'33	39	1/7,100	2/10,600	Formosa
Sailfish-11	Robert E. M. Ward	'35	58	4/13,200	1/2,100	Luzon Strait
Shark II-2	Edward N. Blakely	'34	50	zero	zero	Bonins
Spadefish-1	Gordon W. Underwood	'32	59	6/40,000	6/31,500	Luzon Strait
Sterlet-1	Orme C. Robbins	'34	53	4/14,200	zero	Bonins
Tambor-11	William J. Germershausen	'35	47	1/4,000	1/2,300	Polar circuit

SUBMARINE WAR PATROLS DEPARTING PEARL HARBOR, JULY–AUGUST 1944 (Cont.)

Boat, Patrol Number	Skipper and Class	Days	Ships/Tonnage		Area
			Wartime Credit	JANAC Credit	
Tuna-11	James T. Hardin	'29	51	zero	zero	Empire
Shifted to Australia						
Seawolf	Albert M. Bontier	'35				
AUGUST						
Albacore-10	James W. Blanchard	'27	49	3/11,000	2/1,050	Empire
Archerfish-4	William H. Wright	'36	53	zero	zero	Empire
Bang-3	Anton R. Gallaher	'33	32	5/31,400	3/4,200	Empire
Barb-9	Eugene B. Fluckey	'35	59	4/42,100	3/36,800	Luzon Strait
Barbero-1	Irvin S. Hartman	'33	55	zero	zero	→Fremantle
Batfish-4*	John K. Fyfe	'36	41	2/2,900	1½/1,500	→Fremantle
Cavalla-2	Herman J. Kossler	'34	52	zero	zero	→Fremantle
Finback-10	Robert R. Williams, Jr.	'34	50	2/1,900	1/1,390	Bonins
Gar-13	Maurice Ferrara	'37	54	zero	zero	→Brisbane
Grouper-10	Frederick H. Wahlig	'33	62	zero	zero	Palau
Growler-10	Thomas B. Oakley, Jr.	'34	45	5/22,800	2/2,800	→Fremantle
Guardfish-9	Norvell G. Ward	'35	62	1/3,100	1/873	East China Sea
Hawkbill-1†	Francis W. Scanland, Jr.	'34	53	2/11,500	1/5,075	→Fremantle
Baya-1	Arnold H. Holtz	'31	57	1/7,500	½/4,204	→Fremantle
Becuna-1	Henry D. Sturr	'33	56	2/10,000	½/871	→Fremantle
Pampanito-3	Paul E. Summers	'36	42	3/23,600	2/15,600	Luzon Strait
Pipefish-2	William N. Deragon	'34	52	1/4,000	1/1,000	Empire
Piranha-2	Harold E. Ruble	'33	56	zero	zero	Philippine Sea

Plaice-2	Clyde B. Stevens, Jr.	'30	56	2/10,600	1/800	Empire
Queenfish-1	Charles E. Loughlin	'33	59	6/48,800	3/14,800	Luzon Strait
Razorback-1	Roy S. Benson	'29	55	zero	zero	Philippine Sea
Scabbardfish-1	Frederick A. Gunn	'34	56	zero	zero	Empire
Seahorse-6	Charles W. Wilkins	'24	71	1/1,700	1/800	Luzon Strait
Seal-11	John H. Turner	'36	41	3/7,700	2/6,330	Polar circuit
Sealion II-2	Eli T. Reich	'35	44	6/51,700	3/19,100	Luzon Strait
Searaven-12	Melvin H. Dry	'34	52	1/5,100	1/4,700	Polar circuit
Segundo-1	James D. Fulp, Jr.	'34	60	zero	zero	Philippine Sea
Shad-7	Lawrence V. Julihn	'37	50	3/6,900	1/900	Empire
Sunfish-8	Edward E. Shelby	'33	38	4/33,500	2/11,100	East China Sea
Tang-4	Richard H. O'Kane	'34	34	5/22,500	2/11,500	Empire
Tarpon-12	Saverio Filippone	'37	45	zero	zero	Truk
Thresher-14	John R. Middleton, Jr.	'35	50	3/20,600	3/9,170	East China Sea
Tunny-7	George E. Pierce	'32	44	zero	zero	South China Sea
Whale-9	James B. Grady	'33	68	1/10,000	1/10,200	Philippine Sea

Shifted to Australia

Stingray Sam C. Loomis, Jr.

TOTALS: 117/660,900   66½/302,517

* Shared ½ credit with carrier-based aircraft

† Shared ½ credit with *Baya* and ½ credit with *Becuna*

SUBMARINE WAR PATROLS DEPARTING AUSTRALIA, JULY–AUGUST 1944

Boat, Patrol Number	Skipper and Class		Days	Ships/Tonnage		Area
				Wartime Credit	JANAC Credit	
JULY—FREMANTLE						
Aspro-4	William A. Stevenson	'34	41	4/19,500	1/2,300	South China Sea
Bluefish-6‡	Charles M. Henderson	'34	54	2½/34,500	1½/9,067	→Pearl Harbor
Cabrilla-5	William C. Thompson, Jr.	'35	47	4/27,900	1/3,145	South China Sea
Cod-4	James A. Adkins	'26	53	4/9,000	2/1,708	South China Sea
Guitarro-2	Enrique D. Haskins	'33	48	5/11,800	4/11,200	South China Sea
Gunnel-6	Guy E. O'Neil, Jr.	'37	54	zero	zero	Manila
Gurnard-6	Charles H. Andrews	'30	59	zero	zero	Celebes
Rasher-5	Henry G. Munson	'32	43	5/55,700	5/52,600	→Pearl Harbor
Raton-5	Maurice W. Shea	'37	55	zero	zero	Manila
Ray-5	William T. Kinsella	'34	52	4/36,400	5/26,000	South China Sea
Sandlance-3	Malcolm E. Garrison	'32	45	1/7,500	1/3,000	→Pearl Harbor
Puffer-5‡	Frank G. Selby	'33	48	4½/37,700	1½/7,680	→Pearl Harbor
Nautilus-11	George A. Sharp	'29	27	zero	zero	special mission
JULY—BRISBANE						
Bluegill-2	Eric L. Barr, Jr.	'34	49	3/8,600	3/6,950	Davao
Bream-2	Wreford G. Chapple	'30	48	zero	zero	Davao
AUGUST—FREMANTLE						
Flier-2	John D. Crowley	'31	lost	zero	zero	South China Sea
Haddo-7	Chester W. Nimitz, Jr.	'36	52	5½/17,100	5/14,460	South China Sea
Hake-6	Frank E. Haylor	'36	50	1/1,500	zero	South China Sea
Harder-6	Samuel D. Dealey	'30	lost	1½/3,200	2/1,760	South China Sea

Jack-6	Arthur E. Krapf	'34	48	2/8,200	2/6,287	Celebes
Mingo-5	John R. Madison	'37	46	zero	zero	Celebes
Muskallunge-4	Michael R. Russillo	'27	54	1/800	zero	Indochina
Paddle-5*	Byron H. Nowell	'35	34	1/5,000	1½/5,000	Sulu Sea
Redfin-4†	Marshall H. Austin	'35	57	1/5,100	zero	Celebes
Narwhal-13	Jack C. Titus	'33	27	zero	zero	special mission
Seawolf-14	Albert M. Bontier	'35	24	zero	zero	→Brisbane
Stingray-12	Sam C. Loomis, Jr.	'35	35	zero	zero	→Brisbane
AUGUST—BRISBANE						
Bashaw-3	Richard E. Nichols	'34	55	1/7,700	1/2,800	Davao
Flounder-3	James E. Stevens	'30	61	zero	zero	Davao
Flying Fish-11	Robert D. Risser	'34	80	zero	zero	→Pearl Harbor
Guavina-3	Carl Tiedeman	'33	44	3/3,000	1/1,500	Davao
S-42-6	Paul E. Glenn	'39	29	zero	zero	special mission
			TOTALS:	54/300,200	37½/155,457	

* Shared credit with carrier-based aircraft
† Laid minefield
‡ Bluefish and Puffer shared credit

931

SUBMARINE WAR PATROLS DEPARTING PEARL HARBOR, SEPTEMBER–OCTOBER 1944

Boat, Patrol Number	Skipper and Class		Days	Ships/Tonnage		Area
				Wartime Credit	JANAC Credit	
SEPTEMBER						
Apogon-5	Arthur C. House, Jr.	'34	46	1/6,300	1/2,000	Polar circuit
Barbel-2	Robert A. Keating, Jr.	'33	40	3/6,100	1/1,200	Empire
Bergall-1	John M. Hyde	'34	60	3/21,500	2/14,700	→Fremantle
Besugo-1	Thomas L. Wogan	'30	39	1/700	zero	Empire
Blackfin-1	George H. Laird, Jr.	'33	60	1/4,000	2/2,700	→Fremantle
Blackfish-9	Robert F. Sellars	'34	60	zero	zero	Luzon Strait
Burrfish-4	William B. Perkins, Jr.	'32	69	1/7,600	zero	Empire
Cobia-2	Albert L. Becker	'34	57	zero	zero	→Fremantle
Croaker-2	John E. Lee	'30	48	4/16,600	3/5,800	East China Sea
Drum-11	Maurice H. Rindskopf	'38	59	4/25,100	3/18,500	Luzon Strait
Escolar-1	William J. Millican	'28	lost	zero	zero	East China Sea
Gabilan-3	Karl R. Wheland	'31	46	1/2,200	1/100	Empire
Icefish-1	Richard W. Peterson	'31	61	2/13,300	2/8,400	Luzon Strait
Parche-3	Lawson P. Ramage	'31	77	zero	zero	Luzon Strait
Perch II-3	Blish C. Hills	'33	48	zero	zero	East China Sea
Pomfret-2	Frank C. Acker	'32	30	1/7,500	1/6,900	Luzon Strait
Rock-4	John J. Flachsenhar	'35	61	zero	1/834	→Fremantle
Ronquil-2	Henry S. Monroe	'33	57	zero	zero	Empire
Sailfish-12	Robert E. M. Ward	'35	70	1/800	zero	Luzon Strait
Salmon-11*	Harley K. Nauman	'34	38	1/3,300	1/3,333	Empire
Saury-11	Richard A. Waugh	'37	65	zero	zero	Empire
Sawfish-8	Alan B. Banister	'28	58	2/17,900	2/13,400	Luzon Strait
Sea Devil-1	Ralph E. Styles	'33	51	1/1,900	1/1,000	Empire

Boat	Commander					Area
Sea Dog-1	Vernon L. Lowrance	'30	53	1/4,000	2/7,400	East China Sea
Seadragon-11	James H. Ashley, Jr.	'34	44	3/13,500	3/15,700	Luzon Strait
Shark II-3	Edward N. Blakely	'34	lost	zero	zero	Luzon Strait
Silversides-11	John S. Coye, Jr.	'33	60	zero	zero	Formosa
Skate-6	Richard B. Lynch	'35	54	1/4,000	1/3,700	Empire
Snapper-11	William W. Walker	'34	52	1/4,000	2/2,720	Bonins
Snook-7	George H. Browne	'34	63	3/22,500	3/16,600	Luzon Strait
Sterlet-2*	Orme C. Robbins	'34	64	3⅓/21,900	1⅓/13,833	Empire
Tang-5	Richard H. O'Kane	'34	lost	13/107,324	7/21,772	Formosa
Tilefish-3	Roger M. Keithly	'35	44	4/8,100	zero	Polar circuit
Trepang-1	Roy M. Davenport	'33	36	3/22,300	2/1,750	Empire
Trigger-10*	Frederick J. Harlfinger II	'35	49	⅓/3,300	⅓/3,333	Empire

OCTOBER

Boat	Commander					Area
Albacore-10	Hugh R. Rimmer	'37	lost	zero	zero	Empire
Archerfish-5	Joseph F. Enright	'33	43	1/28,000	1/59,000	Empire
Atule-1	John H. Maurer	'35	60	5/26,700	4/25,691	Luzon Strait
Bang-4	Anton R. Gallaher	'33	40	4/18,400	2/5,200	Formosa
Barb-10	Eugene B. Fluckey	'35	30	5/28,900	2/15,200	East China Sea
Barbel-3	Robert A. Keating, Jr.	'33	38	2/9,400	2/8,800	→Fremantle
Billfish-6	Vernon C. Turner	'33	53	zero	zero	Empire
Greenling-11	John D. Gerwick	'35	48	3/9,900	3/2,695	Empire
Haddock-10	John P. Roach	'32	60	zero	zero	Luzon Strait
Halibut-10	Ignatius J. Galantin	'33	49	1/10,000	1/1,900	Luzon Strait
Jallao-1	Joseph B. Icenhower	'36	61	1/5,200	1/5,200[1]	Luzon Strait
Kete-1	Royal L. Rutter	'30	60	zero	zero	Empire
Kingfish-9	Talbot E. Harper	'37	46	2/7,500	3/3,737	Bonins
Pampanito-4	Frank W. Fenno	'25	59	1/7,500	1/1,200	→Fremantle

* Salmon, Sterlet, and Trigger shared credit

[1] The light cruiser Tama, previously damaged by naval aircraft

SUBMARINE WAR PATROLS DEPARTING PEARL HARBOR, SEPTEMBER–OCTOBER 1944 (Cont.)

BOAT, Patrol Number	Skipper and Class	Days	Ships/Tonnage		Area
			Wartime Credit	JANAC Credit	
Peto-7	Robert H. Caldwell, Jr. '36	43	4/28,000	3/12,600	East China Sea
Picuda-4	Evan T. Shepard '35	35	4/35,300	3/21,600	East China Sea
Pilotfish-3	Allan G. Schnable '34	56	zero	zero	Bonins
Pintado-3	Bernard A. Clarey '34	74	4/21,300	3/5,100	→Brisbane
Pipefish-3	William N. Deragon '34	70	zero	1/800	Luzon Strait
Pogy-7	Peter G. Molteni, Jr. '37	48	zero	zero	Bonins
Pomfret-3	John B. Hess '37	45	2/2,600	3/14,000	Luzon Strait
Queenfish-2	Charles E. Loughlin '33	35	4/38,500	4/14,300	East China Sea
Redfish-2	Louis D. McGregor, Jr. '30	64	3/36,100	2/20,800	East China Sea
Sargo-12	Philip W. Garnett '33	53	zero	zero	Bonins
Scamp-8	John C. Hollingsworth '31	lost	zero	zero	Empire
Sea Cat-1*	Rob Roy McGregor '29	58	1½/15,000	zero	Indochina
Sea Fox-1	Roy C. Klinker '35	49	2/8,000	zero	Empire
Seal-12	John H. Turner '36	50	2/10,000	1/5,700	Polar circuit
Skipjack-10	Richard S. Andrews '31	49	zero	zero	Polar circuit
Spadefish-2	Gordon W. Underwood '32	49	4/33,200	4/39,400	East China Sea
Sunfish-9	Edward E. Shelby '33	56	4/23,800	3/16,200	East China Sea
Tambor-12	William J. Germershausen '35	55	2/5,200	zero	Empire
Tuna-12	Edward F. Steffanides, Jr. '31	52	zero	zero	→Brisbane
Sealion II-3	Eli T. Reich '35	32	1/30,000	2/32,900	East China Sea
Shad-8	Lawrence V. Julihn '37	63	zero	zero	East China Sea
	TOTALS:	121½	784,200	91/468,885	

* Shared credit with *Searaven*

934

SUBMARINE WAR PATROLS DEPARTING AUSTRALIA, SEPTEMBER–OCTOBER 1944

Boat, Patrol Number	Skipper and Class		Days	Ships/Tonnage		Area
				Wartime Credit	JANAC Credit	
SEPTEMBER—FREMANTLE						
Angler-5	Franklin G. Hess	'35	50	1/4,000	1/2,400	Manila
Aspro-5	William A. Stevenson	'34	46	4/25,500	2/10,900	→Pearl Harbor
Bluegill-3	Eric L. Barr, Jr.	'34	64	5/23,300	3/19,630	Manila
Bonefish-6	Lawrence L. Edge	'35	62	3/22,000	2/4,500	→Pearl Harbor
Cabrilla-6	William C. Thompson, Jr.	'35	43	5/29,900	4/24,557	→Pearl Harbor
Cod-5	James A. Adkins	'26	59	1/10,000	1/6,900	→Pearl Harbor
Crevalle-5	Francis D. Walker	'35	20	zero	zero	Java Sea
Flasher-4	Reuben T. Whitaker	'34	51	4/23,000	3/18,610	Manila
Hammerhead-2	John C. Martin	'34	54	6/41,500	5/25,178	South China Sea
Hoe-6	Victor B. McCrea	'32	37	2/15,000	1/2,500	South China Sea
Lapon-6	Donald G. Baer	'37	56	4/25,600	3/14,170	South China Sea
Narwhal-14	Jack C. Titus	'33	22	zero	zero	special mission
Nautilus-12	George A. Sharp	'29	19	zero	zero	special mission
Pargo-5	Davis B. Bell	'37	34	1/4,000	2/2,200	South China Sea[1]
Ray-6*	William T. Kinsella	'34	70	6½/35,100	5⅓/12,645	→Pearl Harbor
Stingray-13	Sam C. Loomis, Jr.	'35	9	zero	zero	special mission
Stingray-14	Sam C. Loomis, Jr.	'35	22	zero	zero	→Brisbane
SEPTEMBER—BRISBANE						
Cero-6	Edward F. Dissette	'34	62	zero	zero	→Pearl Harbor
Dace-5	Bladen D. Claggett	'35	60	3/30,000	3/25,141	South China Sea
Darter-4	David H. McClintock	'35	lost	1/12,500	1/12,000	South China Sea
Permit-14	Donald A. Scherer	'34	50	1/500	zero	→Pearl Harbor
Seawolf-15	Albert M. Bontier	'35	lost	zero	zero	special mission

* Shared credit with *Bream* and *Guitarro*

[1] Laid minefield

935

Boat, Patrol Number	Skipper and Class		Days	Ships/Tonnage		Area
				Wartime Credit	JANAC Credit	
OCTOBER—FREMANTLE						
Barbero-2	Irvin S. Hartman	'33	65	4/21,700	3/9,200	South China Sea
Bashaw-4	Richard E. Nichols	'34	63	zero	zero	South China Sea
Batfish-5	John K. Fyfe	'36	53	2/5,000	zero	→Pearl Harbor
Bream-3*	Wreford G. Chapple	'30	50	½/5,000	⅓/2,270	South China Sea
Growler-11	Thomas B. Oakley, Jr.	'34	lost	zero	zero	Celebes
Guavina-4†	Carl Tiedeman	'33	60	3½/24,800	2/6,117	South China Sea
Guitarro-3*	Enrique D. Haskins	'33	38	3½/28,200	2⅓/10,999	South China Sea
Gunnel-7	Guy E. O'Neil, Jr.	'37	65	3/14,600	3/6,795	→Pearl Harbor
Gurnard-7	Norman D. Gage	'35	38	1/5,000	1/6,900	South China Sea[1]
Haddo-8	Frank C. Lynch, Jr.	'38	60	3/9,000	1/860	→Pearl Harbor
Hake-7	Frank E. Haylor	'36	57	zero	zero	South China Sea
Hardhead-2	Francis A. Greenup	'36	45	2/9,800	2/6,100	South China Sea
Jack-7	Albert S. Fuhrman	'37	58	1/4,000	2/12,200	→Pearl Harbor
Muskallunge-5	Leonce A. Lajaunie, Jr.	'37	56	zero	zero	→Pearl Harbor
Narwhal-15	William G. Holman	'36	22	zero	zero	special mission
Nautilus-13	George A. Sharp	'29	41	zero	zero	special mission
Paddle-6	Joseph P. Fitz-Patrick	'38	29	2/1,100	zero	Celebes
Pargo-6	David B. Bell	'37	53	1/10,000	1/5,200	South China Sea
Raton-6	Maurice W. Shea	'37	55	8/57,200	4/12,300	→Pearl Harbor
Redfin-5	Marshall H. Austin	'35	68	1/10,000	1/5,300	→Pearl Harbor
OCTOBER—BRISBANE						
Flounder-4	James E. Stevens	'30	46	1/700	½/2,849	South China Sea
		TOTALS:		84/508,000	59½/268,495	

* Bream, Guitarro, and Ray shared credit
† Shared credit with carrier-based aircraft (½) and Flounder (½) and sank one ship independently

[1] Laid minefield

SUBMARINE WAR PATROLS DEPARTING PEARL HARBOR, NOVEMBER–DECEMBER 1944

Boat, Patrol Number	Skipper and Class	Days	Ships/Tonnage		Area
			Wartime Credit	JANAC Credit	
NOVEMBER					
Apogon-6	Arthur C. House, Jr.	'34	46	zero	zero	Polar circuit
Besugo-2	Thomas L. Wogan	'30	23	2/8,000	1/1,000	→Fremantle
Blenny-1	William H. Hazzard	'35	62	2/11,100	2/4,950	→Fremantle
Caiman-1	Frederic C. Lucas, Jr.	'30	62	zero	zero	→Fremantle
Dragonet-1	Jack H. Lewis	'27	49	zero	zero	Polar circuit
Finback-11	Robert R. Williams, Jr.	'34	50	1/5,000	1/2,100	Bonins
Grouper-11	Frederick H. Wahlig	'33	54	zero	zero	Empire
Guardfish-10	Douglas T. Hammond	'31	60	zero	zero	Luzon Strait
Piranha-3	Harold E. Ruble	'33	52	zero	zero	East China Sea
Plaice-3	Clyde B. Stevens, Jr.	'30	39	zero	zero	East China Sea
Razorback-2*	Charles D. Brown	'38	47	3½/20,800	1½/4,287	Luzon Strait
Scabbardfish-2	Frederick A. Gunn	'34	47	3/8,600	2/2,345	Empire
Sea Devil-2	Ralph E. Styles	'33	54	2/17,500	2/16,300	Empire
Sea Dog-2	Vernon L. Lowrance	'30	68	zero	zero	Luzon Strait
Sea Owl-1	Carter L. Bennett	'33	54	1/1,600	zero	East China Sea
Sea Poacher-1	Francis M. Gambacorta	'35	52	zero	zero	East China Sea
Segundo-2†	James D. Fulp, Jr.	'34	49	2½/20,200	1/6,363	Luzon Strait
Searaven-13‡	Raymond Berthrong	'38	52	2½/25,800	zero	South China Sea

* Shared ½ credit with *Segundo*
† Shared ½ credit with land-based aircraft and ½ credit with *Razorback*
‡ Shared credit with *Sea Cat*

SUBMARINE WAR PATROLS DEPARTING PEARL HARBOR, NOVEMBER–DECEMBER 1944 (Cont.)

BOAT, PATROL NUMBER	SKIPPER AND CLASS		DAYS	SHIPS/TONNAGE		AREA
				Wartime Credit	JANAC Credit	
Sea Robin-1	Paul C. Stimson	'36	62	1/4,000	1/5,600	→Fremantle
Spearfish-12	Cyrus C. Cole	'35	64	zero	zero	Empire
Spikefish-1	Nicholas J. Nicholas	'32	47	zero	zero	Polar circuit
Tilefish-4	Roger M. Keithly	'35	48	1/9,000	1/527	Polar circuit
Trepang-2	Roy M. Davenport	'33	35	4/35,000	3/13,048	Luzon Strait
Whale-10	James B. Grady	'33	54	zero	zero	Empire
"Burt's Brooms"	(Thomas Burton Klakring)					
Ronquil	Henry S. Monroe					
Saury	Richard A. Waugh					
Tambor	William J. Germershausen					
Sterlet	Orme C. Robbins					
Burrfish	William B. Perkins, Jr.					
Silversides	John S. Coye					
Trigger	Frederick J. Harlfinger II					
DECEMBER						
Aspro-6*	William A. Stevenson	'34	59	1/8,000	½/4,000	Luzon Strait
Balao-7	Marion Ramirez DeArellano	'35	42	2/11,200	1/5,200	East China Sea
Barb-11†	Eugene B. Fluckey	'35	56	8/60,000	4⅓/24,197	East China Sea
Blueback-1	Merrill K. Clementson	'33	61	zero	zero	→Fremantle
Boarfish-1‡	Royce L. Gross	'30	52	1½/9,800	1½/10,445	→Fremantle
Charr-1	Francis D. Boyle	'34	63	zero	zero	→Fremantle
Croaker-3	William B. Thomas	'36	60	zero	zero	→Fremantle
Devilfish-1	Edward C. Stephan	'29	41	zero	zero	Empire
Drum-12	Frank M. Eddy	'37	42	zero	zero	Empire

Boat-patrol	Commander	Class	Age	*	†	Area
Greenling-12	John D. Gerwick	'35	45	zero	zero	Empire
Icefish-2	Richard W. Peterson	'31	42	zero	zero	East China Sea
Kingfish-10	Talbot E. Harper	'37	40	2/15,500	2/3,800	Empire
Kraken-1	Thomas H. Henry	'35	64	zero	zero	→Fremantle
Parche-4	Woodrow W. McCrory	'38	53	1/2,000	1/1,000	Empire
Perch II-4	Blish C. Hills	'33	59	zero	zero	→Fremantle
Picuda-5	Evan T. Shepard	'35	48	3/22,500	1 1/3/6,448	East China Sea
Pogy-8	Peter G. Molteni, Jr.	'37	46	zero	zero	Empire
Puffer-6	Carl R. Dwyer	'38	30	4/18,900	1/800	Empire
Queenfish-3	Charles E. Loughlin	'33	32	1/10,100	1/3/951	East China Sea
Sawfish-9	Douglas H. Pugh	'38	47	zero	zero	Luzon Strait
Seadragon-12	James H. Ashley, Jr.	'34	60	zero	zero	Bonins
Sea Fox-2	Roy C. Klinker	'35	46	zero	zero	Empire
Sealion II-4	Charles F. Putman	'37	43	1/15,800	1/7,000	→Fremantle
Silversides-12	John C. Nichols	'34	50	zero	1/4,500	East China Sea
Snook-8	John F. Walling	'35	54	zero	zero	Polar circuit
Spot-1	William S. Post, Jr.	'30	55	4/11,200	zero	East China Sea
Swordfish-13	Keats E. Montross	'35	lost	zero	zero	Empire
Tautog-13	Thomas S. Baskett	'35	42	3/8,500	2/3,300	East China Sea
Threadfin-1	John J. Foote	'35	54	1/2,000	1/1,800	Empire
Tinosa-8	Richard C. Latham	'34	56	zero	zero	Empire
Trigger-11	Frederick J. Harlfinger II	'35	37	zero	zero	Empire

Shifted to Australia

| Gabilan | William B. Parham | '36 | | | | |

TOTALS: 58/362,100   33 1/2/129,961

* Shared credit with carrier-based aircraft

† Shared credit with *Picuna* and *Queenfish*

‡ Shared credit with land-based aircraft

939

SUBMARINE WAR PATROLS DEPARTING AUSTRALIA, NOVEMBER–DECEMBER 1944

Boat, Patrol Number	Skipper and Class	Days	Ships/Tonnage Wartime Credit	JANAC Credit	Area
NOVEMBER—FREMANTLE					
Baya-2	Arnold H. Holtz '31	55	zero	zero	South China Sea
Becuna-2	Henry D. Sturr '33	53	1/1,100	zero	South China Sea
Flasher-5	George W. Grider '36	48	5/41,700	6/42,800	South China Sea
Hammerhead-3†	John C. Martin '34	52	1/5,000	½/1,427	South China Sea
Hawkbill-2	Francis W. Scanland, Jr. '34	50	1/1,300	1/760	South China Sea
Hoe-7	Miles P. Refo III '38	50	zero	zero	South China Sea
Lapon-7	Donald G. Baer '37	56	zero	zero	→Pearl Harbor
Mingo-6	John R. Madison '37	52	1/10,000	1/9,500	South China Sea
Paddle-7†	Joseph P. Fitz-Patrick '38	53	2/10,800	½/1,427	→Pearl Harbor
Cavalla-3	Herman J. Kossler '34	60	3/6,300	3/4,180	South China Sea
NOVEMBER—BRISBANE					
Gar-14	Maurice Ferrara '37	26	1/1,000	zero	special mission
DECEMBER—FREMANTLE					
Angler-6	H. Bissell, Jr. USNR	72	zero	zero	→Pearl Harbor
Bergall-2*	John M. Hyde '34	21	1/12,500	zero	South China Sea
Besugo-3	Thomas L. Wogan '30	53	2/11,000	2/10,800	South China Sea
Bluegill-4	Eric L. Barr, Jr. '34	52	zero	zero	South China Sea
Bream-4	James L. P. McCallum '35	52	zero	zero	South China Sea
Cobia-3	Albert L. Becker '34	54	1/700	1/720	South China Sea
Dace-6*	Otis R. Cole, Jr. '36	56	1/4,000	1/1,000	→Pearl Harbor
Guitarro-4	Thomas B. Dabney '36	83	zero	zero	South China Sea
Gurnard-8	Norman D. Gage '35	51	zero	zero	South China Sea
Hardhead-3	Francis R. Greenup '36	53	1/2,500	1/834	South China Sea
Rock-5	John J. Flachsenhar '35	63	zero	zero	South China Sea

DECEMBER—BRISBANE

Boat	Skipper	Class	Days	Wartime	JANAC	Area
Gabilan-4	William B. Parham	'36	48	zero	zero	South China Sea
Gar-15	Maurice Ferrara	'37	24	zero	zero	→Pearl Harbor
Stingray-15	Howard F. Stoner	'32	27	zero	zero	special mission
			TOTALS:	21/107,900	17/73,448	

* Laid minefield
† *Hammerhead* and *Paddle* shared credit

SUBMARINE WAR PATROLS DEPARTING PEARL HARBOR, JANUARY–MARCH 1945

BOAT, PATROL NUMBER	SKIPPER AND CLASS		Days	SHIPS/TONNAGE		AREA
				Wartime Credit	JANAC Credit	
JANUARY						
Archerfish-6	Joseph F. Enright	'33	49	1/1,100	zero	South China Sea
Atule-2	John H. Maurer	'35	59	1/6,700	1/6,888	East China Sea
Bang-5	Anton R. Gallaher	'33	50	zero	zero	East China Sea
Batfish-6	John K. Fyfe	'36	61	3/4,500	3/3,262	South China Sea
Blackfish-10	Robert F. Sellars	'34	50	zero	zero	South China Sea
Blower-1	James H. Campbell	'33	60	zero	zero	→Fremantle
Bowfin-7	Alexander K. Tyree	'36	56	2/2,700	1/750	Empire
Brill-1	Harry B. Dodge	'30	62	zero	zero	→Fremantle
Burrfish-5	Morton H. Lytle	'37	48	zero	zero	Empire
Finback-12	Robert R. Williams, Jr.	'34	62	zero	zero	East China Sea
Gato-11	Richard M. Farrell	'35	45	2/4,700	2/3,125	East China Sea
Haddock-11	William H. Brockman, Jr.	'27	51	zero	zero	Empire
Jallao-2	Joseph B. Icenhower	'36	65	zero	zero	East China Sea
Lagarto-1	Frank D. Latta	'32	55	1/900	2/1,845	→Fremantle
Peto-8	Robert H. Caldwell, Jr.	'36	67	zero	zero	Luzon Strait

SUBMARINE WAR PATROLS DEPARTING PEARL HARBOR, JANUARY–MARCH 1945 (*Cont.*)

Boat, Patrol Number	Skipper and Class		Days	Ships/Tonnage		Area
				Wartime Credit	JANAC Credit	
Pilotfish-4	Allan G. Schnable	'34	64	zero	zero	East China Sea
Pipefish-4	William N. Deragon	'34	53	zero	zero	Empire
Piper-1	Bernard F. McMahon	'31	60	1/2,000	zero	Empire
Plaice-4	Clyde B. Stevens, Jr.	'30	58	zero	zero	Luzon Strait
Pomfret-4	John B. Hess	'37	62	zero	zero	Empire
Pompon-7	Stephen H. Gimber	'35	34	zero	zero	Yellow Sea
Rasher-6	Benjamin E. Adams, Jr.	'35	53	zero	zero	East China Sea
Ronquil-3	Robert B. Lander	'37	43	1/10,100	zero	Bonins
Scabbardfish-3	Frederick A. Gunn	'34	52	zero	zero	Luzon Strait
Sennet-1	George E. Porter, Jr.	'32	25	1/500	zero	Bonins
Shad-9	Lawrence V. Julihn	'37	57	zero	zero	South China Sea
Spadefish-3	Gordon W. Underwood	'32	38	4/16,400	4/13,423	East China Sea
Spikefish-2	Nicholas J. Nicholas	'32	51	zero	zero	Empire
Sterlet-3	H. H. Lewis	USNR	66	2/15,000	1/1,148	East China Sea
Sunfish-10	Edward E. Shelby	'33	37	zero	zero	East China Sea
Thresher-15	John R. Middleton, Jr.	'35	82	zero	zero	Luzon Strait
Tilefish-5	Walter F. Schlech, Jr.	'36	56	1/700	1/492	Empire
Trepang-3	Allen R. Faust	'36	57	1/6,100	2/2,261	Empire
FEBRUARY						
Balao-8	Robert K. Worthington	'38	40	3/20,300	2/11,293	East China Sea
Bluefish-7	Charles M. Henderson	'34	42	zero	zero	Empire
Bugara-1	Arnold F. Schade	'33	54	zero	zero	→Fremantle
Chub-1	Cassius D. Rhymes, Jr.	'35	64	zero	zero	→Fremantle
Drum-13	Frank M. Eddy	'37	51	zero	zero	Empire

942

Guardfish-11	Douglas T. Hammond	'31	44	zero	zero	Empire
Icefish-3	Richard W. Peterson	'31	57	zero	zero	East China Sea
Lamprey-1	William T. Nelson	'30	59	zero	zero	→Fremantle
Piranha-4	Donald G. Irvine	'34	69	zero	zero	Luzon Strait
Puffer-7	Carl R. Dwyer	'38	70	zero	zero	→Fremantle
Queenfish-4	Charles E. Loughlin	'33	46	1/12,000	1/11,600	Formosa Strait
Razorback-3	Charles D. Brown	'38	53	zero	zero	East China Sea
Sea Cat-2	Richard H. Bowers	'38	52	1/2,000	zero	East China Sea
Sea Devil-3	Ralph E. Styles	'33	63	6/17,600	3/10,017	East China Sea
Sea Owl-2	Carter L. Bennett	'33	70	1/2,800	1/889	South China Sea
Sea Poacher-2	Francis M. Gambacorta	'35	48	zero	zero	Formosa Strait
Segundo-3	James D. Fulp, Jr.	'34	54	1/4,000	1/3,087	East China Sea
Sennet-2	George E. Porter, Jr.	'32	30	1/2,000	1/720	Empire
Spot-2*	William S. Post, Jr.	'30	61	2/11,700	1½/4,592	East China Sea
Springer-1	Russell Kefauver	'33	48	1/1,500	1/1,500	Empire
Tench-1	William B. Sieglaff	'31	55	1/4,300	zero	Empire
Tunny-8	George E. Pierce	'32	52	zero	zero	Empire

"Mac's Mops" (Bernard F. McMahon)
Bowfin   Alexander K. Tyree
Piper (flag)
Pomfret   John B. Hess
Sterlet   H. H. Lewis
Trepang   Allen R. Faust

"Latta's Lances" (Frank D. Latta)
Haddock   William H. Brockman
Lagarto (flag)
Sennet   George E. Porter, Jr.

---

* Shared credit with naval land-based aircraft

SUBMARINE WAR PATROLS DEPARTING PEARL HARBOR, JANUARY–MARCH 1945 (Cont.)

BOAT, PATROL NUMBER	SKIPPER AND CLASS	DAYS	SHIPS/TONNAGE		AREA
			Wartime Credit	JANAC Credit	
MARCH					
Bang-6	Oliver W. Bagby	'38	55	zero	zero	Luzon Strait
Blackfish-11	Robert F. Sellars	'34	50	zero	zero	South China Sea
Bullhead-1	Walter T. Griffith	'34	37	zero	zero	→Fremantle
Burrfish-6	Morton H. Lytle	'37	49	zero	zero	Formosa Strait
Cabrilla-7	Henry C. Lauerman	'38	48	zero	zero	→Fremantle
Cero-7	Raymond Berthrong	'38	56	4/9,800	3/8,834	Empire
Cod-6	James A. Adkins	'26	65	3/5,000	1/492	→Fremantle
Crevalle-6	Everett H. Steinmetz	'35	46	1/1,300	zero	East China Sea
Devilfish-2	Stephen S. Mann, Jr.	'38	21	zero	zero	Empire
Grouper-12	Frederick H. Wahlig	'33	54	zero	zero	East China Sea
Hackleback-1	Frederick E. Janney	'37	51	zero	zero	Empire
Kete-2	Edward Ackerman	'39	lost	3/12,000	3/6,875	East China Sea
Kingfish-11	Talbot E. Harper	'37	50	zero	zero	Empire
Parche-5	Woodrow W. McCrory	'38	42	3/5,200	1/615	Empire
Picuda-6	Evan T. Shepard	'35	63	zero	zero	Empire
Pogy-9	John M. Bowers	'38	61	zero	zero	Empire
Pompon-8	John A. Bogley	'38	52	zero	zero	East China Sea
Ronquil-4	Robert B. Lander	'37	45	zero	zero	Bonins
Sawfish-10	Douglas H. Pugh	'38	47	zero	zero	Formosa
Sea Dog-3	Earl T. Hydeman	'32	47	1/6,700	1/6,850	Empire
Sea Fox-3	Roy C. Klinker	'35	59	zero	zero	East China Sea
Seahorse-7	Harry H. Greer, Jr.	'34	46	zero	zero	Empire
Silversides-13	John C. Nichols	'34	50	1/2,000	zero	Empire
Snook-9	John F. Walling	'35	lost	zero	zero	Luzon Strait

Boat, Patrol Number	Skipper	Class	Days	Wartime Credit	JANAC Credit	Area
Spadefish-4	William J. Germershausen	'35	35	1/7,000	1/4,127	East China Sea
Sunfish-11	John W. Reed	'38	29	4/13,200	4/5,461	Empire
Threadfin-2	John J. Foote	'35	51	zero	1/900	Empire
Tigrone-1	Hiram Cassedy	'31	43	zero	zero	East China Sea
Tinosa-9	Richard C. Latham	'34	30	zero	zero	East China Sea
Tirante-1	George L. Street III	'37	52	8/28,300	6/12,621	East China Sea
Trigger-12	David R. Connole	'36	lost	1/4,000	2/2,576	Empire
Trutta-1	Arthur C. Smith	'34	42	zero	zero	East China Sea
TOTALS:				68/244,100	51½/126,243	

SUBMARINE WAR PATROLS DEPARTING AUSTRALIA, JANUARY–AUGUST 1945

Boat, Patrol Number	Skipper and Class		Days	Ships/Tonnage		Area
				Wartime Credit	JANAC Credit	
JANUARY—FREMANTLE						
Bashaw-5	H. S. Simpson	USNR	47	1/10,700	1/10,016	South China Sea
Bergall-3	John M. Hyde	'34	28	1/900	2/974	South China Sea
Blackfin-2	William L. Kitch	'38	45	1/1,500	1/1,580	South China Sea
Flasher-6	George W. Grider	'36	75	1/2,100	1/850	South China Sea
Flounder-5	James E. Stevens	'30	42	zero	zero	South China Sea
Guavina-5	Ralph H. Lockwood	'38	42	2/20,000	2/15,565	South China Sea
Hake-8	Frank E. Haylor	'36	61	zero	zero	→Pearl Harbor
Nautilus-14	Willard D. Michael	'38	28	zero	zero	special mission
Pampanito-5	Paul E. Summers	'36	20	2/12,500	2/10,488	South China Sea
Stingray-16	Howard F. Stoner	'32	34	zero	zero	special mission
Pargo-7	David B. Bell	'37	54	3/14,800	1/1,300	→Pearl Harbor

SUBMARINE WAR PATROLS DEPARTING AUSTRALIA, JANUARY–AUGUST 1945 (*Cont.*)

Boat, Patrol Number	Skipper and Class	Days	Ships/Tonnage Wartime Credit	Ships/Tonnage JANAC Credit	Area
January—Brisbane					
Pintado-4	Bernard A. Clarey '34	51	zero	zero	→Pearl Harbor
Tuna-13	Edward F. Steffanides, Jr. '31	64	zero	zero	special mission
February—Fremantle					
Barbel-4	Conde L. Raguet '38	lost	zero	zero	South China Sea
Baya-3	Benjamin C. Jarvis '39	46	3/13,500	2/5,760	South China Sea
Becuna-3	Henry D. Sturr '33	46	1/7,500	1/1,945	South China Sea
Blenny-2	William H. Hazzard '35	49	4/25,500	4/12,611	South China Sea
Caiman-2	William L. Fey, Jr. '37	48	zero	zero	South China Sea
Cavalla-4	Herman J. Kossler '34	46	zero	zero	South China Sea
Cobia-4	Albert L. Becker '34	51	zero	zero	South China Sea
Hammerhead-4	George H. Laird, Jr. '33	22	1/800	1/900	South China Sea
Hawkbill-3	Francis W. Scanland, Jr. '34	58	2/12,800	3/5,596	South China Sea
Hoe-8	Miles P. Refo III '38	46	1/2,300	1/900	→Pearl Harbor
Mingo-7	John R. Madison '37	76	zero	zero	→Pearl Harbor
Pampanito-6	Paul E. Summers '36	57	zero	zero	South China Sea
Sealion II-5	Charles F. Putman '37	47	1/7,300	1/1,458	South China Sea
Sea Robin-2	Paul C. Stimson '36	66	5/15,900	4/7,113	→Pearl Harbor
March—Fremantle					
Bashaw-6	H. S. Simpson USNR	33	zero	zero	South China Sea
Bergall-4	John M. Hyde '34	43	zero	zero	South China Sea
Besugo-4	Herman E. Miller '38	54	3/2,700	1/630[1]	South China Sea
Blackfin-3	William L. Kitch '38	36	zero	zero	South China Sea
Blueback-2	Merrill K. Clementson '33	44	zero	zero	South China Sea
Bluegill-5	Eric L. Barr, Jr. '34	37	1/5,700	1/5,542	South China Sea

946

Boat	Commander					Area
Boarfish-2	Royce L. Gross	'30	42	zero	zero	South China Sea
Bream-5	James L. McCallum	'35	16	1/2,600	zero	Java Sea
Charr-2*†	Francis D. Boyle	'34	51	2/5,700	½/2,850	South China Sea
Croaker-4	William B. Thomas	'36	42	zero	zero	South China Sea
Flounder-6	James E. Stevens	'30	38	zero	zero	South China Sea
Gabilan-5†	William B. Parham	'36	60	3/6,800	1½/3,612	→Pearl Harbor
Guavina-6	Ralph H. Lockwood	'38	48	zero	zero	South China Sea
Gurnard-9	George S. Simmons III	'39	59	zero	zero	→Pearl Harbor
Hammerhead-5	Frank M. Smith	'35	28	1/1,800	1/1,000	South China Sea
Hardhead-4*	Francis A. Greenup	'36	56	1/10,300	1/6,886	Siam Gulf
Kraken-2	Thomas H. Henry	'35	43	zero	zero	South China Sea
Perch II-5	Blish C. Hills	'33	10	1/600	zero	Java Sea
Rock-6	Robert A. Keating, Jr.	'33	58	zero	zero	→Pearl Harbor
APRIL—FREMANTLE						
Bergall-5	John M. Hyde	'34	37	zero	zero	South China Sea
Blackfin-4	William L. Kitch	'38	31	zero	zero	→Pearl Harbor
Blueback-3	Merrill K. Clementson	'33	62	1/1,100	1/300	Java Sea
Bluegill-6	Eric L. Barr, Jr.	'34	41	zero	zero	South China Sea
Boarfish-3	Edward C. Blonts, Jr.	'39	23	zero	zero	Java Sea
Bugara-2	Arnold F. Schade	'33	40	zero	zero	South China Sea
Bullhead-2	Walter T. Griffith	'34	43	2/1,800	zero	South China Sea
Chub-2	Cassius D. Rhymes, Jr.	'35	38	3/2,700	1/492	Java Sea
Cobia-5	Albert L. Becker	'34	40	2/15,100	2/4,675	South China Sea
Croaker-5	William B. Thomas	'36	22	2/5,800	zero	Java Sea
Hawkbill-4	Francis W. Scanland, Jr.	'34	44	1/2,400	1/1,500	South China Sea
Kraken-3	Thomas H. Henry	'35	45	3/3,000	zero	South China Sea
Lamprey-2	Lucien B. McDonald	'38	40	zero	zero	South China Sea

* Laid minefields
† *Charr* and *Gabilan* shared credit
¹ Plus *U-183*

BOAT,				SHIPS/TONNAGE		
PATROL NUMBER	SKIPPER AND CLASS		Days	Wartime Credit	JANAC Credit	AREA

MAY—FREMANTLE

Baya-4	Benjamin C. Jarvis	'39	28	3/13,000	1/2,500	South China Sea
Becuna-4	Henry D. Sturr	'33	39	zero	zero	South China Sea
Blenny-3	William H. Hazzard	'35	55	1/800	1/524	South China Sea
Blower-2	James H. Campbell	'33	40	zero	zero	South China Sea
Bream-6*	James L. McCallum	'35	54	1/10,000	1/1,230	→Pearl Harbor
Brill-2	Harry B. Dodge	'30	41	zero	zero	South China Sea
Caiman-3	William L. Fey, Jr.	'37	62	zero	zero	South China Sea
Cavalla-5	Herman J. Kossler	'34	38	zero	zero	→Pearl Harbor
Guitarro-5*	Thomas B. Dabney	'36	61	zero	zero	South China Sea
Hammerhead-6	Frank M. Smith	'35	25	2/8,500	2/6,823	South China Sea
Lagarto-2	Frank D. Latta	'32	lost	zero	1/5,819	South China Sea
Perch II-6	Charles D. McCall	'39	53	zero	zero	→Pearl Harbor
Sealion II-6	Charles F. Putman	'37	62	zero	zero	South China Sea

JUNE—FREMANTLE

Baya-5	Benjamin C. Jarvis	'39	41	1/700	1/595	Java Sea
Becuna-5	William J. Bush	'38	36	zero	zero	South China Sea
Besugo-5	Herman E. Miller	'38	42	zero	zero	South China Sea
Blower-3	Nelson P. Watkins	'37	35	zero	zero	South China Sea
Bluefish-9	George W. Forbes, Jr.	'39	33	1/2,000	2/2,750	South China Sea
Hammerhead-7	Frank M. Smith	'35	60	1/1,100	2/1,734	South China Sea
Hardhead-5	Francis A. Greenup	'36	33	2/2,500	3/500	South China Sea
Lizardfish-2	Ovid M. Butler	'36	39	zero	zero	South China Sea

Cod-7	Edwin M. Westbrook, Jr.	'38	47	zero	zero	South China Sea
Charr-3	Francis D. Boyle	'34	42	zero	zero	South China Sea
JULY—FREMANTLE						
Blenny-4	William H. Hazzard	'35	40	1/5,700	zero	South China Sea
Boarfish-4	Edward C. Blonts, Jr.	'39	36	zero	zero	South China Sea
Brill-3	Harry B. Dodge	'30	37	zero	zero	South China Sea
Bugara-3	Arnold F. Schade	'33	34	zero	zero	South China Sea
Bullhead-3	Edward R. Holt, Jr.	'39	lost	zero	zero	South China Sea
Bumper-2	Joseph W. Williams, Jr.	'33	34	2/2,500	1/1,189	South China Sea
Caiman-4	William L. Fey, Jr.	'37	28	zero	zero	South China Sea
Chub-3	Cassius D. Rhymes, Jr.	'35	33	1/1,500	zero	South China Sea
Cobia-6	Frederick N. Russell	'39	34	zero	zero	South China Sea
Croaker-6	William B. Thomas	'36	47	zero	zero	South China Sea
Hardhead-6	John L. Haines	'38	24	1/1,800	1/200	South China Sea
Hawkbill-5	Francis W. Scanland, Jr.	'34	31	1/700	zero	South China Sea
Icefish-5	Richard W. Peterson	'31	24	zero	zero	South China Sea
Kraken-4	Thomas H. Henry	'35	23	zero	zero	Java Sea
Lamprey-3	Lucien B. McDonald	'38	25	zero	zero	South China Sea
AUGUST—FREMANTLE						
Capitaine-2	Ernest S. Friedrick	'37	14	zero	zero	South China Sea
Carbonero-2	Charlton L. Murphy, Jr.	'32	15	zero	zero	South China Sea
Loggerhead-2	Ralph M. Metcalf	'35	9	zero	zero	South China Sea
Puffer-9	Carl R. Dwyer	'38	14	zero	zero	South China Sea
	TOTALS:			74/267,000	54/128,407	

* Laid minefields

SUBMARINE WAR PATROLS DEPARTING PEARL HARBOR, APRIL 1945

BOAT, PATROL NUMBER	SKIPPER AND CLASS	DAYS	SHIPS/TONNAGE Wartime Credit	JANAC Credit	AREA
Atule-3	John H. Maurer '35	59	zero	zero	Empire
Billfish-7	L. C. Farley, Jr. USNR	54	2/7,800	2/3,211	Empire
Bluefish-8	George W. Forbes, Jr. '39	38	zero	zero	→Fremantle
Bonefish-7	Lawrence L. Edge '35	31	zero	zero	East China Sea
Bowfin-8	Alexander K. Tyree '36	23	2/9,300	2/3,599	Empire
Bumper-1	Joseph W. Williams, Jr. '33	53	zero	zero	→Fremantle
Dragonet-2	Jack H. Lewis '27	50	zero	zero	East China Sea
Gato-12	Richard Holden '37	52	zero	zero	Empire
Haddock-12	Albert R. Strow '39	42	zero	zero	Empire
Jack-8	Albert S. Fuhrman '37	51	zero	zero	Empire
Jallao-3	Joseph B. Icenhower '36	55	zero	zero	Empire
Lionfish-1	Edward D. Spruance '37	51	zero	zero	East China Sea
Lizardfish-1	Ovid M. Butler '36	52	zero	zero	→Fremantle
Pipefish-5	William N. Deragon '34	47	zero	zero	Empire
Piper-2	Bernard F. McMahon '31	47	1/2,000	zero	Polar circuit
Plaice-5	Richard S. Andrews '31	47	zero	zero	Polar circuit
Pomfret-5	John B. Hess '37	42	zero	zero	Polar circuit
Rasher-7	Charles D. Nace '39	44	zero	zero	→Fremantle
Raton-7	Maurice W. Shea '37	47	3/14,500	3/5,758	→Fremantle
Ray-7	William T. Kinsella '34	49	zero	zero	→Fremantle
Sandlance-4	Malcolm E. Garrison '32	54	1/2,000	zero	Empire
Scabbardfish-4	Frederick A. Gunn '34	53	zero	zero	East China Sea
Sea Cat-3	Richard H. Bowers '38	57	zero	zero	East China Sea
Sea Poacher-3	Charles F. Leigh '39	24	1/700	zero	Polar circuit

Boat, Patrol Number	Skipper and Class		Days	Wartime Credit	JANAC Credit	Area
Segundo-4	James D. Fulp, Jr.	'34	54	4/13,800	1/1,578	East China Sea
Sennet-3	George E. Porter, Jr.	'32	43	3/8,700	2/3,901	Empire
Spikefish-3	Robert R. Managhan	'38	52	zero	zero	Empire
Springer-2	Russell Kefauver	'33	28	3/4,300	3/2,440	East China Sea
Sterlet-4	H. H. Lewis	USNR	42	1/4,000	2/4,155	Polar circuit
Tinosa-10	Richard C. Latham	'34	19	zero	zero	Truk
Toro-1	James D. Grant	'31	54	zero	zero	Empire
Torsk-1	Bafford E. Lewellen	'31	63	zero	zero	Empire
Trepang-4	Allen R. Faust	'36	32	3/11,600	3/6,159	East China Sea
			TOTALS:	24/78,700	18/30,801	

SUBMARINE WAR PATROLS DEPARTING PEARL HARBOR, MAY 1945

Boat, Patrol Number	Skipper and Class		Days	Ships/Tonnage		Area
				Wartime Credit	JANAC Credit	
Apogon-7	Arthur C. House	'34	48	4/12,700	1/2,614	Polar circuit
Balao-9	Robert K. Worthington	'38	35	zero	zero	Empire
Bonefish-8	Lawrence L. Edge	'35	lost	2/14,000	2/12,380	Japan Sea
Bowfin-9	Alexander K. Tyree	'36	37	2/6,300	2/2,785	Japan Sea
Cabezon-1	George W. Lautrup, Jr.	'34	46	1/4,000	1/2,631	Polar circuit
Capitaine-1	Ernest S. Friedrick	'37	62	zero	zero	→Fremantle
Carbonero-1	Charlton L. Murphy, Jr.	'32	42	zero	zero	→Fremantle
Crevalle-7	Everett H. Steinmetz	'35	38	4/8,500	3/6,643	Japan Sea
Dace-7	Otis R. Cole, Jr.	'36	46	1/4,400	1/1,391	Polar circuit
Dentuda-1	John S. McCain, Jr.	'31	58	1/4,000	zero	East China Sea
Devilfish-3	Stephen S. Mann, Jr.	'38	47	zero	zero	Empire

SUBMARINE WAR PATROLS DEPARTING PEARL HARBOR, MAY 1945 (*Cont.*)

Boat, Patrol Number	Skipper and Class		Days	Ships/Tonnage		Area
				Wartime Credit	JANAC Credit	
Flying Fish-12	Robert D. Risser	'34	36	2/3,200	2/4,113	Japan Sea
Guardfish-12	Douglas T. Hammond	'31	49	zero	zero	Empire
Hackleback-2	Frederick E. Janney	'37	49	zero	zero	Empire
Haddo-9	Frank C. Lynch, Jr.	'38	46	6/18,600	3/6,126	East China Sea
Icefish-4	Richard W. Peterson	'31	50	zero	zero	→Fremantle
Lapon-8	Donald G. Baer	'37	50	zero	zero	Empire
Loggerhead-1	Ralph M. Metcalf	'35	64	zero	zero	→Fremantle
Manta-1	Edward P. Madley	'37	46	zero	zero	Polar circuit
Muskallunge-6	William H. Lawrence	'34	52	zero	zero	East China Sea
Paddle-8	Joseph P. Fitz-Patrick	'38	60	zero	zero	East China Sea
Parche-6	Woodrow W. McCrory	'38	59	2/7,200	2/3,669	Empire
Peto-9	Robert H. Caldwell, Jr.	'36	44	zero	zero	Empire
Pilotfish-5	Allan G. Schnable	'34	51	zero	zero	Empire
Piranha-5	Donald G. Irvine	'34	49	3/9,800	zero	Empire
Puffer-8	Carl R. Dwyer	'38	53	zero	zero	→Fremantle
Queenfish-5	Frank N. Shamer	'37	69	zero	zero	East China Sea
Quillback-1	Richard P. Nicholson	'37	53	zero	zero	Empire
Razorback-4	Charles D. Brown	'38	50	zero	zero	Empire
Redfin-6	Charles K. Miller	'39	36	zero	zero	Empire
Ronquil-5	Robert B. Lander	'37	67	1/4,000	zero	East China Sea
Sea Devil-4	Charles F. McGivern	'38	54	1/2,500	1/2,211	East China Sea
Sea Dog-4	Earl T. Hydeman	'32	39	6/29,500	6/7,186	Japan Sea
Sea Owl-3	Warren C. Hall, Jr.	'37	67	1/2,600	1/800	Empire
Shad-10	Donald L. Mehlop	'37	45	3/13,500	2/5,309	East China Sea

Silversides-14	John C. Nichols	'34	59	zero	zero	Empire
Skate-7	Richard B. Lynch	'35	49	5/8,700	4/6,398	Japan Sea
Spadefish-5	William J. Germershausen	'35	39	6/26,100	5/8,578	Japan Sea
Steelhead-7	Robert B. Byrnes	'38	74	zero	zero	Empire
Tench-2	Thomas S. Baskett	'35	37	4/15,800	4/5,069	Empire
Tigrone-2	Hiram Cassedy	'31	44	zero	zero	Empire
Tinosa-11	Richard C. Latham	'34	37	4/12,100	4/6,701	Japan Sea
Tirante-2	George L. Street III	'37	57	3/7,400	2/3,265	East China Sea
Tunny-9	George E. Pierce	'32	49	zero	zero	Japan Sea
			TOTALS:	62/213,900	46/87,869	

SUBMARINE WAR PATROLS DEPARTING PEARL HARBOR, JUNE 1945

Boat, Patrol Number	Skipper and Class		Days	Ships/Tonnage		Area
				Wartime Credit	JANAC Credit	
Angler-7	H. Bissell	USNR	56	zero	zero	Empire
Argonaut II-1	John S. Schmidt	'37	52	zero	zero	East China Sea
Aspro-7	James H. Ashley, Jr.	'34	49	1/500	zero	Empire
Barb-12	Eugene B. Fluckey	'35	54	3/11,200	2/3,620	Empire
Batfish-7	Walter L. Small	'38	58	zero	zero	Empire
Blackfish-12	Robert C. Gillette	'39	57	zero	zero	East China Sea
Cabrilla-8	Henry C. Lauerman	'38	58	zero	zero	→Fremantle
Carp-1	J. L. Hunnicutt	USNR	54	5/9,800	zero	Empire
Cero-8	Raymond Berthrong	'38	33	zero	zero	Empire
Gabilan-6	William B. Parham	'36	56	zero	zero	Empire

SUBMARINE WAR PATROLS DEPARTING PEARL HARBOR, JUNE 1945 (Cont.)

Boat, Patrol Number	Skipper and Class		Days	Ships/Tonnage		Area
				Wartime Credit	JANAC Credit	
Gunnel-8	Guy E. O'Neil, Jr.	'37	41	zero	zero	Empire
Haddock-13	Albert R. Strow	'39	51	zero	zero	Empire
Kingfish-12	Thomas D. Keegan	'39	55	zero	zero	Polar circuit
Lionfish-2	Bricker M. Ganyard	'38	58	1/1,400	zero	Empire
Moray-1	Frank L. Barrows	'35	52	1/600	zero	Empire
Pintado-5	Romondt Budd	'35	41	zero	zero	Empire
Pompon-9	John A. Bogley	'38	34	zero	zero	Truk
Rasher-8	Charles D. Nace	'39	53	zero	zero	→Fremantle
Raton-8	Guy F. Gugliotta	'38	32	zero	zero	→Fremantle
Runner II-1	Raymond H. Bass	'31	30	1/600	1/630	Empire
Sea Fox-4	Roy C. Klinker	'35	49	zero	zero	Empire
Sea Poacher-4	Charles F. Leigh	'39	54	zero	zero	East China Sea
Sea Robin-3	Paul C. Stimson	'36	65	4/5,600	1/1,224	East China Sea
Spot-3	Jack M. Seymour	'35	58	zero	zero	Empire
Springer-3	John F. Bauer	'38	40	zero	zero	Empire
Thornback-1	Ernest P. Abrahamson	'32	52	zero	zero	Empire
Threadfin-3	John J. Foote	'35	53	1/5,200	1/630	East China Sea
Trepang-5	Allen R. Faust	'36	47	3/3,700	1/606	Empire
Trutta-2*	F. P. Hoskins	USNR	46	zero	zero	East China Sea
Whale-11	Freeland H. Carde, Jr.	'38	68	zero	zero	Empire
			TOTALS:	20/38,600	6/6,710	

* Supported Japan Sea operations

SUBMARINE WAR PATROLS DEPARTING PEARL HARBOR, JULY 1945

Boat, Patrol Number	Skipper and Class		Days	Ships/Tonnage		Area
				Wartime Credit	JANAC Credit	
Archerfish-7	Joseph F. Enright	'33	59	zero	zero	Empire
Atule-4	John H. Maurer	'35	51	1/800	1/800	Empire
Balao-10	Robert K. Worthington	'38	47	zero	zero	Empire
Billfish-8	L. C. Farley, Jr.	USNR	44	2/5,200	1/1,091	East China Sea
Catfish-1	William A. Overton	'33	40	zero	zero	Empire
Blackfin-5	William L. Kitch	'38	37	zero	zero	East China Sea
Dragonet-3	Gerald G. Hinman	'38	50	zero	zero	Empire
Entemedor-1	William R. Smith, Jr.	'37	30	zero	zero	Empire
Gato-13	Richard Holden	'37	61	1/800	zero	Empire
Hake-9	Frank E. Haylor	'36	49	zero	zero	Empire
Jack-9	Albert S. Fuhrman	'37	48	zero	zero	Formosa
Jallao-4	Joseph B. Icenhower	'36	51	1/4,000	1/5,795	Japan Sea
Macabi-1	Anthony H. Dropp	'32	42	zero	zero	Truk
Muskallunge-7	William H. Lawrence	'34	40	zero	zero	Polar circuit
Pargo-8	David B. Bell	'37	41	2/7,200	1/5,454	Japan Sea
Perch II-7	Charles D. McCall	'39	47	zero	zero	Empire
Peto-10	Robert H. Caldwell, Jr.	'36	47	zero	zero	Empire
Pipefish-6	A. L. Redon	USNR	42	zero	zero	Empire
Piper-3	Edward L. Beach	'39	46	zero	zero	Japan Sea
Plaice-6	Richard S. Andrews	'31	35	zero	zero	East China Sea
Pogy-10	John M. Bowers	'38	47	2/12,500	2/4,668	Japan Sea
Pomfret-6	John B. Hess	'37	59	zero	zero	East China Sea
Ray-8	William T. Kinsella	'34	30	zero	zero	→Fremantle

SUBMARINE WAR PATROLS DEPARTING PEARL HARBOR, JULY 1945 (Cont.)

Boat, Patrol Number	Skipper and Class	Days	Ships/Tonnage Wartime Credit	JANAC Credit	Area
Razorback-5	Charles D. Brown '38	39	zero	zero	Polar circuit
Redfin-7	Charles K. Miller '39	34	zero	zero	South China Sea
Sandlance-5	James G. Glaes '39	54	zero	zero	Empire
Scabbardfish-5	Frederick A. Gunn '34	51	zero	zero	Empire
Seahorse-8	Harry H. Greer, Jr. '34	38	zero	zero	Empire
Sennet-4	Charles R. Clark, Jr. '39	34	4/24,500	4/13,105	Japan Sea
Shad-11	Donald L. Mehlop '37	41	zero	zero	Marcus Island
Spikefish-4	Robert R. Managhan '38	54	1/1,800	1/1,660	East China Sea
Sterlet-5	H. H. Lewis USNR	48	zero	zero	Empire
Tench-3	Thomas S. Baskett '35	49	zero	zero	Empire
Tigrone-3	Vincent E. Schumacher '38	41	zero	zero	Empire
Toro-2	James D. Grant '31	36	zero	zero	Empire
Torsk-2	Bafford E. Lewellen '31	50	4/6,000	3/2,476	Japan Sea
	TOTALS:		18/62,600	14/35,049	

SUBMARINE WAR PATROLS DEPARTING PEARL HARBOR, AUGUST 1945

Boat, Patrol Number	Skipper and Class	Days	Ships/Tonnage Wartime Credit	JANAC Credit	Area
Apogon-8	Arthur C. House, Jr. '34	26	zero	zero	Marcus Island
Cavalla-6	Herman J. Kossler '34	36	zero	zero	Empire

Cutlass-1	Herbert L. Jukes	'32	22	zero	zero	Polar circuit
Devilfish-4	Stephen S. Mann, Jr.	'38	20	zero	zero	Empire
Haddo-10	Frank C. Lynch, Jr.	'38	31	zero	zero	Empire
Pilotfish-6	Allan G. Schnable	'34	32	zero	zero	Empire
Pintado-6	Romondt Budd	'35	19	zero	zero	Empire
Runner II-2	Raymond H. Bass	'31	29	zero	zero	Empire
Sea Cat-4	Richard H. Bowers	'38	27	zero	zero	Polar circuit
Sea Devil-5	Charles F. McGivern	'38	25	zero	zero	East China Sea
Segundo-5	Stephen L. Johnson	'39	30	zero	zero	Polar circuit
Stickleback-1	Harley K. Nauman	'34	34	zero	zero	Japan Sea
Tilefish-6	Walter F. Schlech, Jr.	'36	33	zero	zero	Empire

PRESENT AT SURRENDER CEREMONY, TOKYO BAY, SEPTEMBER 2, 1945

Proteus	Lewis S. Parks, Commander, Squadron Twenty
Runner II	Raymond H. Bass
Archerfish	Joseph F. Enright
Haddo	Frank C. Lynch, Jr.
Gato	Richard Holden
Sea Cat	Richard H. Bowers
Muskallunge	William H. Lawrence
Tigrone	Vincent E. Schumacher
Razorback	Charles D. Brown
Pilotfish	Allan G. Schnable
Hake	Frank E. Haylor
Segundo	Stephen L. Johnson
Cavalla	Herman J. Kossler

Top Skippers of World War II
By Number of Confirmed Ships Sunk†

Asterisk indicates Medal-of-Honor winner

	Number of Patrols	Ships/Tons Credited	Ships/Tons JANAC
1. Richard H. O'Kane, 1934* *Tang*	5	31/227,800	24/93,824
2. Slade D. Cutter, 1935 *Seahorse*	4	21/142,300	19/72,000
3. Dudley W. Morton, 1930 *R-5, Wahoo*	6	17/100,500	19/55,000
4. Eugene B. Fluckey, 1935* *Barb*	5	25/179,700	16⅓/95,360
5. Samuel D. Dealey, 1930* *Harder*	6	20½/82,500	16/54,002
6. Reuben T. Whitaker, 1934 *S-44, Flasher*	5	18½/111,500	14½/60,846
7. Gordon W. Underwood, 1932 *Spadefish*	3	14/89,600	14/75,386
8. Royce L. Gross, 1930 *Seawolf, Boarfish*	7	13½/80,500	14/65,735
9. Charles O. Triebel, 1929 *S-15, Snook*	8	13/83,300	14/58,837
10. John S. Coye, Jr., 1933 *Silversides*	6	14/71,700	14/39,000
11. William B. Sieglaff, 1931 *Tautog, Tench*	7	15/63,500	13/32,886
12. Thomas S. Baskett, 1935 *S-37, Tautog, Tench*	7	13/50,700	12/27,273
13. Henry C. Bruton, 1926 *Greenling*	4	11/82,600	11/54,564
14. Bafford E. Lewellen, 1931 *Pollack, Torsk*	6	11/38,200	11/23,685
15. Charles H. Andrews, 1930 *Gurnard*	6	11/71,500	10/57,243‡
16. Robert E. Dornin, 1935 *Trigger*	3	13/96,500	10/54,595

† Skippers who sank fewer than five ships are not listed.
‡ Including German ship, not listed in JANAC but officially credited.

	Number of Patrols	Ships/Tons Credited	Ships/Tons JANAC
17. Eric L. Barr, Jr., 1934 *Bluegill*	6	12/51,200	10/46,212
18. Ralph M. Metcalf, 1935 *Pogy, Loggerhead*	5	10/54,800	10/40,040
19. Raymond H. Bass, 1931 *Plunger, Runner II*	8	12/70,300	10/37,977
20. Malcolm E. Garrison, 1932 *Sandlance*	4	11/60,100	10/37,368
21. Thomas B. Klakring, 1927 *S-17, Guardfish*	5	11/76,900	10/33,122
22. John A. Moore, 1932 *Grayback*	3	12½/63,500	9½/45,757
23. Glynn R. Donaho, 1927 *Flying Fish, Picuda*	7	14/71,400	9½/29,870
24. Eli T. Reich, 1935 *Sealion II*	3	11/101,400	9/59,839
25. Walter T. Griffith, 1934 *Bowfin, Bullhead*	5	17/106,300	9/45,874
26. Edward E. Shelby, 1933 *Sunfish*	5	14/106,200	9/45,613
27. Robert D. Risser, 1934 *Flying Fish*	5	8/33,500	9/40,931
28. Norvell G. Ward, 1935 *Guardfish*	5	14/90,200	9/39,302
29. Willard R. Laughon, 1933 *Rasher*	3	10/60,200	9/38,340
30. George E. Porter, Jr., 1932 *Bluefish, Sennet*	6	14/70,300	9/30,940
31. John E. Lee, 1930 *S-12, Grayling, Croaker*	10	16/74,100	9/28,562
32. Russell Kefauver, 1933 *Tambor, Springer*	6	13/64,000	9/23,081
33. William J. Germershausen, 1935 *Tambor, Spadefish*	4	10/42,300	9/16,277
34. William S. Post, Jr., 1930 *Gudgeon, Spot*	7	19/110,900	8½/54,213
35. William T. Kinsella, 1934 *Ray*	4	10½/80,500	8½/34,101
36. Charles E. Loughlin, 1933 *S-14, Queenfish*	8	12/109,400	8⅓/41,718

	Number of Patrols	Ships/Tons Credited	Ships/Tons JANAC
37. Enrique D. Haskins, 1933 Guitarro	3	11½/61,200	8⅓/25,400
38. Henry G. Munson, 1932 S-38, Crevalle, Rasher	9	13/113,400	8/67,630
39. Creed C. Burlingame, 1927 Silversides	5	11/71,700	8/46,865
40. Bernard A. Clarey, 1934 Pintado	4	13/98,600	8/42,956
41. Thomas M. Dykers, 1927 Jack	4	10/77,900	8/42,417
42. Lowell T. Stone, 1929 Lapon	4	10/68,600	8/39,266
43. Robert H. Rice, 1927 Drum, Paddle	5	8/49,000	8/39,100
44. Donald F. Weiss, 1929 Tinosa	3	9/67,100	8/39,047
45. Vernon L. Lowrance, 1930 Kingfish, Sea Dog	7	9/62,200	8/34,199
46. Roy M. Davenport, 1933 Haddock, Trepang	6	17/151,900	8/29,662
47. Charles C. Kirkpatrick, 1931 Triton	3	10/44,600	8/22,749
48. Anton R. Gallaher, 1933 Bang	5	15/94,000	8/20,181
49. George L. Street III, 1937* Tirante	2	11/35,700	8/15,886
50. John A. Tyree, Jr., 1933 Finback	5	8½/55,900	7½/39,371
51. Frank G. Selby, 1933 Puffer	4	9½/78,600	7½/38,159
52. Lawson P. Ramage, 1931* Trout, Parche	7	10/77,600	7½/36,681
53. Robert J. Foley, 1927 Gato	6	10/66,000	7½/26,235
54. George W. Grider, 1936 Flasher	2	6/43,800	7/43,718
55. John C. Broach, 1927 Hake	5	8/51,400	7/37,923
56. Thomas W. Hogan, 1931 Bonefish	4	15/105,500	7/34,329

	Number of Patrols	Ships/Tons Credited	Ships/Tons JANAC
57. James C. Dempsey, 1931 S-37, Spearfish, Cod	10	9/52,100	7/30,794
58. William H. Hazzard, 1935 Blenny	4	8/43,100	7/18,087
59. Francis A. Greenup, 1936 Hardhead	4	6/25,100	7/14,246
60. Earl T. Hydeman, 1932 Sea Dog	2	7/36,200	7/14,036
61. Thomas L. Wogan, 1930 S-34, Tarpon, Besugo	9	9/51,700	6/46,730†
62. Louis D. McGregor, Jr., 1930 Pike, Redfish	4	9/74,600	6/44,637
63. William C. Thompson, Jr., 1935 Cabrilla	4	10/66,300	6/36,062
64. John H. Maurer, 1935 Atule	4	7/34,200	6/33,379
65. Joseph H. Willingham, 1926 Tautog, Bowfin	5	11/55,500	6/25,636
66. Howard W. Gilmore, 1926* Growler	4	8/37,300	6/22,681
67. Duncan C. MacMillan, 1926 Thresher	3	10/61,400	6/22,277
68. Frederick B. Warder, 1925 Seawolf	7	8/38,900	6/18,719
69. William H. Brockman, 1927 Nautilus, Haddock	6	8/29,500	5½/23,829
70. Walter G. Ebert, 1930 Scamp	6	6/49,000	5/34,108
71. James W. Coe, 1930 S-39, Skipjack, Cisco	7	7/45,300	5/26,130
72. John R. Moore, 1929 S-44, Sailfish	6	3/10,100	5/23,978
73. Philip H. Ross, 1927 Halibut, Golet	6	6/45,400	5/23,226

† Including the German raider Michel.

	NUMBER OF PATROLS	SHIPS/TONS CREDITED	SHIPS/TONS JANAC
74. William J. Millican, 1928 S-18, Thresher, Escolar	7	6/40,000	5/21,525
75. Roy S. Benson, 1929 Trigger, Razorback	5	6/36,900	5/17,652
76. Chester W. Nimitz, Jr., 1936 Haddo	3	5½/17,600	5/14,636

Best War Patrols by Number of Ships Sunk

Boat and Patrol No.	Skipper	Ships Sunk*	Tonnage
1. Tang-3	Richard H. O'Kane	10	39,100
2. Wahoo-4	Dudley W. Morton	9	20,000
3. Tang-5	Richard H. O'Kane	7	21,772
4. Flasher-5	George W. Grider	6	42,800
5. Spadefish-1	Gordon W. Underwood	6	31,500
6. Silversides-10	John S. Coye, Jr.	6	14,141
7. Tirante-1	George L. Street III	6	12,621
8. Sea Dog-4	Earl T. Hydeman	6	7,186
9. Ray-6	William T. Kinsella	5⅓	12,645
10. Rasher-5	Henry G. Munson	5	52,600
11. Seahorse-2	Slade D. Cutter	5	27,579
12. Bowfin-2	Walter T. Griffith	5	26,458
13. Ray-5	William T. Kinsella	5	26,000
14. Hammerhead-2	John C. Martin	5	25,178
15. Tang-1	Richard H. O'Kane	5	21,400
16. Pogy-5	Ralph M. Metcalf	5	21,150
17. Snook-5	Charles O. Triebel	5	21,046
18. Seahorse-3	Slade D. Cutter	5	20,900
19. Seahorse-4	Slade D. Cutter	5	19,374
20. Sandlance-2	Malcolm E. Garrison	5	18,328
21. Guardfish-1	Thomas B. Klakring	5	16,709
22. Triton-3	Charles C. Kirkpatrick	5	15,843
23. Barb-8	Eugene B. Fluckey	5	15,472
24. Harder-2	Samuel D. Dealey	5	15,272
25. Haddo-7	Chester W. Nimitz, Jr.	5	14,460
26. Spadefish-5	William J. Germershausen	5	8,578

* According to JANAC figures.

Appendix I

Best War Patrols by Tonnage of Ships Sunk

Boat and Patrol No.	Skipper	Ships Sunk*	Tonnage
1. *Archerfish*-5	Joseph F. Enright	1	59,000
2. *Rasher*-5	Henry G. Munson	5	52,600
3. *Flasher*-5	George W. Grider	6	42,800
4. *Tang*-3	Richard H. O'Kane	10	39,100
5. *Barb*-9	Eugene B. Fluckey	3	36,800
6. *Sealion II*-3	Eli T. Reich	2	32,900
7. *Albacore*-9	James W. Blanchard	2	32,000
8. *Spadefish*-1	Gordon W. Underwood	6	31,500
9. *Spadefish*-2	Gordon W. Underwood	4	30,400
10. *Cavalla*-1	Herman J. Kossler	1	30,000
11. *Gurnard*-5	Charles H. Andrews	4	29,700
12. *Sailfish*-10	Robert E. M. Ward	3	29,571
13. *Tarpon*-6	Thomas L. Wogan	2	27,910
14. *Silversides*-4	Creed C. Burlingame	4	27,798
15. *Seahorse*-2	Slade D. Cutter	5	27,579
16. *Trigger*-6	Robert E. Dornin	4	27,095
17. *Bowfin*-2	Walter T. Griffith	5	26,458
18. *Ray*-5	William T. Kinsella	5	26,000
19. *Seawolf*-12	Royce L. Gross	4½	25,793
20. *Atule*-1	John H. Maurer	4	25,691
21. *Hammerhead*-2	John C. Martin	5	25,178
22. *Dace*-5	Bladen D. Claggett	3	25,141
23. *Flasher*-3	Reuben T. Whitaker	4½	24,949
24. *Pintado*-2	Bernard A. Clarey	2	24,663
25. *Cabrilla*-6	William C. Thompson	4	24,557
26. *Bonefish*-1	Thomas W. Hogan	3	24,206
27. *Barb*-11	Eugene B. Fluckey	4⅓	24,197

* According to JANAC figures.

Top Submarines by Number of Ships Sunk

BOAT	SKIPPERS	SHIPS SUNK*
1. *Tautog*	Willingham, Sieglaff, Baskett	26
2. *Tang*	O'Kane	24
3. *Silversides*	Burlingame, Coye, J. C. Nichols	23
4. *Flasher*	Whitaker, Grider	21
5. *Spadefish*	Underwood, Germershausen	21
6. *Seahorse*	Cutter, Wilkins	20
7. *Wahoo*	Kennedy, Morton	20
8. *Guardfish*	Klakring, N. G. Ward	19
9. *Rasher*	Hutchinson, Laughon, Munson	18
10. *Seawolf*	Warder, Gross	18
11. *Trigger*	Benson, Dornin, Harlfinger, Connole	18
12. *Barb*	Waterman, Fluckey	17
13. *Snook*	Triebel, Browne	17
14. *Thresher*	W. L. Anderson, Millican, H. Hull, MacMillan, Middleton	17
15. *Bowfin*	Willingham, Griffith, Corbus, A. K. Tyree	16
16. *Harder*	Dealey	16
17. *Pogy*	Wales, Metcalf, Bowers	16
18. *Sunfish*	R. W. Peterson, Shelby, Reed	16
19. *Tinosa*	Daspit, Weiss, Latham	16
20. *Drum*	Rice, McMahon, Williamson, Rindskopf	15
21. *Flying Fish*	Donaho, Watkins, Risser	15
22. *Greenling*	Bruton, Grant, Gerwick	15
23. *Jack*	Dykers, Krapf, Fuhrman	15
24. *Grayback*	Saunders, Stephan, J. A. Moore	14
25. *Kingfish*	Lowrance, Jukes, Harper	14

* According to JANAC figures.

Appendix K

Top Submarines by Tonnage of Ships Sunk

BOAT	SKIPPERS	TONNAGE*
1. *Flasher*	Whitaker, Grider	100,231
2. *Rasher*	Hutchinson, Laughon, Munson	99,901
3. *Barb*	Waterman, Fluckey	96,628
4. *Tang*	O'Kane	93,824
5. *Silversides*	Burlingame, Coye, J. C. Nichols	90,080
6. *Spadefish*	Underwood, Germershausen	88,091
7. *Trigger*	Benson, Dornin, Harlfinger, Connole	86,552
8. *Drum*	Rice, McMahon, Williamson, Rindskopf	80,580
9. *Jack*	Dykers, Krapf, Fuhrman	76,687
10. *Snook*	Triebel, Browne	75,473
11. *Tautog*	Willingham, Sieglaff, Baskett	72,606
12. *Seahorse*	Cutter, Wilkins	72,529
13. *Guardfish*	Klakring, N. G. Ward	72,424
14. *Seawolf*	Warder, Gross	71,609
15. *Gudgeon*	Grenfell, Stovall, Post	71,047
16. *Sealion II*	Reich, Putman	68,297
17. *Bowfin*	Willingham, Griffith, Corbus, A. K. Tyree	67,882
18. *Thresher*	W. L. Anderson, Millican, H. Hull, MacMillan, Middleton	66,172
19. *Tinosa*	Daspit, Weiss, Latham	64,655
20. *Grayback*	Saunders, Stephan, J. S. Moore	63,835
21. *Pogy*	Wales, Metcalf, Bowers	62,633
22. *Bonefish*	Hogan, Edge	61,345
23. *Wahoo*	Kennedy, Morton	60,038
24. *Sunfish*	R. W. Peterson, Shelby, Reed	59,815
25. *Archerfish*	Wright, Enright	59,800

* According to JANAC figures.

Appendix L
Submarine Losses in World War II

In Pacific Unless Otherwise Noted

SOURCE: *U.S. Submarine Losses in WW II*

SUBMARINE	SKIPPER	DATE	
1941			
1. *Sealion*	Richard G. Voge	12-10-41	
1942			
2. *S-36*	John R. McKnight, Jr.	1-20-42	
3. *S-26*	Earle C. Hawk	1-24-42	(Atlantic)
4. *Shark*	Louis Shane, Jr.*	2- 42	
5. *Perch*	David A. Hurt	3-3-42	
6. *S-27*	Herbert L. Jukes	6-19-42	
7. *S-39*	Francis E. Brown	8-14-42	
8. *Grunion*	Mannert L. Abele*	7/8 -42	
1943			
9. *Argonaut*	John R. Pierce*	1-10-43	
10. *Amberjack*	John A. Bole, Jr.*	2-16-43	
11. *Grampus*	John R. Craig*	3/5 -43	
12. *Triton*	George K. MacKenzie, Jr.*	3-15-43	
13. *Pickerel*	Augustus H. Alston, Jr.*	4-3-43	
14. *Grenadier*	John A. Fitzgerald	4-22-43	
15. *Runner*	Joseph H. Bourland*	5-28/7-4-43	
16. *R-12*	Edward E. Shelby	6-12-43	(Atlantic)
17. *Grayling*	Robert M. Brinker*	9-9/9-12-43	
18. *Pompano*	Willis M. Thomas*	8-29/9-27-43	
19. *Cisco*	James W. Coe*	9-28-43	
20. *S-44*	Francis E. Brown*	10-7-43	
21. *Dorado*	Earle C. Schneider*	10-12-43	(Atlantic)
22. *Wahoo*	Dudley W. Morton*	10-11-43	
23. *Corvina*	Roderick S. Rooney*	11-16-43	
24. *Sculpin*	Fred Connaway*	11-19-43	
25. *Capelin*	Elliott E. Marshall*	11-23/12-9-43	
1944			
26. *Scorpion*	Maximilian G. Schmidt*	1-5/2-24-44	
27. *Grayback*	John A. Moore*	2-26-44	

* Killed in action.

Submarine	Skipper	Date
28. *Trout*	Albert H. Clark*	2-29-44
29. *Tullibee*	Charles F. Brindupke*	3-26/27-44
30. *Gudgeon*	Robert A. Bonin*	4-7/5-11-44
31. *Herring*	David Zabriskie, Jr.*	6-1-44
32. *Golet*	James S. Clark*	6-14-44
33. *S-28*	J. G. Campbell*	7-4-44
34. *Robalo*	Manning M. Kimmel*	7-26-44
35. *Flier*	John D. Crowley	8-13-44
36. *Harder*	Samuel D. Dealey*	8-24-44
37. *Seawolf*	Albert M. Bontier*	10-3-44
38. *Darter*	David H. McClintock	10-24-44
39. *Shark II*	Edward N. Blakely*	10-24-44
40. *Tang*	Richard H. O'Kane	10-24-44
41. *Escolar*	William J. Millican*	10-17/11-3-44
42. *Albacore*	Hugh R. Rimmer*	11-7-44
43. *Growler*	Thomas B. Oakley, Jr.*	11-8-44
44. *Scamp*	John C. Hollingsworth*	11-9/16-44

1945

45. *Swordfish*	Keats E. Montross*	1-12-45
46. *Barbel*	Conde L. Raguet*	2-4-45
47. *Kete*	Edward Ackerman*	3-20/31-45
48. *Trigger*	David R. Connole*	3-26/28-45
49. *Snook*	John F. Walling*	4-8/20-45
50. *Lagarto*	Frank D. Latta*	5-3-45
51. *Bonefish*	Lawrence L. Edge*	6-18-45
52. *Bullhead*	Edward R. Holt, Jr.*	8-6-45

* Killed in action.

Sources

I. General Bibliography

The books and periodicals listed here deal with the history of submarines, torpedoes, diesel engines, World War I, the naval policy in the peacetime years 1918 to 1939, and general studies of World War II. All proved useful in writing this book. In particular, the author is indebted to Samuel Eliot Morison for his magnificent fifteen-volume naval history of World War II and to specialized articles in the quasi-official naval journal *United States Naval Institute Proceedings,* published at Annapolis, Maryland, and identified below as *U.S.N.I.P.*

Alden, Carroll Storrs. "American Submarine Operations in the War," *U.S.N.I.P.,* June 1920.

Barnes, Robert Hatfield. "Japan's First Submarines," *U.S.N.I.P.,* February 1943.

———. *United States Submarines.* New Haven, Conn.: H. F. Morse Associates, 1946.

Braisted, William R. *United States Navy in the Pacific 1909–1922.* Austin, Tex.: University of Texas Press, 1971.

Cable, F. T. *The Birth and Development of the American Submarine.* New York: Harper & Brothers, 1924.

Churchill, Winston S. *The Second World War.* 6 vols. Boston: Houghton Mifflin Company, 1948–53.

Cohen, Jerome B. *Japan's Economy in War and Reconstruction* (Institute of Pacific Relations). Minneapolis, Minn.: University of Minnesota Press, 1949.

Corbett, Sir Julian. *Naval Operations.* 3 vols. London: Longmans, Green & Company, 1920–23.

Craven, Francis S. "The Painful Development of a Professional Navy," *U.S.N.I.P.,* May 1966.

Craven, Wesley F., and James L. Cate, eds. *Army Air Forces in World War II.* 7 vols. Chicago: University of Chicago Press, 1948–58.

Cross, Wilbur. *Challengers of the Deep.* New York: William Sloane Associates, 1959.

Davis, Vincent. *The Admiral's Lobby.* Chapel Hill, N.C.: University of North Carolina Press, 1967.

Dictionary of American Naval Fighting Ships, Vol. 1 (A-B), Vol. 2 (C-F), Vol. 3 (G-K), Vol. 4 (L-M), Vol. 5 (N-Q), Vol. 6 (R-S) not yet published, Vol. 7 (T-Z) not yet published. Washington, D.C.: U.S. Government Printing Office.

Doenitz, Karl. *Memoirs: Ten Years and Twenty Days.* New York: World Book Company, 1959.

Douglas, Lawrence Henry. "Submarine Disarmament 1919–36." Unpublished dissertation on file in Navy Library, Washington, D.C.

Frothingham, Thomas G. *The Naval History of the World War.* 3 vols. Cambridge, Mass.: Harvard University Press, 1927.

Fuchida, Mitsuo, and Okumiya Masatake. *Midway: The Battle That Doomed Japan.* Annapolis, Md.: U.S. Naval Institute, 1955.

Fukaya, Hajime. "Japan's Wartime Carrier Construction," *U.S.N.I.P.,* September 1955.

———. "The Shokakus—Pearl Harbor to Leyte Gulf," *U.S.N.I.P.,* June 1952.

———. "Three Japanese Submarine Developments," *U.S.N.I.P.,* August 1952.

General Board, U.S. Navy, Minutes, 1930–38. Unpublished, on file in the Classified Operational Archives, Building 210, Navy Yard, Washington, D.C. A priceless source on U.S. submarine developments.

Gibson, R. H., and Maurice Prendergast. *The German Submarine War.* New York: R. R. Smith, 1931.

Hara, Tameichi, Fred Saito, and Roger Pineau. *Japanese Destroyer Captain.* New York: Ballantine Books, 1961.

Hashimoto, Mochitsura. *Sunk: The Story of the Japanese Submarine Fleet 1941–45.* New York: Henry Holt & Company, 1954.

Herzog, Bob, and Allison W. Saville. "Top Submarines in Two World Wars," *U.S.N.I.P.,* September 1961.

Hezlet, Arthur. *The Submarine and Sea Power.* New York: Stein and Day, 1967. A brilliant study of European submarine development.

Howard, Warren S. "The Dragon Puts to Sea," *U.S.N.I.P.,* August 1951.

———. "Japanese Destroyers in World War II," *U.S.N.I.P.,* January 1952.

———. "Japan's Heavy Cruisers in the War," *U.S.N.I.P.,* May 1950.

———. "The Kongos [Japanese battleships] in World War II," *U.S.N.I.P.,* November 1948.

———. "The Mogamis: Cheat Cruisers Extraordinary," *U.S.N.I.P.,* November 1949.

Interrogations of Japanese Officials. 2 vols. U.S. Strategic Bombing Survey (Pacific). Washington, D.C.: U.S. Government Printing Office.

Irwin, Mariette W., and Julie A. Joa, eds. *Dolphin Tales.* Norfolk, Va.: Teagle and Little, 1971.

Ito, Masanori, with Roger Pineau. *The End of the Imperial Japanese Navy.* New York: W. W. Norton & Company, 1956.

Jameson, William, K.B.E. *Most Formidable Thing*. London: Rupert-Hart-Davis, 1965.

Karig, Walter. *Battle Report*. 6 vols. New York: Rinehart & Company, 1944–52.

——— with Russell Harris and Frank A. Manson. "Battleship Banzai," *U.S.N.I.P.*, October 1949. The *Yamato* sortie.

King, Ernest J., and Walter M. Whitehill. *Fleet Admiral King—A Naval Record*. New York: W. W. Norton & Company, 1952.

Kittredge, G. W. "Stalking the *Takao* in Singapore Harbor," *U.S.N.I.P.*, April 1957.

Kuenne, Robert E. *The Attack Submarine*. New Haven, Conn.: Yale University Press, 1965.

Lake, Simon. *The Submarine in War and Peace*. Philadelphia: J. B. Lippincott Company, 1918.

Lockwood, Charles A., and Hans C. Adamson. *Hell at 50 Fathoms*. Philadelphia: Chilton Books, 1962.

Long, E. John. "Japan's Underseas Carriers," *U.S.N.I.P.*, June 1950.

Lord, Walter. *Day of Infamy*. New York: Henry Holt & Company, 1957.

———. *Incredible Victory*. New York: Harper & Row, 1967.

Lundeberg, Philip K. "American Anti-Submarine Operations in the Atlantic, May 1943–May 1945." Ph.D. thesis, Harvard University, 1953.

Maas, Peter. *The Rescuer*. New York: Harper & Row, 1967.

MacArthur, Douglas. *Reports of General MacArthur*. 4 vols. Washington, D.C.: U.S. Government Printing Office, 1966.

Magdeburger, E. C. "Diesel Engines in Submarines," *A.S.N.E.*, Vol. 37, 1925.

Masland, John W. "Japanese-German Naval Collaboration in World War II," *U.S.N.I.P.*, February 1949.

Matsumoto, Kitaro, and Chihaya Masataka. "Design and Construction of Yamato and Musashi," *U.S.N.I.P.*, October 1953.

Meigs, J. F. "Japanese Sea Power," *U.S.N.I.P.*, February 1944.

Moore, Lynn L. "Shinano: The Jinx Carrier," *U.S.N.I.P.*, February 1953.

Morison, Samuel Eliot. *History of United States Naval Operation in World War II*. 15 vols. Boston: Little, Brown and Company, 1947–62.

Morris, Richard K. *John P. Holland, 1841–1914*. Annapolis, Md.: U.S. Naval Institute Press, 1966.

Morton, Louis. *The Fall of the Philippines*. Washington, D.C.: Office of the Chief of Military History, Department of the Army, 1953.

———. "The Japanese Decision for War," *U.S.N.I.P.*, December 1954.

Nakayama, Sadayoshi. "Japan's Phenomenal Shipbuilders," *U.S.N.I.P.*, August 1966.

Nimitz, Chester, and E. B. Potter. *The Great Sea War*. Englewood Cliffs, N.J.: Prentice-Hall, 1960.

Niven, John, Courtlandt Canby, and Vernon Welsh, eds. *Dynamic America: A History of the General Dynamics Corporation and Its Predecessor Companies*. Garden City, N.Y.: Doubleday & Company, 1958.

Ofstie, R. A. *The Campaigns of the Pacific War*. U.S. Strategic Bombing Survey (Pacific). Washington, D.C.: U.S. Government Printing Office.

Perry, Milton F. *Infernal Machines*. Baton Rouge, La.: Louisiana State University Press, 1965.

Possony, Stefan T. "Japanese Naval Strategy," *U.S.N.I.P.*, May 1944.

Potter, E. B. "The Navy's War Against Japan—A Strategic Analysis," *U.S.N.I.P.*, August 1950.

Powel, R. J. H., "Newport Torpedo Station." Unpublished monograph, U.S. Navy Library, Washington, D.C.

Prange, Gordon W. "Miracle at Midway," *Reader's Digest*, November 1972.

Reinertson, J. H. "The Bureau of Ships' Part in the Development of a Diesel Engine for the U.S. Navy," A.S.N.E. paper no. 58-OGP-9.

———, L. E. Alsager, and T. J. Morley. "The Submarine Propulsion Plant—Development and Prospects," *Naval Engineer Journal*, May 1963.

Robinson, Walton L. "Akagi—Famous Japanese Carrier," *U.S.N.I.P.*, May 1948.

Roskill, Stephen W. *Naval Policy Between the Wars*. London: William Collins Sons & Co., 1968.

———. *The War at Sea 1939–1945*. 3 vols. London: H.M. Stationery Office, 1954–61.

Rowland, Buford, and William B. Boyd. *U.S. Navy Bureau of Ordnance in World War II*. Washington, D.C.: U.S. Government Printing Office.

Saville, Allison W. "German Submarines in the Far East," *U.S.N.I.P.*, August 1961.

Sherrod, Robert. *History of Marine Corps Aviation in World War II*. Washington, D.C.: Combat Forces Press, 1952.

Ships' Data, U.S. Naval Vessels. Washington, D.C.: U.S. Government Printing Office, January 1, 1938.

Sims, W. S. *The Victory at Sea*. Garden City, N.Y.: Doubleday, Page, 1921.

Smith, S. E., ed. *The United States Navy in World War II*. New York: William Morrow & Company, 1966.

Sprout, Harold and Margaret. *The Rise of American Naval Power*. Princeton, N.J.: Princeton University Press, 1939.

Stafford, Edward P. *The Far and the Deep*. New York: G. P. Putnam's Sons, 1967.

Sternhell, Charles M., and Alan M. Thorndike. *ASW in World War II*. Washington, D.C.: Navy Department, 1946.

Tanabe, Yabachi. "I Sank the Yorktown at Midway," *U.S.N.I.P.*, May 1963.

Taylor, John C. *German Warships of World War I*. Garden City, N.Y.: Doubleday & Company, 1970.

Toland, John. *The Rising Sun*. New York: Random House, 1970.

Torisu, Kennosuke, and Chihaya Masataka. "Japanese Submarine Tactics," *U.S.N.I.P.*, February 1961.

"U.S. Naval Administration in World War II." Bureau of Ordnance. Unpublished manuscript on file in the Navy Library, Washington, D.C.

U.S. Submarine Data Book. Submarine Force Library and Museum, Naval Submarine Base, New London, Conn.

Von Tirpitz, Alfred P. *My Memoirs.* New York: AMS Press, 1919.

Von der Porten, Edward P. *The German Navy in World War II.* New York: Thomas Y. Crowell Company, 1969.

Wilkinson, J. Burke. "Sneak Craft Attack in the Pacific," *U.S.N.I.P.*, March 1947.

Yokoi, Toshiyuki. "Thoughts on Japan's Naval Defeat," *U.S.N.I.P.*, October 1960.

Yokota, Yutaka. *The Kaiten Weapon.* New York: Ballantine Books, 1962.

Yoshida, Mitsuru. "The End of Yamato," *U.S.N.I.P.*, February 1952.

II. Submarine Operations

1. *Patrol Reports, Ship's Histories, and Log Books*

Every submarine making a war patrol turned in an official patrol report. The bulk of the material for this book was drawn directly from the patrol reports. In all, there were 1,682 patrols. The reports, often one hundred pages or more, contain a daily log of noteworthy events, plus (in some cases) track charts, supplements on torpedo attacks, machinery failure, ship and aircraft sightings, weather and other technical data. Usually, a Special Mission or an Ultra contact produced a separate—more highly classified—supplement because it dealt with intelligence matters. In the preparation of this book, the author consulted all 1,682 patrol reports and the endorsements to these reports appended by the division, squadron, and force commanders.

The patrol reports may be consulted at two locations: the Classified Operational Archives at Building 210, the Navy Yard, Washington, D.C., and in the Submarine Force Library, U.S. Submarine Base, New London, Connecticut. All have been declassified. The Special Mission supplements have been—or may be—declassified under new declassification rules. They are on file in the Classified Operational Archives, but not in New London. The Ultra supplements have not been declassified.

Many of the patrol reports have been summarized in chronological order and produced as "Ship's Histories" in multilith form. Some of these histories are excellent and accurate; others are not and must be used with care. These may be obtained for a small fee from the Department of the Navy, Naval History Division, Washington Navy Yard, Washington, D.C. 20390.

The Ship's Histories are further summarized in the *Dictionary of American Naval Fighting Ships* already listed with the exception of volumes 6 and 7, which have not yet been published. Some of the errors in the multilith ship's histories have been carried forward to the *Dictionary*. The submarine histories summarized in volume 1 (A to B) are hopelessly brief. This same volume contains a valuable index listing submarine contracts and characteristics (size, armament, engines) from 1900 to 1953.

The Classified Operational Archives also has on file ship's deck logs kept by the quartermaster of the watch. These are highly detailed, hour-by-hour—sometimes minute-by-minute—records of events on each submarine at sea and in port. The logs provided much of the raw material for the patrol reports. In addition, there are on file "sailing lists," a list of all personnel sailing with the boat.

2. Lockwood Papers

Admiral Lockwood left his official papers, personal diaries, speeches, correspondence, and other items to the Library of Congress. In all, there are twelve lineal feet of papers, covering the years from about 1925 to 1945. The official correspondence (and personal diaries) for the war years is an indispensable source for anyone writing a history of the submarine war. There are hundreds of letters from Lockwood to Christie and Fife and vice versa. The author drew heavily on this material for this book.

3. Christie Papers

Admiral Christie, who was living in Hawaii at the time this book was completed, has not yet consigned his papers to a repository. However, he made available to the author considerable official correspondence on specific subjects and responded to many queries. He also made available his personal diary for the years 1943–44, a detailed day-by-day account of his activities, problems, and other matters.

4. Biographies

Fortunately for the researcher, the Navy Department has on file brief—but officially correct—biographies of all Naval Academy graduates, compiled from information supplied by each officer. These contain names of parents, birthplace, schooling, maiden name of wife, names of children, a detailed chronological summary of naval service, and promotions and awards with abbreviated citations. The author made use of over five hundred such biographies for this book, all kindly furnished by the navy. Biographies may be obtained by writing Biographies Branch, Department of the Navy, Office of Information, Washington, D.C. 20350.

In addition, the United States Naval Academy Alumni Association, Inc., annually publishes a highly useful document, *Register of Alumni*. This is a thoroughly indexed list of all Naval Academy graduates and nongraduates, living or deceased. Officers are listed by class in order of their standing at graduation, and the entries include the current address of each officer or widow, if any. The author has made use of this document in countless ways and through it was able to establish direct contact with scores of retired officers (see below). A copy may be obtained by writing The U.S. Naval Academy Alumni Association, Inc., Alumni House, Annapolis, Maryland.

Finally, the Naval Academy Yearbook *The Lucky Bag* proved useful in some cases. Issues are on file in Annapolis, the Library of Congress, and the Navy Library in Washington.

5. Interviews, Letters, Special Reports

During World War II, Admiral Lockwood assigned several men to conduct classified taped interviews with some staff officers and submarine skippers. These interviews, now declassified, transcribed, and filed in the Classified Operational Archives, proved useful as source material.

In addition, several key officers submitted special reports on certain phases of the war, notably Admiral Thomas C. Hart and his submarine commander, John Wilkes (whose report was actually written by James Fife). Both were indispensable in sorting out the complex retreat of the Asiatic Fleet (and submarines) from Manila to Australia. Their reports are on file in the Classified Operational Archives.

In 1971, 1972 and 1973, the author conducted numerous and exhaustive taped interviews with scores of staff officers and skippers or their widows. These interviews covered the peacetime years, the evolution of the submarine, diesel engines and torpedoes, and the Submarine School, as well as the war. In addition, he mailed extensive questionnaires to many skippers who were invited to respond on tape —in effect a taped self-interview. Finally, he corresponded by mail

with scores of officers and widows on various points. These sources
provided much material for this book. The tapes and letters will be
turned over to officials at the Archive of Contemporary History, University of Wyoming, Laramie.

The men—or in some cases their widows—who contributed material in wartime reports and interviews and letters to the author are
listed below.

Mrs. Mannert L. Abele

Frank C. Acker

Stephen H. Ambruster

William L. Anderson

William R. Anderson

Charles H. Andrews

Theodore C. Aylward

John B. Azer

Barton E. Bacon, Jr.

Eric L. Barr, Sr.

Thomas S. Baskett

Raymond H. Bass

Edward L. Beach

Rafael C. Benitez

Carter L. Bennett

Roy S. Benson

Leon N. Blair

James W. Blanchard

John H. Brady

William H. Brockman

Henry C. Bruton

Eliot H. Bryant

Creed C. Burlingame

Mrs. John L. Burnside, Jr.

Joseph A. Callaghan

Gordon Campbell

Edward S. Carmick

Bruce L. Carr

Wreford G. Chapple

Ralph W. Christie

Bladen D. Claggett

Frederic B. Clarke

Robert H. Close

Merrill Comstock

John S. Coye

Mrs. John R. Craig

George C. Crawford

John D. Crowley

Slade D. Cutter

Lawrence R. Daspit

Roy M. Davenport

James W. Davis

Samuel D. Dealey

Glynn R. Donaho

Robert E. Dornin

Willard M. Downes

Claren E. Duke

Thomas M. Dykers

Ian C. Eddy

William C. Eddy

Mrs. Robert H. English

Joseph F. Enright

William E. Ferrall

James Fife

John A. Fitzgerald

Clifton W. Flenniken, Jr.

Eugene B. Fluckey

Robert J. Foley

John J. Foote

Charles L. Freeman

John K. Fyfe

Ignatius J. Galantin

Philip W. Garnett

Malcolm E. Garrison

Richard S. Garvey
William J. Germershausen
James D. Grant
Louis P. Gray III
Richard V. Gregory
Elton W. Grenfell
George W. Grider
John B. Griggs, Jr.
John B. Griggs III
Royce L. Gross
William P. Gruner, Jr.
Mrs. Robert Lakin Gurnee
Oscar E. Hagberg
John L. Haines
John M. Haines
Warren C. Hall, Jr.
Edward R. Hannon
James T. Hardin
Frederick J. Harlfinger II
Brooks J. Harral
Thomas C. Hart
Earle C. Hawk
William H. Hazzard
Charles M. Henderson
Thomas H. Henry
Karl G. Hensel
Franklin G. Hess
John B. Hess
James M. Hingson
Thomas W. Hogan
George M. Holley
William G. Holman
Martin P. Hottel
Leon J. Huffman
Jesse L. Hull
Adrian M. Hurst
Tyrrell D. Jacobs
Benjamin C. Jarvis
Carl A. Johnson
James L. Jordan

Allen R. Joyce
Roger M. Keithly
Marvin G. Kennedy
Thomas K. Kimmel
Robert D. King
Oliver G. Kirk
William T. Kinsella
Charles C. Kirkpatrick
Thomas B. Klakring
Robert A. Knapp
Herman J. Kossler
H. J. Kuehn
Richard C. Latham
John E. Lee
William R. Lefavour
Bafford E. Lewellen
James W. Liddell
Mrs. Charles A. Lockwood
Frederick K. Loomis
Charles E. Loughlin
Vernon L. Lowrance
Frederic C. Lucas, Jr.
Nicholas Lucker, Jr.
Frank C. Lynch, Jr.
Ralph C. Lynch, Jr.
Hyland B. Lyon
Edgar J. MacGregor III
Duncan C. MacMillan
Harry C. Maynard
John S. McCain, Jr.
Allan R. McCann
David H. McClintock
Victor B. McCrea
Louis D. McGregor, Jr.
Eugene B. McKinney
Heber H. McLean
Bernard F. McMahon
Fitzhugh McMaster
Ralph M. Metcalf
Leonard S. Mewhinney

Peter G. Molteni
Keats E. Montross
John R. Moore
Raymond J. Moore
Dudley W. Morton
Henry G. Munson
John W. Murphy, Jr.
Walter P. Murphy, Jr.
Stuart S. Murray
William T. Nelson
John C. Nichols
Philip G. Nichols
Stanley G. Nichols
Chester W. Nimitz, Jr.
Richard H. O'Kane
Robert I. Olsen
Frank M. Parker
Lewis S. Parks
Richard W. Peterson
George E. Pierce
Mrs. John R. Pierce
William S. Post, Jr.
Roland F. Pryce
Lawson P. Ramage
Robert P. Ramsey
Eli T. Reich
James R. Reynolds
Cassius D. Rhymes, Jr.
Robert A. Rinehart
Robert D. Risser
Orme C. Robbins
Samuel M. Robinson
J. D. Roche
Francis W. Rockwell
Philip H. Ross
Royal L. Rutter
Mrs. Willard A. Saunders
Kenneth G. Schacht

Paul R. Schratz
John A. Scott
Frank G. Selby
Robert F. Sellars
Jack M. Seymour
Mrs. Louis Shane, Jr.
William B. Sieglaff
Arthur C. Smith
Chester C. Smith
Joseph J. Staley
Harry C. Stevenson
William A. Stevenson
Mrs. John J. Broderick
  (Mrs. Vard A. Stockton)
Augustus R. St. Angelo
William S. Stovall, Jr.
George L. Street III
Charles W. Styer
Paul E. Summers
Arthur H. Taylor
William C. Thompson, Jr.
Charles O. Triebel
John A. Tyree, Jr.
Gordon W. Underwood
George H. Wales
Edward K. Walker
Francis D. Walker, Jr.
Norvell G. Ward
Robert E. M. Ward
Frederick B. Warder
David L. Whelchel
Reuben T. Whitaker
Bruce E. Wiggin
John Wilkes
Charles W. Wilkins
Delbert F. Williamson
William H. Wright
Lloyd V. Young

6. *War Diaries, Operational Orders, Submarine Bulletins*

Each of the three submarine commands kept a War Diary. This was a day-by-day account of the command activities (mostly listings of submarines going on or arriving from patrol and the claimed results). These diaries—on file in the Classified Operational Archives—proved invaluable for compiling the sailing charts of war patrols (Appendix F). They were also useful in many other ways.

Every submarine going on patrol was issued an Operational Order, a lengthy document giving specific instructions about where and how to conduct the war patrol. These documents are also on file in the archives.

From time to time, the Pacific submarine force issued Submarine Bulletins. These documents—classified at the time—contain information on Japanese antisubmarine tactics, technical gear (sonar, radar), outstanding (or unusual) U.S. submarine war patrols, and so on. By 1945, the Bulletin had assumed the form of a classified magazine. Bulletins—now declassified—are on file in the Classified Operational Archives.

7. *Official Administrative and Operational History*

During the closing stages of the war, Lockwood detailed his operations officer, Richard Voge, to write an official administrative and operational history of the submarine war. Voge was assisted in this large undertaking by W. J. Holmes, W. H. Hazzard, D. S. Graham, and H. J. Kuehn.

The Administrative History forms a portion of the navy's unpublished series known as "United States Naval Administration in World War II." It is subtitled "Submarine Commands, Volumes 1 and 2." Copies are on file in the Navy Library, Washington, D.C., and at the Submarine Force Library and Museum, Submarine Base, New London. The Administrative History deals with personnel, bases, submarine construction, repair and refit, communications, and other matters. The author made extensive use of these volumes and is grateful to the Submarine Force Library for their long-term loan.

The Operational History produced by Voge et al. is a massive document of more than 1,500 pages dealing with every conceivable operational aspect of the submarine war. No one attempting a serious submarine history should begin without consulting it. Generally, it tells a positive story; the "skipper problem," for example, is not dealt with. However, the torpedo section contains a long and frank account of torpedo problems which the author has consulted extensively, along with other sources. Copies of the Operational History are on file in the Classified Operational Archives. It contains, among other valuable information, a complete copy of JANAC, with sinkings credited to each submarine.

8. Published Books and Articles

After the war, John M. Will, while attached to the Bureau of Personnel (Assistant Director of Training), hired a writer, Theodore Roscoe, to reduce the Operational History to publishable form. The result was *United States Submarine Operations in World War II*, published in 1949 by the U.S. Naval Institute, Annapolis, Maryland. It is in effect a truncated version of the Operational History (sometimes reproduced word for word). Since it was produced by the navy, it too is a positive story—the Operational History in more manageable form. This work was published in condensed form in paperback by Bantam Books, under the title *Pigboats*.

Wilfred Jay Holmes, who had worked on most of these projects and, in addition, compiled a book titled *U.S. Submarine Losses in World War II*, wrote his own version of the submarine war. Called *Undersea Victory*, it was published by Doubleday & Company in 1966. This is an excellent distillation of preceding official accounts and benefits from Holmes's intelligence, keen insight, and his knowledge of codebreaking—about which, however, he was regrettably denied permission to write. For anyone undertaking a history of the submarine war, Holmes is an indispensable source.

Finally, Lockwood himself published two books that are pertinent. The first, *Sink 'Em All* (New York: E. P. Dutton & Company, 1951) is a personal account of the submarine war, from his arrival in Australia in 1942 to war's end. The second, *Down to the Sea in Subs* (New York: W. W. Norton & Company, 1967) is an autobiography including a brief section on the war, drawn in part from *Sink 'Em All*. Both proved useful, although Lockwood deals with neither the "skipper problem" nor codebreaking nor many other controversial matters.

In addition to the foregoing, the author has consulted other published works on World War II submarine operations (some by sub-mariners). These were:

Beach, Edward L. *Dust on the Sea* (a novel). New York: Holt, Rinehart & Winston, 1972.

——. *Run Silent, Run Deep* (a novel). New York: Henry Holt & Company, 1955.

——. *Submarine!* New York: Henry Holt and Company, 1952.

——. "Unlucky in June: *Hiyo* Meets *Trigger*," *U.S.N.I.P.*, April 1957.

Benitez, Ralph C. "Battle Stations Submerged," *U.S.N.I.P.*, January 1948.

Bowers, Richard H. "Servicing the Silent," *U.S.N.I.P.*, November 1943.

Carmer, Carl. *The Jesse James of the Java Sea*. New York: Rinehart, 1945.

Chambliss, William C. *The Silent Service*. New York: New American Library, 1959.

Cope, Harley F., and Walter Karig. *Battle Submerged—Submarine Fighters in World War II*. New York: W. W. Norton & Company, 1957.

Davis, H. F. D. "Building U.S. Submarines in World War II," *U.S.N.I.P.*, July 1946.

Frank, Gerald, and James D. Horan. *U.S.S. Seawolf*. New York: G. P. Putnam's Sons, 1945.

Grider, George, and Lytel Sims. *War Fish*. Boston: Little, Brown and Company, 1958.

Horie, Y. "The Failure of the Japanese Convoy Escort," *U.S.N.I.P.*, October 1956.

Lockwood, Charles A., and Hans C. Adamson. *Battles of the Philippine Sea*. New York: Thomas Y. Crowell Company, 1967.

—— and ——. *Hellcats of the Sea*. New York: Greenberg, Publisher, 1956.

—— and ——. *Through Hell and Deep Water*. New York: Greenberg, Publisher, 1956.

—— and ——. *Zoomies, Subs and Zeroes*. New York: Greenberg, Publisher, 1956.

Oi, Atsughi. "Why Japan's Anti-submarine Warfare Failed," *U.S.N.I.P.*, June 1952.

Oil in Japan's War. U.S. Strategic Bombing Survey. Washington, D.C.: U.S. Government Printing Office.

Pratt, Fletcher. "Two Little Ships," *U.S.N.I.P.*, July 1947. About *Harder* and destroyer *England*.

Sheridan, Martin. *Overdue and Presumed Lost: The Story of the U.S.S. Bullhead*. Francestown, N.H.: Marshall Jones Co., 1947.

Sterling, Forest J. *Wake of the Wahoo*. Philadelphia: Chilton Books, 1960.

Trumbull, Robert. *Silversides*. New York: Henry Holt & Company, 1945.

Underbrink, Robert L. *Destination Corregidor*. Annapolis, Md.: U.S. Naval Institute, 1971.

U.S. Submarine Losses in World War II (prepared initially by W. J. Holmes). Washington, D.C.: U.S. Government Printing Office, 1946, 1963.

Voge, Richard G., "A Case of Too Much Accuracy," *U.S.N.I.P.*, March 1950. About *Queenfish* and *Awa Maru*.

War Against Japanese Transportation. U.S. Strategic Bombing Survey. Washington: U.S. Government Printing Office, 1947.

Withers, Thomas C. "Preparing SubPac for War," *U.S.N.I.P.*, April 1950.

Zimmerman, Sherwood R. "Operation Forager," *U.S.N.I.P.*, August 1964.

III. Codebreaking

Since the beginning of the enterprise, anything having to do with the breaking of Japanese codes has been classified. During the preparation of this book, the author requested the U.S. government to declassify certain documents and unit histories. After considering the request for eighteen months, the government declined.

1. *Interviews and Letters*

Most of the codebreaking information in this book was gathered through interviews or letters—with submarine skippers and submarine staff officers and with nine codebreakers willing to talk on a background or off-the-record basis. The codebreakers—who cannot be named—provided the author with information on the history of breaking the Japanese codes, on personnel, on the Japanese Language Program, on specific examples of codebreaking triumphs in World War II, on organization, and other matters. The author is grateful to the unnamed codebreakers who were willing to cooperate.

2. *Other Sources*

The author made use of two additional primary sources for Ultra information to submarines: the Pacific and Australian War Diaries for the first year of the war, which contain numerous summaries of Ultra dispatches, and the patrol reports in which some submarine skippers inadvertently included specific mention of Ultra dispatches (by number). The Pearl Harbor hearings conducted after the war contain many hundreds of pages of testimony on breaking the Japanese codes. And in published memoirs and books, some naval leaders have mentioned the contribution of codebreaking to the overall conduct of the war.

In addition, the author consulted the following books, manuscripts, and articles which deal in whole or in part with breaking Japanese codes:

Ardman, Harvey. "U.S. Code-Breakers vs. Japanese Code-Breakers in World War II," *American Legion Magazine*, May 1972.

Davis, Burke. *Get Yamamoto*. New York: Random House, 1969.

Dyer, George C. *The Amphibians Came to Conquer: The Story of Admiral Richmond Kelly Turner*. 2 vols. Washington, D.C.: U.S. Government Printing Office, 1972. (Contains detailed Ultra on Guadalcanal.)

Farago, Ladislas. *The Broken Seal*. New York: Random House, 1967.

Kahn, David. *The Codebreakers*. New York: The Macmillan Company, 1967.

Kimmel, Husband E. *Admiral Kimmel's Story*. Chicago: Henry Regnery Co., 1955.

"New Pearl Harbor Facts, Full Story: How U.S. Got Jap Secrets." *Chicago Tribune*, special supplement, December 7, 1966.

Operational History of Naval Communications (Japanese), prepared by Military History Section H.Q. Army Forces, Far East. Army Library, Washington, D.C. Manuscript.

Stark, Harold R. Unpublished manuscript, Classified Operational Archives.

Thorpe, Elliott R. *East Wind, Rain*. Boston: Gambit, Inc., 1969.

Tuchman, Barbara. *The Zimmermann Telegram*. New York: Viking Press, 1958.

Wohlstetter, Roberta. *Pearl Harbor Warning and Decision*. Stanford, Cal.: Stanford University Press, 1962.

Zacharias, Ellis M., and Ladislas Farago. *Secret Missions: The Story of an Intelligence Officer*. New York: G. P. Putnam's Sons, 1946.

Index

Hunnicutt, James L., in *Carp*, 772*n*, 793

Hunter, Samuel Howard, Jr., 109–11

Hurana, Japanese battleship, 843

Hurd, Kenneth Charles, 264, 325, 789; in *Seal*, 1942 patrols, 120, 129, 132, 142; defense of Java, 161, 164, 175*n*; patrols from Fremantle, 266, 328

Hurst, Adrian Melvin, 261, 313, 438; in *Permit*, patrols, 121–22, 142, 143; in Lingayen Gulf, 124, 127

Hurt, David Albert, 157, 161, 294, 572*n*; in *Perch*, patrols, 122, 129, 142, 162; loses *Perch*, captured by Japanese, 165–66

Hutchinson, Edward Shillingford, 189; in *Grampus*, 262–63; in *Rasher*, 463

Hyde, John Milton, 788; in *Bergall*, 1944 patrols, 726, 756, 771–73; refuses to destroy *Bergall*, 773; 1945 patrols, 822, 826

Hydeman, Earl Twining, in *Sea Dog*, patrol and wolf pack, 804, 834–36, 838, 839

Hydrophone, 18

Hypo codebreaking unit, *see* Codebreaking

Hyuga, Japanese battleship–aircraft carrier, 723, 736, 737, 739, 741, 752, 769, 770, 773, 833; pursuit of, 821–22, 823 (map), 824–25; destroyed, 843

Hyuga Maru, Japanese freighter, 354

I class, Japanese submarines, 479, 636, 740, 779, 780, 847; human torpedoes (*kaiten*) used, 741

I-1, 344; I-7, 391, 565; I-15, 277; I-18, 317; I-19, 276; I-21, 304; I-24, 391, 448, 523; I-25, 247*n*; I-26, 312; I-28, 208, 210; I-29, 652; I-31, 391; I-36, 741;

I-37, 741; I-38, 741; I-42, 547; I-43, 620; I-47, 741; I-58, 845; I-64, 210; I-122, 838; I-168, 215–16; I-173, 94–96; I-175, 479, 532; I-176, 304, 494; I-182, 523; I-183, 563; I-365, 753; I-373, 845

IBM punch cards, 42

Icefish, patrols and wolf packs, 705, 721, 723, 744, 745, 809

Icenhower, Joseph Bryan: in *Jallao*, 1944 patrols and wolf packs, 705, 745, 746; in Battle of Leyte Gulf, 737; 1945 patrol and wolf pack, 815, 845

ICPOA (Intelligence Center, Pacific Ocean Area), 238

Ikomasaw Maru, Japanese transport, 810

Illustrious, British aircraft carrier, 602

Ilmen, Russian freighter, 378

Inazuma, Japanese destroyer, 598

Inchon, 842

Independence, aircraft carrier, 372*n*, 395, 479

India: Japanese raid on, 169; British forces in, 529, 602

Indian Ocean, 190, 829; German submarines in, 761*n*

Indianapolis, cruiser, 40–41; Spruance's flagship, 804; sunk, 844

Indochina, 142, 169, 769; Japanese bases in, 55, 56, 105, 112, 141, 142, 159; 1942–1943 patrols near, 261, 265–66, 324, 325, 328–29, 331, 458, 459, 461, 466–67, 469; 1944 patrols near, 584, 589, 591, 598, 600, 604, 605, 660, 688, 760, 769, 771; *see also* Camranh Bay

Inland Sea, 721, 724, 753, 799; Japanese forces in, 720; U.S. bombing of Japanese fleet, 803, 843

Innis, Walter Deane, 244–45

Internal combustion engine, 6, 8

About the Author

Clay Blair, Jr., was born in Lexington, Virginia, in 1925. He served in the U.S. Navy in World War II, volunteering for submarine service. He attended submarine school (including a cruise on an S-boat) and was attached to the tender *Sperry* for four months at the advance submarine base, Apra Harbor, Guam. In 1945 he made the last two long war patrols of *Guardfish,* the first off Honshu, February to April, the second off Honshu and Hokkaido during May and June. Rising to the rank of Quartermaster 2nd Class, he qualified in submarines and was decorated with the Submarine Combat Insignia and the Asiatic-Pacific Theater medal with three battle stars. After the war, Mr. Blair joined a submarine reserve unit, making a summer cruise in a newer fleet submarine.

As a Washington journalist for Time-Life and the *Saturday Evening Post* from 1950 to 1960, Mr. Blair followed submarine developments closely and came to know many wartime submarine skippers with whom he spent many hours "diving the boats" and analyzing the submarine war. He was the first journalist to go to sea on the new *Tang*-class submarine *Trigger,* the guided missile submarine *Barbero,* and the first to write about the nuclear-powered submarine *Nautilus,* and her "father," Captain Hyman G. Rickover. He led a successful journalistic crusade to retain Rickover in the navy and subsequently was one of the first journalists to make a sea voyage on *Nautilus.* In later years he inspected and wrote about nuclear-powered Polaris submarines and the new nuclear-powered attack submarine *Guardfish.*

Mr. Blair has published three previous books on submarines: *The Atomic Submarine and Admiral Rickover; Nautilus 90 North,* the best-selling account of the *Nautilus* voyage beneath the Arctic ice cap, which was published in twenty-six countries; and *Pentagon Country,* a novel centering on the controversy over the navy's submarine weapons system of the near future, Trident.